PSYCHOTHERAPIES

FOURTH EDITION

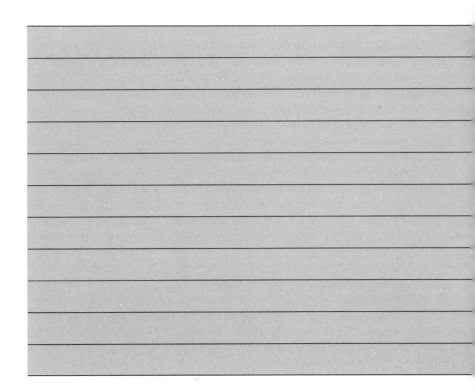

To My Teachers

RUDOLF DREIKURS
J. L. MORENO
CARL ROGERS

–RJC–

Contents

Outline of Book

Contributors

JACOB A. ARLOW, M.D., Clinical Professor of Psychiatry, New York University College of Medicine, New York, NY

AARON T. BECK, M.D., University Professor of Psychiatry, University of Pennsylvania, Philadelphia, PA

ADAM BLATNER, M.D., Professor of Psychiatry, School of Medicine, University of Louisville, Louisville, KY

RAYMOND J. CORSINI, Ph.D., Professor, University of Hawaii, Honolulu, HI

JOHN M. DUSAY, M.D., Private Practice, San Francisco, CA

KATHERINE MULHOLLAND DUSAY, Ph.D., Private Practice, San Francisco, CA

ALBERT ELLIS, Ph.D., Institute for Rational-Emotive Therapy, New York, NY

VINCENT D. FOLEY, Ph.D., Private Practice, Jamaica Estates and Manhattan, NY

YORAM KAUFMANN, Ph.D., Private Practice, New York, NY

ALEXANDER LOWEN, M.D., Director, International Institute for Bioenergetic Analysis, New York, NY

ARNOLD A. LAZARUS, Ph.D., Distinguished Professor, Graduate School of Applied and Professional Psychology, Rutgers University, Piscataway, NJ

ROLLO MAY, Ph.D., Private Practice, Tiburon, CA; Director of the Rollo May Center for Humanistic Studies

HAROLD H. MOSAK, Ph.D., Private Practice, Chicago, IL

NATHANIEL J. RASKIN, Ph.D., Professor of Psychiatry and Behavioral Sciences, Northwestern University Medical School, Chicago, IL

CARL R. ROGERS, Ph.D., Deceased

JAMES S. SIMKIN, Ph.D., Deceased

ROBERT L. TAYLOR, M.D., California State University, Northridge, CA

ROGER WALSH, M.D., Ph.D., Professor of Psychiatry, Social Sciences, and Philosophy, University of California, Irvine, CA

MARJORIE E. WEISHAAR, Ph.D., Private Practice, Providence, RI

G. TERENCE WILSON, Ph.D., Oscar K. Buros Professor of Psychology, Rutgers University, Piscataway, NJ

GARY M. YONTEF, Ph.D., Private Practice, Santa Monica, CA

IRVIN YALOM, M.D., Professor of Psychiatry and Behavioral Sciences, Stanford University School of Medicine, Stanford, CA

A Note to the Reader

Several years ago, having reached the biblical age of threescore and ten, I decided that to ensure its continuation, *Current Psychotherapies* needed a younger editor.

Selecting a collaborator was easy. Dr. Danny Wedding, while a graduate student at the University of Hawaii, had helped write the manual for my *Current Personality Theories*. Impressed with his high standards, I invited him to co-edit *Great Cases in Psychotherapy* (the original reader for the present volume). Further impressed with the quality of his work, I asked him to assist in the editing of the third edition of *Current Psychotherapies*.

One reason for recruiting Dr. Wedding is that philosophically and theoretically he balances my training, experience, and orientation. I am an Adlerian psychologist, while he is a behavior therapist. I have an ideographic orientation, and my primary source of confirmation for the value of counseling and psychotherapy comes from my personal experiences and those of my clients; Danny, who has a more nomothetic orientation, is convinced that outcome research is a critical component in the evaluation of psychotherapy. My training was with humanistic therapists. Danny's training was primarily in behavior modification. Philosophically I represent what the Germans call the *Geistenswissenschaften* viewpoint (a social psychology orientation); Danny represents the *Naturwissenschaften* viewpoint (a physical sciences orientation).

I believe our collaboration leads to a more balanced presentation of psychotherapy.

Raymond J. Corsini
Honolulu, Hawaii

Preface

Current Psychotherapies fulfills a need for a comprehensive introduction to the numerous and varied activities included under the general heading of psychotherapy. Its continuing favorable reception is primarily due to four factors:

1. Chapters are carefully selected to reflect changes in a constantly evolving field. Final decisions about what to include and what to delete with each new edition are guided by professors who reply to surveys designed to help us identify new, important systems and to eliminate chapters no longer found helpful.

2. Leading figures in psychotherapy are recruited as authors. Chapters devoted to recently developed systems are written by their founders; chapters on more established psychotherapies are written by the most qualified individuals available.

3. Chapter authors accept the discipline of working within the constraints of an established format, using a common outline and structured sections that permit students to compare and contrast various aspects of different systems.

4. Each new edition is carefully edited. Multiple revisions are required of almost every chapter to ensure simple and clear writing.

Dr. Corsini has reviewed and edited every word in this fourth edition of *Current Psychotherapies*. However, the final responsibility for this edition is mine.

Dr. Judith McMahon, who teaches from this book at Lindenwood College, served as an editorial consultant. Her critical scrutiny has resulted in fewer redundancies, an improved glossary, and a stronger index.

Our survey of professors' attitudes yielded 74 separate recommendations for new chapters. We rejected recommendations for chapters linked to specific populations and problems (e.g., feminist therapy, sex therapy) as well as recommendations for chapters limited to specific techniques (e.g., implosive therapy, hypnotherapy). None of these are systems of psychotherapy in the sense that we use the term. We believe a psychotherapeutic system must have a broad theoretical base that relates to the procedures employed.

I had initially wanted to include a section on research with every chapter. However, virtually every chapter author maintained that the research base of his or her system was not sufficiently well developed to justify an exclusive section devoted to research findings.

Every chapter retained from the third edition has been revised and updated. We have included a new chapter on *Cognitive Therapy*, the single most-often requested addition. *Person-Centered Therapy* has been completely rewritten. The final chapter introduces three approaches that cannot be covered more completely due to space limitations: *Asian Psychotherapy, Psychodrama,* and *Bioenergetics.* An appendix discusses conditions that may indicate a need for preliminary medical examination of clients, the glossary has been expanded and updated, and photographs of major historical figures associated with the various systems are included for the first time.

Brief case studies are found in every chapter. However, serious students will prefer to study more extensive case histories. Recommendations for case readings are found at the end of every chapter, and illustrative cases can be found in *Case Studies in Psychotherapy,* the reader for *Current Psychotherapies.*

Current Psychotherapies will continue to reflect the concept of disparate systems of therapy described by leading authorities following a preestablished outline. I hope that the current edition maintains the standard of excellence set by previous editions.

Danny Wedding
Huntington, West Virginia

Acknowledgments

Every project of this type involves the efforts of dozens of people; this book is no different. We especially appreciate the recommendations of the hundreds of college professors who responded to our survey.

The following professors are noted for their special assistance in planning this fourth edition:

Betty J. Bosdell	Northern Illinois University
Mary E. Bredemeier	Montclair State University
Jan S. Cavanaugh	University of Delaware
Steve Cody	Marshall University
Gerald Corey	California State University
Ronald L. Dodge	Delta State University
Robert L. Frank	University of Northern Iowa
Donald K. Fromme	Oklahoma State University
Barbara L. Ingram	Pepperdine University
James W. Lichtenberg	University of Kansas
John King McComb	Johns Hopkins University
Peter Madison	University of Arizona
Anthony Marsella	University of Hawaii
Stewart Moore	University of Windsor
Maggie Mulqueen	Lesley College
Robert L. Peterson	Metropolitan State University
Roderick W. Pugh	Loyola University
Catherine M. Reinhardt	Assumption College
Hugh Rosen	Hahneman University
Jerome Siller	New York University
Norman Silverman	Loyola University
Alan Simpkins	University of Hawaii
Genevieve E. Thompson	California Baptist College
Otto Zinser	East Tennessee State University

Clerical assistance was provided by Carolyn Endicott and her staff, Lisa Hunt, Karen Bledsoe, Kelly Webster, Pam Davis, and Barbara Cubic. Jan Lazarus of the History of Medicine Section in the National Library of Medicine helped locate photographs suitable for inclusion in this edition.

Finally we wish to acknowledge our wives, Dr. Kleona Rigney and Cynthia Wedding, who support our editing efforts with their good humor and patience.

CURRENT PSYCHOTHERAPIES

1

Introduction

RAYMOND J. CORSINI

Psychotherapy cannot be defined with any precision. A dictionary definition might go as follows:

Psychotherapy is a formal process of interaction between two parties, each party usually consisting of one person but with the possibility that there may be two or more people in each party, for the purpose of amelioration of distress in one of the two parties relative to any of the following areas of disability or malfunction: cognitive functions (disorders of thinking), affective functions (suffering or emotional discomforts), or behavioral functions (inadequacy of behavior), with the therapist having some theory of personality's origins, development, maintenance and change along with some method of treatment logically related to the theory and professional and legal approval to act as a therapist.

This definition may appear rather comprehensive but as will soon be evident, some modes of therapy will not fit it.

Would the system of psychotherapy that Sigmund Freud underwent, about which Karen Horney (1942) wrote a book, and which Theodore Reik (1948) claimed to be the best of all therapies fit this definition? The system is *self-therapy*. In self-therapy there is only one party; there is no formality and no professional or legal approval, and yet it certainly is therapy.

If we examine various theories and procedures in psychotherapy, we find a truly bewildering set of ideas and behaviors, some of which appear quite bizarre. There have been systems of therapy that had no therapist (Schmidhoffer, 1952); systems in which the therapist says and does nothing (Bion, 1948); systems in which patients are symbolically rebirthed (Bindrim, 1981; Orr & Ray, 1977); systems in which patients are asked to scream or to strike out (Bach & Goldberg, 1975; Janov, 1970); methods that call for meditation or imaging (Ahnsen, 1965; Cautela, 1981; Shorr, 1972; Wolpe, 1958); methods in which the therapist makes fun of the patient, treating him or her with apparent disrespect (Farrelly & Brasma, 1974), and methods that treat the patient or client with utmost respect, attempting to encourage through kindness (Losoncy, 1981); methods in which patients are treated as children (Painter & Vernon, 1981); methods that stress re-

1

ligion (Lair & Lair, 1973; van Kaam, 1976); and methods that are composites or conglomerates of a wide variety of procedures (Gazda, 1981; Shostrom & Montgomery, 1978).

Many other strange procedures have been employed in what is called psychotherapy. What one authority considers to be psychotherapy may be completely different from how other authorities see the process. There is no way at present to settle any differences; so even though A and B may be doing completely different and contradictory things, both are doing psychotherapy. We come to the same conclusion as Lewis Carroll in *Through the Looking Glass:* A word means what you want it to mean.

A comment about counseling and psychotherapy: They are the same qualitatively; they differ only quantitatively. I realized some years ago (Corsini, 1968) that there was nothing that a psychotherapist did that a counselor did not do. Table 1.1 illustrates this basic point:

Table 1.1
Estimation of Percent of Time Spent by
"Counselors" and "Psychotherapists"
in Professional Activities*

Process	Counseling	Psychotherapy
Listening	20	60
Questioning	15	10
Evaluating	5	5
Interpreting	1	3
Supporting	5	10
Explaining	15	5
Informing	20	3
Advising	10	3
Ordering	9	1

*Based on "Counseling and Psychotherapy" in E. F. Borgatta and W. W. Lambert (Eds.), *Handbook of Personality Theory and Research* (Chicago, Rand McNally, 1968).

From Table 1.1, which attempts to generalize about all counseling methods and all verbal psychothera-

peutic procedures, it can be seen that differences are quantitative rather than qualitative and that there is really no fundamental difference between counseling and psychotherapy.

This position will be strongly resisted by many on various grounds, but I maintain that no definition can be made which will include all psychotherapies and exclude all counseling methods. The various attempts to separate the psychotherapies and exclude all counseling methods have failed. The concept that psychotherapy goes into depth while counseling does not is gainsaid by such procedures as behavior modification which operates at the level of symptom removal. Behavior modifiers could hardly be called counselors, because they do not counsel. And when we have a term such as *nondirective counseling,* we have a semantic absurdity if we think about it long enough.

All modes of trying to help people improve themselves via symbolic methods can be called psychotherapy just as all methods to help improve psychological functioning through medications, surgery, electric shock, and other somatic procedures may be called psychiatry. Consequently, the interview, hypnosis, roleplaying, projective techniques, and the like that we shall take up in this book can be considered procedures in counseling/ psychotherapy, but it is best, in my judgment, to call them all processes of psychotherapy. Therefore, when Carl Rogers repeats what you have said, using his own terminology (as he did with me when I was in therapy with him), *this is psychotherapy;* and when Rudolph Dreikurs, an Adlerian, points out basic life-style errors (as he did for me when I was in therapy with him), *this is psychotherapy;* and when

Albert Ellis contradicts your point of view (as he often has with me), *this is psychotherapy;* and when J. L. Moreno has people play different roles in front of a group (as I did many times when working with him) then *this is psychotherapy.*

A number of years ago, in Paris, at an outdoor cafe, I met with a French colleague, and during the course of our conversation I mentioned psychotherapy. "Ah," she said, "*Psychothérapie comme ça—ou comme ça?*" (Psychotherapy like this—or like this?) At the first *ça* she put the palms of her hands about an inch apart, and at the second *ça* she moved her hands out as far as she could, with the palms still facing each other. She was asking me whether I had a narrow conception of psychotherapy or a wide one. We can do the same thing with the hands vertically and ask about the depth of psychotherapy. Essentially, depth is a function of time spent rather than a matter of technique, and two people with the same theory and technique will vary with respect to depth, depending primarily on the time spent with the client. (Incidentally, I call the subjects of psychotherapy *clients* if one sees them in a private office and *patients* if they are in a hospital or institution.)

AN UNUSUAL EXAMPLE OF PSYCHOTHERAPY

About 40 years ago, when I was working as a psychologist at Auburn Prison in New York, I participated in what I believe was the most successful and most elegant psychotherapy I have ever done. One day an inmate, who had made an appointment to see me, came into my office. He was a fairly attractive man in his early 30s. I pointed to a chair, he sat down, and I waited to

find out what he wanted. The conversation went somewhat as follows:

Prisoner: I am leaving on parole Thursday.
Corsini: Yes?
P: I did not want to leave until I thanked you for what you had done for me.
C: What was that?
P: When I left your office about two years ago, I felt like I was walking on air. When I went into the prison yard, everything looked different, even the air smelled different. I was a new person. Instead of going over to the group I usually hung out with—they were a bunch of thieves—I went over to another group of square Johns [prison jargon for noncriminal types]. I changed from a cushy job in the kitchen to the machine shop, where I could learn a trade. I started going to the prison high school and I now have a high school diploma. I took a correspondence course in drafting and I have a drafting job when I leave Thursday. I started back to church even though I had given up my religion many years ago. I started writing to my parents and to my family again, and they have come up to see me and they remember you in their prayers. I now have hope. I know who and what I am. I know I will succeed in life. I plan to go to college. You have freed me. I used to think you bug doctors [prison slang for psychologists and psychiatrists] were for the birds, but now I know better. Thanks for changing my life.

I listened to this tale in wonderment, because to the best of my knowledge I had never spoken with him. I looked at his folder and the only notation there was that I had given him an IQ test about two years before.

"Are you sure it was me?" I finally said. "I am not a psychotherapist, and I have no memory of ever having spoken to you. What you are reporting is the sort of personality and behavior change that takes many years to accomplish—and I certainly haven't done anything of the kind."

"It was you alright," he replied with

great conviction, "and I will never forget what you said to me. It changed my life."

"What was that?" I asked in wonderment.

"You told me I had a high IQ," he replied.

With one sentence of five words I had (inadvertently) changed this person's life.

Let us try to understand this event. If you are clever enough to understand why this man changed so drastically as a result of hearing these five words, my guess is that you have the capacity to be a good therapist.

Intrigued by his reaction to these words, I asked him why this sentence about his IQ had such a profound effect. I learned that up to the time that he heard these five words he had always thought of himself as "stupid" and "crazy"—terms that had been applied to him many times by his family, teachers, and friends. In school, he had always gotten poor grades, which confirmed his belief in his mental subnormality. His friends did not approve of the way he thought and called him crazy. And so he was convinced that he was both an ament (low intelligence) and a dement (insane). But when I said, "You have a high IQ," he had an AHA experience that explained *everything*. In a flash he understood why he could solve crossword puzzles better than any of his friends. He now knew why he read Sinclair Lewis rather than Edgar Rice Burroughs, why he preferred to play chess rather than checkers, why he liked symphonies rather than jazz. With great and sudden intensity he realized through my five words that he was really normal and bright and not crazy or stupid. No wonder he felt as if

he were walking on air when he left my office two years before!

His interpretation of my five words generated a complete change of self-concept—and consequently a change in both his behavior and his feelings about himself and others.

In short, I had performed psychotherapy in a completely innocent and informal way. Even though what happened in no way accords to the definition given earlier, even though there was no agreement between us, no theory, no intention of changing him—the five-word comment had a most pronounced effect, and so it *was* psychotherapy, even though there was no intention on my part or his to achieve the profound personality changes that did occur.

And I have had two long-term clients—each was seen for over 10 years—and in neither case did I do much for them as far as I can tell.

COMPARISONS OF THEORIES

Karl Popper (1968), the philosopher of science who wrote *Conjectures and Refutations*, makes the very astute observation that Marxists, Freudians, and Adlerians are all able to find evidence of the validity of their theories in any aspect of human behavior. In this book he states:

During the summer of 1919 . . . I began to feel more and more dissatisfied with these theories . . . and I began to feel dubious about their claim to scientific status. . . . Why are they so different from Newton's theory and especially from the theory of relativity? . . . It was not my doubting the truth of these theories which bothered me . . . what worried me was . . . that these . . . theories, though posing as sciences, had in fact more in common with primitive myths than with science: that they resembled astrology more than astronomy. (p.34)

Popper goes on to say that he at the time had no reason to believe that Einstein's theory was correct, but Eddington's observation that light did not travel in a straight line but was bent by the sun due to gravitational attraction gave proof of the incorrectness of previous theories (such as Newton's) and so established Einstein's theory as superior to Newton's theory. Popper concluded: (1) it is easy to find confirmation of the validity of theories, (2) confirmation should only be considered if it results from a *risky prediction*, (3) the more a theory "forbids," the better it is, (4) a theory that is not possibly refutable is a poor theory, (5) genuine tests of theories are attempts to refute them, and (6) the only good evidence is negative evidence—i.e., an unsuccessful attempt to refute a particular theory.

Unfortunately, if we accept Popper's contention that the scientific status of any theory rests on its potential for falsification, few theories of psychotherapy qualify as scientific. This may be inevitable.

MODES OF PSYCHOTHERAPY

All psychotherapies are methods of learning. All psychotherapies are intended to change people: to make them think differently (cognition), to make them feel differently (affection), and to make them act differently (behavior). Psychotherapy is learning: it may be learning something new or relearning something one has forgotten; it may be learning how to learn or it may be unlearning; paradoxically, it may even be learning what one already knows.

COGNITION

There are two general ways we learn: directly by experience or indirectly by symbols.

To give a simple example: A child about three years old sees the toast shooting up from a toaster and goes to touch the shiny gadget. The child has no idea that the toaster is hot. Now, how can the child learn that a toaster can be hot and can hurt? One way would be for the child to touch the toaster, thus learning by direct experience. Another way is by symbols (words), by being told: "When we use the toaster, it gets hot, and if you touch it you will be burned."

In both cases, the child learns—in one case, actively (through experience) and in another case, passively (through information).

Some therapists tend to use "active" methods and their clients essentially learn on their own, while some therapists tend to make their clients passive learners. Two strongly contrasting learning styles are represented by Carl Rogers' and Albert Ellis's methodologies. In psychoanalysis, both modes occur. For example, while free associating, the patient may be said to be learning actively. Let us show this by a hypothetical example:

Patient: "And I really think my mother liked my brother more than she liked me. I can't understand why. I tried so hard to win her affection, but somehow I never was able to make her really like me. But recently when I spoke about this with my brother, he told me he always thought that I was mother's favorite. How could this be? Could I have misinterpreted my mother? He thought I was the favorite and I thought he was. Who was? Maybe no one? Maybe we're both pessimists and think that no one can like us? Maybe Mamma liked us both equally, or as equally as possible. How did we come to have opposite conclusions? I think we are just both pessimists, that's what it is! I am sure of it, both of us misinterpreted Mother. . . ."

This is an example of someone talking to himself, conducting a self-analysis, engaged in active learning.

An example of passive learning follows:

C: I had the funniest dream. I was being chased by a rooster, and I was running for my life, and I knew if I got to Lokonner Bay that I would be safe.

T: How do you spell that?

C: I don't know. It is pronounced LOKONNER BAY.

T: And you don't know any such place?

C: No.

T: Can you figure out what Lokonner means?

C: I have been thinking all day about it. It makes no sense to me.

T: Should I tell you what I think it means?

C: Please. I have absolutely no idea.

T: Well, dreams are all symbols. The rooster that is chasing you is a symbol of the male sexual organ, so you are running away from sex. But you believe you will be safe if you can get to Lokonner Bay.

C: But what does Lokonner Bay mean? I have never heard of such a place.

T: Lokonner is probably a contraction for "Love, honor, and obey." What you are saying in your dream is this: Some man is pressuring you to have sex and you want him to marry you. You are afraid to have sex, but if you can get him to marry you (love, honor, and obey), you will be safe.

The examples illustrate two general ways of learning in psychotherapy: actively through self-analysis and passively through being helped to understand the meaning of a dream.

BEHAVIOR

Learning can also occur through action. For example, during World War I, Ernst Simmel was a German army psychiatrist, concerned with curing severely neurotic German soldiers who were suffering from what was then called shell shock (Simmel, 1949). Believing that their condition was caused by repressed hatred of their officers, he gave these men bayoneted rifles and had them attack straw-filled dummies dressed as German officers.

If we had looked on during this psychotherapeutic treatment, we would have seen soldiers repeatedly stabbing mannequins. The modality of treatment was physical action. Plain physical exercise is believed to be psychotherapeutic by some people. Action is used in a number of psychotherapies, especially those that call for body work, such as Bioenergetic Analysis.

One argument for body therapies is that there is no mind. If we can affect the body, that is all that is needed: the body learns, the body is real, all else is an illusion. A contrary argument for body therapies is that the mind does exist, that conditions of the body affect the mind, and that if we work from the outside in, by changing the body we can change the mind. An example might be plastic surgery. Changing someone's looks can affect how that person views himself or herself.

Other examples of physical behavior as psychotherapy would include complex physical activities, such as roleplaying, or doing therapeutic "homework," that is, doing under direction things one would not ordinarily do, such as asking for a date or looking for a job. As in the case of cognitive therapies, behavioral work in therapy can range from active to passive. In examining the various systems in this book, the reader may want to consider how much physical behavior is called for in the particular therapy.

AFFECTION

A third modality in psychotherapy is affection, known more popularly as emotions or feelings. The therapist may believe that this modality will be most effective with a particular client or patient, and so will do things to stir up the person: to raise the individual's emotional state through attempts to make him or her fearful, anxious, angry, hopeful, and so on. We cannot really work directly with the emotions and must reach them indirectly through the intellect or the body.

Emotions are an important part of human psychology. However, the therapist and the client can reach them only indirectly. Consequently, we cannot manipulate emotions in the sense that we can manipulate thinking or behaving. Some systems of psychotherapy are intended to reduce or negate emotions, seeing them as hindering the therapeutic process. Adlerian psychotherapy, for example, is essentially a cognitive therapy, and Adlerians usually see emotions as sabotaging efforts in the therapeutic process. However, in psychodrama, for example, both the words that the therapist will employ and the behavior directed by the other actors are intended to generate strong emotions.

Some people see emotions as epiphenomena accompanying but not affecting therapeutic change, while others see emotions as a powerful agent leading to change and still others see emotions as evidence of change. The whole issue of the relationship of emotions to psychotherapy is unsettled. The reader would do well to attempt to see the place of emotions in the various systems described.

All therapies are essentially combinations of all three of these modalities. While some are rather pure in that they attempt to deal only with the body, the intellect, or the emotions, elements of each apply in most cases. Thus, for example, in Rational-Emotive Therapy, even though rational thinking is utilized for the most part in dealing with the patient, the therapist may give the client direct orders to do certain things (homework) and thus there will be a strong behavioral component. And in a cognitive therapy such as Transactional Analysis, emotionally upsetting situations will develop.

A therapist may think that improvement is a function of one element, but the curative process may actually be something else. It may not be a message that generates a change, but rather the interpretation that the client gives to being handled. Were exactly the same treatment to be done by a robot, it might not have any beneficial psychological effect. Change may well result from the interpretation, "Someone cares for me enough to do this to me."

One final common pathway for all therapies is a new way of seeing life, a reevaluation of self and others. If so, then all therapies are essentially cognitive. Still another way of considering psychotherapy is to see it as a process of "selling"—of trying to help a person to accept a new view of self and of others. From this point of view the psychotherapist is a persuader or a facilitator in attempting to change opinions.

A clear-cut example of persuasion would be attempting to do psychotherapy with someone with a fixed paranoid delusion. A more common example is dealing with a person with incapacitating feelings of inferiority by trying "to sell him" on the notion that he is really OK. Another common example would be dealing with someone with mistaken ideas of marriage or parenting. In all these cases, the therapist is, in a real sense, a salesperson attempting to sell new ideas, new concepts, and new behaviors.

MECHANISMS OF THERAPY

One of the most exciting meetings I ever attended included a major presentation by Carl Rogers on the necessary and sufficient conditions for psychotherapy. It was a most logical and impressive speech and it deeply affected me. However, the next speaker was Albert Ellis, who had been asked to comment on Rogers' paper. Ellis stated that in 25 years of clinical experience he had had many successful cases and that *none* of Rogers' criteria seemed to him to be either necessary or sufficient.

There was not then and there is not now any consensus about what constitutes the basis for change in psychotherapy. Each contributor to this volume uses a section titled *Mechanisms of Psychotherapy* to discuss what makes psychotherapy work. However, I have my own ideas, which I would like to share with readers at this point.

Some 30 years ago, with a psychiatrist colleague, Dr. Bina Rosenberg, I searched through over 300 articles to identify the critical elements necessary for changing people (Corsini & Rosenberg, 1955). We found 220 statements such as "People change when they think that others believe in them" and "The realization that they are not alone makes the difference." We eliminated redundant items and performed a "clinical factor analysis" that identified nine factors.

COGNITIVE FACTORS

Universalization. Clients improve when they realize that they are not alone, that others have similar problems, and that human suffering is universal.

Insight. Growth occurs as clients increasingly come to understand themselves and others and gain different perspectives on their own motives and behavior.

Modeling. People benefit from watching other people. In group therapy both the therapist and other group members may serve as models.

AFFECTIVE FACTORS

Acceptance. This factor reflected the sense of being part of the group and getting unconditional positive regard, especially from the therapist.

Altruism. Change can result from the recognition that one is the recipient of the love and care of the therapist or other members of the group or from being the one who provides love and care to others.

Transference. This factor identifies the emotional bond that occurs between the therapist and the client or between clients in a group setting.

BEHAVIORAL FACTORS

Reality testing. Change becomes possible when clients experiment with new behaviors in the safety of the therapy hour, receiving support and feedback from the therapist and other group members.

Ventilation. This factor encompassed those statements attesting to the value of "blowing off steam" through shouting, crying, or displaying anger in a context in which one could still feel accepted.

Interaction. Clients improve when they are able to openly admit to the group that there is something wrong with themselves or their behavior.

I believe these nine factors encapsulate the basic mechanisms of therapeutic change. Close examination of this model reveals that the cognitive factors imply "Know yourself," the affective factors tell us "Love your neighbor," and the behavioral factors essentially suggest "Do good works." Perhaps there is nothing new under the sun, for this is what philosophers have told us for millenia: know thyself, love thy neighbor, and do good works.

THE CURRENT SITUATION IN PSYCHOTHERAPY

Corsini (1981) lists 250 different systems of psychotherapy. Just as there are some religions that are well known and well accepted, so too, some psychotherapies are well known and well accepted. And just as there are religions viewed as unorthodox and absurd, there are systems of psychotherapy that exist on the fringe of traditional approaches.

I was originally trained as a Rogerian therapist (which I believe is probably the best way for a would-be therapist to start training—and for some people, the best way to remain). After 10 years' experience with this mode of therapy, I applied for a job at a prestigious institute, and while being interviewed I was asked how I dealt with the problem of transference. I think I could not have shocked my learned colleagues more had I slapped them on the face, when I replied, "To the best of my knowledge, none of my clients ever formed a transference relationship with me." They held their mouths open, staring first at me and then at each other, unable to believe what they had heard me say. For this particular group, transference was a necessary factor in psychotherapy, and for someone who claimed to be a psycho-

therapist to deny transference was unthinkable.

In psychotherapy, ideological enclaves are found. Some enclaves consist of people who believe that they have the right, the final, the complete, and the only answer—and that all other systems are incomplete, tentative, weak, or simply mistaken.

People within these enclaves (better known as schools of therapy) tend to communicate mostly with others they meet at conventions. They read each other's writings, and they tend over time to develop specialized vocabularies. They reinforce one another by recounting their successes with the former clients of therapists of different persuasions, "proving" to one another the superiority of their way of thinking and acting. As time goes on, within any particular method of psychotherapy, alternative positions tend to develop, schismatic groups begin to form, and then these groups are either expelled from the original enclave or take off on their own. This has happened many times in the case of people originally trained as Freudian psychoanalysts.

I believe this situation is changing and these ideological boundaries are becoming more permeable. Garfield and Bergin state: "A decisive shift in opinion has quietly occurred; and it has created an irreversible change in professional attitudes about psychotherapy and behavior change. The new view is that the long-term dominance of the major theories is over and that an eclectic position has taken precedence" (1986, p. 7).

I would go even further and state that *all* good therapists are eclectic. This does not mean that they do not follow a particular theory or use specific methods associated with particular approaches to therapy; it does mean that technique and method are always secondary to the clinician's sense of what is the right thing to do with a given client at a given moment in time, irrespective of theory. Put more simply, psychotherapy remains an art. So if formal eclecticism is on the rise, this is all to the good: it shows the maturing of psychotherapy.

Why then, a book such as this? In order to be effectively eclectic, one needs to know as many different theories and systems as possible, from which one can develop a personal theory, a personal system, and an integrated approach. Initially, the neophyte therapist is best served by operating as strictly as possible within the limits of a given system, with close supervision by a skilled practitioner of that system. Later, and with experience, one can begin to develop one's own individual style of therapy.

THE WHOHOWWHOM FACTOR

I have come to believe that what counts in psychotherapy is *who* does it and *how* and to *whom* it is done: the *whohowwhom* factor. This belief developed from my experiences in a small group practice in which all the therapists had the same basic theoretical and operational concepts. We consulted on each other's cases, worked together in co-therapy, met weekly to discuss difficult cases, and came to know each other quite well over a six-year period. However, although we all shared the same theoretical position and generally operated in the same manner, any two new clients who came to our clinic were likely to get entirely different kinds of therapy due to the *whohowwhom* factor. One thera-

pist liked to tell stories to make various points. Another liked to ask Socratic questions. Still another would frequently interrupt to demonstrate errors in the client's thinking and behavior. One played the role of the loving father while another was quite sarcastic. Some were friendly while others were distant. Some saw clients as equals while others saw clients as students who needed to be taught more effective ways to operate. So even in this particular group with a *shared* theory and methodology, there were wide variations in therapy practice and style. The senior therapist, who had trained the others, was in a good position to decide which new client was to go to which therapist. For example, I tended to be assigned difficult adult clients but no adolescents.

Sometimes the *how* variable will be of less importance than the match between *who* and *whom*, because differences in actual technique may be relatively small for some systems. However, at times an apparently limited method, such as the person-centered approach, may achieve superior results for some people when other more complex methods will fail. I am reminded of the fable of the cat and the fox. The fox bragged about how he had so many ways of escaping from dogs. The cat had only one: to climb a tree. Both the cat and the fox were chased by dogs. The cat went up the tree and remained there until the dogs went away. The fox used up all his tricks but eventually was caught. So too, sometimes something simple is superior to something complex, and even in psychotherapy, less can be more.

Research

Many people in the recent history of psychotherapy have wondered about the effectiveness of counseling and psychotherapy. As Dr. Wedding mentions in his preface, he wanted to include a section in every chapter of this book examining relevant research findings for each system, but practically every contributor was against the idea. Nonetheless, the sentiment expressed by Strupp and Bergin (1969, p. 20) is very much on the minds of people:

The problem of psychotherapy research in its most general terms should be reformulated as a standard scientific question: What specific therapeutic interventions produce specific changes in specific patients under specific conditions?

The best and most complete answer I know of was given by C. H. Patterson (1987, p. 247):

Before this model (relative to research) could be implemented we would need (1) a taxonomy of client problems or psychological disorders . . . ; (2) a taxonomy of client personalities; (3) a taxonomy of therapeutic techniques . . .; (4) a taxonomy of therapists; and (5) a taxonomy of circumstances. . . . If we did have such systems of classification, the practical problems would be insurmountable. Assuming five classes of variables, each with ten classifications, . . . a research design would require $10 \times 10 \times 10 \times 10 \times 10$ or 100,000 cells. . . . So, I conclude we don't need complex multivariate analyses and should abandon any attempt to do the crucial, perfect study of psychotherapy. It simply is not possible.

It is difficult for me or anyone else brought up with nomothetic approaches, imbued with Edward Lee Thorndike's concept that anything that exists can be measured, to accept this pessimistic point of view, but I contend that Patterson, who has studied this issue intensively and written widely on the problems of research in counseling and psychotherapy, is essentially correct.

Psychotherapy is an art based on science, and as is true for any art, there can be no simple measures of so complex an activity.

CORRECTION OF A HISTORICAL ERROR

In many historical accounts found in textbooks, an essentially incorrect view of the early years of psychotherapy is recounted. The story given generally goes as follows: In the beginning Sigmund Freud started a brand new system of psychotherapy called psychoanalysis. A number of other people learned about it and became his students. In later years, for a variety of reasons, they decided to separate from him and went on to start their own systems of thought.

In reality, numerous people preceded Freud, doing psychotherapy in a variety of ways. We may start with the Swiss physician, Paul Dubois (1848–1918), one of the first psychotherapists in the modern sense of the term, because his method of treating psychotics was to talk with them in a reasonable manner. Still another person to be considered is Pierre Janet (1859–1947), referred to by Ellenberger as "the first person to found a new system of dynamic psychiatry aimed at replacing those of the nineteenth century" (1970, p. 331). Janet, at about the time that Sigmund Freud began his work, was the best-known and most respected psychotherapist of his time.

There was a great deal of interest and activity in psychotherapy prior to Freud, and there were already the conflicts, schisms, claims, and jealousies that were also to be found later. The whole history of psychotherapy is replete with personality clashes and other signs of struggles for superiority.

In 1902, Sigmund Freud invited several colleagues to meet with him to discuss personality theory. The group was later to be called the Wednesday Psychological Society. Some of the members were independent thinkers, each with his own position; Freud, the oldest, the best known, and the most published, was the host. It is important to understand that some members of this group were *psycho-analysts* and not *psychoanalysts*. Hyphenated, this word meant that these people were interested in the analysis of the psyche; spelled as one word it meant that they were followers of Sigmund Freud.

Three members of this Wednesday night group are the subjects of the next three chapters: Sigmund Freud, Alfred Adler, and Carl Jung. From the beginning, these three moved in quite different directions. Freud was a mechanistic deterministic thinker who developed a system of psychology with essentially biological and hydraulic elements: a system of stresses and strains, conflicts and tensions, with a dynamic interaction between biological instinctive drives and social demands. Adler was essentially a commonsense thinker with a shrewd understanding of people's motivations. Jung was an internalized person, mystical, religious, creative. Freud was the ideal German scientist, a keen student of minutiae, a pedant; Adler was a man of the people, socially oriented and concerned; Jung was an introverted, distant but friendly person. Their theories of personality and their psychotherapeutic systems can be seen as direct extensions of their manifest personalities.

Since the deaths of Freud in 1939, Adler in 1937, and Jung in 1961, the theories of the latter two have remained more or less constant. On the other hand, the theory of Freud has divided into a number of different approaches, some quite different from Freud's original thinking. There are now a variety of psychoanalytic groups with varying orientations. To make a religious analogy, psychoanalysis may be likened to Christianity, with various groups using the same ultimate authority (the *Bible*) but having different interpretations of these basic writings.

During the period 1910 to about 1939, these big three dominated psychotherapy in Europe and the United States. However, a number of other points of view existed at that time, most of which have either disappeared or have been incorporated into eclectic thinking, including the theories of such people as Pierre Janet, Jules Déjèrine, Trigant Burrow, Albert Korzybski, Otto Rank, and Wilhelm Reich. However, a number of theories and methodologies that are considered to be deviations from pure Freudian psychoanalysis, such as the therapies of Harry Stack Sullivan, Karen Horney, and Theodore Reik, are still very much alive.

Since 1940, when Carl Rogers gave his historic Psi Chi paper in Minnesota, a considerable number of alternative systems of psychotherapy have begun. It is difficult to establish the dates of their beginnings because there is generally a considerable lapse of time between when a system starts and when publications about it first appear. But it might not be too far off to say that from about 1900 to 1939 there were three major points of view and about a dozen minor ones in psychotherapy and that during the next 50 years there were a dozen major points of view (including the original three) and perhaps two dozen other ones of consequence.

This situation leads to the speculation that as time goes on there may continue to be an expanding universe of major and minor systems of psychotherapy. If psychotherapy is essentially a matter of philosophy, then ultimately there will be multiple systems; if it is essentially a matter of science, then ultimately there will be one eclectic system.

PSYCHOTHERAPY AND PSYCHOTHERAPIST

There appears to be a concordance between the personality of a psychotherapy innovator and the system he or she has developed. In an article called "Freud, Rogers and Moreno" (Corsini, 1956), I made a comparison between the manifest personalities of these three men and their systems of psychotherapy. I never met Freud, but there is a good deal of biographical information about him, and there seems to be no question that his personality and his method of psychoanalysis were congruent. Freud was a rather shy person, uncomfortable with people, a pedantic bookish type, an intellectual. His methodology—having people lie down, with him sitting behind them and out of sight while he listened intently to what they said—fits exactly his manifest personality. The system and the man seem identical.

I got to know Carl Rogers quite well. As a graduate student at the University of Chicago (1953–55), I was in contact with him both as a client and as a student. In later years I met him on many occasions socially and at professional meetings. Rogers, whether in his social life, as a teacher, or as a therapist, was exactly the same. He and his system were identical.

I also got to know J. L. Moreno, the founder of psychodrama, quite well. I listened to him lecture many times, I was often on the psychodrama stage with him, and we had a social relationship. There was no question at all about the congruence of Moreno's unique personality and his methodology. Again, the system and the man were identical.

What is the implication of these similarities for the reader? I believe that if one is to go into the fields of counseling and psychotherapy, then the best theory and methodology to use have to be one's own! The reader will not be either successful or happy using a method not suited to his or her own personality. The really successful therapist either adopts or develops a theory and methodology congruent with his or her own personality.

In reading these accounts, in addition to attempting to determine which school of psychotherapy seems most sensible, the reader should also attempt to find one that fits his or her philosophy of life, one that seems most right in terms of its theory, and one with a method of operation that appears most appealing in use.

A final value of this book lies in the greater self-understanding that may be gained by close reading. This book about psychotherapies may be psychotherapeutic for the reader. Close reading vertically (chapter by chapter) and then horizontally (section by section) may well lead to personal growth as well as better understanding of the current psychotherapies.

ANNOTATED BIBLIOGRAPHY

Adler, A. (1958). *What life should mean to you.* New York: Capricorn Books.

Adler has special meaning for me because I am both an Adlerian and the co-author of the first textbook on Adlerian psychology written in English (Manaster & Corsini, 1982). *What Life Should Mean to You* converted me, even though by consensus other of Adler's books are more important. I recommend this book as easy reading through which one can learn about a simple and good man and his penetrating thinking about topics of importance. You will learn that a good many so-called modern ideas about the sexes and the environment were topics of concern to Adler.

Corsini, R. J. (1981). *Handbook of innovative psychotherapies.* New York: John Wiley.

In close to 1000 double-columned pages, a total of 66 systems of psychotherapy are systematically summarized, as in *Current Psychotherapies,* generally by the innovators of these systems or by major interpreters. While in the present volume a dozen innovative systems are included, a much broader scope is found in the *Handbook,* which is aimed at the professional therapist rather than the student. The *Handbook* would follow quite well after *Current Psychotherapies* for those who want a more complete and detailed understanding of psychotherapy as a whole.

Ellenberger, H. F. (1970). *The discovery of the unconscious.* New York: Basic Books.

One of the most readable and yet most thoroughly researched volumes, this is in my judgment the number one book in the field. Its subtitle, *The History and Evolution of Dynamic Psychiatry,* explains the book quite well. I recommend it to all who enjoy reading good writing and who can be excited by the evolutionary history of psychotherapy as one of the greatest creations of the human mind.

Frank, J. D. (1961). *Persuasion and healing.* Baltimore: Johns Hopkins Press.

Frank's book stands out for its simplicity and good sense. Frank, who is an outstanding therapist and researcher, is a leading figure in psychotherapy today. This book should be read by all interested in psychotherapy.

Freud, S. (1961). *The psychopathology of everyday life. Complete psychological works of Sigmund Freud (Vol. 6).* London: Hogarth Press. (Originally published 1901)

It would be a major loss to anyone interested in psychotherapy not to read at least this volume. Freud is thrilling to read, for one can almost see how he thinks. The clarity of his position and the forcefulness of his arguments have materially affected all people in the field of applied psychology, and, in a sense, practically every contemporary system of psychotherapy in existence today owes its existence to psychoanalysis in that the new system was developed as an extension of, or as a reaction to, Freud's thinking.

Rogers, C. R. (1942). *Counseling and psychotherapy.* Boston: Houghton Mifflin.

There is a joke about an imaginary

book with the title *Brain Surgery Self-Taught*. Well, no doubt thousands of other psychologists as well as I began with Rogers' book in front of them while talking with clients. From being directive counselors we became nondirective therapists. In 1943, when I first read this book, I was a directive vocational and educational counselor. Within a few months of following the book, I was in deep trouble in my attempt to be a therapist. I wrote to Carl Rogers, who at that time was at Ohio State and who generously helped me. Later, I became his student at the University of Chicago. Over 40 years we maintained our correspondence and our friendship. It is my judgment that this is a fundamental book that every person interested in psychotherapy should read and understand. No matter where one will move to later in one's career, there is no better way to begin as a psychotherapist than by following Rogers' direction.

REFERENCES

Ahnsen, A. (1965). *Eidetic psychotherapy.* Lahore, Pakistan: Nai Mat Booat.

Bach, G. R., & Goldberg, H. (1975). *Creative aggression.* Garden City, NY: Doubleday.

Bindrim, P. (1981). Aqua-energetics. In R. J. Corsini (Ed.), *Handbook of innovative psychotherapies.* New York: John Wiley.

Bion, J. (Ed.) (1948). *Therapeutic social clubs.* London: Lewis.

Cautela, J. (1981). Covert conditioning. In R. J. Corsini (Ed.), *Handbook of innovative psychotherapies.* New York: John Wiley.

Corsini, R. J., & Rosenberg, B. (1955). Mechanisms of group psychotherapy. *Journal of Abnormal and Social Psychology, 51*, 406–411.

Corsini, R. J. (1968). Counseling and psychotherapy. In E. F. Borgotta & W. W. Lambert (Eds.), *Handbook of personality theory and research.* Chicago, IL: Rand McNally.

Corsini, R. J. (1956). Freud, Rogers and Moreno. *Group Psychotherapy, 9*, 274–281.

Corsini, R. J. (Ed.) (1981). *Handbook of innovative psychotherapies.* New York: John Wiley.

Ellenberger, H. (1970). *The discovery of the unconscious.* New York: Basic Books.

Farrelly, F., & Brasma, J. (1974). *Provocative therapy.* Cupertino, CA: Meta.

Garfield, S. L., & Bergin, A. E. (1986). *Handbook of psychotherapy and behavior change.* New York: John Wiley.

Gazda, G. M. (1981). Multiple impact training. In R. J. Corsini (Ed.), *Handbook of innovative psychotherapies.* New York: John Wiley.

Horney, K. (1942). *Self-analysis.* New York: Norton.

Janov, A. (1970). *The primal scream.* New York: Vintage Books.

Lair, J., & Lair, J. C. (1973). *Hey, God, what should I do now?* New York: Doubleday.

Losoncy, L. (1981). *Encouragement therapy.* Englewood Cliffs, NJ: Prentice-Hall.

Manaster, G. J., & Corsini, R. J. (1982). *Individual psychology.* Itasca, IL: F. E. Peacock.

Orr, L., & Ray, S. (1977). *Rebirthing in the new age.* Milbrae, CA: Celestial Arts.

Painter, G., & Vernon, S. (1981). Primary relationship therapy. In R. J. Corsini (Ed.), *Handbook of innovative psychotherapies.* New York: John Wiley.

Patterson, C. H. (1987). Comments. *Person-Centered Review, 1*, 246–248.

Popper, K. R. (1968). *Conjectures and refutations.* Oxford: Oxford University Press.

Reik, T. (1948). *Listening with the third ear.* New York: Farrar and Strauss.

Schmidhoffer, E. (1952). Mechanical group therapy. *Science, 115*, 120–123.

Shorr, J. E. (1972). *Psychoimagination ther-*

apy. New York: Intercontinental Medical Book Co.

Shostrom, E. L., & Montgomery, D. (1978). *Healing love.* Nashville: Abington.

Simmel, E. (1949). War neuroses. In S. Lorand (Ed.), *Psychoanalysis today.* New York: International Universities Press.

Strupp, H. H., & Bergin, A. E. (1969). Some empirical and conceptual bases for coordinated research in psychotherapy. *International Journal of Psychiatry, 1,* 18–90.

van Kaam, A. (1976). *The dynamics of spiritual self-direction.* Denville, NY: Dimension Books.

Wolpe, J. (1958). *Psychotherapy by reciprocal inhibition.* Stanford, CA: Stanford University Press.

SIGMUND FREUD, 1856–1939

2

Psychoanalysis

JACOB A. ARLOW

OVERVIEW

Psychoanalysis is a system of psychology derived from the discoveries of Sigmund Freud. Originating as a method for treating certain psychoneurotic disorders, psychoanalysis has come to serve as the foundation for a general theory of psychology. Knowledge derived from the treatment of individual patients has led to insights into art, religion, social organization, child development, and education. In addition, by elucidating the influence of unconscious wishes on the physiology of the body, psychoanalysis has made it possible to understand and treat many psychosomatic illnesses.

BASIC CONCEPTS

According to Ernst Kris (1950), psychoanalysis may be defined as human nature seen from the vantage point of conflict. Psychoanalysis views the mind as the expression of conflicting forces. Some of these forces are conscious; others, perhaps the major ones, are unconscious. Psychoanalysis emphasizes the importance of unconscious forces in mental life.

Conflict is an inexorable dimension of the human condition. It reflects the contradiction inherent in humans as biological animals and social beings. Each human infant has to be civilized and acculturated to incorporate and integrate the ideals and values, the inhibitions and the taboos, of society. The primary instrument in this process is the family. Later, the more formalized institutions of society take over much of the responsibility for acculturating the individual. In this development, frustration, anger, disappointment, and conflict are inevitable.

The functioning of the mind is related to events in the body. The body is the substrate of all psychology, including psychoanalysis. Basic responses to stimuli are part of man's biological inheritance. These responses, phylogenetically determined, undoubtedly were of evolutionary significance in the struggle of the species to survive. A fundamental principle of psychoanalytic theory is that human psychology is governed by a tendency to seek pleasure and to avoid pain: the *pleasure principle* (Freud, 1911). Although this principle is operative throughout life, it is patently and overwhelmingly dominant in the first few years of existence. The earliest experiences of pleasure and pain play a crucial role in shaping each individual's psychological structure. (The term *structure*, as used in psychoanalysis, pertains to the repetitive, relatively stable, organized forms of mental responses and functioning.) The impact of the earliest experiences is intensified in the case of the human infant, because in contrast to animals, the human has a much longer period of dependence upon adults. Without their care and solicitude, he could not survive. This fact of biology eventuates in an early and abiding attachment to others.

Freud's revolutionary perceptions represent a fusion of the most advanced humanistic and scientific ideas of the late nineteenth and early twentieth centuries. In psychoanalysis, he combined the liberal ideal of respect for the integrity of each individual with a rigorous attempt to establish a scientific method for studying the individual as a living, social entity. He emphasized clinical observation. Theory for Freud was a superstructure erected on clinical observation that could be altered by new findings. Accordingly, it was essential to establish an objective method by which reliable observations could be made. This prerequisite Freud met in his formulation of the psychoanalytic situation which is at the same time a form of therapy and a method of investigation.

Psychoanalysis is the most extensive, inclusive, and comprehensive system of psychology. It encompasses humans' inner experiences and outer behavior, their biological nature and social roles, how they function individually and how they function in groups.

Essentially, psychoanalysis continues the rationalist spirit of Greek philosophy, to "know thyself." Knowing one's self, however, is understood in quite a different way. It is not to be found in the pursuit of formal, logical analysis of thinking. As far as the individual is concerned, the sources of his neurotic suffering are by their very nature "unknowable." They reside outside the realm of consciousness, barred from awareness by virtue of their painful, unacceptable quality. By enabling the patient to understand how his neurotic symptoms and behavior represent derivatives of unconscious conflicts, psychoanalysis permits the patient to make rational choices instead of responding automatically. Self-knowledge of a very special kind strengthens the individual's ability to control his fate and his happiness. For the successfully analyzed individual, freedom from neurotic inhibition and suffering is often experienced as a liberating, self-fulfilling transformation, which enables him not only to actualize his own potential but to contribute to the advancement and happiness of others. Knowing one's self may have far-reaching social implications. It is important to bear this in mind, because even under the best of circumstances, because of practical difficulties, only a relatively small number of people at best can or will be analyzed.

OTHER SYSTEMS

Almost every form of modern psychotherapy owes some debt to psychoanalysis. As Leo Rangell (1973) has shown, most forms of psychotherapy now widely practiced are based on some element of psychoanalytic theory or technique. Usually some procedure or a particular concept is borrowed from psychoanalysis and used as the rationale for a particular treatment. This is not to imply that other forms of therapy are invalid or ineffectual. Quite the contrary. Although there are many ways to treat neuroses, there is but one way to understand them—psychoanalysis (Fenichel, 1945). It has been stated in many quarters that psychoanalysts believe their method is the only worthwhile form of treatment. This is not true. There are many situations where a nonanalytic treatment is preferable to an analytic one. For many forms of mental illness, psychoanalysis is inadvisable or contraindicated. However, psychoanalysis is the only approach that makes clear what is going on in neurosis; it is the one theory that gives a scientific explanation to the effectiveness of all psychotherapies.

Historically, the line of descent of *Jungian analysis* and *Adlerian therapy* from psychoanalysis is clear. Both Carl Jung and Alfred Adler broke with Freud early in the history of the psychoanalytic movement. Jung had serious differences with Freud concerning the nature of drives. His approach places less emphasis on maturational and developmental processes. Jung emphasized the significance of culturally determined, unconsciously transmitted symbolic representations of the principal themes of human existence. Behind the transformations of individual experience, Jung and his followers see the constant recurrence of mythic themes common to all humanity. Jung's concept of the transmission of unconscious fantasies through a collective unconscious has been criticized as being too mystical. In some respects, Jung's views on the collective unconscious correspond to the Freudians' concept of primitive universal fantasy, but the latter regard these only as vehicles for derivatives of the instinctual drives of childhood rather than original determinants of behavior. They are secondary rather than primary factors in shaping personality. Some of Jung's concepts are particularly useful in elucidating the more regressed manifestations seen in schizophrenic patients (Jung, 1909).

Adler (Ansbacher & Ansbacher, 1956) believed the role of social and political pressures was underestimated by Freudian psychoanalysts. There was considerable validity to this criticism, analysts having concentrated primarily on the transformation of the derivatives of the energy of the sexual drive, the *libido*. To Adler, the cause of conflicts was determined by factors such as inferiority over social status, inadequate physical endowment, sexual weakness, and discrimination. Many of his concepts presaged later psychoanalytic contributions concerning the role of self-esteem, particularly in relation to the so-called narcissistic personality disorders.

Recent years have seen the burgeoning of many forms of therapy in which the central aspect of the treatment consists of self-expression, releasing emotion, overcoming inhibitions, and articulating in speech and behavior the fantasies or impulses previously suppressed. The *encounter movement* (Burton, 1969; Schultz, 1967) represents one such school. *Primal scream therapy* is another. These forms of treatment represent exaggerations and caricatures of the principle of emotional catharsis that Freud advanced in his early studies of hysteria (Freud, 1895). At that time, he thought that discharge of pent-up emotion could have a beneficial therapeutic effect. Subsequent experience with the treatment of neurotic patients, however, convinced Freud that this method was limited and, in the long run, ineffectual, since it did not give sufficient weight to the needs of self-punishment and the various defenses the ego uses to ward off anxiety. In the expressive forms of treatment, the group experience plays an enormous role in mitigating anxiety. Expressing in the presence of others what is ordinarily inexpressible can go far in ameliorating a sense of guilt. The burden of guilt, furthermore, is lightened by the knowledge that other members of the group admit to the same or similar feelings and impulses. Everyone's guilt is no one's guilt (Sachs, 1942). The effect of such treatment, however, depends to a large extent on the continuity of contact with the group experience. Since no essential insight or psychological restructuring has taken place, the tendency for relapse once the group experience is discontinued is very strong. Furthermore, there are cases in which the individual perceives the temptation and the opportunity to express derivatives of forbidden impulses as so overwhelming a danger that he is unable to cope with it and in some instances may suffer a psychotic break.

Mitigating the influence of the superego on the total psychological equilibrium seems to be the essential feature of the *rational-emotive system* of Albert Ellis (1970). Ellis attempts to get the patient to change his values, particularly in regard to sexuality, helping relieve the patient of irrational guilt that may have inhibited many as-

pects of his life and behavior. When this treatment is effective, it can be understood in terms of the patient's having made an identification with the therapist's personality and values. The therapist comes to serve as an auxiliary superego that may replace or alter the patient's patterns of judgment, self-evaluation, and ideal aspirations. This is similar to what one observes in cases where individuals are "cured" of their difficulties through religious conversion, usually as the result of an attachment to some charismatic religious (sometimes political) figure.

As part of the psychoanalytic situation, the analyst listens patiently, sympathetically, uncritically, and receptively. This aspect of psychoanalytic technique forms the core of the nondirective listening of Carl R. Rogers (1951). In other forms of treatment, sympathetic listening may be combined with counseling, trying to guide the patient in a rational manner through the real and imaginary pitfalls of living. Otto Fenichel (1945) pointed out that verbalization of vaguely felt anxieties may bring relief because the individual can face concretized, verbalized ideas better than unclear, emotional sensations. Transference also plays a role. The fact that a therapist spends time and shows interest and sympathy reawakens echoes of previous situations of having been helped by friends or relatives. For lonely people it can be a substantial relief to have someone to talk with. When the patient can see some connection between his worries and other patterns of behavior, he feels an accession of strength in relation to the deeper unconscious forces within his personality.

All the foregoing forms of therapy make use of one or more of the fundamental features of psychoanalytic therapy, namely, a setting in which the patient can express thoughts and feelings spontaneously and freely to an uncritical, receptive observer; the achievement of insight through interpretation; and finally, and perhaps most important, an awareness of the power of the transference relationship.

Other forms of therapy such as *Gestalt therapy* (Perls, Hefferline & Goodman, 1951), *reality therapy* (Glasser, 1967), and *behavior therapy* (Wolpe, 1958) illustrate the principles just mentioned. Essentially, the therapist is unconsciously cast in the role of serving as a model or acting as the transference instrument in an effort either to deny or to project the effects of internal conflicts. The therapist unconsciously joins the patient in a pattern of playing out some derivative of the patient's childhood fantasies. Accordingly, such forms of therapy play into the patients' tendency to try to act out expressions of their unconscious conflicts. For this reason, one can expect that such forms of therapy can have only limited usefulness and short-term effectiveness.

HISTORY

PRECURSORS

Psychoanalysis, as originated by Sigmund Freud (1856–1939), represented an integration of the major European intellectual movements of his time. This was a period of unprecedented advance in the physical and biological sciences. A new liberal humanism was abroad, a humanism based on materialist philosophy and the free exercise of thought. The crucial issue of the day was Darwin's theory of evolution. A group of young biologists, deeply influenced by the teachings of Hermann Helmholtz (Berenfeld, 1944), took it as a matter of principle to explain biological phenomena solely in terms of physics and chemistry. One member of that group was Ernst Brücke (Jones, 1953), later chief of the biological research laboratories at the University of Vienna, where Freud went to pursue a career as a research biologist. Models borrowed from physics, chemistry, and the theory of evolution recur regularly throughout Freud's writings, but most strikingly in his early psychological works.

Freud came to psychoanalysis by way of neurology. During his formative years, great strides were being made in neurophysiology and neuropathology. Freud himself contributed to the advancement of the science with original work on the evolution of the elements of the central nervous system, on aphasia, on cerebral palsy, and on the physiological functions of cocaine. In *The Interpretation of Dreams*, he offered a model of the human mind based on the physiology of the reflex arc.

This was also the time when psychology separated from philosophy and began to emerge as an independent science. Freud was interested in both fields. He knew the works of the "association" school of psychologists (J. F. Herbart, Alexander von Humboldt, and Wilhelm Wundt), and he had been impressed by the way Gustav Fechner (Freud, 1894) applied concepts of physics to problems of psychological research. Ernest Jones (1953) has suggested that the idea of using free association as a therapeutic technique may be traced to the influence of Herbart. In the mid-nineteenth century, there was great interest in states of split consciousness (Zilboorg & Henry, 1941). The French neuropsychiatrists had taken the lead in studying conditions such as somnambulism, multiple personalities, fugue states, and hysteria. Hypnotism was one of the principal methods used in studying these conditions. The leading figures in this field of investigation were Jean Charcot, Pierre Janet, Hippolyte Bernheim, and Ambrose Liebault. Freud had the opportunity to work with several of them and was particularly influenced by Charcot.

BEGINNINGS

Freud wrote two essays on the history of psychoanalysis: *The History of the Psychoanalytic Movement* (1914a) and *An Autobiographical Study* (1925). Both works concerned primarily how Freud's theories evolved. In what follows, this evolution is traced by organizing developments around Freud's major works:

1. *Studies on Hysteria (1895)*
2. *The Interpretation of Dreams*
3. *On Narcissism*
4. *Papers on Metapsychology*
5. *Dual Instinct Theory*
6. *Structural Theory*

Studies on Hysteria (1895)

The history of psychoanalysis proper begins when Josef Breuer, a Viennese physician with research interests, told Freud about a remarkable experience he was having with a patient (Anna O.) who seemed to be curing herself of the symptoms of hysteria by means of talking. Breuer had observed that when he placed his patient into a hypnotic trance and had her relate what was oppressing her mind, she would tell of some highly emotional fantasy or event in her life. If the telling of this material was accompanied by a massive outburst of emotion, the patient would be relieved of her symptoms. Once awake, the patient was totally unaware of the "traumatic event" she had related or of its connection to her disability. Freud tried the same procedure on other patients and was able to confirm Breuer's findings. They summarized their findings in a publication entitled *Studies on Hysteria* (1895), in which they reasoned that the symptoms of hysteria were the result of an undischarged quantity of emotion, connected with a very painful memory. These memories have been split off from their connection with the rest of the mind but they continue to exert a dynamic, intrusive effect in the form of symptoms. The task of therapy was to bring about recollection of the forgotten event together with a cathartic abreaction of the undischarged emotion. Working independently, Freud came to the conclusion that the traumatic events involved in causing hysteria took place in childhood and were regularly of a sexual nature. Because at the time it was generally believed that children before the age of puberty had no sexual drives, Freud was led to the conclusion that the patients he observed had all been seduced by an older person. Further investigation demonstrated that this was not always true. Freud unknowingly had come upon the data that were to serve him as the basis for the discovery of childhood sexuality.

The Interpretation of Dreams (1900)

The second phase of Freud's discoveries concerned a solution to the riddle of the dream. The idea that dreams could be understood occurred to Freud when he observed how regularly they appeared in the associations of his neurotic patients. *Dreams and symptoms*, he came to realize, had a similar structure. They were both the end product of a compromise between two sets of conflicting forces in the mind, between unconscious childhood sexual wishes seeking discharge and the repressive activity of the rest of the mind. In effecting this compromise, an inner censor disguised and distorted the representation of the unconscious sexual wishes from childhood. This process makes dreams and symptoms unintelligible. The kind of wishes that entered into the formation of dreams were connected with the pleasurable sensations that children get from stimulating the mouth, anus, skin, and genitals, and resembled the various forms of overt sexual activity typical for the perversions.

The Interpretation of Dreams was at the same time a partial record of Freud's own self-analysis. In it Freud first described the Oedipus complex, perhaps the most striking of his many ideas destined to disturb the sleep of the world. In addition, in the concluding chapter of this work, Freud attempted to elaborate a theory of the human mind that would encompass dreaming, psychopathology, and normal functioning. The central principle of this theory is that mental life represents an unrelenting conflict between the conscious and unconscious parts of the mind. The unconscious parts of the mind contain the biological, instinctual sexual drives, impulsively pressing for discharge. Opposed to these elements are forces that are conscious or readily available to consciousness, functioning at a logical, realistic, and adaptive level. Because the fundamental principle of this conceptualization of mental functioning concerned the depth or "layer" of an idea in relationship to consciousness, this theory was called the topographic theory.

In the years that followed the publication of The Interpretation of Dreams, Freud used the concepts of unconscious conflict, infantile sexuality, and the Oedipus complex to attain new insights into the psychology of religion, art, character formation, mythology, and literature. These ideas were published in a group of major contributions: The Psychopathology of Everyday Life (1901), Jokes and Their Relationship to the Unconscious (1905a), Three Essays on Sexuality (1905b), and, somewhat later, Totem and Taboo (1913).

On Narcissism (1914)

The next phase in the development of Freud's concepts came when he attempted to apply methods of psychoanalysis to understanding the psychoses. Up to this point, Freud saw the major conflict in mental life as a struggle between the energy of the sexual drive (libido), which was directed towards preserving the species, and the ego, the self-preservative drives. This frame of reference did not seem adequate to elucidate the symptoms of psychosis. These phenomena, Freud felt, could be better understood in terms of a conflict between libidinal energies vested in the self and libidinal energies vested in the representation of objects of the external world. The concept of narcissism proved useful, in addition, in explaining such phenomena as falling in love and pride in one's own children (Freud, 1914a, 1921).

The Metapsychological Papers (1915)

From his clinical observations, Freud came to recognize certain inconsistencies in his topographical model of the mind. He noted, for example, that many unconscious mental contents were, in fact, anti-instinctual and self-punitive; clearly, a strict qualitative differentiation of mental phenomena according to the single criterion of accessibility to consciousness was no longer tenable. In several papers, notably *Repression* (1915a) and *The Unconscious* (1915b), Freud tried to synthesize his psychological concepts under the heading of *metapsychology*. By this term he meant "describing a mental process in all of its aspects—dynamic, topographic, and economic." The papers written during this period represent a transitional phase in Freud's thinking before he embarked upon a major revision of his theory.

The Dual Instinct Theory (1920)

The role of aggression in mental life convinced Freud that he had to revise his theory of drives. He observed how self-directed aggression operated in depression, masochism, and, generally, in the many ways people punish themselves. Individuals wrecked by success, persons who commit crimes out of a sense of guilt in the hope of being punished, and patients in therapy who respond negatively to the insight they achieve during treatment are typical of this category. In 1920, in his essay *Beyond the Pleasure Principle*, Freud extended his dualistic concept by putting forward the notion of two instincts, libido and aggression, both derived in turn from broader, all-pervading biological principles—an instinct of love (Eros) and an instinct towards death and self-destruction (Thanatos).

The Structural Theory (1923)

Having recognized that in the course of psychic conflict, conscience may operate at both conscious and/or unconscious levels, and having perceived that even the methods by which the mind protects itself from anxiety may be unconscious, Freud reformulated his theory in terms of a structural organization of the mind. Mental functions were grouped according to the role they played in conflict. The three major subdivisions of the psychic apparatus he called the ego, the id, and the superego. The ego comprises a group of functions that orient the individual toward the external world and mediates between it and the inner world. It acts, in effect, as an executant for the drives and correlates these demands with a proper regard for conscience and the world of reality. The id represents the organization of the sum total of the instinctual pressures on the mind, basically the sexual and aggressive impulses. The superego is a split-off portion of the ego, a residue of the early history of the individual's moral training and a precipitate of the most important childhood identifications and ideal aspirations. Under ordinary circumstances, there is no sharp demarcation among these three major components of the mind. Intrapsychic conflict, however, makes the differences and the demarcations stand out clearly.

One of the major functions of the ego is to protect the mind from internal dangers, from the threat of a breakthrough into consciousness of conflict-laden impulses. The difference between mental health and illness depends upon how well the ego can succeed in this responsibility. In his monograph *Inhibitions, Symptoms and Anxiety* (1926), Freud detailed that the key to the problem is the appearance of the unpleasant affective state of anxiety, perhaps the most common symptom of psychoneurosis. Anxiety serves as a warning signal alerting the ego to the danger of over-whelming anxiety or panic that may supervene if a repressed, unconscious wish emerges into consciousness. Once warned, the ego may undertake any of a wide array of defenses. This new view had far-reaching implications for both theory and practice.

CURRENT STATUS

Since Freud, developments in psychoanalysis have been many and varied. Under the leadership of Melanie Klein (1932), the English school of psychoanalysis has emerged. It emphasizes the importance of primitive fantasies of loss (the *depressive* position) and persecution (the *paranoid* position) in the pathogenesis of mental illness. This school is particularly influential in Europe and South America.

When Nazi persecution forced many of the outstanding European analysts to migrate to this country, the United States became the world center for psychoanalysis. The leading figures in this movement were Heinz Hartmann, Ernst Kris, and Rudolph Loewenstein. These three collaborators (1946, 1949) tried to establish psychoanalysis as a general psychology. They did so by extending Hartmann's concepts of the adaptive function of the ego (Hartmann, 1939) and clarifying fundamental working hypotheses concerning drives and development of the psychic apparatus. Their theories integrated the invaluable contributions of Anna Freud (1936, 1951) derived from studies of long-term child development. In the course of these investigations, several questions concerning the sense of self were posed. How and when does the sense of self develop and what are the consequences to the individual if the

process miscarries? Edith Jacobson (1954), D. W. Winnicott (1953), and John Bowlby (1958) were among those who contributed to the clarification of the problem. The most cogent studies in the field, however, come from the meticulous clinical and developmental observations conducted by Margaret Mahler (1975) and her coworkers. All of these studies underline the importance of the early attachment to the mother and the vicissitudes of the processes of separation and individuation.

These early experiences seem to play a crucial role in the development of self-esteem. Considerations of self-esteem are central in the psychology of narcissistic character disorders and borderline personalities. Clinical and theoretical illumination of these conditions were offered in the writings of Annie Reich (1973) and have been extended in an original way by Heinz Kohut (1971) and Otto Kernberg (1968).

More recent developments in the field are too numerous to describe. David Rapaport (1951) and several of his students have integrated psychoanalytic theories with broad psychological principles and findings. Jacob Arlow and Charles Brenner (1964) have attempted to synthesize newer clinical findings into the framework of the structural theory. Other authors, critical of some of the propositions of psychoanalysis, are attempting to reformulate psychoanalytic theory in terms of communications theory (Peterfreund, 1971; Schafer, 1976) and neurophysiology (Rubenstein, 1967). Some authors have emphasized the importance of interpersonal relationships (Sullivan, 1953) and the role of identification and the transformations of the personality during the life cycle

(Erikson, 1968). Karen Horney (1940) and Erich Fromm (1955) have stressed the social, political, and cultural factors in the development of the individual.

The American Psychoanalytic Association is the largest and most prestigious of psychoanalytic societies in the United States. It consists of almost 2,500 members and affiliates. It comprises 33 affiliate societies and conducts centers for the professional training of psychoanalysts in 26 institutes in the United States. With the exception of some recent changes, admission to training in affiliate institutes and to membership in the American Psychoanalytic Association is restricted to members of the medical profession. (This condition does not hold in the other affiliate societies of the International Psychoanalytical Association.) Standards for training in psychoanalysis are set by the Board on Professional Standards of the American Psychoanalytic Association. In addition to the requirement of an M.D. degree, a candidate must have had residency training in psychiatry. The course of study is from four to eight or more years and consists of three parts: (1) the training analysis, (2) formal courses in the literature and technique of psychoanalysis, and (3) the treatment of at least three or four patients under the supervision of a training analyst.

There are many other psychoanalytic organizations in the United States. The American Academy of Psychoanalysis is a scientific organization that has not in the past conducted programs of training. Although many of its members belong to the American Psychoanalytic Association, membership in the academy is not restricted to physicians. There are, in addition, several societies composed of physicians, psychologists, social workers, and other professionals who have received training at either the William Alanson White Institute or other centers for training in the United States. Perhaps the largest of these is the National Psychological Association for Psychoanalysis.

Recent years have witnessed a rich burgeoning of the psychoanalytic literature. In addition to the long-standing major publications in the field, such as the *American Psychoanalytic Association Journal*, the *International Journal of Psychoanalysis*, the *Psychoanalytic Quarterly*, the *Psychoanalytic Study of the Child*, the *Psychoanalytic Review*, and *Psychiatry*, many new journals have appeared, such as the *International Psychoanalytic Review*, the *Chicago Annual of Psychoanalysis*, the *International Journal of Psychoanalytic Psychotherapy*, *Psychoanalysis and Contemporary Science*, and *Psychological Issues*.

The 24-volume *Standard Edition of the Complete Works of Sigmund Freud* is the basic source for theory and instruction in psychoanalysis. In 1954 Fenichel wrote *The Psychoanalytic Theory of Neurosis*, the closest work to a textbook in psychoanalysis. Unfortunately, this valuable source book has not been brought up to date. The 3-volume biography of Freud by Ernest Jones (1953–57) contains a comprehensive overview of Freud's contributions. The most concise, accurate, and readable statement of current psychoanalytic theory is to be found in Charles Brenner's (1973) *An Elementary Textbook of Psychoanalysis*. Alexander Grinstein (1971) has been editing *The Index of Psychoanalytic Writings*. Consisting of 14 volumes, it covers all the psychoanalytic literature up to and including the year 1969.

PERSONALITY

THEORY OF PERSONALITY

The psychoanalytic theory of personality is based on a number of fundamental principles. The first and foremost is determinism. Psychoanalytic theory assumes that mental events are not random, haphazard, accidental, unrelated phenomena. Thoughts, feelings, and impulses are events in a chain of casually related phenomena. They result from antecedent experiences in the life of the individual. Through appropriate methods of investigation, the connection between current mental experience and past events can be established. Many of these connections are unconscious.

The second principle is the topographic viewpoint. Every mental element is judged according to its accessibility to consciousness. The process by which certain mental contents are barred from consciousness is called repression, an active effort to keep certain thoughts out of awareness to avoid pain or unpleasure. Psychoanalytic investigation of normal and pathological phenomena has demonstrated the important role unconscious forces play in the behavior of the individual. Some of the most important decisions in one's life may be determined by unconscious motives.

The third basic approach is the dynamic viewpoint. This pertains to the interaction of libidinal and aggressive impulses. Because of their biological roots, these impulses have been loosely and inaccurately referred to as instincts. The correct term in psychoanalytic theory, translated from the German Treib, is drives. Because this has become common usage, instinct and drive will be used interchangeably in the rest of this chapter.

It is important to distinguish drives in humans from instinctive behavior in animals. Instinct in animals is a stereotyped response, usually with clear survival value evoked by specific stimuli in particular settings. As used in psychoanalysis, drive is a state of central excitation in response to stimuli. This sense of central excitation impels the mind to activity, with the ultimate aim of bringing about the cessation of tension, a sense of gratification. Drives in humans are capable of a wide variety of complex transformations. Drive theory in psychoanalysis is intended to account for the psychological findings gathered in the clinical setting. Biology supports many of the formulations regarding the libidinal drive. This is not so in the case of the aggressive drive, a concept founded almost exclusively on psychological data (Brenner, 1971).

The fourth approach to personality theory has been called the genetic viewpoint, tracing the origins of later conflicts, character traits, neurotic symptoms, and psychological structure to the crucial events and wishes of childhood and the fantasies they generated. The genetic approach is not a theory; it is an empirical finding confirmed in every psychoanalysis. In effect, it states that in many ways, we never get over our childhood. We do not have a complete answer to the question why we fail to do so. One factor undoubtedly resides in the long period of biological dependence characteristic of the human infant. There seems to be a broad tendency in the higher forms of life for the earliest experiences to have a persistent and crucial effect on later development. Freud's observations about the crucial role of events in early childhood in shaping later behavior have been confirmed by ethologists in their studies of other forms of life (Lorenz, 1952; Tinbergern, 1951).

Personality evolves out of the interaction between inherent biological factors and the vicissitudes of experience. For any individual, given an average expectable environment, one may anticipate a more or less predictable sequence of events constituting the steps in the maturation of the drives and the other components of the psychic apparatus. Whatever happens to the individual—illness, accidents, deprivation, abuse, seduction, abandonment—in some way will alter the native endowment and will contribute towards determining the ultimate personality structure.

The terminology used for describing the development of the drives originally applied only to the libidinal drives. Freud had conceptualized them first and did not postulate an independent aggressive drive until later. The early phases of the libidinal drives are quite distinct and clearly relate to specific zones of the body. The somatic substrate of aggression is not so clearly defined. Psychoanalysis postulates that whenever drive activity is involved, some mixture or fusion of the sexual and the aggressive drive energies has taken place. Ordinarily one of the component elements is more dominant than the other.

VARIETY OF CONCEPTS

Oral Phase

The earliest phase of instinctual life is oral. This phase extends from birth to approximately 18 months. The chief source of libidinal gratification centers around feeding and the organs connected with that function—the mouth, the lips, and the tongue. Gratification of oral needs in the form of sa-

tiety brings about a state of freedom from tension and induces sleep. Many disturbances of sleep seem to be connected with unconscious fantasies of an oral libidinal nature (Lewin, 1946, 1949). Biting and sucking serve both to gratify oral drives and to "explore" the world. During the oral phase, the basic orientation of the psychic apparatus is to take in what is pleasurable and to expel what is unpleasant. According to Karl Abraham (1924), people whose early oral needs have been excessively frustrated turn out to be pessimists. On the other hand, individuals whose oral needs have been gratified tend to have a more optimistic view of the world.

Anal Phase

Between the ages of 18 months and 3 years, the main source of pleasure and libidinal gratification comes from retaining and passing feces. The fundamental instinctual orientation concerns what is to be retained and is therefore valuable, and what is to be expelled and ultimately becomes worthless. During the anal phase, interest in the bodily processes, in smelling, touching, and playing with feces, are paramount. Regarded for a while as an extruded portion of one's self, the feces are considered as a particularly valuable and highly prized possession. The disgust that those who train the child evince and the shame the child is made to feel may contribute toward a lowered sense of self-esteem. In reaction, the child may respond by stubborn assertiveness, contrary rebelliousness, and the determination to be in control of whatever happens to him. Through reaction formation the child may overcome the impulse to soil by becoming meticulously clean, excessively punctual, and quite parsimonious in handling possessions (Freud, 1917).

Phallic Phase

After the third year, the main area of libidinal gratification shifts to the genitals. For both boys and girls, the penis becomes the principal object of interest in the phallic phase. At this time the clitoris, embryologically an analogue of the penis, begins to be appreciated for the pleasurable sensations evoked by stimulation. Some awareness of the pleasure potential of the vagina is present at this phase in many little girls (Greenacre, 1967). Also prominent in the phallic phase are exhibitionistic and voyeuristic wishes.

By the time children have reached the phallic phase, they have made marked advances in the complexity of their psychological structure. The basic orientation during this phase is therefore much more subtle and complicated. Although children remain basically self-centered, their relations with others in the environment take on a rich texture. They love and want to possess those who give them pleasure; they hate and want to annihilate those who stand in their way and frustrate them. They become curious about sexual differences and about the origin of life and in a primitive childlike way fashion their own answers to these important questions. They want to love and to be loved, to be admired and to be like those they admire. They may overidealize themselves or share a sense of power by feeling at one with those they idealize. During this time, children may entertain intensely hostile wishes with the penis serving as an instrument for aggression. This gives rise to intense fears of retaliation, usually directed against the penis. It is also the era of the discovery of the anatom-

ical distinction between the sexes, a phase from which the fear of the female genital and envy of the male genital originate.

Three salient features in the development of the drives must be mentioned here. First is the concept of autoerotism. When gratification of a particular instinctual urge is not forthcoming, it is always possible for children to gratify themselves by stimulating the appropriate zones of their bodies, combining such activities with appropriate fantasies. This evolves into the more common forms of childhood masturbation. Second, as the individual passes from one libidinal phase to another, the interest in the gratification of the preceding phase is not completely surrendered. It is only partially superseded by the succeeding libidinal gratification. When there is a particularly strong and persistent attachment to libidinal gratification from a particular object of infancy, one speaks of fixation. Fixations are usually unconscious and often serve as a focus for symptom formation later in life. A third feature of libidinal development is the potentiality for regression, the reactivation of or the return to an earlier mode of libidinal gratification. Regressive reactivation of earlier modes of mental functioning is common and not necessarily pathological. Usually the regression reactivates some childhood libidinal impulse that had been involved in the process of fixation.

For each of the aforementioned phases of development, there is a characteristic danger. During the oral phase, the greatest danger is that the mother will not be available. This is usually referred to as the danger of loss of the (need-satisfying) object. During the anal phase, after the concept of the mother as an independent entity has crystallized, *losing the mother's love* constitutes the danger. Typical of the phallic phase is fear of retaliation or punishment for forbidden sexual and aggressive wishes. The kind of punishment usually fantasied by both boys and girls takes the form of injury to the body, specifically to the genitals. For this reason, the danger characteristic of the phallic phase is referred to as the *fear of castration*. Later in life, after external prohibitions and threats of punishment have been internalized into the personality in the form of the superego, *fear of conscience* takes its place among the danger situations. Each one of these situations evokes anxiety as a signal alerting the ego to set in motion various mental maneuvers to eliminate or minimize the danger. These maneuvers Anna Freud (1936) called the *mechanisms of defense*, because they protect the rest of the personality from the unpleasant affect of anxiety.

The combined influence on the mind of the libidinal and aggressive wishes constitute the id. The other components of the mind are the ego and the superego. It will be possible to present only a few observations on the development of these psychological structures. The earliest psychological experience of the infant is most likely one of global sensory impingement (Spitz, 1955). The infant makes no differentiation between self and the rest of the world, between what is in the body and what is outside of it. The inherent capacities to perceive, to move, and later to speak mature gradually. The concept of the self as an independent entity develops over a period of two to three years (Jacobson, 1954; Mahler, 1975). There is evidence that for a certain period during the first

year of life, the child is unable to distinguish between himself and the person who cares for him. Certain objects in the external world, for example, a blanket or a stuffed animal toy, may be experienced at times as being part of the self and at other times as part of the external world (Winnicott, 1953).

At first the instinctual drives center mainly on the self—a state called *narcissism*. As other people come to be appreciated as sources of sustenance, protection, and gratification, some of the energy of the libidinal drive settles (is vested) on mental representations of others. Technically, these others are referred to as *love objects*, or *objects* for short. At its core, the human personality retains a considerable complement of childish self-centeredness. The capacity to need others, to love, to want to please, and to want to become like others is one of the most significant indicators of psychological maturity. In addition to constitutional factors, the quality of experience with objects during the early years is decisive in shaping the all-important capacity to love and identify with others. Disturbances in this process because of traumatic experiences or poor object relations contribute to the severe forms of pathology known as narcissistic character disorders, borderline states, and the psychoses.

Needing, wanting, and identifying with valued persons are fraught with the dangers of frustration, disappointment, and, inevitably, conflict. The imperious wishes of childhood can never be gratified in full. Inexorably, relations with the important objects become a mixture of love and hatred. Such feelings come to a climactic crisis with the oedipal longings of the phallic phase. As a rule during the ages of three to six, the child develops intense erotic longings for the parent of the opposite sex and a hostile competitive orientation toward the parent of the same sex. Circumstances may induce enormous variations in this basic pattern, including a total inversion of the choice of sexual object. It is the responsibility of the ego to deal with these conflicts. Under favorable circumstances, oedipal wishes are given up, repressed. They become unconscious. They are, however, not totally obliterated but continue as a potential source of instinctual pressure in the form of unconscious fantasies. Disguised versions of these fantasies may persist in consciousness as the familiar daydreams of childhood. They continue to exert an important influence on nearly every aspect of mental life: on the forms and objects of adult sexuality; on creative, artistic, vocational, and other sublimated activity; on character formation; and on whatever neurotic symptoms the individual may develop later (Brenner, 1973).

Under favorable circumstances, the child relinquishes most of the hostile and neurotic impulses of the Oedipus complex and identifies with the parent of the same sex, especially with his or her moral standards and prohibitions. This is the matrix of the moral part of the personality called the superego. This agency observes the self and judges its thoughts and actions in terms of what it considers right and wrong. It may prescribe punishment, reparation, or repentance for wrongdoing or may reward the self with heightened esteem and affection for virtuous thought and action. The superego is the seed of the conscience and the source of guilt. Under certain conditions, its functioning may be as impulsive and demanding as any primitive instinctual wish of the id.

This is particularly true in states of depression.

Latency Period

With the passing of the Oedipus complex and the consolidation of the superego, a relatively quiescent phase ensues, called the *latency period*. Children now can be socialized and they can direct their interests to the larger world, where the process of education becomes a more formalized experience. This state prevails until the onset of *puberty and adolescence*. The transformations that take place during this period are crucial in establishing the adult identity. As a result of the physiological and psychological changes involved in assuming the adult role, the conflicts of childhood are evoked anew. Variations of fantasies that originally served as vehicles for the drives during childhood become the conscious concomitants of adolescent masturbation. Guilt over masturbation derives primarily from the unconscious wishes that find substitute expression in the masturbation fantasies. During adolescence, a second attempt is made to master the conflicts arising from childhood wishes. (Through the successful resolution of these conflicts, individuals consolidate their adult identity about their sexual role, more responsibility, and choice of work or profession.)

Conflicts stemming from some phase of life are part of normal human development. Uncontrolled expression of certain instinctual impulses could have calamitous consequences for the individual. Free expression of drives represents a major confrontation with one's morality and could, under certain circumstances, provoke a severe superego response in the form of guilt or self-punishment. It falls upon the ego to mediate the demands made upon it by the id and the superego with due consideration for the exigent needs of reality. All of mental life represents a shifting balance, a tenuously stable equilibrium between the pressures of the id, the superego, and reality. Presumably, the most effective way to deal with a conflict would be to bar the impulse permanently from consciousness. When this occurs, one may speak of successful repression. In most instances, however, the victory is by no means one-sided. By their very nature, unconscious wishes remain dynamic and from time to time threaten to overcome the repression instituted to constrain them. Such intrusion may precipitate attacks of panic or, in lesser form, anxiety. Under such circumstances, the ego undertakes fresh measures to ward off the unpleasant affect of anxiety. If successful repression cannot be maintained, various compromises have to be effected by calling into play the different mechanisms of defense, which may become permanent features of the individual's character.

Unsuccessful resolution of intrapsychic conflicts eventuates in neurotic illness and neurotic character traits, inhibitions, sexual perversions, and patterns of behavior of a neurotic or self-defeating nature. In all these instances, a price has been paid in terms of suffering and restriction of the individual's capacities and freedom.

PSYCHOTHERAPY

THEORY OF PSYCHOTHERAPY

The principles and techniques of psychoanalysis as therapy are based upon the psychoanalytic theory of neurosis. As the theory of neurosis changed, so did the technique of therapy. Origi-

nally, Freud felt that neurotic symptoms were the result of pent-up, undischarged emotional tension connected with the repressed memory of a traumatic childhood sexual experience. At first, he used hypnosis to bring about emotional catharsis and abreaction of the trauma. Because many of his patients could not be hypnotized, he dropped hypnosis in favor of forced suggestion, a technique of recollection fostered by the insistent demanding pressure of the therapist. Among other things, this technique produced artifacts in the form of sexual fantasies about childhood, which the patient offered the therapist as if they were recollections of actual events. Taking advantage of his new operational concepts of the dynamic unconscious and the principle of strict psychic determinism, Freud reduced the element of suggestion to a minimum by a new technical procedure in which he asked his patients to report freely and without criticism whatever came into their minds. Thus, the technique of *free association* evolved.

During the period when the topographic model of the psychic apparatus was paramount in Freud's mind, the principal technical goal was to make the contents of the unconscious conscious. The patient's productions were interpreted according to principles very similar to those used in *The Interpretation of Dreams*. The most striking discovery Freud made during this period was that of *transference,* a highly emotional attitude the patient develops towards the analyst which represents a repetition of the individual's fantasy wishes concerning objects of the past, foisted onto the analyst. The discovery that the anti-instinctual forces of the mind, such as the defense mechanisms, guilt, and self-punishment, could operate at an unconscious level contributed to the elaboration of the structural theory. The structural theory pointed to the need to analyze the functioning of the defense mechanisms and the self-punitive trends. Elucidating the nature of the unconscious danger and the quality of the anxiety attendant upon its appearance have since become central points of analytic technique.

In later years, in an attempt to apply psychoanalytic therapy to types of cases that have heretofore been refractory to treatment, newer techniques were suggested. Franz Alexander (1932) felt that because most patients had been traumatized by parental mismanagement during childhood, it was necessary for the analyst to arrange "a corrective emotional experience" to counteract the effects of the original trauma. A more recent elaboration of these ideas has been proposed by E. R. Zetzel (1970) and Ralph Greenson (1967), who emphasized particular measures required to instill confidence to create a proper alliance between therapist and patient. Greenson emphasizes the importance of the real personality of the analyst. Some analysts, influenced by Melanie Klein, see in the analyst's emotional reaction a mirror of what the patient is experiencing consciously or unconsciously (Racker, 1953; Weigert, 1970). Heinz Kohut (1971) has suggested strengthening the self-esteem of patients with narcissistic personality disorders.

Recent years have seen the development of major innovations and changes in the psychoanalytic theory of pathology and treatment. The teachings of Kohut have become the basis for a school known as self psychology. According to this approach, the regulation of self-esteem and the

vicissitudes of what is called the "self state" are perhaps the primary factors in pathology and dictate in many ways the analyst's approach to the treatment of the patient. Very early dissonance in a mother/child interaction creates the basis for narcissistic vulnerability, the untoward effects of which have to be compensated for during treatment. Another major development may be seen in the theories concerning object relations. These theories, as well as those of Kohut, developed out of experience with so-called borderline and narcissistic personality disorders. A preeminent spokesman for the object relations school is Kernberg, who emphasizes in his writings how the relations with the earliest significant objects in the individual's life leave a residue of internalized relationship concepts that may continue throughout the individual's life. In addition, later trauma may evoke latent object relations and lead the individual to respond in an unrealistic way to present-day situations. In addition, the combination of psychoanalysis with other modalities of treatment, such as drugs, group therapy, and family interaction, has been advanced.

Onset of Neurosis

In the genesis of neurotic disorders, the conflicts of childhood are of critical importance. By far the most common and most significant conflicts involve the wishes of the oedipal phase. All children have conflicts and most of them develop some kind of childhood neurosis. Usually childhood neurosis assumes the form of general apprehensiveness, nightmares, phobias, tics, mannerisms, or ritualistic practices. Most primary behavior disorders of children represent disguised forms of neurosis from which the element of manifest fear has disappeared. Phobia is probably the most frequent symptom of childhood neurosis. In most cases, with the passage of the oedipal phase, the disturbances caused by instinctual conflicts have been sufficiently ameliorated to permit the child to progress normally. In some cases, a childhood neurosis continues with relatively little change into adult life.

Neurosis in adults may develop anew when the balance between the pressures of the drives and the defensive forces of the ego is upset. There are three typical situations in which this may occur.

1. An individual may be unable to cope with the additional psychological burden of normal development. The unconscious significance of becoming an adult and assuming responsibilities of marriage and undertaking the competitive and aggressive challenges of maturity may prove too much for the ego.

2. Disappointment, defeat, loss of love, physical illness, or some other consequence of the human condition may lead an individual to turn away from current reality and unconsciously seek gratification in the world of fantasy. This usually involves a reactivation (regression) of the fantasy wishes of the oedipal phase. As these wishes are regressively reactivated, the conflicts and anxieties of childhood are revived and the process of symptom formation begins. The fantasy wishes that are regressively reactivated are the ones that earlier had been the subject of fixation.

3. By a combination of circumstances, an individual may find himself in adult life in a situation that corresponds in its essential features to some childhood trauma or conflict-laden fantasy. Current reality is then misperceived in terms of the childhood conflict and the individual responds as he did in childhood, by forming symptoms.

PROCESS OF PSYCHOTHERAPY

The standard technical procedure of psychoanalysis for studying the functioning of the mind is known as the *psychoanalytic situation*. The patient is asked to assume a recumbent position on the couch, looking away from the analyst. The patient is asked to express in words whatever thoughts, images, or feelings come to mind, and to express these elements without distortion, censorship, suppression, or prejudgment concerning the significance or insignificance of any particular idea. Seated behind the couch, the analyst listens in an uncritical, nonjudgmental fashion, maintaining an attitude of benign curiosity. The analyst's values and judgments are strictly excluded from the therapeutic interaction.

From time to time the analyst interrupts the patient's associations. In doing so, he momentarily interferes with the patient's role as a passive reporter and makes him observe and reflect upon the significance and possible connections among his associations. The analyst's interventions momentarily change the patient's role from passive reporter to active observer and, at times, interpreter. The principle of free association is somewhat modified in connection with the interpretation of dreams. In this instance, the analyst may ask the patient to tell him whatever comes to mind in connection with this or that particular image of the dream.

The practical conditions of the treatment are also strictly regulated. A fixed schedule of fees and appointments is maintained. Any attempt by the patient to deviate from the basic understanding of the analytic situation calls for investigation and analysis. Changes in the basic conditions of the treatment are inadvisable and when necessary are effected by mutual consent between the patient and the analyst after the problem has been analyzed.

The analyst attempts to create a set of conditions in which the patient's mind, thoughts, and images are endogenously determined. The patient's thoughts and associations should come primarily from persistent dynamic internal pressure of the drives as organized in unconscious fantasies. Thoughts and associations should not represent responses to external manipulation, exhortation, stimulation, or education. This is what is uniquely psychoanalytic in the therapeutic interaction. Under the conditions of the analytic situation, the influence of inner mental forces can be more easily and clearly observed than in more usual situations. It becomes possible for the material hitherto suppressed or repressed to be verbalized and examined. This presupposes the strictest adherence to professional principles on the part of the analyst. Everything done must be in the interest of advancing the patient's insight through the process of analysis. There is no greater responsibility in the analytic situation than strict preservation of the patient's confidentiality. Communication of any material of the analysis to any source is contrary to the spirit of the analytic situation, even when the patient believes a breach of confidentiality is in his own best interests.

Psychoanalysis involves a commitment to change through critical self-examination. To maintain continuity of the analytic process, at least four sessions a week are indicated. Each session lasts at least 45 minutes. The course of treatment may run for several years. Undertaking psychoanalytic treatment involves considerable sacrifice in time, effort, and money. These are not conditions into which one may enter lightly.

The psychoanalytic situation has been structured in this manner with the intention of making it possible to accomplish the goal of psychoanalytic therapy, namely, to help the patient achieve a resolution of intrapsychic conflict through understanding conflicts and dealing with them in a more mature manner. Because the analytic situation is relatively uncontaminated by the intrusion of ordinary interpersonal relationships, the interaction of the three components of the mind—the ego, the id, and the super-ego—may be studied in a more objective way, making it possible to demonstrate to the patient what parts of thought and behavior are determined by inner wishes, conflicts, and fantasies and what parts represent a mature response to objective reality.

MECHANISMS OF PSYCHOTHERAPY

The treatment process may be divided into four phases:

1. Opening phase
2. Development of transference

3. Working through
4. Resolution of transference

The Opening Phase

Psychoanalytic observation begins with the very first contact. Everything the patient says and does is noted for possible significance and use later in the treatment. The initial set of interviews is part of the opening phase. During these interviews, the nature of the patient's difficulty is ascertained and the decision is reached whether analysis is indicated. To determine this, it is necessary for the analyst to learn as much as possible about the patient; for example, his current life situation and difficulties, what he has accomplished, how he relates to others, and the history of his family background and childhood development. Formalized history taking, following a prescribed outline, is not encouraged. Priorities in the subjects to be discussed should be left to the patient's intuition. Much is learned from how the patient approaches the practical task of making his problems known to the therapist and how he responds to the delineation of the analytic contract. The understanding of the analytical situation must be clearly defined from the very beginning and the respective responsibilities of both parties explicitly stated.

After a few sessions of face-to-face interviews, the second part of the opening phase begins when the patient assumes the couch. No two patients begin treatment in the same way. Some find it difficult to lie on the couch and say whatever comes to mind; others take readily to this new set of conditions. Everything the patient says and does— the position assumed on the couch, the clothes worn, characteristic phrases, what the patient chooses to present as

the opening statement of the session, and punctuality—are all clues to unconscious mental processes.

During the opening phase, the analyst learns more about the patient's history and development. He gets to understand in broad outline the nature of the patient's unconscious conflicts and has an opportunity to study the characteristic ways by which the patient resists revealing himself or becoming aware of repudiated thoughts and feelings. Gradually the analyst is able to detect a continuous thread of themes that follow relatively uniform sequences and repeat themselves in a variety of meaningful configurations. These productions can be understood in terms of the persistent, unconscious fantasy representing wishes from childhood, dynamically active in the patient's current life in disguised and distorted ways. In the early phases, the analyst deals almost exclusively with the superficial aspects of the patient's material. He tries to demonstrate to the patient significant correlations in the material presented but restricts himself primarily to those elements that are readily accessible to consciousness and that are not too close to the patient's basic conflicts. In ordinary cases, the initial phase of the treatment lasts from three to six months.

The Development of Transference

The next two phases of treatment, the transference and working through, constitute the major portion of the therapeutic work and actually overlap. At a certain stage in the treatment, when it appears the patient is just about ready to relate his current difficulties to unconscious conflicts from childhood concerning wishes over some important person or persons in his life, a new and interesting phenomenon emerges. Emotionally, the analyst assumes major significance in the life of the patient. The patient's perceptions of and demands upon the analyst become inappropriate, out of keeping with reality. The professional relationship becomes distorted as he tries to introduce personal instead of professional considerations into their interaction. Understanding transference was one of Freud's greatest discoveries. He perceived that in the transference, the patient was unconsciously reenacting a latter-day version of forgotten childhood memories and repressed unconscious fantasies. *Transference*, therefore, could be understood as a form of memory in which repetition in action replaces recollection of events.

Analysis of the transference is one of the cornerstones of psychoanalytic technique. It helps the patient distinguish fantasy from reality, past from present, and it makes real to the patient the force of the persistent unconscious fantasy wishes of childhood. Analysis of transference helps the patient understand how one misperceives, misinterprets, and relates to the present in terms of the past. In place of the automatic, uncontrolled, stereotyped ways through which the patient unconsciously responds to unconscious fantasies, the patient is able to evaluate the unrealistic nature of impulses and anxieties and to make appropriate decisions on a mature and realistic level. In this way, analysis helps the patient achieve a major realignment in the dynamic equilibrium between impulse and conflict that ultimately leads to a satisfactory resolution of the pathogenic conflict once the patient comes to understand not only the nature of the fears that motivate his defenses, but self-

punitive trends as well. For the most part, these are also unconscious.

Working Through

This phase of the treatment coincides with and continues the analysis of transference. One or two experiences of insight into the nature of one's conflicts are not sufficient to bring about change. Analysis of the transference has to be continued many times and in many different ways. The patient's insight into problems by way of the transference is constantly deepened and consolidated by working through, a process that consists of repetition, elaboration, and amplification. Working through acts as a kind of catalyst between analysis of transference and the overcoming of the amnesia for crucial childhood experiences (Greenacre, 1956). Usually the experience of successful analysis of a transference phenomenon is followed by the emergence into memory of some important event or fantasy from the patient's past. Analysis of the transference facilitates recall. Recall illuminates the nature of the transference. This reciprocal interplay between understanding the transference and recollecting the past consolidates the patient's insight into conflicts and strengthens his conviction concerning the interpretive reconstructions made in the course of treatment.

Resolution of Transference

The resolution of transference is the termination phase of treatment. When the patient and the analyst are satisfied that the major goals of the analysis have been accomplished and the transference is well understood, a date is set for ending treatment. Technically, the analyst's aim is to resolve the patient's unconscious neurotic attachment to him. There are a number of striking features typical of this phase of treatment. Most characteristic and dramatic is a sudden and intense aggravation of the very symptoms for which the patient sought treatment. It seems as if all the analytic work had been done in vain. Upon further analysis, this turn of events can be understood as a last-ditch effort on the part of the patient to convince the analyst that he is not yet ready to leave treatment and that he should be permitted to continue the relationship indefinitely. There are many motives for this unconscious attitude. In part, the patient is unwilling to surrender so gratifying and helpful a relationship. In part, it continues a continuation of some passive, dependent orientation from childhood. But most of all, it represents a last-chance endeavor to get the analyst to fulfill the very unconscious, infantile fantasy wishes that were the source of the patient's conflicts to begin with.

Another interesting thing that happens during the termination phase of treatment is the emergence of hitherto repressed memories that confirm or elaborate the reconstructions and interpretations made earlier in the treatment. It is as if the patient presents new insight or findings to the analyst as a parting gift of gratitude. Unconsciously, it often has the significance of presenting the analyst with a child, a gift of new life, as a form of thanks for the new life that analysis has made possible for the patient.

Finally, during the closing phase of treatment, the patient may reveal a hitherto concealed group of wishes amounting to a desire to be magically transformed into some omnipotent or omniscient figure, a striving kept secret throughout the analysis but that the patient had quietly hoped would be fulfilled by the time the treatment was over. It is important during this phase to analyze all the fantasies the patient has about how things will be after the analysis is over (Schmideberg, 1938). If one fails to deal with all the problems mentioned above, the possibilities of relapse remain high.

APPLICATIONS

PROBLEMS

From the description of psychoanalysis as therapy, it should be clear that any potential patient must be able to fulfill certain objective as well as personal requirements. Essentially, patients must be strongly motivated to overcome their difficulties by honest self-scrutiny. Because it is difficult at the beginning to predict how long treatment will last, individuals must be in a position to commit a considerable period in advance for the purpose of carrying the analysis through to successful termination. In addition, psychoanalysis patients must accept the discipline of the conditions proposed by the psychoanalytic contract. The psychoanalytic dialogue is an unusual form of communication, inevitably entailing frustration of transference wishes. Patients must be able to accept such frustration and to express thoughts and feelings in words rather than action. Impulsive, willful, self-centered, and highly narcissistic individuals may not be able to accommodate themselves to such structures. People who are basically dishonest, psychopathic, or pathological liars obviously will not be equal to the task of complete and unrelenting self-revelation. Furthermore, because cooperation with the analyst in an enterprise of self-exploration requires some degree of objectivity and reality testing, functions severely impaired in the psychoses, psychoanalysis can rarely be used in the treatment of such conditions except under very special circumstances.

Because psychoanalysis is a time-consuming, expensive, and arduous form of treatment, it is not indicated when difficulties are minor. Genuine suffering and pain are the most reliable allies of the analytic process. Through insight, psychoanalysis hopes to enable the patient to overcome inner conflicts. This can be helpful only insofar as such insights can be put to constructive use in altering one's life situation. If the person's objective situation is so bad that there is nothing one can do about it, psychoanalysis will be of no avail. This can be seen, for example, where the analyst recognizes how the story the patient presents reflects a lifelong struggle against murderous, destructive, and self-destructive impulses, the psychological consequences of severe congenital deformity or crippling disease early in childhood. No psychological insight can compensate for the injustices of fate.

Because so much of psychoanalytic technique depends on analysis of the transference, psychoanalysis is best suited for conditions in which transference attachments tend to be strong. This is true in the classical psychoneurotic entities—hysteria, anxiety hysteria, obsessive-compulsive neurosis, and a variety of states characterized by anxiety. In actual practice, the symptomatologies of the psychoneuroses tend to overlap. The diagnostic label attended to a particular condition usually reflects the major mechanism of defense characteristically employed to ward off anxiety. In hysteria, for example, by a process called *conversion*, the energy of a sexual wish that the ego was unable to repress successfully may be transformed into alterations of body functions, such as paralysis, absence of sensation, and abnormal sensations. An unconscious fantasy of sucking on a penis or swallowing it may manifest itself consciously in the feeling that there is an abnormal lump in the throat that cannot be swallowed–the classical globus hystericus. A symptom is compromise formation. Unconsciously, it gratifies the wish and the need for punishment at the same time.

Phobias are typical of anxiety hysteria. The phobic patient wards off anxiety by treating some other external object or situation as the representative of the unconscious impulse. In one form of *agoraphobia*, a patient may become anxious whenever she goes out on the street, the street representing the place where it is possible to realize her unconscious wish to be a prostitute. The mechanism of defense is a double one. The internal (sexual) danger is projected onto the street, an external situation. By avoiding the external object, the patient controls an internal danger. The mechanisms of defense represent a combination of projection and avoidance.

Psychoanalysis is also applicable for character disorders that represent substitutes for psychoneurotic symptoms. For a person whose unconscious fantasies lead him unconsciously to misconstrue dancing as indulgence in dangerous sexual activity, it may prove much more acceptable just to avoid dancing than to experience blushing, palpitations, and sweating whenever he attempts it. Such a person may be diagnosed as suffering from phobic character disorders.

There are many forms of character disorders of this type—hysterical, obsessive, compulsive, depressive, and so on. Arlow (1972) has demonstrated how certain character traits may represent transformations from what originally had been transient perversions. Petty liars, hoaxers, and unrealistic personalities may be said to be suffering from character perversions.

Sexual difficulties, like premature ejaculation, and psychoneurotic depressions are ordinarily quite amenable to psychoanalytic treatment. More generalized patterns of behavior that interfere with the patient's conscious goals for happiness and success can be traced to unconscious conflicts and can be treated psychoanalytically. Some men, for example, repeatedly fall in love with and marry the same kind of woman, although they know from previous experience that the marriage will end disastrously. Similarly, certain women seem incapable of choosing men other than those who will hurt, abuse, and humiliate them. Other people will unconsciously arrange their lives so any success is followed by an even greater failure. In these cases, their normal way of life or choice of love object or self-engineered fate is the equivalent of a psychoneurotic disorder.

In recent years, many patients seeking psychoanalytic treatment seem to be suffering from masochistic character disorders or from narcissistic neuroses. Into this latter category fall those paradoxical combinations of low self-esteem and heightened grandiosity. Mood swings, depression, tendencies toward drug dependence, compulsive strivings for recognition and success, and patterns of promiscuous sexuality are not uncommon. Such pa-

tients often complain of inner emptiness, lack of goals, hypochondriasis, and an inability to make lasting attachments or love relationships. Because of new contributions to the technical management of these problems, the prognosis of their treatment by psychoanalysis seems much better today than in previous years.

A number of conditions may be helped by psychoanalysis under specially favorable conditions. Among these are some cases of drug addiction, perversions, borderline personalities, and, on rare occasions, psychoses. Pioneering work applying psychoanalytic principles, if not the complete technique, to the treatment of psychotics has been done by Paul Federn (1952), Frieda Fromm-Reichmann (1950), H. Rosenfeld (1954), and H. F. Searles (1965).

EVALUATION

Unfortunately, there exists no adequate study evaluating the results of psychoanalytic therapy. In a general way, this is true of almost all forms of psychotherapy. There are just too many variables to be taken into account to make it possible to establish a controlled, statistically valid study of the outcome of the therapy. Several attempts have been made in this direction beginning with Otto Fenichel (1930), including studies by Fred Feldman (1968), H. J. Eysenck (1965), Julian Meltzoff and Melvin Kornreich (1970), R. S. Wallerstein and N. J. Smelser (1969), and A. Z. Pfeffer (1963), as well as several studies by the American Psychoanalytic Association. None of the findings of these studies has proven definitive and irrefutable. By and large, the number of "cures" range from 30 to 60 percent, depending on the studies and the criteria employed.

In any individual case, evaluation of the outcome of treatment has to be judged in a global fashion. Comparisons are made between the situation at the beginning of treatment and the alteration in the patient's life and symptoms at termination. The patient may have been cured of more conditions than initially complained about; previously unforeseen possibilities of self-fulfillment may have been realized. On the other hand, unrecognized complicating difficulties and intercurrent events may have changed the total configuration of the patient's life. In the face of objective reality, the claims of psychoanalysis must be modest. At best, psychoanalysis tries to help the patient effect the best possible solution of difficulties that circumstances will allow. It seeks to achieve the most stable equilibrium possible between the various forces at conflict in the mind. How well that equilibrium is sustained will also depend on how favorably life treats the patient during and after treatment. Freud himself was quite modest about the therapeutic claims of psychoanalysis (Freud, 1937). The validity of what psychoanalysis has discovered concerning human nature and the functioning of the human mind are not necessarily related to the effectiveness of psychoanalysis as treatment. Nonetheless, the fact remains that when properly applied to the appropriate condition, psychoanalysis remains the most effective mode of therapy yet devised.

TREATMENT

Freud compared writing about psychoanalysis to explaining the game of chess. It is easy to formulate the rules of the game, to describe the opening phases, and to discuss what has to be done to bring a chess game to a close. What happens in between is subject to infinite variation. The same is true of psychoanalysis. The analytic contract, the opening phase, and the tasks of termination can be described definitively. The analysis of the transference and the process of working through consist of countless bits of analytic work. Rudolf Loewenstein (1958) approached the problem by distinguishing between tactical and strategic goals in psychoanalytic technique. *Tactical* concerns involve the analysis of the immediate presenting material in terms of some conflict, usually involving the analyst. The *strategic* goal is to elucidate the nature of the unconscious childhood fantasy and to demonstrate the many ways in which it affects the patient's current life.

How this appears in actual practice may be demonstrated in the following illustration. The patient is a middle-aged businessman whose marriage has been marked by repeated strife and quarrels. His sexual potency has been tenuous. At times he has suffered from premature ejaculation. At the beginning of one session, he began to complain about having to return to treatment after a long holiday weekend. He said, "I'm not so sure I'm glad to be back in treatment even though I didn't enjoy my visit to my parents. I feel I just have to be free." He then continued with a description of his visit home, which he said had been depressing. His mother was bossy, aggressive, manipulative, as always. He feels sorry for his father. At least in the summertime, the father can retreat to the garden and work with the flowers, but the mother watches over him like a hawk. "She has such a sharp tongue and a cruel mouth. Each time I see my father he seems to be getting smaller and smaller; pretty soon he will disappear and there will be nothing left of him. She does that to people. I always feel that she is hovering over me ready to swoop down on me. She has me intimidated just like my wife."

The patient continued, "I was furious this morning. When I came to get my car, I found that someone had parked in a way that hemmed it in. It took a long time and lots of work to get my car out. During the time I realized how anxious I was; the perspiration was pouring down the back of my neck.

"I feel restrained by the city. I need the open fresh air; I have to stretch my legs. I'm sorry I gave up the house I had in the country. I have to get away from this city. I really can't afford to buy another house now, but at least I'll feel better if I look for one.

"If only business were better, I could maneuver more easily. I hate the feeling of being stuck in an office from nine until five. My friend Bob had the right idea—he arranged for retirement. Now he's free to come and go as he pleases. He travels, he has no boss, no board of directors to answer to. I love my work but it imposes too many restrictions on me. I can't help it, I'm ambitious. What can I do?"

At this point, the therapist called to the patient's attention the fact that throughout the material, in many different ways, the patient was describing how he feared confinement, that he had a sense of being trapped.

The patient responded, "I do get symptoms of claustrophobia from time to time. They're mild, just a slight anxiety. I begin to feel perspiration at the back of my neck, and I have a sense of restlessness. The hair seems to stand up on the back of my neck. It happens when the elevator stops between floors or when a train gets stuck between stations. I begin to worry about how I'll get out."

The fact that he suffered from claustrophobia was a new finding in the analysis. The analyst noted to himself that the patient felt claustrophobic about the analysis. The conditions of the analytic situation imposed by the analyst were experienced by the patient as confining. In addition, the analyst noted, again to himself, these ideas were coupled with the idea of being threatened and controlled by his mother.

The patient continued, "You know I have the same feeling about starting an affair with Mrs. X. She wants to and I guess I want to also. Getting involved is easy. It's getting uninvolved that concerns me. How do you get out of an affair once you're in it?"

In this material, the patient associates being trapped in a confined space with being trapped in the analysis and with being trapped in an affair with a woman.

The patient continued, "I'm really chicken. It's a wonder I was ever able to have relations at all and to get married. No wonder I didn't have intercourse until I was in my twenties. My mother was always after me, 'Be careful about getting involved with girls; they'll get you into trouble. They'll be after you for your money. If you have sex with them, you can pick up a disease. Be careful when you go to public toilets; you can get an infection, etc., etc., etc.' She made it all sound dangerous. You can get hurt from this, you can get hurt from that. It reminds me of the time I saw two dogs having intercourse. They were stuck together and couldn't separate—the male dog was yelping and screaming in pain. I don't even know how old I was then, maybe five or six or perhaps seven, but I was definitely a child and I was frightened."

At this point, the analyst is able to tell the patient that his fear of being trapped in an enclosed space is the conscious derivative of an unconscious fantasy in which he imagines that if he enters the woman's body with his penis, it will get stuck; he will not be able to extricate it; he may lose it. The criteria used in making this interpretation are clear: they consist of the sequential arrangement of the material, the contiguity of related themes, the repetition of the same or analogous themes, and the convergence of the different elements into one common hypothesis that encompasses all the data, namely, an unconscious fantasy of danger to the penis once it enters a woman's body. This is the tactical goal that can be achieved on the basis of this material. In this instance, it constitutes an important step toward the strategic goal, which, in this case, would consist of making the patient aware of childhood sexual strivings toward the mother, of a wish to have relations with her, and of a concomitant fear growing out of the threatening nature of her personality, and that, like a hawk, she would swoop down upon him and devour him. These interpretations would give him insight into the causes of his impotence and his stormy relations with women, particularly his wife. The material also demonstrates how a neurotic person misperceives, misinterprets, and responds inappropriately to current experience in terms of his unconscious fantasy. To this patient, having to keep a definite set of appointments with the analyst, having his car hemmed in between two other cars,

being responsible to authorities, and getting stuck in elevators or in trains were all experienced as dangerous situations that evoked the symptoms of anxiety. Consciously, he experienced restrictions by rules and confinement within certain spaces. Unconsciously, he was thinking in terms of experiencing his penis inextricably trapped inside a woman's body.

This is the essence of the neurotic process—the persistent unconscious fantasies of childhood serve to create a mental set according to which the individual in a selective and idiosyncratic way interprets everything that happens to him. Therefore, neurotic conflicts do not represent conflicts with reality. They are intrapsychic conflicts (Arlow, 1963).

The material of any one analytic session is by no means always so dramatic. Yet one must be careful not to prejudge the significance and possible ramifications of any event or session, no matter how trivial it may appear at first. A seemingly insignificant interaction between the patient and the analyst may lead to very important discoveries illuminating the origins and the meaning of the neurosis. For the most part, however, the major portion of the analytic work is directed toward understanding the patient's defenses and overcoming resistances. It is not always easy to distinguish between mechanisms of defense and resistances. Typically, the *mechanisms of defense* are repetitive, stereotyped, automatic means used by the ego to ward off anxiety. A *resistance* is any one of a wide range of phenomena distracting the patient from pursuing the requirements of the analytic situation.

It may seem strange that a patient who has made so serious a commitment to self-understanding should not follow the course of action in treatment that is intended to bring relief. However, this is not at all unexpected. Because the mind characteristically turns away from or tries to repress unpleasant feelings and thoughts and because the neurotic process develops when it has been unable to accomplish this end successfully, it should come as no surprise that the endeavor to both fulfill and control forbidden impulses should continue into analytic experience. Herman Nunberg (1926) showed how the patient unconsciously brings into the analysis a wish to preserve intact those very infantile strivings that caused his difficulties in the first place.

The analysis of defenses and resistances is slow, piecemeal work. Nevertheless, from it, much can be learned about how the patient's character was shaped in response to the critical events and object relations of childhood. A particularly difficult resistance to overcome during treatment comes from the use of the mechanism known as *isolation*. This is the tendency for the patient to deal with his thoughts as if they were empty of feeling or unrelated to other ideas or to his behavior. A patient may begin a session, for example, by mentioning in two or three short sentences an incident that took place on his way to the session. He had passed a man on the street who suddenly, without cause or warning, extended his arm in such a way that he almost struck the patient. This reminded the patient of an incident some years earlier when he saw someone actually being hit in this very same manner. On this occasion, as in the past, the patient, not a native New Yorker, shrugged the incident off with the reassuring judgment, "Well, that's New York for you. It's a good thing he

didn't have a knife." All of this was stated in an even, flat, unemotional tone.

With no transition, the patient turned to matters of closer concern to him. He described at great length, and again in an even-tempered way, how his boss had criticized his work in front of his colleagues. Many of the criticisms, he felt, were unjustified, but mindful of his position, he had maintained a calm, respectful demeanor. Even when recounting the incident, in the session, he showed little sign of anger. When this was called to his attention, he admitted that indeed he had been angry and was surprised that he had not transmitted that feeling to the therapist. At this point, the therapist made the connection for the patient between his opening report of a near-assault on the street and the experience with his boss. Actually, the patient had been saying, "There are dangerous people abroad. If one is not careful, they may strike you, even kill you. They have murderous impulses." The incident in the street served as a convenient locus onto which the patient projected his own murderous wishes to retaliate against the boss. He dealt with these impulses in an isolated way, an intellectual judgment he made about someone else's motives.

At this stage of the treatment, he could grasp only intellectually, by inference, the intensity of his vengeful wishes. Much could be learned from the analysis of this experience beyond illustrating how the patient manages to control and to suppress his feelings. This patient was particularly vulnerable to any assault on his pride, any humiliation of his narcissism, especially if it occurred as part of a public spectacle. Later in the analysis, it was possible to demonstrate the connection between these components of the patient's character and the feelings of defeat, insignificance, and humiliation he experienced during the oedipal phase while watching his parents having intercourse in the bedroom he shared with them.

It would be impossible to catalogue all the forms that resistance can take. Some of the more usual ones may be noted here. The most direct and unequivocal form of resistance occurs when the patient finds he has nothing to say. The patient may remain silent on the couch for minutes on end. Even a trivial lateness of a few minutes may carry some hidden meaning. Often a patient may miss sessions, forget them, or oversleep. He may be tardy in paying the bill for treatment, giving very realistic explanations to account for the tardiness. Sometimes patients will talk endlessly about trivial day-to-day events revealing little or nothing that can be used to understand their problems. A patient may introduce a dream at the beginning of a session and make no reference to it for the rest of the analytic hour. On the other hand, the patient may fill the entire session with dreams, making it impossible to learn more than the facade of what had been recorded of the night's experience. Some patients report how they have become ardent advocates of psychoanalysis, proselytizing their friends and relatives, urging all of them to enter into treatment, at the very time when they themselves are making little effort or progress in the analytic work.

The important principle governing all manifestations of resistance is that they must be analyzed like everything else that happens in the course of analysis. What must be understood is why the patient is behaving the way he is at a particular moment. What is the motive behind his unconscious wish to break off the analytic work? What conflict is he trying to evade? Exhortation, suggestion, encouragement, prohibitions —any of a number of educational procedures that in other forms of therapy may be introduced at such a time must be carefully avoided. No matter how provocative, frustrating, or irritating the patient's behavior may be, the analyst never departs from the responsibility to make the patient understand his behavior. His attitude must remain at all times analytic.

How the analyst works can best be understood by examining three aspects of treatment: empathy, intuition, and introspection. An analyst must be capable of empathizing with his patient. Empathy is a form of "emotional knowing," the experiencing of another's feelings. It is a special mode of perceiving. It presupposes an ability on the analyst's part to identify with the patient and to share the patient's experience affectively as well as cognitively. The empathic process is central to the psychotherapeutic relationship and is also a basic element in all human interaction. It finds its highest social expression in the aesthetic experience of the artist as well as in religion and other group phenomena. It is based upon the dynamic effect of unconscious fantasies shared in common (Beres & Arlow, 1974). Two features characterize empathy. First, the identification with the patient is only transient. Second, the therapist preserves separateness from the object (the person being analyzed). The analyst's empathy makes it possible to receive and perceive both the conscious and unconscious processes operating in the patient.

It is impossible for the analyst at any one time to keep in the foreground of his thinking everything the patient has shared. How then does he arrive at an understanding of the patient? This is done intuitively. The myriad data communicated by the patient are organized in the analyst's mind into meaningful configurations outside the scope of consciousness. What the analyst perceives as his understanding of the patient is actually the end product of a series of mental operations carried out unconsciously. He becomes aware of this by the process of introspection when the interpretation comes to his mind in the form of a free association. Not everything that comes to the analyst's mind in the course of a session is necessarily the correct interpretation. If he is working properly, it is usually some commentary on the patient's material. After introspection presents to the analyst's consciousness the result of his intuitive work, he does not necessarily impart this information to the patient immediately. He checks his idea with what he has learned from the patient and judges its validity in terms of contiguity, repetition, coherence, consistency, and convergence of theme, as outlined earlier. Intuition gives way to cognitive elaboration. In the long run, the validity of the interpretation is confirmed by the dynamic impact it has upon the patient's productions, that is, how it affects the equilibrium between impulse and defense in the patient's mind.

MANAGEMENT

Much has been written about the analyst's emotional response to the patient. The analyst is not an unfeeling, neutral automaton as presented in caricatures of psychoanalysis. He does respond emotionally to the therapeutic interaction, but he keeps these responses to himself. He regards them as a form of affective monitoring of the patient's productions. He uses his feelings as clues to understanding the direction that the patient's thoughts are taking. If he feels angry, sexually aroused, or frustrated, he must always consider the possibility that this is precisely the mood the patient wants to generate in him. It behooves the therapist to uncover the patient's motive in doing so.

There is much disagreement in analytic literature about the analyst's emotional response to the patient. Sometimes this is referred to as countertransference, the counterpart of the patient's transference onto the analyst. These issues have been revived by Annie Reich (1960). Strictly speaking, countertransference should be reserved for those situations in which a patient and his productions evoke in the analyst conflicts relating to some unresolved childhood fantasy of his own, causing him to misperceive, misinterpret, and misrespond to the analysand in terms of his own difficulties. Some analysts see the therapist's feelings as the operation of a mechanism known as projective identification (Little, 1951; Tower, 1956). They interpret the analyst's feelings as identical with those the patient is experiencing and they feel it beneficial to the course of the analysis for the analyst to discuss these feelings with the patient. For some analysts, this is the principal mode of treatment. Most analysts in the United States do not agree with this point of view. They try to understand the significance of what they feel about the patient. They do not discuss it with the patient.

Neurotic countertransference to the patient on the part of the analyst can constitute a real problem. Ordinarily the analyst will try to analyze the problem for himself. If this is ineffective, he may seek a consultation with a colleague. If the problem persists, or if it can be demonstrated to be more pervasive than had been suspected before and to apply to other patients as well, it indicates a need for the analyst to undergo further psychoanalysis himself. When the analyst finds that he cannot control his counter transference responses, he discusses the issues honestly and frankly with the patient and arranges for transfer to another analyst.

CASE EXAMPLE

It is impossible to capture in any condensed presentation the essence of the psychoanalytic experience. The course of an analysis proceeds unevenly. Seemingly fragmented material, arduously assembled over long periods, incompletely comprehended, suddenly may be brilliantly illuminated in a few dramatic sessions, when thousands of disparate threads organize themselves into a tapestry of meaning. Accordingly, any effort to describe in an overall way the course of psychoanalysis inevitably must sound oversimplified and slick. For practical purposes, only the main trends and conclusions can be described. The taxing day-to-day struggle with resistances and defenses has to be inserted by one's imagination. With these warnings in mind, let us proceed to the description of a relatively uncomplicated case.

The patient, whom we will call Tom, was a junior faculty member in a prominent eastern university. At age 30 he was still unmarried, although recently he had begun to live with a woman who had studied under him when she was a graduate student. Although Tom was a popular and successful teacher, much admired and appreciated by his students, he was unable to advance professionally because he could not fulfill the requirements for the Ph.D. degree. He had passed the requisite courses and had completed his doctoral thesis except for a few notes and bibliographical references. The next step was to defend his thesis before the committee, but he could not do so as long as he had not put the final touches on his thesis. This he seemed unable to do. Several years had gone by and he was afraid that all the work he had done might have been in vain.

Tom had another problem that concerned his difficulties with women. He did not seem to be able to maintain a long-term relationship with any woman. For almost a year, he had been genuinely fond of a woman, whom we will call Anita, and at her urging, had finally decided to let her live with him. That was four months ago, and since that time, he had become increasingly irritable and found himself quarreling with Anita, criticizing many of the things she did around the house. He would have liked her to move out but he was not quite sure how to tell her. Since she had moved in with him, his sexual performance had deteriorated. Whereas previously he had suffered from premature ejaculation after entry, in the past few months he had had difficulty getting and maintaining an erection. The only times he had been able to perform well sexually were with women he knew to be frigid.

Tom's father, a practical and industrious man, operated a small business.

Through judicious and conservative investments, he was able to acquire a comfortable fortune. Although he was proud of Tom, he was unable to share his son's intellectual interests. Tom's mother was a delicate, sensitive, somewhat hypochondriacal woman. As a child, she had had rheumatic fever, which had left her with a mild case of mitral stenosis. Her doctors had advised her not to have any children. But her wish for a child overrode her doctor's admonition, and after a rather difficult labor, which left her exhausted for several months, she gave birth to Tom. When Tom was five years old, she had a miscarriage. She was much concerned with Tom's development. She saw to it that he was well fed and clean. He was toilet trained by 18 months and seemed to thrive in all ways.

During the preliminary interviews, Tom stated that he was not aware of any neurotic problems he may have had in childhood. He recalled no phobias or nightmares but had been told that at the age of five he was something of a behavior problem. He had become contrary and disobedient toward his mother and had refused to let her kiss him good night. Once when his mother was out of the kitchen for a while, he had emptied the contents of the refrigerator on the kitchen floor. However, after a few months, he seemed to change. He reverted to the obedient child he had been before but became a finicky eater and remained so.

Tom was not happy about starting school. Because his mother was ill, a favorite aunt accompanied him on the first day. He was quite shy and fearful of the other children. Once he learned how to read, however, things began to change. He was clearly the best student in the class and was well liked be-cause he generously helped slower students with their work. Through various activities, he soon became the most popular student in each class. He could keep his classmates amused by inventing funny stories. At lunchtime, he would readily share his sandwiches with his friends. In spite of this, he was quite fearful of the other children. He avoided contact sports and never got involved in a fistfight. He welcomed the frequent absences from school occasioned by repeated respiratory infections. He could stay in bed, munch crackers, and eat to his heart's delight.

Tom's academic progress was not as good as his teachers and parents had expected. Being naturally gifted, it was easy for him in the lower grades to be outstanding without exerting any real effort. In high school and college, he refused to be "a greasy grind." No one was going to accuse him of putting in extra effort just to get good marks. Repeatedly, his teachers informed him and his parents that he was not working up to his potential. When he had to recite in class, his heart would pound and his face would flush even though he knew the answers to the questions posed by the teacher. On two occasions in college, on crucial examinations, he made gross blunders in interpreting the questions. Ordinarily, he should have failed, but his teachers, cognizant of his abilities, after discussing the matter with him, gave him passing grades. In the Ph.D. program, he fulfilled the requirements at a satisfactory level. It was when he had to work independently that his performance faltered.

Although he liked girls, he never seemed to get along well with them. When he was 5½ years old, he pinched the infant sister of a friend when no one was looking. When she began to cry, he disclaimed any knowledge of why she might be doing so. When he was 12 or 13, he recalled having a crush on a lovely girl who lived next door, but he never did anything about it. At 14 he was extremely disappointed when a girl he took to a party spent most of the evening in the company of his best friend. He never dated the girl again, but, surprisingly, his relationship with his friend remained unchanged. He felt a definite antagonism toward attractive girls, thinking they were all vain and self-centered. With those girls he did date, he maintained a haughty, condescending air. He would rupture the relationship through some seemingly inadvertent act that hurt the girl's feelings. He came to realize on his own that there was something malicious about his gaucherie. On several occasions, while talking to one girl, he would address her with the name of another, a slip of the tongue hardly flattering to the girl involved.

From the very beginning, Tom was a "good patient." He followed the rules of the analytic situation and was agreeable and deferential. He soon began to display the vast fund of knowledge he had on a great variety of subjects. In the course of some observation, I made a comment indicating some familiarity with one of the subjects Tom was discussing. This proved very upsetting to him. For a few days, he became anxious and depressed. Intellectually, he was convinced he was superior to everyone else, at least in the areas of his expertise. He believed the only reason it was not generally acknowledged was that he did not try hard enough. He realized that he wanted me, as his analyst, to admire him, but he had not realized that be-

hind his deferential facade, he was intensely competitive. A few days later, he reported a recurrent fantasy. He imagined what would happen if a holdup man confronted him with a gun. He would tell the villain, "My life is too important to me. Money doesn't mean anything to me—just don't hurt me," and he would passively hand over his wallet.

In the clothes closet, Tom noted a fur coat belonging to the patient who preceded him. He left the door of the waiting room open a fraction and placed his chair in a position where he could see the patient as she left the consulting room. She was an attractive woman with blonde ringlets, just the type he despised. In the sessions, he began to make disparaging comments concerning her. "How easy it is to be a woman. You just have to be attractive and everything is taken care of for you." He was certain that I was more interested in her and that I would be taken in by her self-centered complacency and smugness. It would be impossible for him to compete with her for my attention. She had the inside track. He began to realize some of the reasons for his antagonism towards such women. He felt that a woman so attractive would never pay any attention to him.

Tom began one session in a state of almost uncontrollable fury. I had begun his session seven minutes later than usual. Although this was due to my lateness in arriving at the office, he was certain that I had done so because I was too fascinated with what my previous patient was telling me to let her go on time. He began the session by saying that while he was in the clothes closet, he had had the impulse to take the coat belonging to the previous patient and throw it on the floor. On the way to his appointment that morning, the bus was very crowded and he had become quite anxious. People jostled him and he felt he could not breathe. He became so uncomfortable that he left the bus and walked the rest of the way to the office. He thought the city was getting overcrowded, with too many people on the relief rolls who had to be supported by hard-working citizens like himself. They were all parasites like my previous patient, who probably lived luxuriously on her husband's hard-earned income.

In the ensuing weeks, he began to talk about his relationship with Anita. Her presence in his house had been intrusive. She did not contribute sufficiently to the maintenance of the household. At night, after they had had intercourse, he would want to get as far away from her as possible. In fact, it would have been better if he could have told her to leave the bed completely. Several times he had a fantasy of choking her. He recalled a definite sense of pleasure when he saw her leaving the house. The thing that seemed to irritate him most, however, was how careless Anita was with food. She would take a portion of meat larger than she could eat, so much had to be thrown out. In addition, she used to leave the refrigerator door open for long periods. He would have to dispose of the milk that had gone sour. He did make the observation, "After all, I'm an only child. It never was easy for me to share." He remembered that when he was six years old, a friend of his and his friend's sister had received a play house for Christmas and the two had fought over who should occupy the house. He then remembered reading in the Bible years later how Jacob and Esau had fought with each other inside their mother's womb.

During this phase of the analysis, he began to have nightmares. The following dream is typical. The patient reported, "I was swimming in the lake, the water was dark and murky. Suddenly, I was surrounded by a school of small fish, the kind I used to raise when I was a kid. They seemed prepared to lunge at me as if to bite me. I woke up gasping for breath."

Tom learned to swim late. He was most comfortable in a pool. In an ocean, he feared being bitten by a large fish or being stung by an eel. Worst of all was swimming in a lake, where the reeds growing from the muddy bottom could tangle him, draw him down, and drown him. Between the ages of 8 and 12, he raised tropical fish. He was always careful to be present when the baby fish were hatched to remove them from the tank so the other fish would not eat them.

Shortly before he was five, his mother told him that he might be getting a baby sister or brother. She explained that his father had introduced something like an egg into her that had hatched, and a future baby was swimming around in a special fluid inside her body. Clearly this news did not please Tom, for the story goes that he pointed his ray gun at his mother's abdomen. During the same period he emptied the contents of the refrigerator onto the kitchen floor. The pregnancy did not come to term. A few months later, the mother began to bleed and she was taken to the hospital. Tom saw some of the blood on the bathroom floor. From the behavior of the grown-ups, Tom could conclude that something terrible was happening. His mother did not come home from the hospital with a baby. Tom was relieved that he had his mother back again and that he did not have to share her and the food with a younger sibling. But unconsciously, he imagined that he was responsible for the baby's death. He fantasized that when he was inside the mother's body, he had destroyed the potential sibling, lacerating it with his teeth. About this time, he developed an aversion to eating eggs or fish, a characteristic that persisted into his adult life. Unconsciously, he feared that these representatives of siblings whom he had destroyed within his mother's body would retaliate by destroying him from within his own body. The attractive patient in the consultation room, the grimy welfare recipients in the bus, and the sloppy Anita in his apartment all represented potential siblings he wanted to oust and destroy because they threatened to invade his territory and rob him of his mother's love and food. He feared they in turn would do to him exactly what he intended to do to them, namely, destroy them with his mouth. As he overcame these fears, he became more giving with Anita. He invited her to share his apartment again. Sexually, his potency began to improve.

His former rival, the attractive blonde with the fur coat, began to intrigue him. What kind of sexual life did she lead? Through the partially open doorway of the waiting room he observed her comings and goings. Perhaps the analyst was interested in her sexually. She seemed the type to go for older men.

Before his session one day, Tom went to the bathroom and forgot to lock the door. As he was standing urinating, the blonde patient entered. Surprised and embarrassed, she withdrew in great confusion. Somehow Tom found the incident amusing and gratifying.

A short time later, he had the following dream, "I get up at night and go to the bathroom. I sit on the toilet and masturbate, looking at the pictures in some porno girlie magazine. Suddenly I notice that there are two sets of large french windows. They swing open, people are passing by on what seems to be a boardwalk. I'm angry and embarrassed because they're all looking in on me. In the background I hear the sounds of a choo-choo train going by."

Immediately, he related the dream to the experience with the previous patient. From the french windows, he could place the setting of the dream exactly. There were such windows in a room he and his parents had occupied in a rooming house at the Jersey shore, where they had gone for a two-week vacation. He was four and a half years old at the time and he was much intrigued by what was going on in the adjoining room at the rooming house. Two young women shared the room. It had a sliding door that did not close completely. Through the half-inch-wide space, little Tom tried to watch the girls getting undressed, and he was especially curious when their boyfriends came to visit them over the weekend.

There had been a wreck on the Asbury Park railroad just before he and his parents had arrived at the seashore. Several people had been killed and the derailed cars had not yet been removed. He recalled for the first time that as a child he had had frequent nightmares in which he heard the huffing and puffing of a locomotive train, the volume and pitch of the noise increasing in unbearable intensity until he awoke in great anxiety. As it turned out, the room he used to occupy at home was next to his parents' bedroom and from time to time he had been aware of strange noises coming from their room.

Going to the bathroom in the dream reminded him of a number of "dirty habits" he had. After his bowels moved, he was not too meticulous about wiping himself, so frequently there were stains on his underwear. His mother used to scold him about this. When he undressed at night, he would let his dirty clothes pile up on the floor for his mother to pick up in the morning. Later when he began to masturbate, he would ejaculate onto the bedsheet, leaving a stain that his mother would have to notice when she changed the bedding. He did something similar when he began to entertain girlfriends in his bedroom. In no way did he try to conceal from his parents, who often were home, what was going on in his bedroom, and if any doubt lingered in their minds, he left unambiguous evidence in the form of a rumpled bed and a stained sheet, making clear to them exactly what had been taking place. He defended his life-long pattern of masturbating. "To begin with," he said, "I'm completely in control. No girl can disappoint me; I have all the satisfaction I want and I get it by myself."

Working through the themes suggested in this material was very rewarding. It was clear that the patient had witnessed his parents having intercourse during that summer vacation. His response was as complex as it was long-lasting. He felt left out, betrayed, and humiliated. In his mind, his mother became a whore who did dirty things and who preferred his father because he was more powerful and had a bigger penis, while he was so small and insignificant. In his subsequent nightmares of the sounds of the locomotive, he feared his own wishes that his parents would die during the act as the people had perished in the railroad accident. He no longer trusted his mother, and this affected his attitude toward all women, especially after his sweetheart had turned her affections to his best friend when he was 12 years old. He became convinced that no woman would be interested in him and he decided "to show them." He would grow up, become outstanding and famous, and show that he had no use for them. He would take his vengeance by doing to his mother (and women in general) what she had done to him. He would flaunt before her the signs of his own dirty sexual activity and he would leave her and other women embarrassed, angered, and confused, as he had left the blonde patient who had come into the bathroom while he was urinating. After some of these conflicts had been worked through, the blonde patient no longer seemed so haughty, and if Anita did not close the door to the refrigerator so promptly, it no longer seemed catastrophic.

Tom's interests now turned to his professional work, which for a long time he had been treating lightly. He became more demanding of his students and less deferential to the chairman of his department. In fact, he realized how often he had thought of becoming the chairman himself. Behind his "good-guy" affability, he could see how competitive and ambitious he really was. He decided that he was being underpaid, that he needed more money, and that the thing to do was to get on with his work and earn the Ph.D. degree. Without the Ph.D., he felt like a boy. It was time to become a man.

No sooner had he begun to work on his thesis than the old inhibition returned. He blocked on using key references from important authorities in the field. He thought that I would accuse him of being a plagiarist, stealing his teacher's ideas. Guilt over stealing was not a new theme in his life. During his latency years, for a few months, in the company of a friend, he went on a stealing spree. He took some of the small change his father had left on the dresser and went to his mother's pocketbook looking for bills he knew his father had put there. From the most popular boy in his class, a born leader, he stole a fountain pen, which he hid under his shirt. From a cousin whom he admired for his strong physique and athletic ability, he stole a textbook of an advanced grade. As he put it, "I devoured the book voraciously."

From childhood on, stealing was prominent in his fantasy life. His favorite story was "Jack and the Beanstalk." "I loved to hear again and again how Jack ran off with the giant's money." His favorite movie was The Thief of Baghdad. The most exciting part was where the thief, Ali, goes to the mountains, climbs the great statue of the god, and steals from his forehead the largest jewel in the world, one that bestows on its owner magic, knowledge, and wealth. It reminded him of the myth of Prometheus, who stole knowledge from the gods, and of his own Promethean wish for omniscience. In this connection, he remembered that he had forgotten to return some books he had borrowed from the university library several years back. He recalled going with his father, at the age of four, to a turkish bath. He was awed by the gigantic size of his father's penis and wanted to reach up and touch it.

Coming a bit late for his session one day, he saw the blonde patient walking toward him on the street. He nodded to her and she acknowledged his greeting with a friendly smile. He felt he should have stopped to talk with her; perhaps he could have arranged for a date that ultimately could lead to an affair. As he entered the lobby of the building, he found himself caught up in a fantasy of a violent quarrel with me because I was forbidding him to have anything to do with the patient. Going up, he thought the elevator man seemed ominously threatening. This material led to the theme that I was standing in the way of his sexual freedom and of his achieving manhood, just as earlier in life, he had felt his father had stood in the way.

On two occasions, he lost the bill for the previous month's analysis and brought in a check for several sessions fewer than he was actually supposed to pay. He came to realize that he wanted to steal from me not just my money, but also my profession and my powers. He developed a craving for food before he came to the sessions; he was particularly fond of hot dogs and chocolate bars. For a while, he thought it would be a good idea to become an analyst himself. He could do as well, if not better. During this time, he became increasingly irritable and anxious, and the work he had undertaken to complete his Ph.D. thesis came to a complete standstill.

The anxiety that appeared during this phase of the analysis was connected to three types of dreams or fantasies. They were (1) dreams in which there was a danger of being devoured by sharks, dogs, or lions roaming in the jungle; (2) fantasies of a confrontation with a holdup man (only now Tom would often see himself fighting back); and (3) fantasies and dreams of struggle with an adversary in an enclosed space: the lobby of my building, a tunnel, or the basement of his childhood home. He had several dreams in which he saw himself perched at the window of his basement with a gun ready to defend the house against assault by intruders.

From his associations, it became clear in time that the feared adversary who threatened to mutilate him physically represented at different times myself, his father, the chief of his department, and the man who was to serve as chairman of the oral examining board for the Ph.D. examination. An examination represented to him a bloody, competitive struggle in which one either kills or is killed. It also had the unconscious significance of a trial where one is pronounced innocent or guilty. To pass the examination was to be permitted to enter the council of elders, to have the rights to be sexual, to have a woman, and to become a father. He told Anita that until he got the Ph.D., he could not think of marrying her, but would do so as soon as he passed. Unconsciously he felt he could not become a husband or father as long as he was in analysis, which meant to him as long as his father was alive. Accordingly, successful termination of treatment had the unconscious significance of killing his father. Fear of retaliation for his murderous wishes against authority figures intensified. His impotence grew more severe; unconsciously he imagined that within the woman's vagina was the adversary who would kill or mutilate him. During this period, he recapitulated the events and fantasies of his childhood in which he competed with his father for his mother's attention. The experiences between the ages of four and five proved to be the crucial ones. They centered around the boy's hostility

and envy of the father due to having slept in the same room with his parents at the Jersey coast. He recollected and reexperienced surges of tender loving feelings for his mother, who risked her life giving birth to him. He felt he had to repay her in kind. If only he could restore her heart to its original condition. As a child, he would fantasize about giving her new life in the form of a child.

After many months of working through the anxieties of these unconscious fantasies of childhood, the patient began to make progress in his work and he became potent again. He was well prepared for his Ph.D. oral exam. The day before he took the examination, confident that he would pass, while giving a talk before a large audience in a lecture hall, he had the following fantasy: his eye had fastened on the elaborate chandelier that hung from the ceiling. He imagined himself reaching up with one hand and tearing the chandelier out of the ceiling. He recalled how as a child he had been greatly impressed when he saw his father, seemingly gigantic, standing on a ladder reaching up to the ceiling to change an electric bulb. His Promethean wish was about to be fulfilled. Indeed, he did succeed.

Tom married Anita after he got the Ph.D. Five years after finishing the analysis, he reported that he was doing well in his work. He had been promoted and would soon be eligible for tenure. He was the proud father of a daughter and his wife was expecting a second child. Anita continued to forget to close the refrigerator door.

SUMMARY

As a system of thought and a technique for dealing with mental illness, psychoanalysis has been developing and changing over the years. What seemed at first a monolithic theory is now being examined critically from many different points of view. Technical innovations and reformulations of theoretical concepts are appearing in ever-increasing numbers. In addition, the literature of psychoanalysis has expanded enormously and there are special volumes dedicated to psychoanalysis and sociology, anthropology, history of childhood, aesthetics, developmental psychology, religion, and biography. Clinical investigation in the therapeutic setting according to the rules of the psychoanalytic situation remains the fundamental base of psychoanalytic knowledge and will clearly continue to be so in the future. Many alternative forms of psychotherapy appear from time to time on the horizon, draw great attention to themselves, but soon fade from the scene. Psychoanalysis has remained a steady, reliable, and growing discipline.

Two points have to be borne in mind about the position of psychoanalysis as therapy and as a system of thought. Not all forms of mental disturbance can or should be treated by psychoanalysis. Paradoxically, the demands of psychoanalysis require the coopera-tion of a patient with a fairly healthy ego who is well motivated to change and capable of facing himself honestly. For properly selected patients, psychoanalysis can offer the promise of help in attaining the best possible solution that can be realized from overcoming inner conflicts. It does not pretend to create perfectly balanced super-humans, in harmony with themselves and the universe.

The second point to be emphasized is that the reliability of the conclusions of psychoanalytic investigation diminishes the further one gets away from the clinical base of the psychoanalytic situation. Whenever psychoanalytic knowledge and insights are applied outside the analytic situation, one must take into consideration the possibility of innumerable alternative hypotheses and influences.

Because of the changing nature of the psychopathology of our time, notably the great increase in patients suffering from narcissistic, neurotic, and character disorders, and from mild perversions and addictions, one can anticipate new discoveries, fresh observations, original theoretical formulations, and innovative technical procedures.

ANNOTATED BIBLIOGRAPHY

The following books are recommended for those who want to attain deeper knowledge of psychoanalysis as theory and practice:

Brenner, C. (1973). *An elementary textbook of psychoanalysis.* New York: International Universities Press.
There is no better presentation of current psychoanalytic theory than this volume, which has become a worldwide introduction to psychoanalysis and has been translated into nine languages. It is the most comprehensive, systematic, and intelligible presentation of the subject, a worthy companion piece to Anna Freud's *The Ego and the Mechanisms of Defense.*

The theoretical development flows smoothly, logically, and cautiously. In addition to the basic theory of psychoanalysis, the book describes the part played by unconscious forces in day-to-day living and surveys the remarkable contribution of psychoanalysis to human knowledge. Current trends in the field are assessed and problems still requiring exploration are examined.

Freud, A. (1966). *The ego and the mechanisms of defense. The writings of Anna Freud (Vol. 2).* New York: International Universities Press. (Originally published 1936.)

Perhaps the finest and clearest writing style in psychoanalysis belongs to Anna Freud. *The Ego and the Mechanisms of Defense* is an established classic for its lucidity in portraying the theoretical implications of the structural theory and its application to problems of technique. In a relatively small volume, the author offers a definitive presentation of the psychoanalytic concept of conflict, the functioning of the anxiety signal, and the many ways in which the ego attempts to establish a stable homeostasis between impulse and defense. The sections on the origin of the superego, identity, and the transformations in adolescence afford the best picture of how the postoedipal child becomes an adult.

Freud, S. (1915–1917). *Introductory lectures on psychoanalysis.* London: Hogart Press.

These lectures make up volumes 15 and 16 of *The Complete Psychological Works of Sigmund Freud.* The books constitute a set of lectures Freud gave at the University of Vienna. His lectures are a model of lucidity, clarity, and organization. Introducing a new and complicated field of knowledge, Freud develops his thesis step by step, beginning with simple, acceptable, commonsense concepts, and advancing his argument consistently until the new and startling ideas that he was to place before his audience seem like the inevitable and logical consequences of each individual's own reflection. *The Introductory Lectures on Psychoanalysis* remains to this day the easiest and most direct approach to the understanding of psychoanalysis.

Hartmann, H. (1964). *Essays on ego psychology.* New York: International Universities Press.

For the advanced reader who is interested in the broadest theoretical applications of psychoanalysis to psychology, science, and sociology, there is no more authoritative exposition than this book of essays by the outstanding American psychoanalytic theoretician of the twentieth century. Hartmann discusses the concept of health, rational and irrational action, and the application of psychoanalytic concepts to social science and developmental psychology. This is not an easy set of essays to read, but the meticulous student who wants to be exposed to the broadest and highest level of analytic theory will be well rewarded for his or her efforts.

Jones, E. (1953–1975). *The life and work of Sigmund Freud.* New York: Basic Books.

This three-volume biography of Freud is one of the great biographies of our time. It captures the intellectual and spiritual ambience of Freud's period in history. It is a remarkable portrayal of the personality and thought of a genius. In addition, this book contains an accurate and readable summary of almost all of Freud's important contributions. It traces the history and the personalities of the psychoanalytic movement to the death of Freud in 1939.

CASE READINGS

Arlow, J. A. (1976). Communication and character: A clinical study of a man raised by deaf-mute parents. *Psychoanalytic Study of the Child, 31,* 139–163.

The adaptive capacities of the individual, even under difficult environmental circumstances, are illustrated in this well-documented case of someone raised by deaf-mute parents. In many respects, overcoming real hardships and conquering shame contributed to the character development of this person. In addition, one can observe how more than adequate mothering was possible on the part of a woman handicapped by deafness, as well as being educationally deprived.

Boyer, L. B. (1977). Working with a borderline patient. *The Psychoanalytic Quarterly, 46,* 389–420. [Reprinted in D. Wedding and R. J. Corsini (Eds.) (1989). *Case studies in psychotherapy.* Itasca, IL: F. E. Peacock.]

This is a teaching case that illustrates the application of psychoanalytic techniques in the treatment of a patient with a severe character disorder. Dr. Boyer describes his long relationship with this patient with considerable humor and sensitivity. The case provides vivid examples of many of the issues discussed in the current chapter.

Bornstein, B. (1949). The analysis of the phobic child, some problems of theory and technique in child analysis. *Psychoanalytic Study of the Child, 4,* 181–226.

This case represents an illustration of the classical technique of child analysis, as practiced by one of Anna Freud's principal collaborators and pupils. The relationship between theory and clinical technique is clearly expounded.

Freud, S. (1963). The rat man. In S. Freud, *Three case histories.* New York: Crowell-Collier. [Reprinted in D. Wedding and R. J. Corsini (Eds.) (1979). *Great cases in psychotherapy.* Itasca, IL: F. E. Peacock.]

The case of the "rat man" was a landmark in Freud's developing theory of psychoanalysis. In precise, clinical reporting, Freud outlined the role of the primary process, magical thinking, of ambivalence and anal fixation in the structure of the obsessive-compulsive neurosis. Although, in his later writings, Freud expanded his clinical theory and metapsychology, this case report represents a prime example of how Freud utilized the data of his observation to elucidate new findings and to shed light on problems hitherto obscure.

Winnicott, D. W. (1972). Fragment of an analysis. In P. L. Giovacchini, *Tactics and technique in psychoanalytic therapy* (pp. 455–493). New York: Science House.

Winnicott's approach to psychoanalytic theory and practice represented an important turning point in psychoanalysis. This case report demonstrates his special approach to problems of pathogenesis and treatment, an approach which emphasizes the influence of interpersonal interactions and feelings. Winnicott's technical precepts have had a strong and lasting effect on psychoanalytic practice.

REFERENCES

Abraham, K. (1924). The influence of oral erotism on character formation. Selected papers of Karl Abraham (Vol. 1, pp. 393–496). London: Hogarth Press.

Alexander, F. (1932). The medical value of psychoanalysis. New York: Norton.

Ansbacher, H., & Ansbacher, R. (Eds.) (1956). The individual psychology of Alfred Adler. New York: Basic Books.

Arlow, J. A. (1963). Conflict, regression and symptom formation. International Journal of Psychoanalysis 44, 12–22.

Arlow, J. A. (1972). Character perversion. In I. M. Marcus (Ed.), Currents in psychoanalysis. (pp. 317-336). New York: International Universities Press.

Arlow, J. A., & Brenner, C. (1964). Psychoanalytic concepts in the structural theory. New York: International Universities Press.

Berenfeld, S. (1944). Freud's earliest theories and the school of Helmholtz. Psychoanalytic Quarterly, 13, 341–362.

Beres, D., & Arlow, J. A. (1974). Fantasy and identification in empathy. Psychoanalytic Quarterly, 43, 4–25.

Bowlby, J. (1958). The nature of the child's ties to the mother. International Journal of Psychoanalysis, 39, 350–373.

Brenner, C. (1971). The psychoanalytic concept of aggression. International Journal of Psychoanalysis, 52, 137–144.

Brenner, C. (1973). An elementary textbook of psychoanalysis. New York: International Universities Press.

Breuer, J., & Freud, S. (1895). Studies on hysteria. Standard edition of the complete psychological works of Freud (Vol. 2). London: Hogarth Press.

Burton, A. (Ed.). (1969). Encounter. San Francisco: Jossey-Bass.

Ellis, A. (1970). Reason and emotion in psychotherapy. New York: Lyle Stuart.

Erikson, E. (1968). Identity, youth and crisis. New York: Norton.

Eysenck, H. J. (1965). The effects of psychotherapy. International Journal of Psychiatry, 1, 99–142.

Federn, P. (1952). Ego psychology and the psychoses. New York: Basic Books.

Feldman, F. (1968). Results of psychoanalysis in clinic case assignments. Journal of the American Psychoanalytic Association, 16, 274–300.

Fenichel, O. (1930). Zehn Jahre Berliner psychoanalytischer Institut. Vienna: International Psychoanalytischer Verlag.

Fenichel, O. (1945). The psychoanalytic theory of neurosis. New York: Norton.

Freud, A. (1936). The ego and mechanisms of defense. New York: International Universities Press.

Freud, A. (1951). Observations on child development. Psychoanalytic Study of the Child, 6, 18–30.

Freud, S. (1894).[1] The neuropsychoses of defense. (Standard Edition Vol. 3).

Freud, S. (1895). Studies on hysteria. (Standard Edition Vol. 2).

Freud, S. (1900). The interpretation of dreams. (Standard Edition Vol. 4).

Freud, S. (1901). The psychopathology of everyday life. (Standard Edition Vol. 6).

Freud, S. (1905a). Jokes and their relationship to the unconscious. (Standard Edition Vol. 8).

Freud, S. (1905b). Three essays on sexuality. (Standard Edition Vol. 7).

Freud, S. (1911). Formulations regarding the two principles of mental functioning. (Standard Edition Vol. 12).

Freud, S. (1913). Totem and taboo. (Standard Edition Vol. 13).

Freud, S. (1914a). The history of the psychoanalytic movement. (Standard Edition Vol. 14).

Freud, S. (1914b). On narcissism: An introduction. (Standard Edition Vol. 14).

Freud, S. (1915a). Repression. (Standard Edition Vol. 14).

Freud, S. (1915b). The unconscious. (Standard Edition Vol. 14).

Freud, S. (1917). On transformations of instinct as exemplified in anal erotism. (Standard Edition Vol. 17).

---

[1]All references to Sigmund Freud are from the Complete Psychological Works of Sigmund Freud, edited by James Strachey and published by Hogarth Press, London.

Freud, S. (1920). *Beyond the pleasure principle. (Standard Edition Vol. 18).*

Freud, S. (1921). *Group psychology and the analysis of the ego. (Standard Edition Vol. 18).*

Freud, S. (1923). *The ego and the id. (Standard Edition Vol. 19).*

Freud, S. (1925). An autobiographical study. (*Standard Edition Vol. 20*).

Freud, S. (1926). *Inhibitions, symptoms and anxiety. (Standard Edition Vol. 20).*

Freud, S. (1937). *Analysis terminable and interminable. (Standard Edition Vol. 23).*

Fromm, E. (1955). *The sane society.* New York: Holt, Rinehart and Winston.

Fromm-Reichmann, F. (1950). *Principles of intensive psychotherapy.* Chicago: University of Chicago Press.

Glasser, W. (1967). *Reality therapy.* New York: Julian Press.

Greenacre, P. (1956). Re-evaluation of the process of working through. *International Journal of Psychoanalysis, 37,* 439–444.

Greenacre, P. (1967). The influence of infantile trauma on genetic pattern. *Emotional Growth, 1,* 216–299.

Greenson, R. (1967). *The technique and practice of psychoanalysis.* New York: International Universities Press.

Grinstein, A. (Ed.) (1971). *The index of psychoanalytic writings.* New York: International Universities Press.

Hartmann, H. (1939). *Ego psychology and the problem of adaptation.* New York: International Universities Press.

Hartmann, H., & Kris, E. (1945). The genetic approach to psychoanalysis. *Psychoanalytic Study of the Child, 1,* 11–30.

Hartmann, H., Kris, E., & Loewenstein, R. N. (1946). Comments on the formation of psychic structure. *Psychoanalytic Study of the Child, 2,* 11–38.

Hartmann, H., Kris, E., & Loewenstein, R. N. (1949). Notes on the theory of aggression. *Psychoanalytic Study of the Child, 4,* 9–36.

Horney, K. (1940). *New ways in psychoanalysis.* New York: Norton.

Jacobson, E. (1954). The self and the object world: Vicissitudes of their infantile cathexes and their influence on ideational and affective development. *Psychoanalytic Study of the Child, 9,* 75–127.

Jones, E. (1953). *The life and work of Sigmund Freud.* New York: Basic Books.

Jung, C. (1909). *The psychology of dementia praecox.* New York & Washington: Nervous and Mental Disease.

Kernberg, O. (1968). The therapy of patients with borderline personality organization. *International Journal of Psychoanalysis, 49,* 600–619.

Klein, M. (1932). *The psychoanalysis of children.* London: Hogarth Press.

Kohut, H. (1971). *The analysis of the self. Monograph Series of the Psychoanalytic Study of the Child (No. 4).* New York: International Universities Press.

Kris, E. (1950). Preconscious mental processes. *Psychoanalytic Quarterly, 19,* 540–560.

Lewin, B. D. (1946). Sleep, the mouth and the dream screens. *Psychoanalytic Quarterly, 15,* 419–434.

Lewin, B. D. (1949). Mania and sleep. *Psychoanalytic Quarterly, 18,* 419–433.

Little, M. (1951). Countertransference and the patient's response to it. *International Journal of Psychoanalysis, 32,* 321–340.

Loewenstein, R. (1958). Remarks on some variations in psychoanalytic technique. *International Journal of Psychoanalysis, 39,* 202–210.

Lorenz, C. (1952). *King Solomon's ring.* New York: Crowell.

Mahler, M., Pine, F., & Bergman, A. (1975). *The psychological birth of the human infant.* New York: Basic Books.

Meltzoff, J., & Kornreich, M. (1970). *Research in psychotherapy.* New York: Atherton Press.

Nunberg, H. (1926). The will to recovery. *International Journal of Psychoanalysis, 7,* 64–78.

Perls, F., Hefferline, R., & Goodman, P. (1951). *Gestalt therapy.* New York: Julian Press.

Peterfreund, E. (1971). Information systems and psychoanalysis. *Psychological Issues Monograph (Nos. 25–26).* New York: International Universities Press.

Pfeffer, A. Z. (1963). The meaning of the analyst after analysis: A contribution to the theory of therapeutic results. *Journal of the American Psychoanalytic Association, 11*, 229–244.

Racker, E. (1953). A contribution to the problem of countertransference. *International Journal of Psychoanalysis, 34*, 313–324.

Rangell, L. (1973). On the cacophony of human relations. *Psychoanalytic Quarterly, 42*, 325–348.

Rapaport, D. (1951). *The organization and pathology of thought.* New York: Columbia University Press.

Reich, A. (1960). Further remarks on countertransference. *International Journal of Psychoanalysis, 41*, 389–395.

Reich, A. (1973). *Psychoanalytic contributions.* New York: International Universities Press.

Rogers, C. (1951). *Client-centered therapy.* New York: Houghton Mifflin.

Rosenfeld, H. (1954). Consideration concerning the psychoanalytic approach to acute and chronic schizophrenia. *International Journal of Psychoanalysis, 35*, 135–140.

Rubenstein, B. B. (1967). Explanation and mere description: A metascientific examination of certain aspects of the psychoanalytic theory of motivation in motives and thought. Psychoanalytic essays in honor of David Rapaport. *Psychological Issues Monograph (Nos. 18–19).* New York: International Universities Press.

Sachs, H. (1942). *The creative unconscious.* Cambridge, MA: Sci-Art Publishers.

Schafer, R. (1976). *A new language of psychoanalysis.* New Haven & London: Yale University Press.

Schmideberg, M. (1938). After the analysis. *Psychoanalytic Quarterly, 7*, 122–142.

Schultz, W. C. (1967). *Joy.* New York: Grove Press.

Searles, H. F. (1965). *Collected papers on schizophrenia and related subjects.* New York: International Universities Press.

Spitz, R. (1955). The primal cavity: A contribution to the genesis of perception and its role in psychoanalytic theory. *Psychoanalytic Study of the Child, 10*, 215–240.

Sullivan, H. S. (1953). *The interpersonal theory of psychiatry.* New York: Norton.

Tinbergern, N. (1951). *The study of instinct.* London: Oxford University Press.

Tower, L. E. (1956). Countertransference. *Journal of the American Psychoanalytic Association, 4*, 224–265.

Wallerstein, R. S., & Smelser, N. J. (1969). Articulations and applications. *International Journal of Psychoanalysis, 50*, 693–710.

Weigert, E. (1970). *The courage to love.* New Haven: Yale University Press.

Winnicott, D. W. (1953). Transitional objects and transitional phenomena: A study of the first not-me possession. *International Journal of Psychoanalysis, 34*, 89–97.

Wolpe, J. (1958). *Psychotherapy by reciprocal inhibition.* Stanford, CA: Stanford University Press.

Zetzel, E. R. (1970). *The capacity for emotional growth: Theoretical and clinical contributions to psychoanalysis.* New York: International Universities Press.

Zilboorg, G., & Henry, G. W. (1941). *A history of medical psychology.* New York: Norton.

ALFRED ADLER, 1870–1937

3

Adlerian Psychotherapy

HAROLD H. MOSAK

OVERVIEW

Adlerian psychology (Individual Psychology), the personality theory and therapeutic system developed by Alfred Adler, views the person holistically as a creative, responsible, "becoming" individual moving toward fictional goals within his or her phenomenal field. It holds that one's lifestyle is sometimes self-defeating because of inferiority feelings. The individual with "psychopathology" is discouraged rather than sick, and the therapeutic task is to encourage the person, to activate his or her social interest, and to develop a new life-style through relationship, analysis, and action methods.

Basic Concepts

Adlerian psychology is predicated upon assumptions that differ in significant ways from the Freudian "womb" from which it emerged. Adler throughout his lifetime credited Freud with primacy in the development of a dynamic psychology. His debt to Freud for explicating the purposefulness of symptoms and for ex-

pressing the notion that dreams were meaningful was consistently acknowledged. The influence of early childhood experiences in personality development constitutes still another point of agreement. Freud emphasized the role of psychosexual development and the Oedipus complex while Adler focused upon the effects of children's perceptions of their family constellation and their struggle to find a place of significance within it.

Adlerian basic assumptions can be expressed as follows:

1. All behavior occurs in a social context. Humans are born into an environment with which they must engage in reciprocal relations. The oft-quoted statement by the Gestalt psychologist Kurt Lewin that "behavior is a function of person and environment" bears a striking parallel to Adler's contention that people cannot be studied in isolation (1929).

2. Individual Psychology is an interpersonal psychology. How individuals interact with the others sharing "this crust of earth" (Adler, 1958, p. 6) is paramount. Transcending interper-

sonal transactions is the development of the feeling of being a part of a larger social whole, the feeling of being socially embedded, the willingness to contribute in the communal life for the common weal—movements that Adler (1964b) incorporated under the heading of Gemeinschaftsgefühl, or social interest.

3. Adlerian psychology rejects reductionism in favor of holism. Jan Smuts (1961), who introduced the concept of holism, and Adler engaged in a correspondence that unfortunately has never been published. The Adlerian demotes part-functions from the central investigative focus in favor of studying the whole person and how he or she moves through life. This renders the polarities of conscious and unconscious, mind and body, approach and avoidance, ambivalence and conflict meaningless except as subjective experiences of the whole person. That is, people behave as if the conscious mind moves in one direction while the unconscious mind moves in another. From the external observer's viewpoint, all part-functions are subordinate functions of the individual's goals and style of life.

4. Conscious and unconscious are both in the service of the individual, who uses them to further personal goals. Adler (1963a) treats unconscious as an adjective rather than a noun, thus avoiding reifying the concept. That which is unconscious is the nonunderstood. Like Otto Rank, Adler felt that humans know more than they understand. Conflict, defined as intrapersonal by others, is defined as a "one step forward and one step backward movement," the net effect being to maintain the individual at a point "dead center." Although people experience themselves in the throes of a

conflict, unable to move, in reality they create these antagonistic feelings, ideas, and values because they are unwilling to move in the direction of solving their problems (Mosak & LeFevre, 1976).

5. The understanding of the individual requires the understanding of his or her cognitive organization, the life-style. The latter concept refers to the convictions individuals develop early in life to help them organize experience, to understand it, to predict it, and to control it. Convictions are conclusions derived from the individual's apperceptions, and they constitute a biased mode of apperception. Consequently, a life-style is neither right nor wrong, normal or abnormal, but merely the "spectacles" through which people view themselves in relationship to the way in which they perceive life. Subjectivity rather than so-called objective evaluation becomes the major tool for understanding the person. As Adler wrote, "We must be able to see with his eyes and listen with his ears" (1958, p. 72).

6. Behavior may change throughout a person's life span in accordance with both the immediate demands of the situation and the long-range goals inherent in the life-style. The life-style remains relatively constant through life unless the convictions change through the mediation of psychotherapy. Although the definition of psychotherapy customarily refers to what transpires within a consulting room, a broader view of psychotherapy would include the fact that life in itself may often be psychotherapeutic.

7. According to the Adlerian conception, people are not pushed by causes; that is, they are not determined by heredity and environment. "Both are giving only the frame and the influ-

ences which are answered by the individual in regard to his styled creative power" (Ansbacher & Ansbacher, 1956). People move toward self-selected goals, which they feel will give them a place in the world, will provide them with security, and will preserve their self-esteem. Life is a dynamic striving. "The life of the human soul is not a 'being' but a 'becoming' " (Adler, 1963a, p. ix).

8. The central striving of human beings has been variously described as completion (Adler, 1958), perfection (Adler, 1964a), superiority (Adler, 1926), self-realization (Horney, 1951), self-actualization (Goldstein, 1939), competence (White, 1957), and mastery (Adler, 1926). Adler distinguishes among such strivings in terms of the direction a striving takes. If strivings are solely for the individual's greater glory, he considers them socially useless and, in extreme conditions, characteristic of mental problems. On the other hand, if the strivings are for the purpose of overcoming life's problems, the individual is engaged in the striving for self-realization, in contributing to humanity, and in making the world a better place to live.

9. Moving through life, the individual is confronted with alternatives. Because Adlerians are either non-determinists or soft determinists, the conceptualization of humans as creative, choosing, self-determined decision makers permits them to choose the goals they want to pursue. Individuals may select socially useful goals or they may devote themselves to the useless side of life. They may choose to be task-oriented or they may, as does the neurotic, concern themselves with their own superiority, protecting themselves from threats to their sense of personal worth.

10. The freedom to choose (McArthur, 1958) introduces the concepts of value and meaning into psychology. These were unpopular concepts at the time (1931) that Adler wrote What Life Should Mean to You. The greatest value for the Adlerian is Gemeinschaftsgefühl, or social interest (Ansbacher, 1968). Although Adler contends that it is an innate feature of human beings, at least as potential, acceptance of this criterion is not absolutely necessary. People possess the capacity for coexisting and interrelating with others. Indeed, the "iron logic of social living" (Adler, 1959) demands that we do so. Even in severe psychopathology, total extinction of social interest does not occur. Even the psychotic retains some commonality with "normal" people.

As Rabbi Akiva noted two millennia ago, "The greatest principle of living is to love one's neighbor as oneself." If we regard ourselves as fellow human beings with fellow feeling, we are socially contributive people interested in the common welfare and, by Adler's pragmatic definition of normality, mentally healthy (Dreikurs, 1969; Shoben, 1957).

If my feeling derives from my observation and conviction that life and people are hostile and I am inferior, I may divorce myself from the direct solution of life's problems and strive for personal superiority through over-compensation, wearing a mask, withdrawal, attempting only safe tasks where the outcome promises to be successful, and other devices for protecting my self-esteem. Adler said the neurotic in terms of movement displayed a "hesitating attitude" toward life (1964a). Also, the neurotic was described as a "yes-but" personality (Adler, 1934); at still other times, the neurotic was described as an "if only . . ." personality (Adler, 1964a): "If only I didn't have these symptoms, I'd. . . ." The latter provided the rationale for "The Question," a device Adler used for differential diagnosis as well as for understanding the individual's task avoidance.

11. Because Adlerians are concerned with process, little diagnosis is done in terms of nomenclature. Differential diagnosis between functional and organic disorder does often present a problem. Because all behavior is purposeful, a *psychogenic* symptom will have a psychological or social purpose and an *organic* symptom will have a somatic purpose. An Adlerian would ask "The Question" (Adler, 1964a; Dreikurs, 1958, 1962), "If I had a magic wand or a magic pill that would eliminate your symptom immediately, what would be different in your life?" If the patient answers, "I'd go out more often socially" or "I'd write my book," the symptom would most likely be psychogenic. If the patient responds, "I wouldn't have this excruciating pain," the symptom would most likely be organic.

12. Life presents challenges in the form of the life tasks. Adler named three of these explicitly but referred to two others without specifically naming them (Dreikurs & Mosak, 1966). The original three tasks were those of *society, work,* and *sex.* The first has already been alluded to. Because no person can claim self-sufficiency, we are all interdependent. Important in the social sphere, it also means that each of us is dependent upon the labor of other people and they, in turn, are dependent upon our contribution. Work thus becomes essential for human survival. The cooperative individual assumes this role willingly and cheer-

fully accepts a part in the human enterprise. In the sexual realm, because two different sexes exist, we must also learn how to relate to that fact. We must define our sex roles, partly on the basis of cultural definitions and stereotypes, and train ourselves to relate to the *other,* not the *opposite,* sex. Other people, of either sex, do not represent the enemy. They are our fellows, with whom we must learn to cooperate.

Fourth (Dreikurs & Mosak, 1967) and fifth tasks (Mosak & Dreikurs, 1967) have been described. Although Adler alluded to the *spiritual,* he never specifically named it (Jahn & Adler, 1964; Adler, 1987). But each of us must deal with the problem of defining the nature of the universe, the existence and nature of God, and how to relate to these concepts. Finally, we must address the task of *coping with ourselves.* William James (1890) made the distinction between the self as subject and the self as object, and it is as imperative, for the sake of mental health, that good relations exist between the "I" and the "me" as between the "I" and other people.

13. Because life is bigger than we are and constantly provides challenges, living demands courage (Neuer, 1936). Courage is not an *ability* one either possesses or lacks. Nor is courage synonymous with bravery, like falling on a grenade to save one's buddies from injury or death. *Courage* refers to the *willingness* to engage in risk-taking behavior when one either does not know the consequences or when the consequences might be adverse. We are all *capable* of courageous behavior provided that we are *willing.* Our willingness will depend upon many variables, internal and external, such as our life-style convictions, our

degree of social interest, the extent of risk as we appraise it, and whether we are task-oriented or prestige-oriented. Given that life offers few guarantees, all living requires risk taking. It would require very little courage to live if we were perfect, omniscient, or omnipotent. The question we must each answer is whether we have the courage to live despite the knowledge of our imperfection (Lazarsfeld, 1966).

14. Life has no intrinsic meaning. We give meaning to life, each of us in our own fashion. We declare it to be meaningful, meaningless, an absurdity, a prison sentence (cf., the adolescent's justification for doing as he pleases—"I didn't ask to be born"), a vale of tears, a preparation for the next world, and so on. Dreikurs (1957, 1971) maintained that the meaning of life resided in doing for others and in contributing to social life and social change. Viktor Frankl (1963) believes the meaning of life lies in love, expressing a psychological variation of the popular 1950s song, "Nature Boy," in which the refrain went, "The greatest thing you'll ever learn is to love and be loved in return." The meaning we attribute to life will "determine" our behavior. We will behave *as if* life were really in accord with our perceptions, and, therefore, certain meanings will have greater practical utility than others. Optimists will live an optimistic life, take their chances, and not be discouraged by failure and adversity. They will be able to distinguish between failing and being a failure. Pessimists will refuse to be engaged with life, refuse to try, sabotage their efforts if they do make an attempt, and, through their methods of operation, endeavor to confirm their preexisting pessimistic anticipations (Krausz, 1935).

OTHER SYSTEMS

Students often have asked, "Do you Adlerians believe in sex too?" The question is not always asked facetiously. Freud accorded sex the status of the master motive in behavior. Adler merely categorized sex as one of several tasks the individual was required to solve. Freud employed esoteric jargon and Adler favored common sense language. One story has it that a psychiatrist took Adler to task after a lecture, denigrating his approach with the criticism, "You're only talking common sense," to which Adler replied, "I wish more psychiatrists did." We can place other differences between these two men in columnar form, as shown in Table 3.1.

A more extended comparison of Freud's and Adler's concepts of humankind may be found in articles by H. W. von Sassen (1967) and Otto Hinrichsen (1913).

Adler and the neo-Freudians

Adler once proclaimed that he was more concerned that his theories survived than that people remembered to associate his theories with his name. His wish apparently was granted. In discussing Adler's influence upon contemporary psychological theory and practice, Henri Ellenberger commented, "It would not be easy to find another author from which so much has been borrowed from all sides without acknowledgment than Adler" (1970, p. 645). Many neo-Freudians have credited Adler with contributing to and influencing their work. In her last book, Karen Horney wrote of "neurotic ambition," "the need for perfection," and "the category of power." "All drives for glory have in common the reaching out for greater knowledge, wisdom, virtue or powers than

Table 3.1
Comparison of Freud's and Adler's Concepts

Freud	*Adler*
1. Objective	1. Subjective
2. Physiological substratum for theory	2. A social psychology
3. Emphasized causality	3. Emphasized teleology
4. Reductionistic. The individual was divided into "parts" that were antagonistic toward each other: e.g., id-ego-superego, Eros vs. Thanatos, conscious vs. unconscious.	4. Holistic. The individual is indivisible. He or she is a unity and all "parts" (memory, emotions, behavior) are in the service of the whole individual.
5. The study of the individual centers about the intrapersonal, the intrapsychic.	5. People can only be understood interpersonally, and as social beings moving through and interacting with their environment.
6. The establishment of intrapsychic harmony constitutes the ideal goal of psychotherapy. "Where id was, there shall ego be."	6. The expansion of the individual, self-realization, and the enhancement of social interest represent the ideal goals for the individual.
7. People are basically "bad." Civilization attempts to domesticate them, for which they pay a heavy price. Through therapy the instinctual demands may be sublimated but not eliminated.	7. People are neither "good" nor "bad," but as creative, choosing human beings, they may choose to be "good" or "bad" or both, depending upon their life-style and their appraisal of the immediate situation and its payoffs. Through the medium of therapy people can choose to actualize themselves.
8. People are victims of both instinctual life and civilization.	8. People, as choosers, can shape both their internal and their external environments. Although they are not the complete masters of their fate and cannot always choose what will happen to them, they can always choose the posture they will adopt toward life's stimuli.
9. Description of child development was postdictive and not based upon direct observation of children but upon the free associations of adults.	9. Children were studied directly in families, in schools, and in family education centers.
10. Emphasis upon the Oedipus situation and its resolution	10. Emphasis upon the family constellation
11. People are enemies. Others are our competitors, and we must protect ourselves from them. Theodore Reik quotes Nestroy, "If chance brings two wolves together, . . . neither feels the least uneasy because the other is a wolf; two human beings, however, can never meet in the forest, but one must think: That fellow may be a robber" (1948, p. 477).	11. Other people are *mitmenschen*, fellow human beings. They are our equals, our collaborators, our cooperators in life.
12. Women feel inferior because they envy men their penises. Women are inferior. "Anatomy is destiny."	12. Women feel inferior because in our cultural milieu women are undervalued. Men have privileges, rights, preferred status, although in the current cultural ferment, these roles are being reevaluated.
13. Neurosis has a sexual etiology.	13. Neurosis is a failure of learning, a product of distorted perceptions.
14. Neurosis is the price we pay for civilization.	14. Neurosis is the price we pay for our lack of civilization.

are given to human beings; they all aim at the *absolute*, the unlimited, the infinite" (1951, pp. 34–35). Those familiar with Adler's writings on the neurotic's perfectionistic, godlike striving will immediately be struck with the similarity in viewpoint.

Horney (1951) rejected Freud's pessimism, "his disbelief in human goodness and human growth," in favor of the Adlerian view that a person could grow and could "become a decent human being" and that a person's potentialities "deteriorate if this relationship to others and hence to himself is, and continues to be, disturbed."

Others have also remarked upon the resemblance between the theories of Horney and Adler; the reviewer of one Horney book wrote that Karen Horney had just written a new book by Alfred Adler (Farau, 1953).

Erich Fromm also expresses views similar to those of Adler. According to Fromm, people make choices. The attitude of the mother in child rearing is of paramount importance. Life fosters feelings of powerlessness and anxiety. Patrick Mullahy (1955) indicates that

The only adequate solution, according to Fromm, is a relationship with man and nature, chiefly by love and productive work, which strengthens the total personality, sustains the person in his sense of uniqueness, and at the same time gives him a feeling of belonging, a sense of unity and common destiny with mankind. (pp. 251–252)

Although Harry Sullivan places greater emphasis upon developmental child psychology than does Adler, Sullivan's "person" moves through life in much the same manner as does Adler's. Thus, Sullivan (1954) speaks of the "security operations" of the individual, a direct translation of Adler's and Lene Credner's (1930)

Sicherungen. His "good me" and "bad me" dichotomy, in expression if not in manner of development, is essentially the same as that described by Adlerians.

So many similarities between Adler and the neo-Freudians have been noted that Gardner Murphy concluded, "If this way of reasoning is correct, neurosis should be the general characteristic of man under industrialism, a point suspected by many Freudians and, in particular, by that branch of the Freudian school (Horney and her associates) that has learned most from Adler" (1947, p. 569). A summary of such resemblances appears in Heinz and Rowena Ansbacher's *Individual Psychology of Alfred Adler* (1956) as well as in an article by Walter James (1947). Fritz Wittels (1939) has proposed that the neo-Freudians should more properly be called "neo-Adlerians," and a study by Heinz Ansbacher (1952) suggests that many traditional Freudians would concur.

Adler and Rogers

Although the therapies of Adler and Carl Rogers are diametrically opposed, their theories share many commonalities. Both are phenomenological, goal-directed, and holistic. Each views people as self-consistent, creative, and capable of change. To illustrate, Rogers (1951) postulates the following:

1. The organism reacts as an organized whole to the phenomenal field (p. 486).
2. The best vantage point for understanding behavior is from the internal frame of reference of the individual himself (p. 494).
3. The organism reacts to the field as it is experienced and perceived (p. 484-85).

4. The organism has one basic tendency and striving—to actualize, maintain, and enhance the experiencing organism (p. 487).

Much of the early research on non-directive and client-centered therapy used as a criterion measure the discrepancy between *self-concept* and *self-ideal*. The Adlerian would describe the extent of discrepancy as a measure of inferiority feelings.

Adler and Ellis

Both cognitive psychologies, the theories of Adler and Ellis exhibit many points of convergence. Albert Ellis (1970, 1971) finds his rational-emotive psychology to parallel that of Adler's. What Adler calls basic mistakes, Albert Ellis refers to as irrational beliefs or attitudes. Both accept the notion that emotions are actually a form of thinking and that people create or control their emotions by controlling their thinking. They agree that we are not victims of our emotions but their creators. In psychotherapy, they (1) adopt similar stances with respect to unconscious motivation, (2) confront patients with their irrational ideas (basic mistakes or internalized sentences), (3) counterpropagandize the patient, (4) insist upon action, and (5) constantly *encourage* patients to assume responsibility for the direction of their lives in more positive channels. The last phrase seems to reflect the major disagreement between Adler and Ellis, namely, what is "positive." Ellis argues,

Where Adler writes, therefore, that "All my efforts are devoted towards increasing the social interest of the patient," the rational therapist would prefer to say, "Most of my efforts are devoted towards increasing the self-interest of the patient." He assumes that if the individual possesses ra-

tional self-interest he will, on both biological and logical grounds, almost invariably tend to have a high degree of social interest as well. (1957, p. 43)

Adler and Other Systems

The many points of convergence and divergence between Adler and several of the existentialist thinkers have been noted by many writers (Birnbaum, 1961; Farau, 1964; Frankl, 1970). Phyllis Bottome had written in 1939 that "Adler was the first founder of an existence psychology" (p. 199). Given that existential psychology is not a school but a viewpoint, it is difficult to make comparisons, but interested readers may discover for themselves in an editorial by Ansbacher (1959) the lines of continuity between Adler and current existential thought.

The recognition of Adler as one of the earliest humanistic psychologists is clear. Ellis pays homage to Adler as "one of the first humanistic psychologists" (1970, p. 32). Abraham Maslow (1962, 1970) published five papers in Adlerian journals over a period of 35 years. As we have already observed, many of Adler's ideas have been incorporated by the humanistic psychologists with little awareness of Adler's contributions. "The model of man as a composite of part functions" that James Bugental (1963) questions has been repudiated by Adlerians for almost half a century. Bugental proposes "that the defining concept of man basic to the new humanistic movement in psychology is that *man is the process that supersedes the sum of his part functions.*" We may compare this proposal with that of Dreikurs: "The whole is more than a sum total of its parts; therefore, it cannot be explained by any number of qualities but only understood as an indivisible whole in motion toward a goal" (1960a, p. 194).

Adlerian psychology is a value psychology (Adler wrote *What Life Should Mean to You* in 1931), as Viktor Frankl and Rollo May, among others, acknowledge in their debt to Adler. Frankl wrote:

What he [Adler] ... achieved and accomplished was no less than a Copernican switch.... Beyond this, Alfred Adler may well be regarded as an existential thinker and as a forerunner of the existential-psychiatric movement. (1970, p. 38)

May expresses his debt as follows:

I appreciate Adler more and more.... Adler's thoughts as I learned them in studying with him in Vienna in the summers of 1932 and 1933 led me indirectly into psychology, and were very influential in the later work in this country of Sullivan and William Alanson White, etc. (1970, p. 39)

Abraham Maslow wrote:

For me Alfred Adler becomes more and more correct year by year. As the facts come in, they give stronger and stronger support to his image of man. I should say that in one respect especially the times have not yet caught up with him. I refer to his holistic emphasis. (1970, p. 39)

HISTORY

PRECURSORS

Adler's insistence that people cannot be studied in isolation but only in their social context was previously expressed by Aristotle who referred to the human being as a *zoon politikon*, a political animal (Adler, 1959). Adler exhibits his affinity with the philosophy of stoicism, as both Ellenberger (1970) and H. N. Simpson (1966) point out. Other commentators have noted the resemblance of Adler's writings to Kant's philosophy, especially with respect to the categorical imperative, private logic, and overcoming. Adler and Nietzsche have often been compared,

and much has been made of their common usage of the concept of the *will to power*. However, Adler spoke of it in terms of the normal strivings for competence, while Nietzsche's references to this concept referred to what Adler would call the "useless side of life." Nietzsche stressed the *Übermensch* (Superman) and Adler spoke of equality. Adler further stressed *social feeling*, a concept totally alien to the Nietzschian philosophy.

Throughout history, philosophers have struggled with the mind-body problem, and at one point, Adler related his description of personality types to Hippocrates' humoral theory, but after 1927 made no further mention of it. At the dawn of the modern scientific era, the rationalistic and empirical schools of philosophy were providing explanations for the connections between mind and body. The issue lay relatively dormant within psychology and experienced a renaissance when psychologists and psychiatrists began to address themselves to the study of psychosomatic syndromes. Psychosomatic and somatopsychic hypotheses were advanced to explain how emotions could influence the production of symptoms and how bodily states might create emotional or mental illness. Adler rejected such divisions. Like Kurt Lewin (1935), he rejected categorization and dichotomies. Like Jan Smuts (1961), he was a holist; *Individual Psychology* was not meant to describe the psychology of the individual. It referred rather to Adler's holistic stance, that a person could be understood only as a whole, an indivisible unity. To study people atomistically was to not capture fully the nature of humanity. For Adler, the question was neither "How does mind affect body?" nor "How does body affect mind?" but rather "How does the individual use body and mind in the pursuit of goals?" Although Adler's *Study of Organ Inferiority and Its Psychical Compensation* (1917) might seem to contradict such statements by expressing a causalistic viewpoint, this highly original theory was formulated during the period when Adler was a member of the Freudian circle. Later Adler added the subjective factor:

It might be suggested, therefore, that in order to find out where a child's interest lies, we need only to ascertain which organ is defective. But things do not work out quite so simply. The child does not experience the fact of organ inferiority in the way that an external observer sees it, but as modified by his own scheme of apperception. (1969)

Perhaps the greatest influence upon Adler was Hans Vaihinger's (1965) "philosophy of 'as if.' " According to Vaihinger, a fiction is "a mere piece of imagination" that deviates from reality but that is nevertheless utilitarian for the individual. Both the concept of the world and the concept of the self are subjective, that is, fictional, and therefore in error. *Truth* is "only the most expedient error, that is, the system of ideas which enables us to act and to deal with things most rapidly, neatly, and safely, and with the minimum of irrational elements" (p. 108).

Finally, Adler's psychology has a religious tone (Adler, 1958; Jahn & Adler, 1964; Mosak, 1987c). His placement of social interest at the pinnacle of his value theory is in the tradition of those religions that stress people's responsibility for each other. Indeed, Adler maintained that "Individual Psychology makes good religion if you are unfortunate enough not to have another" (Rasey, 1956, p. 254).

BEGINNINGS

Adler was born near Vienna on February 7, 1870, and died while on a lecture tour in Aberdeen, Scotland, on May 27, 1937. After graduating from the University of Vienna in 1895, Adler entered private practice as an ophthalmologist in 1898. He later switched to general practice and then to neurology. During this period, Adler gave portents of his later social orientation by writing a book on the health of tailors (1898). In this respect, he may be regarded as the progenitor of industrial medicine.

In 1902, Adler, at Freud's invitation, joined in the latter's Wednesday evening discussion circle. Biographers agree that Adler wrote two defenses of Freud's theories that may have gained him the invitation. Although textbooks frequently refer to Adler as a student of Freud, Adler was actually a colleague who had already established his own place as a physician (Ansbacher, 1962; Ellenberger, 1970; Federn, 1963; Maslow, 1962). Through the next decade, Adler had one foot in and one foot out of the Freudian circle. Although his *Study of Organ Inferiority* won Freud's unqualified endorsement, Adler's introduction of the aggression instinct in 1908 met with Freud's disapproval. Not until 1923, long after Adler had discarded instinct theory, did Freud incorporate the aggressive instinct into psychoanalysis (Sicher & Mosak, 1967), at which time Adler declared, "I enriched psychoanalysis by the aggressive drive. I glady make them a present of it!" (Bottome, 1939, p. 63).

Adler's increasing divergence from Freud's viewpoint led to discomfort and disillusion in the Vienna Society. Adler criticized Freud's sexual stance; Freud condemned Adler's ego psychology. They disagreed on (1) the unity of neuroses, (2) penis envy (sexual) versus the masculine protest (social), (3) the defensive role of the ego in neuroses, and (4) the role of the unconscious. Freud did not think Adler had discovered anything new but had merely reinterpreted what psychoanalysis had already said. He believed that what Adler discovered was "trivial," and that it was "methodologically deplorable and condemns his whole work to sterility" (Colby, 1951). After a series of meetings where these issues were discussed in an atmosphere of fencing, heckling, and vitriol (Brome, 1968), Adler in 1911 resigned as president of the Vienna Psychoanalytic Society. Later that year, Freud forced the choice between Adler and himself. Several members of the circle expressed their sympathy for Adler by resigning and forming the Society for Free Psychoanalytic Research.

During the next decade, with the exception of the war period, Adler and his co-workers developed the social view of the neuroses. Their focus was primarily clinical, although Adler (1914) as early as 1908 had demonstrated an interest in children and in education. In 1922 Adler initiated what was perhaps the first community-outreach program, child-guidance centers within the community. These centers were located in public schools and were directed by psychologists who served without pay. The method, for which Adler drew much criticism, was that of public family education, a method still used in Adlerian family education centers. Twenty-eight such centers existed in Vienna until 1934, when an unfriendly government closed them. This form of center was transported to the United States by Rudolf Dreikurs and his students (Dreikurs, Corsini, Lowe & Sonstegard,

1959). The success of these centers motivated the Vienna School authorities to invite several Adlerians to plan a school along Adlerian lines, and from this invitation emerged the school described in Oskar Spiel's *Discipline without Punishment* (1962). The school emphasized encouragement, class discussions, democratic principles, and the responsibility of children for themselves and for each other, educational methods that are still in use.

The social orientation of Individual Psychology inevitably led to interest in group methods and Adler's introduction of family therapy (1922). Dreikurs (1959) is credited with the first use of group psychotherapy in private practice.

Between World Wars I and II, Adlerian groups existed in 20 European countries and in the United States. In 1926 Adler was invited to the United States to lecture and demonstrate, and until 1934, when fascism took hold in Austria, he divided his time between the United States, where he was on the medical faculty of the Long Island College of Medicine, and abroad. Two of his children, Alexandra and Kurt, now practice psychiatry in New York City. With the march of Nazism, many Adlerians were forced to flee their European homelands, and after many hardships, Adlerians made the United States the center of their activities. Today Individual Psychology societies exist in the United States, England, Canada, France, Denmark, Switzerland, Germany, Austria, the Netherlands, Greece, Italy, Israel, and Australia.

CURRENT STATUS

The resurgence of the Adlerian school after the dispersion from Europe was an uphill effort. Personal hardships of refugee Adlerians were compounded by the existing psychological climate in this country. The economic depression still prevailed. The Freudian school held a near monopoly, both in the treatment area and with respect to appointments in medical schools. Some Adlerians defected; others became crypto-Adlerians. However, others persevered in retaining their identity and their optimism. Local societies were founded and 1952 saw the formation of the American Society of Adlerian Psychology (now the North American Society of Adlerian Psychology). Several journals appeared; the major American one is *Individual Psychology*, formerly called the *Journal of Individual Psychology*, which itself was the successor to the *Individual Psychology Bulletin*, of which Dreikurs was for many years the editor. The International Association of Individual Psychology also publishes the *Individual Psychology Newsletter*.

Training institutes that offer certificates in psychotherapy, counseling, and child guidance are found in New York, Chicago, Minneapolis, Berkeley, San Francisco, Cincinnati, St. Louis, Dayton, Fort Wayne, Cleveland, Vancouver, Montreal, and Toronto. Individual courses and programs of study are offered at many universities, such as Oregon, Arizona, West Virginia, Vermont, Governors State, Southern Illinois, and Georgia State. Masters degrees based on an Adlerian curriculum are offered by Bowie State College and by the Alfred Adler Institute of Chicago. The latter has been accredited to offer a doctoral program in clinical psychology.

Although Adlerian psychology was once dismissed as moribund, superficial (i.e., an "ego psychology"), and suitable mainly for children, it is today a viable psychology that pioneered in the holistic, phenomenological, social, teleological view of human beings.

Today's Adlerian may operate as a traditional clinician but remains innovative. Joshua Bierer has been a pioneer in social psychiatry (1969) and a leader in the day-hospital movement (1951). Therapeutic social clubs have been in operation at the Alfred Adler Mental Hygiene Clinic in New York and at Saint Joseph Hospital in Chicago. Dreikurs originated multiple psychotherapy (1950), and he, Harold Mosak, and Bernard Shulman have contributed to its development (1952a, 1952b, 1982). Rudolf Dreikurs, Asya Kadis, Helene Papanek, and Bernard Shulman have made extensive contributions to group therapy. In a joint research project with the Counseling Center (Rogerian) of the University of Chicago, John Shlien, Mosak, and Dreikurs (1962) investigated the effects of time limits in therapy. Because they prefer the goal of prevention to that of healing, Adlerians function extensively in the area of education. Manford Sonstegard, Raymond Lowe, Bronia Grunwald, Oscar Christensen, Raymond Corsini, and Loren Grey are among those responsible for applying Adlerian principles in the schools. Mosak (1971) has participated in a program that introduced Adlerian methods into an entire school system. All of these have been students of Dreikurs, who transported the tradition from Vienna, and who himself made a great contribution in this area. In the Adlerian social tradition, Adlerians may be involved in community outreach programs or dedicating their efforts to the study of subjects such as drugs, aging, delinquency, religion, and poverty.

A new development in the field of

education may be seen in the work of Corsini and his associates (1977, 1979). Corsini C4R Schools implement the philosophy of Adler in education. The contemporary Adlerian finds the growth model of personality infinitely more congenial than the sickness model. The Adlerian is not interested in curing sick individuals or a sick society, but in reeducating individuals and in reshaping society so all people can live together as equals in a free society.

PERSONALITY

THEORY OF PERSONALITY

Adlerian psychology is a psychology of use rather than of possession. This assumption decreases the importance of the question, "How do heredity and environment shape the individual?" and "How much of intelligence is hereditary and how much is due to environment?" The functionalist, holistic Adlerian asks instead, "How does the individual use heredity and environment?"

For Adler, the family constellation constitutes the primary social environment. Every child searches for significance in this environment and competes for position within the family constellation. One sibling becomes the "best" child, another the "worst" one. Being favored, being one of the favored sex within the family, adopting the family values, or identifying or allying oneself with a parent or sibling may provide the grounds for the feeling of having a place. Handicaps, organ inferiorities, or being an orphan are other "position makers" for some children.

Of supreme importance is the child's position in the family constellation. Thus, it would appear that the first child usually is a conservative and the second is often a rebel. The baby is ordinarily either everyone's darling or one who stands on tiptoes to see above the preceding siblings. If these general characteristics possess any validity, at best they exist as statistical probabilities and not as defining traits. Considering the family constellation in terms of birth order or ordinal position creates the problem of characterizing, let us say, the fifth child in the family. Although the fifth child is often encountered in the therapy situation, he or she never receives any attention in the literature. Birth order, per se, also ignores the gender position of the child. The children in two-sibling families in which the possible configurations are boy-boy, girl-girl, boy-girl, and girl-boy do not possess similar characteristics based upon ordinal position alone (Shulman & Mosak, 1977).

The Adlerian prefers to study the family constellation in terms of the *psychological* position. A simple example illustrates this point of view. Take two siblings separated in age by 10 years. In birth order research, these would be treated as a first child and a second child. From the Adlerian point of view the psychological position of each would *most likely* be that of an only child with *perhaps* the older child functioning as an additional parent figure for the younger. The italicized terms *most likely* and *perhaps* are used expressly to indicate that: (1) Adlerians do not recognize a causalistic, one-to-one relationship between family position and sibling traits; and (2) whatever relationship exists can only be understood in context, that is, when one knows the family climate and the total configuration of factors in the family constellation. Adler, whenever he generalized or ventured a prediction, was fond of reminding his students, "Everything could also be quite different."

The search for significance and the consequent sibling competition reflect the values of the competitive society in which we live. We are encouraged to be first, to excel, to be popular, to be athletic, to be a "real" man, to "never say die," to recall that "practice makes perfect," and to "dream the impossible dream." Consequently, each child must stake out a piece of "territory" that includes the attributes or abilities that are hoped will give a feeling of worth. If through their evaluations of their own potency (abilities, courage, and confidence) children are convinced that they can achieve this place through useful endeavor, they will pursue "the useful side of life." Should children feel that they cannot attain the goal of having a "place" in this fashion, they will become discouraged and engage in disturbed or disturbing behavior in their efforts to find a place. For the Adlerian the "maladjusted" child is not a "sick" child. He or she is a "discouraged" child. Dreikurs (1948, 1949) classifies the goals of the discouraged child into four groups—attention getting, power seeking, revenge taking, and declaring deficiency or defeat. Dreikurs is speaking of immediate rather than long-range goals. These are the goals of children's "misbehavior," not of all children's behavior (Mosak & Mosak, 1975).

In the process of becoming socialized human beings, children form conclusions on the basis of their subjective experiences. Because judgment and logical processes are not highly developed in young children, many of their growing convictions contain errors or only partial "truths." Neverthe-

less, they accept these conclusions about themselves and others *as if* they were true even though they are "fictions." They are subjective evaluations, biased apperceptions of themselves and of the world, rather than objective "reality." Thus, one can be truly inferior without feeling inferior. Conversely, one can feel inferior without being inferior.

The child creates a cognitive map, the life-style that will assist "little me" in coping with the "big" world. The life-style includes the aspirations, the long-range goals, and a "statement" of the conditions, personal or social, that are requisite for the individual's "security." The latter are also fictions and are stated in therapy as "If only . . . , then I. . . ." Mosak (1954) divided life-style convictions into four groups:

1. The *self-concept*—the convictions I have about who I am.
2. The *self-ideal* (Adler coined this phrase in 1912)—the convictions of what I should be or am obliged to be to have a place.
3. The *Weltbild,* or "picture of the world"—convictions about the not-self (world, people, nature, and so on) and what the world demands of me.
4. The *ethical convictions*—the personal "right-wrong" code.

When there is a discrepancy between self and ideal-self convictions ("I am short; I should be tall"), *inferiority feelings* ensue. Although an infinite variety of inferiority feelings exist, one should be mentioned that Adler discussed while he was still in the Freudian Society, which eventuated in the rift between himself and Freud. It assumes monumental importance in some circles today—the masculine protest. In a culture that places a premium on masculinity, some women feel inferior because they have not been accorded the prerogatives or privileges of men ("I am woman; I should be equal to man"). But men also suffered from the masculine protest because being a man is not sufficient to provide a "place" for some men ("I am a man; but I should be a *real* man"). Because Adler believed in the equality of the sexes, he could not accept these fictions (Mosak & Schneider, 1977).

Lack of congruence between convictions in the self-concept and those in the *Weltbild* ("I am weak and helpless; life is dangerous") also results in inferiority feelings. Discrepancies between self-concept and ethical convictions ("One should always tell the truth; I lie") lead to inferiority feelings in the moral realm. Thus, the guilt feeling is merely a variant of the inferiority feeling (Mosak, 1987b).

These variations of inferiority feelings in and of themselves are not "abnormal." It would be difficult to quarrel with Adler's observations that to live is to *feel* inferior. It is only when individuals act *as if* they were inferior, develop symptoms, or behave as "sick" that we see evidences of what in the medical model would be called *pathology* and what Adlerians call *discouragement* or the *inferiority complex*. To oversimplify, the *inferiority feeling* is universal and "normal"; the *inferiority complex* reflects the discouragement of a limited segment of our society and is usually "abnormal." The former may be masked or hidden from the view of others; the latter is an open demonstration of inadequacy, or "sickness."

Using their "maps," people facilitate their movement through life. This permits them to evaluate, understand, experience, predict, and control experi-ence. Lawrence Frank writes in this connection:

The personality process might be regarded as a sort of rubber stamp which the individual imposes upon every situation by which he gives it the configuration that he, as an individual, requires; in so doing he necessarily ignores or subordinates many aspects of the situation that for him are irrelevant and meaningless and selectively reacts to those aspects that are personally significant. (1939, p. 392)

Although the life-style is the instrument for coping with experience, it is very largely nonconscious. The life-style comprises the cognitive organization of the individual rather than the behavioral organization. As an illustration, the conviction "I require excitement" may lead to the vocational choices of actor, racing car driver, explorer, or to "acting out" behavior. Such a conviction may further lead to getting into jams or exciting situations, or engaging in creative acts, or discovery.

Within the same life-style, one can behave usefully or uselessly. The above distinction permits Adlerians (e.g., Dreikurs, 1961; Nikelly, 1971a) to distinguish between *psychotherapy* and *counseling*. The former, they maintain, has as its aim the change of life-style; the latter has as its goal the change of behavior within the existing life-style.

Because the Adlerian literature discusses the life tasks of occupation, society, and love so extensively, these tasks of life will not be elaborated upon here, except for some brief comments. Lewis Way points out that "The problems they pose can never be solved once and for all, but demand from the individual a continuous and creative movement toward adaptation" (1962, pp. 179–80).

Love, as an emotion, is like other

emotions, cognitively based. People are not "victims" of their emotions or passions. They create emotions to assist them in the attainment of their goals. Love is the conjunctive emotion we create when we want to move toward people.

Although the life tasks of love, occupation, and society demand solution, it is possible to avoid or postpone them if one can compensate in other areas. "Even successful persons fall into neurosis because they are not more successful" (Way, 1962, p. 206). The neurotic symptom is an expression of "I can't because I'm sick"; the person's movement betrays the "I won't because my self-esteem might get hurt" (Krausz, 1959, p. 112). Although neurotics' movements are consonant with their "private logic" (Nikelly, 1971b), they still cling to "common sense." They know what they should do or feel, but they "can't." Adler referred to them as "yes-but" personalities. Eric Berne (1964) has graphically described their interpersonal maneuvers in the "Why don't you—Yes, but" game. The genesis of neurosis lies in discouragement. People avoid and postpone or take circuitous routes to solutions so they can "save face." Even when they expect or arrange to fail, they try to salvage some self-esteem. Students, fearful of failing examinations, will refrain from studying. In the event they do fail, they merely have to hold that they were lazy or neglectful but not stupid.

The psychotic's goal of superiority is often loftier than that which can be achieved by mere humans. "Individual Psychology has shown that the goal of superiority can only be fixed at such attitudes when the individual has, by losing interest in others, also lost interest in his own reason and un-

derstanding . . . common sense has become useless to him" (Adler, 1964a, pp. 128–29). Adler used "common sense" in much the same manner that Sullivan spoke of "consensual validation." In the pseudo work area, the psychotic becomes superintendent of the mental hospital. In the pseudo social area, the hypomanic patient resembles the cheerful extrovert and the more acutely manic patient becomes a "name dropper" and "swallows up" people (Shulman, 1962). The paranoid patient pictures people as threatening and manifests a "search for glory," to use Karen Horney's (1951) phrase, by the persecutory delusion that they are conspiring to do something to me. The delusions of grandeur of the psychotic depressive patients ("I'm the worst sinner of all time") and of the schizophrenic who claims to be Christ are some other "solutions" to the spiritual pseudo tasks. The reifying hallucinations of talking with the devil fall in this category (Adler, 1963b; Mosak & Fletcher, 1973).

The psychologically healthy or normal individual has developed social interest and is willing to commit to life and the life tasks without evasion, excuse, or "side shows" (Wolfe, 1932). This person proceeds with confidence and optimism about meeting life's challenges. There is a sense of belonging and contributing, the "courage to be imperfect," and the serene knowledge that one can be acceptable to others, although imperfect. Above all, this person rejects the faulty values that culture projects and attempts to substitute for them values more consonant with the "ironclad logic of social living." Such a person does not exist, nor will psychotherapy produce such a person. Yet this is the Adlerian ideal, and because Adler's intent was to substitute small errors for larger errors, many of these goals can be approximated in psychotherapy. Many fortunate people have the courage (Adler, 1928) and social interest to do this for themselves without therapeutic assistance.

VARIETY OF CONCEPTS

The simplicity of the Adlerian vocabulary renders definition and interpretation generally unnecessary. Yet some differences of opinion and emphasis about Adlerian concepts remain unresolved. In terms of *life-style*, Adlerians disagree with respect to what it describes—behavioral or cognitive organization. *Social interest* (Bickhard & Ford, 1976; Crandall, 1981; Edgar, 1975; Kazan, 1978) apparently is not a unitary concept but a cluster of feelings and behaviors (Ansbacher, 1968). Although social interest is often described as "innate," many Adlerians wonder what makes it so, given that it appears to be neither genetic nor constitutional. As one looks at the theories of Adler, Freud, and Jung, one is struck with the effort on the part of all three to "biologize" their theories. Perhaps it was the temper of the times. Perhaps it was because all three were physicians. Perhaps it resulted from the need to make their theories respectable during a period when psychoanalysis was held in low esteem. None of these theories would incur any great damage if "instincts," "social interest," and "racial unconscious" were treated as psychological constructs rather than as biological processes. Adler, having introduced the concept of *organ inferiority* with its consequent compensation, actually had proposed a biopsychological theory, but it must be recalled that this transpired during his "Freudian period." Later he substituted the *social inferiority feeling* for actual organ inferiority, and with the exception of one important article (Shulman & Klapman, 1968), Adlerians have published little on organ inferiority. Although people undoubtedly do compensate for organ inferiority, the latter is no longer the cornerstone of the Adlerian edifice.

Gardner Murphy (1947) took issue with Adler's use of compensation as the only defense mechanism. Literally, Adler's writings do read that way. On the other hand, if one reads more closely, compensation becomes an umbrella to cover all coping mechanisms. Thus, Adler speaks of safeguards, excuses, projection, the depreciation tendency, creating distance, and identification. Although a Freudian might view these as defense mechanisms the ego employs in its warfare with the instinctual drives, the Adlerian prefers to view them as problem-solving devices the person uses to protect self-esteem, reputation, and physical self rather than as defense mechanisms. Because Adlerians do not accept the concept of *the* unconscious, such mechanisms as repression and sublimation become irrelevant in the Adlerian framework. Adlerian theory has no room for instincts, drives, libido, and other alleged movers.

The *Journal of Individual Psychology* (now *Individual Psychology*) referred to itself as being "devoted to a holistic, phenomenological, teleological, field-theoretical, and socially oriented approach," placing it closer to Rogers, Maslow, the existential humanists, and some of the neo-Freudians than to the one-to-one (cause-effect, stimulus-response) psychologies. Because of the emphasis on behavior (movement),

Adlerian psychology and behavior-modification theory have been equated. This is an error. Adlerians, although interested in changing behavior, have as their major goal not behavior modification, but motivation modification. Dreikurs writes: "We do not attempt primarily to change behavior patterns or remove symptoms. If a patient improves his behavior because he finds it profitable at the time, without changing his basic premises, then we do not consider that as a therapeutic success. We are trying to change goals, concepts, and notions" (1963, p. 79).

PSYCHOTHERAPY

THEORY OF PSYCHOTHERAPY

All scientific schools of psychotherapy have their shares of successes and failures. A considerable number of therapies based upon nonscientific foundations probably reach equal success levels. Consequently, we may conclude that the validity of a psychodynamic theory bears no direct relationship to its therapeutic effectiveness. Like their predecessors, modern theories may also vanish from practice to appear only in the textbooks of future generations. In any event, regardless of its validity or endurance, any theory must be implemented within the context of the therapist-patient relationship. As Fred Fiedler (1950) has shown, therapeutic success is a function of the expertness of the therapist rather than of the therapist's orientation. This may help to explain the successes of modern and primitive theories.

Given that the underlying psychodynamic theory is not the crucial factor in therapy, perhaps it is the special techniques that contribute to therapeutic effectiveness. This would certainly seem to have been Rogers' early position before nondirective therapy became person-centered therapy. For the early nondirective school, the creation of a warm, permissive, nonjudgmental atmosphere; reflection of feeling; and avoidance of interpretation, advice, persuasion, and suggestion were paramount in the therapeutic situation.

The Freudian assigns central importance to transference, but behavior modification therapists ignore it. To many directive therapists, content and manner of interpretation are crucial. The Adlerian emphasizes interpretation of the patient's life-style and movement.

Criteria for "getting well" correspond to the particular therapeutic emphasis. Some therapists propose depth of therapy as the decisive factor. For most Adlerians, depth of therapy does not constitute a major concern. In this connection, therapy is neither deep nor superficial except as the patient experiences it as such.

If neither theory nor the use of prescribed techniques is decisive, is it the transference relationship that makes cure possible? Or the egalitarian relationship? Or the warm, permissive atmosphere with the nonjudgmental therapist accepting the patient as is? Because all of these relationships are involved in various forms of both effective and noneffective therapy, we must hypothesize either that therapeutic effectiveness is a matter of matching certain therapeutic relationships to certain patients or that all therapeutic relationships possess common factors. These factors, variations on the Christian virtues of faith, hope, and love, appear to be necessary, but not sufficient, conditions of effective therapy.

Faith

D. Rosenthal and Jerome D. Frank (1956) discuss the implications of faith in the therapeutic process. Franz Alexander and Thomas French state:

As a general rule, the patient who comes for help voluntarily has this confidence, this expectation that the therapist is both able and willing to help him, before he comes to treatment; if not, if the patient is forced into treatment, the therapist must build up this feeling of rapport before any therapeutic change can be effected. (1946, p. 173)

Many therapeutic mechanisms may enhance the patient's faith. A simple explanation clarifies matters for some patients, a complex interpretation for others. The therapist's own faith in him- or herself, the therapist's appearance of wisdom, strength, and assurance, and the therapist's willingness to listen without criticism may all be used by patients to strengthen their faith.

Hope

Patients seek treatment with varying degrees of hope, running the gamut from complete hopelessness to hope for (and expectation of) everything, including a miracle. Because of the efficacy of the self-fulfilling prophecy, people *tend* to move in the direction of making their anticipations come true. Therefore, the therapist must keep the patient's hope elevated.

Because the Adlerian holds that the patient suffers from discouragement, a primary therapeutic technique lies in encouragement. Expression of faith in the patient, noncondemnation, and avoidance of being overly demanding may give the patient hope. The patient may also derive hope from feeling understood. Accordingly, the construction of therapy as a "we" experience where patients do not feel they stand alone, where they feel security in the strength and competency of their therapist, and where they feel some symptom alleviation may all prove helpful. They may also gain hope from attempting some course of action they feared or did not know was available to them. Humor assists in the retention of hope (Mosak, 1987a). Lewis Way comments, "Humor such as Adler possessed in such abundance, is an invaluable asset, since, if one can occasionally joke, things cannot be so bad" (1962, p. 267). Each therapist has faith in his methods for encouraging and sustaining hope. They are put to the most severe test in patients who are depressed or suicidal.

Love

In its broadest sense, the patient must feel that the therapist cares (Adler, 1963a, 1964a). The mere act of treating the patient may furnish such evidence by using techniques such as empathic listening, "working through" together, or having two therapists in multiple psychotherapy offering interest in the patient. Transfer of a patient to another therapist or from individual to group therapy may have a contrary effect unless it is "worked through."

But the therapist must avoid pitfalls such as infantilizing, oversupporting, or becoming a victim of the patient when the patient accuses the therapist of not caring enough. In Adlerian group therapy, the group is conceptualized as a "reexperiencing of the family constellation" (Kadis, 1956). Thus, the therapist may be accused of playing favorites, of caring too much for one or too little for another patient.

The Adlerian theory of psychotherapy rests on the notion that psychotherapy is a cooperative educational enterprise involving one or more therapists and one or more patients. The goal of therapy is to develop the patient's social interest. To accomplish this, therapy involves a changing of faulty social values (Dreikurs, 1957). The subject matter of this course in reeducation is the patient—the lifestyle and the relationship to the life tasks. Learning the "basic mistakes" in the cognitive map, the patient has the opportunity to decide whether to continue in the old ways or move in other directions. "The consultee must under all circumstances get the conviction in relation to treatment that he is absolutely free. He can do, or not do, as he pleases" (Ansbacher & Ansbacher, 1956, p. 341). The patient can make the decision between self-interest and social interest. The educational process has as its goals:

1. The fostering of social interest.
2. The decrease of inferiority feelings, the overcoming of discouragement, and the recognition and utilization of one's resources.
3. Changes in the person's life-style, that is, perceptions and goals. The therapeutic goal, as has been mentioned, involves transforming big errors into little ones (as with automobiles, some persons need a "tune-up"; others require a "major overhaul").
4. Changing faulty motivation that underlies even acceptable behavior or changing values.
5. Encouraging the individual to recognize equality among people (Dreikurs, 1971).
6. Helping the person to become a contributing human being.

"Students" who reach these educational objectives will feel belonging and acceptant of themselves and others. They will feel that they can ar-range, within life's limits, their own destinies. Such patients eventually come to feel encouraged, optimistic, confident, courageous, secure—and asymptomatic.

PROCESS OF PSYCHOTHERAPY

The process of psychotherapy, as practiced by the Adlerian, has four aims: (1) establishing and maintaining a "good" relationship; (2) uncovering the dynamics of the patient, including lifestyle and goals, and how they affect life movement; (3) interpretation culminating in insight; and (4) reorientation.

Relationship

A "good" therapeutic relationship is a friendly one between equals. Both the Adlerian therapist and the patient sit facing each other, their chairs at the same level. Many Adlerians prefer to work without a desk because distancing and separation may engender undesirable psychological sets. Having abandoned the medical model, the Adlerian looks with disfavor upon casting the doctor in the role of the actor (omnipotent, omniscient, and mysterious) and the patient in the role of the acted-upon. Therapy is structured to inform the patient that creative human beings play a role in creating their problems, that one is responsible (not in the sense of blame) for one's actions, and that one's problems are based upon faulty perceptions and inadequate or faulty learning, especially of faulty values (Dreikurs, 1957). If this is so, one can assume responsibility for change. What has not been learned can be learned. What has been learned "poorly" can be replaced by better learning. Faulty perception and values can be altered and modified. From the initiation of treatment, the patient's efforts to remain passive are discouraged. The patient has an active role in the therapy. Although assuming the role of student, the patient is still an active learner responsible for contributing to his or her own education.

Therapy requires cooperation, which means alignment of goals. Noncoincidence of goals may not permit the therapy to get off the ground, as, for example, when the patient denies the need for therapy. The initial interview(s) must not, therefore, omit the consideration of initial goals and expectations. The patient may wish to overpower the therapist or to make the therapist powerful and responsible. The therapist's goal must be to avoid these traps. The patient may want to relinquish symptoms but not underlying convictions, and may be looking for a miracle. In each case, at least a temporary agreement upon goals must be arrived at before the therapy can proceed. Way cautions:

A refusal to be caught in this way [succumbing to the patient's appeals to the therapist's vanity or bids for sympathy] gives the patient little opportunity for developing serious resistances and transferences, and is indeed the doctor's only defence against a reversal of roles and against finding that he is being treated by the patient. The cure must always be a cooperation and never a fight. It is a hard test for the doctor's own balance and is likely to succeed only if he himself is free from neurosis. (1962, p. 265)

Adler (1963a) offers similar warnings against role reversal.

Because the problems of resistance and transference are defined in terms of patient-therapist goal discrepancies, throughout therapy the goals will diverge and the common task will consist of realigning the goals so patient and therapist move in the same direction.

The patient, in bringing a life-style to therapy, expects from the therapist the kind of response expected from all others. The patient may feel misunderstood, unfairly treated, or unloved and may anticipate that the therapist will behave accordingly. Often the patient unconsciously creates situations to invite the therapist to behave in this manner. For this reason, the therapist must be alert to what Alderians call "scripts," and to what Eric Berne (1964) calls "games," and foil the patient's expectations. A patient, for example, will declare, "Have you ever seen a patient like me before?" to establish uniqueness and to challenge the therapist's competence. The therapist's response may just be a straightforward, but nonsarcastic, "Not since the last hour," followed by a discussion of uniqueness. Because assessment begins with the first moment of contact, the patient is generally given some interpretation, usually phrased as a guess, during the first interview. This gives the patient something to think about until the next interview. The therapist will soon find it possible to assess how the patient will respond to interpretation, to therapy, and to the therapist, and will gain some glimpse of the life-style framework. The therapist does not play the patient's game because at that game the patient is the professional, having played it successfully since childhood (although often in self-defeating fashion), whereas the therapist is a relative amateur. The therapist does not have to win the game but merely does not play it. Only one side wins in a tug-of-war. However, in this case, one side (the therapist) is uninterested in victories or defeats and merely does not pick up the end of the rope. This renders the "opponent's" game ineffective and the two can proceed to play more productive, cooperative games.

The whole relationship process increases the education of the patient. For some patients it is their first experience of a good interpersonal relationship, a relationship of cooperation and mutual respect and trust. Despite occasional bad feelings, the relationship can endure and survive. The patient learns that good and bad relationships do not merely happen—they are products of people's efforts—and that poor interpersonal relationships are products of misperceptions, inaccurate conclusions, and unwarranted anticipations incorporated in the life-style.

Analysis

Investigation of a patient's dynamics is divided into two parts. First, the therapist wants to understand the patient's life-style and, second, aims to understand how the life-style affects current function with respect to the life tasks. Not all suffering stems from the patient's life-style. Many patients with adequate life-styles develop problems or symptoms in the face of intolerable or extreme situations from which they cannot extricate themselves.

Analytic investigation begins with the first moment. The way a patient enters the room, posture, and choice of seating (especially important in family therapy) all provide important clues. What the patient says and how it is said expand the therapist's understanding, especially when the therapist interprets the patient's communications in interpersonal terms, or "scripts," rather than in descriptive terms. Thus, the Adlerian translates the descriptive statement, "I am confused" into the admonition, "Don't pin me down." "It's a habit," conveys the declaration, "And that's another thing you're not going to get me to change," as the patient attempts erroneously to convince the therapist that habits are unchangeable (Mosak & Gushurst, 1971). As therapy progresses, the therapist assesses, follows up, and juxtaposes clues in patterns, and accepts some hypotheses and rejects others in an effort to understand the patient. As therapy progresses, the patient offers information one way or another, and the therapist pieces it together bit by bit like a jigsaw puzzle.

The Life-style Investigation

In formal assessment procedures, the patient's family constellation is explored to ascertain conditions prevailing when the child was forming life-style convictions. We obtain glimpses of what position the child found in the family and how he or she went about finding a place within the family, in school, and among peers. The second portion of the assessment consists of interpreting the patient's early recollections. An *early recollection* occurs in the period before continuous memory and may be inaccurate or a complete fiction. It represents a single event ("One day I remember . . .") rather than a group of events ("We used to . . ."). Adlerians refer to the latter as a *report* rather than a recollection. Recollections are treated as a projective technique (Mosak, 1958). If one understands the early recollections, one understands the patient's "Story of My Life" (Adler, 1958), because people selectively recollect from their past incidents consonant with their life-styles. The following recollection of Adler's (1947) may serve to illustrate the consonance between his earliest recollection and his later psychological views:

One of my earliest recollections is of sitting on a bench, bandaged up on account of rickets, with my healthy elder brother sitting opposite me. He could run, jump, and move about quite effortlessly, while for me movement of any sort was a strain and an effort. Everyone went to great pains to help me, and my mother and father did all that was in their power to do. At the time of this recollection I must have been about two years old. (p. 9)

In a single recollection, Adler refers to organ inferiority, the inferiority feeling, the emphasis upon "my desire to move freely—to see all psychic manifestations in terms of movements" (p. 10), and social feeling (Mosak & Kopp, 1973).

The summary of early recollections, the story of the patient's life, permits the derivation of the patient's "basic mistakes." The life-style can be conceived as a personal mythology. The individual will behave *as if* the myths were true because, for him or her, they are true. When the Greeks believed that Zeus lived on Olympus, they regarded it as truth and behaved as if it were true, although we have now consigned this belief to the realm of mythology. Although it was not true that Zeus existed, it is true that Olympus exists. So there are "truths" or partial "truths" in myths and there are myths we confuse with truth. The latter are *basic mistakes*.

Basic mistakes may be classified as follows:

1. *Overgeneralizations.* "People are hostile." "Life is dangerous."
2. *False or impossible goals of "security."* One false step and you're dead." "I have to please everybody."
3. *Misperceptions of life and life's demands.* Typical convictions might be "Life never gives me any breaks" and "Life is so hard."
4. *Minimization or denial of one's worth.* "I'm stupid" and "I'm un-

deserving" or "I'm *just* a housewife."
5. *Faulty values.* "Be first even if you have to climb over others."

Finally, the therapist is interested in how the patient perceives his or her assets.

The following sample life-style summary is not intended to be a complete personality description, but it does offer patient and therapist initial hypotheses.

SUMMARY OF FAMILY CONSTELLATION

John is the younger of two children, the only boy, who grew up fatherless after age nine. His sister was so precocious that John became discouraged. Because he felt he would never become famous, he decided perhaps he could at least be notorious, and through negative behavior brought himself to the attention of others. He acquired the reputation of a "holy terror." He was going to do everything his way, and nobody was going to stop him. He followed the guiding lines of a strong, masculine father from whom he learned that the toughest man wins. Because notoriety came with doing the disapproved, John early became interested in and engaged in sex. This also reinforced his feelings of masculinity. Because both parents were handicapped and yet still "made it," John apparently decided that without any physical handicaps, the sky would be the limit for him.

SUMMARY OF EARLY RECOLLECTIONS

"I run scared in life, and even when people tell me there's nothing to be scared of, I'm still scared. Women give men a hard time. They betray them, they punish them, and they interfere with what men want to do. A real man takes no crap from anybody. Somebody always interferes. I am not going to do what others want me to do. Others call that bad and want to punish me for it, but I don't see it that way. Doing what I want is merely part of being a man."

"BASIC MISTAKES"

1. John exaggerates the significance of masculinity and equates it with doing what he pleases.
2. He is not on the same wavelength as women. They see his behavior as "bad"; he sees it as only "natural" for a man.
3. He is too ready to fight, many times just to preserve his sense of masculinity and not because of the issue he is allegedly fighting over.
4. He perceives women as the enemy, even though he looks to them for comfort.
5. Victory is snatched from him at the last moment.

ASSETS

1. He is a driver. When he puts his mind to things, he makes them work.
2. He engages in creative problem solving.
3. He knows how to get what he wants.
4. He knows how to ask a woman "nicely."

During the course of the treatment, other forms of analysis will occur. Because the therapist views the life-style as consistent, it will express itself in all of the patient's behavior—physical behavior, language and speech, fantasy productions, dreams, and interpersonal relationships, past and present. Because of this consistency, the patient may choose to express self in any or all of these media because they all express life-style. The therapist observes behavior, speech, and language closely during each interview. Sometimes the dialogue will center on the present, sometimes on the past, often on the future. Free association and chitchat, except when the latter serves a therapeutic purpose, are mostly discouraged. Although dream analysis is an integral part of psychotherapy, the patient who speaks only of dreams receives gentle dissuasion (Alexandra Adler, 1943). The analysis proceeds with an examination of the interplay between life-style and the life tasks— how the life-style affects the person's function and dysfunction vis-a-vis the life tasks.

Dreams

Adler saw the dream as a problem-solving activity with a future orientation, in contrast to Freud's view that it was an attempt to solve an old problem. The dream is seen by Adlerians as a rehearsal of possible future courses of action. If we want to postpone action, we forget the dream. If we want to dissuade ourselves from some action, we frighten ourselves with a nightmare.

The dream, Adler said, was the "factory of the emotions." In it we create moods that move us toward or away from the next day's activities. Commonly, people say, "I don't know why but I woke up in a lousy mood today." The day before Adler died, he told friends, "I woke smiling . . . so I knew my dreams were good although I had forgotten them" (Bottome, 1939, p. 240). Just as early recollections reflect long-range goals, the dream experiments with possible answers to immediate problems. In accord with the view of the individual's uniqueness, Adlerians reject the theory of fixed symbolism. One cannot understand a dream without knowing the dreamer, although Adler (1936) and Erwin Wexberg (1929) do address themselves to some frequently encountered dream themes. Way admonishes:

One is reminded again of two boys, instanced by Adler [1964a, p. 150], each of whom wished to be a horse, one because he would have to bear the responsibility for his family, the other to outstrip all the others. This should be a salutary warning against making dictionary interpretations. (1962, pp. 282–84)

The interpretation of the dream does not terminate with the analysis of the content but must include the purposive function. Dreams serve as weathervanes for treatment, bringing problems to the surface and pointing to the patient's movement. Dreikurs describes a patient who related recurrent dreams that were short and actionless, reflecting his life-style of figuring out "the best way of getting out of a problem, mostly without doing anything. . . . When his dreams started to move and become active he started to move in his life, too" (1944, p. 26).

Reorientation

All reorientation in all therapies proceeds from persuading the patient, gently or forcefully, that change is in his or her best interest. The patient's present manner of living accords "safety" but not happiness. Because neither therapy nor life offers *guarantees*, one must risk some "safety" for the possibility of greater happiness and self-fulfillment. This dilemma is not easily solved. Like Hamlet, the patient wonders whether it is better to "bear those ills we have than fly to others that we know not of."

Insight

Analytic psychotherapists frequently assign central importance to insight, upon the assumption that "basic change" cannot occur in its absence. The conviction that insight must precede behavioral change often results in extended treatment, in encouraging some patients to become "sicker" to avoid or postpone change, and in increasing their self-absorption rather than their self-awareness. Meanwhile patients relieve themselves from the responsibility of living life until they have achieved insight.

A second assumption, treasured by therapists and patients alike, distinguishes between *intellectual* and *emotional* insight (Ellis, 1963; H. Papanek, 1959), a dualism the holistic Adlerian experiences difficulty in accepting. This and other dualisms, such as conscious versus unconscious, undeniably exist in the patient's subjective experience. But these antagonistic forces are creations of the patient that delay action. Simultaneously the patient can maintain a good conscience because he or she is the victim of conflicting forces or an emotional block. Solving problems is relegated to the future while the patient pursues insight. *Insight*, as the Adlerian defines it, is understanding translated into constructive action. It reflects the patient's understanding of the purposive nature of behavior and mistaken apperceptions as well as an understanding of the role both play in life movement. So-called intellectual insight merely reflects the patient's desire to play the game of therapy rather than the game of life.

Interpretation

The Adlerian therapist facilitates insight mainly by interpretation of ordinary communications, dreams, fantasies, behavior, symptoms, the patient-therapist transactions, and the patient's interpersonal transactions. The emphasis in interpretation is on purpose rather than cause, on movement rather than description, on use rather than possession. Through interpretation the therapist holds up a mirror for the patient.

The therapist relates past to present only to indicate the continuity of the maladaptive life-style, not to demonstrate a causal connection. The therapist may also use humor or illustrate with fables (Pancner, 1978), anecdotes, and biography. Irony may prove effective but it must be handled with care. The therapist may "spit in the patient's soup," a crude expression for exposing the patient's intentions in such a way as to make them unpalatable. The therapist may offer the interpretation directly or in the form of "Could it be that. . .?" or may invite the patient to make interpretations. Although timing, exaggeration, understatement, and accuracy are technical concerns of any therapist, they are not too important for the Adlerian therapist, who does not view the patient as fragile.

Other Verbal Techniques

Advice is often frowned upon by therapists. Hans Strupp relates, "It has been said that Freud, following his own recommendations, never gave advice to an analysand on the couch but did not stint with the commodity from the couch to the door" (1972, p. 40). Wexberg (1970) frowned on giving advice to a patient, but the Adlerian therapist freely gives advice, as did Freud, taking care, however, not to encourage dependency. In practice the therapist may merely outline the alternatives and let the patient make the decision. This invitation develops faith in self rather than faith in the therapist. On the other hand, the therapist may offer direct advice, taking care to encourage the patient's self-directiveness and willingness to stand alone.

Given that Adlerians consider the patient discouraged rather than sick, it is no surprise that they make extensive use of encouragement. Enhancing the patient's faith in self, "accentuating the positive and eliminating the negative," and keeping up the patient's hope all contribute to counteracting the patient's discouragement. The patient

who "walks and falls" learns it is not fatal and can get up and walk again. Therapy also counteracts the patient's social values, thus altering his or her view of life and helping give meaning to it. Moralizing is avoided, although therapists must not deceive themselves into believing their system has no value orientation. The dialogue concerns "useful" and "useless," rather than "good" or "bad" behavior.

The therapist avoids rational argument and trying to "out-logic" the patient. These tactics are easily defeated by the patient who operates according to the rules of *psychologic* (private) logic rather than formal logic. Catharsis, abreaction, and confession may afford the patient relief by freeing him or her from carrying the burden of "unfinished business," but as has been noted (Alexander & French, 1946), these may also be a test of whether the patient can place trust in the therapist.

Action Techniques

Adlerians regularly use roleplaying, talking to an empty chair (Shoobs, 1964), the Midas technique (Shulman, 1962), the behind-the-back technique (Corsini, 1953), and other action procedures to assist the patient in reorientation. The extent of use is a function of the therapist's preference, training, and readiness to experiment with the novel.

MECHANISMS OF PSYCHOTHERAPY

The Therapist as Model

The therapist represents values the patient may attempt to imitate. Adlerian therapists represent themselves as "being for real," fallible, able to laugh at themselves, caring—models for social interest. If the therapist can possess these characteristics, perhaps the patient can, too, and many patients emulate their therapists, whom they use as referents for normality (Mosak, 1967).

Change

There comes a time in psychotherapy when analysis must be abandoned and the patient must be encouraged to act in lieu of talking and listening. Insight has to give way to decisive action.

Some of the techniques Adlerians use to elicit change are described below. They are not panaceas, nor are they used indiscriminately. The creative therapist will improvise techniques to meet the needs of the therapeutic moment, and remember, above all, that people are more important than techniques and strategies. Losing sight of these cautions, the therapist is a technician who does all the "right" things but is never engaged in human encounter with another human being.

Acting "as if"

A common patient refrain in treatments is "If only I could . . ." (Adler, 1963a). We often request that for the next week the patient act "as if." The patient may protest that it would only be an act and therefore phony. We explain that all acting is not phony pretense, that one can try on a role as one might try on a suit. It does not change the person wearing the suit, but sometimes with a handsome suit of clothes, one may feel differently and perhaps behave differently, thus becoming a different person.

Task Setting

Adler (1964a) gave us the prototype for task setting in his treatment of depressives, writing:

To return to the indirect method of treatment: I recommend it especially in melancholia. After establishing a sympathetic relation I give suggestions for a change of conduct in two stages. In the first stage my suggestion is "Only do what is agreeable to you." The patient usually answers, "Nothing is agreeable." "Then at least," I respond, "do not exert yourself to do what is disagreeable." The patient, who has usually been exhorted to do various uncongenial things to remedy this condition, finds a rather flattering novelty in my advice, and may improve in behavior. Later I insinuate the second rule of conduct, saying that "it is much more difficult and I do not know if you can follow it." After saying this I am silent, and look doubtfully at the patient. In this way I excite his curiosity and ensure his attention, and then proceed, "If you could follow this second rule you would be cured in fourteen days. It is—to consider from time to time how you can give another person pleasure. It would very soon enable you to sleep and would chase away all your sad thoughts. You would feel yourself to be useful and worthwhile."

I receive various replies to my suggestion, but every patient thinks it is too difficult to act upon. If the answer is, "How can I give pleasure to others when I have none myself?" I relieve the prospect by saying, "Then you will need four weeks." The more transparent response, "Who gives me pleasure?" I encounter with what is probably the strongest move in the game, by saying, "Perhaps you had better train yourself a little thus: do not actually DO anything to please anyone else, but just think out how you COULD do it!" (pp. 25–26)

The tasks are relatively simple and are set at a level at which patients can sabotage the task, but they cannot fail and then scold the therapist.

The patient must understand that not the physician but life itself is inexorable. He must understand that ultimately [he will have] to transfer to practical life that which has been theoretically recognized. . . . But from the physician he hears no word of reproach or of impatience, at most an occasional kindly, harmless, ironical remark. (p. 101)

A 50-year-old man who professed "genuine" intention to get married but simultaneously avoided women was instructed to seek one meaningful contact with a woman (how to do so was up to him) every day. After raising many objections, he complained, "But it's so hard! I'll get so tired out I won't be able to function." The therapist good-humoredly relented and informed him, "Since God rested on the seventh day, I can't ask you to do more than God. So you need carry out the task only six days a week."

One form of task setting Adler introduced is called *antisuggestion* by Wexberg (1929) and *paradoxical intention* by Frankl (1963). This method used nonclinically by Knight Dunlap (1933) was labeled *negative practice.* The symptomatic patient unwittingly reinforces symptoms by fighting them, by saying, "Why did this have to happen to *me?* The insomniac keeps one eye open to observe whether the other is falling asleep and then wonders at the difficulty in falling asleep. To halt this fight, the patient is instructed to intend and even increase that which he or she is fighting against.

Creating Images

Adler was fond of describing patients with a simple phrase, for example, "The beggar as king." Other Adlerians give patients similar shorthand images that confirm the adage that "one picture is worth a thousand words." Remembering this image, the patient can remember goals, and in later stages, can learn to use the image to laugh at self. One overambitious patient, labeled "Superman," one day began to unbutton his shirt. When the therapist made inquiry, the patient laughingly replied, "So you can see my blue shirt with the big 'S' on it." Another patient, fearing sexual impotence, concurred with the therapist's observation that he had never seen an impotent dog. The patient advanced as explanation, "The dog just does what he's supposed

to do without worrying about whether he'll be able to perform." The therapist suggested that at his next attempt at sexual intercourse, before he made any advances, he should smile and say inwardly, "Bowwow." The following week he informed the members of his group, "I bowwowed."

Catching Oneself

When patients understand personal goals and want to change they are instructed to catch themselves with their hand in the cookie jar" as it were. Patients may catch themselves in the midst of their old behavior but still feel incapable of doing anything about it at the moment. With additional practice, they learn to anticipate situations before their occurrence.

The Push-Button Technique

This method, effective with people who feel they are victims of their disjunctive emotions, involves requesting patients to close their eyes, recreate a pleasant incident from past experience, and to note the feeling that accompanies this image. Then they are asked to recreate an unpleasant incident of hurt, humiliation, failure, or anger and to note the accompanying feeling. Following this the patient recreates the first scene again. The lesson Adlerians try to teach clients is that they can create whatever feeling they wish merely by deciding about what they will think. She is the creator, not the victim, of emotions. To be depressed, for example, requires *choosing* to be depressed. We try to impress the patient with their power for self-determination. This method, devised for clinical use by Mosak (1985), has been the subject of experimental investigation by Brewer (1976), who found it an effective technique in treating state depression.

The "Aha" Experience

The patient who gains awareness in treatment and increases participation in life recurrently has "aha" or "eureka" experiences. With this greater understanding, the patient generates self-confidence and optimism, resulting in increased encouragement and willingness to confront life's problems with commitment, compassion, and empathy.

Posttherapy

After therapy is over the patient can implement newly acquired learning to serve both self and others. Operationally, the goal of therapy may be defined as that of making the therapist superfluous. If therapist and patient have both done their jobs well, the goal will have been achieved.

APPLICATIONS

Problems

Although Adler, like the other Nervenärzte ("nerve doctors") of his era, conducted one-to-one psychotherapy, his own social outlook moved him out of the consulting room and into the community. Although he never relinquished his clinical interests, he concurrently was an educator and a social reformer. Joost Meerloo, a Freudian, eulogizes Adler with his confession:

As a matter of fact, the whole body of psychoanalysis and psychiatry is imbued with Adler's ideas, although few want to acknowledge this fact. We are all plagiarists, though we hate to confess it. . . . The whole body of social psychiatry would have been impossible without Adler's pioneering zest. (1970, p. 40)

Clinical

All the early pioneers in psychotherapy treated neurotics. However, psychotics were considered not amenable to psychotherapy because they could not enter into a transference relationship. Adlerians, unencumbered by the concept of transference, treated psychotics regularly. Henri Ellenberger (1970) suggests that "among the great pioneers of dynamic psychiatry, Janet and Adler are the only ones who had personal clinical experience with criminals, and Adler was the only one who wrote something on the subject from his direct experience." An Adlerian, Ernst Papanek (1971), of whom Claude Brown (1965) wrote so glowingly in his Manchild in the Promised Land, was director of Wiltwyck School (a reform school), and Mosak set up a group therapy program at Cook County Jail in Chicago employing paraprofessionals as therapists (O'Reilly, Cizon, Flanagan & Pflanczer, 1965). The growth model implicit in Adlerian theory has prompted Adlerians to see human problems in terms of people's realizing themselves and becoming fellow human beings. Much "treatment" then is of "normal" people with "normal" problems. A therapy that does not provide the client with a philosophy of life, whatever else it may accomplish in the way of symptom eradication or alleviation, behavior modification, or insight, is an incomplete therapy. Hence the Adlerian is concerned with the client's problems of living and existence. Deficiency, suffering, and illness do not constitute the price of admission to Adlerian therapy. One may enter therapy to learn about oneself, to grow, and to actualize oneself.

Social

Adler's interests were rather catholic. In the area of education, he believed in prevention rather than cure and founded family education centers in the community where parents and teachers could receive direct advice on child rearing. Dreikurs and his students (Dreikurs et al., 1959) have founded family education centers throughout the world. Offshoots of these centers are the hundreds of parent study groups where parents can share problems and solutions with other parents under guidance of a paraprofessional leader (Soltz, 1967). In addition, professional therapists have used a variety of methods for teaching child-rearing practices (Allred, 1976; Beecher & Beecher, 1966; Corsini & Painter, 1975; Dreikurs, 1948; Dreikurs & Soltz, 1964; Painter & Corsini, 1989).

Adler himself wrote on social issues and problems such as crime, war, religion, group psychology, Bolshevism, leadership, and nationalism. Among contemporary Adlerians (Angers 1960; Clark 1965, 1967a, 1967b; Elam 1969a, 1969b; Gottesfeld 1966; Hemming 1956; La Porte 1966; Lombardi 1969; and Nikelly 1971c) the "newer" social problems of protest, race, drugs, social conditions, and the "newer" views of religion (Mosak, 1987b) have been added to the Adlerians' previous interests.

EVALUATION

Until very recently, little research had emerged from the Adlerian group. As was the case with most European clinicians, European Adlerians were suspicious of research based upon statistical methods. A complicating factor was the *idiographic* (case method) approach upon which Adlerians relied. Statistical methods are more appropriate for *nomothetic* (group) research. Even now statisticians have not developed appropriate sophisticated methods for idiographic studies. The research methods lent themselves well to studies of "causal" factors, but the Adlerian rejected causalism, feeling

that causes can only be imputed (and therefore disputed) in retrospective fashion but that they contributed little to the understanding of humans.

The most often-cited studies involving Adlerian psychology were conducted by non-Adlerians. Fred Fiedler (1950) compared therapeutic relationships in psychoanalytic, nondirective, and Adlerian therapy. He found there was greater similarity between therapeutic relationships developed by experts of the three schools than between expert and less expert therapists within the same school. Recently Crandall (1981) has presented the first large-scale investigation of an Adlerian construct. Using his Social Interest Scale, Crandall found positive correlations between social interest and optimism about human nature, altruism, trustworthiness, being liked, and several measures of adjustment and wellbeing. Because of the number of ways social interest has been defined (Bickhard & Ford, 1976; Crandall, 1981; Edgar, 1975; Kazan, 1978), his study represents a valuable contribution to the understanding of this concept.

A joint research study conducted by the (Rogerian) Counseling Center of the University of Chicago and the Alfred Adler Institute of Chicago examined the effects of time limits in psychotherapy (Shlien, Mosak & Dreikurs, 1962). Patients of both groups of therapists were given 20 interviews, and the groups were compared with each other and with two control groups. The investigators reported changes in self-ideal correlations. These correlations improved significantly and, according to this measure, suggest that time-limited therapy "may be said to be not only *effective,* but also twice as *efficient* as time-unlimited therapy." Follow-up of these patients in both experimental groups indicated that the gains were retained when measured one year later.

Much of the research in family constellation has also been done by non-Adlerians. Charles Miley (1969) and Lucille Forer (1977) have compiled bibliographies of this literature. The results reported are contradictory probably because non-Adlerians treat birth order as a matter of ordinal position and Adlerians consider birth order in terms of psychological position (Mosak, 1972). Walter Toman (1970) recognized this distinction in his many studies of the family constellation.

Ansbacher (1946) and Mosak (1958) have also distinguished between Freudian and Adlerian approaches to the interpretation of early recollections. Robin Gushurst (1971) provides a manual for interpreting and scoring one class of recollections. His reliability studies demonstrate that judges can interpret early recollection data with high interjudge reliability. He also conducted three validity studies to investigate the hypothesis that life goals may be identified from early recollections data and found that he could do this with two of his three experimental groups. While Fiedler compared therapists of different orientations, Heine (1953) compared patients' reports of their experiences in Adlerian, Freudian, and Rogerian therapy.

Adlerian psychology would undoubtedly benefit from more research. With the shift in locus from Europe to the United States, with the accelerated growth of the Adlerian school in recent years, with the introduction of more American-trained Adlerians into academic settings, and with the development of new research strategies suitable for idiographic data, there is increasing integration of Adlerians into research activities. A summary of these activities appears in two articles by Watkins (1982, 1983).

TREATMENT

One can hardly identify a mode of treatment in which some Adlerian is not engaged. From a historical viewpoint the initial Adlerian modality was one-to-one psychotherapy. Many Adlerians still regard individual psychotherapy as the treatment of choice. But they did not accept some of the therapeutic conventions of the times and discounted the value of prognosis. Adlerians demonstrated willingness to undertake treatment with any who sought their services.

Dreikurs, Mosak, and Shulman (1952a, 1952b, 1982) introduced *multiple psychotherapy*, a format in which several therapists treat a single patient. It offers constant consultation between therapists, prevents the emotional attachment of a patient to a single therapist, and obviates or dissolves impasses. Countertransference reactions are minimized. Flexibility in the number of therapist roles and models is increased. Patients are more impressed or reassured when two therapists independently agree. The patient also may benefit from the experience of observing disagreement between therapists and learn that people can disagree without loss of face.

Multiple therapy creates an atmosphere that facilitates learning, permitting patient interaction with two different personalities with two different approaches. Therapeutic impasses and problems of dependency are resolved more easily. These include the responsibility for self, absence of the therapist-transference reactions, and termination. In the event that therapist and patient do not hit it off, the patient does not become a therapeutic casualty and is merely transferred to the second therapist.

Dreikurs (1959) in the mid-1920s initiated group therapy in private practice. This application was a natural evolution from the Adlerian axiom that people's problems were always social problems. Group therapy finds considerable adherents among Adlerians. Some Adlerian therapists regard group therapy as the method of choice either on practical grounds (e.g., fees, large numbers of patients to be treated, etc.) or because they believe that because human problems are primarily social problems, they are most effectively handled in the group social situation. Others use group therapy as a preface to individual therapy or to taper patients off from intensive individual psychotherapy. A number of therapists combine individual and group psychotherapy in the conviction that this combination maximizes therapeutic effect (H. Papanek, 1954, 1956). Still other therapists visualize the group as assisting in the solution of certain selected problems or with certain types of populations. Co-therapist groups are very common among Adlerians.

An offshoot of group treatment is the therapeutic social club in a mental hospital as initiated by the British Adlerian, Joshua Bierer. Although these clubs possess superficial similarities to Abraham Low's recovery groups (Low, 1952) and to halfway houses in that all attempt to facilitate the patient's reentrance into society, the therapeutic social club emphasizes the "social" rather than the "therapeutic" aspects of life, taking the "healthy" rather than the "sick" model. Psychodrama has been used by Adlerians, sometimes as separate therapy, sometimes in conjunction with another therapeutic modality (Starr, 1977).

Marriage counseling has figured prominently in Adlerian activities. Adlerians defied the trend of the times and preferred to treat the couple as a unit rather than as separate individuals. To "treat" merely one mate may be compared to having only half the dialogue of a play. Seeing the couple together suggests that they have a joint relationship problem rather than individual problems and invites joint effort in the solution of these problems. The counselor can observe and describe their interaction (Mozdzierz & Lottman, 1973; Pew & Pew, 1972). Married couples group therapy (Deutsch, 1967) and married couples study groups constitute two more settings for conducting marriage counseling. Phillips and Corsini (1982) have written a self-help book to be used by married people who are experiencing trouble in their marriage.

In the early 1920s, Adler persuaded the Viennese school administration to establish child-guidance centers in the schools. The social group was the primary vehicle for treatment (Adler, 1963a; Alexandra Adler, 1951; Seidler & Zilahi, 1949). Dreikurs wrote several popular books and many articles (Dreikurs, 1948; Dreikurs & Grey, 1968; Dreikurs & Soltz, 1964) to disseminate this information to parents and teachers, and currently thousands of parents are enrolled in study groups where they obtain supplementary information on child rearing.

The preventive methods in schools as started by Adler were adopted by educators and school counselors who used them in individual classes, schools, and in one instance in an entire school system (Mosak, 1971a). The methods were originally applied in the Individual Psychological Experimental School in Vienna (Birnbaum, 1935; Spiel, 1962) and have been elaborated upon in this country by many educators (Corsini, 1977, 1979; Dinkmeyer & Dreikurs, 1963; Dreikurs, 1968, 1972; Dreikurs, Grunwald & Pepper, 1982; Grunwald, 1954).

With respect to broader social problems, Dreikurs devoted the last part of his life to the problem of interindividual and intergroup conflict resolution. Much of this work was performed in Israel and has not been reported. Kenneth Clark, a former president of the American Psychological Association, has devoted much of his career to studying and providing recommendations for solutions for problems of black people, as have Harry Elam (1969a, 1969b) and Jacqueline Brown (1976).

MANAGEMENT

The Setting

Adlerians function in every imaginable setting: the private-practice office, hospitals, day hospitals, jails, schools, and community programs. Offices do not need any special furnishing, but reflect either the therapist's aesthetic preferences or the condition of the institution's budget. No special equipment is used, except perhaps for special projects. Although voice recordings are a matter of individual choice, they are sometimes maintained as the patient's file. Some therapists ask their patients to listen to these recordings during or between interviews. Some voice recordings and videotape recordings have also been made for demonstration and teaching purposes.

In the initial interviews, the therapist generally obtains the following kinds of information (in addition to demographic information):

1. Was the patient self-referred? If not, he or she may continue treatment only for the duration of the "sentence." Reluctant adolescents may punish their parents by failing to keep appointments for which they know the parents must pay. For that matter, the patient who is sent may merely be the identified patient, so labeled by someone, usually parents. This is one reason why, when a child is referred, Adlerians prefer to see the entire family.

2. Is the patient negative about treatment? If the patient is reluctant, "conversion" is necessary if therapy is to proceed.

3. What does the patient come for? Is it treatment to alleviate suffering? If so, suffering from what? Does the patient make the implicit demand that the therapist legitimize or confirm an already made decision? Is the patient there to get others off his back? May he think that as long as he is in therapy, he does not have to accept responsibilities or make decisions? After all, he may be designated by himself or others as "sick" or "confused."

Some new patients are "supermarket shoppers" who announce the number of therapists who have helped them already. Their secret goal is to be perfect. Unless such a patient's fictional goal is disclosed, today's therapist may be the latest of many therapists about whom the patient will be telling the next therapist. Adler (1935/1982) describes such a person as belonging to the ruling type, one who must conquer. Others are scalp collectors who spend their lives defeating therapists, winning Pyrrhic victories. Therapists of any orientation will recognize many such recurring types (Mosak, 1971b; Mosak & Shulman, 1963).

4. What are the patient's expectations about treatment? A patient may check the therapist's diplomas and credentials to make sure he or she is not a quack or may worry if there is no couch in the room. Some viewers of psychological movies will think that free association is the order of the day.

5. What are the patient's expectations? Perfection? Failure? A solution for a specific problem without any major personality alterations? Immediate cure?

6. What are the patient's goals in psychotherapy? We must distinguish between stated goals—to get well, to learn about self, to be a better spouse and parent, to gain a new philosophy of life—and nonverbalized goals—to remain sick, to punish others, to defeat the therapist and sabotage therapy, to maintain good intentions without changing ("Look how hard I'm trying and the money I'm spending on therapy"). The importance of this determination cannot be overstated. The Adlerian defines resistance as that which occurs when the patient's goals and those of the therapist do not coincide. Consequently, the therapist who fails to understand the patient's goals may be operating at cross-purposes, and the therapeutic effort may deteriorate into a vicious circle of resistance-overcoming resistance-resistance rather than the cooperative effort for which the Adlerian therapist aims. The best technique for handling resistance is to avoid fostering it, to listen attentively and empathetically to the patient, to follow movement in therapy, to understand goals and strategies, and to encourage the development of therapy as a "we" endeavor.

The patient may also resist in order to depreciate or defeat the therapist because the patient lacks the courage to live on the useful side of life and fears that the therapist might nudge in that direction. The intensification of such escape methods may become most pronounced during the termination phase of treatment when the patient realizes he or she must soon face the realistic tasks of life without the therapist's support.

Tests

Routine physical examinations are not required by Adlerians in view of the therapy's educational orientation. Nevertheless, many patients do have physiological problems and Adlerians are trained to be sensitive to the presence of these problems. The therapist who suspects such problems will make referrals for physical examination.

Adlerians are divided on the issue of psychological testing. Most Adlerians avoid nosological diagnosis, except for nontherapeutic purposes, such as filling out insurance forms. Labels are static descriptions and ignore the *movement* of the individual. They describe what the individual *has*, but not how he or she *moves* through life.

Older, European-trained therapists eschewed psychological testing. Apparently Adler himself, although he developed the first projective test, Early Recollections, had little use for testing. Dreikurs was distrustful of tests, his opinion of them being that they were relatively unnecessary because "the test situation indicates what is probably true. Observation permits us to determine what is true" (Dinkmeyer & Dreikurs, 1963, p. 10). Dreikurs also felt tests were unreliable because they could provide deceptive results and, thus, might be harmful

(Dreikurs, 1968). Dreikurs did refer patients for testing, nevertheless.

Regine Seidler placed more faith in projective testing than in so-called objective tests, maintaining that the latter are actually subjective tests because "the *subjective attitude* of each and every individual toward any given test necessarily renders the test non-objective" (1967, p. 4). Objective tests were more useful to her as measures of test-taking attitude than of what the test was purportedly measuring.

Early recollections serve as a test for Adlerians, assisting them in the life-style assessment. Younger Adlerians employ many conventional tests and some nonconventional ones for diagnostic and differential diagnostic purposes as well as in the treatment of the patient.

The Therapist

The Adlerian therapist ideally is an authentically sharing, caring person. Helene and Ernst Papanek write: "The therapist participates actively. Without playing any sharply defined 'role,' he shows warmth toward and a genuine interest in the patient and encourages especially his desire for change and betterment. The relationship itself has a purpose: to help the patient help himself" (1964, p. 117). Adler relates how he treated a mute schizophrenic patient who after three months of silence assaulted him and "I instantly decided not to defend myself. After a further attack, during which a window was smashed, I bound up his slightly bleeding wound in the friendliest way" (1924, p. 24). Because the ideal goal in psychotherapy is to encourage the development of social interest, therapists must be models for social interest themselves.

Adlerian therapists remain free to have feelings and opinions and to express them. Such expression in a spontaneous way permits patients to view therapists as human beings, discouraging any perceptions of omnipotence or perfection with which patients may invest them. If therapists err, they err—but then the patient may learn the courage to be imperfect from this experience (Lazarsfeld, 1966). The experience may also facilitate therapy.

Therapists must not inject evaluation of their worth into the therapy, doing their therapeutic job without concern for prestige, not reveling in successes or becoming discouraged by failures. Otherwise, they may bounce like a rubber ball from therapy hour to therapy hour or perhaps even within the same hour. The therapist's worth does not depend upon external factors but rather on what lies within the self. The therapist is task-oriented rather than self-oriented.

Therapists reveal themselves as persons. Because therapists are authentic, patients have the opportunity to appraise them as genuine human beings. These perceptions may combine realistic judgments as well as judgments stemming from the patient's life-style. The concept of the *anonymous therapist* is foreign to Adlerian psychology. Such a role would increase social distance between therapist and patient, interfering with the establishment of the egalitarian, human relationship that Adlerians regard as indispensable. The "anonymous therapist" role was created to facilitate the establishment of a transference relationship, and because the Adlerian rejects the transference concept as Freud formulated it, the maintenance of such a posture is considered irrelevant, if not harmful to the relationship the therapist wants to establish with the patient. Dreikurs (1961) deplored the prevalent attitude among therapists of not coming too close to patients because it might affect the therapeutic relationship adversely. Shulman (Wexberg, 1929/1970, p. 88) defines the role of the therapist as that of "a helping friend." Self-revelation can only occur when therapists feel secure, at home with others, unafraid to be human and fallible, and thus unafraid of their patients' evaluations, criticism, or hostility (cf. Rogers' "congruence"). For these and other reasons, Adlerian training institutes customarily require a "didactic analysis" of their candidates.

Is the Adlerian therapist judgmental? In a sense all therapists are judgmental in that therapy rests upon some value orientation: a belief that certain behavior is better than other behavior, that certain goals are better than other goals, that one organization of personality is superior to another form of organization. Dreikurs states, "There is always a value and moral problem involved in the cure [in all therapy]" (1961, p. 93). On the other hand, the patient who seeks help is often a discouraged human being. To criticize would merely reinforce discouragement, reduce personal worth, and perhaps confirm life-style convictions (e.g., "People are unfair" or "I am unlovable" or "I do everything wrong"). Given that two cardinal principles of the Adlerian intervention are caring and encouragement, such judgments are best avoided.

Patient Problems

If the therapist does not like the patient, it raises problems for a therapist of any persuasion (Fromm-Reichman, 1949). Some therapists merely do not accept such patients. Still others feel they ought not to have or ought to overcome such negative feelings and accept the patient for treatment, leading to both participants' "suffering." It appears difficult to possess "unconditional positive regard" for a patient you dislike. Adlerians meet this situation in the same manner other therapists do.

Seduction problems are treated as any other patient problem. The secure therapists will not frighten, panic, or succumb. If the patient's activities nevertheless prevent the therapy from continuing, the patient may be referred to another therapist, a transfer easily accomplished in multiple psychotherapy. Flattery problems are in some ways similar and have been discussed elsewhere (Berne, 1964; Mosak & Gushurst, 1971).

Suicide threats are always taken seriously (Ansbacher, 1961, 1969). Alfred Adler warned, however, that our goal is "to knock the weapon out of his hand" so the patient cannot make us vulnerable and intimidate us at will with his threats. As an example, he narrates, "A patient once asked me, smiling, 'Has anyone ever taken his life while being treated by you?' I answered him, 'Not yet, but I am prepared for this to happen at any time' " (Ansbacher & Ansbacher, 1956, pp. 338–39).

Kurt Adler postulates "an underlying rage against people" in suicide threats and that this goal of vengefulness must be uncovered. He "knocks the weapon out of the patient's hand" as follows:

Patients have tested me with the question of how would I feel if I were to read of their suicide in the newspaper. I answer that it is possible that some reporter hungry for news would pick up such an item from a police blotter. But, the next day, the paper will already be old, and only a dog perhaps may honor their suicide notice by lifting a leg over it in some corner. (1961, p. 66)

Alexandra Adler (1943), Lazarsfeld (1952) and Oscar Pelzman (1952) discuss problems beyond the scope of this chapter.

CASE EXAMPLE

BACKGROUND

The patient was a 53-year-old, Viennese-born man, in treatment almost continuously with Freudian psychoanalysts, here and abroad, since he was 17. With the advent of tranquilizers, he had transferred his allegiances to psychiatrists who treated him with a combination of drugs and psychotherapy and finally with drugs alone. When he entered Adlerian treatment, he was being maintained by his previous therapist on an opium derivative and Thorazine. He failed to tell his previous therapist of his decision to see us and also failed to inform us that he was still obtaining medication from his previous therapist.

The treatment process was atypical in the sense that the patient's "illness" hampered us from following our customary procedure. Having over the years become therapy-wise, he invested his creativity in efforts to run the therapy. Cooperative effort was virtually impossible. In conventional terms, the co-therapists, Drs. A and B, had their hands full dealing with the patient's resistances and "transference."

PROBLEM

When the patient entered treatment, he had taken to bed and spent almost all his time there because he felt too weak to get up. His wife had to be constantly at his side or he would panic. Once she was encouraged by a friend to attend the opera alone. The patient wished her a good time and then told her, "When you return, I shall be dead." His secretary was forced into conducting his successful business. Everyone was forced into "the emperor's service." The price he paid for this service was intense suffering in the form of depression, obsessive-compulsive behavior, phobic behavior, especially agoraphobia, divorce from the social world, somatic symptoms, and invalidism.

TREATMENT

The patient was seen in multiple psychotherapy by Drs. A and B, but both therapists were not present at each interview. We dispensed with the lifestyle assessment because the patient had other immediate goals. It seemed to us from the patient's behavior that he probably had been raised as a pampered child and that he was using "illness" to tyrannize the world and to gain exemption from the life tasks. If these guesses were correct, we anticipated he would attempt to remain "sick," would resist giving up drugs, and would demand special attention from his therapists. As part of the treatment strategy, the therapists decided to wean him from medication, to give him no special attention, and not to be manipulated by him. Given that he had undergone analysis over a period of more than three decades, the therapists thought he could probably produce a better analysis of his problems than they could. For this reason, interpretation was kept at a minimum. The treatment plan envisaged a tactical and strategic, rather than interpretive, approach. Some excerpts from the early part of treatment are reproduced on the following pages.

March 8

Dr. B wanted to collect life-style information but the patient immediately complained that he wanted to terminate. He said his previous therapist, Dr. C, had treated him differently. Therapist B was too impersonal. "You won't even give me your home phone number. You aren't impressed by my illness. Your treatment is well meaning but it won't help. Nothing helps. I'm going back to Dr. C and ask him to put me in the hospital. He gave me advice and you are so cruel by not telling me what to do."

March 19

Relatively calm. Compares B with Dr. C. Later compares B with A. Favors B over Dr. C because he respects former's strength. Favors B over A because he can succeed in ruffling latter but not former. Talk centers about his use of weakness to overpower others.

March 22

Telephones to say he must be hospitalized. Wife left him [untrue] and secretary left him [it turns out she went to lunch]. Would B come to his office to see him? B asks him to keep appointment in B's office. Patient races about office upset. "I'm sweating water and blood." When B remains calm, patient takes out bottle of Thorazine and threatens to take all. Next he climbs up on radiator, opens window (17th floor), jumps back, and says, "No, it's too high."

"You don't help me. Why can't I have an injection?" Then he informs B that B is a soothing influence. "I wish I could spend the whole day with you." B speaks softly to patient and patient speaks quietly. Patient asks for advice about what to do this weekend. B gives antisuggestion and tells him to try to worry as much as he can. He is surprised and dismisses it as "bad advice."

March 29

B was sick on March 26, so patient saw A. "It was useless." No longer worried about state hospital. Thinks he will now wind up as bum because he got drunk last week. His secretary gave him notice but he hopes to keep her "by taking abuse. No one treats a boss like she treats me." Got out of bed and worked last week. Went out selling but "everyone rejected me." When B indicates that he seems to be better, he insists he's deteriorating. When B inquired how, he replies paradoxically, "I beat out my competitors this week."

April 2

Has habit of sticking finger down throat to induce vomiting. Threatens to do so when enters office today. B tells patients about the logical consequences of his act—he will have to mop up. Patient withdraws finger. "If you would leave me alone, I'd fall asleep so fast." B leaves him alone. Patient angrily declaims, "Why do you let me sleep?"

April 9

Too weak even to telephone therapist. If wife goes on vacation, he will kill himself. How can he survive with no one to tell him to eat, to go to bed, to get up? "All I do is vomit and sleep." B suggests that he tyrannizes his wife as he did his mother and sister. He opens window and inquires, "Shall I jump?" B recognizes this as an attempt to intimidate rather than a serious threat and responds, "Suit yourself." Patient closes window and accuses, "You don't care either." Asks whether he can see A next time and before receiving answer, says, "I don't want him anyway."

Follows this with, "I want to go to the state hospital. Can you get me a private room?" At end of interview falls to knees and sobs, "Help me! Help me to be a human being."

April 12

Enters, falls to knees, encircles therapist's knees, whimpers, "Help me!" So depressed. If only he could end it all. B gives him Adler's suggestion to do one thing each day that would give someone pleasure. Patient admits behaving better. Stopped annoying secretary and let her go home early because of bad weather. Agitation stops.

April 15

Didn't do anything this weekend to give pleasure. However, he did play cards with wife. Took her for drive. Sex with wife for "first time in a long time." B gives encouragement and then repeats "pleasure" suggestion. He can't do it. Calm whole hour. Says his wife has told him to discontinue treatment. Upon inquiry, he says she didn't say exactly that but had said, "I leave it up to you."

April 19

Wants B to accompany him back to his office because he forgot something. Wants shorter hour this week and longer one next week. "Dr. C let me do that." When B declines, he complains, "Doctor, I don't know what to do with you anymore."

April 23

Wouldn't consider suicide. "Perhaps I have a masochistic desire to live." B suggests he must be angry with life. He responds that he wants to be an infant and have all his needs gratified. The world should be a big breast and he should be able to drink without having to suck [probably an interpretation he had received in psychoanalysis]. Yesterday he had fantasy of destroying the whole city.

This weekend he helped his wife work in the garden. He asks for suggestions for weekend. B and patient play "yes-but." B does so deliberately to point out game (cf. Berne's "Why don't you...? Yes but" [1964]) to patient. Patient then volunteers possibility of clay modeling. B indicates this may be good choice in that patient can mold, manipulate, and "be violent."

April 29

Had birthday last week and resolved to turn over new leaf for new year but didn't. Cries, "Help me, help me." Depreciates B. "How much would you charge me to come to my summer home? I'm so sick, I vomited blood." When B tells him if he's that sick, hospitalization might be advisable, he smiles and says, "For money, you'd come out." B and patient speak of attitude toward B and attitude toward his father. Patient depreciates both, possibly because he could not dominate either.

May 1

Didn't think he could make it today because he was afraid to walk on street. Didn't sleep all night. So excited, so upset [he seems calm]. Perhaps he should be put in hospital, but then what will happen to his business?

"We could sit here forever and all you would tell me is to get clay. Why don't you give me medicine or advice?" B points out that the patient is much stronger than any medication, as evidenced by number of therapists and treatments he has defeated.

He says he is out of step with world. B repeats an earlier interpretation by A that the patient wants the world to conform to him and follows with statement about his desire to be omnipotent, a desire that makes him feel weak and simultaneously compensates for his feelings of weakness. He confirms with "All Chicago should stand still so I could have a holiday. The police should stop at gunpoint anyone who wants to go to work. But I don't want to. I don't want to do anything anymore. I want a paycheck but I don't want to work." B remarks on shift from "I can't" to "I don't want to." Patient admits and says, "I don't want to get well. Should I make another appointment?" B refers decision back to him. He makes appointment.

May 6

"I'm at the end, dying with fear [enumerates symptoms]. Since 5 this morning I'm murdering ——— and ———. Such nice people and I'm murdering them and I'm electrocuted. And my secretary and wife can't stand it anymore. Take me to a state hospital. I don't want to go. Take me. I'm getting crazy and you don't help me. Help me, *Lieber Doktor!* I went to the ladies' room twice today to get my secretary and the girls complained to the building office. I'm not above the rules. I knew I violated them. My zipper was down again [he frequently "forgets"] and I just pulled it up before you came in today." B agrees that state hospital might be appropriate if he is becoming "crazier." "Then my wife will divorce me. It's terrible. They have bars there. I won't go. I'm not that bad yet. Why, last week I went out and made a big sale!" B suggests he "practice" his fears and obsessions.

May 8

Seen by A and B, who did summary of his family constellation. It was done very tentatively because of the meager information elicited.

May 13

Complains about symptoms. He had taken his wife to the movie but "was too upset to watch it." He had helped with the raking. Returns to symptoms and begging for Thorazine. "How will I live without Thorazine?" B suggests they ought to talk about how to live. He yells, "With your quiet voice, you'll drive me crazy." B asks, "Would you like me to yell at you like your father did?" "I won't talk to you anymore."

"*Lieber Gott,* liberate me from the evil within me." Prays to everyone for help. B counters with, "Have you ever solicited your own help?" Patient replies, "I have no strength, I could cry. I could shout. I don't have strength. Let me vomit."

May 15

Demands Thorazine or he will have heart attack. B requests a future autobiography. Responds "I don't anticipate anything" and returns to Thorazine question. B points out his real achievement in staying off Thorazine. Patient mentions price in suffering. B points out that this makes it an even greater achievement. Patient accepts idea reluctantly. B points out that they are at cross-purposes because patient wants to continue suffering but have pills; B's goal is to have him stop his suffering. "I want pills." B offers clay. "Shit on your clay."

May 20

Must have Thorazine. Has murderous and self-castrating fantasies. Tells A that A doesn't know anything about medicine. Dr. C did. Why don't we let him go back to Dr. C? A leaves room with patient following. After three to four minutes patient returns and complains, "You call this treatment?" Dr. A points out demand of patient to have own way. He is a little boy who wants to be big but doesn't think he can make it. He is a pampered tyrant. A also refers to patient's favorite childhood game of lying in bed with sister and playing "Emperor and Empress."

Patient points out innate badness in himself. A points out he creates it. Patient talks of hostility and murder. A interprets look on his face as taking pride in his bad behavior. Patient picks up letter opener, trembles, then grasps hand with other hand but continues to tremble. A tells him that this is a spurious fight between good and evil, that he can decide how he will behave.

He kneaded clay a little while this weekend.

May 22

Last weekend he mowed lawn, tried to read but "I'm nervous. I'm talking to you like a human being but I'm not really a human being." Raw throat. Fears might have throat cancer. Stopped sticking finger down throat to vomit as consequence. Discussion of previously expressed idea of "like a human being." Fantasy of riding a boat through a storm. Fantasy of A being acclaimed by crowd and patient in fantasy asking B, "Are you used to A getting all the attention?"

Complains about wife and secretary, neither of whom will any longer permit tyrannization.

June 3

Relates fantasy of being magician and performing unbelievable feats at the White House. He asked the president whether he was happily married and then produced the president's ring. Nice weekend. Made love to wife at his initiative. Grudgingly admits enjoying it.

June 10

"Ignored my wife this week." Yet he took initiative and they had sex again. Both enjoyed it but he was afraid because he read in a magazine that sex is a drain on the heart. At work secretary is angry. After she checks things, he rechecks. Pledged his God today he wouldn't do it anymore. He'll only check one time more. Outlines several plans for improving business "but I don't have the strength." Wants to cut down to one interview per week because he doesn't get well and can't afford to pay. B suggests that perhaps he is improving if he wants to reduce the number of sessions. Patient rejects and agrees to two sessions weekly.

June 24

Talks about fears. B tells him he will go on vacation next week. He accepts it calmly although he had previously claimed to be unendurably upset. Patient tells B that he has given up vomiting and masturbation, saying, "You have enormous influence on me." B encourages by saying patient made the decision by himself.

Sept. 4

[Patient was not seen during August because he went on a "wonderful" vacation.] Stopped all medication except for occasional use of a mild tranquilizer his family physician prescribed. Able to read and concentrate again. Has surrendered his obsessive ruminations. He and his secretary get along without fighting although she doesn't like him. He is punctual at the office. He and wife get along well. He is more considerate of her. Both are sexually satisfied.

B and patient plan for treatment. Patient expresses reluctance, feeling that he has gone as far as he can. After all, one psychoanalyst said that he was hopeless and had recommended a lobotomy, so this was marked improvement. B agreed, telling patient that if he had considered the patient hopeless, he would not have undertaken treatment, nor would he now be recommending continuation. "What kind of treatment?" B tells him that no external agent (e.g., medicine, lobotomy) will do it, that his salvation will come from within, that he can choose to live life destructively (and self-destructively) or constructively. He proposes to come weekly for four weeks and then biweekly. B does not accept the offer.

Sept. 17

Since yesterday his symptoms have returned. Heart palpitations.

Sept. 25

Took wife to dinner last night. Very pleasant. Business is slow and his obligations are heavy but he is working. He has to exert effort not to backslide. B schedules double interview. Patient doesn't want to see A. It will upset him. He doesn't see any sense in seeing B either but since B insists . . . Heart palpitations disappeared after last interview. Expresses realistic concerns today and has dropped usual frantic manner. Wants biweekly interviews. B wants weekly. Patient accepts without protest.

As therapy continued, the patient's discussion of symptoms was superseded by discussion of realistic concerns. Resistance waned. When he entered treatment, he perceived himself as a good person who behaved badly because he was "sick." During therapy, he saw through his pretenses and settled for being "a bad guy." However, once he understood his tyranny and was able to accept it, he had the oppor-

tunity to ask himself how he preferred to live his life—usefully or uselessly. Because the therapists used the monolithic approach (Alexander & French, 1946; Mosak & Shulman, 1963), after resolving the issue of his tyranny, therapy moved on to his other "basic mistakes," one at a time. The frequency of interviews was decreased and termination was by mutual agreement.

FOLLOW-UP

The patient improved, remaining off medication. When he devoted himself to his business, it prospered to the point where he could retire early. He moved to a university town, where he studied archaeology, the activity he liked best in life. The relationship with his wife improved and they traveled abroad. Because of the geographical distance between them, the therapists and the patient had no further contact.

SUMMARY

Adlerian psychology as a theory of personality may be described as follows:

1. Its approach is social, teleological, phenomenological, holistic, idiographic, and humanistic.

2. Its underlying assumptions are (a) the individual is unique, (b) the individual is self-consistent, (c) the individual is responsible, (d) the person is creative, an actor, a chooser, and (e) people in a soft-deterministic way can direct their own behavior and control their destinies.

3. Its personality theory takes as its central construct the life-style, a system of subjective convictions held by the individual that contains his self-view and world view. From these convictions, other convictions, methods of operation, and goals are derived.

The person behaves *as if* these convictions were true and uses his life-style as a cognitive map with which he explores, comprehends, prejudges, predicts, and controls the environment (the life tasks). Because the person cannot be understood *in vacuo* but only in his social context, the interaction between the individual and his life tasks, his line of movement, is indispensable for the purpose of fully comprehending the individual.

4. "Psychopathology," "mental illness," and similar nomenclature are reifications and perpetuate the nominal fallacy, "the tendency to confuse naming with explaining" (Beach, 1955). The "psychopathological" individual is a discouraged person. Such people have either never developed or have lost their courage with respect to meeting the life tasks. With their pessimistic anticipations, stemming largely from their life-style, they create "arrangements,"—evasions, excuses, sideshows, symptoms—to protect their self-esteem, or they may "cop out" completely.

5. Because people's difficulties emanate from faulty perceptions, learnings, values, and goals that have resulted in discouragement, therapy consists of an educative or reeducative endeavor in which two equals cooperatively tackle the educational task. Many of the traditional analytic methods have been retained, although they are understood, and sometimes used, differently by the Adlerian. The focus of the therapy is the encouragement of the individual, the experience of encouragement coming from many avenues in the therapy. The individual learns to have faith in self, to trust, and to love. The ultimate, *ideal* goal of psychotherapy is to release people's social interest so they may become fellow human beings, cooperators, contributors to the creation of a better society, people who feel they belong to and are at home in the universe. Such patients can be said to have actualized themselves. Because therapy is learning, everyone can change. On the entrance door of the Guidance Clinic for Juvenile Delinquency in Vienna was the inscription, "IT IS NEVER TOO LATE" (Kramer, 1947).

Adlerian psychology has become a viable, flourishing system. Neglected for several decades, it has in recent years acquired respectability. Training institutes, professional societies, family-education centers, and study groups continue to proliferate. With Adlerians being trained in universities rather than solely in institutes, they are writing more and doing research. Non-Adlerians are also engaged in Adlerian research. The previously rare Adlerian dissertation has become more commonplace. Currently Adlerians in greater numbers are moving out of the clinic and into society to renew their attention to the social issues and problems Adler raised 50 years ago—poverty, war, conflict resolution, aggression, religion, and social cooperation. As Way apprises, "We shall need not only, as Adler says, more cooperative individuals, but a society better fitted to fulfill the needs of human beings" (1962, p. 360).

Complementing the Adlerians' endeavors are individuals and groups who have borrowed heavily from Adler, often without acknowledgment or awareness. Adlerian formulations are so often discovered in the writing of non-Adlerians that they have become part of what Adler might have called "the common sense." Keith Sward, for example, reviewed Alexander and

French's *Psychoanalytic Therapy* (1946), writing:

The Chicago group would seem to be Adlerian through and through.... The Chicago Institute for Psychoanalysis is not alone in this seeming rediscovery of Rank and Adler. Psychiatry and psychology as a whole seem to be drifting in the same direction. Adler has come to life in other vigorous circles, notably in the publications of the "Horney" school. (1947, p. 601)

We observe glimpses of Adler in the Freudian ego-psychologists, in the neo-Freudians, in the existential systems, in the humanistic psychologies, in client-centered theory, in rational-emotive therapy, in integrity therapy, in transactional analysis, and in reality therapy. This is not an augury of the eventual disappearance of Adlerian psychology through absorption into other schools of psychology, for, as the motto of the Rockford, Illinois, Teacher Development Center claims, "Education is like a flame.... You can give it away without diminishing the one from whom it came." As Joseph Wilder writes in his introduction to *Essays in Individual Psychology* (Adler & Deutsch, 1959), "most observations and ideas of Alfred Adler have subtly and quietly permeated modern psychological thinking to such a degree that the proper question is not whether one is Adlerian but how much of an Adlerian one is" (p. xv).

ANNOTATED BIBLIOGRAPHY

Adler, A. (1964). *Social interest: A challenge to mankind.* New York: Capricorn Books. (Originally published 1929).

This is the last exposition of Adler's thought and provides an easily read overview of Adlerian psychology.

Adler, A. (1964). *Problems of neurosis: A book of case-histories.* New York: Harper Torchbooks. (Originally published 1929.)

Adler presents his theory of neurotic development, illustrating with many case examples. H. L. Ansbacher has written an excellent introduction to the paperback edition that concisely covers the basic theory of Adlerian psychology.

Ansbacher, H. L. (1983). Individual Psychology. In R. J. Corsini & A. J. Marsella (Eds.), *Personality theories, research and assessment.* Itasca, IL: F. E. Peacock.

Ansbacher's chapter is the twin of this one, compactly summarizing the theory of Individual Psychology while this chapter concentrates on Adlerian psychotherapy. Ansbacher's summary is probably one of the most satisfactory short explications of both the history and the theory of Individual Psychology by one who is acknowledged to be the dean of Adlerian theoreticians.

Ansbacher, H. L., & Ansbacher, R. (Eds.) (1964). *The individual psychology of Alfred Adler.* New York: Harper Torchbooks.

An almost encyclopedic collection of Adler's writings, this volume displays both the great variety of topics that commanded his attention and the evolution of his thinking through the years. Because of the nature of the construction of this book, it is imperative that the reader read the preface.

Dreikurs, R., & Soltz, V. (1964). *Children: The challenge.* New York: Duell, Sloan & Pearce.

Dreikurs and Soltz have written *the* Adlerian book on child rearing. It is the book most often studied in university training programs and parent study groups. While Adlerians have made extensive contributions to the fields of education and parent education, these are not within the purview of a chapter on Adlerian psychotherapy. Further references may be found in the two volumes of the Mosak and Mosak bibliography.

Manaster, G. J., & Corsini, R. J. (1982). *Individual psychology.* Itasca, IL: F. E. Peacock.

This is the first textbook of Adlerian psychology written in English by two students of Rudolf Dreikurs. Corsini was the former editor of the *Journal of Individual Psychology* and Manaster succeeded him. Written in a much simpler style than the Ansbacher and Ansbacher text (1956), this book covers more or less the same materials. Two features make it unique: it contains the single most complete Adlerian psychotherapy case summary published to date and there is a section abstracting the more important research studies published in the field of Adlerian psychology.

Mosak, H. H. (Ed.) (1973). *Alfred Adler: His influence on psychology today.* Park Ridge, NJ: Noyes Press.

Written to commemorate the centennial year of Adler's birth, this volume contains chapters by Rudolf Dreikurs, Alexandra Adler, Lewis Way, Erwin Krausz, Willard and Marguerite Beecher, and others. These papers cover topics such as neurosis, black pride, Shakespeare, logical consequences, family therapy, the Oedipus myth, and sociometry.

Mosak, H., & Mosak, B. (1975). *A bibliography of Adlerian psychology.* Washington, DC: Hemisphere Publishing.

This volume contains almost 10,000 references to the literature of Adlerian psychology and is valuable to the researcher in helping to locate Adlerian writings.

Mosak, B., & Mosak, H. H. (1985). *A bibliography of Adlerian psychology (Vol. 2).* Washington, DC: Hemisphere Publishing.

This second volume of this bibliography covers all publications by Adlerians from 1973 to 1977.

CASE READINGS

Adler, A. (1929). *The Case of Miss R. The interpretation of a life study.* New York: Greenberg.

Adler does an interlinear interpretation of the case study of a patient who in his time would have been labeled "psychoasthenic." The patient is also agoraphobic.

Since Adler did not treat this patient, the course of therapy is unknown. However, we can observe how Adler constructs a life-style as well as his understanding of the patient's approach to the life tasks.

Adler, A. (1964). *The case of Mrs. A.: The diagnosis of a life style.* In H. L. Ansbacher & R. R. Ansbacher (Eds.), *Superiority and social interest* (pp.

159-190). Evanston, IL: Northwestern University Press; (1969). Chicago: Alfred Adler Institute. Reprinted in D. Wedding & R. J. Corsini (Eds.) (1979). *Great cases in psychotherapy*. Itasca, IL: Peacock. (Original work published in 1931)

This publication is similar to the above and interprets the case study of an obsessive-compulsive woman who fears that she will kill her children.

Ansbacher, H. L. (1966). Lee Harvey Oswald: An Adlerian interpretation. *Psychoanalytic Review*, 53, 379–390.

The psychodynamics of John F. Kennedy's assassin are presented from the Adlerian point of view.

Dreikurs, R. (1959). A record of family counseling sessions. In R. Dreikurs, R. Lowe, M. Sonstegard, & R. J. Corsini (Eds.), *Adlerian family counseling* (pp. 109–152). Eugene, OR: University of Oregon Press.

Two sessions of family counseling conducted by Rudolf Dreikurs and Stefanie Necheles are presented. The identified patient, a nine-year-old boy, is described by his parents as an angry child.

Frank, I. (1981). My flight toward a new life. *Journal of Individual Psychology*, 37(1), 15–30.

A young anorexic woman describes the course of her eating problem as well as the various treatments, Adlerian and non-Adlerian, which she underwent until the problem was resolved.

Manaster, G. J., & Corsini, R. J. (1982). *Individual Psychology*. Itasca, IL: Peacock.

Chapter 17 offers verbatim excerpts of a course of therapy of a man who in dualistic fashion perceives himself in conflict, ambivalent, and self-contradictory.

Mosak, H. H. (1972). Life style assessment: A demonstration based on family constellation. *Family of Individual Psychology*, 28, 232–247.

A verbatim description of a life style assessment done in public demonstration is presented. The subject is a teenage girl who feels that she is the sole "non-very" person in a "very" family.

Mosak, H. H., & Maniacci, M. (1989). The case of Roger. In D. Wedding & R. J. Corsini (Eds.), *Case studies in psychotherapy*. Itasca, IL: F. E. Peacock.

This case history was specifically written to complement the current chapter and it illustrates many of the methods, techniques, and principles of Adlerian psychotherapy. Careful reading of the case should help the student more fully appreciate how the Adlerian actually proceeds in therapy.

REFERENCES

Adler, Alexandra (1943). Problems in psychotherapy. *American Journal of Individual Psychology*, 3, 1–5.

Adler, Alexandra (1951). Alfred Adler's viewpoint in child guidance. In E. Harms (Ed.), *Handbook of child guidance*. New York: Child Care Publications.

Adler, A. (1898). *Gesundheitsbuch für das Schneidergewerbe*. Berlin: C. Heymanns.

Adler, A. (1914). Das Zärtlichkeitsbedürfnis des Kindes. In A. Adler & C. Furtmuller (Eds.), *Heilen und Bilden*. München: Reinhardt.

Adler, A. (1917). *Study of organ inferiority and its psychical compensation*. New York: Nervous & Mental Disease Publishing Co.

Adler, A. (1922). Erziehungsberatungsstellen. In A. Adler & C. Furtmüller (Eds.), *Heilen und Bilden*. München: Bergmann.

Adler, A. (1924). Progress in individual psychology. *British Journal of Medical Psychology*, 4, 22–31.

Adler, A. (1972). *The neurotic constitution*. Freeport, NY: Books for Libraries Press. (Originally published 1926.)

Adler, A. (1928). On teaching courage. *Survey Graphic*, 61, 241–242.

Adler, A. (1929). Position in family influences lifestyle. *International Journal of Individual Psychology*, 3, 211–227.

Adler, A. (1930). Individual psychology. In Carl Murchison (Ed.), *Psychologies of*

1930. Worcester, MA: Clark University Press.

Adler, A. (1934). Lecture to the Medical Society of Individual Psychology, London. *Individual Psychology Pamphlets, 13*, 11–24.

Adler, A. (1982). The fundamental views of Individual Psychology. *Individual Psychology, 38*(1) 3–6. (Reprinted from *International Journal of Individual Psychology*, 1935, *1*(1) 5–8.)

Adler, A. (1936). On the interpretation of dreams. *International Journal of Individual Psychology, 2*, 3–16.

Adler, A. (1947). How I chose my career. *Individual Psychology Bulletin, 6*, 9–11.

Adler, A. (1958). *What life should mean to you*. New York: Capricorn Books.

Adler, A. (1959). *Understanding human nature*. New York: Premier Books.

Adler, A. (1963a). *The practice and theory of individual psychology*. Paterson, NJ: Littlefield, Adams.

Adler, A. (1963b). *The problem child*. New York: Capricorn Books.

Adler, A. (1964a). *Problems of neurosis*. New York: Harper & Row.

Adler, A. (1964b). *Social interest: A challenge to mankind*. New York: Capricorn Books.

Adler, A. (1969). *The science of living*. New York: Doubleday Anchor Books.

Adler, K. A. (1961). Depression in the light of individual psychology. *Journal of Individual Psychology, 17*, 56–67.

Adler, K. A., & Deutsch, D. (1959). *Essays in individual psychology*. New York: Grove Press.

Alexander, F., & French, T. M. (1946). *Psychoanalytic therapy*. New York: Ronald Press.

Allred, G. H. (1976). *How to strengthen your marriage and family*. Provo, UT: Brigham Young University Press.

Angers, W. P. (1960). Clarifications toward the rapprochement between religion and psychology. *Journal of Individual Psychology, 16*, 73–76.

Ansbacher, H. L. (1946). Adler's place today in the psychology of memory. *Journal of Personality, 15*, 197–207.

Ansbacher, H. L. (1952). "Neo-Freudian" or "Neo-Adlerian"? *American Journal of Individual Psychology, 10*, 87–88. (Also in *American Psychologist* (1953), *8*, 165–166.)

Ansbacher, H. L. (1959). A key to existence. *Journal of Individual Psychology, 15*, 141–142.

Ansbacher, H. L. (1961). Suicide: Adlerian point of view. In N. L. Farberow & E. S. Schneidman (Eds.), *The cry for help*. New York: McGraw-Hill.

Ansbacher, H. L. (1962). Was Adler a disciple of Freud? A reply. *Journal of Individual Psychology, 18*, 126–135.

Ansbacher, H. L. (1967). Life style: A historical and systematic review. *Journal of Individual Psychology, 23*, 191–212.

Ansbacher, H. L. (1968). The concept of social interest. *Journal of Individual Psychology, 24*, 131–141.

Ansbacher, H. L. (1969). Suicide as communication: Adler's concept and current applications. *Journal of Individual Psychology, 25*, 174–180.

Ansbacher, H. L., & Ansbacher, R. (Eds.). *The individual psychology of Alfred Adler*. New York: Basic Books.

Beach, F. A. (1955). The descent of instinct. *Psychological Review, 62*, 401–410.

Beecher, W., & Beecher, M. (1966). *Parents on the run*. New York: Agora Press.

Berne, E. (1964). *Games people play*. New York: Grove Press.

Bickhard, M. H., & Ford, B. L. (1976). Adler's concept of social interest. *Journal of Individual Psychology, 32*, 27–49.

Bierer, J. (1951). *The day hospital, an experiment in social psychiatry and synthoanalytic psychotherapy*. London: H. K. Lewis.

Bierer, J., & Evans, R. I. (1969). *Innovations in social psychiatry*. London: Avenue Publishing.

Birnbaum, F. (1935). The Individual-Psychological Experimental School in Vienna. *International Journal of Individual Psychology, 1*, 118–124.

Birnbaum, F. (1961). Frankl's existential psychology from the viewpoint of Individual Psychology. *Journal of Individual Psychology, 17*, 162–166.

Bottome, P. (1939). *Alfred Adler: A biography*. New York: Putnam.

Brewer, D. H. (1976). *The induction and alteration of state depression: A comparative study*. Unpublished doctoral dissertation. University of Houston.

Brome, V. (1968). *Freud and his early circle*. New York: William Morrow.

Brown, C. (1965). *Manchild in the promised land.* New York: Signet Books.

Brown, J. F. (1976). Parallels between Adlerian psychology and the Afro-American value system. *Individual Psychologist, 13,* 29–33.

Bugental, J. F. T. (1963). Humanistic psychology: A new breakthrough. *American Psychologist, 18,* 563–67.

Clark, K. B. (1965). Problems of power and social change: Toward a relevant social psychology. *Journal of Social Issues, 21,* 4–20.

Clark, K. B. (1967a). *Dark ghetto.* New York: Harper Torchbooks.

Clark, K. B. (1967b). Implications of Adlerian theory for understanding of civil rights problems and action. *Journal of Individual Psychology, 23,* 181–190.

Colby, K. M. (1951). On the disagreement between Freud and Adler. *American Image, 8,* 229–238.

Corsini, R. J. (1953). The behind-the-back technique in group psychotherapy. *Group Psychotherapy, 6,* 102–109.

Corsini, R. J. (1967). Let's invent a first-aid kit for marriage problems. *Consultant,* (Smith, Klein & French Laboratories) *7,* 40.

Corsini, R. J. (1979). Individual education. In E. Ignas & R. J. Corsini (Eds.), *Alternative educational systems* (pp. 200–256). Itasca, IL: F. E. Peacock.

Corsini, R. J. (1977). Individual education. *Journal of Individual Psychology, 33,* 295–349.

Corsini, R. J., & Painter, G. (1975). *The practical parent.* New York: Harper & Row.

Crandall, J. E. (1981). *Theory and measurement of social interest.* New York: Columbia University Press.

Credner, L. (1930). Sicherungen. *Internationale Zeitschrift für Individualpsychologie, 8,* 87–92. (Translated as Safeguards (1936). *International Journal of Individual Psychology, 2,* 95–102.)

Deutsch, D. (1967). Group therapy with married couples. *Individual Psychologist, 4,* 56–62.

Dinkmeyer, D., & Dreikurs, R. (1963). *Encouraging children to learn: The encouragement process.* Englewood Cliffs, NJ: Prentice-Hall.

Dreikurs, R. (1944). The meaning of dreams. *Chicago Medical School Quarterly, 3,* 4–6, 25–26.

Dreikurs, R. (1949). The four goals of children's misbehavior. *Nervous Child, 6,* 3–11.

Dreikurs, R. (1948). *The challenge of parenthood.* New York: Duell, Sloan & Pearch.

Dreikurs, R. (1950). Techniques and dynamics of multiple psychotherapy. *Psychiatric Quarterly, 24,* 788–799.

Dreikurs, R. (1957). Psychotherapy as correction of faulty social values. *Journal of Individual Psychology, 13,* 150–158.

Dreikurs, R. (1958). A reliable different diagnosis of psychological or somatic disturbances. *International Record of Medicine, 171,* 238–242.

Dreikurs, R. (1959). Early experiments with group psychotherapy. *American Journal of Psychotherapy, 13,* 882–891.

Dreikurs, R. (1960a). The current dilemma in psychotherapy. *Journal of Existential Psychiatry, 1,* 187–206.

Dreikurs, R. (1960b). *Group psychotherapy and group approaches. Collected papers.* Chicago: Alfred Adler Institute.

Dreikurs, R. (1961). The Adlerian approach to therapy. In Morris I. Stein (Ed.), *Contemporary psychotherapies* (pp. 80–94). Glencoe, IL: The Free Press.

Dreikurs, R. (1962). Can you be sure the disease is functional? *Consultant* (Smith, Kline & French Laboratories).

Dreikurs, R. (1963). Psychodynamic diagnosis in psychiatry. *American Journal of Psychiatry, 119,* 1045–1048.

Dreikurs, R. (1968). *Psychology in the classroom.* New York: Harper & Row.

Dreikurs, R. (1969). Social interest: The basis of normalcy. *The Counseling Psychologist, 1,* 45–48.

Dreikurs, R. (1971). *Social equality: The challenge of today.* Chicago: Henry Regnery.

Dreikurs, R. (1972). Technology of conflict resolution. *Journal of Individual Psychology, 28,* 203–206.

Dreikurs, R., Corsini, R. J., Lowe, R., & Sonstegard, M. (1959) *Adlerian family counseling.* Eugene, OR: University of Oregon Press.

Dreikurs, R., & Grey, L. (1968). *Logical consequences*. New York: Meredith.

Dreikurs, R., Grunwald, B., & Pepper, F. C. (1982). *Maintaining sanity in the classroom (2nd ed.)*. New York: Harper & Row.

Dreikurs, R., & Mosak, H. H. (1966). The tasks of life I. Adler's three tasks. *Individual Psychologist, 4*, 18–22.

Dreikurs, R., & Mosak, H. H. (1967). The tasks of life II. The fourth life task. *Individual Psychologist, 4*, 51–55.

Dreikurs, R., Mosak, H. H., & Shulman, B. H. (1952a). Patient-therapist relationship in multiple psychotherapy. I. Its advantages to the therapist. *Psychiatric Quarterly, 26*, 219–227.

Dreikurs, R., Mosak, H. H., & Shulman, B. H. (1952b). Patient-therapist relationship in multiple psychotherapy. II. Its advantages for the patient. *Psychiatric Quarterly, 26*, 590–596.

Dreikurs, R., Shulman, B. H., & Mosak, H. H. (1982). *Multiple psychotherapy*. Chicago: Alfred Adler Institute.

Dreikurs, R., & Soltz, V. (1964). *Children: The challenge*. New York: Duell, Sloan & Pearch.

Dunlap, K. (1933). *Habits: Their making and unmaking*. New York: Liveright.

Edgar, T. (1975). Social interest—another view. *Individual Psychologist, 12*, 16–24.

Elam, H. (1969a). Cooperation between African and Afro-American, cultural highlights. *Journal of the National Medical Association, 61*, 30–35.

Elam, H. (1969b). Malignant cultural deprivation, its evolution. *Pediatrics, 44*, 319–326.

Ellenberger, H. F. (1970). *The discovery of the unconscious*. New York: Basic Books.

Ellis, A. (1957). Rational psychotherapy and Individual Psychology. *Journal of Individual Psychology, 13*, 38–44.

Ellis, A. (1963). Toward a more precise definition of "emotional" and "intellectual" insight. *Psychological Reports, 13*, 125–126.

Ellis, A. (1970). Humanism, values, rationality. *Journal of Individual Psychology, 26*, 37–38.

Ellis, A. (1971). Reason and emotion in the Individual Psychology of Adler. *Journal of Individual Psychology, 27*, 50–64.

Farau, A. (1953). The influence of Alfred Adler on current psychology. *American Journal of Individual Psychology, 10*, 59–76.

Farau, A. (1964). Individual psychology and existentialism. *Individual Psychologist, 2*, 1–8.

Federn, E. (1963). Was Adler a disciple of Freud? A Freudian view. *Journal of Individual Psychology, 19*, 80–81.

Fiedler, F. E. (1950). A comparison of therapeutic relationships in psychoanalytic, non-directive and Adlerian therapy. *Journal of Consulting Psychology, 14*, 436–445.

Forer, L. K. (1977). Bibliography of birth order literature of the 1970s. *Journal of Individual Psychology, 33*, 122–141.

Frank, L. K. (1939). Projective methods for the study of personality. *Journal of Personality, 8*, 389–413.

Frankl, V. E. (1963). *Man's search for meaning*. New York: Washington Square Press.

Frankl, V. E. (1970). Forerunner of existential psychiatry. *Journal of Individual Psychology, 26*, 38.

Fromm-Reichman, F. (1949). Notes on personal and professional requirements of a psychotherapist. *Psychiatry, 12*, 361–378.

Goldstein, K. (1939). *The organism*. New York: American Book Co.

Gottesfeld, H. (1966). Changes in feelings of powerlessness in a community action program. *Psychological Reports, 19*, 978.

Grunwald, B. (1954). The application of Adlerian principles in a classroom. *American Journal of Individual Psychology, 11*, 131–141.

Gushurst, R. S. (1971). The reliability and concurrent validity of an idiographic approach to the interpretation of early recollections. Unpublished doctoral dissertation. University of Chicago.

Heine, R. W. (1953). A comparison of patients' reports on psychotherapeutic experience with psychoanalytic, nondirective, and Adlerian therapists. *American Journal of Psychotherapy, 7*, 16–23.

Hemming, J. (1956). *Mankind against the killers*. London: Longmans, Green.

Hinrichsen, O. (1913). Unser Verstehen

der seelischen Zusammenhänge in der Neurose und Freud's und Adler's Theorien. *Zentralblätter für Psychoanalyse, 3,* 369–393.

Horney, K. (1951). *Neurosis and human growth.* London: Routledge & Kegan Paul.

Ignas, E., & Corsini, R. J. (Eds.) (1979). *Alternative educational systems.* Itasca, IL: F. E. Peacock.

Jahn, E., & Adler, A. (1964). Religion and Individual Psychology. In H. L. Ansbacher & R. Ansbacher (Eds.), *Superiority and social interest.* Evanston, IL: Northwestern University Press. (Adler's essay is reprinted in *Individual Psychology,* 1987, 43(4), 522–526).

James, W. T. (1947). Karen Horney and Erich Fromm in relation to Alfred Adler. *Individual Psychology Bulletin, 6,* 105–116.

James, W. (1890). *Principles of psychology.* New York: Holt.

Kadis, A. L. (1956). Re-experiencing the family constellation in group psychotherapy. *American Journal of Individual Psychology, 12,* 63–68.

Kazan, S. (1978). Gemeinschaftsgefühl means caring. *Journal of Individual Psychology, 34,* 3–10.

Kramer, H. D. (1947). Preventive psychiatry. *Individual Psychology Bulletin, 7,* 12–18.

Krausz, E. O. (1935). The pessimistic attitude. *International Journal of Individual Psychology, 1,* 86–99.

Krausz, E. O. (1959). The commonest neurosis. In K. A. Adler & D. Deutsch (Eds.), *Essays in individual psychology.* (pp. 108–118). New York: Grove Press.

La Porte, G. H. (1966). Social interest in action: A report on one attempt to implement Adler's concept. *Individual Psychologist, 4,* 22–26.

Lazarsfeld, S. (1952). Pitfalls in psychotherapy. *American Journal of Individual Psychology, 10,* 20–26.

Lazarsfeld, S. (1966). The courage for imperfection. *Journal of Individual Psychology, 22,* 163–165.

Lewin, K. (1935). *A dynamic theory of personality.* New York: McGraw-Hill.

Lombardi, D. M. (1969). The special language of the addict. *Pastoral Psychology, 20,* 51–52.

Low, A. A. (1952). *Mental health through will training.* Boston: Christopher.

Manaster, F. J., & Corsini, R. J. (1982). *Individual psychology.* Itasca, IL: F. E. Peacock.

Maslow, A. H. (1962). Was Adler a disciple of Freud? A note. *Journal of Individual Psychology, 18,* 125.

Maslow, A. H. (1970). Holistic emphasis. *Journal of Individual Psychology, 26,* 39.

May, R. (1970). Myth and guiding fiction. *Journal of Individual Psychology, 26,* 39.

McArthur, H. (1958). The necessity of choice. *Journal of Individual Psychology, 14,* 153–157.

Meerloo, J. A. M. (1970). Pervasiveness of terms and concepts. *Journal of Individual Psychology, 26,* 40.

Miley, C. H. (1969). Birth-order research, 1963–1967: Bibliography and index. *Journal of Individual Psychology, 25,* 64–70.

Mosak, B., & Mosak, H. H. (1975a). *A bibliography of Adlerian Psychology* (Vol. 2). Washington, DC: Hemisphere.

Mosak, B., & Mosak, H. H. (1975b). Dreikurs' four goals: The clarification of some misconceptions. *Individual Psychologist, 12,* 14–16.

Mosak, H. H. (1954). The psychological attitude in rehabilitation. *American Archives of Rehabilitation Therapy, 2,* 9–10.

Mosak, H. H. (1958). Early recollections as a projective technique. *Journal of Projective Techniques, 22,* 302–311. [Also in G. Lindzey & C. S. Hall (Eds.) (1965). *Theories of Personality: Primary sources and research.* New York: Wiley.]

Mosak, H. H. (1967). Subjective criteria of normality. *Psychotherapy, 4,* 159–161.

Mosak, H. H. (1971a). Strategies for behavior change in schools: Consultation strategies. *Counseling Psychologist, 3,* 58–62.

Mosak, H. H. (1971b). Lifestyle. In A. G. Nikelly (Ed.), *Techniques for behavior change* (pp. 77–81). Springfield, IL: Charles C Thomas.

Mosak, H. H. (1972). Life style assessment: A demonstration based on family constellation. *Journal of Individual Psychology, 28,* 232–247.

Mosak, H. H. (1980). *A child's guide to parent rearing.* Chicago: Alfred Adler Institute.

Mosak, H. H. (1985). Interrupting a depression: The pushbutton technique. *Individual Psychology, 41(2),* 210–214.

Mosak, H. H. (1987a). *Ha Ha and Aha: The role of humor in psychotherapy.* Muncie, IN: Accelerated Development.

Mosak, H. H. (1987b). Guilt, guilt feelings, regret and repentance. *Individual Psychology, 43(3),* 288–295.

Mosak, H. H. (1987c). Religious allusions in psychotherapy. *Individual Psychology, 43(4),* 496–501.

Mosak, H. H., & Dreikurs, R. (1967). The life tasks III. The fifth life task. *Individual Psychologist, 5,* 16–22.

Mosak, H. H., & Fletcher, S. J. (1973). Purposes of delusions and hallucinations. *Journal of Individual Psychology, 29,* 176–181.

Mosak, H. H., & Gushurst, R. S. (1971). What patients say and what they mean. *American Journal of Psychotherapy, 3,* 428–436.

Mosak, H. H., & Kopp, R. (1973). The early recollections of Adler, Freud, and Jung. *Journal of Individual Psychology, 29,* 157–166.

Mosak, H. H., & LeFevre, C. (1976). The resolution of "intrapersonal conflict." *Journal of Individual Psychology, 32,* 19–26.

Mosak, H. H., & Mosak, B. (1975). *A bibliography for Adlerian psychology.* Washington, DC: Hemisphere.

Mosak, H. H., & Schneider, S. (1977). Masculine protest, penis envy, women's liberation and sexual equality. *Journal of Individual Psychology, 33,* 193–201.

Mosak, H. H., & Shulman, B. H. (1963). *Individual psychotherapy: A syllabus.* Chicago: Alfred Adler Institute.

Mozdzierz, G. J., & Lottman, T. J. (1973). Games married couples play: Adlerian view. *Journal of Individual Psychology, 29,* 182–194.

Mullahy, P. (1955). *Oedipus: Myth and complex.* New York: Evergreen.

Murphy, G. (1947). *Personality: A biosocial approach to origins and structure.* New York: Harper.

Murphy, G., Murphy, L. B., & Newcomb, T.

M. (1937). *Experimental social psychology (Rev. ed.).* New York: Harper.

Neuer, A. (1936). Courage and discouragement. *International Journal of Individual Psychology, 2,* 30–50.

Nikelly, A. G. (1971a). Basic processes in psychotherapy. In A. G. Nikelly (Ed.), *Techniques for behavior change* (pp. 27–32). Springfield, IL: Charles C Thomas.

Nikelly, A. G. (1971b). Developing social feeling in psychotherapy. In A. G. Nikelly (Ed.), *Techniques for behavior change* (pp. 91–95). Springfield, IL: Charles C Thomas.

Nikelly, A. G. (1971c). The protesting student. In A. G. Nikelly (Ed.), *Techniques for behavior change.* Springfield, IL: Charles C Thomas.

O'Reilly, C., Cizon, F., Flanagan, J., & Pflanczer, S. (1965). *Men in jail.* Chicago: Loyola University.

Orgler, H. (1965). *Alfred Adler: The man and his work.* New York: Capricorn Books.

Painter, G., & Corsini, R. J. (1989). *Effective discipline in the home and the school.* Muncie, IN: Accelerated Development.

Pancner, K. R. (1978). The use of parables and fables in Adlerian psychotherapy. *Individual Psychologist, 15,* 19–29.

Papanek, E. (1971). Delinquency. In A. G. Nikelly (Ed.), *Techniques for behavior change* (pp. 177–183). Springfield, IL: Charles C Thomas.

Papanek, H. (1954). Combined group and individual therapy in private practice. *American Journal of Psychotherapy, 8,* 679–686.

Papanek, H. (1956). Combined group and individual therapy in the light of Adlerian psychology. *International Journal of Group Psychotherapy, 6,* 135–146.

Papanek, H. (1959). Emotion and intellect in psychotherapy. *American Journal of Psychotherapy, 13,* 150–173.

Papanek, H., & Papanek, E. (1961). Individual Psychology today. *American Journal of Psychotherapy, 15,* 4–26.

Pelzman, O. (1952). Some problems in the use of psychotherapy. *Psychiatric Quarterly Supplement, 26,* 53–58.

Pew, M. L., & Pew, W. (1972). Adlerian marriage counseling. *Journal of Individual Psychology, 28,* 192–202.

Phillips, C. E., & Corsini, R. J. (1982). *Give in or give up.* Chicago: Nelson-Hall.

Rasey, M. I. (1956). Toward the end. In C. E. Moustakas (Ed.), *The self: Explorations in personal growth* (pp. 247–260). New York: Harper.

Reik, T. (1948). *Listening with the third ear.* New York: Farrar, Straus & Cudahy.

Rogers, C. R. (1951). *Client-centered therapy.* Boston: Houghton Mifflin.

Rosenthal, D., & Frank, J. D. (1956). Psychotherapy and the placebo effect. *Psychological Bulletin, 53,* 294–302.

Seidler, R. (1967). The individual psychologist looks at testing. *Individual Psychologist, 5,* 3–6.

Seidler, R., & Zilahi, L. (1949). The Vienna child guidance clinics. In A. Adler & Associates, *Guiding the child.* (pp. 9–27). London: Allen & Unwin.

Shlien, J. M., Mosak, H. H., & Dreikurs, R. (1962). Effect of time limits: A comparison of two psychotherapies. *Journal of Counseling Psychology, 9,* 31–34.

Shoben, E. J., Jr. (1957). Toward a concept of normal personality. *American Psychologist, 12,* 183–189.

Shoobs, N. E. (1964). Role-playing in the individual psychotherapy interview. *Journal of Individual Psychology, 20,* 84–89.

Shulman, B. H. (1960). A psychodramatically oriented action technique in group psychotherapy. *Group Psychotherapy, 22,* 34–39.

Shulman, B. H. (1962). The meaning of people to the schizophrenic and the manic-depressive. *Journal of Individual Psychology, 18,* 151–156.

Shulman, B. H. (1964). Psychological disturbances which interfere with the patient's cooperation. *Psychosomatics, 5,* 213–220.

Shulman, B. H., & Mosak, H. H. (1977). Birth order and ordinal position. *Journal of Individual Psychology, 33,* 114–121.

Shulman, B. H., & Klapman, H. (1968). Organ inferiority and psychiatric disorders in childhood. In E. Harms (Ed.), *Pathogenesis of nervous and mental diseases* (pp. 49–62). New York: Libra.

Sicher, L., & Mosak, H. H. (1967). Aggression as a secondary phenomenon. *Journal of Individual Psychology, 23,* 232–235.

Simpson, H. N. (1966). *Stoic apologetics.* Oak Park, IL: Author.

Smuts, J. C. (1961). *Holism and evolution.* New York: Viking Press.

Soltz, V. (1967). *Study group leader's manual.* Chicago: Alfred Adler Institute.

Spiel, O. (1962). *Discipline without punishment.* London: Faber & Faber.

Starr, A. (1977). *Psychodrama.* Chicago: Nelson-Hall.

Strupp, H. H. (1972). Freudian analysis today. *Psychology Today, 6,* 33–40.

Sullivan, H. S. (1954). *The psychiatric interview.* New York: Norton.

Sward, K. (1947). Review (Review of *Our inner conflicts*). *Science,* December 1, 600–601.

Toman, W. (1970). Never mind your horoscope, birth order rules all. *Psychology Today, 4,* 45–48, 68–69.

Vaihinger, H. (1965). *The philosophy of "as if."* London: Routledge & Kegan Paul.

Von Sassen, H. W. (1967). Adler's and Freud's concepts of man: A phenomenological comparison. *Journal of Individual Psychology, 23,* 3–10.

Watkins, C. E., Jr. (1982). A decade of research in support of Adlerian psychological theory. *Individual Psychology, 38*(1), 90–99.

Watkins, C. E., Jr. (1983). Some characteristics of research on Adlerian theory, 1970–1981. *Individual Psychology, 39*(1), 99–110.

Way, L. (1962). *Adler's place in psychology.* New York: Collier Books.

Wexberg, E. (1929). *Individual Psychology.* London: Allen & Unwin.

Wexberg, E. (1970). *Individual psychological treatment.* Chicago: Alfred Adler Institute. (Original published in 1929).

White, R. W. (1957). Adler and the future of ego psychology. *Journal of Individual Psychology, 13,* 112–124.

Wittels, F. (1939). The neo-Adlerians. *American Journal of Sociology, 45,* 433–445.

Wolfe, W. B. (1932). *How to be happy though human.* London: Routledge & Kegan Paul.

CARL G. JUNG, 1875–1961

4

Analytical Psychotherapy

YORAM KAUFMANN

OVERVIEW

Analytical psychotherapy is an attempt to create, by means of a symbolic approach, a dialectical relationship between consciousness and the unconscious. The *psyche* is seen as a self-regulating system whose functioning is purposive, with an internally imposed direction toward a life of fuller awareness. In psychotherapy a dialogue ensues, via dreams, fantasies, and other unconscious products, between the conscious state of the analysand and his or her personal, as well as the collective, unconscious.

BASIC CONCEPTS

The last millennium in Western culture can be characterized as a period of increased rationality. In the attempt to master nature and fate, humans have tried to discard fantasies, superstitions, and flights of fancy, replacing them with a more objective vision. The resulting viewpoint made possible technology and scientific knowledge that brought much material comfort. It was inevitable that this approach,

therefore, gradually would outweigh all others. Freud's contribution to civilization was to suggest that rationality and consciousness form but one aspect of the totality of human experience and to postulate another realm of the psyche, namely, the *unconscious*. This major assumption Jung shares with Freud. Neither of them sought to depreciate consciousness. Certainly the primary effort in life and in analysis is to become more conscious, to gain more awareness. Nonetheless, consciousness is but a small boat on the vast sea of the unconscious. We have to face the unpleasant fact that we are not masters in our own houses, but are ruled by forces and sources of energy operating through us, rather than ruled by us. These unconscious forces Jung saw as being both destructive and creative, but dangerous if ignored and unheeded. The unconscious is not just the sum total of everything that has been repressed in the course of one's development; it also contains wellsprings of creativity and sources of guidance and meaning.

Structurally, the *unconscious* and

the *conscious* constitute two subsystems of the psyche. These two compensate each other; the more one-sided an attitude is in one system, the more pronounced its opposite is in the other.

Jung postulated, in addition to the usual instincts of sex, aggression, hunger, and thirst, an instinct toward *individuation.* Jung believed an autonomous force exists that persistently pushes us to achieve wholeness (not perfection!), much like the physiological force that guides our physical development. This force is constantly trying to launch us on a process of fulfilling our truest self, thereby finding our own wholeness and particular meaning in life.

All our behavior is both consciously and unconsciously motivated. We behave partly because of reasons of which we are aware and partly because of reasons of which we are unaware. One of the most fruitful ways to understand a person's unconscious is through dreams. A dream is posited to contain a message to the dreamer's awareness from the unconscious. The message is not expressed in our everyday language, but is veiled. If the veil is lifted, the dream is interpreted or translated. Analytical psychology attaches a great deal of importance to the interpretation of dreams. This process is usually the backbone of a person's analysis.

To the average modern rationalist, all this may seem ludicrous and foggy. To other civilizations, these ideas are a matter of course, an obvious aspect of life. The Naskapi Indian, for example, carries within himself, in his heart, an inner companion whom he calls the Great Man, who is immortal and toward whom an attitude of total honesty is required. He communicates with the Great Man via dreams and inner voices. Life is viewed as a deepening communication with this inner companion.

This view posits that the unconscious has an existence of its own not reducible to other modes of psychic activity. The guiding and directing quality imputed to the unconscious implies a prospective, teleological aspect. The past determines the present to a large extent, but primarily, our actions are geared with a view toward the future: we act not only because of the past but for the sake of the future.

The unconscious is our storehouse of energy, the psychic sphere within which transformations and metamorphoses are made possible. One can decide to stop acting under compulsion but to no avail; no matter how resolute the decision, compulsion reappears. Take for example the case of a young man valiantly wrestling with a potential psychotic process. He tells the following recurrent childhood dream:

I am standing alone on a beach facing the Pacific Ocean. The ocean has huge waves, which come rolling on and engulf me.

The clinical picture is clear: The ego is threatened by an invasion from the unconscious. A possibility of a psychotic process is indicated.

After several months of analysis in which close attention was given to unconscious material, the patient dreams:

I am on the beach in Acapulco with a lot of people around me having a good time. I sense turbulence in the ocean, but I know that it will not reach me; I sense very strongly the boundary between the ocean and the beach.

To *Acapulco* the patient associated the popular resort where everyone goes. The possibility of a transformation is indicated. Turbulence is still there but the patient feels more secure. Note the change from the lonely and isolated feeling of the childhood dream to this dream, which has the feeling of belonging.

Later he brought in the following dream:

I am on a ship on a cruise. We are at the middle of the ocean. A plank is lowered, and we are invited to swim. The water is beautifully blue and clear. At first I am slightly anxious, but I jump in and swim, and then return safely to the ship.

What is the language of communication between consciousness and the unconscious? The unconscious is not directly available to consciousness. The only communication seemingly available is the symbol. Symbols are attempts to express something essentially unexplainable but nevertheless existing. One can have the greatest understanding of the cross as a symbol, but the cross itself, emerging in a dream, carries profound meaning to the dreamer unexplainable in rational terms. *It is a basic tenet of Jungian therapy that all products of the unconscious are symbolic* and can be taken as guiding messages.

What is the source of power of the unconscious? Jung came to the conclusion that the part of the unconscious which is a direct result of each individual's particular life situation represents only a small though important part of a larger totality, which he named the *collective unconscious*. The first part is called the *personal* level of the unconscious, the second the *nonpersonal* (or transpersonal) level. What is meant here is that all human beings, from the most remote past to our present days and into the foreseeable future, share the same inherited predispositions for psychic functioning.

As an analogy, compare the libido with water and the unconscious to a flat plane. If the water were to cover that plane, there would be no differentiation in the way the water is distributed; it would also form a flat plane. If we assume, however, that the plane is covered with rocks, causing depressions and protrusions of various shapes and sizes, the water flow now is along certain *gradients*. These rocks and craters are somewhat akin to the *archetypes*. The archetypes are a priori ordering principles, but over the ages, personalities. Archetypes have given rise to equivalent forms of imagery in myths, fairy tales, and works of art in many cultures. Motifs include transformation, death and rebirth, the hero struggle, the mother, the divine child. Archetypes exist in us as potentialities; our life circumstances (our particular culture, our family, and our environment) determine in which way and which of the archetypes are actualized. The archetype, or psychic propensity, has to be activated (or evoked) by an experiential reality, which endows it with its specific form. For instance, we all participate in the heroic struggle, but each of us experiences it differently according to our talents, temperament, and environment.

The archetypes are carriers of energy; the emergence of an archetype brings forth an enormous amount of energy. Conversely, all genuine creativity is archetypal in nature (cf., Neumann, 1955). Under normal circumstances the archetypal images express contemporary motifs; a modern man is not likely to dream about slaying a dragon (the archetypal imagery in Greek and Norse mythology), but rather about fighting with his mother-in-law, walking through a dark tunnel, and so on. The more archaic representations are usually activated when the life-force encounters a powerful obstruction, either through a life situation (loss of a leg, death of the beloved, a circumstance that does not allow for an acceptable solution) or contrived through various methods of meditation. In both cases, a profound introversion results in a regression of the libido to more primitive levels. The archetypal realm, in its capacity as an ordering principle, provides us with a sense of meaning. If we understand all suffering as losses of meaning, the archetype can provide the healing-power principles.

OTHER SYSTEMS

The Jungian point of view accords easily with other contributions to the understanding of the psyche, such as Gestalt and Adlerian theories and even some aspects of behavior modification, especially as far as technique is concerned. But it is most edifying to contrast it with traditional psychoanalysis. To illustrate some of the differences between the Jungian and Freudian approaches, we have chosen examples of dreams discussed in Greenson's book, The Technique and Practice of Psychoanalysis (1968). It is dangerous to analyze dreams of patients one does not know. Nevertheless for heuristic purposes, some conclusions may be formulated. The first dream is that of a male patient (p. 40):

I am waiting for a red traffic light to change when I feel that someone has bumped into me from behind. I rush out in fury and find out, with relief, it was only a boy on a bicycle. There was no damage to my car.

Greenson concludes that a comparison with his father in terms of sexual ability is involved. The boy on a bicycle is interpreted as masturbation and the red light as prostitution. Greenson comes to one conclusion that the patient has a wish-fulfilling fantasy that mother doesn't want sex with father, who is not very potent. Jungians would take the dream more phenomenologically. The red traffic light is taken to symbolize the laws of society, some general, conventional code, a collective prohibition; the little boy is an infantile, childish force within the dreamer, something not in full control; the being bumped, uncontrolled juvenile impatience, with no harm done. The message is, "You are up against the need to control your childish, infantile side, which urges you to break accepted conventions that must be respected."

A woman patient in her fourth year of analysis dreams (p. 143):

(1) I am being photographed in the nude, lying on my back in different positions; legs closed, legs apart. (2) I see a man with a curved yardstick in his hand; it had writing on it which was supposed to be erotic. A red, spiny-backed little monster was biting this man with sharp, tiny teeth. The man was ringing a bell for help, but no one heard it but me and I didn't seem to care.

Greenson feels the dream points out the dreamer's resistance to her recognition of a deep-seated hostility to a man's penis and disgust towards her own vagina. With the red monster, she associates menstrual blood, a medieval fiend out of Hieronymus Bosch. We see this dream as possibly expressing criticism of the analysis. The patient feels she is being photographed in the nude in all positions, with special interest in the area between her legs: this seems to be her experiential feeling about her analysis. Dream 2 emphasizes this point even further: the man, with whom she later associates her analyst, is judging her by bookish (writing), distorted (curved), rigid (yardstick), and erotic standards. Furthermore, the analyst seems to be bitten, "bugged" as it were, by something out of Hieronymus Bosch. Bosch depicted in his paintings the two instincts that the Church, in the name of Christianity, was trying to suppress: sexuality and aggression in their various forms. If a Jungian analyst were handed this dream, he or she would in all probability be wondering whether the patient's unconscious was not picking up a sore spot of the analyst's own repressed sexuality and/or aggression. This is not at all uncommon. We often get patients who hit us in our blind spots, and we end up treating our patients and ourselves at the same time.

If we want to be completely phenomenological and empirical, this interpretation is only a *possibility* suggested by the patient's association. The man in the dream is unknown. The patient could very well have dreamt the same dream with Dr. Greenson as the man holding the yardstick, and then we would have been more justified in our interpretation. As it is, it must be taken as a possible suggestive line of inquiry. We are on safer ground if we see this dream on a subjective level, taking the man with the yardstick as an inner man, an animus figure (see page 128). On that level, the dream has a paradoxical message indeed: the dreamer is excessively preoccupied with sexuality. This distorted, moralistic view of herself is in itself a result of a repression of deep-seated drive elements. Hence this interpretation would be in opposition to Greenson's formulation.

Sexuality, for Jung, is more than mere instinctuality; it is also creative power, a bridge between the sacred and the profane. In many religions, sexual symbolism is used to express humans' complex relationship to God. With the advent of Christianity, this aspect of sexuality was repressed and what remained was mere body function. Rollo May (1961) gives an example in which church spires appearing in a dream were interpreted by a Freudian as phallic symbols and by a Jungian as spirituality.

Analytical psychotherapy strongly differentiates itself from other systems in its emphasis on the purposive, prospective functioning of the psyche. What it objects to in other dynamic systems of psychotherapy is the exaggerated emphasis on reductive, causal thinking. One can trace human behavior to genetic antecedents, but these account for only a portion of our nature; we not only react to our past, we also live and relate in the present and take the future into account.

In its emphasis on the prospective and meaningful aspect of the psyche, analytical psychotherapy anticipated a lot of common ground with existential psychotherapy and logotherapy, perhaps most fundamentally in the fact that these therapies are philosophical rather than merely biological therapies. Although one cannot deal with the data of the human psyche without theories, one can minimize the theoretical restrictions imposed upon an interpretive system. Analytical psychology considers itself to be empirical and phenomenological in that the therapist is required to lay aside various preconceptions about human behavior and be ready to follow the vicissitudes and serpentine ways of the psyche wherever they might lead.

HISTORY

PRECURSORS

C. G. Jung was born in Kesswil, Switzerland, and received most of his education in Basel. In contrast to Freud, who was primarily influenced by the scientific, positivistic, and materialistic philosophy of his time, Jung grew up in a cultural tradition that constituted a reaction to the Enlightenment movement.

The hallmark of the Enlightenment was its unswerving optimism. It sought to establish reason as the prime mover, admitting the existence of emotion but seeing it as an element primarily distracting to the rational process. It was believed that by the application of the analytical method all questions ultimately could be resolved.

Gradually, the Enlightenment gave way to a cultural climate in many ways its antithesis (Ellenberger, 1970). Reason began to be dethroned, and in contrast to the positing of a split between nature and human, the unity of the two was postulated, as well as the unity of reason and emotion. The world began to be seen as the arena for the interaction of polar oppositions, in chemistry and physiology as well as in philosophy and psychology. It followed naturally that consciousness could not be the only state extant in human beings. A hundred years after G. W. Leibnitz postulated it, the unconscious was again thrust into prominence. Its manifestations were recognized as legitimate sources of inquiry, mysticism was not frowned upon, and parapsychology was earnestly studied. G. F. Creuzer (1810) published an exhaustive work on mythology and folktales, trying to understand them as symbolical productions rather than as undeveloped ways of thinking. Life was understood as a series of transformations from primordial phenomena, and analogy was given a prominent place as a scientific tool. Outstanding and influential personalities of that time included the philosophers Friedrich Von Schelling, Eduard von Hartmann, and Arthur Schopenhauer and the physician-psychologist Carl Gustav Carus. The latter especially influenced Jung's work. Not only did Carus treat the unconscious with the utmost respect, he also imputed to it a creative and healing ability (an essential element in Jungian psychology) and he divided the unconscious into several parts, one of which, the "general unconscious," foreshadows Jung's concept of the collective unconscious.

Some of Jung's ideas can be traced even further back. His concept of the archetypes is adumbrated by Immanuel Kant's notion of a priori universal forms of perception. We can never perceive reality as it actually is, but have to impose upon the perceptual process a set of imperatives that determine what we actually see. Jung translated the concept of philosophical imperatives into archetypes in the psychological realm.

Dream interpretation, an important part of analytic psychotherapy, was used in ancient times. Particularly famous are Joseph's interpretation of his own dream (the first "self-analysis"), the dreams of his cell mates, and, finally, those of the Pharaoh. The Talmud also devotes a great deal of attention to dreams, and several dream books are known to us, notably the Egyptian, the Chaldean, and one by the Greek, Artemidorus.

BEGINNINGS

It is generally assumed that both Alfred Adler and Carl Jung began their psychoanalytic careers with their association with Freud; that they started as his students, went with him some of the way, and then "deviated" from orthodox psychoanalytic theory. (The reason this version persists is probably that it agrees with the myth of the rebellious son deposing the father.) In both cases, however, the situation was quite different. Both Adler and Jung had formulated some of their major ideas before they came to know Freud. At that time, Jung was writing his medical thesis on the so-called occult phenomena (Jung, 1902). A careful reading of that initial statement of Jung's shows that it contains most of his major ideas in embryonic form.

It is ironic that Jung, later to be called vague, mystical, and abstruse, made as his next step a study bridging the gap between experimental and depth psychology. Jung was assigned by Eugen Bleuler (the head of the Burghölzli Clinic) the task of studying the association test, originally developed by Francis Galton. In this test, people are asked to respond to chosen words with the first word that comes spontaneously. Jung discovered that each person tended to respond to specific words, varying from person to person, either too quickly or too slowly, relative to an average response time for the rest of the words. From this Jung assumed that these particular words carried special meaning for that person—that the words led to some idea accompanied by affect, which Jung then called the *complex*. These complexes were usually unknown to the subject. Jung then postulated the notion that they were unconscious by virtue of repression. It seemed as if Jung had in this way adduced "proof" of the unconscious and the process of repression, both key concepts in Freud's budding theories.

Moreover, it was an *empirical* confirmation, and it is important to note that all his life, Jung considered himself an empiricist, an observer of psychological data.

These discoveries resulted in a warm correspondence between Jung and Freud. The exchange of letters brought about in 1907 the meeting of Jung and Freud in Vienna. Freud was immediately captivated by Jung's tremendous energy and rich imagination. To the annoyance of his own inner circle, who felt that Jung would eventually go his own way, Freud appointed Jung the first president of the International Psychoanalytic Association.

Jung's publication of *The Psychology of Dementia Praecox* (1907) considerably heightened his growing reputation and recognition. It was an application of psychoanalytic principles to schizophrenia, and although it contained serious misgivings about some of Freud's ideas, it was considered an important psychoanalytic contribution.

Jung began to formulate the idea of archetypes after a patient reported a hallucination in which the sun had a phallus that moved from side to side, causing a wind. Jung was forcibly struck by the fact that this imagery was also used in ancient times, mentioned in sources of which this uneducated man had had no knowledge. This and similar incidents led Jung to postulate a level of primordial imagery in the unconscious common to all humanity. He called this the *collective unconscious*, and the primordial images were designated as *archetypes*. Note that Jung started out with empirical clinical data and that theory followed. Jung thought the data were important and basic, whereas theory could be tentative and susceptible to change.

By identifying main themes in psychological material and amplifying them with parallel motifs culled from mythology, comparative religion, and literature, Jung forged a new way of looking at clinical material. He used this method first on a series of fantasies of a young woman, Miss Miller, reported by Theodore Flournoy in 1906. Out of this grew Jung's *Symbols of Transformation* (1911). This book marked a final break with Freud. Not only did it suggest a new method for a psychological approach to clinical material, it also challenged some of Freud's most basic ideas. Jung identified *libido* as general psychic energy rather than as sexual energy, thus dethroning sexuality as the all-encompassing causative element in things psychic. Disturbances in sexuality he viewed as the expression and reflection of more basic psychological conflicts—as the symptom, the outer manifestation, rather than the origin.

In contrast to the clear, persuasive writing of Freud, Jung's manner of writing presents problems to the uninitiated. Jung wrote in the way he believed the psyche functioned, and sometimes tended to assume all readers were familiar with the necessary cultural background. Furthermore, Jung believed the psychic realities never can be completely grasped by consciousness. We can understand some of their manifestations, some of their characteristics, but inherently, they are beyond our ken. We cannot, therefore, delineate them precisely, but must be content with approximations and analogies. Jung's style is mosaic-like and allusive. One illustration leads to another. If, however, one follows his train of thought carefully, a definite pattern emerges, centering around a common theme, and the seeming digressions fall into place, elucidating and elaborating the main idea. The most rewarding way to read Jung is to let oneself actively associate to the images presented; the material then comes alive and becomes meaningful.

CURRENT STATUS

The Jungian movement originally tended to attract primarily introverted people who shied away from proselytizing. Jung was extremely reluctant to give his assent for the establishment of an institute to teach and spread his ideas. New movements tend to attract unfavorable projections, and the Jungian movement has been no exception; until about 1960, it was virtually ignored in the United States. Jung's influence, however, has been enormous, although mostly unacknowledged, and recently there has been a reawakening to his ideas. Calvin Hall and Gardner Lindzey (1962) and Ruth Munroe (1955) include remarkably favorable chapters on Jung in their respective books. A recent book by a classical Freudian, Nerville Symington, devoted a whole chapter to Jung which was quite sympathetic. Some existential therapists write and speak as underground Jungians. Jungian training institutes have been established in the United States in New York, Los Angeles, Chicago, Seattle, Boston, and San Francisco. The number of Jungian analysts has been steadily growing all over the world. There are important centers in Switzerland, Britain, Germany, Israel, France, and Italy. Since 1958, international congresses have been held every two years, and several centers publish periodicals. The oldest is *Spring*, published by the New York Analytical Psychology Club. Others are the annual *British Journal of Analytical Psychology, Psychological Per-*

spectives (Los Angeles), *Zeitschrift für Analytisch Psychologie und Ihre Grenzgebite* (Berlin), *La Rivista di Psicologia Analitica* (Rome), and *Quaternio* (Rio de Janeiro). In most centers, the emphasis is on work with adults, but in Israel and England, a considerable contingent of analysts works with children. Group work has only recently been introduced in New York, the West Coast, and Zurich.

Requirements for entry into the training institutes vary from place to place. Jung's original intention was to train any mature individual with an open relationship to his unconscious. He himself trained philosophers, philologists, artists, and mathematicians, recognizing that academic education contributes very little to one's ability to function as a therapist. The training institutes, however, consider that academic standards are necessary to give proof of seriousness of purpose as well as to meet outer standards of certification. Prospective analysts are allowed a range of related fields of academic endeavor, but the final criterion of acceptance as a candidate for training comes after at least 100 hours of qualified personal analysis, recommendation of the analyst, and interviews by three analysts of the training board. At present there are about 400 qualified Jungian analysts, members of the International Association for Analytic Psychology.

PERSONALITY

THEORY OF PERSONALITY

Analytical psychology does not possess a detailed personality theory equivalent to the topographic, genetic, economic, dynamic, and structural views of psychoanalytic theory. The psyche is viewed as composed of several subsystems, each autonomous yet interdependent: the ego, the personal unconscious, and the nonpersonal (collective) unconscious.

The Ego

The ego is the center of consciousness, the experiential being of the person. It is the sum total of thoughts, ideas, feelings, memories, and sensory perceptions.

The Personal Unconscious

This consists of everything repressed during one's development. The *personal unconscious* is composed of elements that had once been conscious and are relatively easily available to consciousness. These elements are clustered around complexes defined as emotionally toned ideas and behavioral impulses. The complex may be thought of as having a core, which is archetypal, and which therefore will lie outside the sphere of the personal unconscious, and a shell, which is the particular form it takes in a given individual. For instance, several people may have a father complex. The complex will take different guises with different people.

The Nonpersonal Unconscious

This part of the unconscious includes the archetypes, which are inborn psychic predispositions to perception, emotion, and behavior. This layer of the unconscious is not directly amenable to consciousness, but can be observed indirectly through its manifestations in eternal themes in mythology, folklore, and art. Some archetypes, due to their importance and frequency, have been documented more than others. For instance, Joseph Campbell (1956) has documented extensively the hero archetype. Other archetypes include rebirth, the Great Mother, the Wise Old Man, the trickster, the divine child, wholeness, and God. Not all of these archetypes are actualized at all times and with the same intensity. Some archetypes play an important role in the development of the personality—the persona, the shadow, the animus or anima, and the Self.

The persona. The persona is the archetype of adaptation. The word originally meant the actor's mask, but it is not used here in the negative sense. We need mediation between our inner psychic life and the outside world, as much as we need a skin for the same purpose for our physical being. It would be destructive if we behaved in the same way under all situations, as a teacher in front of a class, at a cocktail party, among close friends, and in bed. This, indeed, is the case if we have not developed a viable persona. The persona may become rigid, as with the physician, lawyer, or minister who cannot stop being their roles. Ideally, the persona is flexible; that is, different circumstances evoke within us different qualities and aspects that are adaptive within the given context. People often mistake this phenomenon and take it to mean that they are different people in different places.

The shadow. The shadow is our "other side," all that we would like not to be. It is the compensatory side to our conscious ego, as seen in the case of Dr. Jekyll and Mr. Hyde. It is all those things we would never recognize in ourselves and what we are particularly allergic to in others. Because the shadow is unconscious, it is experienced as a projection onto others. Projection is the main mechanism of the psyche. The dynamics of projection seen this way are more encompassing

than in the customary form. Here, they do not necessarily involve an erroneous attribution of feelings or qualities to another person, but a mirror of ourselves. We might very well be correct in our perception (e.g., the other person might indeed be angry), but if it stirs strong emotions in us, that person reflects our own anger. An encounter with the shadow is the sine qua non of every analysis and is generally very painful.

The shadow is always symbolized by figures of the same sex. As always in Jungian thought, the shadow is not all negative; if accepted and assimilated, it can become a source of creativity. In people whose conscious experience of themselves is very negative, the shadow, being a compensatory figure, will include all their positive qualities, and they will meet successful and talented people in their dreams.

The animus and anima. Two central elements in Chinese philosophy are the Yin and Yang. The Yin represents the feminine principle: the world of nature, creation and life, earthiness and concreteness, receptivity and yielding, the dark and containing, the collective and undifferentiated, the unconscious. The Yang is its opposite—the masculine principle, the driving energy, the creative and initiating, the light and hot, the penetrating, stimulating and dividing, the principle of separation and differentiation, restriction and discipline, the arousing and phallic, aggression and enthusiasm, spirit and heaven. These two principles do not oppose but complement each other. The Yin without the Yang is the status quo, inertia, and the Yang without the Yin is the enthusiastic rushing forward without the solid base of correctness and solidity. Every element contains these two principles to varying degrees and proportions. These proportions are not unalterably fixed, they change with necessity; a given situation will require more of the Yin, and another will require more of the Yang.

The concept of anima and animus is similar to and is much harder to grasp than that of the shadow or the persona. Rationality fails us here, but the animus-anima experience is very real nonetheless, as we will try to illustrate.

Human beings are potentially bisexual, biologically as well as psychologically. During our development one side comes to predominate over the other, the other side existing in an inferior form. Thus, males have usually the preponderance of the Yang principle in their consciousness, women the Yin. Contrasexual aspects coexist in the unconscious. Thus, the male has an unconscious Yin side, the *anima*, and the woman has an unconscious Yang aspect, the *animus*. On the positive side, a woman's animus is responsible for her ability to discriminate and differentiate, to judge and to act, for discipline and aggressiveness. If a positive conscious relationship cannot be maintained toward the animus, we meet the notorious animus-ridden woman, whose hallmarks are argumentativeness, dogmatism, and behavior on the basis of prejudices and preconceived notions. Briefly, a woman's animus is the sum total of her expectations, a system of unconscious criteria with which the world is judged and experienced. The animus is symbolized by male figures appearing in a woman's dreams and fantasies, as a husband, son, father, lover, Prince Charming, the neighbor next door, and so on.

Conversely, for a man the anima embodies the Yin aspect. This accounts for a man's capacity for relatedness, emotionality, involvement with people and ideas, a spontaneous and unplanned approach to life and its experiences, sensuality, and instinctuality. The anima is symbolized by female figures in a man's unconscious products, appearing as the beloved one, the princess, priestess, witch, prostitute, nymph. If the anima is not related to and consciously integrated, the man appears barren, abstract, and detached, as if lacking some vital element. On the other hand, an anima-possessed man is swayed by moods, depressions, and anxieties, and tends to be withdrawn and detached.

The animus and anima seem to operate like autonomous personalities. We experience them, but cannot control them. They are the guides to the collective unconscious, leading to the other side. Through painful encounter with them we gain some acquaintance with their mode of being, but never total control.

The self. The archetype of the *Self* is an expression of our inherent psychic predisposition to experience wholeness, centeredness, and meaning in life. The Self is our god within ourselves—although it must immediately be added that the psychological existence of such an element does not affirm or deny the metaphysical question of whether there is also a God outside of ourselves. It is the Great Man of the Naskapi Indian, the internal embodiment of ancient and timeless wisdom. We come in contact with the Self when we are faced with problems of eternal validity, with paradox, with absurd situations that admit of no rational solutions; when we are at the end of our tether about what to do; when we have recognized that ego adaptation is not enough and have to surrender to a higher authority, transcending the ego. At the moment of birth, ego and Self appear as one. The first half of life is devoted to their separation, requiring heroic attitudes and ego reliance. Then the process reverses itself, as the ego attitude is revealed as incomplete and insufficient, and the striving for realization of the Self begins.

The process by which this goal is achieved is called individuation, separating oneself from the collective and finding one's own unique way. The Self is symbolized as the Wise Old Man, the figure of Christ, Buddha, the treasure hard to attain, the jewel, and the Philosopher's stone.

VARIETY OF CONCEPTS

Sexuality

Freud equated libido with sexual energy. To Jung, libido was *psychic energy* in any manifestation, including sexual and power drives. Psychic energy operates by archetypal fields analogous to the instincts on the biological level. Thus the archetypes pertain to the same realm as the instincts while being at the same time paradoxically their polar opposites, because the instincts are energy carriers on the biological level while the archetypes are energy carriers on the spiritual level.

Sexuality is the biological manifestation of the union of two opposites, male and female. The union of opposites, or their reconciliation, is the life goal. We have to reconcile good and evil, active and passive, life and death, and, most importantly, the personal

and the transpersonal. The last pair, which can be formulated also as the union of the ego and the Self, means experiencing the religious dimension of the psyche. This is *not* to be understood as saying that religion is nothing but sublimation of sexuality. What it *does* mean is that both sexuality and religion are expressions of the phenomenon of the reconciliation of the opposites, two realms of experience expressing different levels of the same basic reality.

The Oedipus Complex

Freud initially came upon this concept from his own self-analysis. Later he presumably found the same mechanism in his patients.

That the unconscious seems to have a mythological layer is one of the mainstays of Jungian psychology. The Oedipus story is seen as but one mythological pattern among many. The Jungian approach to mythology is symbolic, whereas Freud reduced the mythologem to a literal interpretation. From our point of view, Freud seems to have missed the point about this myth.

The story can carry quite a different flavor from that imputed to it by Freud. The main theme might be that we *cannot escape our fate.* Both Oedipus and his parents try to thwart fate, with disastrous results. Countless mythologems repeat that motif. For example, Jonah refuses to obey God's command, tries to escape, and is swallowed by the whale. Oedipus must face up to the mystery of his tragic fate, the mystery of the Sphinx—to murder his father, marry his mother—and *then consciously accept the inevitable tragic guilt!* Oedipis is thus a hero who has partially failed through his unconsciousness. This "blinds" him and makes him rejoin the Furies, the angry mothers. It is to be noted that the incest is only incidental to the main theme. Also, the incest itself is *not* desired by Oedipus, nor is he punished for it.

Racial Unconscious

Jung never used this term. It was introduced by his opponents and detractors to imply a racist coloration to Jung's theories. As pointed out earlier, various archetypes are inherent in all of us but only a few are evoked in each of us, the others lying dormant in the deep reaches of the psyche. Which of the archetypes are actualized depends on a variety of factors: the historical period, the cultural environment, and the particular life situation of the individual. Jung used the term *collective unconscious* for the world of the archetypes, then the term *objective psyche* was introduced as a more accurate description of the idea, and finally the concept was termed the *transpersonal unconscious*, which we consider the most apt.

Organ Inferiority

This Adlerian concept refers to the notion that most people have, or feel themselves subjectively to have, a part of the body that is inferior. This feeling of inferiority causes them to overcompensate and put much emphasis on the inferior organ. We have no quarrel with the fact that people tend to experience bodily parts as inadequate and that this may bring about suffering leading to overcompensation. We contend, however, that the real or imagined deformity usually serves only as a hook for a projection. This projection will occur only if there exists an initial predisposition for it, that is, if there is an appropriate archetypal activation as can be seen from the fact that two people with the same deformity may react very differently to their problem. One might treat it purely as a physical handicap that must be overcome realistically and appropriately, and the other might see it as the source of all his troubles or an indication that life is against him. We would then say that in the first case, the deformity has not fallen within an activated archetype, and in the second case, we see the archetype of the victim (the martyr or the Isaac Complex).

Defense Mechanism

The Jungian position generally views *defense mechanisms* as expressions of psychic necessity based upon projections of judgmental or hostile dynamics upon the other person. Projection plays a crucial part in Jungian thinking, and to a lesser extent, so does identification, but both tend to be seen not as defenses against anxiety but as processes, inevitable because of a state of primary unconsciousness.

The Pleasure Principle

Jungians do not consider pleasure to be the ultimate drive, although we do not minimize its importance. It is seen as one drive among several.

Environment and Conditioning

The analytical approach, despite what seems to be the general belief, places a great deal of importance on the effects of *environment* and *conditioning*. We stress that these two factors do not operate on a tabula rasa, but interact with the archetypal predispositions of the individual. The same environment will evoke different responses from different individuals. Given an archetypal constellation, conditioning can be very effective, but one cannot condition people to responses that will run counter to their given predisposition, as has been convincingly demonstrated even in animals (Breland & Breland, 1961).

Psychopathology

Analytical psychology does not view psychopathology as a disease or a deviation from a "normal" state. Symptoms are considered to be unconscious messages to the individual that something is awry, presenting a task that demands to be fulfilled. The person is not allowed to go on living comfortably but is summoned, as it were, by a voice within, urgently demanding to be heard. Why some people are called and others left alone is impossible to say. The explanation can be ascribed only partially to causal etiological factors, for very often the same traumatic conditions affect one person in one way and another in a totally different way. The symptoms themselves, viewed symbolically, frequently provide the clue to precisely that which is missing and must be developed. Our infirmities, our inferior side, provide us ultimately with the way to meaning and wholeness.

PSYCHOTHERAPY

THEORY OF PSYCHOTHERAPY

Analytical therapy does not possess a specific theory of psychotherapy. Jung conceived therapy as a process of self-knowledge, a reconstruction of the personality, or even as education. He emphasized the empirical, tentative nature inherent in any therapeutic approach, objecting strenuously to any premature attempt to cast psychotherapy into a fixed structure: "Theories in psychology are the very devil. It is true that we need certain points of view for orienting and heuristic value; but they should always be regarded as mere auxiliary concepts that can be laid aside any time" (Jung, 1954, p. 7). This is easier said than done. But Jung, for one, lived this principle as fully as possible.

Jung is known for his revolutionary theoretical insights, but it is sometimes forgotten what a superb therapist he was as well. People who had doubts about his theoretical conceptualizations did not hesitate to consult him therapeutically. Jung as a therapist was unorthodox, doing one thing in a given case and doing the opposite in the next one; ready to modify, change, and create; constantly aware of the vagaries of human nature. He was a pragmatist whose motto was, "Anything goes, as long as it works." Thus, when confronted in an initial interview by a woman whose main symptom was that she had not slept for several weeks, Jung sang a lullaby, putting her to sleep! In another case, faced with a woman unable to get in touch with her own inner religious function, Jung taught her the scriptures, each session handing her an assignment and testing her the next session. In Jung's consulting room, people danced, sang, acted, mimed, played musical instruments, painted, and modeled with clay, the procedures limited only by Jung's inventiveness and ingenuity. It is not surprising, therefore, that Jung distrusted theory, endlessly cautioning against falling prey to its rigidities and limitations. "Learn your theories as well as you can, but put them aside when you touch the miracle of the living soul" (Jung, 1954). With this caveat firmly fixed in our minds, we will attempt to delineate several general principles applicable to the therapeutic procedure, always mindful that these should be overruled when the occasion arises.

As a general rule, therapy starts with a thorough investigation of the patient's conscious state. Given that the unconscious is viewed as compensatory to the conscious state, the latter has to first be established. The same dream, for example, can have quite different interpretations with differing conscious attitudes. The investigation will include the past history of the patient, various important influences in his or her life, attitudes, values, and ideas. The analyst then is able to point out inconsistencies and contradictions, peculiar reactions, and behavior patterns. Most important, patients are thus taught the slow and difficult road to their inner world. Confronted with unexpected questions and observations, they find many of their tacit assumptions challenged and questioned. They start to learn to introspect. A not unusual result of this period is a sense of tremendous confusion, following the initial sense of relief that accompanies the onset of therapy.

With most people, dreamwork is then cautiously introduced. Patients are thus launched on the awesome encounter with their unconscious. If patients are in any way receptive to this new way, they are soon confronted with the disagreeable realization that they are not masters of their own house, and that they have to contend with forces over which they have little control. To typical, rational citizens of the Western world, this is a jarring proposition. With this encounter with the workings of their unconscious side, patients become acquainted with the compensatory nature of the unconscious. No sooner has a firm attitude been established in consciousness than the unconscious seems to bring out the opposite one, and patients soon find themselves caught between pairs of opposites. This position creates tension and anxiety, but also the possibility of transformation and the resolution of the opposites by the emergence of a third entity that transcends the two poles.

An important principle is that of the quasi-intentionality of the psyche. The person's unconscious products (dreams, fantasies, artistic productions) are interpreted not only in terms of antecedent causes—although this may also apply—but primarily as pointing out the way to further development. Thus, a patient brings in the following dream:

I am in a gym, performing various exercises, with some other men. They are arranged in a line, in which they perform the exercises. I try to join the line at the head, but am rejected. I then try for the second place, and am rejected again. I try one place after the other till coming to the end of the line, and am rejected from every one of them.

At first the dreamer has difficulty associating to the dream. The analyst points out that the dream seems to involve men only. The dreamer then realizes that the men in the dream were actually boys from his all-male Catholic primary school, a place dominated by "oughts" and "shoulds." With this come unpleasant memories of the gym class, which the dreamer hated passionately. The only reason he attended was because he was forced to; had it been left up to him, he would not have shown up at any of the classes. As an afterthought, he adds that his mother also thought "it was good for you." The imagery of the dream is direct and clear—the dreamer is being rejected from the line; he does not belong there.

Although for most people, the initial

period of therapy is devoted to helping them get in touch with their inner world, for people who are overly absorbed in their introversion, an attempt is made to put them in touch with external reality. The analysis always tries to compensate for attitudes that are too one-sided.

The major principle of analytical therapy is for the analyst to follow scrupulously the direction and guidance of the unconscious, to abandon, as far as possible, all preconceptions and fixed ideas. For instance, it might be an analyst's clinical judgment that a patient is caught in a mother problem, but the dreams might stress a problem with the older brother. For the analyst to put aside his or her own judgment is a tall order, given that our major way of coping with the unknown is to cling to ready-made formulas. In addition, the analyst may be presented with the necessity of not being judgmental towards lines of conduct that violate his or her inner moral code. By doggedly following the wisdom of the unconscious, the patient slowly learns to accept that within him- or herself there exists a guiding force, the Self, that points the way, painful though it might be, to a mode of being more meaningful and more whole. This force may appear in the guise of a simple "solution" to a complicated situation (e.g., a way to overcome a nagging compulsion) or it may point to a considerable complication of what seems like a simple problem. It may tell the patient that there is a way out of his dilemma if he but changes his attitude, or, on the contrary, that nothing can be done about it, that he is "fated" to live with it. Dreams determine primarily the *timing* of what is being interpreted in addition to the content of the interpretation. The ana-

lyst is quite often aware of possibilities about what is going on in the patient long before the patient is. As a general rule, a Jungian analyst will refrain from introducing these interpretations unless a dream heralds the patient's readiness to assimilate them. Case management in general is based upon the direction of the unconscious.

Psychotherapy ideally takes into consideration three modes: the *fate element* (which determines, for instance, what cannot be changed but has to be accepted); *skill* (the sum total of techniques that can be consciously formulated, taught, and communicated); and *art*, that intangible something (related to intuition and feeling) that weaves everything together. An exclusive emphasis on fate is likely to lead to fortune telling and card reading. A stress on mere skill entails a typical mechanical and barren approach. And if the art is overplayed, we get the "wild analyst."

PROCESS OF PSYCHOTHERAPY

People who have only a vague familiarity with Jung, based primarily on his more theoretical writings, tend to have a rather distorted view of Jungian therapy. They conceive of it either as an endless concatenation of symbols leading far back to antiquity or as a spinning out of esoteric fantasies. Nothing is farther from the truth. People listening in on an analytic hour are liable to hear the most mundane issues being discussed, including budgets, relationships with in-laws or bosses, and so on. The cardinal rule in Jungian analysis is that *the basis of any analysis is experiencing; mere intellectual understanding is insufficient.* This is not to minimize the important role of intellectual understanding, but to emphasize the importance of experiencing a psychic reality. Thus, the analyst may discourage the attempt of a patient to do away with depression. Rather, the patient will be asked to stay with the depression, to let it be, accepting it as an unconscious message.

Generally speaking, the therapeutic encounter in a Jungian setting involves an active interchange between analyst and patient. Depending on the patient's development, the state of the transference and various other factors, the analyst will exchange feelings, experiences, and even dreams. In principle, the nature of the interchange is limited only by the analyst's imagination. The mood of the hour may veer from highly serious to humorous. The analyst may teach, suggest, cajole, give advice, reflect feelings, or give support. The main emphasis is on the conscious assimilation of the immediate experience, using as well techniques that have now become the stock in trade of Gestalt therapy and the encounter movement (breathing methods and what are now called sensitivity training activities were in use by Jungian analysts in the early 1920s).

However, interpretation is the main work of the analytic process. *Interpretation* is the process of enlarging upon given data in a way that makes it possible for patients to perceive connections, motivations, and feelings of which they have been unaware. The main thrust of the analytical process may be summarized as an attempt to make conscious as much as possible what has been unconscious. After the reality situation and the patient's phenomenological world have been established, dream interpretation is undertaken.

Dreamwork is the core of Jungian therapy. Individuals vary considerably in their capacity to remember dreams. There are some who never remember any, but they are rare in the typical patient population. The constant reinforcement of the importance attached to dreams by the analyst and the seriousness with which even the most trivial dream is treated, usually brings about a change even in those people who seem to have difficulty in remembering their dreams. We will focus here on dream interpretation, because all unconscious products (fantasies, paintings, daydreaming) are treated essentially in the same way.

Dream Interpretation

The most profitable way to look at a dream is to see it as a metaphorical drama unfolding before our eyes. In a well-conceived play, the setting is first established, physically as well as psychologically; the mood is suggested and possible conflicts are hinted at. This may be called the *exposition.* Then a *crisis* develops and the conflict is thrust to the fore. The various forces hinted at in the exposition emerge fully and we have the unfolding of the drama. Then, as a general rule, a *solution* is introduced, sometimes in the form of there being no solution, but a stalemate, or an impasse. These dynamics apply equally well to any unconscious product, such as daydreams, fantasies, and fairy tales.

The main difference between a classical Freudian approach to a dream and a Jungian one is based on *repression.* To Freudians a dream is the result of the emergence of repressed contents from the unconscious. As a result, it is viewed, essentially, as a distortion that must be unraveled. Thus the actual drama of the dream is referred to as the *manifest* contents of the dream, behind which there lurks the *latent* content. A Jungian views the dream phenomenologically. The drama of the dream *is* the unconscious message expressed in symbolic form, a message not necessarily repressed or hidden, but rather trying to reveal itself.

In Freudian psychoanalysis, the dreamer would be asked to "free" associate to any given symbol in the dream. Assume, for instance, that a dream in which a wheel appears is reported. The dreamer might say that the wheel reminds him of a tractor, then a tractor toy he had in childhood. A whole slew of memories pertaining to that particular period might emerge, taking the dreamer farther and farther away from the original symbol, namely, the wheel. If the dreamer is persistent in his associative process, he will ultimately reach a painful point, concerning perhaps his mother, his older brother, or perhaps a homosexual experience. Naturally these are relevant domains for psychological inquiry, but in all probability they would have little to do with that specific dream.

A Jungian, on the other hand, would consider it of paramount importance that the specific symbol used by the unconscious is a wheel, not a tractor. The patient could have dreamt directly about the tractor, but did not. The symbol of the wheel emerged in his dream. The *association* to the tractor and that childhood period is, of course, not to be ignored. An *association* is a connection, not necessarily causal, by virtue of contiguity. Thus, the dreamer in Jungian analysis is asked to say what comes first to his mind when he thinks about, or pictures, the wheel of his dream. It could be his childhood tractor toy, his grandma's parakeet, or an ancient cart he had seen once in a movie. This is done

for every symbol in the dream, for inanimate objects as well as for people. It is also done for the major occurrences in the dream. If, for instance, the dreamer is promised something in the dream, he will be asked to associate to a promise. Thus is the *associative context* of the dream established. But this is not sufficient for interpretation. The *amplifications* must be kept in mind as well. An amplification is what an object actually *is*. For example, the dreamer may associate his cousin to a lamp appearing in his dream, but essentially, a lamp is something that gives light in the darkness. Likewise, a pen might remind a dreamer of a penis (especially if he is a product of our culture), but primarily a pen is an instrument for writing. Amplification may come from yet another source. Because of the hypothesis of the archetypal nature of the unconscious, the analyst will bear in mind all possible parallels he or she can find (from mythology, fairy tales, literature, and so forth) to the various symbols and dramas featured in the specific dream. The more precise the equivalence, the more pertinent the amplification. Amplifications that are too general can easily lead one astray.

Dreams have logic of their own. Usually it may be assumed that if the dream drama includes two events that follow each other, it is implied that the second happening occurred *because* of the first. A woman dreamt that she saw a snake on the ground, that she jeered at the snake, and the snake then attacked her. We may conclude that the snake attacked her *because* she jeered at it. A more appropriate response would have been either to flee the scene as soon as possible or to try to kill the snake. The dream implies that the dreamer is jeering at the very powerful unconscious content that, as a result of this attitude, is threatening to annihilate her. (In this specific case, the woman had just recently overcome a serious alcoholism problem. She was supremely confident of her ability not to succumb to it anymore and was recklessly playing with dangerous temptations. The snake represents the addiction potentiality, which was still lurking.)

These examples, chosen for their relative clarity and simplicity, might easily mislead the uninitiated to believe that dreams are easily interpreted. This is far from the case. Every therapist is chagrined to discover that there are many leads and possibilities, and the ambiguity of dreams might very well allow for two completely contradictory understandings. This is why a dream series is of such paramount importance. A dream can be likened to a mathematical equation with many unknowns; the "solution," therefore, is at best tentative. A series of dreams supplies many more equations with the same unknowns and can be assumed to deal with the same conflict from many different angles. By finding parallels between dreams, one can often discern one's way in what might otherwise have been a jungle. At our present state of knowledge, dream interpretation is a trial-and-error process. The therapist is often aware that a dream may be understood along different, even contradictory lines. Sometimes the therapist needs to take a risk and follow one line of interpretation rather than another, and then wait for the following dream for corroboration or disapproval.

A dream can be interpreted on the objective or the subjective level. The *objective level* refers to people (or events) outside of the dreamer. For instance, if one dreams about his wife, the dream is then taken to express something about the actual relationship between husband and wife. On the other hand, the *subjective level* entails relating to all figures and activities in the dreams as pertaining to the dreamer's "inner" psyche, that is, the inner wife, friend, boss, struggle, and so on.

For example, a young man is about to get married, although he is uncertain about his feelings about his future wife. He dreams he is about to embrace her passionately when a friend rings the doorbell. His wife-to-be answers the door and stays to talk with her friend, completely ignoring her fiancé, who is left frustrated and angry. On the objective level, this dream bodes ill for the relationship, the dream implying that the bride-to-be is far from being really related to the patient. On the subjective level, however, the dream seems to be saying that the dreamer and his feminine side are not well related; that is, he has difficulty relating to people and being intimate with them. Accordingly, interpretation on the objective level would thrust the burden of the problematic relationship onto the woman's shoulders; the subjective interpretation would implicate the dreamer's own capacity for relatedness.

Sometimes a dream that has to be understood subjectively is mistakenly taken on the objective level. A patient dreams that his wife has been sleeping with an ex-boyfriend of hers. The dreamer, impulsive and given to literal interpretations, gets furious and berates his wife for infidelity, to her utter bafflement, because she has not seen this boyfriend for years. Moreover, he lives thousands of miles away. The next night our patient has the same dream, but this time it is not the boyfriend who is involved but some unknown man. Obviously the first dream was suggesting that his inner wife, the anima, was having an affair with someone else, rather than actually implicating his wife.

Let us consider another example. After six months in therapy, Miriam brings in the following dream:

I am in a classroom at my alma mater with Professor P. My father is standing beside me. Professor P. is explaining how to evaluate determinants. He says that a determinant always reduces to a fraction and another number, which he does not know whether to put in the numerator or the denominator. My father says it is not important where this number is put, while I passionately insist that it is very important indeed.

Miriam has a doctoral degree in mathematics, and the dream involves mathematical symbols. To the professor she associates the first course she took with him, on the functions of a real variable. The dream, therefore, is concerned with the determination and evaluation of reality. The professor, who is a loved and respected authority for her, explains that reality always reduces to a fraction, namely, to a situation where someone is above and someone below; that is, life is a power struggle or a battle for dominance (who is above and who under). Her father, an animus figure, claims that it should not matter. This brings to light Miriam's belief that an attempt to dominate and control is to be despised, an attitude forcibly inculcated into her by her rational, intellectual father. But the dream bares her unconscious wish to dominate and control.

When the interpretation of the dream was offered to her, she burst into tears and said that the previous night she and her husband had sexual intercourse, she being in the dominant position, and for the first time in her life she really enjoyed herself, an experience that frightened her so much she had blocked it completely out of her memory until the interpretation recalled it to mind. She then recalled several instances in her life when her natural ambitions and assertiveness had been rudely repressed so that she was forced to adopt a passive-aggressive mode of behavior to avoid being crumbled and trodden upon by her environment.

Dream interpretation, regardless of how phenomenologically done, is still, unfortunately, a reductive procedure. The symbol is a mediator between consciousness and the unconscious, conveying much more than can be rationally expressed. When we interpret a dream we are, in effect, reducing a highly graphic and symbolic imagery to a verbal, that is, rational, statement. Something is lost in this reduction. It is incumbent, therefore, to make this statement more experiential to the dreamer. Miriam was asked to keep the imagery of the dream vividly in mind and to be reminded of it when confronted by a situation that seemed to her to involve issues of control and dominance. In therapy she might be asked to paint the dream or to carry on a conversation with the father figure in the dream. Other means might also be employed. The dream or fantasy might be enacted in a group, with various members taking different roles, generating a psychodrama.

MECHANISMS OF PSYCHOTHERAPY

Obviously the analytical process is not a simple one and does not lend itself to a clear explication. It is not easy to demonstrate precisely what factors are involved in a successful (or unsuccessful, for that matter) analysis. We can only try to establish tentative guidelines.

Acceptance

This is probably the sine qua non of any depth therapy. During the course of the therapy, it is essential that the patient feel accepted by the therapist. This is done not so much by what the therapist actually says as it is by genuine openness. All Jungian analysts are required to undergo a thorough analysis. They therefore experience the difference between acceptance and non-acceptance by their own analysts and get a personal understanding of its profound importance. They learn that the relationship between the analyst and the analysand is not between the "healthy" and the "sick," but between someone who has delved into his or her own psyche and has come out of this experience not only unscathed but enhanced, and as a result has established an ongoing dialogue with his or her unconscious, and someone who has not undergone this voyage. This voyage, ideally, has not inflated the analyst and led to feelings of superiority but rather has given the analyst an enormous respect for the intricacy and complexity of the human psyche and, consequently, a healthy humility in the face of hidden resources and potentialities inherent in the human being confronted.

The idea of psychic lameness may be acknowledged, but taken as a challenge to further psychic development and enrichment. One is crippled not so much because of what has happened in the past but because one is being called from within to enlarge one's horizons, to become more of a person.

A person's neurotic symptoms may present an important and difficult task. This is expressed in the mythologem of Jonah, called by God to prophesy doom to Ninevah. Jonah refused and as a result was swallowed by a whale, or, psychologically stated, he was inflicted by a neurotic or psychotic depression. The neurotic is someone trying to escape his fate, but this fate, once recognized, accepted, assimilated, and actively participated in, could lead to a life of fuller meaning and greater wholeness—although not necessarily less suffering.

Relationship to the Inner World

Western civilization, goal- and achievement-oriented, places a great deal of emphasis on the outside world. This is to the detriment of our other reality, the inner one, which is at least as important as the outer one. Most of the people applying for therapy have lost touch with their inner world; some of them are barely aware of its existence. One of the profound consequences of analytical therapy is the rebridging of the gap between the outer and inner worlds. Patients are gently but persistently encouraged to pay heed to and value their inner world. The power and vicissitudes of inner psychic life are demonstrated over and over, and they come to respect it.

On the other hand, some people seem to come for therapy not because they are out of touch with their inner world but because, or so it seems, they are too much in touch with it. In fact, they seem to be flooded with unconscious fantasies. Here the analytic task is different. To establish a viable dialogue between consciousness and unconsciousness, the two have to be clearly separated from each other. The integrity of an independent conscious position needs to be established. As with human beings, real communication exists only between distinctly different positions.

Transference

Transference is a special instance of the more general phenomenon of projection. Unconscious contents, because unconscious, are subject to projection. The subject experiences that part of the psyche of which he or she is not aware by attributing it to the object. In general, this object can be both human as well as inanimate.

Transference is the sum total of all the projections with which the patient endows the analyst. Jung's attitude toward the role that the transference plays during analysis underwent drastic changes. At the beginning, he tended to agree with Freud upon the all-important function of the transference for a therapeutic cure. As Jung became more and more involved with the archetypal nature of the psyche, however, he came to minimize the role of transference as an essential element in the therapeutic process. At this intermediate period, Jung maintained that therapy could go on comfortably without transference, that, in fact, it proceeded much more smoothly without it. It was a nuisance, he averred, and, moreover, it was a result of insufficient rapport between therapist and patient. Where this rapport has been established, he thought, there was no need for a transference. Yet ultimately Jung had to bow to the force of the clinical evidence and recognize the profound effect of the transference as well as the therapeutic value of the analysis of the transference.

Countertransference is the analyst's projection on the patient. This phenomenon is not viewed as a hindrance to be avoided or minimized, but as a necessary concomitant that may be fruitfully used by the therapist as a guide during the course of therapy. On a more general level, countertransference is the complementary part of the total archetype that manifests itself in the guise of various polar opposites: guru-disciple, savior-sinner. The analyst can use his or her own reactions as a therapeutic tool. Those reactions provide information about what is going on in the analytic process. If, for instance, the analyst perceives in herself a spontaneous urge to bully her patient, she will know the master-slave configuration is operating.

APPLICATIONS

PROBLEMS

Jung devoted a great deal of energy to religion. Religion is the expression of an archetypal need to endow our human existence with meaning. An understanding of the various archetypal form elements as expressed in the study of comparative religions, therefore, is crucial to a thorough understanding of how, for various peoples in different epochs, this need found its realization. Mythology in particular and folklore in general are domains in which archetypal imagery and archetypal motifs appear in practically pure form. Both myth and folktale are part of an essentially oral tradition that has handed these motifs down from generation to generation. That which survives such a prolonged process of erosion and distortion are the archetypal motifs in a clear and accessible form.

Art is another domain to which analytical psychology can contribute specific insights. All too often, artistic products are analyzed reductively, traced to the family constellation of the artist or to childhood traumata. Inspired art, however, is more than that. It is a personal expression of something universal and timeless, existing in each of us, the giving of a specific and personal form to an archetypal motif. It is a common hypothesis that creativity is the product of neurotic suffering—take away the neurosis and the art disappears. To this, analytic psychology takes exception. Creativity involves the ability to give realistic and visible expression to archetypal drives without being inundated by them. Artists are different from other people in that they are burdened, as it were, with the additional energy charge of archetypal forces that press for visible manifestation. They do not create because they are neurotic, but may be neurotic because they are creative and have to contend with powerful forces within themselves. Genuine artists will not be robbed of their creativity by Jungian analysis; rather, they will be more adequately able to contend with their potent resources. Only where "artistic" endeavors are used as cover-ups or escape mechanisms will analysis undo them.

EVALUATION

The Jungian analyst evaluates a prospective patient's readiness for therapy along the same lines used by other clinicians—by assessing the person's emotional maturity, the kind of adjustment made, the level of functioning, and so forth. The analyst will, however, place primary importance on the person's relationship with the unconscious. Using knowledge of archetypal patterns, the therapist will often be able to gauge the patient's stage of development and base decisions accordingly. Some examples will illustrate.

A highly intellectualized patient who seems to have difficulty in delv-

ing into himself and who experiences analysis as a humiliating process brings, after several months, this initial dream:

I stand on the shore, under the watchful eye of the Queen and King. I am given to understand that a treasure is buried on the island facing us and that I am to find it. I swim across to the island. On it there is a transparent wall that has to be climbed. It is covered by venetian blinds. I peer through and see young children carrying guns. I recoil and swim back to the mainland.

In this dream, the atmosphere and the presence of the King and Queen clearly indicate its archetypal nature (the dreamer, musically inclined, associated Wagnerian figures to the King and Queen). Because this was an initial dream, it assumes an additional importance, possibly representing the life myth of the dreamer. Here he is presented with the hero's task, to uncover the "treasure hard to attain," a motif appearing in countless myths and fairy tales. As usual, the path to the treasure is not smooth. Here, besides swimming to the island without apparent difficulties, our dreamer has to overcome a wall. As he looks through it, he sees that this would entail confronting his infantile aggressive impulses and he draws back. Prognostically, this does not augur well for the analysis and the patient's ability or willingness to see it through. The treasure, which on the archetypal level is our very essence, seems to be beyond the reach of his effort. As a matter of fact, the patient stayed in therapy for six months, then took a job in another city and stopped therapy without having touched on any deep issue in himself.

Another example is of a different kind. The patient has come to therapy in a crisis situation and has made substantial progress both in solving his current conflicts and in bringing about what seems a real change in his personality. He is toying with the idea of terminating and "being on his own." Now, this is a classical dilemma for the therapist who has no objective standards to determine when the analysis is to be terminated. Is the patient's wish to leave the analysis a genuinely healthy decision, or is it an urge born out of the anticipatory anxiety of delving into deeper material? In the latter case, should the therapist let the patient go, hoping he will come back at a future time when he is more secure and ready, or should he confront the patient and analyze his "resistance"? In other words, is the patient requesting an honorable discharge or is he shirking? In the actual case, the analyst presented the patient two alternatives, explained that he had no way of making the decision, and asked the patient to mull it over, bearing the alternatives in mind. The next session, the patient, not a prolific dreamer, brought the following dream:

I see a girl that I know. I want to approach her and talk to her, because I really like her, but when I half-heartedly attempt to do so, she suddenly vanishes.

To the girl he associates independence, autonomy, and self-reliance. Obviously the message of the dream is: "Your own independence, autonomy, and self-reliance still elude you." The therapist then took the stand that the patient's decision was precipitous and advised that he stay with the analysis.

Often, when the patient's grasp of reality is more or less tenuous, the therapist is involved in a different kind of problem. Thus, a patient who has been in therapy for several months dreams:

I am standing near the ocean. It is night, and there is a full moon. Suddenly, the moon starts swinging from side to side, in bigger and bigger arcs, until it falls into the ocean. There it explodes like a hydrogen bomb with a big mushroom cloud. The radiation made me evaporate like powder.

The dream shows a tendency toward ego disintegration. A psychotic episode is foreshadowed. Indeed, upon further inquiry the therapist learned that on the day before the dream, the patient felt he could not get up from a chair on which he had been sitting. Something was pulling him back and only the strongest effort managed to get him up. The therapist then confronted the patient with the fact that he was being threatened by a catatonic episode and the two calmly discussed the alternatives involved, including hospitalization. They both finally decided to try to work at it together outside a hospital. For the next two weeks they were in close contact. It was touch and go whether the psychotic elements or the conscious ones would prevail. Fortunately, the latter won.

TREATMENT

Analytical psychology originally was considered applicable primarily to persons who had adjusted to the outer world very well, had accomplished what was expected of them by society, but who, entering the second half of life, found themselves listless and dissatisfied. Thus, at its inception, analytical psychotherapy was an attempt to find meaning and was primarily geared for the "adjusted" middle-aged man or woman.

More than two-thirds of Jung's patients were in their second half of life. Most had paid society its due by raising a family and finding a vocation and were now confronted with the task of finding a meaning in life. In his earlier writings, Jung stressed this division between the first "half" and the second "half" of life, maintaining that different modes of treatment were called for according to which "half" one is dealing with.

Group Psychotherapy

It is useful to recall, whenever one deals with Jung, the background against which he practiced and wrote. The beginning of the twentieth century brought in its wake a psychology that defined normality in terms of a collective average. Pathology was still being conceptualized in terms of deviation from a statistical norm. Jung's basic Swiss temperament rebelled against this tendency toward conformity and collectivization, and during all his lifetime, he remained a steadfast guardian of individuality.

It is not surprising, then, that Jung distrusted group therapy. To Jung, one of the most important aspects of the therapeutic process was the encounter with one's inner religion, one's sense of the divine within oneself. In a group, where so many emotions vie for attention, such an experience is harder to come by, unless the analyst is aware of this problem and takes direct actions to facilitate such experiences.

Yet there is nothing in Jung's psychotherapeutic concepts that is counterindicative of group analysis. Quite the opposite is the case: analytical concepts lend themselves admirably to the group process (Whitmont, 1964). Judiciously applied, they can turn the analytical group into a potent instrument yielding unexpected rewards.

Inherent in the group process is the enhancing of the experiential dimension. Instead of discussing the shadow

abstractly in an individual hour, the shadow is lived and felt in the group. Something that may have been thrashed around for months in individual sessions becomes suddenly a gut experience in the group. Issues come to the fore that would be unlikely to arise in individual sessions. The group experience is, therefore, a complementary workshop experience to the individual analysis; each is enriched by the other.

The group experience often challenges one's relation to the mother archetype in its protecting or devouring aspect, thus reflecting one's relationship with one's personal mother. The group is also an excellent vehicle to constellate other archetypal dimensions. The transformation motif, death and rebirth, initiation, the twin brothers—all these can be evoked by various techniques as their possibilities arise spontaneously from the living situation. Psychodrama, Gestalt techniques, sensitivity training, and ritualizations may be employed. The analyst may be more active in group sessions than he or she could allow in individual sessions, and the transference to the analyst is lessened considerably. The analyst can be responded to more like the human being he or she is rather than the archetypal role thrust upon him or her in individual analysis. Often this permits negative attitudes to surface in the group, attitudes that the analysand was too frightened of to raise individually.

Family Therapy

Often analytic work with only one member of a couple will lead to the dissolution of the relationship. Although this is inevitable in some cases, it is destructive and unnecessary in others. Considerations like these may make it desirable that the same analyst work with the two members individually or even treat them as a couple. Very often the archetypal situation in which the patient is found lends itself to more effective handling in the family constellation, and then the entire family should be treated as a unit. With very severely disturbed people, family intervention may be indicated.

MANAGEMENT

Jungians do not, as a rule, differ to any marked degree from other therapists working within a dynamic depth-psychological framework as far as management is concerned.

The Setting

The analyst may work in a clinic or an office, or often in his or her own home. No special trappings are necessary. The emphasis is on intimacy: the analyst may sit beside a desk or table, but nothing separates the analyst from the analysand, and they confront each other directly. The analyst may or may not take notes. In some cases the session takes place in a hospital. The patient is assured absolute confidentiality. Special equipment is rarely used, although in this electronic age some people express the desire to record the sessions so they can listen to them at home in leisure.

The intensity and effectiveness of the analysis are not simple and direct functions of the frequency of the sessions. One can work in depth even if one sees a patient once a month. Most analysts, however, prefer to see their patients once or twice a week, at least in the beginning. A growing number of analysts show a marked predilection for working on a once-a-week basis, increasing the number only if absolutely necessary.

The Relationship

Analysts differ widely in how they conduct the first interview. Some prefer to plunge into the thick of the problem, and others insist on a thorough anamnesis starting from earliest memories and going systematically and methodically through the various life stages and emotional development of the patient. Most analysts devote the first few sessions to a mutual evaluation of the patient and the therapist. A basic mutual liking and respect are necessary for a meaningful analysis. If the initial antagonism is too pronounced (on either side), the patient will be transferred. Analysts are aware that initial negative reactions are projections and that attitudes and feelings toward patients will undergo change. However, from their own personal analyses, analysts have gained sufficient awareness of their own blind spots and know that even in the most thorough analysis, these cannot be completely worked through. One is never perfect, and allowances for one's weaknesses are a crucial characteristic of a good therapist. As a general rule, it is not advisable to work in a relationship with an analysand who is a forcible reminder of the analyst's own mother or father, and this holds true even if the parental complex was thoroughly thrashed out during the analyst's own analytical work.

The major importance of the initial sessions lies in taking stock of the unconscious reactions of analyst and analysand to each other.

No routine demand for psychological testing or physical examination is usually made. If the analyst is presented with a symptom that might prove organic, a physical checkup is in order. Flexibility and an intuitive-feeling approach are the hallmarks of the good clinician.

The nature of the relationship between analyst and analysand is determined more by the nature of the two participants than by the specific school of thought to which the analyst belongs. Analysts differ in their personalities and temperaments. Some will tend to be more cerebral and aloof, others more feeling and warm, some more talkative, others more reticent, some more therapeutically active, some less. Broadly speaking, however, an analyst would tend to be more a listener, less active and less sharing of self at the early stages of analysis. It is by dint of cooperating fruitfully in the analytic process that a growing intimacy and a friendship are established. As time goes on the analyst generally shares more of self and the relationship becomes more of a peer confrontation, rather than a healer-patient one.

Patient Problems

Very little can be said regarding the kind of patient behaviors likely to cause problems to the analyst. The way in which a given analyst reacts to a specific development is more a function of personality than of theoretical persuasion. Some therapists will exclude a certain category of patients on an a priori basis, such as alcoholics, drug addicts, and suicidal risks. By these exclusions, the therapist recognizes his or her personal limitations. The analytical orientation as such does not preclude any given situation, and the way in which an analyst may deal with a particular kind of behavior is determined by the analyst's personality, understanding of the situation, and relationship with the patient.

CASE EXAMPLE

Michael is in his early 20s, the third son in a midwestern family that had four sons. He is attractive, bright, introspective, and highly sensitive to the world around him. Mood and atmosphere affect him profoundly. This sensitivity allows him to feel the implicit and unexpressed needs of other people, a quality he is able to use creatively as well as destructively in a peer group. He tends to react in an extreme and absolutist fashion, betraying an inner insecurity that comes occasionally to the surface. He can be honest with himself and with others and is deeply committed to finding his true meaning.

Michael came to therapy because of his homosexuality. Refreshingly free from the common guilt feelings aroused by societal strictures (both his and his wife's families were aware of the state of affairs), he nevertheless had failed to find satisfaction in the homosexual world. Michael expected therapy to help him form lasting and meaning relationships in the homosexual or heterosexual world.

This was not Michael's first attempt at therapy. He had attempted to work through his problem in college, when his homosexual feelings intensified. The counselor refused to get involved with Michael's feeling and fantasy world, saying it was like a ball of yarn that was better left alone. He advised Michael to concentrate on his behavior rather than on his fantasies and attempted, as Michael experienced it, to "butch him up." As a result, he got married to a sexually shy girl, a virgin like himself. A baby girl was soon born, but the marriage rapidly deteriorated, resulting in a temporary separation. Michael came into the present therapy expecting to be told to "make a man of himself" and, in effect, to be rejected for what he was. That would have clinched his negative relationship toward the adult male world.

The first dream Michael presented was the following:

I am in the kitchen with my mother. Upstairs I can hear the sound of heavy chains clanking across the floor. Mother tells me not to worry, that father has gone insane, but that they had chained him upstairs so that he can't hurt me. She intimately places her hand over mine on the table and caresses it.

The dream seems to correspond to the actual family constellation. Michael experiences his father as weak, given to ineffectual violent rages that only emphasize his impotence. The mother stands always on the side of the children, effectively lessening any impact the father might have had. She is also seductive toward her children, especially towards Michael, her favorite. However, it would be a mistake to understand this dream as simply repeating the family psychology, the so-called oedipal character of which Michael is quite aware, for on that level the dream is adding nothing. What the dream is probably describing is the archetypal constellation of someone caught in the grips of homosexuality. The assertive capacity of the ego is under the seductive dominance of the mother archetype, hence his masculinity is chained and not trusted. The dream does not say anything about the outcome of this situation. That we are here dealing with a potentially difficult state of affairs is demonstrated in the second dream:

My father, brother, and I are peddling out to sea in water bikes. The water is choppy and threatening. I see my father dipping my baby into the shark-infested water.

Clearly, his anima is yet in an infantile ("baby") stage; that is, his feeling side, his capacity for emotional relatedness, is still undeveloped and threatened by the dangers of the deep, the regressive urges (sharks). He will have to derive masculine strength from an inner source, one hopes as a result of the analytical relationship. Indeed, sometime later we have the third dream:

I follow Y (the analyst) in climbing a difficult terraced mountain. Y is surprised that there is a physical side to my nature and says he enjoys my company.

Michael, who had suppressed his physical side as a result of ridicule, or lack of trust, rediscovers it in the company of his spiritual guide. Climbing the mountain can be archetypically taken as the road of individuation, the analyst representing an aspect of the Self. A further progress is made when the symbolism is more personal in the fourth dream:

Keith boasts about how many girls he has dated. Under his braggadocio I sense his insecurity, to which I respond in a fatherly way. Suddenly, we are romantically kissing. We are equals. I am transported. Mother tries to find out what has happened between Keith and me.

Keith is a high school friend Michael had not seen since that time. He had idolized Keith, seeing in him that aspect of masculinity he himself so lacked. Here, Keith is to be taken as a positive shadow figure, and the dream foresees the possibility of Michael's getting in touch with his repressed masculinity. Now that this has happened, we can expect a new attitude toward the anima, the feminine side.

Fifth dream: I am teaching my baby girl to talk.

The anima is still a baby, but the ego is developing a positive relationship to her. In the meantime, Michael had decided to reestablish his relationship with his wife, and she had returned to him. Michael had also joined a group run by his analyst. The atmosphere in the sessions became more and more charged. Obviously something was afoot.

Sixth dream: I am in the group and suddenly I discover to my horror that I am dressed in a way that looks very gay. I feel ridiculous and say so to one of the girls. She is not concerned and does not take my dress as an indication of my character, just an accident. She simply rolls down the sleeves and makes minor adjustments, and the clothes look normal. A guy who is sitting behind me is dressed in a gay manner. He tries to pull me away from the girl and embraces me. His clothing is full of curved needles that jut outward and they pierce me. I struggle and free myself. The girl's clothing is also full of pins, but they are safety pins and they are closed.

The girl in question embodies to Michael the essence of femininity and her acceptance of him as a man is of prime importance. The conflict depicted here is between the homosexual and heterosexual sides in Michael. The homosexual side, although potent, proves to be "prickly" and disagreeable, according to his dream. We can thus conclude that potentially Michael is able to free himself from his homosexual side. It is worthwhile to note that in this dream, the dream ego (the dreamer) has made an active choice, which involved a struggle he initiated and out of which he came victorious.

For Michael to be able actively to challenge the destructive aspect of the mother, he will have to get sustenance and support from the father world. In myths this usually takes the form of some heavenly intervention—Hercules is helped in his labors by Zeus, his divine father; Perseus is provided with the necessary gear (an invisible helmet and a shield) to fight the Gorgon (the Great Mother in her terrible aspect), who turns all who gaze upon her into stone. Consciously, Michael feels helpless. How will he be able to find his own masculinity when he has not had a strong father as a model? This is, indeed, difficult. Michael will have to find his father within himself, a search that one hopes will be aided by the relationship with the male analyst. In Michael's specific case, it means establishing contact with his spiritual side first, namely, broaching the religious question.

Seventh dream: The setting of this dream is a large church. In the rear Y (the analyst) is sitting behind an old wooden table reading from an ancient book. The letters are shaped like old German runes, long and narrow. But when I look close, I see that it could also be Chinese. Y is translating to a group of people, including me.

This dream had a profound effect on Michael. He was awed and puzzled by the church setting. His conflict with religion first arose when he came into puberty and started masturbating. In a characteristic absolutistic fashion, he decided that sex and religion were mutually exclusive, given that the latter seemed to negate the former. He therefore discarded his religious beliefs and considered himself an atheist. Until the appearance of this dream, the religious function in him seemed to be successfully repressed. The dream imagery, however, awakened strong positive feelings, not necessarily for the collective form of institutionalized religion, but for an individual, inner experience. The dream casts the analyst as a translator and transmitter of ancient wisdom, of both

Western (the runes) and Eastern traditions. There could hardly be a better description of the analytical process from a Jungian point of view. In a further scene in the dream (not reported here), a wind, a traditional symbol of the spirit, blows through the church. The symbolism is very rich, which made the analyst decide that the analytic sessions by themselves could not support the heavy symbolic load because their duration was too short to permit more than a hint at the depth and amplitude of the issues raised by this dream. Up to this point, Michael did not know of the analyst's specific theoretical orientation. The issue had never arisen, as Michael did not come to him looking specifically for a Jungian analyst. No professional terminology was ever used. With Michael's intellectual bent, the analyst had decided that overemphasis on the intellectual side would be detrimental to the course of his analysis. (With another patient it might prove important to introduce an intellectual framework at the outset of the therapy.) The analyst now suggested several books about the symbolism of church and spirit. In this he was also guided by considerations having to do with the archetypal nature of the dream. In Norse mythology, the runes (the alphabet, knowledge, consciousness) were given as a gift to Odin when he sacrificed himself on the ash tree as a symbol of transmittable culture and knowledge.

There is now a new element with which Michael must contend: the religious dimension, the spiritual side of the father archetype. The assimilation of a father figure on a more personal level will have to wait and will come only much later.

Eighth dream: I am with my father. A coarse brutish guy appears and insults my father. I wait confidently for my father to hit him but he is afraid; he is too weak. Thereupon I hit the guy.

Here the dreamer recognizes that he has to assume masculine qualities himself, rather than look for them in vain in other people who are unable to provide them. Meanwhile, on the level of outer reality, the changes that the unconscious heralds are taking place at a very slow rate. Michael is very anxious to get on with it and be "quickly transformed." He then has the ninth dream:

It is a warm summery day. I find a cocoon hanging on a vine and pick it up. The covering is a delicate green color. Its transparency allows me to see the orange wings of the butterfly inside and I realize that it is a monarch butterfly. I cup my hands together to provide warmth for the cocoon, hoping that the warmth of my hands will help it emerge sooner. Then I realize it won't help. I must simply wait for it to emerge by itself.

The graphic beauty of this dream is breathtaking. The dreamer is knowledgeable about butterflies and knows that the monarch, a king, is a very unusual butterfly. In the fall, the monarchs fly together from all over, congregating and migrating to the South for the winter, after which they return. Butterfly is psyche in Greek and is an archetypal image for the Self, the goal of the individuation process. Michael spontaneously said that this is an initiation dream, in which he is initiated into manhood. To the monarch he associated his masculinity "hang-up," which, initially ugly, is transformed into something beautiful that is part of the collective sense of virility. But, says the dream, the process cannot be deliberately rushed; the natural rhythms of growth have to be respected.

We realize that our presentation of Michael's case is at best an abstraction. Any attempt to communicate an alive, intense, deep relationship between two people over a few pages is impossible; only a few broad strokes out of the whole picture can be delineated. We focused on a segment as it was reflected primarily in the unconscious process. We did not dwell on the outside reality or on the vicissitudes of the analyst-analysand relationship. We depicted the most salient dreams, omitting scores of others, not all of which were understood. The overall pattern is discernible more in retrospect than in situ; certainly, no conscious plan was followed. Finally, let us again emphasize that dreams point to possibilities, not actualities. Michael's concrete problems are far from solved.

SUMMARY

Analytical psychotherapy attempts to deal with the human psyche in a phenomenological-existential way using a few basic assumptions as guideposts. The psyche includes consciousness, the center of which is the ego, and the unconscious, which comprises two spheres—the personal unconscious, the sum total of everything that has been repressed during one's lifetime, and the collective unconscious, or nonpersonal psyche. Archetypes are instinctlike ordering patterns of behavior, emotion, and perception. They can never be apprehended directly but are accessible to us through their effect on our behavior, feeling, or the emergence of images and representations in dreams, myths, folklore, and creative art.

Jung imputed to the psyche an inherent urge toward wholeness or individuation, the state of being what one was meant to become. The psyche is assumed to function in a purposive way toward the goal and thus operates as a self-regulating compensatory system. All unconscious products are, therefore, interpreted as messages guiding us to that goal. The emphasis is not only on the inhibiting forces of the past, but primarily on the creative potential of the present.

The psyche contains several elements worthy of special consideration. The Self is the archetype of centeredness. It is the agency that directs total functioning in a holistic way. The shadow is that part of the personality at variance with the ego ideal. The anima in men and the animus in women are our countersexual parts, the experience of the "other," the guide to what we might potentially be.

Jung has left us with theoretical foundations that, although far from exhausted, are firmly established and can be successfully applied in most cases. The technical side of psychotherapy, on the other hand, has not fared as well, and there is little doubt that this is the arena where future efforts must be directed. It has always been known, but is becoming increasingly crucial, that an adequate interpretation and understanding of unconscious material, although of utmost importance, are, by themselves, not enough. One is confronted more and more in one's clinical practice by instances where the dream, the fantasy, the drawing, the very nature of the problem is understood, both by the analyst and the analysand, and still no progress seems to be made. What we still sorely lack are effective means by which to translate the hard-won intellectual-theoretical understanding into an experiential phenomenon so that behavioral change is possible.

The verbal dimension by itself is decidedly not enough. The primitives intuited this and instituted rituals to enhance psychic phenomena. Analytical psychotherapy is also attempting to cope with this problem. To that effect, various nonverbal techniques are being incorporated into traditional practice. Groups and movement, sensitivity training, and rituals are being employed so psychic facts may be experienced more deeply and hitherto unlocked doors may be thrust open.

ANNOTATED BIBLIOGRAPHY

Jung, C. G. (1933). Modern man in search of a soul. New York: Harcourt Brace.

This collection of essays illustrates Jung's creative approach to psychotherapy, the role of dreams, and man's spiritual nature. It is written in a clear, engaging style, which makes for easy, enjoyable reading.

Jung, C. G. (1956). Two essays on analytical psychology. New York: Meridian Books.

This book, on a higher level of sophistication than Man and his symbols, presents the core ideas of Jungian thought. These issues are the structure of the personal and transpersonal unconscious; the incompleteness of Freud's and Adler's viewpoints; persona, anima and animus; and Jung's psychotherapeutic approach.

Jung, C. G. (1963). Memories, dreams, reflections. Recorded and edited by Aniela Jaffé. New York: Pantheon Books.

This is the closest thing to an autobiography Jung ever wrote. It details the relationship between his inner, personal struggles and his discoveries. The least intellectual of his books, it is personal and warm and makes for absorbing reading.

Jung, C. G. (1964). Man and his symbols. Garden City, NY: Doubleday.

This is the easiest of Jung's books to understand. Jung himself wrote only the first chapter, which he completed a few months before his death. It can, therefore, be taken as a final, authoritative statement of his ideas. The other chapters are written by his followers and students, under his supervision. In contrast to some of his other, specialized writings, this book is addressed to the intelligent lay reader. In the hardcover edition, there is a wealth of pertinent illustrations. The book presents Jung's basic ideas in an easily understandable way.

Whitmont, E. C. (1969). The symbolic quest. New York: Putnam.

This textbook presents a lucid exposition of Jung's major ideas, drawing upon clinical material for illustration. Particularly useful is the seventh chapter, which explains the way an archetypal theme is expressed in a person's life.

CASE READINGS

Adler, G. (1961). *The living symbol: A case study in the process of individuation.* New York: Pantheon Books.

This is a whole book devoted to an analysis of a woman suffering from claustrophobia. The material is used as a stepping stone for examining Jung's particular contribution to the process of analysis. It is worthwhile to gain the flavor of the experience in Jungian analysis.

Baynes, H. G. (1969). *Mythology of the soul: A research into the unconscious from schizophrenic dreams and drawings.* London: Riders & Company.

A massive book containing two case histories of people we would classify today as borderline, this is a highly readable account of analytical psychotherapy by a very gifted teacher. One of the patients is an artist, thus providing a case that is rare in the literature.

Hillman, J. (1972). Archetypal psychology. In A. Burton (Ed.), *Operational theories of personality.* (pp. 65-98). New York: Brunner/Mazel.

This case history offers a useful illustration for teaching purposes.

Jacobi, J. (1969). A case of homosexuality. *Journal of Analytical Psychology, 14,* 48-64. [Reprinted in D. Wedding & R. J. Corsini (Eds.) (1989). *Case studies in psychotherapy.* Itasca, IL: F. E. Peacock.]

This classic case illustrates many of the principles of Analytical Psychotherapy discussed in the preceding chapter. The serious student will find the case both fascinating and illuminating.

Jung, C. G. (1968). An analysis of a patient's dream. *Analytical psychology: Its theory and practice.* New York: Pantheon. [Reprinted in D. Wedding and R. J. Corsini, (Eds.) (1979). *Great cases in psychotherapy.* Itasca, IL: F. E. Peacock.]

This brief interpretation of a dream is taken from one of Jung's speeches and demonstrates how he used dreams to make clinical inferences.

Lockhart, R. A. (1975). Mary's dog is an ear mother: Listening to the voices of psychosis. *Psychological Perspectives, 6,* 144-160.

This case provides an example of a brief, intensive psychotherapy with a young psychotic man who was hospitalized for hallucinations.

Ross, E. L. (1972). *Dreams and the growth of personality: Expanding awareness in psychotherapy.* New York: Pergamon Press.

Part 2 of this book contains a relatively full case history of a young woman. It is well written by a Jungian analyst who sees himself primarily as a "growth therapist."

Sullwood, E. (1971). Eagle eye. In Hilde Krisch (Ed.), *The well-tended tree.* (pp. 235-253). New York: Putnam.

This lovely analysis of a six-year-old Indian boy offers an example of an analysis with children using a sandbox.

REFERENCES

Breland, K., & Breland, M. (1961). The misbehavior of organisms. *American Psychologist, 16,* 681-684.

Campbell, J. (1956). *The hero with the thousand faces.* New York: Meridian.

Campbell, J. (1968). *The masks of gods.* New York: Viking Press.

Creuzer, G. F. (1810). *Symbolik and mythologie der alten völker.* Leipzig: Leske.

Ellenberger, H. F. (1970). *The discovery of the unconscious.* New York: Basic Books.

Flournoy, T. (1906). *Miss Frank Miller* "Quelfues faits d'imagination créatrice subconsciente." *Archives de psychologie, 1,* 36-51.

Greenson, R. R. (1968). *The technique and practice of psychoanalysis.* New York: International Universities Press.

Hall, C., & Lindzey, G. (1962). *Theories of personality.* New York: Wiley.

Jaffé, A. (1971). *From the life and work of C. G. Jung.* New York: Harper.

Jung, C. G. (1957). On the psychology and pathology of so-called occult phenomena. In *Psychiatric studies. Collected Works (Vol. 1). Bollingen Series XX.* Princeton, NJ: Princeton University Press. (Originally published 1902.)

Jung, C. G. (1960). The psychology of dementia praecox. In *The psychoanalysis of mental disease. Collected Works (Vol. 3). Bollingen Series XX.* Princeton, NJ: Princeton University Press. (Originally published 1907.)

Jung, C. G. (1964). *The development of personality. Collected Works (Vol. 17). Bollingen Series XX.* Princeton, NJ: Princeton University Press. (Originally published 1954.)

Jung, C. G. (1967). *Symbols of transformation. Collected Works (Vol. 5). Bollingen Series XX.* Princeton, NJ: Princeton University Press. (Originally published 1911.)

Jung, C. G. (1968). *The archetypes and the collective unconscious. Collected Works (Vol. 9, Part I). Bollingen Series XX.* Princeton, NY: Princeton University Press. (Originally published 1934.)

May, R. (Ed.) (1961). *Existential psychology.* New York: Random House.

Munroe, R. (1955). *Schools of psychoanalytic thought.* New York: Rinehart and Winston.

Neumann, E. (1955). *The archetypal world of Henry Moore. Bollingen Series LXI.* Princeton, NJ: Princeton University Press.

Whitmont, E. (1964). Group therapy and analytical psychology. *Journal of Analytical Psychology, 9,* 1–21.

Whitmont, E. (1970). *The symbolic quest.* New York: Putnam.

CARL R. ROGERS, 1902–1987

5

Person-Centered Therapy

NATHANIEL J. RASKIN and CARL R. ROGERS[1]

OVERVIEW

Person-centered therapy is an approach to helping individuals and groups in conflict. Its essentials were formulated by psychologist Carl R. Rogers in 1940. A clearly stated theory, accompanied by the introduction of verbatim transcriptions of psychotherapy, stimulated a vast amount of research on a revolutionary hypothesis: that a self-directed growth process

would follow the provision and reception of a particular kind of relationship characterized by genuineness, nonjudgmental caring, and empathy. This hypothesis has been tested over decades in situations involving teachers and students, administrators and staffs, facilitators and participants in cross-cultural groups, as well as psychotherapists and clients.

BASIC CONCEPTS

Perhaps the most fundamental and pervasive concept in person-centered therapy is trust. The foundation of Rogers' approach is an *actualizing tendency* present in every living organism —in human beings, a trust in a constructive directional flow toward the realization of each individual's full potential. Rogers (1980) has described this actualizing force as part of a *formative tendency*, observable in the movement toward greater order, complexity, and interrelatedness that can be observed in stars, crystals, and microorganisms, as well as in human beings.

[1]Carl Rogers died on February 4, 1987, at the age of 85. He remained active until a few days before his death. This chapter was one of the many projects on which Carl was working at the time of his death.

At a conference in 1986 Carl responded to all manner of questions, including one on his feelings about dying. He said he was not afraid of death, but would hate to live for an extended period in a confused state. In this respect, he died as he wished. He spoke passionately about his distaste for being idolized, agreeing with the notion, "if you meet the Buddha on the road; kill him." As always, he displayed his characteristic attitude of genuine respect for other individuals, independent of age, experience, and especially status, and he participated as an equal.

This chapter summarizes Rogers' preeminent contributions as a twentieth-century social scientist and, as a joint effort, culminates a collaborative association of 47 years. - NJR.

On a more basic level, there is a trust that individuals and groups can set their own goals and monitor their progress toward these goals. This has special meaning in relation to children, students, and workers, who are often viewed as requiring detailed and constant guidance and supervision. In the context of psychotherapy, a person-centered approach assumes that clients can be trusted to select their own therapists, to choose the frequency and length of their therapy, to talk or to be silent, to decide what needs to be explored, to achieve their own insights, and to be the architects of their own lives. Groups are believed to be capable of developing the processes that are right for them, and of resolving conflicts within the group.

One particular person-centered application of trust relates to the therapist or facilitator. In the early days of the movement, the focus was entirely on the client. The therapist provided continuous and consistent empathy for the client's perceptions, meanings, and feelings. With experience came growing recognition that it was important for the therapist to be appreciated as a person in the relationship and to be regarded with trust, as is the client.

Eugene Streich formulated one of the earliest statements of this trust:

When the therapist's capacity for awareness is thus functioning freely and fully without limitations imposed by theoretical formulations of his role, we find that we have, not an individual who may do harm, not a person who must follow certain procedures, but a person able to achieve, through the remarkable integrative capacity of his central nervous system, a balanced, therapeutic, self-growing, other-growth facilitating behavior as a result of all these elements of awareness. To put it another way, when the therapist is less than fully himself—when he denies to awareness various aspects of his ex-

perience—then indeed we have all too often to be concerned about his effectiveness, as our failure cases would testify. But when he is most fully himself, when he is his most complete organism, when awareness of experience is most fully operating, then he is to be trusted, then his behavior is constructive. (1951, pp. 8–9)

Some 30 years later Rogers, in more intuitive and spiritual language, expressed such trust in the therapist or group facilitator, referring to it as "one more characteristic" of a growth-promoting relationship, supplementing the classical conditions of congruence, unconditional positive regard, and empathy:

When I am at my best, as a group facilitator or a therapist, I discover another characteristic. I find that when I am closest to my inner, intuitive self, when I am somehow in touch with the unknown in me, when perhaps I am in a slightly altered state of consciousness in the relationship, then whatever I do seems to be full of healing. Then simply my *presence* is releasing and helpful. (1986a, p. 198)

Congruence, unconditional positive regard, and *empathy* represent basic concepts of person-centered therapy. These are qualities the therapist provides. While distinguishable, these three concepts are intimately related (Rogers, 1957). Congruence refers to the correspondence between the thoughts and the behavior of the therapist; thus, genuineness describes this characteristic. The therapist does not put up a professional front or personal facade.

The therapist also possesses unconditional positive regard for the client. The client may be reserved or talkative, address any issue of choice, and come to whatever insights and resolutions are personally meaningful. The therapist's regard for the client will not be affected by these particular choices, characteristics, or outcomes.

The therapist expresses this quality of genuine regard through *empathy*. Being empathic reflects an attitude of profound interest in the client's world of meanings and feelings as the client is willing to share this world. The therapist receives these communications and conveys appreciation and understanding, with the effect of encouraging the client to go further or deeper. The notion that this involves nothing more than a repetition of the client's last words is erroneous. Instead, an interaction occurs in which one person is a warm, sensitive, respectful companion in the typically difficult exploration of another's emotional world. The therapist's manner of responding should be individual, natural, and unaffected. When empathy is at its best, the two individuals are participating in a process which may be compared to that of a couple dancing, the client leading, the therapist following: the smooth, spontaneous back-and-forth flow of energy in the interaction has its own aesthetic rhythm.

Basic concepts on the client side of the process include *self-concept, locus-of-evaluation*, and *experiencing*. In focusing on what is important to the person seeking help, client-centered therapists soon discovered that the person's perceptions and feelings about self were of central concern (Raimy, 1948). A client might think there was something wrong with her because men chose not to continue their relationships with her. Or a client might see himself as deficient for not being able to select an occupation and stick to it. In one way or another, the concept of self was found to be wanting or in conflict. A major component of self-concept is self-regard. Clients typically lacked self-esteem.

Some of the earliest psychotherapy research projects showed that when clients were rated as successful in therapy, their attitudes toward self became significantly more positive (Sheerer, 1949).

Successful clients were also found to progress along a related dimension, *locus-of-evaluation*. At the same time that they gained in self-esteem, they tended to shift the basis for their standards and values from other people to themselves. People commonly began therapy overly concerned with what others thought of them—their locus-of-evaluation was external. With success in therapy, their attitudes toward others, as toward themselves, became more positive and they were less dependent on others for their values and standards (Raskin, 1952).

A third central concept in person-centered therapy is *experiencing*, a dimension along which successful clients improved (Rogers, Gendlin, Kiesler & Truax, 1967), shifting from a rigid mode of experiencing self and world to a mode characterized by openness and flexibility.

The three therapist qualities and the three client constructs described in this section have been carefully defined, measured, and studied in scores of research projects relating therapist practice to the outcome of psychotherapy. There is considerable evidence that when clients receive congruence, unconditional positive regard, and empathy, their self-concepts become more positive and realistic, they become more self-expressive and self-directed, they become more open and free in their experiencing, their behavior is rated as more mature, and they deal better with stress (Rogers, 1986a).

OTHER SYSTEMS

Person-centered therapy evolved predominantly out of Rogers' own experience. However, there are both important differences and conceptual similarities between the person-centered approach and other personality theories.

Self-actualization, a concept central to person-centered theory, was advanced most forcefully by Kurt Goldstein. His holistic theory of personality emphasizes that individuals must be understood as totalities and that they strive to actualize themselves (Goldstein, 1959). Goldstein's work and ideas preceded those of Abraham Maslow, a founder of humanistic psychology, who was opposed to the Freudian and behavioral interpretations of human nature.

Heinz Ansbacher, a leading proponent of Adlerian theory, joined A. Maslow (1968) and Floyd Matson (1969) in recognizing a host of theories and therapists "united by six basic premises of humanistic psychology":

1. People's creative power is a crucial force, in addition to heredity and environment.

2. An anthropomorphic model of humankind is superior to a mechanomorphic model.

3. Purpose, rather than cause, is the decisive dynamic.

4. The holistic approach is more adequate than an elementaristic one.

5. It is necessary to take humans' subjectivity, their opinions and viewpoints, and their conscious and unconscious fully into account.

6. Psychotherapy is essentially based on a good human relationship (Ansbacher, 1977, p. 51).

Among those subscribing to such beliefs were Alfred Adler, William Stern, Gordon Allport, the Gestalt psychologists (Max Wertheimer, Wolfgang Kohler, and Kurt Koffka), the neo-Freudians (Franz Alexander, Erich Fromm, Karen Horney, and Harry Stack Sullivan), post-Freudians, such as Judd Marmor and Thomas Szasz, phenomenological and existential psychologists, such as Rollo May, the cognitive theorist George A. Kelly, and of course, Carl Rogers (Ansbacher, 1977).

While some fundamental person-centered concepts and values are consonant with the proponents of other systems, Rogers and Sanford (1985) have listed a number of distinctive characteristics of client-centered therapy. These include:

1. The hypothesis that certain attitudes in therapists constitute the necessary and sufficient conditions of therapeutic effectiveness

2. The concept of therapists being immediately present and accessible to clients, relying on their moment-to-moment experiencing in the relationships

3. The *intensive and continuing* focus on the phenomenological world of the client (hence the term "client-centered")

4. A developing theory that the therapeutic process is marked by a change in the client's manner and immediacy of experiencing with increasing ability to live more fully in the moment

5. A concern with the process of personality change, rather than with the structure of personality

6. Emphasis on the need for continuing research to learn more about psychotherapy

7. The hypothesis that the same principles of psychotherapy apply to all

persons, whether they are categorized as psychotic, neurotic, or normal

8. A view of psychotherapy as one specialized example of all constructive interpersonal relationships with the consequent generalized applicability of all knowledge gained from the field of psychotherapy

9. A determination to build all theoretical formulations out of the soil of experience, rather than twisting experience to fit a preformed theory and

10. A concern with the philosophical issues that derive from the practice of psychotherapy.

Meador and Rogers (1984) distinguished person-centered therapy from psychoanalysis and from behavior modification in these terms:

In psychoanalysis the analyst aims to interpret connections between the past and the present for the patient. In person-centered therapy, the therapist facilitates the client's discoveries of the meanings of his or her own current inner experiencing. The psychoanalyst takes the role of a teacher in interpreting insights to the patient and encouraging the development of a transference relationship, a relationship based on the neurosis of the patient. The person-centered therapist presents him- or herself as honestly and transparently as possible and attempts to establish a relationship in which he or she is authentically caring and listening.

In person-centered therapy, transference relationships may begin, but they do not become full-blown. Rogers has postulated that transference relationships develop in an evaluative atmosphere in which the client feels the therapist knows more about the client than the client knows about him- or herself, and therefore the client becomes dependent. Person-centered therapists tend to avoid evaluation. They do not interpret for clients, do not question in a probing manner, and do not reassure or criticize clients. Person-centered therapists have not found the transference relationship, central to psychoanalysis, a necessary part of a client's growth or change.

In behavior therapy, *behavior change* comes about through external control of associations to stimuli and the consequences of various responses. In practice, if not in theory, behavior therapy *does* pay attention to the therapy relationship; however, its major emphasis is on specific changes in specific behaviors. In contrast, person-centered therapists believe behavior change evolves from within the individual. Behavior therapy's goal is symptom removal. It is not particularly concerned with the relationship of inner experiencing to the symptom under consideration, or with the relationship between the therapist and the client, or with the climate of their relationship. It seeks to eliminate the symptom as efficiently as possible using the principles of learning theory. Obviously, this point of view is quite contrary to person-centered therapy, which maintains that fully functioning people rely on inner experiencing to direct their behavior. (1984, p. 146)

Raskin (1974), in a comparison of Rogers' practice with those of leaders of five other orientations, found that client-centered therapy was distinctive in providing empathy and unconditional positive regard. Psychoanalytically oriented and eclectic psychotherapists agreed with client-centered theory on the desirability of empathy, warmth, and unconditional positive regard, but examples of rational-emotive, psychoanalytically oriented, and Jungian interviews were ranked low on these qualities.

This study provided a direct comparison of audiotaped samples of therapy done by Rogers and by Albert Ellis, the founder of rational-emotive therapy (RET). Among 12 therapist variables rated by 83 therapist-judges, the only one on which Rogers and Ellis were alike was Self-Confident. Rogers' therapy sample received high ratings on the following dimensions: Empathy, Unconditional Positive Regard, Congruence, and Ability to Inspire Confidence. The interview by Ellis was rated high on the Cognitive and Therapist-Directed dimensions. Rogers was rated low on Therapist-Directed, while Ellis received a low rating on Unconditional Positive Regard.

This research lends support to the following differences between person-centered therapy and rational-emotive therapy.

1. Unlike RET, the person-centered approach greatly values the therapeutic relationship.

2. Rational-emotive therapists provide much direction, both during the therapeutic contact and outside of it; the person-centered approach encourages the client to determine direction, both in and out of therapy.

3. Rational-emotive therapists work hard to point out deficiencies in their clients' thought processes; person-centered therapists accept and respect their clients' ways of thinking and perceiving.

4. Person-centered therapy characteristically leads to actions chosen by the client; rational-emotive methods include "homework" assignments by the therapist.

5. The person-centered therapist will relate to the client on a feeling level, and in a respectful and accepting way; the rational-emotive therapist will be inclined to interrupt this affective process to point out the irrational harm that the client may be doing to self and interpersonal relationships.

While Rogers and Ellis have very different philosophies and methods of trying to help people, they share some very important beliefs and values:

1. A great optimism that people can change, even when they are deeply disturbed

2. A perception that individuals are often unnecessarily self-critical, and that negative self-attitudes can become positive

3. A willingness to put forth great effort to try to help people, both through individual therapy and through professional and popular writing

4. A willingness to demonstrate their methods publicly

5. A respect for science and research

Similar differences and commonalities will be found when Rogers is compared to other cognitive therapists like Aaron Beck.

HISTORY

PRECURSORS

One of the most powerful influences on Carl Rogers was learning that traditional child-guidance methods in which he had been trained did not work very well. At Columbia University's Teachers College he had been taught testing, measurement, diagnostic interviewing, and interpretive treatment. This was followed by an internship at the psychoanalytically oriented Institute for Child Guidance, where he learned to take exhaustive case histories and do projective personality testing. It is important to note that Rogers originally went to a Rochester child-guidance agency believing in this diagnostic, prescriptive, professionally impersonal approach, and it was only after actual experience that he concluded that it was not effective. As an alternative, he tried listening and following the client's lead rather than assuming the role of the expert. This worked better, and he discovered some theoretical and applied support for this alternative approach in the work of Otto Rank and his followers at the University of Pennsylvania School of Social Work and the Philadelphia Child Guidance Clinic. One particularly important event was a three-day seminar in Rochester with Rank (Rogers & Haigh, 1983). Another was his association with a Rankian-trained social worker, Elizabeth Davis, from whom "I first got the notion of responding almost entirely to the feelings being expressed. What later came to be called the reflection of feeling sprang from my contact with her" (Rogers & Haigh, 1983, p. 7).

Rogers' methodology and, later, his theory, grew out of the soil of his own experience and from learning what worked for him. At the same time, a number of links to Otto Rank are apparent in Rogers' early work.

Elements of Rankian theory that bore a close relationship to principles of nondirective therapy include:

1. The individual seeking help is not simply a battleground of impersonal forces such as id and superego, but has personal creative powers.

2. The aim of therapy becomes the acceptance by the individual of self as unique and self-reliant.

3. In order to achieve this goal, the client rather than the therapist must become the central figure in the therapeutic process. The client is his or her own therapist and has powers of self-creation as well as of self-destruction. The former can be brought into play if the therapist will play the role not of authority, but of ego-helper.

4. The therapist can be neither an instrument of love, which would make the patient more dependent, nor an instrument of education, which attempts to alter the individual.

5. The goals of therapy are achieved by the patient not through an explanation of the past, which the client would resist if interpreted, and which, even if accepted by the client, would serve to lessen responsibility for present adjustment, but rather through the experiencing of the present in the therapeutic situation (Raskin, 1948, pp. 95–96).

Rank explicitly, eloquently, and repeatedly rejected therapy by technique and interpretation, stating:

Every single case, yes every individual hour of the same case, is different, because it is derived momentarily from the play of forces given in the situation and immediately applied. My technique consists essentially in having no technique, but in utilizing as much as possible experience and understanding that are constantly converted into skill but never crystallized into technical rules which would be applicable ideologically. There is a technique only in an ideological therapy where technique is identical with theory and the chief task of the analyst is interpretation (ideological), not the bringing to pass and granting of experience. (1945, p. 105)

Rank is obscure about his actual practice of psychotherapy, particularly the amount and nature of his activity during the treatment hour. Unsystematic references in *Will Therapy* (1945) reveal that, despite his criticism of educational and interpretive techniques and his expressed value of the patient being his or her own therapist, he assumed a position of undisputed power in the relationship.

BEGINNINGS

Carl Ransom Rogers was born in Oak Park, Illinois, on January 8, 1902. Rogers' parents believed in hard work, responsibility, and religious fundamentalism and frowned on activities like drinking, dancing, and card playing. The family was characterized by closeness and devotion but did not openly display affection. While in high school, Carl worked on the farm, and he became interested in experimentation and the scientific aspect of agriculture while still maintaining his love of reading and nature. Later he entered the University of Wisconsin, following his parents and older siblings, as an agriculture major. Rogers also carried on his family's religious tradition. He was active in the campus YMCA and was chosen to be one of ten American youth delegates to the World Student Christian Federation's Conference in Peking, China, in 1922. At that time he switched his major from agriculture to history, which he thought would better prepare him for a career as a minister. After graduating from Wisconsin in 1924 and marrying Helen Elliott, a childhood friend, he entered the Union Theological Seminary. Two years later, and in part as a result of taking several psychology courses, Rogers moved "across Broadway" to Teachers College, Columbia University, where he was exposed to what he later described as "a contradictory mixture of Freudian, scientific, and progressive education thinking" (Rogers & Sanford, 1985, p. 1374).

After Teachers College Rogers worked for 12 years at a child-guidance center in Rochester, New York, where he soon became an administrator as well as a practicing psychologist. He began writing articles and became active at a national level. His book The Clinical Treatment of the Problem Child was published in 1939, and he was offered a professorship in psychology at Ohio State University.

Once at Ohio State, in a climate of great excitement among the growing number of graduate students who chose to work with him, Rogers began to teach newer ways of helping problem children and their parents.

In 1940, Rogers was teaching an enlightened distillation of child-guidance practices described in The Clinical Treatment of the Problem Child. From his point of view, this approach represented a consensual direction in which the field was moving and was evolutionary rather than revolutionary. The clinical process began with an assessment, including testing of children and interviewing of parents, and the results of assessment provided the basis for a treatment plan. Once in treatment, nondirective principles were followed.

Rogers' views became more radical. His presentation at the University of Minnesota, on December 11, 1940, entitled "Some Newer Concepts in Psychotherapy," is the single event most often identified with the birth of client-centered therapy.

Rogers decided to expand this talk into a book titled Counseling and Psychotherapy, over one-third of which consisted of the verbatim transcript of an electronically recorded eight-interview case. The book described the generalized process in which a client begins with a conflict situation and a predominance of negative attitudes and moves toward insight, independence, and positive attitudes. Rogers hypothesized that the counselor promoted such a process by avoiding advice and interpretation and by consistently recognizing and accepting the client's feelings. Research corroboration of this new approach to counseling and psychotherapy was offered, including the first (Porter, 1943) of what soon became a series of pioneering doctoral dissertations on the process and outcomes of psychotherapy. In a very short time, an entirely new approach to psychotherapy was born, as was the field of psychotherapy research. This approach and its accompanying research led to the eventual acceptance of psychotherapy as a primary professional function of clinical psychologists.

After serving as Director of Counseling Services for the United Service Organizations during World War II, Rogers was appointed Professor of Psychology at the University of Chicago and became head of the university's counseling center. The 12 years that Rogers remained at Chicago were a period of tremendous growth in client-centered theory, philosophy, practice, research, applications, and implications. In 1957, Rogers published a classic "necessary and sufficient conditions" paper in which congruence and unconditional positive regard were added to empathy as three essential therapist-offered conditions of therapeutic personality change. This was followed by a comprehensive and rigorous theory of therapy, personality, and interpersonal relationships (Rogers, 1959b). Rogers' philosophy of the "exquisitely rational" nature of the behavior and growth of human beings was further articulated and related to the thinking of Søren Kierkegaard, Abraham Maslow, and others. The practice of client-centered therapy both deepened and broadened; more profound self-exploration resulted in longer cases. The therapist was also more fully appreciated as a person in the therapeutic relationship. Psychotherapy research, which had begun so auspiciously at Ohio State, continued with investigations by Godfrey T.

Barrett-Lennard (1962), John Butler and Gerard Haigh (1954), Desmond Cartwright (1957), Eugene Gendlin (1961), Nathaniel Raskin (1952), Julius Seeman (1959), John Shlien (1964), and Stanley Standal (1954), among others.

At Ohio State, there was a sense that client-centered principles had implications beyond the counseling office. At Chicago, this was made most explicit by the empowerment of students and the counseling center staff. About half of Rogers' *Client-Centered Therapy* (1951) was devoted to applications of client-centered therapy, with additional chapters on play therapy, group therapy, and leadership and administration.

In 1957, Rogers accepted a professorship in psychology and psychiatry at the University of Wisconsin. With the collaboration of associates and graduate students, a massive research project was mounted, based on the hypothesis that hospitalized schizophrenics would respond to a client-centered approach (Rogers, Gendlin, Kiesler & Truax, 1967). Two relatively clear conclusions emerged from a complex maze of results: (1) the most successful patients were those who had experienced the highest degree of accurate empathy, and (2) it was the client's, rather than the therapist's, judgment of the therapy relationship that correlated more highly with success or failure.

CURRENT STATUS

Rogers left the University of Wisconsin and full-time academia and began living in La Jolla, California, in 1964. He was a resident fellow for four years at the Western Behavioral Sciences Institute and then, starting in 1968, at the Center for Studies of the Person. In more than two decades in California, Rogers wrote books on a person-centered approach to teaching and educational administration, on encounter groups, on marriage and other forms of partnership, and on the "quiet revolution" that he believed would emerge with a new type of "self-empowered person." Rogers believed this revolution had the potential to change "the very nature of psychotherapy, marriage, education, administration, and politics" (Rogers, 1977). These books were based on observations and interpretations of hundreds of individual and group experiences.

A special interest of Rogers and his associates was the application of a person-centered approach to international conflict resolution. This resulted in trips to South Africa, Eastern Europe, and the Soviet Union, as well as in meetings with Irish Catholics and Protestants and with representatives of nations involved in Central American conflicts (Rogers & Ryback, 1984). In addition to Rogers' books, a number of valuable films and videotapes have provided data for research on the basic person-centered hypothesis that individuals and groups which have experienced empathy, congruence, and unconditional positive regard will go through a constructive process of self-directed change.

A current thrust of the person-centered approach is international. This is expressed in many ways:

1. The client-centered approach is an important orientation to the practice of psychotherapy in Japan, Germany, Switzerland, Italy, and other European countries.

2. Since the early 1970s, Charles Devonshire, Alberto Zucconi, and others have initiated person-centered training programs for psychologists, teachers, physicians, and other professionals throughout Europe.

3. Reinhard Tausch (1978), Germain Lietaer (1981), and Godfrey Barrett-Lennard (1986) have organized and disseminated client-centered literature and research internationally.

4. Rogers' basic attitude of trust in the positive nature and self-directive capacities of the human species has influenced people on every continent, and Rogers' writings have been translated and disseminated worldwide.

5. There is international participation in client-centered activities through the facilitator-training effort known as the La Jolla Program and through a European cross-cultural workshop organized annually.

6. International forums on the Person-Centered Approach have been held in Oaxtepec, Mexico; Norwich, England; and La Jolla, California. Two internationally attended meetings of the Association for the Development of the Person-Centered Approach were held in Chicago and New York in 1986 and 1988.

7. There has been a passionate interest in peace and international conflict resolution reflected in Rogers' meetings with Irish Catholics and Protestants; his visits to South Africa and the Soviet Union; cross-cultural workshops in Brazil, Dublin, and Hungary; and a person-centered workshop on the "Central American Challenge" (Rogers, 1986e).

8. The *Person-Centered Review,* "an international journal of research, theory, and application," was initiated by David Cain in 1986. Half of its 24 editorial board members reside outside of the United States.

Since 1980, when a group called Carl Rogers and Associates was formed to implement the theory and application of the person-centered approach, a number of institutions have been established to further this orientation. The *Person-Centered Review* is one expression of this shift, which Rogers explained in the first issue:

I have always opposed the institutionalization of a client-centered "school"—the founding of institutes, the granting of certificates of completion, the setting of standards for membership. Although well intentioned, such institutionalization leads almost inevitably to an increasingly narrow, rigid, bureaucratic point of view. . . .

There is a second element to be considered. . . . The approach . . . emphasizes shared values, yet encourages uniqueness . . . it encourages those [with person-centered] values to develop their own special and unique ways of being, their own ways of implementing this shared philosophy.

These two factors—my refusal to institutionalize and the paradoxical nature of the approach—have meant that the impact of my work has been primarily pervasive rather than affecting only the field of psychology.

There has thus developed a large number of people in many nations—therapists, teachers, business people, doctors, social workers, researchers, lay people, family counselors, pastors—who have a strong interest in the continuing development of a client-centered/person-centered approach. All too often these persons work alone and feel alone. . . . Here is where I see the exciting function of the new *Person-Centered Review*. . . . It will help to tie together the global network that already exists but lacks an awareness of itself. The *Review* can be a vehicle for new ideas, innovative methods, thoughtful critiques, new models of research, and integrative philosophical and theoretical thinking. (Rogers, 1986b, pp. 3–5)

PERSONALITY

THEORY OF PERSONALITY

Rogers moved from an openly scornful attitude toward psychological theory to the development of a rigorous 19-proposition "theory of therapy, personality, and interpersonal relationships" (Rogers, 1959b). On one level, this signified a change in Rogers' respect for theory. On another, this comprehensive formulation can be understood as a logical evolution evident in Rogers since childhood: his interest in nature and in how things grew and the pleasure he derived from viewing the order in natural processes. His belief in the importance of the child's conscious attitudes toward self and self-ideal was central to the test of personality adjustment he later devised for children (Rogers, 1931). The portrayal of the client's growing through a process of reduced defensiveness and of self-directed expansion of self-awareness was described in a paper on the processes of therapy (Rogers, 1940). Rogers wrote here of a gradual recognition and admission of a real self with its childish, aggressive, and ambivalent aspects as well as more mature components. As data on personality changes in psychotherapy started to accumulate rapidly, with the objective analyses of verbatim interviews, Rogers found support for his belief that the facts are always friendly, despite some negative results.

As outgoing president of the American Psychological Association, Rogers summed up this perspective:

Client-centered therapy has led us to try to adopt the client's perceptual field as the basis for genuine understanding. In trying to enter this internal world of perception . . . we find ourselves in a new vantage point for understanding personality dynamics. . . . We find that behavior seems to be better understood as a reaction to this reality-as-perceived. We discover that the way in which the person sees himself, and the perceptions he dares not take as belonging to himself, seem to have an important relationship to the inner peace which constitutes adjustment. We discover . . . a capacity for the restructuring and reorganization of self, and consequently the reorganization of behavior, which has profound social implications. We see these observations, and the theoretical formulations which they inspire, as a fruitful new approach for study and research in various fields of psychology. (1947, p. 368)

Rogers expanded his observations into theory of personality and behavior, which was included in the book *Client-Centered Therapy* (1951). This theory is based on 19 basic propositions:

1. Every individual exists in a continually changing world of experience of which he is the center.

2. The organism reacts to the field as it is experienced and perceived. This perceptual field is, for the individual, "reality."

3. The organism reacts as an organized whole to this phenomenal field.

4. The organism has one basic tendency and striving—to actualize, maintain, and enhance the experiencing organism.

5. Behavior is basically the goal-directed attempt of the organism to satisfy its needs as experienced, in the field as perceived.

6. Emotion accompanies and in general facilitates such goal-directed behavior, the kind of emotion being related to the seeking versus the consummatory aspects of the behavior, and the intensity of the emotion being related to the perceived significance of the behavior for the maintenance and enhancement of the organism.

7. The best vantage point for understanding behavior is from the internal frame of reference of the individual himself.

8. A portion of the total perceptual field gradually becomes differentiated as the self.

9. As a result of interaction with the environment, and particularly as a result of evaluational interaction with others, the structure of self is formed—an organized, fluid, but consistent conceptual pattern of perceptions of characteristics and relationships of the "I" or the "me," together with values attached to these concepts.

10. The values attached to experiences, and the values which are a part of the self structure, in some instances are values experienced directly by the organism, and in some instances are values introjected or taken over from others, but perceived in distorted fashion, as if they had been experienced directly.

11. As experiences occur in the life of the individual, they are either (a) symbolized, perceived, and organized into some relationship to the self, (b) ignored because there is no perceived relationship to the self-structure, or (c) denied symbolization or given a distorted symbolization because the experience is inconsistent with the structure of the self.

12. Most of the ways of behaving which are adopted by the organism are those which are consistent with the concept of self.

13. Behavior may, in some instances, be brought about by organic experiences and needs which have not been symbolized. Such behavior may be inconsistent with the structure of the self, but in such instances the behavior is not "owned" by the individual.

14. Psychological maladjustment exists when the organism denies to awareness significant sensory and visceral experiences, which consequently are not symbolized and organized into the gestalt of the self-structure. When this situation exists, there is a basis for potential psychological tension.

15. Psychological adjustment exists when the concept of the self is such that all the sensory and visceral experiences of the organism are, or may be, assimilated on a symbolic level into a consistent relationship with the concept of self.

16. Any experience which is inconsistent with the organization or structure of self may be perceived as a threat, and the more of these perceptions there are, the more rigidly the self-structure is organized to maintain itself.

17. Under certain conditions, involving primarily complete absence of any threat to the self-structure, experiences which are inconsistent with it may be perceived and examined, and the structure of self re-

vised to assimilate and include such experiences.

18. When the individual perceives and accepts into one consistent and integrated system all his sensory and visceral experiences, then he is necessarily more understanding of others and is more accepting of others as separate individuals.

19. As the individual perceives and accepts into his self-structure more of his organic experiences, he finds that he is replacing his present value system—based so largely upon introjections which have been distortedly symbolized—with a continuing organismic valuing process. (pp. 481–533)

Rogers comments that

This theory is basically phenomenological in character, and relies heavily upon the concept of the self as an explanatory construct. It pictures the end-point of personality development as being a basic congruence between the phenomenal field of experience and the conceptual structure of the self—a situation which, if achieved, would represent freedom from internal strain and anxiety, and freedom from potential strain; which would represent the maximum in realistically oriented adaptation; which would mean the establishment of an individualized value system having considerable identity with the value system of any other equally well-adjusted member of the human race. (p. 532)

Further investigation of these propositions were conducted at the University of Chicago Counseling Center in the early 1950s in carefully designed and controlled investigations of personality changes in psychotherapy. Stephenson's (1953) Q-technique was used to measure changes in self-concept and self-ideal during and following therapy and in a no-therapy control period. Many results confirmed Rogers' hypotheses, e.g., a significant increase in congruence between self and ideal occurred during therapy, and changes in the perceived self were toward better psychological

adjustment (Rogers & Dymond, 1954).

Rogers' personality theory has been described as growth-oriented rather than developmental. While this is accurate, it does not acknowledge Rogers' sensitivity to the attitudes with which children are confronted, beginning in infancy:

While I have been fascinated by the horizontal spread of the person-centered approach into so many areas of our life, others have been more interested in the vertical direction and are discovering the profound value of treating the *infant*, during the whole birth process, as a person who should be understood, whose communications should be treated with respect, who should be dealt with empathically. This is the new and stimulating contribution of Frederick Leboyer, a French obstetrician who . . . has assisted in the delivery of at least a thousand infants in what can only be called a person-centered way. (Rogers, 1977, p. 31)

Rogers goes on to describe the infant's extreme sensitivity to light and sound, the rawness of the skin, the fragility of the head, the struggle to breathe, etc., and the specific ways in which Leboyer has taught parents and professionals to provide a beginning life experience that is caring, loving, and respectful.

This sensitivity to children was further expressed in Rogers' explanation of his fourth proposition (*The organism has one basic tendency and striving—to actualize, maintain, and enhance the experiencing organism*):

The whole process (of self-enhancement and growth) may be symbolized and illustrated by the child's learning to walk. The first steps involve struggle, and usually pain. Often it is true that the immediate reward involved in taking a few steps is in no way commensurate with the pain of falls and bumps. The child may, because of the pain, revert to crawling for a time. Yet the forward direction of growth is more powerful than the satisfactions of remaining infantile. Children will actualize themselves, in spite of the painful experiences of so doing. In the same way, they will become independent, responsible, self-governing, and socialized, in spite of the pain which is often involved in these steps. Even where they do not, because of a variety of circumstances, exhibit the growth, the tendency is still present. Given the opportunity for clear-cut choice between forward-moving and regressive behavior, the tendency will operate. (Rogers, 1951, pp. 490–91)

One of Rogers' hypotheses about personality (Proposition 8) was that a part of the developing infant's private world becomes recognized as "me," "I," or "myself." Rogers described infants, in the course of interacting with the environment, as building up concepts about themselves, about the environment, and about themselves in relation to the environment.

Rogers' next suppositions are crucial to his theory of how development may proceed either soundly or in the direction of maladjustment. He assumes that very young infants are involved in "direct organismic valuing," with very little or no uncertainty. They have experiences such as "I am cold, and don't like it," or "I like being cuddled," which may occur even though they lack descriptive words or symbols for these examples. The principle in this natural process is that the infant positively values those experiences that are perceived as self-enhancing and places a negative value on those that threaten or do not maintain or enhance the self.

This situation changes once children begin to be evaluated by others (Holdstock & Rogers, 1983). The love they are given and the symbolization of themselves as lovable children become dependent on behavior. To hit or to hate a baby sibling may result in the child's being told that he or she is bad and unlovable. The child, to preserve a positive self-concept, may distort experience.

It is in this way . . . that parental attitudes are not only introjected, but . . . are experienced . . . in distorted fashion, as if based on the evidence of one's own sensory and visceral equipment. Thus, through distorted symbolization, expression of anger comes to be "experienced" as bad, even though the more accurate symbolization would be that the expression of anger is often experienced as satisfying or enhancing. . . . The "self" which is formed on this basis of distorting the sensory and visceral evidence to fit the already present structure acquires an organization and integration which the individual endeavors to preserve. (Rogers, 1951, pp. 500–501)

This type of interaction may sow the seeds of confusion about self, self-doubt, and disapproval of self, and reliance upon the evaluation of others. Rogers indicated that these consequences may be avoided if the parent can accept the child's negative feelings and the child as a whole while refusing to permit certain behaviors, like hitting the baby.

VARIETY OF CONCEPTS

Various terms and concepts appear in the presentation of Rogers' theory of personality and behavior that often have a unique and distinctive meaning in this orientation.

Experience

Experience refers to the private world of the individual. At any moment, some of this is conscious. A lot is available to consciousness, like the pressure of the pen against our fingers as we write. Some of it may be difficult to bring into awareness, like the idea, "I am an aggressive person." While people's actual awareness of their total experiential field may be limited, each individual is the only one who can know it completely.

Reality

For psychological purposes, reality is basically the private world of individual perceptions, though for social purposes reality consists of those perceptions which have a high degree of communality among various individuals" (Rogers, 1951, p. 485). Two people will agree on the reality that a particular person is a politician. One sees her as a good woman who wants to help people and, based on this reality, votes for her. The other person's reality is that the politician appropriates money to get elected, and therefore this person votes against her. In therapy, changes in feelings and perceptions and, therefore, reality may occur. The client may begin with the belief that the therapist is mostly interested in fees. This reality may change to a perception of the therapist as primarily caring.

The Organism Reacting as an Organized Whole

A person may be hungry, but because of a report to complete, will skip lunch. In psychotherapy, clients often become more clear about what is most important to them, resulting in behavioral changes then directed toward the clarified goals. A politician may decide not to run for office because he decides that his family life is more important.

The Organism's Actualizing Tendency

This is a central tenet in the writings of Kurt Goldstein, Hobart Mowrer, Harry Stack Sullivan, Karen Horney, and Andras Angyal, to name just a few. The child's painful struggle to learn to walk is an example. It is Rogers' belief, and the belief of most other personality theorists that, given a free choice and in the absence of external force, individuals prefer to be healthy rather than sick, to be independent rather than dependent, and in general to further the optimal development of the total organism.

The Internal Frame of Reference

This is the perceptual field of the individual. It is the way the world appears and the meanings attached to experience and feelings. From the person-centered point of view, this internal frame of reference provides the fullest understanding of why people behave as they do. It is to be distinguished from external judgments of behavior, attitudes, and personality.

The Self, Concept of Self, Self-structure

"These terms refer to the organized, consistent, conceptual Gestalt composed of perceptions of the characteristics of the 'I' or 'me' and the perceptions of the relationships of the 'I' or 'me' to others and to various aspects of life, together with the values attached to these perceptions. It is a Gestalt available to awareness although not necessarily in awareness. It is a fluid and changing process, but at any given moment it . . . is at least partially definable in operational terms" (Meador & Rogers, 1984, p. 158).

Symbolization

This is the process by which the individual becomes aware or conscious of an experience. There is a tendency to deny symbolization to experiences at variance with the concept of self—e.g., people who think of themselves as truthful will tend to resist the symbolization of an act of lying. Ambiguous experiences tend to be symbolized in ways that are consistent with self-concept. A person lacking in self-confidence may symbolize a silent audience as unimpressed; one who is confident may symbolize such a group as attentive and interested.

Psychological Adjustment or Maladjustment

This refers to the consistency, or lack of consistency, between an individual's sensory and visceral experiences and the concept of self. A self-concept that includes elements of weakness and imperfection facilitates the symbolization of failure experiences. The need to deny or distort such experiences does not exist and therefore fosters a condition of psychological adjustment.

Organismic Valuing Process

This is an ongoing process in which individuals freely rely on the evidence of their own senses for making value judgments. This is in distinction to a fixed system of introjected values characterized by "oughts" and "shoulds" and by what is supposed to be right or wrong. The organismic valuing process is consistent with the person-centered hypothesis of confidence in the individual and, even though established by each individual, makes for a highly responsible socialized system of values and behavior. The responsibility derives from people making choices on the basis of their direct, organic processing of situations, in contrast to acting out of fear of what others may think of them or what others have taught them is the way to think and act.

The Fully Functioning Person

Rogers defined those who rely on organismic valuing processes as fully functioning people, able to experience all of their feelings, afraid of none of them, allowing awareness to flow freely in and through their experiences. Seeman (1984) has been involved in a 25-year research program to clarify and describe the qualities of such optionally functioning individuals. These empirical studies highlight the possession of a positive self-concept, greater physiological responsiveness, and an efficient use of the environment.

PSYCHOTHERAPY

THEORY OF PSYCHOTHERAPY

The basic theory of person-centered therapy is that if the therapist is successful in conveying genuineness, unconditional positive regard, and empathy, then the client will respond with constructive changes in personality organization. Research has demonstrated that these qualities can be made real in a relationship and can be conveyed and appreciated in a short time. Changes in self-acceptance, immediacy of experiencing, directness of relating, and movement toward an internal locus-of-evaluation may occur in short-term intensive workshops or even in single interviews.

After a four-day workshop of psychologists, educators, and other professionals conducted by Rogers and R. C. Sanford in Moscow, participants reported their reactions. The following is a typical response:

This is just two days after the experience and I am still a participant. I am a psychologist, not a psychotherapist. I have known Rogers' theory but this was a process in which we were personally involved. I didn't realize how it applied. I want to give several impressions. First was the effectiveness of this approach. It was a kind of process in which we all learned. Second, this process was moving, without a motor. Nobody had to lead it or guide it. It was a self-evolving process. It was like the Chekhov story where they were expectantly awaiting the piano player and the piano started playing itself. Third, I was impressed by the manner of Carl and Ruth. At first I felt they were passive. Then I realized it was the silence of understanding. Fourth, I want to mention the penetration of this process into my inner world. At first I was an observer, but then the approach disappeared altogether. I was not simply surrounded by this process, I was absorbed into it! It was a revelation to me. We started moving. I wasn't simply seeing people I had known for years, but their feelings. My fifth realization was my inability to control the flow of feelings, the flow of the process. My feelings tried to put on the clothes of my words. Sometimes people exploded; some even cried. It was a reconstruction of the system of perception. Finally, I want to remark on the high skill of Carl and Ruth [Sanford], of their silences, their voices, their glances. It was always some response and they were responded to. It was a great phenomenon, a great experience. (Rogers, 1987, pp. 298–99)

This kind of experience speaks against the perception of the person-centered approach as a safe, harmless, innocuous, and unproductive form of therapy. It is intended to be safe, but clearly it can also be powerful.

Empathy

Empathy, in person-centered therapy, is an active, immediate, continuous process. The counselor makes a maximum effort to get under the skin of the client, to get within and to live the attitudes expressed instead of observing them, to catch every nuance of their changing nature, to absorb him- or herself completely in the attitudes of the other. In struggling to do this, if one is attempting to live the attitudes of others, one cannot be diagnosing them or thinking of making the process go faster. Such understanding must be acquired through intense, continuous,

and active attention to the feelings of others to the exclusion of any other type of attention (Rogers, 1951).

The accuracy of the therapist's empathic understanding has often been emphasized, but more important is the therapist's interest in appreciating the world of the client and offering such understanding with the willingness to be corrected. This creates a process in which the therapist gets closer and closer to the client's meanings and feelings, developing an ever-deepening relationship based on respect for and understanding of the other person.

Person-centered therapists vary in their views of the empathic understanding process. Some aim to convey an understanding of just what the client wishes to communicate. For Rogers, it has felt right not only to clarify meanings of which the client is aware, but also those just below the level of awareness. Rogers has been especially passionate about empathy's not being exemplified by a technique such as "reflection of feeling," but by a way of being in which the therapist is sensitively immersed in the client's world of experience.

Unconditional Positive Regard

Other terms for this condition are warmth, acceptance, nonpossessive caring, and prizing.

When the therapist is experiencing a positive, nonjudgmental, acceptant attitude toward whatever the client is at that moment, therapeutic movement or change is more likely. It involves the therapist's willingness for the client to be whatever immediate feeling is going on—confusion, resentment, fear, anger, courage, love, or pride.... When the therapist prizes the client in a total rather than a conditional way, forward movement is likely. (Rogers, 1986a, p. 198)

The roots of this therapist-offered condition are deeply imbedded in the history of this approach, as evidenced by this characterization of "relationship therapy" a half-century ago:

The worker makes no attempt to force conclusions or actions upon the client but rather gives him the fullest opportunity to express feelings usually inhibited, to see and accept himself with all his limitations. Out of such a relationship the individual acquires more realization of what he himself is able to do with his own problems, and the ways in which he can assume his own responsibilities. It is in this relationship with a non-critical, accepting worker that the client achieves an emotional growth that has not been possible for him as he defends himself in other situations. (Rogers, 1937, p. 240)

Congruence

Rogers regards congruence as

the most basic of the attitudinal conditions that foster therapeutic growth.... [it] does not mean that the therapist burdens the client with all of his or her problems or feelings. It does not mean that the therapist blurts out impulsively any attitudes that come to mind. It does mean, however, that the therapist does not deny to himself or herself the feelings being experienced and that the therapist is willing to express and to be open about any persistent feelings that exist in the relationship. It means avoiding the temptation to hide behind a mask of professionalism. (Rogers & Sanford, 1985, p. 1379)

Correspondingly, an effective way of dealing with the common occurrence of therapist fatigue is to express it. This strengthens the relationship because the therapist is not trying to cover up a real feeling. It may also reduce or eliminate the fatigue and restore the therapist to a fully attending and empathic state.

Implied Therapeutic Conditions

There are three other conditions in addition to the "therapist-offered" conditions of empathy, congruence, and unconditional positive regard (Rogers, 1957):

1. The client and therapist must be in psychological contact.

2. The client must be experiencing some anxiety, vulnerability, or incongruence.

3. The client must receive or experience the conditions offered by the therapist.

Rogers describe the first two as preconditions for therapy. The third, the reception by the client of the conditions offered by the therapist, sometimes overlooked, is essential. Research relating therapeutic outcome to empathy, congruence, and unconditional positive regard based on external judgments of these variables is moderately supportive of the person-centered hypothesis. If the ratings are done by clients themselves, the relationship to outcome is much stronger. Orlinsky and Howard (1978) reviewed 15 studies relating client perception of empathy to outcome and found that 12 supported the critical importance of perceived empathy.

PROCESS OF PSYCHOTHERAPY

The practice of person-centered therapy dramatizes its differences from most other orientations. Therapy begins immediately, with the therapist trying to understand the client's world in whatever way the client wishes to share it. The first interview is not used to take a history, to arrive at a diagnosis, to determine if the client is treatable, or to establish the length of treatment.

The therapist immediately shows respect for clients, allowing them to proceed in whatever way is comfortable for them. She listens without prejudice. She does not have her own agenda. She is open to either positive or negative feelings, speech or silence. This first hour may be the first of hundreds or it may be the only one; this is for the client to determine. If the client has questions, the therapist tries to recognize and to respond to whatever feelings are implicit in the questions. "How am I going to get out of this mess?" may be the expression of the feeling, *My situation seems hopeless*. The therapist will convey recognition and acceptance of this attitude. If this question is actually a plea for suggestions, the therapist may reply that she does not have the answers, but hopes she can help the client find the ones that are right for him. There is a willingness to stay with the client in moments of confusion and despair. There is a realization that reassurance and easy answers are not helpful and show a lack of respect for the client.

The therapist looks to the client for decisions about the timing and frequency of therapy. The therapist must respect her own availability, but is guided as much as possible by scheduling that feels right to the client. Person-centered therapists commonly share with their clients the responsibility for fee setting and manner of payment. In a money-oriented society, this is an opportune area for showing respect for the client.

Regard is also demonstrated through discussion of options such as group therapy and family therapy, in contrast to therapists of other orientations who "put" the client in a group or make therapy conditional on involvement of the whole family. This is not to be interpreted as meaning that the client is allowed to dictate the circumstances of therapy, but to make clear that the client is a vital partner in determining these conditions. On many issues, the client is regarded as the expert.

An Interview Illustrating the Process of Therapy

It has always been characteristic of the person-centered approach to illustrate its principles with verbatim accounts. This has the advantage of depicting the interaction between therapist and client more exactly and gives readers the opportunity to agree or to differ with the interpretation of the data.

The following is a demonstration interview carried out by Carl Rogers in 1983. Because of space limitations, the middle third of the interview has been omitted. Asterisks indicate words that could not be made out, in the transcription.

Therapist 1: OK, I think I'm ready. And you ... ready?

Client 1: Yes.

T-2: I don't know what you might want to talk about, but I'm very ready to hear. We have half an hour, and I hope that in that half an hour we can get to know each other as deeply as possible, but we don't need to strive for anything. I guess that's my feeling. Do you want to tell me whatever is on your mind?

C-2: I'm having a lot of problems dealing with my daughter. She's 20 years old; she's in college; I'm having a lot of trouble letting her go. ... And I have a lot of guilt feelings about her; I have a real need to hang on to her.

T-3: A need to hang on so you can kind of make up for the things you feel guilty about—is that part of it?

C-3: There's a lot of that ... Also, she's been a real friend to me, and filled my life ... And it's very hard*** a lot of empty places now that she's not with me.

T-4: The old vacuum, sort of, when she's not there.

C-4: Yes. Yes. I also would like to be the kind of mother that could be strong and say, you know, "Go and have a good life," and this is really hard for me to do that.

T-5: It's very hard to give up something that's been so precious in your life, but also something that I guess has caused you pain when you mentioned guilt.

C-5: Yeah, And I'm aware that I have some anger toward her that I don't always get what I want. I have needs that are not met. And, uh, I don't feel I have a right to those needs. You know . . . She's a daughter; she's not my mother—though sometimes I feel as if I'd like her to mother me . . . It's very difficult for me to ask for that and have a right to it.

T-6: So it may be unreasonable, but still, when she doesn't meet your needs, it makes you mad.

C-6: Yeah, I get very angry, very angry with her.
PAUSE

T-7: You're also feeling a little tension at this point, I guess.

C-7: Yeah. Yeah. A lot of conflict . . .

T-8: Umm-hmm . . .

C-8: A lot of pain.

T-9: A lot of pain. Can you say anything more what that's about?

C-9: [Sigh.] I reach out for her, and she moves away from me. And she steps back and pulls back . . . And then I feel like a really bad person. Like some kind of monster, that she doesn't want me to touch her and hold her like I did when she was a little girl . . .

T-10: It sounds like a very double feeling there. Part of it is, "Damn it, I want you close." The other part of it is, "Oh my God, what a monster I am to not let you go."

C-10: Umm-hum. Yeah. I should be stronger. I should be a grown woman and allow this to happen.

T-11: But instead, sometimes you feel like her daughter.

C-11: Umm-hmm. Yeah. Sometimes when I cuddle her, I feel I'm being cuddled.

T-12: Umm-hmm.
PAUSE
But you place a lot of expectations on yourself: "I should be different."

C-12: Yeah. I should be more mature. I should have my needs met so that I don't have to get anything from her.

T-13: You should find other ways and other sources to meet your needs, but somehow that doesn't seem to be happening?

C-13: Well, I feel I get a lot of my needs met, but the need from her is very strong—it's the need from a woman really, I think . . . It doesn't quite make up for the needs I get from men ****** . . .

T-14: There are some things that you just want from her.

C-14: Umm-hmm. Yeah. Just from her. [Sigh.]

T-15: When she pulls back, that's a very painful experience.

C-15: Yeah, that really hurts. That really hurts. [Big sigh.]
PAUSE

T-16: It looks like you're feeling some of that hurt right now.

C-16: Yeah, I can really feel her stepping back.

T-17: Umm-hmm. Umm-hmm.
PAUSE

T-18: Pulling away from you.

C-17: Yeah . . . . Going away.

T-19: *** you feel her sort of slipping away, and you . . . and it hurts . . . and—

C-18: Yeah. I'm just sort of sitting here alone. I guess like, you know, I can feel her gone and I'm just left here.

T-20: Umm-hmm. You're experiencing it right now: that she's leaving and here you are all alone.

C-19: Yeah. Yeah. Yeah. I feel really lonely. [Cries.]

T-21: Umm-hmm. Umm-hmm. If I understand right, not lonely in every respect, but lonely for her.

C-20: Lonely for her. Yeah. Yeah. [Cries.]

T-22: I'm not a good therapist—I forgot a box of Kleenex, but . . . I think I've got . . . [Laughs.]

C-21: Thank you. [Laughs.] I feel like I could cry a million tears about that. [Laughs.]

T-23: Umm-hmm. It feels as if the tears could just flow and flow on that score.

C-22: Yeah. Never stop.

T-24: That just to have her leave, have her pull away is just more than you can take.

C-23: Yeah. Yeah. It's really hard to go on without her. [Cries.]

T-25: It sounds as though that is almost the center of your life.

C-24: It's very close to that, you know. My husband, my children, my home . . . My work is important too, but there's something about the heart that's connected to her. [Sigh.]

T-26: And there's a real ache in your heart with her leaving.

C-25: Yeah. Yeah. [Cries.]

PAUSE

C-26: Oh . . . I just don't want her to go.

T-27: I want to keep her as my daughter, as my little girl, as the one I can cuddle . . .

C-27: Yeah, yeah. The one I can cuddle. She likes to cuddle too.

T-28: Umm-hmm. Umm-hmm.

C-28: [Cries.] And you know, I'm also scared for her. I'm scared for her out in the world. I'm scared for her to have to go through all the things that I did and how painful that is. I'd like to save her from that.

T-29: You'd like to protect her from that life out there and all the pain that you went through . . .

C-29: Yeah, yeah. And all the new stuff that all the young people are going through . . . It's very hard. She's struggling.

T-30: It's a hard world . . .

C-30: Yeah, very hard . . .

T-31: And you'd like to cushion it for her . . .

C-31: Yeah, make it perfect . . .

[Middle third of interview omitted]

T-73: Does that mean that you feel no one cares, no one accepts?

C-73: No. I feel like now that there are people who do, who care and accept and hear and value me. But there's that little—

T-74: So that the person who can't care and accept and value you is you.

C-74: Umm-hmm. Yeah. It's mostly me.

T-75: The person who sees those things as unforgivable is you.

C-75: Yeah. Yeah. Nobody else is that hard on me.

T-76: Umm-hmm. Nobody could be that cruel to you, or make such awful judgment.

C-76: [Sigh.]

T-77: Or hate you so.

C-77: Or hate me so. Yeah.

T-78: Sounds like you're the judge, the jury, and the executioner.

C-78: Yeah, My own worst enemy.

T-79: You pass a pretty tough sentence on yourself.

C-79: Yeah. Yeah, I do. Not a very good friend to me.

T-80: No.

C-80: ***—

T-81: You're not a very good friend to yourself. Umm-hmm.

C-81: Umm-hmm.

T-82: And you wouldn't think of doing to a friend what you do to yourself.

C-82: That's right. I would feel terrible if I treated anyone the way I treat me.

T-83: Umm-hmm. Umm-hmm. Umm-hmm.

PAUSE

T-84: Because to you, your self is just unlovable.

C-84: Well, there's a part of me that's lovable . . .

T-85: OK. OK.

C-85: Yeah.

T-86: OK. So in some respects you do love yourself.

C-86: Yeah. I love and appreciate the little child part of me—

T-87: Umm-hmm—

C-87: That's really struggled and come through—

T-88: Umm-hmm—

C-88: And survived—

T-89: Umm-hmm—

C-89: An awful lot.

T-90: Umm-hmm. That's a damned nice little girl.

C-90: Yeah. She's really special—

T-91: Umm-hmm.

C-91: She's like my daughter.

T-92: Uh-huh.

C-92: [Sigh.]

T-93: And she's a daughter you can hold on to.

C-93: Yeah. Yeah. I can still cuddle her. And tell her she's beautiful. And love her.

T-94: And she's a survivor, and she's strong, and she's been through a lot, but she's OK.

C-94: Yeah, Yeah, she is. She's real special.

PAUSE

T-95: It must be nice to have such a special person in your life.

C-95: Yeah. It is. That is nice. Yeah. She's very nice.

T-96: Can she care for the other parts of you?

C-96: She's starting to ***—

T-97: She's starting to.

C-97: Yeah.

T-98: Umm-hmm.

C-98: Just beginning.

T-99: Umm-hmm.

T-100: She's not as hard on you as the adult you.

C-99: No. That's right.

T-101: Umm-hmm.

C-100: She's much more understanding.

T-102: Umm-hmm.

C-101: And compassionate.

T-103: Umm-hmm.

C-102: [Sigh.]

PAUSE

T-104: Sounds like she loves you.

C-103: Yeah. She gives me all that unconditional love that I didn't feel like I got.

T-105: Umm-hmm. Umm-hmm. Umm-hmm.

PAUSE

T-106: And she loves all of you.

C-104: Yeah. Yeah. She loves all of me.

T-107: To her, none of it is unforgivable.

C-105: No. It's all OK.

T-108: All OK.

C-106: Yeah. [Sigh.]

PAUSE

T-109: I like her.

C-107: I like her to. [Sigh.] She's going to save me.

T-110: Hmm?

C-108: She's going to save me.

T-111: She's going to save you.

C-109: [Laughs.] From hurting myself anymore.

T-112: Umm-hmm.

PAUSE

T-113: She may really be able to keep you from being so hard on yourself. Really save you.

C-110: Yeah, I think she will; I think she will; I just have to give her a little help too.

T-114: Umm-hmm. Umm-hmm.

C-111: Like we'll work together . . . *** save me.

T-115: She's a good companion to have, isn't she?

C-112: Yeah, she is. [Sigh.]

C-113: It's good to have a friend.

T-116: Yeah. Umm-hmm. To have that kind of a friend inside really touches you.

C-114: Yeah. It really does. It'll never go away.

T-117: Umm-hmm.

C-115: It'll always be there for me.

T-118: Umm-hmm. She's not going to pull away and—

C-116: Go out into the world and do her thing. Laughs. *** gonna stay home with Mama.

T-119: Umm-hmm. Umm-hmm. And be a mother to Mama too, huh?

C-117: Yeah. Yeah.

PAUSE

[Sigh.]

T-120: What's that smile?

C-118: It's your eyes are twinkling.

[Both Laugh.]

T-121: Yours twinkle too.

[Laugh.]

[Sigh.]

Tape Over.[2]

Commentary

The interview illustrates, in concrete form, many principles of the process of person-centered therapy:

In T-2, Rogers makes it clear that he is leaving it up to the client to talk about what she wishes and feels comfortable with. He indicates that this can be a deep exchange but that it does not have to be.

T-1 and T-2 signify that Rogers is ready to enter immediately into a person-to-person exchange in which he will be "very ready to hear" whatever the client chooses to bring up.

After this, his responses are consistent attempts to understand the client and to communicate, or check out, his understanding of her feelings. They show that he is open to whatever kinds of feelings the client verbalizes. In T-6, he recognizes a negative feeling, anger; in T-10, he responds to a mixture of feelings, of her wanting to get close to her daughter and feeling like a terrible person because of her daughter's negative reaction; in T-23, he accepts her feeling that her tears are end-

[2]From a previously unpublished article by Carl Rogers given to me for this chapter. N.J.R.

less; in T-85 and T-86 and many succeeding responses, he conveys his recognition of positive self-attitudes.

The therapist's last two statements (T-120 and T-121) reveal a mutuality in the relationship implicit throughout the interview but often not obvious on the printed page.

The client's tears and frequent expressions of self-depreciation could provide a stimulus for reassurance. However, Rogers consistently does not do this; he is a reliable understanding partner who stays with the client as she lives with her various negative feelings and accompanies her as she finds the strength to rise above them.

MECHANISMS OF PSYCHOTHERAPY

The interview just quoted reveals many examples of the way in which change and growth are fostered in the person-centered approach. Rogers' straightforward statements in opening the interview (T-1 and T-2) allow the client to begin with a statement of the problem of concern to her and to initiate dialogue at a level comfortable for her.

Just as he does not reassure, Rogers does not ask questions. In response to C-2, he does not ask how long the problem has been going on, whether she has other children, the status of her marriage, or any other of the myriad questions that could construct a logical background and case history for dealing with the presenting problem. Rogers does not see himself as responsible for arriving at a solution to the problem as presented, or determining whether this is the problem that will be focused on in therapy, or changing the client's attitudes. The therapist sees the client as having these responsibilities and respects her capacity to fulfill them.

In this excerpt from a person-centered interview are numerous examples of the client's expanding her view of the problem after the therapist recognized her stated percept, accepted it unconditionally, and communicated his understanding to her:

1. Rogers' recognition of the client's stated need to hang on to her daughter (T-3) is followed by the client's recognition that her daughter has been "a real friend to me" (C-3).

2. The therapist's appreciation of the difficulty the client has in letting go of her daughter (T-5) is followed by the revelation of anger felt toward her daughter because "I don't always get what I want" (C-5). The therapist's acceptance of the anger as stated (T-6) helps the client to bring out the extent of the emotion (T-6).

3. The therapist's continued recognition of the client's feelings (T-7 and T-8) help her to express and share the extreme pain she feels (C-8).

The pattern of client-therapist communication leading to constant expansion of attitudes continues throughout the interview. Another result worth noting is the experiencing of emotion in the moment, as distinguished from the recounting of the emotion. This comes out in the exchange (T-15, C-15) and continues into the tears which begin in C-20.

In the final third of the interview, we see another result of the therapist's empathic way of being with the client. She has now shifted from her daughter to herself as the agent of bad self-treatment: "That's right. I would feel terrible if I treated anyone the way I treat me" (C-82).

The mechanism of therapist acceptance leading to change of self-attitude is shown operating powerfully in T-84, C-84: "Because to you, your self is just unlovable." "Well, there's a part of me that's lovable . . . " The client goes on to define that part as "the little child part of me" (C-86), "She's really special" (C-90), relates that part of herself to her daughter (C-91), and sees that she herself can provide all the caring feelings she has been seeking unsuccessfully from her daughter (C-93). The remainder of the interview clarifies a reciprocal relationship in which she sees that a part of herself that she prizes and loves is also a part she can depend on as a permanent source of support.

The interview exemplifies the therapeutic mechanism of empathy backed by genuineness and unconditional positive regard. It helps the client to (1) examine her problems in a way that shifts responsibility from others to herself, (2) experience emotions in the immediacy of the therapy encounter, (3) accept aspects of self formerly denied to awareness, and (4) raise her general level of self-regard.

Therapeutic change involves a blend of cognitive and affective elements. The integration of intellect and feelings is occurring in the therapist and in his relationship with the client. He is grasping her perceptions of her external and internal worlds, doing so with warmth and genuine caring. The client is also looking at some of the most troubling aspects of her life and changes the way she looks at others and self while experiencing anger, pain, loneliness, tearfulness, nurturance, disgust, tenderness, and compassion. The resolution that she introduces toward the end of the interview (C-115), "It'll always be there for me"

[that part of herself which will never let her down], may be seen as the therapeutic blending of conation, cognition, and affect.

AN EARLY FORMULATION

In a paper given at the first meeting of the American Academy of Psychotherapists in 1956, Rogers (1959a) presented "a client-centered view" of "the essence of psychotherapy." He conceptualized a "molecule" of personality change, hypothesizing "therapy is made up of a series of such molecules, sometimes strung rather closely together, sometimes occurring at long intervals, always with periods of preparatory experiences in between" (p. 52). Rogers attributed four qualities to such a "moment of movement":

(1) It is something which occurs in this existential moment. It is not a *thinking* about something, it is an experience of something at this instant, in the relationship. (2) It is an experiencing which is without barriers, or inhibitions, or holding back. She is consciously *feeling* as sorry for herself as she *is* sorry for herself. (3) This is . . . an experience which has been repeated many times in her past, but which has never been completely experienced. In the past she has felt it at some physiological level, but has "covered it up." This is the first time that it has been experienced completely. (4) This experience has the quality of being acceptable. It is . . . not "I feel sorry for myself, and that is reprehensible." It is instead an experience of "My feeling *is* one of sorrow for myself, and this is an acceptable part of me" (pp. 52–53).

This mechanism of psychotherapy described by Rogers in 1956 closely matches the experience of the client just discussed: She has a full, emotional experience of a part of herself, a lovable child, of which she has been aware but also covered up; she now experiences that part of herself, and accepts the child completely as part of a newly integrated self. Her laughter and twinkling eyes express the great emotional gratification that accompanies this reorganization.

APPLICATIONS

PROBLEMS

Person-centered therapists offer the same basic conditions to all prospective clients. These conditions do not include psychological tests, history taking, or other assessment procedures leading to diagnoses and treatment plans. Diagnostic labels take away from the person of the client; assuming a professional posture takes away from the person of the therapist. The therapist's task is uncluttered by the need to be an expert. Rogers clearly stated his position on this issue:

We have come to recognize that if we can provide understanding of the way the client seems to himself at this moment, he can do the rest. The therapist must lay aside his preoccupation with diagnosis and his diagnostic shrewdness, must discard his tendency to make professional evaluations, must cease his endeavors to formulate an accurate prognosis, must give up the temptation to subtly guide the individual, and must concentrate on one purpose only: that of providing deep understanding and acceptance of the attitudes consciously held at this moment by the client as he explores step-by-step into the dangerous areas which he has been denying to consciousness. (1946, p. 420)

A consequence of this position is that the person-centered approach has been used with individuals diagnosed by others as psychotic or retarded as well as with people simple seeking a personal growth experience.

"James" was one of the patients in the Wisconsin study (Rogers et al., 1967). In the course of a detailed description of two interviews with this patient, a "moment in change" is described in which the patient's hard shell is broken by his perception of the therapist's warmth and caring, and he pours out his hurt and sorrow in anguished sobs. This followed an intense effort by Rogers, in two interviews a week for the better part of a year, to reach this 28-year-old man, whose sessions were filled with prolonged silences. Rogers stated, "We were relating as two . . . genuine persons. In the moments of real encounter the differences in education, in status, in degree of psychological disturbance, had no importance—we were two persons in a relationship" (Rogers et al., 1967, p. 411). Eight years later this patient telephoned Rogers and reported continued success on his job and general stability in his living situation, and he expressed appreciation for the therapeutic relationship with Rogers (Meador & Rogers, 1984).

This clinical vignette emphasizes the person-centered rather than problem-centered nature of this approach. All people have feelings, all people like to be understood, and all people have issues of self-concept maintenance and enhancement. The person-centered approach respects the various ways people use to deal with these issues. In this regard, it may work particularly well with people who are "different."

This nonconcern with a person's "category" can be seen in person-centered cross-cultural and international conflict resolution. Empathy is provided in equal measure for the Catholics and Protestants in Northern Ireland (Rogers & Ryback, 1984) and for the oppressed blacks and troubled whites in South Africa (Rogers, 1986c). Conflict resolution is fostered when the facilitator appreciates the attitudes and feelings of opposing parties, and then the stereotyping of one side by the other is broken down by the protagonists' achievement of empathy.

EVALUATION

The heart of evaluation in person-centered therapy is the evaluative process in the client. The client evaluates whether therapy is useful and the specific ways in which he or she can use it. During the course of therapy, the client decides what to bring up, how much to explore any particular issue, the level of emotional intensity, etc. The natural extension of this client-centered responsibility is that the client decides when it is time to terminate therapy. While people share similar kinds of problems, aspirations, and feelings, the differences between clients in what they want and what they get out of therapy are enormous and range from simple problem relief to marked changes in personality organization.

Because the theory of personality development in person-centered therapy is based on how clients experience change, there is a smooth transition from clients' descriptions of change and those of therapists or external judges. Victor Raimy's (1948) pioneering dissertation on self-concept at Ohio State University was based on self-references in counseling interviews and on simple quantitative analysis of changes in self-approval in 14 complete series of counseling interviews. He defined a *self-reference* as "a group of words spoken by the client which directly or indirectly describe him as he appears in his own eyes." Self-ratings of this type were used extensively in the "parallel studies" project analyzing the first 10 completely recorded cases at the University of Chicago Counseling Center (Rogers & Raskin, 1949). Rogers described his experience leading up to the use of the Q-sort:

In my early days as a therapist, I tended to scorn any thinking about the self ... [it] seemed so ephemeral.... Another problem was that it had very different meanings for different people.

But my clients kept pushing me toward its consideration. It cropped up so frequently in therapeutic interviews. "I can't be my real self;" "I think that underneath I have a solid self, if I could get to it;" "I don't understand my self;" "With my mother, I never show my true self;" "I'm always afraid that if I uncover the real me, I'll find there is nothing there." Clearly, it was important to find a way of defining, of thinking about, the *self*. But how? (1986d, p. 1)

Rogers eventually found an answer in William Stephenson's Q-sort technique. It was possible with Stephenson's method to study any subject for which a large population of descriptive statements could be generated. The subject chosen was "the self as perceived by the individual," with items such as "I am assertive," "I feel inadequate," "I am a responsible person," etc. One hundred such items were sorted by the client into nine piles in a continuum from "most like me," to "least like me." This method allowed for quantified descriptions of self-concept and correlations between perceived self before and after therapy, between perceived self and ideal self, etc.

After the formulation of "the necessary and sufficient conditions of constructive personality change" (Rogers, 1957), considerable research was generated on the measurement of empathy, congruence, and unconditional positive regard and their effects on the outcome of psychotherapy. In the early 1970s, the relationship of outcome to the provision of person-centered conditions was generally regarded as impressive (Bergin & Garfield, 1971). By the late 1970s, some psychotherapy researchers concluded that the "potency and generalizability" of the earlier evidence were "not as great as once thought" (Mitchell, Bozarth & Krauft, 1977). More recently, Patterson (1984) and Raskin (1985) have challenged the basis for questioning the strength of the original conclusions.

Through all of these assessments, a consistent finding has been that when the measurement of the therapist-offered conditions is based on client perception rather than external judgment, the relationship to outcome is stronger. Much of this research has utilized the *Relationship Inventory* (Barrett-Lennard, 1986).

TREATMENT

The process of the person-centered approach has been described particularly in the context of individual psychotherapy with adults, its original arena. The broadening of the "client-centered" designation to "person-centered" stemmed from the generalizability of client-centered principles to other areas of human relations.

Play Therapy

Rogers' early clinical experience was in a child-guidance setting and his doctoral dissertation required the development of a personality test for children. The book that led to his appointment at Ohio State was *The Clinical Treatment of the Problem Child* (Rogers, 1939). Rogers deeply admired Jessie Taft's play therapy with children at the Philadelphia Child Guidance Clinic and was specifically impressed by her ability to accept the negative feelings verbalized or acted out by the child, which led the way to the emergence of positive attitudes in the child.

One of Rogers' graduate student associates, Virginia Axline, formulated play therapy as a comprehensive system of treatment for children. Axline shared Rogers' deep conviction about self-direction and self-actualization and, in addition, was passionate in her interest in helping fearful, inhibited, sometimes abused children to develop the courage to express long-buried emotions and to experience the exhilaration of being themselves. She used play when children could not overcome the obstacles to self-realization by words alone.

In addition to the central achievement of formulating the method of nondirective play therapy, Axline made major contributions to research on play therapy, group therapy with children, schoolroom applications, and parent-teacher as well as teacher-administrator relationships. She also demonstrated the value of play therapy for poor readers, for clarifying the diagnosis of mental retardation in children, and for dealing with race conflicts in young children (Axline, 1947; Rogers, 1951).

Client-Centered Group Process

Beginning as a one-to-one method of counseling in the 1940s, client-centered principles were being employed in group therapy, classroom teaching, workshops, organizational development, and concepts of leadership less than ten years later. Individual therapy practice, teaching, and research led to the development of a client-centered philosophy that influenced all of these other areas of human relations.

Classroom Teaching

In Columbus, while Rogers was beginning to espouse the nondirective approach, he accepted the role of the expert who structured classes and graded students. At Chicago, he began to practice a new philosophy, which he later articulated in *Freedom to Learn*:

I ceased to be a *teacher*. It wasn't easy. It happened rather gradually, but as I began to trust students, I found they did incredible things in their communication with each other, in their learning of content material in the course, in blossoming out as growing human beings. Most of all they gave me courage to be myself more freely, and this led to profound interaction. They told me their feelings, they raised questions I had never thought about. I began to sparkle with emerging ideas that were new and exciting to me, but also, I found, to them. I believe I passed some sort of crucial divide when I was able to begin a course with a statement something like this: "This course has the title 'Personality Theory' (or whatever). But what we do with this course is up to us. We can build it around the goals we want to achieve, within that very general area. We can conduct it the way *we* want to. We can decide mutually how we wish to handle these bugaboos of exams and grades. I have many resources on tap, and I can help you find others. I believe I am one of the resources, and I am available to you to the extent that you wish. But this is our class. So what do we want to make of it?" This kind of statement said in effect, "We are *free* to learn *what* we wish, *as* we wish." It made the whole climate of the classroom completely different. Though at the time I had never thought of phrasing it this way, I changed at that point from being a *teacher* and *evaluator*, to being a *facilitator of*

learning—a very different occupation. (1983, p. 26)

The change was not easy for Rogers. Nor was it easy for students who were used to being led and experienced the self-evaluation method of grading as strange and unwelcome.

The Intensive Group

The early 1960s witnessed another important development, the intensive group. This had multiple roots, among them some of Rogers' experiences at the end of his tenure at the University of Wisconsin and the early years of the American Academy of Psychotherapists (AAP). Beginning with the goal of cognitive exchanges among therapists with diverse therapeutic orientations, AAP workshops developed rapidly into close and intensive encounters. Rogers' move to California in 1964 spurred his interest in intensive groups, and in 1970, he published a 15-step formulation of the development of the basic encounter group.

Rogers visualized the core of the process, the "basic encounter," as occurring when an individual in the group responds with undivided empathy to another in the group who is sharing and also not holding back.

Rogers conceptualized the leader or facilitator's role in the group as exemplifying the same basic qualities as the individual therapist; in addition, he thought it important to accept and respect the group as a whole, as well as the individual members. An outstanding example of the basic encounter group can be seen in the film *Journey into Self*, which shows very clearly the genuineness, the spontaneity, the caring, and the empathic behavior of co-facilitators Rogers and Richard Farson (McGaw, Farson & Rogers, 1968).

Peace and Conflict Resolution

Searching for ways to peacefully resolve conflicts between larger groups has become the cutting edge of the person-centered movement, even though it began making contributions decades ago (Axline, 1948; Rogers, 1948). The scope of the person-centered movement's interest in this arena extends all the way to conflicts between nations. In some instances opposing groups have met in an intensive format with person-centered leadership. This has occurred with parties from Northern Ireland, South Africa, and Central America. A meeting in Austria on the "Central American Challenge" included a significant number of diplomats and other government officials (Rogers, 1986e). A major goal accomplished at this meeting was to provide a model for person-centered experiences for diplomats in the hope that they will be strengthened in future international meetings by an increased capacity to be empathic and to participate more fully in human encounters. Rogers (1987) and his associates have also conducted workshops on the Person-Centered Approach in Eastern Europe and the Soviet Union.

Rogers offered a person-centered interpretation of the Camp David accord and a proposal for avoiding nuclear disaster (Rogers & Ryback, 1984). One notion is central to all these attempts at peaceful conflict resolution: When a group in conflict can receive and operate under conditions of empathy, genuineness, and caring, negative stereotypes of the opposition weaken and are replaced by personal, human feelings of relatedness (Raskin & Zucconi, 1984).

MANAGEMENT

A person-centered approach implies maximizing the person-to-person relationship between client and therapist. This means minimizing a professional, impersonal, institutional approach.

Hundreds of tapes, films, and printed interviews document the consistent attention to the feelings of the client in person-centered therapy. Not so apparent are other ways in which the therapist reaches out to meet the client directly and personally. If a receptionist or other staff people are on the scene, they act in a manner that conveys respect for the individual client.

The therapist feels it is important to be punctual with the client, who is entitled to the therapist's continuous and full attention. This means keeping the door closed, not glancing at the mail, and refusing to be interrupted during the therapy session.

The physical aspects of the therapy situation should be comfortable. Informality is generally desirable in both the physical and the psychological climates. First names may be used mutually, if both therapist and client are comfortable with this.

The therapist's specific behaviors communicate respect and maximize the client's opportunity to experience respect. The importance of conveying such respect is shown more forcefully, perhaps, when the client is a child. Elaine Dorfman wrote:

The therapist is ready for the child when he arrives. Regardless of the mess made in previous contacts, the room is in order at the beginning of each new hour. If delayed, the therapist apologizes, just as he would with an adult. Appointments are faithfully kept. If it is necessary to break one, the child is told in advance. If the therapist is unable to let the child know ahead of time, the child receives an apology as soon as possible, in the form of a personal letter of explanation if he can read. The child's confidences are kept, in exactly the same way as are those of the adult client. In these and other ways, the child is told that he is a person worthy of respectful treatment. (1951, pp. 240–41)

It is important for children to know that what they say or do in the playroom will not be communicated to their parents by the therapist. Often children choose to share this kind of information with their parents. When they do not so choose, it is crucial to respect their wishes. Working out negative attitudes toward parents, in words or in play, with an understanding and accepting therapist, can be central to therapeutic progress.

The respect for confidentiality was manifested when Rogers accepted the University of Chicago's offer to establish a counseling center. One of Rogers' conditions was that confidentiality would be maintained and that no reports would be sent to the Dean of Students.

While confidentiality is accorded a very special place, the recording of interviews continues to be encouraged. Confidentiality expresses the profound respect felt for the client. Recording is consistent with the attitudes of openness and interest in research that are hallmarks of the approach. These are not contradictory practices. Recordings are done only with the person's knowledge and permission; microphones and machine are out in the open. Experience with recording taught client-centered therapists that listening to an interview again often helped them to hear client attitudes more clearly. Frequently, the therapist actually heard things that had been missed in the original interview. The

recording is available to the client who wants to hear it and this is often insightful. If the therapist is comfortable in proposing recording and setting up the equipment, the client usually is. If the therapist feels some conflict, this is often communicated to the client. In any event, if there is any question about it, the client's wishes regarding confidentiality and recording are respected.

CASE EXAMPLE[3]

INTRODUCTION

In 1964 Carl Rogers was filmed in a half-hour interview with a woman client for a film series, *Three Approaches to Psychotherapy* (Rogers, 1965). That interview contains many of the elements of person-centered therapy discussed in this chapter and is a typical example of the person-centered way of working. The film gives the reader an opportunity to see and hear Carl Rogers in action.

Rogers had never seen the woman before the interview and knew his contact with her would be limited to a half-hour. In his introduction to the interview, he describes the way he will hope to be with her. He says he will, if he is fortunate, first of all, be real, try to be aware of his own inner feelings and to express them in ways that will not impose these feelings on her. Second, he hopes he will be caring of her, prizing her as an individual and accepting her. Third, he will try to understand her inner world from the inside; he will try to understand not just the surface meanings, but the meanings just below the surface. Rogers says

---

[3]This example is borrowed from Meador & Rogers, 1984, pp. 187–92.

if he is successful in holding these three attitudes, he expects certain things to happen to the client, expectations based on his experience and his research. He expects she will move from a remoteness from her inner experiencing to a more immediate awareness and expression of it; from disapproving of parts of her self to greater self-acceptance; from a fear of relating to relating to him more directly; from holding rigid, black-and-white constructs of reality to holding more tentative constructs; and from seeing the locus-of-evaluation outside herself to finding the locus-of-evaluation in her own inner experiencing.

The fact that the interview lasted for only half an hour and the client was seen by the therapist only this one time emphasizes that the person-centered approach depends on the here-and-now attitudes of the therapist, attitudes as valid and constant in a brief interaction as over a long period.

THE INTERVIEW

The interview is with a young woman, Gloria, a 30-year-old divorcée. The first portion of the interview concerns the problem Gloria presents initially, that she has not been honest with her 9-year-old daughter Pammy about the fact that she has had sexual relationships with men since her divorce. Gloria has always been honest with her children and is feeling great conflict over having lied to Pammy. She wants to know whether telling Pammy the truth about her sexual relationships will affect Pammy adversely.

At the very beginning Gloria tells Rogers, "I almost want an answer from you. I want you to tell me if it would af-

fect her wrong if I told her the truth, or what." Later, on two occasions, she asks again for a direct answer to her question. Clearly, she wants an "authority" to tell her what to do. Rogers' responses assure her that he understands her dilemma and guide her to her own resources for answering. After each time that she asks the question and hears the response, Gloria explores her own feelings a little more deeply.

To her first request, Rogers replies, "And it's this concern about her (Pammy) and the fact that you really aren't—that this open relationship that has existed between you, now you feel it's kind of vanished?" After Gloria's reply, he says, "I sure wish I could give you the answer as to what you should tell her." "I was afraid you were going to say that," she says. Rogers replies, "Because what you really want is an answer."

Gloria begins to explore her relationship with Pammy and concludes that she feels real uncertainty about whether or not Pammy would accept her "devilish" or "shady" side. Gloria finds she is not certain she accepts that part of herself. Again she asks Rogers for an answer: "You're just going to sit there and let me stew in it and I want more." Rogers replies, "No, I don't want to let you just stew in your feelings, but on the other hand, I also feel this is the kind of very private thing that I couldn't possibly answer for you. But I sure as anything will try to help you work toward your own answer. I don't know whether that makes any sense to you, but I mean it." Gloria says she can tell he really does mean it and again begins to explore her feelings, this time focusing more on the conflict she herself feels between her actions and her inner standards. Shortly, she again says, "I want you very much to give me a direct answer."

Rogers replies:

I guess, I am sure this will sound evasive to you, but it seems to me that perhaps the person you are not being fully honest with is you, because I was very much struck by the fact that you were saying, 'If I feel all right about what I have done, whether it's going to bed with a man or what, if I really feel all right about it, then I do not have any concern about what I would tell Pam or my relationship with her.'

To this Gloria answers:

Right. All right. Now I hear what you are saying. Then all right, then I want to work on accepting me then. I want to work on feeling all right about it. That makes sense. Then that will come natural and then I won't have to worry about Pammy. . . .

This statement indicates that Gloria has assimilated a real insight, an understanding that the solution to her problem is in herself rather than in an authoritative opinion on how knowledge of her sex life will affect Pammy.

From this point in the interview she focuses on her inner conflict. She tells Rogers what she "wishes he would tell her" and then says she can't quite take the risk of being the way she wants to be with her children "unless an authority tells me that." Rogers says with obvious feeling, "I guess one thing that I feel very keenly is that it's an awfully risky thing to live. You'd be taking a chance on your relationship with her and taking a chance on letting her know who you are, really." Gloria says she wishes very strongly that she could take more risks, that she could act on her own feelings of rightness without always needing encouragement from others. Again she says what she'd like to do in the situation with Pammy, and then adds, "Now I feel like 'Now that's solved'—and I didn't even solve a thing; but I feel relieved."

Gloria: I do feel like you have been saying to me—you are not giving me advice, but I do feel like you are saying, "You know what pattern you want to follow, Gloria, and go ahead and follow it." I sort of feel a backing up from you.

Rogers: I guess the way I sense it, you've been telling me that you know what you want to do, and yes, I do believe in backing up people in what they want to do. It's a little different slant than the way it seems to you.

Gloria's expressing the feeling, "Now that's solved—and I didn't even solve a thing; but I feel relieved," exemplifies an awareness of inner experiencing, a felt meaning she has not yet put into words. She "feels relieved" as though her problem is solved. Therapeutic movement has occurred in her inner self before she understands its explicit meaning. It is interesting that she says in the same speech, "I feel a backing up from you." She *feels* the support of Rogers' empathic understanding and acceptance of her. From the person-centered point of view there is a relationship between her feeling understood and valued and her movement from seeking the locus-of-evaluation outside herself to depending on her own inner feeling of "rightness" for a solution to her problem.

The next portion of the interview involves Gloria's experience of her own inner valuing processes and the conflicts she sometimes feels. She explains her use of the word *utopia*, which refers to times she is able to follow her inner feelings: "When I do follow a feeling and I feel this good feeling inside of me, that's sort of utopia. That's what I mean. That's the way I like to feel whether it's a bad thing or a good thing. But I feel right about me." Whether the action she takes might be thought of as "good" or "bad," if she feels right about it, that's "utopia."

Rogers' response that in those moments she must feel "all in one piece" brings tears to Gloria's eyes, for those moments are all too few. In the midst of her weeping, she continues speaking.

Gloria: You know what else I was just thinking? I . . . a dumb thing . . . that all of a sudden while I was talking to you, I thought, "Gee, how nice I can talk to you and I want you to approve of me and I respect you, but I miss that my father couldn't talk to me like you are." I mean, I'd like to say, "Gee, I'd like you for my father." I don't even know why that came to me.

Rogers: You look to me like a pretty nice daughter. But you really do miss that fact that you couldn't be open with your own Dad.

Gloria is now quite close to her inner experiencing, allowing her tears to flow as she thinks of her rare moments of "utopia" and then expressing a feeling that comes into awareness of positive affection for Rogers. She then explores her relationship with her father, maintaining the same closeness to her inner feelings, as she says, "You know, when I talk about it, it feels more flip. If I just sit still a minute, it feels like a great big hurt down there."

Gloria looks at and feels her deep inner hurt over her relationship to her father. She has moved significantly from seeking a solution outside herself to a problem with her children to looking inward at a painful hurt. She says she tries to soothe the hurt through relationships with fatherly men, pretending they are her father, as she is doing with Rogers.

Rogers: I don't feel that's pretending.
Gloria: Well, you're *not* really my father.
Rogers: No. I meant about the real close business.
Gloria: Well, see, I sort of feel that's pretending too, because I can't expect you to feel very close to me. You don't know me that well.

Rogers: All I can know is what I am feeling, and that is I feel close to you in this moment.

Here Rogers presents himself as he really is, offering Gloria the experience of genuine caring from another, an experience she missed in her relationship with her real father. Shortly after this exchange, the interview ends.

EVALUATION

It is clear that the therapist's empathy, genuineness, and caring come through and are received by the client throughout the course of the interview. His acceptance helps her make important progress, as can be seen in several places. For instance, she begins the interview looking for an authority to tell her what to do and by its end has much greater faith in her own ability to make decisions. She moves from trying to keep some distance from her emotions to letting them be expressed without inhibition, going so far as to focus directly on the great hurt she feels about her relationship with her father. She also starts off not accepting part of herself, and then sees greater self-acceptance as an important task for future work. Her self-concept becomes more complete, her experiencing becomes less rigid, her locus-of-evaluation moves from external to more internal, and her self-regard increases. All the important qualities of the therapist and client are revealed in this brief interview, as well as the kind of therapeutic movement a person-centered approach is designed to produce.

The intensity of Rogers' genuineness and presence in the relationship is readily apparent from watching the film. The strength of his feelings comes through when he says, "It's an awfully risky thing to live," and when he clearly expresses his inner self, "All I can know is what I am feeling, and that is I feel close to you in this moment."

The therapeutic movement the client makes follows the direction and manner that Rogers initially predicted. First, he says she will move from a remoteness from her feelings to an immediate awareness and expression of them. She does in fact begin the interview wanting an answer to a troubling question and does move to a point toward the end where her feelings are flowing into awareness and she is expressing them as they occur. At one point she says, concerning her wanting a father like Rogers, "I don't even know why that came to me." She is allowing her feelings to come into expression without censoring, questioning, or even knowing where they are coming from.

Rogers also predicts Gloria will move from disapproving of herself toward self-acceptance. In the beginning, Gloria says she is not sure she accepts her "shady" or "devilish" side. Later, she very explicitly asks to work on accepting herself and spends much of the remaining time exploring the nuances of her self-acceptance.

Initially, Gloria believes there is a true answer that will solve her problem. She construes reality in this black-and-white fashion. Later, she tentatively considers relying on her own inner experiencing for solutions as she says, "I wish I could take more risks." Finally, she describes the utopian experience of feeling so sure of herself that whatever she does comes out of her inner experience and feels "right." This same example demonstrates the therapeutic process of moving from finding the locus-of-

evaluation outside oneself to finding it in one's inner self.

The quality of this interview is like a piece of music that begins on a thin persistent note and gradually adds dimensions and levels until the whole orchestra is playing. The intuitive interaction and response of the therapist are not unlike the interplay in a creative improvisation. Whatever wisdom science can bring to how the instruments are made and which combinations make for harmony and growth will greatly enrich the players, but we must never lose sight of the primacy of the creative human beings making the music.

As a result of countless inquiries about Gloria from people who had viewed his interview with her, Rogers (1984) published a historical note in which he stated that for about 10 years after the interview, Gloria wrote to him approximately once or twice a year. Her last letter was written "shortly before her untimely death" 15 years following the interview. He also described her reactions at a weekend conference led by him a year or more after the interview, during which her interviews with Rogers and with Fritz Perls and Albert Ellis were shown. She expressed much anger about the fact that she had done all the things Perls had asked her to do and that she had given over her power to him. Having seen the interview at this point, she did not like it, which contrasted with her positive reaction soon after the interview.

Rogers also described Gloria's request, at the end of a luncheon with him and his wife Helen, during the same weekend, that they allow her to think of them as "parents in spirit," parents she would have liked to have had. "We each replied that we would be pleased and honored to have that status in her life. Her warm feelings for us were reciprocated. . . . In the ensuing years she wrote me about many things in her life. . . . There were very good times, and there were tragic times . . . and she showed sensitivity, wisdom, and courage in meeting the different aspects of her experience." Rogers concludes, "I am awed by the fact that this fifteen-year association grew out of the quality of the relationship we formed in one thirty-minute period in which we truly met as persons. It is good to know that even one half-hour can make a difference in a life" (pp. 423–25).

SUMMARY

The central hypothesis of the person-centered approach is that individuals have within themselves vast resources for self-understanding and for altering their self-concepts, behavior, and attitudes toward others. These resources will become operative in a definable, facilitative, psychological climate. Such a climate is created by a psychotherapist who is empathic, caring, and genuine. The expression of each of these qualities in practice has special significance.

Empathy as practiced in the person-centered approach refers to a consistent, unflagging appreciation of the experience of the client. It involves a continuous process of checking with the client to see if understanding is complete and accurate. It is carried out in a manner that is personal, natural, and free flowing; it is not a mechanical kind of reflection or mirroring. Caring is characterized by a profound respect for the individuality of the client and by unconditional, nonpossessive regard. Genuineness is marked by congruence between what the therapist feels and says, and by the therapist's willingness to relate on a person-to-person basis rather than through a professionally distant role.

The impetus given to psychotherapy research by the person-centered approach has resulted in substantial evidence demonstrating that changes in personality and behavior occur when a therapeutic climate is provided. Two frequent results of successful person-centered therapy are increased self-esteem and greater openness to experience.

The trust in the perceptions and the self-directive capacities of clients expanded client-centered therapy into a person-centered approach to education, group process, organizational development, and conflict resolution. Person-centered leaders facilitate the assumption of responsibility and power by students, workers, group members, and opposing parties in conflict.

The world in the last decades of the twentieth century is characterized by forces of enormous magnitude that threaten life on earth and, at the same time, the significance of the individual. In a narrower perspective, the client and the practitioner within the field of psychotherapy and mental health services are being increasingly hemmed in by economic forces. These magnify the power of institutions, systems, and impersonally determined criteria and reduce the importance of individuals, feelings, and experience. In one sense this weakens the person-centered approach; in another it ensures its continued existence and growth as a scientifically based system prizing individual worth.

ANNOTATED BIBLIOGRAPHY

Rogers, C. R. (1942). *Counseling and psychotherapy*. Boston: Houghton Mifflin.

This was the first book-length presentation of an approach to therapy relying entirely on the client's capacity to construct his or her own personality change. Chapter 2 is a slightly revised version of the talk given by Rogers at the University of Minnesota on December 11, 1940, which is regarded as the beginning of client-centered therapy.

Rogers, C. R. (1951). *Client-centered therapy*. Boston: Houghton Mifflin.

This book describes the orientation of the therapist, the therapeutic relationship as experienced by the client, and the process of therapy. It expands and develops the ideas expressed in the earlier book *Counseling and Psychotherapy*.

Rogers, C. R. (1961). *On becoming a person*. Boston: Houghton Mifflin.

Perhaps Rogers' best-known work, this book helped to make his personal style and positive philosophy known globally. The book includes an autobiographical chapter and sections on the helping relationship; the ways in which people grow in therapy; the fully functioning person; the place of research; the implications of client-centered principles for education, family life, communication, and creativity; and the impact on the individual of the growing power of the behavioral sciences.

Rogers, C. R. (1980). *A way of being*. Boston: Houghton Mifflin.

As the book jacket states, this volume "encompasses the changes that have occurred in Dr. Rogers' life and thought during the decade of the seventies in much the same way *On Becoming a Person* covered an earlier period of his life. The style is direct, personal, clear—the style that attracted so many readers to the earlier book." There is a large personal section, including chapters on what it means to Rogers to listen and to be heard and one on his experience of growing as he becomes older (he was 78 when the book came out), as well as important theoretical chapters. An appendix contains a chronological bibliography of Rogers' publications from 1930 to 1980.

Rogers, C. R. (1983). *Freedom to learn for the 80's*. Columbus, Ohio: Charles E. Merrill.

This is a substantial revision of *Freedom to Learn*, published in 1969. It was Rogers' last full-length book. One of the areas about which Rogers felt most passionately was learning. He was aware of the contrast between the marvelous capacity of children and adults to learn and to grow and the stultifying influence of most educational institutions. This book describes some of his own experiences in facilitating classroom learning and the experiments of others in promoting "responsible freedom."

CASE READINGS

Rogers, C. R. (1942). The case of Herbert Bryan. In C. R. Rogers, *Counseling and psychotherapy* (pp. 261–437). Boston: Houghton Mifflin.

This may be the first publication of a completely recorded and transcribed case of individual psychotherapy that illustrates the new nondirective approach. Rogers provides a summary of the client's feelings after each interview and additional commentary.

Rogers, C. R. (1954). The case of Mrs. Oak. In C. R. Rogers & R. F. Dymond (Eds.), *Psychotherapy and personality change.* Chicago: University of Chicago Press. [Also found in abridged form in C. R. Rogers (1961). *On becoming a person.* Boston: Houghton Mifflin. Also in D. Wedding & R. J. Corsini (Eds.) (1989). *Case Studies in psychotherapy.* Itasca, IL: F. E. Peacock.]

This is a classic case illustrating therapist empathy and client change in terms of Rogers' self-theory.

Rogers, C. R. (1977). A person-centered workshop: Its planning and fruition. In C. R. Rogers, *Carl Rogers on personal power* (pp. 149–185). New York: Dell.

This is an account of a 16-day intensive workshop in the person-centered approach. It is included because so much of the person-centered approach has been expressed in a group context and because it was so meaningful to Rogers, who said, "Of all the ventures in which I have ever been involved, this was the most thoroughly person-centered . . . it has been, for me, a thoroughgoing test of the value of person-centeredness."

Rogers, C. R. (1967). A silent young man. In C. R. Rogers, G. T. Gendlin, D. V. Kiesler, & C. Truax (Eds.), *The therapeutic relationship and its impact: A study of psychotherapy with schizophrenics* (pp. 401–406) Madison, WI: University of Wisconsin Press.

This case consists of two transcribed interviews that were conducted by Rogers as part of a year-long treatment of a very withdrawn hospitalized schizophrenic patient who was part of a client-centered research project on client-centered therapy with a schizophrenic population.

Rogers, C. R. (1986). The dilemmas of a South African white. *Person-Centered Review, 1,* 15–35.

This article includes the transcription of a 30-minute demonstration interview conducted by Rogers. It is followed by the client's and therapist's reactions, a presentation of the themes of the interview, and two follow-up statements from the client, the second one coming three years after the interview.

REFERENCES

Ansbacher, H. L. (1977). Individual psychology. In R. J. Corsini (Ed.), *Current Psychotherapies.* Itasca, IL: F. E. Peacock.

Axline, V. M. (1947). *Play therapy.* Boston: Houghton Mifflin.

Barrett-Lennard, G. T. (1962). Dimensions of therapist response as causal factors in therapeutic change. *Psychological Monographs, 76* (43, Whole No. 562).

Barrett-Lennard, G. T. (1986). The relationship inventory now: Issues and advances in theory, method, and use. In L. S. Greenberg & W. M. Pinsof (Eds.), *The psychotherapeutic process: A research handbook* (pp. 439–476). New York: Guilford.

Bergin, A. E., & Garfield, S. L. (Eds.). (1971). *Handbook of psychotherapy and behavior change: An empirical analysis.* New York: Wiley.

Butler, J. M., & Haigh, G. V. (1954). Changes in the relation between self-concepts and ideal concepts consequent upon client-centered counseling. In C. R. Rogers & R. F. Dymond (Eds.), *Psycho-*

therapy and personality change (pp. 55–75). Chicago: University of Chicago Press.

Cartwright, D. S. (1957). Annotated bibliography of research and theory construction in client-centered therapy. Journal of Counseling Psychology, 4, 82–100.

Dorfman, E. (1951). Play therapy. In C. R. Rogers, Client-centered therapy (pp. 235–277). Boston: Houghton Mifflin.

Gendlin, E. T. (1961). Experiencing: A variable in the process of therapeutic change. American Journal of Psychotherapy, 15, 233–245.

Gendlin, E. T. (1978). Focusing. New York: Everest House.

Goldstein, K. (1959). The organism: A holistic approach to biology derived from psychological data in man. New York: American Book. (Originally published 1934).

Holdstock, T. L., & Rogers, C. R. (1983). Person-centered theory. In R. J. Corsini & A. J. Marsella (Eds.), Personality theories, research and assessment. Itasca, IL: F. E. Peacock.

Lietaer, G. (1981). The client-centered approach in the seventies. Part I. A structured survey of the literature. Tijdschrift voor Psychotherapie (Dutch Journal of Psychotherapy), 7, 81–102.

Maslow, A. H. (1968). Toward a psychology of being (2nd ed.). Princeton, NJ: Van Nostrand.

Matson, F. W. (1969). Whatever became of the Third Force? American Association of Humanistic Psychology Newsletter, 6 (1), 1 & 14–15.

McGaw, W. H., Farson, R. E., & Rogers, C. R. (Producers) (1968). Journey into self [Film]. Berkeley: University of California Extension Media Center.

Meador, B. D., & Rogers, C. R. (1984). Person-centered therapy. In R. J. Corsini (Ed.), Current Psychotherapies (3rd ed.) (pp. 142–195). Itasca, IL: F. E. Peacock.

Mitchell, K. M., Bozarth, J. D., & Krauft, C. C. (1977). A reappraisal of the therapeutic effectiveness of accurate empathy, non-possessive warmth, and genuineness. In A. S. Gurman & A. M. Razin (Eds.), Effective psychotherapy:

A handbook of research (pp. 482–502). New York: Pergamon Press.

Orlinsky, D. E., & Howard, K. L. (1978). The relation of process to outcome in psychotherapy. In S. L. Garfield & A. E. Bergin (Eds.), Handbook of psychotherapy and behavior change: An empirical analysis (2nd ed.) (pp. 283-329). New York: Wiley.

Patterson, C. H. (1984). Empathy, warmth, and genuineness in psychotherapy: A review of reviews. Psychotherapy, 21, 431–438.

Porter, E. H., Jr. (1943). The development and evaluation of a measure of counseling interview procedures. Educational and Psychological Measurement, 3, 105–126, 215–238.

Raimy, V. C. (1948). Self-reference in counseling interviews. Journal of Consulting Psychology, 12, 153–163.

Rank, O. (1945). Will therapy, truth and reality. New York: Knopf.

Raskin, N. J. (1948). The development of nondirective therapy. Journal of Consulting Psychology, 12, 92–110.

Raskin, N. J. (1952). An objective study of the locus-of-evaluation factor in psychotherapy. In W. Wolfe & J. A. Pecker (Eds.), Success in psychotherapy (pp. 143–162). New York: Grune & Stratton.

Raskin, N. J. (1974). Studies of psychotherapeutic orientation: Ideology and practice. Research Monograph No. 1. Orlando, FL: American Academy of Psychotherapists.

Raskin, N. J. (1980). The concept of the self in client-centered therapy and the person-centered approach, 1940–1980. Talk at Northwestern University Psychiatry Grand Rounds. Chicago.

Raskin, N. J. (1985). Client-centered therapy. In S. J. Lynn and J. P. Garske (Eds.), Contemporary psychotherapies: Models and methods (pp. 155–190). Columbus, OH: Charles F. Merrill.

Raskin, N. J. (1986a). Client-centered group psychotherapy. Part I. Development of client-centered groups. Person-Centered Review, 1, 272–290.

Raskin, N. J. (1986b). Client-centered group psychotherapy. Part II. Research on client-centered groups. Person-Centered Review, 1, 389–408.

Raskin, N. J., & Zucconi, A. (1984). Peace, conflict resolution, and the person-centered approach. Program presented at the annual convention of the American Psychological Association, Toronto.

Rogers, C. R. (1931). Measuring personality adjustment in children nine to thirteen. New York: Teachers College, Columbia University, Bureau of Publications.

Rogers, C. R. (1937). The clinical psychologist's approach to personality problems. Family, 18, 233–243.

Rogers, C. R. (1939). The clinical treatment of the problem child. Boston: Houghton Mifflin.

Rogers, C. R. (1940). The process of therapy. Journal of Consulting Psychology, 4, 161–164.

Rogers, C. R. (1942). Counseling and psychotherapy. Boston: Houghton Mifflin.

Rogers, C. R. (1946). Significant aspects of client-centered therapy. American Psychologist, 1, 415–422.

Rogers, C. R. (1947). Some observations on the organization of personality. American Psychologist, 2, 358–368.

Rogers, C. R. (1948) Dealing with social tensions. New York: Hinds, Hayden & Eldredge.

Rogers, C. R. (1951). Client-centered therapy. Boston: Houghton Mifflin.

Rogers, C. R. (1957). The necessary and sufficient conditions of therapeutic personality change. Journal of Consulting Psychology, 21, 95–103.

Rogers, C. R. (1959a). The essence of psychotherapy: A client-centered view. Annals of Psychotherapy, 1, 51–57.

Rogers, C. R. (1959b). A theory of therapy, personality and interpersonal relationships as developed in the client-centered framework. In S. Koch (Ed.), Psychology: A study of science: Formulations of the person and the social context (pp. 184–256). New York: McGraw-Hill.

Rogers, C. R. (1961). On becoming a person. Boston: Houghton Mifflin.

Rogers, C. R. (1965). Client-centered therapy. Part I. In E. Shostrom (Ed.), Three approaches to psychotherapy. [Film]. Santa Ana, CA: Psychological Films.

Rogers, C. R. (1970). Carl Rogers on encounter groups. New York: Harper and Row.

Rogers, C. R. (1977). Carl Rogers on personal power. New York: Delacorte Press.

Rogers, C. R. (1980). A way of being. Boston: Houghton Mifflin.

Rogers, C. R. (1983). Freedom to learn for the 80's. Columbus, OH: Charles E. Merrill.

Rogers, C. R. (1984). A historic note— Gloria. In R. F. Levant & J. M. Shlien (Eds.), Client-centered therapy and the person-centered approach (pp. 423–425). New York: Praeger.

Rogers, C. R. (1986a). Client-centered therapy. In I. L. Kutash & A. Wolf (Eds.), Psychotherapist's casebook: Therapy and technique in practice (pp. 197–208). San Francisco: Jossey-Bass.

Rogers, C. R. (1986b). A comment from Carl Rogers. Person-Centered Review, 1, 3–5.

Rogers, C. R. (1986c). The dilemmas of a South African white. Person-Centered Review, 1, 15–35.

Rogers, C. R. (1986d). Measuring the self and its changes: A forward step in research. Archives of Humanistic Psychology, 1–13.

Rogers, C. R. (1986e). The Rust workshop: A personal overview. Journal of Humanistic Psychology, 26, 23–45.

Rogers, C. R. (1987). Inside the world of the Soviet professional. Journal of Humanistic Psychology, 27, 277–304.

Rogers, C. R., & Dymond, R. F. (Eds.). (1954). Psychotherapy and personality change. Chicago: University of Chicago Press.

Rogers, C. R., Gendlin, G. T., Kiesler, D. V., & Truax, C. (Eds.) (1967). The therapeutic relationship and its impact: A study of psychotherapy with schizophrenics. Madison: University of Wisconsin Press.

Rogers, C. R., & Haigh, G. (1983). I walk softly through life. Voices: The Art and Science of Psychotherapy, 18, 6–14.

Rogers, C. R., & Raskin, N. J. (1949). A coordinated research in psychotherapy. Journal of Consulting Psychology, 13, 149–220.

Rogers, C. R., & Ryback, D. (1984). One alternative to nuclear planetary suicide. In R. F. Levant & J. M. Shlien (Eds.), *Client-centered therapy and the person-centered approach: New directions in theory, research, and practice* (pp. 400–422). New York: Praeger.

Rogers, C. R., & Sanford, R. C. (1985). Client-centered psychotherapy. In H. I. Kaplan, B. J. Sadock, & A. M. Friedman (Eds.), *Comprehensive textbook of psychiatry (4th ed.)* (pp. 1374–1388). Baltimore: William & Wilkins.

Seeman, J. (1959). Toward a concept of personality integration. *American Psychologist, 14,* 794–797.

Seeman, J. (1984). The fully functioning person: Theory and research. In R. F. Levant & J. M. Shlien (Eds.), *Client-centered therapy and the person-centered approach: New directions in theory, research, and practice* (pp. 131–152). New York: Praeger.

Sheerer, E. T. (1949). An analysis of the relationship between acceptance of and respect for others in ten counseling cases. *Journal of Consulting Psychology, 13,* 169–175.

Shlien, J. M. (1964). Comparison of results with different forms of psychotherapy. *American Journal of Psychotherapy, 28,* 15–22.

Standal, S. (1954). *The need for positive regard: A contribution to client-centered theory.* Unpublished Ph.D. dissertation, University of Chicago.

Stephenson, W. V. (1953). *The study of behavior.* Chicago: University of Chicago Press.

Streich, E. R. (1951). The self-experience of the client-centered therapist. Unpublished paper. Chicago: The University of Chicago Counseling Center.

Tausch, R. (1978). Facilitative dimensions in interpersonal relations: Verifying the theoretical assumptions of Carl Rogers. *College Student Journal, 12,* 2–11.

ALBERT ELLIS

6

Rational-Emotive Therapy

ALBERT ELLIS

OVERVIEW

Rational-emotive therapy (RET), a theory of personality and a method of psychotherapy developed in the 1950s by Albert Ellis, a clinical psychologist, holds that when a highly charged emotional consequence (C) follows a significant activating event (A), A may seem to, but actually does not, cause C. Instead, emotional consequences are largely created by B—the individual's *belief system*. When an undesirable emotional consequence occurs, such as severe anxiety, this can usually be traced to the person's irrational beliefs, and when these beliefs are effectively disputed (at point D), by challenging them rationally and behaviorally, the disturbed consequences become minimal and largely cease to recur. From its inception, RET has viewed cognition and emotion integratively, with thought normally including and being sparked by some degree of desire or feeling and with feeling significantly including cognition (Ellis, 1962). It is therefore a comprehensive cognitive-affective behavioral theory and practice of psychotherapy.

BASIC CONCEPTS

The main propositions of rational-emotive therapy (RET) are:

1. People are born with a potential to be rational as well as irrational. They have predispositions to be self-preserving, to think about their thinking, to be creative, to be sensuous, to be interested in their fellows, to learn by mistakes, and to actualize their potentials for life and growth. They also have propensities to be self-destructive, to be short-range hedonists, to avoid thinking things through, to procrastinate, to repeat the same mistakes, to be superstitious, to be intolerant, to be perfectionistic and grandiose, and to avoid actualizing their potentials for growth.

2. People's tendency to irrational thinking, self-damaging habituations, wishful thinking, and intolerance is frequently exacerbated by their culture and their family group. Their suggestibility (or conditionability) is greatest during their early years, and

consequently they are then most influenced by family and social pressures.

3. Humans tend to perceive, think, emote, and behave simultaneously. They therefore, at one and the same time, are cognitive, conative, and motoric. They rarely act without also cognizing, because their present sensations or actions are apprehended in a network of prior experiences, memories, and conclusions. They seldom emote without thinking, because their feelings include, and are usually triggered by, an appraisal of a given situation and its importance. They rarely act without perceiving, thinking, and emoting, because these processes provide them with reasons for acting. Just as their "normal" behavior is a function of their perceiving, thinking, emoting, and acting, so, too, is their disturbed behavior. To understand self-defeating conduct, therefore, we had better understand how people perceive, think, emote, and act. To help them change their malfunctioning, it is usually desirable to use a variety of perceptual-cognitive, emotive-evocative, and behavioristic-reeducative methods in a full therapeutic armamentarium (Bernard, 1986; Dryden, 1984; Dryden & Trower, 1986; Ellis, 1971, 1977a, 1985a, 1987a, 1988; Ellis & Becker, 1982; Ellis & Bernard, 1983, 1985; Ellis & Grieger, 1986; Ellis & Dryden, 1987).

4. Although all the major psychotherapies employ a variety of cognitive, emotive, and desensitizing techniques, and although all (including many unscientific methods like witch doctoring) may help individuals who have faith and who work at applying them, they are probably not equally effective in terms of time and effort nor in terms of the elegance and length of the "solutions." Highly cognitive, active-directive, homework-assigning, and discipline-oriented therapies like RET are likely to be more effective, usually in briefer periods and with fewer sessions, than therapies that include less cognitive-active-disciplining methodologies.

5. Rational-emotive therapists do not believe a warm relationship between counselee and counselor is a necessary or a sufficient condition for effective personality change. They believe it is desirable for therapists to fully accept clients but criticize and point out the deficiencies of their *behavior.* RET therapists accept clients as fallible humans without necessarily giving *personal* warmth. They may use a variety of impersonal therapeutic methods, including didactic discussion, behavior modification, bibliotherapy, audiovisual aids, and activity-oriented homework assignments. To keep clients from becoming and remaining unduly dependent, RET therapists often deliberately use hardheaded methods of convincing clients that they had damned well better resort to more self-discipline.

6. Rational-emotive therapists use roleplaying, assertion training, desensitization, humor, operant conditioning, suggestion, support, and a whole bag of other "tricks." As A. A. Lazarus (1981) points out in presenting "multimodal" therapy, such wide-ranging methods are most effective in helping the client achieve deep-seated cognitive change. RET is not really oriented toward symptom removal, except when it seems that this is the only kind of change likely to be accomplished with clients. It is primarily designed to induce people to examine and change some of their most basic values—particularly those values that keep them disturbance prone. If clients have a serious fear of failing on the job, the rational-emotive therapist does

not merely help them to give up this particular symptom. Instead, the therapist usually tries to show them how to minimize their basic awfulizing tendencies. The usual goal of RET, therefore, is not merely to eliminate clients' presenting symptoms but to help rid them of other symptoms as well and, more importantly, to modify their underlying symptom-creating propensities. There are really two basic forms of RET: (a) general RET, which is almost synonymous with cognitive-behavior therapy; and (b) preferential RET, which includes general RET but which also emphasizes cognitive or philosophic restructuring and which strives for the most elegant solution to emotional disturbance. General RET tends to teach clients rational or appropriate behaviors. Preferential RET teaches them how to dispute irrational ideas and inappropriate behaviors and to internalize rules of logic and scientific method.

7. RET holds that virtually all serious emotional problems directly stem from magical, empirically unvalidatable thinking and that if disturbance-creating ideas are vigorously disputed by logico-empirical thinking, they can be eliminated or minimized and will ultimately cease to reoccur. No matter how defective people's heredity may be, and no matter what trauma they may have experienced, the main reason they now overreact or underreact to obnoxious stimuli (at point A) is that they now have some dogmatic, irrational, unexamined beliefs (at point B). Because these beliefs are unrealistic, they will not withstand objective scrutiny. They are essentially deifications or devilifications of themselves or others, and when empirically checked and logically assailed, they tend to evaporate. Thus, a woman with severe emotional difficulties does not merely believe it is undesirable if her lover is rejecting. She tends to believe, also, that (a) it is awful; (b) she cannot stand it; (c) she should not, must not be rejected; (d) she will never be accepted by any desirable partner; (e) she is a worthless person because one lover has rejected her; and (f) she deserves to be damned for being so worthless. Such common covert hypotheses are nonsensical and devoid of empirical referents. They can be elicited and demolished by any scientist worth his or her salt, and the rational-emotive therapist is exactly that: an exposing and nonsense-annihilating scientist.

8. Rational-emotive psychology asserts that insights often do not lead to major personality change because, at best, they help people see that they do have emotional problems and that these problems have dynamic antecedents—presumably in the experiences that occurred during childhood. According to RET theory, this kind of insight is largely misleading. It is not the activating events (A) of people's lives that "cause" dysfunctional emotional consequences (C); it is that they interpret these events unrealistically and therefore have irrational beliefs (B) about them. The "real" cause of upsets, therefore, is themselves and not what happens to them (even though the experiences obviously have some influence over what they think and feel). In RET, insight number 1 —namely, that the person's self-defeating behavior is related to antecedent and understandable causes—is duly stressed, but clients are led to see these antecedents largely in terms of their own beliefs and not in terms of past or present activating events. Their therapist, moreover, also presses them to see and to employ additional insights.

Insight number 2 is the understanding that although they became emotionally disturbed (or, more accurately, *made* themselves disturbed) in the past, they are *now* upset because they *keep indoctrinating themselves* with the same kind of magical beliefs. These beliefs do not continue because people were once "conditioned" and so hold them "automatically." No! They still, here and now, *actively reinforce them* by mixed-up thinking and foolish actions (or inactions) and it is their own present active self-propagandizations that truly keep them alive. Unless they fully admit and face their own responsibilities for the continuation of these irrational beliefs, it is unlikely they will uproot them.

Insight number 3 is people's acknowledgment that because it is their own tendency to think crookedly that created emotional malfunctioning and that because it is their own continuous reindoctrinations and habituations that keep this magical thinking extant, *only hard work and practice* will correct these irrational beliefs—and keep them corrected. They had better admit that insights 1 and 2 are not enough! Only repeated rethinking of their irrational beliefs and repeated actions designed to undo them are likely to extinguish or minimize them.

OTHER SYSTEMS

RET, which is different from most other schools of psychotherapy, largely eschews free association, gathering of material about the client's past history, and dream analysis, all of which are considered to be mostly sidetracking and thus ineffectual. RET is not concerned with the presumable sexual origins of disturbance or with the Oedipus complex. When transference does

occur in therapy, the rational therapist is likely to attack it, showing clients that transference phenomena tend to arise from the irrational belief that they must be loved by the therapist (and others) and that they had better surrender this foolish belief. Although RET practitioners are much closer to modern neoanalytic schools, such as those of Karen Horney, Erich Fromm, Wilhelm Stekel, Harry Stack Sullivan, and Franz Alexander, than to the Freudian school, they employ considerably more persuasion, philosophical analysis, homework activity assignments, and other directive techniques than practitioners of these schools generally use.

RET overlaps significantly with Adlerian theory, but departs from the Adlerian practices of stressing early childhood memories, making considerable use of dream material, and insisting that social interest is the heart of therapeutic effectiveness. RET is much more specific than Adler's Individual Psychology in disclosing, analyzing, and attacking the concrete internalized beliefs that clients keep telling themselves to create and perpetuate their disturbance, and so it is closer in this respect to general semantic theory and philosophical analysis than it is to Individual Psychology.

Adler contended that people have basic fictional premises and goals and that they generally proceed quite logically on the basis of these false hypotheses. RET, on the other hand, holds that people, when disturbed, may have both irrational premises and illogical deductions from these premises. Thus, in Individual Psychology, a male who has the unrealistic premise that he *should* be the king of the universe, but actually has only mediocre abilities, is shown that he is "logically" concluding that he is an utterly inferior person. But in RET this same individual, with the same irrational premise, is shown that in addition to this "logical" deduction he may also be making several other illogical conclusions, for example, (a) he should be king of the universe because he was once king of his own family; (b) his parents will be impressed by him only if he is outstandingly achieving and therefore he must achieve outstandingly; (c) if he cannot be king of the universe, he might as well do nothing and get nowhere in life; and (d) he deserves to suffer for not being the noble king that he should be.

RET has much in common with parts of the Jungian therapeutic outlook, especially in that it views clients holistically rather than only analytically, holds that the goal of therapy would better be growth and achievement of potential as well as relief of disturbed symptoms, and emphasizes individuality. In practice, however, RET deviates radically from Jungian treatment because Jungians are fairly psychoanalytic and are preoccupied with dreams, fantasies, symbol productions, and the mythological or archetypal contents of their clients' thinking—most of which the RET practitioner deems a waste of time, given that these techniques are not too effective in showing clients what their irrational philosophic assumptions are and how these can be radically challenged and changed.

RET is in close agreement with person-centered or relationship therapy in one—and perhaps only one— way: They both emphasize what Stanley Standal and Carl Rogers call unconditional positive regard and what in rational-emotive psychology is called full acceptance or tolerance. Harry Bone (1968) points out that both

RET and client-centered therapy have basically the same goal: helping people to refuse to condemn themselves even though they may be utterly unenthusiastic about some of their behavior. Rational therapists differ radically from the Rogerian therapist in that they actively teach (a) that blaming is the core of emotional disturbance; (b) that it leads to dreadful results; (c) that it is possible, although difficult, for humans to learn to avoid rating themselves even while continuing to rate their performances; and (d) that they can give up self-rating by challenging their magic-based (musturbatory), self-evaluating assumptions and by deliberately risking (through homework activity assignments) possible failures and rejections. The rational-emotive practitioner is more persuading, more didactic, and more information giving than the person-centered practitioner, and in these respects they are probably almost at opposite ends of the therapeutic continuum.

RET is in many respects an existential phenomenologically oriented therapy because rational-emotive goals overlap with the usual existentialist goals of helping clients to define their own freedom, cultivate individuality, live in dialogue with others, accept their experiencing as highly important, be fully present in the immediacy of the moment, and learn to accept limits in life. Many who call themselves existential therapists, however, are rather anti-intellectual, prejudiced against the technology of therapy, and confusingly nondirective, while RET makes much use of incisive logical analysis, clear-cut techniques (including behavior modification procedures), and a great deal of directiveness and teaching by the therapist.

RET has much in common with behavior modification. Many behavior therapists, however, are mainly concerned with symptom removal and ignore the cognitive aspects of conditioning and deconditioning. RET is therefore closer to broad-spectrum or multimodal behavior modifiers—such as A. T. Beck (1976), M. R. Goldfried and G. C. Davison (1976), A. A. Lazarus (1981), M. J. Mahoney (1985), and D. H. Meichenbaum (1977)—than to therapists who mainly stick to classical forms of operant conditioning or symptom desensitization.

HISTORY

PRECURSORS

The philosophic origins of rational-emotive therapy (RET) go back to the Stoic philosophers, particularly Epictetus and Marcus Aurelius. Although most early Stoic writings have been lost, their gist has come down to us through Epictetus, who in the first century A.D. wrote in *The Enchiridion*, "People are disturbed not by things, but by the view which they take of them."

The modern psychotherapist who was the main precursor of RET was Alfred Adler. "I am convinced," he stated, "that *a person's behavior springs from his ideas*" (1964a, italics in original). And:

The individual . . . does not relate himself to the outside world in a predetermined manner, as is often assumed. He relates himself always according to his own interpretation of himself and of his present problem. . . . It is his attitude toward life which determines his relationship to the outside world. (1964b)

Adler (1931) put the A-B-C or S-O-R theory of human disturbance very neatly:

No experience is a cause of success or failure. We do not suffer from the shock of our experiences—the so-called *trauma*—but we make out of them just what suits our purposes. We are *self-determined* by the meaning we give to our experiences; and there is probably something of a mistake always involved when we take particular experiences as the basis of our future life. Meanings are not determined by situations, but we determine ourselves by the meanings we give to situations.

In his first book on individual psychology, Adler's motto was *Omnia ex opionione suspensa sunt* (Everything depends on opinion). It would be hard to state one of the essential tenets of RET more succinctly and accurately.

Other important precursors of the rational-emotive approach are Paul Dubois, Jules Dejerine, and Ernest Gaukler, who used persuasive forms of psychotherapy with their clients. Alexander Herzberg was one of the inventors of homework assignments. Hippolyte Bernheim, Andrew Salter, and a host of other therapists have employed hypnosis and suggestion in a highly active-directive manner. Frederick Thorne created what he once called directive therapy. Franz Alexander, Thomas French, John Dollard, Neal Miller, Wilhelm Stekel, and Lewis Wolberg all practiced forms of psychoanalytically oriented psychotherapy that actually diverged so far in practice from the mainstays of Freudian theory that they more properly can be classified in the active-directive therapy column and can in many ways be identified with RET.

In addition, a large number of individuals during the early 1950s, when RET was first being formulated, independently began to arrive at some theories and methodologies that significantly overlap with the methods outlined by Ellis (1962, 1971). These include Eric Berne, Rogelio Diaz-Guerrero, Jerome Frank, George Kelly, Abraham Low, E. Lakin Phillips, Julian Rotter, and Joseph Wolpe.

BEGINNINGS

After practicing classical psychoanalysis and psychoanalytically oriented psychotherapy for several years, during the late 1940s and early 1950s, Ellis discovered that no matter how much insight his clients gained or how well they seemed to understand the events of their early childhood, they rarely lost their symptoms and they still retained strong tendencies to create new ones. He eventually realized this was because they were not merely indoctrinated with irrational, mistaken ideas of their own worthlessness when they were very young, but that they actively *reindoctrinated themselves* with the original taboos, superstitions, and irrationalities they had picked up (and *invented* as well as easily learned) during childhood.

Ellis also discovered that as he pressed his clients to surrender the few basic irrational premises that invariably seemed to underlie their disturbed symptoms, they often tended to resist giving up these ideas. This was not, as the Freudians hypothesized, because they hated the therapist, or wanted to destroy themselves, or were still resisting parent images, but because they *naturally,* one might say *normally,* tended to musturbate, to absolutistically demand (a) that they do well and win others' approval, (b) that people act considerately and fairly, and (c) that environmental conditions be unfrustrating and gratifying. Ellis concluded that humans are *self-talking* and *self-evaluating* and *self-sustaining.* They frequently take simple preferences—such as desires for love, approval, success, and pleasure—and misleadingly define them as needs. They thereby create "emotional" difficulties.

Ellis thus found that people are not exclusively the products of social learning but rather that their so-called pathological symptoms are the result of biosocial learning. *Because they are human* (and not because they are reared in specific family-centered ways), they tend to have strong, irrational, empirically unvalidatable ideas; and as long as they hold on to these ideas—which nearly all of them fairly consistently do—they tend to be what is commonly called "neurotic." These main irrational ideologies are not infinitely varied or hard to discover. They can be listed under a few simple headings and once understood, they can be quickly uncovered by using RET.

Ellis also discovered these irrational assumptions were so biosocially deep-rooted and so difficult for people to surrender that weak methods were unlikely to budge them. Passive, non-directive methodologies (such as reflection of feeling and free association) rarely changed them. Warmth and support often helped clients live more "happily" with unrealistic notions. Suggestion or "positive thinking" sometimes enabled them to cover up and live more "successfully" with underlying negative self-evaluations. Abreaction and catharsis frequently helped them to feel better but tended to reinforce rather than eliminate their demands. Classic desensitizing sometimes relieved clients of anxieties and phobias but did not elegantly undermine their anxiety-arousing, phobia-creating fundamental philosophies.

What would work effectively, Ellis

found in the early days of RET, was an active-directive, cognitive-emotive-behavioristic attack on major self-defeating musts and commands. The essence of effective psychotherapy according to RET is full tolerance of people *as individuals* combined with a campaign against their self-defeating *ideas, traits, and performances.*

As Ellis abandoned his previous psychoanalytic approaches to become much more philosophical and behavioral, he obtained significantly better results (Ellis, 1962). Other therapists who began to employ RET in their own practice also found that when a difficult client, with whom various methods had been ineffectively employed, switched to rational-emotive procedures, more progress was made in a few weeks than in months or years of prior treatment (Ellis, 1985a, 1988; Ellis & Dryden, 1987).

CURRENT STATUS

The Institute for Rational-Emotive Therapy, Inc., a nonprofit scientific and educational organization, was founded in 1959 to teach the principles of rational living. With headquarters in New York City and branches in several cities in the United States and other countries, it disseminates the rational-emotive approach, through (1) adult education courses in the principles of rational living, (2) postgraduate training programs, (3) moderately priced clinics for individual or group therapy, (4) special workshops, seminars, practica, and training marathons for professionals, offered regularly in various parts of the world, and (5) the publication of books, monographs, pamphlets, and a journal, the *Journal of Rational-Emotive Therapy*, in which the latest developments in RET are published.

The Institute for Rational-Emotive Therapy, 45 East 65th Street, New York, N.Y. 10021, has a register of hundreds of psychotherapists who have received training in RET. In addition, hundreds of other therapists follow primarily RET principles, and a still greater number use some of the major aspects of RET in their work. Cognitive restructuring, employed by almost all cognitive-behavior therapists today, stems mainly from RET. But RET also includes several other emotive and behavioral methods.

Research Studies

Many experiments have validated the main therapeutic hypotheses of RET. Ellis found the vast majority of these studies support important RET contentions. For example, (a) clients tend to receive more effective help from a highly active-directive, strongly disputing psychotherapeutic approach than from a more passive approach; (b) efficient therapy includes activity-oriented homework assignments; (c) people largely choose to disturb themselves and can intentionally choose to surrender these disturbances; (d) a great deal of psychotherapy consists of cognitive diversion or distraction, which can be used for significant, if often inelegant, personality change; (e) helping clients modify their beliefs helps them to make significant changes, which are more enduring than those achieved through other methods of therapy; and (f) many effective methods of cognitive therapy exist, including modeling, roleplaying, skill training, and problem solving.

In addition, hundreds of clinical and research papers have appeared that present empirical evidence of the validity of RET's main theories of personality. Most of the experimental studies in this area have been done by psychologists who have no stake in substantiating RET. Many of these studies are reviewed and listed in Ellis and Whiteley (1979). These research studies substantiate the following hypotheses: (a) Human thinking and emotion do not constitute two disparate or different processes, but significantly overlap. (b) Although activating events (A) significantly contribute to emotional and behavioral consequences (C), people's beliefs (B) about A more importantly and more directly "cause" C. (c) The kinds of things people say to themselves, as well as the form in which they say these things, significantly affect their emotions and behavior and often lead them to feel emotionally disturbed. (d) Humans not only think and think about their thinking but also think about thinking about their thinking. Whenever they have strong feelings at C (consequence) after something has happened in their lives at A (activating events), they tend to make C into a new A—to perceive and think about their emotions (and emotional disturbances) and thereby significantly escalate, diminish, or otherwise modify these emotions and create new ones. (e) People not only think about what happens to them in words, phrases, and sentences but also do so by images, fantasies, dreams, and other kinds of representations. These nonverbal cognitions contribute significantly to their emotions and behaviors and can be used to change such behaviors. (f) Just as cognitions importantly contribute to emotions and actions, emotions also significantly contribute to or "cause" cognitions and actions, and actions contribute to or "cause" cognitions and emotions. When people change one of these three modalities of behav-

ing they concomitantly tend to change the other two.

PERSONALITY

THEORY OF PERSONALITY

Physiological Basis of Personality

Unlike most modern systems of psychotherapy, RET emphasizes the biological aspects of human personality. Obliquely, most other systems do this, too, given that they say, at bottom, something like this: "Humans are easily influenced by their parents during early childhood and thereafter remain similarly influenced for the rest of their lives, unless some intervention, such as years of psychotherapy, occurs to enable them to give up this early ingrained influenceability and to start thinking much more independently." These psychotherapeutic systems implicitly state an "environmentalist's" position, which is really physiologically and genetically based, because only a *special, innately predisposed* kind of animal would be so prone to be "environmentally determined."

Although RET holds that people have vast untapped resources for growth and that they are in many important ways able to change their social and personal destinies, it also holds that they have exceptionally powerful innate tendencies to think irrationally and to harm themselves (Ellis, 1976b).

Most of these human tendencies may be summarized by stating that humans are born with an exceptionally strong tendency to want, to "need," and to roundly condemn (1) themselves, (2) others, and (3) the world when they do not immediately get what they supposedly "need." They consequently think "childishly" (or "humanly") all their lives and are able only with enormous difficulty to achieve and maintain "mature" or realistic behavior. This is not to deny, as Abraham Maslow and Carl Rogers have pointed out, that humans have impressive self-actualizing capacities. They do, and these are strong inborn propensities, too. But, alas, they frequently defeat themselves by their inborn and acquired self-sabotaging ways.

Social Aspects of Personality

Humans are reared in social groups and spend much of their lives trying to impress, live up to the expectations of, and outdo the performances of other people. On the surface, they are "ego-oriented," "identity seeking," or "self-centered." Even more importantly, however, they usually define their "selves" as "good" or "worthwhile" when they are successfully other-directed—that is, when they believe that others accept and approve of them. It is realistic and sane for people to find or fulfill "themselves" in their interpersonal relations and to have a considerable amount of what Adler calls "social interest." For, as John Donne beautifully expressed it, practically no one is an island. The healthy individual *does* find it enjoyable to love and be loved by significant others and to relate reasonably well to almost everyone he or she encounters. In fact, the better one's interpersonal relations are, the happier one is likely to be.

However, what we call *emotional disturbance* is frequently associated with people's caring *too much* about what others think and stems from their believing they can accept themselves *only* if others think well of them. When disturbed, they escalate their desire for others' approval, and the practical advantages that normally go with such approval, into an absolutistic *dire need* to be liked, and, doing this, they can hardly avoid becoming anxious and prone to depression (Bernard, 1986; Ellis, 1962, 1987a, 1988; Ellis & Dryden, 1987; Ellis & Harper, 1975). Given that we have our being-in-the-world, as the existentialists point out, it is quite *important* that others to some degree value us. But it is not *all*-important that they regard us very highly, and it is our tendency to exaggerate the importance of others' acceptance that often causes our inappropriate emotions (Ellis 1985a, 1985b; Ellis & Becker, 1982, Ellis & Dryden, 1987).

Psychological Aspects of Personality

How, specifically, do people become psychologically disordered? According to RET, they usually needlessly upset themselves as follows:

When individuals feel upset at point C, after experiencing an obnoxious occurrence at point A, they almost always convince themselves of highly inappropriate, irrational beliefs (iB's), such as: "I *can't stand* this Activating Event! It is *awful* that it exists! It *shouldn't* exist! I am a *worthless person* for not being able to ward it off or immediately get rid of it. And you are a louse for inflicting it on me!" This set of beliefs is irrational because: (a) People *can* stand the noxious activating event, even though they may never like it and (b) it is hardly *awful* because *awful* is an essentially undefinable term, with surplus meaning and no empirical referent. By calling the noxious activating event *awful*, the disturbed individual means (1) it is highly inconvenient, and (2) it is *more than* inconvenient, disadvantageous, and unbeneficial. But what noxious stimulus can be, in point of fact, *more than* inconvenient, disadvantageous, and unbeneficial? (c) By holding that the noxious happening in their lives *should not* exist, people really contend that they have godly power and that whatever they *want* not to exist *must* not. This hypothesis is, to say the least, highly unprovable! (d) By contending that they are *worthless persons* because they have not been able to ward off an unfortunate activating event, people hold that they should be able to control the universe and that because they are not succeeding in doing what they cannot do, they are obviously worthless. They thereby posit *two* unvalidatable premises.

The basic tenet of RET is that emotional *upsets*, as distinguished from feelings of sorrow, regret, annoyance, and frustrations, are caused by irrational beliefs. These beliefs are irrational because they magically insist that something in the universe *should*, *ought*, or *must* be different from the way it indubitably is. Although these irrational beliefs are ostensibly connected with reality (the activating events at point *A*), they are magical ideas beyond the realm of empiricism and are established by arbitrary fiat. They generally take the form of the statement, "Because I *want* something, it is not only desirable or preferable that it exist, but it absolutely *should*, and it is *awful* when it doesn't!" No such proposition, obviously, can ever be validated, and yet, oddly enough, such propositions are devoutly held, every day, by literally billions of human beings. That is how incredibly disturbance-prone people are!

Once people become emotionally upset—or, rather, upset themselves!— another peculiar thing frequently occurs. Most of the time, they know they are anxious, depressed, or otherwise agitated, and also generally know that their symptoms are undesirable and (in our culture) socially disapproved. For who approves or respects highly agitated or "crazy" people? They therefore make their emotional consequence (C) or symptom into another activating event (A^2) and create a secondary symptom (C^2) about this new A!

Thus, if you originally start with something like (A): "I did poorly on my job today." (B): "Isn't that horrible!" you will wind up with (C): feelings of anxiety, worthlessness, and depression. You may now start all over with (A^2): "I feel anxious and depressed, and worthless!" (B^2): "Isn't *that* horrible!" Now you end up with (C^2): even greater feelings of anxiety, worthlessness, and depression. In other words, once you become anxious, you frequently make yourself anxious about *being* anxious; once you become depressed, you make yourself depressed about *being* depressed; and so on. You now have two consequences or symptoms for the price of one, and you often go around and around, in a vicious cycle of (a) condemning yourself for doing poorly at some task, (b) feeling guilty or depressed because of this self-condemnation, (c) condemning yourself for your feelings of guilt and depression, (d) condemning yourself for condemning yourself, (e) condemning yourself for seeing that you condemn yourself and for still not stopping condemning yourself, (f) condemning yourself for going for psychotherapeutic help and still not getting better, (g) condemning yourself for being more disturbed than other individuals, (h) concluding that you are indubitably hopelessly disturbed and that nothing can be done about it; and so on, in an endless spiral.

No matter what your original damning is about—and it hardly matters what it is about, because the activating event (A) is not really that important—you eventually tend to end up with a chain of disturbed reactions only obliquely related to the original "traumatic events" of your life. That is why the psychoanalytic psychotherapies are quite misleading—they wrongly emphasize these "traumatic events" rather than your self-condemnatory attitudes about these events—and that is why these therapies are virtually powerless to help you with any secondary disturbance, such as anxiety about being anxious. Most major psychotherapies also concentrate either on A, the activating events in the individual's life, or on C, the emotional consequences experienced subsequent to the occurrence of these events, and rarely consider B, the belief system, which is the vital factor in the creation of disturbance.

Even assuming, moreover, that activating events and emotional consequences are important, there is not too much we can do by concentrating our therapeutic attention on these two things. The activating events belong to the past by the time we see clients. Sometimes it was many years ago that they were criticized by their parents, rejected by their mates, or lost a series of jobs. There is nothing that anyone can do to change those prior happenings.

As for clients' present feelings, the more we focus on them, the worse they are likely to feel. If we keep talking about their anxiety, getting them to reexperience this feeling, they can easily become more anxious. The most logical point to interrupt their disturbed process is to get them to focus on their anxiety-creating belief system—point B.

If, for example, a male client feels anxious during a therapy session and the therapist reassures him that there is nothing for him to be anxious about, he may become more anxious or may achieve a palliative "solution" to his problem by convincing himself, "I am afraid that I will act foolishly right here and now, and wouldn't that be awful! No, it really wouldn't be awful, because *this* therapist will accept me, anyway."

Or the therapist can concentrate on the activating events in the client's life, which are presumably making him anxious—by, for instance, showing him that his mother used to point out his deficiencies in making an impression on others, that he was always afraid his teachers would criticize him for reciting poorly, that he is still afraid of speaking to authority figures who might disapprove of him, and that, *therefore*, because of all his prior and present fears, in situations A^1, A^2, A^3 ... A^n, he is *now* anxious with the therapist. Whereupon the client might convince himself, "Ah! Now I see that I am generally anxious when I am faced with authority figures. No wonder I am anxious even with my own therapist!" In which case, he might feel much better and temporarily lose his anxiety.

It would be much better for the therapist to show this client that he was anxious as a child and is still anxious with various kinds of authority figures not because they are authorities or do have some power over him, but because he has always believed, and still believes, that he *must* be approved, that it is *awful* when an authority figure disapproves of him, and that he will be destroyed if he is criticized.

Whereupon the anxious client would tend to do two things: (a) He would become diverted from A (criticism by an authority figure) and from C (his feelings of anxiety) to a consideration of B (his irrational belief system). This diversion would help him become immediately nonanxious—for when he is focusing on "What am I telling myself (at B) to make myself anxious" he cannot too easily focus upon the self-defeating, useless thought, "Wouldn't it be terrible if I said something stupid to my therapist and if even he disapproved of me!" (b) He would begin actively to dispute (at point D) his anxiety-creating irrational beliefs, and not only could he then temporarily change them (by convincing himself, "It would be unfortunate if I said something stupid to my therapist and he disapproved of me, but it would hardly be terrible or catastrophic!"), but he would also tend to have a much weaker allegiance to these self-defeating beliefs the next time he was with an authority figure and risked criticism by this individual. So he would obtain, by the therapist's getting him to focus primarily on B rather than on A and C, curative and preventive, rather than palliative, results in connection with his anxiety.

This is the basic personality theory of RET: Human beings largely (although not entirely) create their own emotional consequences. They are born with a distinct proneness to do so and learn, through social conditioning, to exacerbate (rather than to minimize) that proneness. They nonetheless have considerable ability to understand what they are foolishly believing to cause their distress (because they have a unique talent for thinking about their thinking) and to train themselves to change their self-sabotaging beliefs (because they also have a unique capacity for self-discipline or self-reconditioning). If they think and work hard at understanding and contradicting their musturbatory belief systems, they can make amazing palliative, curative, and preventive changes in their disturbance-creating tendencies. And if they are helped to zero in on their crooked thinking and inappropriate emoting and behaving by a highly active-directive, didactic, philosophic, homework-assigning therapist, they are more likely to change their symptom-creating beliefs than if they mainly work with a dynamically oriented, client-centered, conventional existentialist, or classical behavior-modification-centered therapist.

Although RET is mainly a theory of personality change, it is also a personality theory in its own right (Ellis, 1978, 1985a, 1987a; Ellis & Dryden, 1987). Many of its hypotheses have been validated by scores of controlled experiments, as indicated in the "Evaluation" section of this chapter.

VARIETY OF CONCEPTS

RET largely tends to agree with Sigmund Freud that the pleasure principle (or short-range hedonism) tends to run most people's lives; with Karen Horney and Erich Fromm that cultural influences as well as early family influences tend to play a significant part in bolstering people's irrational thinking; with Alfred Adler that fictitious goals tend to order and to run human lives; with Knight Dunlap and Gordon Allport that once individuals begin to think and act in a certain manner, they find it very difficult to think or act differently, even when they want strongly to do so; with Ivan Pavlov that humans' large cerebral cortices provides them with a secondary signaling system through which they often become cognitively conditioned; with Jerome Frank that people are exceptionally prone to the influence of suggestion; with Jean Piaget that active teaching is much more effective than passive learning; with Freud and his daughter Anna that people frequently refuse to acknowledge their mistakes and resort to defenses and rationalizations that cover up underlying feelings of shame and self-deprecation; and with Abraham Maslow and Carl Rogers that humans, however disturbed they may be, have great untapped growth forces.

On the other hand, RET has serious objections to certain aspects of many popular personality theories:

1. It opposes the Freudian concept that people have clear-cut libidinous instincts, which if thwarted must lead to emotional disturbances. It also objects to the views of William Glasser that all humans have needs to be approved and to succeed—and that if these are blocked, they cannot possibly accept themselves or be happy. RET, instead, thinks in terms of human *desires*, which only become *needs* or *necessities* when people foolishly *define* them as such.

2. RET places the Oedipus complex as a relatively minor subheading under people's major irrational belief that they absolutely have to receive the approval of their parents (and others), that they *must not* fail (at lusting or almost anything else), and that when they are disapproved and when they fail, they are totally worthless. Virtually all so-called sexual problems—such as impotence, frigidity, compulsive homosexuality, and nymphomania—partly result from people's irrational beliefs that they *utterly need* approval and success.

3. RET holds that humans' environment, particularly childhood parental environment, *reaffirms* but does not *create* strong tendencies to think irrationally and to over- or underemote. Parents and culture usually teach children standards and values, but they do not usually teach them absolutistic *musts* about these values. People *naturally* and *easily* add rigid commands to socially imbibed standards. Otherwise they would rarely make themselves neurotic.

4. RET looks skeptically at anything mystical, devout, transpersonal, or magical, when these terms are used in the strict sense. It believes that reason itself is limited, ungodlike, and unabsolute (Ellis, 1962, 1985c). It holds that humans may in some ways transcend themselves or experience altered states of consciousness—for example, hypnosis—that may enhance their ability to know themselves and the world and to solve some of their problems. But it does not believe that people can transcend their humanness and become in any way more than or greater than human—that is, superhuman. They can become more adept, competent, and intelligent, but they still remain *fallible* and in no way godly. RET especially holds that minimal disturbance is correlated with people's surrendering all pretensions to superhumanness and with fully accepting their own and the world's intrinsic limitations.

5. RET believes that no part of a human is to be reified into an entity called the unconscious, although it holds that people have many thoughts, feelings, and even acts of which they are unaware. These "unconscious" thoughts and feelings are, for the most part, slightly below the level of consciousness, are not often deeply repressed, and can usually be brought to

consciousness by some brief, incisive probing. Thus, if a wife is more angry at her husband than she is aware of, and if her anger is motivated by the unconscious grandiose thought, "After all I've done for him, he *should be* having sex with me more frequently!" a rational-emotive therapist (who suspects these unconscious feelings and thoughts) can usually induce her to (a) *hypothesize* that she is angry with her husband and look for some evidence with which to test that hypothesis and (b) *check* herself for grandiose thinking whenever she feels angry. In the majority of instances, without resorting to free association, dream analysis, analyzing the transference relationship, hypnosis, or other presumably "depth-centered" techniques for revealing unconscious thoughts and feelings, rational-emotive practitioners can reveal these in short order—sometimes in a matter of minutes. They show the client her unconsciously held attitudes, beliefs, and values and, in addition, teach the client how to bring her hidden ideas to consciousness and to actively dispute them when they are inimical to her appropriately emoting and behaving.

People often see how RET differs significantly from psychoanalysis, Rogerianism, Gestalt therapy, and orthodox behavior therapy but have difficulty seeing how it differs from more closely related schools, such as Adler's Individual Psychology. RET agrees with almost all of Adlerian theory but has a much more hardheaded and behavior-oriented practice (Dryden, 1984; Ellis, 1985a, 1988; Ellis & Bernard, 1983, 1985; Ellis & Dryden, 1987, Ellis, McInerney, DiGiuseppe, & Yeager, 1988). It also minimizes most of the Adlerian emphasis on early childhood memories, life-style, and the importance of birth order.

RET is similar to Jay Haley's strategic therapy in that it is quite active-directive, often gives out homework assignments, and tries to change the system (such as the family system in which clients live) as well as help clients to change themselves. However, it favors direct, clear, and down-to-earth persuasive methods rather than the indirect, clever, and frequently paradoxical methods that Haley (and other strategic therapists) tend to use. Moreover, RET is far more cognitive, disputational, educational, emotive, and behavioral than strategic therapy.

RET overlaps with Beck's (1976) cognitive therapy (CT) in several ways: (a) It usually disputes clients' irrational beliefs more actively, directly, quickly, and forcefully than does CT. (b) It emphasizes absolutist musts more than CT and holds that all the major disturbance-creating irrationalities implicitly stem from dogmatic shoulds and musts. (c) It uses psychoeducational approaches—such as books, pamphlets, audiovisual cassettes, talks, and workshops—as intrinsic elements and stresses their use more than does CT. (d) It clearly distinguishes between appropriate negative feelings (e.g., sadness and frustration) and inappropriate negative feelings (e.g., depression and hostility). (e) RET routinely emphasizes several emotive-evocative methods—such as shame-attacking exercises, rational-emotive imagery, and *strong* self-statements and self-dialogues—that CT ignores. (f) RET favors in vivo desensitization, preferably done implosively, while CT does not. (g) RET often uses penalties as well as reinforcements to help people do their homework (Ellis, 1985a, 1985b, 1987b; Ellis & Dryden, 1987; Ellis, McInerney, DiGiuseppe & Yeager, 1988).

PSYCHOTHERAPY

THEORY OF PSYCHOTHERAPY

According to the theory of RET, emotional disturbance occurs when individuals *demand, insist,* and *dictate* that they must have their wishes satisfied. Thus, they *demand* that they succeed and be approved, they *insist* that others treat them fairly, and they *dictate* that the universe be more pleasant. If people's demandingness (and not their desirousness) gets them into emotional trouble, they can alleviate their pain in several inelegant and elegant ways.

Distraction

Just as a whining child can be temporarily diverted by receiving a piece of candy, so can adult demanders be transitorily sidetracked by distraction. Thus, a therapist who sees a man who is afraid of being rejected (that is, *demands* that significant others accept him) can try to divert him into activities such as sports, aesthetic creation, a political cause, yoga exercises, meditation, or preoccupation with the events of his childhood. While the individual is so diverted, he will hardly have the time, or inclination, to demand acceptance by others and to make himself anxious. Distraction techniques are mainly palliative, given that people are still underlyingly demanders and as soon as they are not diverted they will probably return to their childish dictating.

Satisfying Demands

If a woman's insistences are always catered to, she will tend to feel better (but not necessarily get better). To arrange this kind of "solution," a therapist can give her love and approval, provide her with pleasurable sensations (for example, put her in an encounter group where she is hugged or massaged), teach her methods of succeeding in getting her demands, or give her reassurance that she eventually will be gratified. Many clients will feel immensely better when given this kind of treatment, but most will probably have their demandingness reinforced rather than minimized.

Magic

A boy who demands frequently can be assuaged by magic: by, for example, his parents' saying that a fairy godmother will soon satisfy his demands. Similarly, adolescent and adult demanders can be led to believe (by a therapist or someone else) that God will help them; that if they suffer enough on this earth they will go to heaven and have all their demands satisfied there; that even though they are deprived in one way (say, by being rejected), they are really a *better person* than their rejector and that therefore they can tolerate rejection; that their therapist is a kind of magician who will take away their troubles merely by listening to what bothers them. These magical solutions sometimes work beautifully by getting the true believer to feel better and to give up disturbed symptoms, but they rarely work for any length of time and frequently lead to eventual disillusionment.

Giving up Demandingness

The most elegant solution to the problems that result from irrational demandingness is to induce the individual to become less commanding, godlike, and dictatorial. Normal children in maturing become less childish, less insistent that they must have their desires immediately gratified. The rational psychotherapist tries to induce clients to acquire minimal demandingness and maximum tolerance. RET practitioners may, at times, use temporary "solutions," such as distraction, satisfying the client's "needs," and even (on very rare occasions) magic. But they realize that these are low-level, inelegant, palliative solutions, mainly to be used with clients who utterly refuse to accept a more elegant and permanent resolution of their basic demandingness. Preferably, the rational-emotive therapist strives for the highest order solution: radical minimization of *musturbation*, perfectionism, grandiosity, and intolerance.

In RET, the attempt to help clients minimize their dictatorial, dogmatic, absolutistic core philosophy is attempted in three main therapeutic ways: cognitive, emotive, and behavioristic.

1. *RET cognitive therapy* attempts to show clients that they had better give up perfectionism if they want to lead a happier, less anxiety-ridden existence. It teaches them how to recognize their *shoulds, oughts,* and *musts;* how to separate rational (nonabsolutistic) from irrational (absolutistic) beliefs; how to use the logico-empirical method of science in relation to themselves and their own problems; and how to accept reality, even when it is pretty grim. It assumes that clients can think, can think about their thinking, and can even think about thinking about their thinking; and it consequently helps them to hone and sharpen their cognitive processes. Information-giving, explicatory, and didactic, RET is oriented toward helping people with emotional disturbances philosophize more effectively and thereby uncreate these disturbances. It not only employs a one-to-one Socratic-type dialogue between the client and the therapist, but it also, in group therapy, encourages other members of the group to discuss, explain, and reason with the ineffectually thinking client. It teaches logical and semantic precision—that a man's being rejected does not mean he will *always* be rejected and that a woman's failing does not means she *cannot* succeed. It helps clients to keep asking themselves whether even the worst things that might happen would be really as bad as they melodramatically fantasize that they would be.

2. *Emotive-evocative therapy* employs various means of dramatizing preferences and musts so clients can clearly distinguish between the two. Thus, the therapist may employ *role-playing* to show the clients exactly what their false ideas are and how they affect relations with others; *modeling* to show clients how to adopt different ideas; *humor* to reduce disturbance-creating ideas to absurdity; *unconditional acceptance* to demonstrate that they are acceptable, even with their unfortunate traits, and that they can accept themselves fully; and *strong disputing* to persuade people to give up some of their crazy thinking and replace it with more efficient notions. The therapist may also direct clients, either in individual or group counseling, to take risks (for example, telling another group member what they really think of him) that will prove it is really not that risky; to reveal themselves (for example, give the details of their impotency or homosexuality) to convince themselves that others can accept them with their failings; and to get in touch with their "shameful" feelings (such as hostility) so they can zero in on the exact things they are telling themselves to create

these feelings. The therapist may also use pleasure-giving techniques, such as sensory awareness and being cuddled by another group member, not merely to satisfy clients' unreasonable demands for immediate gratification, but to show them they are capable of doing many pleasant acts that they think, wrongly, they *cannot* do and that they *can* guiltlessly seek mere pleasure for the sake of pleasure, even though others may frown upon them for so doing.

3. *Behavior therapy* is employed in RET not only to help clients change their dysfunctional symptoms and to become habituated to more effective ways of performing, but also to help change their *cognitions*. Thus their demandingness that they perform beautifully may be whittled away by the therapist's giving them assignments, such as risk taking (for example, ask a member of the other sex for a date), deliberately failing at some task (for example, make a real attempt to speak badly in public), imagining themselves in failing situations, and throwing themselves into unusual activities that they consider especially dangerous. Clients' demandingness that others treat them fairly and that the world be kind may be challenged by the therapist's inducing them to stay in poor circumstances and teach themselves, at least temporarily, to accept them; to take on hard tasks (like enrolling in college); to imagine themselves having a rough time at something and not feeling terribly upset or having to "cop out" of it; to allow themselves to do a pleasant thing, such as go to a movie or see their friends, only after they have done unpleasant but desirable tasks, such as studying French or finishing a report for their boss; and so on. RET often employs operant conditioning to reinforce peoples' changing behavior (e.g., smoking or overeating) or changing irrational thinking (e.g., condemning themselves when they smoke or overeat).

The RET theory of psychotherapy asserts that there are many kinds of psychological treatment and that most of them work to some degree. An efficient system of therapy includes (a) economy of time and effort, (b) rapid symptom reduction, (c) effectiveness with a large percentage of different kinds of clients, (d) depth of solution of the presenting problems, and (e) lastingness of the therapeutic results. A therapy with these elements may be labeled "elegant"—that is, approaching the ideal of psychotherapy. Philosophically, RET combats absoluteness more intensively than does any other system (Ellis, 1987a). Realistic and unindulgent, RET gets to the core of and ruthlessly persists at undermining childish demandingness—the main element of serious emotional disturbance.

PROCESS OF PSYCHOTHERAPY

The many roads taken in RET are aimed at one major goal: minimizing the client's central self-defeating outlook and acquiring a more realistic, tolerant philosophy of life. Because some of its methods are similar to methods used by other therapists, they are not detailed in this chapter. Most of the space here is devoted to the cognitive-persuasive aspects of RET, its most distinguishing characteristic.

Rational-emotive therapists generally do not spend a great deal of time listening to the client's history, encouraging long tales of woe, sympathetically getting in tune with emotionalizing, or carefully and incisively reflecting feelings. They may at times use all these methods, but they usually make an effort to keep them short because they consider most long-winded dialogues of this nature a form of indulgence therapy, in which the client may be helped to *feel* better but rarely to *get* better. Even when these methods work, they are often highly inefficient and sidetracking.

Similarly, the rational-emotive therapist makes little use of free association, dream analysis, interpretations of the transference relationship, explanations of the client's present symptoms in terms of past experiences, disclosure and analysis of the so-called Oedipus complex, and other "dynamically" directed interpretations or explanations. When these are employed at all, they are briefly employed to help clients see some of their basic irrational ideas.

Thus, if a male therapist notes that a female client rebels against him, just as she previously rebelled against her father during her childhood, he will not interpret the present rebelliousness as stemming from the prior pattern, but will instead probably say something like:

It looks like you frequently hated your father because he kept forcing you to follow certain rules you considered arbitrary and because you kept convincing yourself: "My father isn't being considerate of me and he *ought* to be! I'll fix his wagon!" I think you are now telling yourself approximately the same thing about me. But your angry rebelliousness against your father was senseless because (a) he was not a *total bastard* for perpetrating a bastardly *act*; (b) there was no reason why he *ought* to have been considerate of you (although there were several reasons why *it would have been preferable* if he had been); and (c) your getting angry at him and trying to "fix his wagon" would not, probably, encourage him to act more kindly, but actually to be more cruel.

You consequently confused—as most children will—being displeased with your father's *behavior* with being "righteously" angry at *him*, and you foolishly and needlessly *made yourself* upset about his supposedly unfair treatment of you. In my case, too, you are probably doing much the same thing. You are taking the restrictions that I place on you and insisting they are *too* onerous (when in point of fact, they are only onerous), and, after assuming that I am wrong in placing them on you (which I indeed may be), you are condemning me for my supposedly wrong deeds. Moreover, you are quite possibly assuming that I am "wrong" and a "louse" for being wrong because I resemble, in some ways, your "wrong" and "lousy" father.

But this is another illogical conclusion (that if I resemble your father in *some* ways, I must resemble him in all ways) and an irrational premise (that I, like your father, am a *bad person* if I do a wrong *act*). So you are not only *inventing* a false connection between me and your father, but you are creating today, as you have done for many years now, a renewed *demand* that the world be an easy place for you and that everyone *ought to* treat you fairly. Now, how are you going to challenge your irrational premises and illogical deductions?

Rational-emotive practitioners often employ a fairly rapid-fire active-directive-persuasive-philosophic methodology. In most instances, they quickly pin the client down to a few basic irrational ideas. They challenge the client to validate these ideas, show that they contain extralogical premises that cannot be validated; logically analyze these ideas and make mincemeat of them; vigorously show why they cannot work and why they will almost inevitably lead to renewed disturbed symptomatology; reduce these ideas to absurdity, sometimes in a highly humorous manner; explain how they can be replaced with more rational theses; and teach clients how to think scientifically, so they can observe, logically parse, and minimize any subsequent irrational ideas and illogical deductions that lead to self-defeating feelings and behaviors.

Lest it be thought that this picture of what the therapist does in RET is exaggerated, a verbatim typescript from the recording of the first part of an initial session with a 25-year-old single woman who works as the head of a computer programmer section is presented:

T-1 [Reading from the biographical information form that the clients at the Institute for Rational-Emotive Therapy in New York City fill out before their first session: Inability to control emotions; tremendous feelings of guilt, unworthiness, insecurity; constant depression; conflict between inner and outer self; overeating; drinking; diet pills.] All right, what would you want to start on first?

C-1: I don't know. I'm petrified at the moment!

T-2: You're petrified—of what?

C-2: Of you!

T-3: No, surely not of me—perhaps of yourself!

C-3: [Laughs nervously.]

T-4: Because of what I am going to do to you?

C-4: Right! You are threatening me, I guess.

T-5: But how? What am I doing? Obviously, I'm not going to take a knife and stab you. Now, in what way am I threatening you?

C-5: I guess I'm afraid, perhaps, of what I'm going to find out—about me.

T-6: Well, so let's suppose you find out something *dreadful* about you—that you're thinking foolishly or something. Now why would that be awful?

C-6: Because I, I guess I'm the most important thing to me at the moment.

T-7: No, I don't think that's the answer. It's, I believe, the opposite! You're really the *least* important thing to you. You are prepared to beat yourself over the head if I tell you that you're acting foolishly. If you were not a self-*blamer*, then you wouldn't care what I said. It would be important to you—but you'd just go around correcting it. But if I tell you something really nega-

tive about you, you're going to beat yourself mercilessly. Aren't you?

C-7: Yes, I generally do.

T-8: All right. So perhaps *that's* what you're really afraid of. You're not afraid of me. You're afraid of *your* own self-criticism.

C-8: [Sighs.] All right.

T-9: So why do you have to criticize yourself? Suppose I find you're the worst person I ever met? Let's just suppose that. All right, now *why* would you have to criticize yourself?

C-9: [Pause.] I'd have to. I don't know any other behavior pattern, I guess, in this point of time. I always do. I guess I think I'm just a shit.

T-10: Yeah. But that, that isn't so. If you don't know how to ski or swim, you could learn. You can also learn not to condemn yourself, no matter what you do.

C-10: I don't know.

T-11: Well, the answer is: You don't know how.

C-11: Perhaps.

T-12: I get the impression you're *saying,* "I *have* to berate myself if I do something wrong." Because isn't that where your depression comes from?

C-12: Yes, I guess so. [Silence.]

T-13: Now, what are you *mainly* putting yourself down for right now?

C-13: I don't seem quite able, in this point of time, to break it down very neatly. The form gave me a great deal of trouble. Because my tendency is to say *everything.* I want to change everything; I'm depressed about everything; etc.

T-14: Give me a couple of things, for example.

C-14: What I'm depressed about? I, uh, don't know that I have any purpose in life. I don't know what I—what I am. And I don't know in what direction I'm going.

T-15: Yeah. but that's—so you're saying, "I'm ignorant!" [Client nods.] Well, what's so awful about being ignorant? It's too bad you're ignorant. It would be nicer if you weren't—if you *had* a purpose and *knew* where you were going. But just let's suppose the worst: for the rest of your life you didn't have a purpose and you stayed this way. Let's suppose that. Now, why would you be so bad?

C-15: Because everyone *should* have a purpose!

T-16: Where did you get the should?

C-16: 'Cause it's what I believe in. [Silence.]

T-17: I know. But think about it for a minute. You're obviously a bright woman. Now, where did that should come from?

C-17: I, I don't know! I'm not thinking clearly at the moment. I'm too nervous! I'm sorry.

T-18: Well, but you can think clearly. Are you now saying, "Oh, it's hopeless! I can't think clearly. What a shit I am for not thinking clearly!" You see: you're blaming yourself for that.

[From C-18 to C-26 the client upsets herself about not reacting well to the session, but the therapist shows her this is not overly important and calms her down.]

C-27: I can't imagine existing, uh, or that there would be any reason for existing without a purpose!

T-28: No, but the vast majority of human beings don't have much purpose.

C-28: [Angrily.] All right, then. I should not feel bad about it.

T-29: No, no, no! Wait a minute, now. You just jumped. [Laughs.] You jumped from one extreme to another! You see, you said a sane sentence and an insane sentence. Now, if we could get you to separate the two—which you're perfectly able to do—you would solve the problem. What you really mean is "It would be better if I had a purpose. Because I'd be happier." Right?

C-29: Yes.

T-30: But then you magically jump to "Therefore I should!" Now do you see the difference between "It would be better if I had a purpose" and "I should, I must, I've got to"?

C-30: Yes, I do.

T-31: Well, what's the difference?

C-31: [Laughs.] I just said that to agree with you!

T-32: Yes! See, that won't be any good. We could go on that way forever, and you'll agree with me, and I'll say, "Oh, what a great woman! She agrees with me." And then you'll go out of here just as nutty as you were before!

C-32: [Laughs, this time with genuine appreciation and good humor.]

T-33: You're perfectly able, as I said, to think—to stop giving up. That's what you've done most of your life. That's why

you're disturbed. Because you refuse to think. And let's go over it again: "It would be better if I had a purpose in life; if I weren't depressed, etc., etc. If I had a good, nice, enjoyable purpose." We could give reasons why it would be better. "It's fairly obvious why it would be better!" Now, why is that a magical statement, that "I should do what would be better"?

C-33: You mean, why do I feel that way?

T-34: No, No. It's a belief. You feel that way because you believe that way.

C-34: Yes.

T-35: If you believed you were a kangaroo, you'd be hopping around and you'd feel like a kangaroo. Whatever you believe, you feel. Feelings come from your beliefs. Now, I'm temporarily forgetting about your feelings, because we really can't change feelings without changing beliefs. So I'm showing you: you have two beliefs—or two feelings, if you want to call them that. One, "It would be better if I had a purpose in life." Do you agree? [Client nods.] Now that's perfectly reasonable. That's quite true. We could prove it. Two, "Therefore, I should do what would be better." Now those are two different statements. They may seem the same, but they're vastly different. Now, the first one, as I said, is sane. Because we could prove it. It's related to reality. We can list the advantages of having a purpose—for almost anybody, not just for you.

C-35: [Calm now, and listening intently to T's explanation.] Uh-huh.

T-36: But the second one, "Therefore, I should do what would be better," is crazy. Now, why is it crazy?

C-36: I can't accept it as a crazy statement.

T-37: Because who said you should?

C-37: I don't know where it all began! Somebody said it.

T-38: I know, but I say whoever said it was screwy!

C-38: [Laughs.] All right.

T-39: How could the world possibly have a should?

C-39: Well, it does.

T-40: But it doesn't! You see, that's what emotional disturbance is: believing in shoulds, oughts, and musts instead of it would be betters. That's exactly what makes people disturbed! Suppose you said to yourself, "I wish I had a dollar in my pocket right now," and you had only ninety cents, how would you feel?

C-40: Not particularly upset.

T-41: Yes, you'd be a little disappointed. *It would be better* to have a dollar. But now suppose you said, "I *should*, I *must* have a dollar in my pocket at all times," and you found you had only ninety cents. Now, how would you feel?

C-41: Then I would be terribly upset, following your line of reasoning.

T-42: But not because you had only the ninety cents.

C-42: Because I thought I *should* have a dollar.

T-43: THAT'S RIGHT! The *should*. And what's more, let's just go one step further. Suppose you said, "I must have a dollar in my pocket at all times." And you found you had a dollar and ten cents. Now how would you feel?

C-43: Superb, I guess.

T-44: No—anxious!

C-44: [Laughs.] You mean I'd be guilty: "What was I doing with the extra money?"

T-45: No.

C-45: I'm sorry, I'm not following you. I—

T-46: Because you're not *thinking!* Think for a minute. Why, if you said, "I *must* have a dollar, I *should* have a dollar," and you had a dollar and ten cents, would you still be anxious? *Anybody* would be. Now why would anybody be anxious if they were saying, "I've got to have a dollar!" and they found they had a dollar and ten cents?

C-46: Because it violated their *should.* It violated their rule of what they thought was right, I guess.

T-47: Well, not at the moment. But they could easily lose twenty cents.

C-47: Oh! Well.

T-48: Yeah! They'd still be anxious. You see, because *must* means, "At *all* times I must—"

C-48: Oh, I see what you mean! All right. I see what you mean. They could easily lose some of the money and would therefore feel insecure.

T-49: Yeah. All anxiety comes from *musts.*

C-49: [Long silence.] Why do you create such an anxiety-ridden situation initially for someone?

T-50: I don't think I do. I see hundreds of people and you're one of the few who *makes* this so anxiety provoking for yourself. The others may do it mildly, but you're making it very anxiety provoking. Which just shows that you carry *must* into *everything*, including this situation. Most people come in here very relieved. They finally got to talk to somebody who knows how to help them, and they're very happy that I stop the horseshit, and stop asking about their childhood, and don't talk about the weather, etc. And I get *right away* to what bothers them. I tell them in five minutes. I've just explained to you the secret of all emotional disturbance. If you really followed what I said, and used it, you'd never be disturbed about practically anything for the rest of your life!

C-50: Uh-huh.

T-51: Because every time you're disturbed, you're changing *it would be better* to a *must.* That's all disturbance is! Very very simple. Now, why should I waste your time and not explain this—and talk about irrelevant things?

C-51: Because perhaps I would have followed your explanation a little better if I hadn't been so threatened initially.

T-52: But then, if I pat you on the head and hold back, etc., then you'll think for the rest of your life you have to be patted on the head! You're a bright woman!

C-52: All right—

T-53: That's another *should.* "He *should* pat me on the head and take it slowly— then a shit like me can understand! But if he goes *fast* and makes me *think*, oh my God I'll make an error—and that is awful!" More horseshit! You don't have to believe that horseshit! You're perfectly able to follow what I say—if you stop worrying about "I *should* do perfectly well!" For that's what you're basically thinking, sitting there. Well, why *should* you do perfectly well? Suppose we had to go over it twenty times before you got it?

C-53: I don't *like* to appear stupid!

T-54: No. See. Now you're lying to yourself! Because you again said a sane thing— and then you added an insane thing. The sane thing was "I don't like to appear stupid, because *it's better* to appear bright." But then you immediately jumped over to the insane thing: "And it's *awful* if I appear stupid—"

C-54: [Laughs appreciatively, almost joyously.]

T-55: "—I *should* appear bright!" You see?

C-55: [With conviction.] Yes.

T-56: The same crap! It's always the same crap. Now if you would look at the crap—instead of "Oh, how stupid I am! He hates me! I think I'll kill myself!" then you'd get better right away.

C-56: You've been listening! [Laughs.]

T-57: Listening to what?

C-57: [Laughs.] Those wild statements in my mind, like that, that I make.

T-58: That's right! Because I know that you have to make those statements—because I have a good *theory*. And according to my theory, people couldn't get upset *unless* they made those nutty statements to themselves.

C-58: I haven't the faintest idea why I've been so upset—

T-59: But you *do* have the faintest idea. I just told you.

C-59: All right, I know!

T-60: Why are you upset? Repeat it to me.

C-60: I'm upset because I know, I—the role that I envisioned myself being in when I walked in here and what I [Laughs, almost joyously.] and what I would do and should do—

T-61: Yeah?

C-61: And therefore you forced me to violate that. And I don't like it.

T-62: "And isn't it *awful* that I didn't come out greatly! If I had violated that *beautifully*, and I gave him the *right* answers immediately, and he beamed, and said 'Boy, what a bright woman this is!' then it would have been all right."

C-62: [Laughing good-humoredly.] Certainly!

T-63: Horseshit! You would have been exactly as disturbed as you are now! It wouldn't have helped you a bit! In fact, you would have got nuttier! Because then you would have gone out of here with the same *philosophy* you came in here with: "That when I act well and people pat, uh, when they pat me on the head and say, 'What a great woman am I!' then everything is rosy!" It's a nutty philosophy! Because even if I loved you madly, the next person you talk to is likely to hate you. So I like brown eyes and he likes blue eyes or something. So you're then dead! Because

you really think: "I've got to be *accepted*! I've got to act intelligently!" Well, why?

C-63: [Very soberly and reflectively.] True.

T-64: You see?

C-64: Yes.

T-65: Now, if you will learn that lesson, then you've had a very valuable session. Because you *don't* have to upset yourself. As I said before, if I thought you were the worst shit who ever existed, well that's my *opinion*. And I'm entitled to it. But does it make you a turd?

C-65: [Reflective silence.]

T-66: *Does* it?

C-66: No.

T-67: *What* makes you a turd?

C-67: *Thinking* that you are.

T-68: That's right! Your *belief* that you are. That's the only thing that could ever do it. And you never have to believe that. See? You control your thinking. I control *my* thinking—*my* belief about you. But you don't have to be affected by that. You *always* control what you think. And you believe you don't. So let's get back to the depression. The depression, as I said before, stems from self-castigation. That's where it comes from. Now what are you castigating yourself for?

C-68: Because I can't live up to— There's a basic conflict in what people appear to think I am and what I think I am.

T-69: Right.

C-69: And perhaps it's not fair to blame other people. Perhaps I thrust myself into a leader's role. But, anyway, my feeling right now is that all my life I've been forced to be something that I'm not, and the older I get the more difficult this *facade*, huh, this *appearance*, uh—that the veneer is coming thinner and thinner and thinner, until I just can't do it any more.

T-70: Well, but really, yeah, I'm afraid you're a little wrong. Because, oddly enough, almost the opposite is happening. You are thrust into this role. That's right: the role of something of a leader. Is that correct?

C-70: Yes.

T-71: And *they* think you're filling it.

C-71: Everyone usually does.

T-72: And it just so happens they're *right*.

C-72: But it's taking more and more out of me.

T-73: Because you're not doing something else. You see, you *are* fulfilling their expectations of you. Because, obviously, they wouldn't think you are a leader, they'd think you were a nothing if you *were* acting like a nonleader. So you are filling their expectations. But you're not fulfilling your own idealistic and impractical expectations of leadership.

C-73: [Verging on tears.] No, I guess I'm not.

T-74: You see that's the issue. So therefore you *are* doing OK by them—by your job, etc. But you're not being an angel, you're not being *perfect!* And you should be, to be a real *leader.* And therefore you're a *sham!* You see? Now, if you give up those nutty expectations of yourself and go back to their expectations, you're in no trouble at all. 'Cause obviously you're doing all right by them and *their* expectations.

C-74: Well, I haven't been. I had to, to give up one very successful situation. And, uh, when I left, they thought it was still successful. But I just could not go on—

T-75: "Because I must, I must *really* be a leader in *my* eyes, be pretty *perfect.*" You see. "If I satisfy the world, but I know I did badly, or less than I *should,* then I'm a slob! And they haven't found me out, so that makes me a *double* slob. Because I'm pretending to them to be a nonslob when I really am one!"

C-75: [Laughs in agreement, then grows sober.] True!

T-76: But it's all your silly *expectations.* It's not *them.* And oddly enough, you are— even with your *handicap,* which is depression, self-deprecation, etc.—you're doing remarkably well. Imagine what you might do *without* this nutty handicap! You see, you're satisfying them while you're spending most of your time and energy flagellating yourself. Imagine what you might do *without* the self-flagellation! Can you see that?

C-76: [Stopped in her self-blaming tracks, at least temporarily convinced, speaks very meaningfully.] Yes!

MECHANISMS OF PSYCHOTHERAPY

From the foregoing partial protocol (which consumed about 15 minutes of the first session with the client), it can be seen that the therapist tries to do several things:

1. No matter what *feelings* the client brings out, the therapist tries to get back to her main irrational *ideas* that most probably lie behind these feelings—especially her ideas that contend that it would be *awful* if someone, including him, disliked her.

2. The therapist does not hesitate to contradict the client, using evidence from the client's own life and from his knowledge of people in general.

3. He usually is a step *ahead* of her—tells her, for example, that she is a self-blamer before she has said that she is. Knowing, on the basis of RET *theory,* that she has *shoulds, oughts,* and *musts* in her thinking if she is becoming anxious, depressed, and guilty, he forces her to admit these *shoulds* and then attacks them (T-16, T-17).

4. He uses the strongest philosophic approach he can think of. "Suppose," he keeps saying to her, "the *worst* thing happened and you really did do badly and others hated you, would you *still* be so bad?" (T-15). He assumes if he can convince her that *none* of her behavior, no matter how execrable, denigrates *her,* he has helped her to make a *deep* attitudinal change.

5. He is not thrown by her distress (C17), is hardly sympathetic about these feelings, but *uses* them to try to prove to her that, right now, she still believes in foolish ideas and thereby upsets herself. He does not dwell on her "transference" feelings, the way she accuses him of acting toward her. He interprets the *ideas* behind these feelings, shows her why they are self-defeating, and indicates why his acting sympathetically would probably reinforce instead of help change her demanding philosophy.

6. He is fairly stern with her but also shows full acceptance and demonstrates confidence in her abilities by insisting that she can do better in her thinking and her behaving if she stops berating herself (T-20, T-33).

7. Instead of merely *telling* her that her ideas are irrational, he keeps trying to get her to see this for herself (T-36). He does, however, *explain* some relevant psychological processes, such as that her *feelings* come from her *thinking* (T-35, T-68).

8. He deliberately, on several occasions, uses strong language (T-18, T-50, T-53, T-56, T-63, T-65). This is done (a) to help loosen up the client, (b) to show that even though he is a professional, he is also a down-to-earth human being, and (c) to give her an emotive jolt or shock, so his words may take more dramatic effect. Note that in this case the client *first* called herself a "shit" (C-9).

9. Although hardly sympathetic to her ideas, he is really quite empathic, for he is listening hard to what she is probably telling herself. In this sense, rational-emotive therapists are very empathic, because they are usually attuned to the client's unexpressed concepts (her negative ideas about herself and the world) rather than to her *superficial* feelings (her perceptions that she is doing poorly or that others are abusing her).

10. The therapist keeps *checking* the client's ostensible understanding of what he is teaching her (T-65, T-67) to make sure she truly does understand and can repeat back his message in her own words.

11. Although a meaningful dialogue obviously takes place, the therapist—as is common in early sessions of RET—does most of the talking and explaining. He gives her plenty of opportunity to express herself, but uses her responses as take-off points for further teaching. At times, he almost seems to be lecturing her. But he tries to make each "lecture" brief and trenchant and to relate it specifically to her problems and feelings. Also, at times he stops to let ideas sink in.

As can be seen from the first part of this initial RET session, the client does not receive feelings of love and warmth from the therapist. Transference and countertransference spontaneously occur, but they are quickly analyzed, the philosophies behind them are revealed, and they tend to evaporate in the process. The client's deep feelings (shame, self-pity, weeping, anger) clearly exist, but the client is not given too much chance to revel in these feelings or to abreact strongly to them. As the therapist points out and attacks the ideologies that appear to underlie these feelings, they swiftly change and are sometimes almost miraculously transformed into other, contradictory feelings (such as humor, joy, and reflective contemplation). On the whole, because of the therapist's "coolness," philosophizing, and insistence that the client can feel something besides anxiety and depression, she tends to change her destructivness into constructive feelings minutes after the session starts.

What the client does seem to experience, as the session proceeds, are (a) full acceptance of herself, in spite of her poor behavior both during the session and in her external life; (b) renewed confidence that she can do certain things—e.g., think for herself—that at first she seems to think she cannot do; (c) a new concept that never or rarely seems to have occurred to her before, namely, that it is her own perfectionistic *shoulds* that are upsetting her and not the attitudes of others (including the therapist); (d) reality testing, in her starting to see that even though she performs inefficiently (with the therapist and with some of the people she works with), she can still recover, try again, and probably do better in the future; and (e) reduction of some of her defenses in that she can stop blaming others (such as the therapist) for her anxiety and can start to admit that she is doing something herself to cause it.

In these 15 minutes the client is getting only *glimmerings* of these constructive thoughts and feelings. The RET intent, however, is that she will *keep* getting insights—that is, *philosophic* rather than merely *psychodynamic* insights—into the self-causation of her disturbed symptoms, that she will use these insights to change some of her most enduring and deep-seated ways of thinking about herself, about others, and about the world, and that she will thereby eventually become ideationally, emotionally, and behaviorally much less self-defeating. Unless she finally makes a thorough-going *attitudinal* (as well as symptom-reducing) change as a result of rational-emotive therapy, although helped considerably, she will still be far from the ideal RET goal of basic personality change.

APPLICATIONS

PROBLEMS

It is easier to state what kind of problems are *not* handled than the kind that *are* handled in RET. Individuals who are out of contact with reality, in a highly manic state, seriously autistic or brain injured, and in the lower ranges of mental deficiency are not normally treated. They are referred for physical treatment, for custodial or institutional care, or for behavior therapy along operant conditioning lines.

Most other individuals with difficulties are treated with RET. These include (1) clients with maladjustment, moderate anxiety, or marital problems, (2) those with sexual difficulties, (3) run-of-the-mill "neurotics," (4) individuals with character disorders, (5) truants, juvenile delinquents, and adult criminals, (6) borderline personalities, (7) overt psychotics, including those with delusions and hallucinations, when they are somewhat in contact with reality, (8) individuals with higher grade mental deficiency, and (9) clients with psychosomatic problems.

Although innumerable kinds of individuals with varying types of problems are treated with RET, no claim is made that they are treated with equal effectiveness. As is the case with virtually all psychotherapies, the rational-emotive approach is significantly more effective with mildly disturbed individuals and those who have a single major symptom (such as sexual inadequacy) than with seriously disordered clients (Ellis, 1962, 1985a). This conforms to the hypotheses of RET theory that the tendency toward emotional distress is largely inborn and not merely acquired, that individuals with serious aberrations are more innately predisposed to have rigid and crooked thinking than are those with lesser aberrations, and that consequently they are less likely to make major advances. Moreover, RET emphasizes hard work at changing one's thinking and at doing homework activity assignments, and it is clinically observable that many of the most dramatically symptom-ridden individuals (such as those who are severely depressed) tend to do considerably less work and more shirking (including shirking at therapy) than those with milder symptoms. Nevertheless, seasoned RET practitioners claim they get better results with a wide variety of clients than do therapists from other schools.

RET is applicable for preventive purposes. Rational-emotive procedures are closely connected to the field of education and have enormous implications for emotional prophylaxis. A number of clinicians have shown how they can help prevent normal children from eventually becoming seriously disturbed. Evidence shows that when nondisturbed grade school pupils are given, along with regular elements of an academic education, a steady process of rational-emotive education, they can learn to understand themselves and others and to live more rationally and happily in this difficult world (Bernard & Joyce, 1985; Ellis, 1969a, 1973; Ellis & Bernard, 1983; Gerald & Eyman, 1985; Knaus, 1974.)

EVALUATION

RET has directly or indirectly inspired scores of experimenters to test its clinical and personality theories and there now are hundreds of research studies that tend to validate its hypotheses (Ellis & Whiteley, 1979). More than 200 outcome studies have been published, showing that RET is effective in changing the thoughts, feelings, and behaviors of groups of individuals with various kinds of disturbances. These studies now tend to show that RET disputing usually works better than no therapy and is often more effective than other methods of psychotherapy (Bernard & DiGiuseppe, in press;

DiGiuseppe, Miller & Trexler, 1979; Ellis, 1979a; Engels & Dieksta, 1986; McGovern & Silverman, 1984; Miller & Berman, 1983; Smith & Glass, 1977). Haaga and Davison (in press) have recently critically reviewed many RET outcome studies and found that it has distinct effectiveness with people suffering from test anxiety, social anxiety, stress and general anxiety, obsessions, stuttering, excessive anger, antisocial behavior, obesity, and type A behavior pattern.

In addition, scores of other outcome studies have been done by other cognitive therapists and their associates—particularly by Bandura (1977) and Beck, Rush, Shaw, and Emery (1979)—that also support the clinical hypotheses of RET. Finally, more than 200 other investigations have shown that the irrationality scales derived from Ellis' original list of irrational ideas significantly correlate with virtually all the diagnostic disorders with which these scales have been tested (Baisden, 1980; DiGiuseppe, Miller & Trexler, 1979; Ellis, 1979a; T. Smith, in press). The research showing of RET, as a theory and a practice of psychotherapy, is a tribute to its effort to state its hypotheses in a clear and highly testable form.

Individual Evaluations

RET therapists may use various diagnostic instruments and psychological tests, and they especially employ tests of irrationality, such as the rational beliefs inventories of Jones (1968); Kassinove, Crisci, and Tiegerman (1977); Baisden (1980); and Shorkey and Whiteman (1977). Many of these tests have been shown to have considerable reliability and validity in controlled experiments (Baisden, 1980; T. Smith, in press).

TREATMENT

RET employs virtually all forms of individual and group psychotherapy. Some of the main methods are these:

Individual Therapy

Most clients with whom RET is practiced are seen for individual sessions, usually on a once-a-week basis, for from 5 to 50 sessions. They generally start off their sessions by telling their most upsetting feelings or consequences (C) during the week. RET therapists then discover what activating events (A) occurred before clients felt so badly and help them to see what rational beliefs (rB) and what irrational beliefs (iB) they held in connection with the activating events. They teach clients to dispute (D) their irrational beliefs and often give them concrete homework activity assignments to help with this disputing. They then check up in the following session, sometimes with the help of an RET Self-Help Report Form (Sichel & Ellis, 1984), to see how the clients have tried to use the RET approach during the week. They keep teaching clients how to dispute their irrational beliefs and giving them new homework assignments until they not only start to lose their presenting symptoms but acquire a saner, more tolerant attitude toward life.

In particular, RET therapists try to show clients how (1) to rid themselves of anxiety, guilt, and depression by fully accepting themselves, as human beings, whether or not they succeed at important tasks and performances and whether or not significant people in their lives approve or love them; (2) to minimize their anger, hostility, and violence by becoming tolerant of other people even when they find these people's traits or performances unappetizing and unfair; and (3) to reduce their low frustration tolerance and inertia by working to change unpleasant reality but learning gracefully to stand it when it is truly inevitable.

Group Therapy

RET is particularly applicable to group therapy. Because group members are taught to apply RET principles to one another, they both help others learn the principles and get practice (under the direct supervision of the group leader) in applying them. In group work, moreover, there is usually more opportunity for the members to be given homework assignments (some of which are to be carried out in the group itself), to get assertion training, to engage in roleplaying, to interact with other people, to take verbal and nonverbal risks, to learn by the experiences of others, to interact therapeutically and socially with each other in after-group sessions, and to have their behavior directly observed by the therapist and other group members (Ellis & Dryden, 1987).

Marathon Encounter Groups

Although RET is one of the most cognitively oriented therapies, it has been successfully modified for what Ellis (1969b) calls "A Weekend of Rational Encounter." In a rational-emotive marathon, the first several hours are spent in having members of the group go through a series of exercises designed to get them to know each other intimately, relate verbally and nonverbally, bring out some of their most harrowing and "shameful" experiences, take unusual risks, and have intense one-to-one personal encounters. During these first hours, problem solving is deliberately eschewed. Then, when the members of the marathon group have gotten to know each other and given up some of their defenses, many hours are spent delving into their deepest problems, so most of them come to understand the philosophic sources of their emotional problems and how they can change themselves by altering these cognitions. Other verbal and nonverbal exercises to encourage encountering and intensive therapy are performed. Specific homework assignments are given to each of the marathon group members. Finally, there are closing exercises.

Brief Therapy

RET is naturally designed for *brief therapy*. It is preferable that individuals with severe disturbances come to individual and/or group sessions for at least six months, so they have an opportunity to practice what they are learning. But for individuals who are going to stay in therapy for only a short while, RET can teach them, in from 1 to 10 sessions, the A-B-C method of understanding any emotional problem, seeing its main philosophic source, and how to start working to change fundamental disturbance-creating attitudes (Ellis, 1985a; Ellis & Dryden, 1987).

This is particularly true for the person who has a specific problem—such as hostility toward a boss or sexual impotency—and who is not too *generally* disturbed. Such an individual can, with the help of RET, be almost completely "cured" in a few sessions. But even clients with long-standing difficulties may be significantly helped as a result of brief therapy using the rational-emotive approach.

Two special devices often employed in RET with regular clients can help speed the therapeutic process and make treatment relatively brief. The first is to tape the entire session. These recordings are then listened to, usually several times, by the clients in their own home, car, or office so they can more incisively see their problems and the rational-emotive way of handling them. Many clients who have difficulty in hearing what goes on during the face-to-face sessions (because they are too intent on talking themselves, are easily distractible, or are too anxious) are able to get more from listening to a recording of these sessions than from the original encounter with the therapist.

Second, an RET Self-Help Form is frequently used with clients to help teach them how to use the method when they encounter emotional problems between therapy sessions or after therapy has ended. This form is reproduced on pages 227–228.

Marriage and Family Therapy

From its very beginnings, RET has been extensively used in marriage and family counseling (Ellis, 1962, 1965, 1975, 1977a; Ellis & Dryden, 1987; Ellis & Harper, 1961, 1975). Usually marital or love partners are seen together. RET therapists listen to their complaints about each other, then try to show that even if the complaints are justified, upsetness is not. Work is done with either or both participants to minimize anxiety, depression, guilt, and—especially—hostility, and a kind of small-group session ensues. As they begin to learn and apply the RET principles, they usually become much less disturbed about their differences, often within a few sessions, and then are much better able to minimize their incompatibilities and maximize their compatibilities. Sometimes, of course, they decide that they would be better off separated or divorced, but usually they decide to work at their individual and collective problems, to tackle some of their basic disturbances, and to achieve a happier marital arrangement. They are frequently taught contracting, compromising, communication, and other relating skills. The therapist is concerned with each of them as individuals who can be helped emotionally, whether or not they decide to stay together. But the more they work at helping themselves, the better their relationship tends to become.

In family therapy, rational-emotive practitioners sometimes see all the members of the same family together, they may see the children in one session and the parents in another, or they may see them all individually. Some joint sessions are usually held to observe the interactions among family members, but there is no fetishistic sticking *only* to joint sessions. Whether together or separately, parents are frequently shown how to accept their children and to stop condemning *them*, no matter how execrable their *behavior* may be, and children are similarly shown that they can accept their parents and their siblings even when their traits and deeds are highly disappointing. The general rational-emotive principles of tolerance for oneself and for others are repeatedly taught, and as these are imbibed and applied, family relationships tend to become remarkably improved. As is common in RET procedures, bibliotherapy supplements counseling and the family participants often significantly help themselves by reading RET materials like *A New Guide to Rational Living* (Ellis & Harper, 1975), *A Rational Counseling Primer* (Young, 1974), *How to Live with—and without—Anger* (Ellis, 1977a), *How to Live with a "Neurotic"* (Ellis, 1975), *A Guide to Successful Marriage* (Ellis & Harper, 1961), *A Guide to Personal Happiness* (Ellis & Becker, 1982), and *How To Stubbornly Refuse To Make Yourself Miserable About Anything—Yes, Anything!* (Ellis, 1988).

MANAGEMENT

The *setting* of rational-emotive sessions is much like that for other types of therapy. Most individual sessions take place in an office, but there may well be no desk between the therapist and the client, and RET therapists tend to be informally dressed and use down-to-earth language. Because they presumably have relatively few ego hang-ups and because they do not care too much what others, including clients, think of them, they tend to be more open, authentic, and less "professional" than the average therapist. The main special equipment used is a cassette tape recorder, with the client being encouraged to bring his or her own cassette, make a recording of the session, and take it home for replaying.

Relationships between client and therapist are somewhat different in RET than in many other forms of therapy. Rational-emotive therapists are highly active, give their own views without hesitations, usually answer direct questions about their personal life, do a good deal of the speaking, particularly during early sessions, and are quite energetic and often directive in group therapy. At the same time, they may engage in considerable explaining, interpreting, and "lecturing"; may be objective and not overly warm to

RET SELF-HELP FORM

Institute for Rational-Emotive Therapy
45 East 65th Street, New York, N.Y. 10021
(212) 535-0822

(A) ACTIVATING EVENTS, thoughts, or feelings that happened just before I felt emotionally disturbed or acted self-defeatingly: _____

_____

(C) CONSEQUENCE or CONDITION—disturbed feeling or self-defeating behavior—that I produced and would like to change: _____

_____

(B) BELIEFS—Irrational BELIEFS (IBs) leading to my CONSEQUENCE (emotional disturbance or self-defeating behavior). Circle all that apply to these ACTIVATING EVENTS **(A).**	**(D) DISPUTES** for each circled IRRATIONAL BELIEF. Examples: *"Why* MUST I do very well?" *"Where is it written* that I am a BAD PERSON?" *"Where is the evidence* that I MUST be approved or accepted?"	**(E) EFFECTIVE RATIONAL BELIEFS (RBs)** to replace my IRRATIONAL BELIEFS (IBs). *Examples: "I'd* PREFER *to do very well but I don't* HAVE TO." *"I am a* PERSON WHO *acted badly, not a BAD PERSON." "There is no evidence that I* HAVE TO *be approved, though I would* LIKE *to be."*
1. I MUST do well or very well!		
2. I am a BAD OR WORTHLESS PERSON when I act weakly or stupidly.		
3. I MUST be approved or accepted by people I find important!		
4. I NEED to be loved by someone who matters to me a lot!		
5. I am a BAD, UNLOVABLE PERSON if I get rejected.		
6. People MUST treat me fairly and give me what I NEED!		

(OVER)

7. People MUST live up to my expectations or it is TERRIBLE!

8. People who act immorally are undeserving, ROTTEN PEOPLE!

9. I CAN'T STAND really bad things or very difficult people!

10. My life MUST have few major hassles or troubles.

11. It's AWFUL or HORRIBLE when major things don't go my way!

12. I CAN'T STAND IT when life is really unfair!

13. I NEED a good deal of immediate gratification and HAVE to feel miserable when I don't get it!

Additional Irrational Beliefs:

(F) FEELINGS and BEHAVIORS I experienced after arriving at my EFFECTIVE RATIONAL BELIEFS: _____

I WILL WORK HARD TO REPEAT MY EFFECTIVE RATIONAL BELIEFS FORCEFULLY TO MYSELF ON MANY OCCASIONS SO THAT I CAN MAKE MYSELF LESS DISTURBED NOW AND ACT LESS SELF-DEFEATINGLY IN THE FUTURE.

some clients; and may easily work with clients they personally do not like, because they are much more interested in helping them with their emotional problems than in relating to them personally. Because they tend to have complete tolerance for all individuals, no matter how execrable their behavior, RET therapists are often seen as warm and caring by clients.

Resistance is usually handled by showing clients that they resist changing their outlook and behavior because they would like to find a magical easy solution rather than work at changing themselves. Resistance is not usually interpreted as their particular feelings about the therapist. If a client tries to seduce a therapist, this is not usually explained in terms of "transference" but in terms of (a) the dire needs for love, (b) normal attraction to a helpful person, and (c) the natural sex urges of two people who have intimate mental-emotional contact. If the therapist is attracted to the client, he or she usually admits the attraction, but explains why it is unethical to have sex relations with a client (Ellis, 1985a).

Client Problems

No matter what the presenting problem, RET therapists do not become overly interested in *it* or devote too much time and energy to trying to induce the client to fully *express* it or the emotions surrounding it. Rather, they try to get the client to see and tackle the basic ideas or philosophies that underlie it. This is notably shown in the course of workshops and seminars for executives. In these workshops, the participating executives constantly bring up business, management, organizational, personal, and other problems. But they are shown that they usually have a problem about the problem and it is *this* (emotional or philosophic) problem that the rational-emotive method zeroes in on and helps the individual quickly and effectively solve. Then he or she usually has little difficulty in solving the original, objective problem (Ellis, 1972).

The main exception to this rule is individuals who are so inhibited or defensive that they do not permit themselves to feel and who therefore may not even be aware of some of their underlying problems. Thus, the successful businessman who only comes for psychological help because his wife insists they have a poor relationship and who claims that nothing really bothers him other than his wife's complaints may have to be jolted out of his complacency by direct confrontation by the rational-emotive therapist or group, and only then may be able to see that he really has a problem. RET group therapy may be particularly helpful for such an individual so that he finally expresses underlying anxieties and resentments and begins to acknowledge he has problems he can work on.

Extreme emotionalism in the course of RET sessions—such as crying, psychotic behavior, and violent expressions of suicidal or homicidal intent— are naturally difficult to handle. But therapists handle them by their own presumably rational philosophy of life and therapy, which includes these ideas: (a) Client outbursts make things difficult, but they are hardly *awful, terrible,* or *catastrophic.* It is merely too bad that they occur. (b) Behind each outburst is some concrete, irrational idea. Now, what is this idea? How can it be forcefully brought to the client's attention and what can be done to help change it? (c) No therapist can possibly help every client all the time. If this particular client cannot be helped and has to be referred elsewhere or lost to therapy, that is unfortunate. But it does not mean that the therapist is a failure with a capital F, and that he or she cannot go on to help others.

Profound depressions are usually handled by the rational-emotive therapist by showing the clients, as quickly, directly, and vigorously as possible, that they are probably causing their depression by (a) blaming themselves for what they have done or not done, (b) castigating themselves for being depressed and inert, and (c) bemoaning their fate because of the hassles and harshness of environmental conditions. This self-condemnation is not only revealed but energetically attacked and, in the meantime, the therapist may give clients reassurance and support, may refer them for supplementary medication, may speak to their relatives or friends to enlist their aid, and may recommend temporary withdrawal from some involved activities. Through an immediate and direct assailing of clients' extreme self-deprecation and self-pity, the therapist often helps deeply depressed and suicidal people in a short period.

The most difficult clients are usually the chronic avoiders or shirkers who keep looking for magical solutions. These individuals are forthrightly shown that no such magic exists; that if they do not want to work hard to get better, it is their privilege to keep suffering; that they are entitled to goof, that they are not *terrible persons* for goofing, but that they could live much more enjoyably if they worked at helping themselves; and that to help them get going a form of people-involved therapy, such as group therapy, is frequently a method of choice. Results with these kinds of individuals are still relatively poor in RET (and virtually all other therapies), but persistence and vigor on the part of the therapist often finally overcome this kind of resistance (Ellis, 1985a).

CASE EXAMPLE

This section is relatively brief because it concerns the 25-year-old computer programmer whose initial session was presented in part earlier in this chapter. Other case material on this client follows.

BACKGROUND

Sara R. came from an orthodox Jewish family. Her mother died in childbirth when Sara was two years of age, so Sara was raised by a loving but strict and somewhat remote, father and a tyrannical paternal grandmother. She did well in school, but had few friends up to and through college. Although fairly attractive, she was always ashamed of her body, did little dating, and occupied herself mainly with her work. At the age of 25, she was head of a section in a data processing firm. She was highly sexed and masturbated several times a week, but she had intercourse with a male only once, when she was too drunk to know what she was doing. She had been overeating and overdrinking steadily since her college days. She had three years of fairly classic psychoanalysis, thought her analyst was "a very kind and helpful man," but got little or no help from the process. She was quite disillusioned about therapy as a result of this experience and came to see the present therapist only because the president of her company, who liked her a great deal, told her that he would no longer put up with her constant drinking and insisted that she come to see the writer.

TREATMENT

Rational-emotive treatment continued for six sessions along the same lines indicated in the transcript included previously in this chapter. This was followed by 24 weeks of RET group therapy and 1 weekend of rational encounter.

Cognitively, the client was repeatedly shown that her central problem was that she devoutly believed she had to be almost perfect and that she must not be criticized in any major way by significant others. She was persistently taught, instead, to refrain from rating her self but only to measure her performances; to see that she could never be, except by arbitrary definition, a worm even if she never rid herself of her overeating, her compulsive drinking, and her other foolish symptoms; to see that it was highly desirable but not necessary that she relate intimately to a man and to win the approval of her peers and her bosses at work; and first to accept herself with her hostility and then to give up her childish demands on others that led her to be so hostile to them. Although she devoutly believed in the "fact" that she and others should be extremely efficient and follow strict disciplinary rules, and although she time and again resisted the therapist's and the group members' assaults against her moralistic shoulds, she was finally induced to replace them, in her vocabulary as well as in her internalized beliefs, with it would be betters. She claimed to have completely overthrown her original religious orthodoxy, but she was

shown that she had merely replaced it with an inordinate demand for certainty in her personal life and in world affairs, and she was finally induced to give this up, too.

Emotively, Sara was fully accepted by the therapist as a person, even though he strongly assailed many of her ideas and sometimes humorously reduced them to absurdity. She was assertively confronted by some of the group members, who took her to task for condemning other members for their stupidities and their shirking, and she was helped to relate to these people in spite of their inadequacies. The therapist and some of the others in her group and in the marathon weekend of rational encounter in which she participated used vigorous, down-to-earth language with her, which she initially disliked but which she later began to use to some extent herself. When she went on a drinking bout for a few weeks and felt utterly depressed and hopeless, two group members brought out their own previous difficulties with alcohol and drugs and showed how they had managed to get through that almost impossible period of their lives. Another member gave her steady support through many phone calls and visits. At times, when she clammed up or sulked, the therapist and other group members forced her to open up and voice her real feelings. Then they went after her defenses with RET analyses and revealed her foolish ideas (especially the idea that she had to be terribly hurt if others rejected her) and how these could be uprooted. During the marathon, she was able, for the first time in her life, to let herself be really touched emotionally by a male who, up to that time, was a perfect stranger to her, and this showed her that she could afford to let down her long-held barriers to intimacy and let herself love.

Behavioristically, Sara was given homework assignments that included talking to attractive males in public places and thereby overcame her fears of being rejected. She was shown how to stay on a long-term diet (which she had never done before) by only allowing herself rewarding experiences (such as listening to classical music) when she had first maintained her diet for a certain number of hours. Through the use of roleplaying with the therapist and other group members she was given training in being assertive with people at work and in her social life without being hostile.

RESOLUTION

Concomitant with her individual and group therapy, and probably as a result of the combination of cognitive, emotive, and behavioristic approaches, Sara progressed in several ways: (1) She stopped drinking completely, lost 25 pounds, and appeared to be maintaining both her sobriety and her weight loss. (2) She became considerably less condemnatory of both herself and others and began to make some close friends. (3) She had satisfactory sex relations with three different males and began to go steadily with the second one of the three. (4) She only rarely made herself guilty or depressed, accepted herself with her failings, and began to focus much more on enjoying than on rating herself.

FOLLOW-UP

Sara had RET individual and group sessions for six months—and occasional follow-up sessions for the next year. She married her steady boyfriend about a year after she had originally begun treatment, having two premarital counseling sessions with him following their engagement. Two and one-half years after the close of therapy, she and her husband visited one of the regular Friday night workshops given by the therapist at the Institute for Rational-Emotive Therapy in New York City and they reported that everything was going well in their marriage, at her job, and in their social life. Her husband seemed particularly appreciative of the use she was making of RET principles and noted that "she still works hard at what she learned with you and the group and, frankly, I think that she keeps improving, because of this work, all the time." She smilingly and enthusiastically agreed.

SUMMARY

Rational-emotive therapy (RET) is a comprehensive system of personality change that includes a large variety of cognitive, emotive, and behavior therapy methods. It is not merely an eclectic or pragmatic psychological treatment but is based on a clear-cut theory of emotional health and disturbance. The many techniques it employs are used in the light of that theory. Its major hypotheses also relate to child-rearing, education, social and political affairs, the extension of people's intellectual-emotional frontiers, and the abetting of their unique potential for growth. Rational-emotive psychology is hardheaded, empirically oriented, rational, and nonmagical. It fosters the use of reason, science, and technology in the straightforward interest of man and woman. It is humanistic, existentialist, and hedonistic. It makes growth and happiness the relevant core of a person's intrapersonal and interpersonal life.

RET theory holds that people are biologically and culturally predisposed to choose, create, relate, and enjoy, but that they are also just as strongly predisposed to conform, be suggestible, hate, and arbitrarily block their enjoying. Although they have remarkable capacities to observe, reason, imaginatively enhance their experiencing, and transcend some of their own essential limitations, they also have an incredibly facile and easy propensity to ignore reality, misuse reason, and rigidly and intolerantly invent gods and demons that frequently sabotage their health and happiness. In the course of their refusals to accept reality, their continual *musturbation*, and their absorption in deifying and devilifying themselves and others, they frequently wind up with fairly severe manifestations of what is called emotional disturbance.

More specifically, when noxious stimuli occur in people's lives at point A (the activating event), they usually observe these events fairly objectively and conclude, at point rB (their rational belief), that this event is unfortunate, inconvenient, and disadvantageous and that they wish it would change. They then appropriately feel, at point C (the consequence), sad, regretful, frustrated, or annoyed. These appropriate feelings usually help them to try to do something about the noxious activating event, so they feel a new consequence, namely, neutrality or joy. Their inborn and acquired hedonistic orientation thereby encourages them to have, in regard to noxious or unpleasant activating events (or activating experiences), thoughts ("I don't like this; let's see what I can do to change it") and feelings (sorrow and annoyance) that enable them to reorder their environment and to live more enjoyably.

Very often, however, when similar noxious activating events occur in people's lives, they observe these events intolerantly and grandiosely and conclude, at point iB (their irrational beliefs), that they are awful, horrible, and catastrophic, that they *must* not exist, and that they absolutely cannot stand them. They then inappropriately feel the consequence, at point C, of worthlessness, guilt, anxiety, depression, rage, and inertia. Their inappropriate feelings usually interfere with their doing something constructive about the noxious activating events, and they tend to condemn themselves for their unconstructiveness and to experience more feelings of shame, inferiority, and hopelessness. Their inborn and acquired person-downing, antihumanistic, deifying and devilifying philosophy encourages them to have, in regard to noxious or unpleasant activating events, foolish thoughts ("How awful this is and I am! There's nothing I can do about it!") and inappropriate feelings (hatred of themselves, of others, and of the world) that drive them to whine and rant and live less enjoyably.

RET is a cognitive-emotive-behavioristic method of psychotherapy uniquely designed to enable people to observe, understand, and persistently attack their irrational, grandiose, perfectionistic *shoulds*, *oughts*, and *musts*. It employs the logico-empirical method of science to encourage people to surrender magic, absolutes, and damnation; to acknowledge that nothing is sacred or all-important (although many things are quite important) and nothing is "awful" or "terrible" (although many things are exceptionally unpleasant and inconvenient); and to gradually teach themselves and to practice the philosophy of desiring rather than demanding and of working at changing what they can change and gracefully putting up with what they cannot.

In conclusion, rational-emotive therapy is a method of personality change that quickly and efficiently helps people resist their tendencies to be too conforming, suggestible, and anhedonic. It actively and didactically, as well as emotively and behaviorally, shows people how to abet and enhance one side of their humanness while simultaneously changing and living more happily with (and not repressing or squelching) another side. It is thus realistic and practical as well as idealistic and future-oriented. It helps individuals more fully to actualize, experience, and enjoy the here and now, but it also espouses long-range hedonism, which includes planning for their own (and others') future. It is what its name implies: rational *and* emotive, realistic *and* visionary, empirical *and* humanistic. As, in all their complexity, are humans.

ANNOTATED BIBLIOGRAPHY

Ellis, A. (1975). *How to live with a "neurotic"* (rev. ed.). New York: Crown Publishers.

This first book published on RET (1957) shows how almost anyone can use RET techniques to cope with and to help disturbed individuals at home or on the job. This is also the first psychology book to use a new linguistic device called E-prime language, or "semantic therapy," which eliminates the use of any form of the verb "to be," thus allowing no implication that human behavior remains fixed or unalterable.

Ellis, A. (1962). *Reason and emotion in psychotherapy.* New York: Lyle Stuart. (Paperback edition, Secaucus, NJ: Citadel, 1977.)

This was the first book to present RET in textbook form, written mainly for therapists and clinicians but also widely used by people who want to help themselves overcome their emotional problems.

Ellis, A. (1971). *Growth through reason: Verbatim cases in rational-emotive therapy.* Hollywood, CA: Wilshire Books.

This book presents verbatim dialogues between rational-emotive therapists and their clients, with Ellis stopping the tape, so to speak, at frequent intervals to explain what is happening—what RET techniques the therapist is using and what growth is taking place. Two of Dr. Ellis' therapy dialogues are included, as well as those by other therapists using RET: Ben N. Ard, Jr.; H. Jon Geis; John M. Gullo; Paul A. Hauck; and Maxie C. Maultsby, Jr.

Ellis, A. (1973). *Humanistic psychotherapy: The rational-emotive approach.* New York: McGraw-Hill Paperbacks.

This book presents, for the public and the profession, an up-to-date version of RET that emphasizes both its humanistic and its active-directive aspects. This approach places humans squarely in the center of the universe and shows how they have responsibility for choosing to make or not to make themselves emotionally disturbed.

Ellis, A., & Grieger, R. (1987). *Handbook of rational-emotive therapy.* 2 vols. New York: Springer.

This sourcebook offers some of the most salient and classic writings on RET, with sections on the theoretical and conceptional foundations of RET, the dynamics of emotional disturbance, the primary techniques and basic process of rational-emotive therapy, and RET with children.

Ellis, A., & Harper, R. A. (1975). *A new guide to rational living.* Englewood Cliffs, NJ: Prentice-Hall; and Hollywood: Wilshire Books.

This completely revised and rewritten version of the RET self-help classic is one of the most widely read self-help books ever published and the one most often recommended by cognitive-behavior therapists to their clients. It is a succinct, straightforward approach to RET based on self-questioning and homework.

CASE READINGS

Ard, B. N. (1971). The case of the black and silver masochist. In A. Ellis, *Growth through reason: Verbatim cases in rational-emotive therapy* (pp. 15–45). Hollywood: Wilshire Books. [Reprinted in D. Wedding & R. J. Corsini (1979). *Great cases in psychotherapy.* Itasca, IL: F. E. Peacock.]

Ard tackles the case of a 24-year-old schizophrenic woman who pays men to beat her with black and silver belts to assuage the guilt feelings that stem from her religious assumptions. By courageously disputing some of her religious and other irrational beliefs, the therapist makes real progress with an unusually disturbed woman who had not previously been helped by shock treatments or other forms of therapy.

Ellis, A. (1971). A twenty-three-year-old woman, guilty about not following her parents' rules. In A. Ellis, *Growth through reason: Verbatim cases in rational-emotive therapy* (pp. 223–286). Hollywood: Wilshire Books. [Reprinted in D. Wedding & R. J. Corsini (Eds.) (1989). *Case studies in psychotherapy.* Itasca, IL: F. E. Peacock.]

Ellis presents a verbatim protocol of the first, second, and fourth sessions with a woman who comes for help because she is self-punishing, impulsive and compulsive, afraid of males, has no goals in life, and is guilty about her relations with her parents. The therapist quickly zeroes in on her main problems and shows her that she need not feel guilty about doing what she wants to do in life, even if her parents keep upsetting themselves about her beliefs and actions.

Maultsby, M. C., Jr. (1971). A relapsed client with severe phobic reactions. In A. Ellis, *Growth through reason: Verbatim cases in rational-emotive therapy* (pp. 179–222). Hollywood: Wilshire Books.

Maultsby presents a verbatim first session and parts of subsequent sessions with a 24-year-old undergraduate student who had been previously hospitalized for a psychotic episode, who had 30 sessions of traditional psychotherapy, who reported significant improvement in most of his problems after 50 sessions of group rational-emotive therapy, but who a year later reported that his gains were being whittled away, that he was becoming afraid of having a concussion and a consequent major loss of intelligence, that he again felt stupid in his schoolwork, and that he blamed many of his personal failings on an automobile accident. Maultsby deals with this relapsed client in an active-directive manner and in relatively few additional sessions helps the client get to the point where he no longer feels disturbed.

Ellis, A. (1977). Verbatim psychotherapy session with a procrastinator. In A. Ellis & W. J. Knaus, *Overcoming procrastination* (pp. 152–167). New York: New American Library.

Ellis presents a single verbatim session with a procrastinator who was failing to finish her doctoral thesis in sociology. He deals with her problems in a direct, no-nonsense manner typical of rational-emotive therapy, and as a result of a single session, she later reports she finished her thesis, although she had previously been procrastinating on it for a number of years.

REFERENCES

Adler, A. (1931). *What life should mean to you.* New York: Blue Ribbon Books.

Adler, A. (1964a). *Superiority and social interest.* Ed. by H. L. Ansbacher & R. R. Ansbacher. Evanston, IL: Northwestern University Press.

Adler, A. (1964b). *Social interest: A challenge to mankind.* New York: Capricorn.

Baisden, H. E. (1980). *Irrational beliefs: A construct validation study.* Unpublished doctoral dissertation. University of Minnesota.

Beck, A. T. (1976). *Cognitive therapy and the emotional disorders.* New York: International Universities Press.

Beck, A. T. Rush, A. J., Shaw, B. F., & Emery, G. (1979). *Cognitive therapy of depression.* New York: Guilford Press.

Bernard, M. E. (1986). *Staying alive in an irrational world: The psychology of Albert Ellis.* South Melbourne, Australia: Carlton and Macmillan.

Bernard, M. E., & DiGiuseppe, R. (Eds.) (1988). *Inside rational-emotive therapy.* Orlando, FL: Academic Press.

Bernard, M. E., & Joyce, M. R. (1985). *Rational-emotive therapy with children and adolescents.* New York: Wiley.

Bone, H. (1968). Two proposed alternatives to psychoanalytic interpreting. In E. Hammer (Ed.), *Use of interpretation in treatment.* New York: Grune and Stratton.

Burns, D. D. (1980). *Feeling good: The new mood therapy.* New York: Morrow.

Corey, G., & Borey, M. S. (1986). *I never knew I had a choice.* Monterey, CA: Brooks/Cole.

DiGiuseppe, R. A., Miller, N. J., & Trexler, L. D. (1979). A review of rational-emotive psychotherapy outcome studies. In A. Ellis & J. M. Whiteley (Eds.), *Theoretical and empirical foundations of rational-emotive therapy* (pp. 218–235). Monterey, CA: Brooks/Cole.

Dryden, W. (1984). *Rational-emotive therapy: Fundamentals and innovations.* Beckenham, England: Croom-Helm.

Dryden, W., & Trower, P. (Eds.) (1986). *Rational-emotive therapy: Recent developments in theory and practice.* Bristol, England: Institute for RET (UK).

Dyer, W. (1976). *Your erroneous zones.* New York: Funk and Wagnalls.

Ellis, A. (1962). *Reason and emotion in psychotherapy.* Secaucus, NJ: Lyle Stuart.

Ellis, A. (1965). *Sex without guilt.* Secaucus, NJ: Lyle Stuart; North Hollywood, CA: Wilshire Books.

Ellis, A. (1969a). A weekend of rational encounter. *Rational Living, 4(2),* 1–8.

Ellis, A. (1969b, November). Teaching emotional education in the classroom. *School Health Review.*

Ellis, A. (1971). *Growth through reason.* North Hollywood, CA: Wilshire Books.

Ellis, A. (1972). *Executive leadership: The rational-emotive approach.* New York: Institute for Rational-Emotive Therapy.

Ellis, A. (1973). *Humanistic psychother-*

apy: *The rational-emotive approach.* New York: McGraw-Hill.

Ellis, A. (1975). *How to live with a neurotic (rev. ed).* North Hollywood, CA: Wilshire Books.

Ellis, A. (1977a). *Anger—how to live with and without it.* Secaucus, NJ: Citadel Press.

Ellis, A. (1977b). *A garland of rational humorous songs.* (Cassette recording). New York: Institute for Rational-Emotive Therapy.

Ellis, A. (1978). Toward a theory of personality. In R. J. Corsini (Ed.), *Readings in current personality theories.* Itasca, IL: Peacock.

Ellis, A. (1979a). Rational-emotive therapy: Research data that support the clinical and personality hypotheses of RET and other modes of cognitive-behavior therapy. In A. Ellis & J. M. Whiteley (Eds.), *Theoretical and empirical foundations of rational-emotive therapy* (pp. 101–173). Monterey, CA: Brooks/Cole.

Ellis, A. (1976b). The biological basis of human irrationality. *Journal of Individual Psychology, 32,* 145–168.

Ellis, A. (1979b). *The intelligent woman's guide to dating and mating.* Secaucus, NJ: Lyle Stuart.

Ellis, A. (1980). Rational-emotive therapy and cognitive behavior therapy: Similarities and differences. *Cognitive Therapy and Research, 4,* 325–340.

Ellis, A. (1985a). *Overcoming resistance: Rational-emotive therapy with difficult clients.* New York: Springer.

Ellis, A. (1985b) Expanding the ABCs of rational-emotive therapy. In M. Mahoney & A. Freeman (Eds.), *Cognition and psychotherapy* (pp. 313–323). New York: Plenum.

Ellis, A. (1985c). Two forms of humanistic psychology: Rational-emotive therapy vs. transpersonal psychology. *Free Inquiry, 15*(4), 14–21.

Ellis, A. (1987a). A sadly neglected cognitive element in depression. *Cognitive Therapy and Research, 11,* 121–146.

Ellis, A. (1987b). The use of rational humorous songs in psychotherapy. In W. F. Fry, Jr., & W. A. Salameh (Eds.), *Handbook of humor and psychotherapy* (pp. 265–286). Sarasota, FL: Professional Resource Exchange.

Ellis, A. (1988). *How to stubbornly refuse to make yourself miserable about anything—yes, anything!* Secaucus, NJ: Lyle Stuart.

Ellis, A., & Becker, I. (1982). *A guide to personal happiness.* North Hollywood, CA: Wilshire.

Ellis, A., & Bernard, M. E. (Eds.) (1983). *Rational-emotive approaches to the problems of childhood.* New York: Plenum.

Ellis, A., & Bernard, M. E. (Eds.) (1985). *Clinical applications of rational-emotive therapy.* New York: Plenum.

Ellis, A., & Dryden, W. (1987). *The practice of rational-emotive therapy.* New York: Springer.

Ellis, A., & Grieger, R. (Eds.) (1986). *Handbook of rational-emotive therapy.* 2 vols. New York: Springer.

Ellis, A., & Harper, R. A. (1961). *A guide to successful marriage.* North Hollywood, CA: Wilshire Books.

Ellis, A., & Harper, R. A. (1975). *A new guide to rational living.* North Hollywood, CA: Wilshire Books.

Ellis, A., McInerney, J. F., DiGiuseppe, R. A., & Yeager, R. (1988). *Rational-emotive treatment of alcoholism and substance abuse.* New York: Pergamon.

Ellis, A., & Whiteley, J. M. (1979). *Theoretical and empirical foundations of rational-emotive therapy.* Monterey, CA: Brooks/Cole.

Engels, G., & Dieksta, R. (1986). A meta-analysis of rational-emotive therapy outcome studies. In P. Eelen & O. Fontaine (Eds.), *Behavior therapy: Beyond the conditioning framework* (pp. 121–140). Leuven: Leuven University Press and Lawrence Erlbaum Associates.

Gerard, M., & Eyman, W. (1985). *Thinking straight and talking sense.* New York: Institute for Rational-Emotive Therapy.

Goldfried, M. R., & Davison, G. C. (1976). *Clinical behavior therapy.* New York: Holt, Rinehart and Winston.

Grieger, R., & Boyd, J. (1980). *Rational-emotive therapy: A skills-based approach.* New York: Van Nostrand Reinhold.

Grieger, R., & Grieger, I. (Eds.) (1982). *Cognition and emotional disturbance.* New York: Human Sciences Press.

Haaga, D. A., & Davison, G. C. (in press). Outcome studies of rational-emotive therapy. In M. E. Bernard & R. DiGiuseppe (Eds.), *Inside rational-emotive therapy.* Orlando, FL: Academic Press.

Hauck, P. A. (1973). *Overcoming depression.* Philadelphia: Westminster.

Hauck, P. A. (1984). *The three faces of love.* Philadelphia: Westminster.

Heesacker, M., Heppner, P. P., & Rogers, M. E. (1982). Classics and emerging classics in psychology. *Journal of Counseling Psychology, 29,* 400–405.

Jakubowski, P., & Lange, A. (1978). *The assertive option.* Champaign, IL: Research Press.

Jones, R. (1968). *A factored measure of Ellis' irrational belief systems with personality and maladjustment correlates.* Ph.D. dissertation. Texas Tech College.

Kassinove, H., Crisci, R., & Tiegerman, S. (1977). Developmental trends in rational thinking: Implications for rational-emotive school mental health programs. *Journal of Community Psychology, 5,* 266–274.

Knaus, W. (1974). *Rational-emotive education.* New York: Institute for Rational-Emotive Therapy.

Knaus, W. (1983). *How to conquer your frustrations.* Englewood Cliffs, NJ: Prentice-Hall.

Knaus, W., & Hendricks, C. (1986). *The illusion trap.* New York: World Almanac.

Lazarus, A. A. (1981). *The practice of multimodal therapy.* New York: McGraw-Hill.

Mahoney, M. J. (1985). Psychotherapy and human change processes. In M. J. Mahoney & A. Freeman (Eds.), *Cognition and psychotherapy* (pp. 3–48). New York: Plenum.

McGovern, T. E., & Silverman, M. S. (1984). A review of outcome studies of rational-emotive therapy from 1977 to 1982. *Journal of Rational-Emotive Therapy, 2*(1), 7–18.

Meichenbaum, D. H. (1977). *Cognitive behavior modification.* New York: Plenum.

Miller, R. C., & Berman, J. S. (1983). The efficacy of cognitive behavior therapies: A quantitative review of the research evidence. *Psychological Bulletin, 94,* 39–53.

Shorkey, C. T., & Whiteman, V. L. (1977). Development of the rational behavior inventory. *Educational and Psychological Measurement, 37,* 527–534.

Sichel, J., & Ellis, A. (1984). *RET self-help form.* New York: Institute for Rational-Emotive Therapy.

Smith, D. (1982). Trends in counseling and psychotherapy. *American Psychologist, 37,* 802–809.

Smith, M. L., & Glass, G. V. (1977). Meta-analysis of psychotherapy outcome studies. *American Psychologist, 32,* 752–760.

Smith, T. W. (in press). Assessment in rational-emotive therapy. In M. E. Bernard & R. DiGiuseppe (Eds.), *Inside rational-emotive therapy.* Orlando, FL: Academic Press.

Spillane, R. (1985). *Achieving peak performance: A psychology of success in the organization.* Sydney, Australia: Harper & Row.

Sprenkle, D. H., Keeney, B. P., & Sutton, P. M. (1982). Theorists who influence clinical members of the AAMFT: A research note. *Journal of Marital and Family Therapy, 8,* 367–369.

Velten, E. (1986). Withdrawal from heroin and methadone with RET: Theory and practice. In W. Dryden and P. Trower (Eds.), *Rational-emotive therapy: Recent developments in theory and practice* (pp. 228–247). Bristol, England: Institute for RET (UK).

Walen, S. R., DiGiuseppe, R., & Wessler, R. L. (1980). *A practitioner's guide to rational-emotive therapy.* New York: Oxford.

Waters, V. (1981). *Rational stories for children.* New York: Institute for Rational-Emotive Therapy.

Wessler, R. A., & Wessler, R. L. (1980). *The principles and practice of rational-emotive therapy.* San Francisco, CA: Jossey-Bass.

Wilson, S. B. (1986). *A journey through the mind's eye.* East Dundee, IL: Mind's Eye Publishing Company.

Wolpe, J. (1982). *The practice of behavior therapy (3rd ed.).* New York: Pergamon.

Young, H. C. (1974). *A rational counseling primer.* New York: Institute for Rational-Emotive Therapy.

IVAN PAVLOV
1849–1936

B. F. SKINNER

ALBERT BANDURA

JOSEPH WOLPE

7

Behavior Therapy

G. TERENCE WILSON

OVERVIEW

Behavior therapy is a relative new-comer on the psychotherapy scene. Not until the late 1950s did it emerge as a systematic approach to the assessment and treatment of psychological disorders. In its early stages of development, behavior therapy was defined as the application of modern learning theory to the treatment of clinical problems. The phrase *modern learning theory* then referred to the principles and procedures of classical and operant conditioning. Behavior therapy was seen as the logical extension of behaviorism to complex forms of human activities.

Behavior therapy has undergone significant changes in both nature and scope. This rapid change and growth is one of the striking features of behavior therapy, which has been responsive to advances in experimental psychology and innovations in clinical practice. It has grown increasingly more complex and sophisticated. As a result, behavior therapy can no longer be simply defined as the clinical application of classical and operant conditioning theory.

Behavior therapy today is marked by a diversity of views. There is now a broad range of heterogeneous procedures with different theoretical rationales and open debate about conceptual bases, methodological requirements, and evidence of efficacy (Kazdin & Wilson, 1978). As behavior therapy has expanded, the degree of overlap with other psychotherapeutic approaches has increased. Nevertheless, the basic concepts characteristic of the approach are clear and its commonalties with and differences from nonbehavioral therapeutic systems can be identified.

BASIC CONCEPTS

The various approaches in contemporary behavior therapy include (a) *applied behavior analysis*, (b) *a neobehavioristic mediational stimulus-response model*, (c) *social learning theory*, and (d) *cognitive behavior modification*. Basically, these four approaches differ in the extent to which they use cognitive concepts and procedures. At one end of this continuum is *applied behavior analysis*, which fo-

241

cuses exclusively on observable behavior and rejects all cognitive mediating processes. At the other end are *social learning theory* and *cognitive behavior modification*, which rely heavily on cognitive theories.

Applied Behavior Analysis

This approach is a direct extension of Skinner's (1953) radical behaviorism, relying on operant conditioning, the fundamental assumption of which is that behavior is a function of its consequences. Accordingly, treatment procedures are based on altering relationships between overt behaviors and their consequences. Applied behavior analysis makes use of techniques based on reinforcement, punishment, extinction, stimulus control, and other procedures derived from laboratory research. Cognitive processes are considered private events and are not regarded as the proper subjects of scientific analysis. Applied behavior analysis is also distinguished by its methodology for evaluating treatment effects. The focus is on the intensive study of the individual subject.

The Neobehavioristic Mediational Stimulus-Response Model

This approach features the application of the principles of classical and avoidance conditioning. It derives from the learning theories of Ivan Pavlov, E. R. Guthrie, Clark Hull, O. H. Mowrer, and N. E. Miller. Unlike the operant approach, the S-R model is mediational, with intervening variables and hypothetical constructs prominently featured. Exemplifying the mediational nature of this approach is the central importance assigned to anxiety. The treatment techniques of systematic desensitization and flooding, which are most closely associated with this model, are both directed toward the extinction of the underlying anxiety that is assumed to maintain phobic disorders. Private events, especially imagery, have been an integral part of this approach, including systematic desensitization and covert conditioning techniques such as covert sensitization. The rationale behind all these methods is that covert processes follow the laws of learning that govern overt behaviors.

Social Learning Theory

The social learning approach to behavior therapy depends on the theory that behavior is based on three separate but interacting regulatory systems (Bandura, 1977). They are (a) external stimulus events, (b) external reinforcement, and most importantly, (c) cognitive mediational processes.

In the social learning approach, the influence of environmental events on behavior is largely determined by cognitive processes, which govern what environmental influences are attended to, how they are perceived, and how the individual interprets them. Social learning theory is based on a reciprocal determinism model of causal processes in human behavior. Psychological functioning, according to this view, involves a reciprocal interaction among three interlocking sets of influences: behavior, cognitive processes, and environmental factors. Bandura put it as follows:

Personal and environmental factors do not function as independent determinants; rather they determine each other. Nor can "persons" be considered causes independent of their behavior. It is largely through their actions that people produce the environmental conditions that affect their behavior in a reciprocal fashion. The experiences generated by behavior also partly determine what individuals think, expect, and can do, which in turn, affect their subsequent behavior. (1977, p. 345)

In social learning theory the person is the agent of change. The theory emphasizes the human capacity for self-directed behavior change.

Cognitive Behavior Modification

This fourth approach encompasses a number of diverse procedures, some of which have developed outside the mainstream of behavior therapy. The techniques most characteristic of cognitive behavior modification are referred to as cognitive restructuring and are drawn largely from the cognitive approaches of Ellis and Beck (see chapters 6 and 8). The basic assumption of this approach is that it is not experience itself, but the person's interpretation of that experience which produces psychological disturbance. Therapy consists of persuasion and argument directed toward altering irrational ideas. Specific behavioral tasks are also used to modify faulty perceptions and interpretations of important life events.

Common Characteristics

Although the four preceding behavior therapy approaches often involve conceptual differences, behavior therapists subscribe to a common core of basic concepts. Two major assumptions are (a) a learning model of human behavior that differs fundamentally from the traditional intrapsychic, psychodynamic, or quasi-disease model of mental illness, and (b) a commitment to the scientific method.

The emphasis on the psychological as opposed to quasi-disease model of abnormal behavior, and on a scientific approach, have the following consequences:

1. Many types of abnormal behavior formerly regarded as illnesses in themselves or as signs and symptoms of illness are better construed as nonpathological "problems of living" (key examples include anxiety reactions, sexual deviance, and conduct disorders).

2. Most abnormal behavior is assumed to be acquired and maintained in the same manner as normal behavior. It can be treated through the application of behavioral procedures.

3. Behavioral assessment focuses on the current determinants of behavior rather than on the analysis of possible historical antecedents. Specificity is the hallmark of behavioral assessment and treatment, and it is assumed that the person is best understood and described by what the person does in a particular situation.

4. Treatment requires a prior analysis of the problem into components or subparts. Procedures are then systematically targeted at specific components.

5. Treatment strategies are individually tailored to different problems in different individuals.

6. Understanding the origins of a psychological problem is not essential for producing behavior change. Conversely, success in changing a problem behavior does not imply knowledge about its etiology.

7. Behavior therapy involves a commitment to the scientific approach. This includes an explicit, testable conceptual framework; treatment either derived

from or at least consistent with the content and method of experimental-clinical psychology; therapeutic techniques that can be described with sufficient precision to be measured objectively and that can be replicated; the experimental evaluation of treatment methods and concepts; and the emphasis on innovative research strategies that allow rigorous evaluation of specific methods applied to particular problems instead of global assessment of ill-defined procedures applied to heterogeneous problems.

OTHER SYSTEMS

Behavior therapy shares many commonalties with other psychological therapies, particularly those that tend to be briefer and more directive. The broader and more complex behavior therapy has become, the greater has been the overlap. In some cases, behavior therapy has "borrowed" treatment concepts and methods from other systems. For example, behavioral marital therapy places great emphasis on communication skills (Jacobson & Margolin, 1979). The reliance upon communication analyses of interpersonal behavior in the treatment of marital conflict was derived not from an operant conditioning viewpoint, but from the clinical tradition of client-centered therapy (Knudson, Gurman & Kniskern, 1979).

Cognitive-behavioral treatment strategies have incorporated some of the concepts and methods of both Albert Ellis' rational-emotive therapy and Aaron Beck's cognitive therapy (Kendall & Hollon, 1979; O'Leary & Wilson, 1987). While such approaches within behavior therapy are proving useful in conceptualizing therapeutic

mechanisms, the evidence shows that the behavioral procedures are the most effective methods for producing psychological change—broad change that includes subjective, emotional, and behavioral components (Bandura, 1986). Because Beck's cognitive therapy emphasizes the importance of behavioral procedures in correcting the dysfunctional cognitions that are assumed to cause emotional distress, his approach overlaps greatly with cognitive-behavioral treatment methods.

In terms of clinical practice, behavior therapy and multimodal therapy are similar. The majority of the techniques that Arnold Lazarus (1981) lists as the most frequently used in multimodal therapy (see chapter 13) are standard behavior therapy strategies. This is not surprising given that Lazarus (1971) was one of the pioneers of clinical behavior therapy, helping to broaden its conceptual bases and introducing innovative clinical methods. Whether or not the multimodal techniques that receive no attention in behavior therapy (e.g., time projection, the empty chair technique) add to therapeutic efficacy is unclear because there are no controlled studies or even acceptable uncontrolled clinical trials to help decide the issue.

Either therapists are guided in their formulations and treatment of different problems on the basis of clearly stated principles or they act as a result of personal experience and intuition. Behavior therapy represents an attempt to move beyond idiosyncratic practices and to base clinical practice on more secure scientific foundations. Of course, this does not mean that clinical practice by behavior therapists is always based on solid empirical evidence. Behavior therapists, not unlike therapists from other approaches, have developed their own clinical lore, much of which owes nothing to experimental research. Lacking sufficient information and guidelines from research, behavior therapists often adopt an informed trial-and-error approach to difficult or unusual problems. Nonetheless, behavior therapy is clearly linked to a specifiable and testable conceptual framework.

Behavior therapy differs fundamentally from psychodynamic approaches to treatment. Based on a learning or educational model of human development, behavior therapy rejects the quasi-disease model of psychoanalytic therapy in which abnormal behavior is viewed as a symptom of underlying unconscious conflicts. Psychoanalytic therapy has difficulty in explaining the well-documented successes of behavior therapy that directly contradict basic concepts that psychoanalysts claim are crucial for therapeutic change. Some psychodynamic therapists have predicted that behavioral treatment will result in symptom substitution because behavioral treatment allegedly overlooks the "real" cause of the problem. Yet the evidence is clear that symptom substitution does not occur as a sequel of successful behavior theory (e.g., Sloane, Staples, Cristol, Yorkston & Whipple, 1975).

Family and systems therapists assert that problems of an individual can best be understood and successfully treated by changing the entire interpersonal system within a family. Behavior therapy has increasingly emphasized the importance of other family members in treatment, especially in the maintenance of therapeutic improvement. However, behavior therapists reject the assumption that every problem requires a broad-scale intervention in the family system. The findings of well-controlled outcome studies clearly show that this is not always necessary (Mathews, Gelder & Johnston, 1981). For example, not only does individual behavior therapy for agoraphobics produce long-term improvement in phobic fear and avoidance behavior, but it often also results in increases in marital satisfaction and other aspects of interpersonal functioning (Marks, 1981). Data such as these discredit some of the claims of the family systems theorists.

Most forms of psychotherapy tend to be limited to specific populations of patients. Traditional psychoanalytic therapy, for instance, has focused predominantly on white, well-educated, socially and economically advantaged, neurotic patients. Behavior therapy is more broadly applicable to the full range of psychological disorders than is traditional psychotherapy (Kazdin & Wilson, 1978). In the Sloane et al. (1975) study, for example, behavior therapy appeared to be more effective than traditional psychotherapy, particularly with the more complex problems in the more severely disturbed patients. Areas of successful application of behavior therapy procedures are found in education, rehabilitation, and even medicine (Franks, Wilson, Kendall & Brownell, 1982; Kazdin, 1978b). Finally, there is evidence showing that behavior therapy is the preferred treatment for certain problems, such as phobic and obsessive disorders, sexual dysfunction, and a number of childhood disorders. Overall evaluation of the comparative efficacy of behavior therapy versus other psychotherapies continues to be uncertain. Nevertheless, in no comparative outcome study to date has behavior therapy been shown to be less effective than any alternative form of psychotherapy (Kazdin & Wilson,

1978). The evidence, unsatisfactory as it still is, indicates that behavior therapy is more effective than psychoanalytic and other verbal psychotherapies (see Andrews & Harvey, 1981; O'Leary & Wilson, 1987; Shapiro & Shapiro, 1983).

HISTORY

PRECURSORS

Two historical events overshadow all others in the development of behavior therapy. The first was the rise of behaviorism in the early 1900s. The key figure in the United States was J. B. Watson, who criticized the subjectivity and mentalism of the psychology of the time and put forward behaviorism as the basis for the objective study of behavior. Watson's emphasis on the overriding importance of environmental events, his rejection of covert aspects of the individual, and his claim that all behavior could be understood as a result of learning became the formal bases of behaviorism.

Watson's extremist position has been widely rejected, and more refined versions of behaviorism have been developed. Preeminent in this regard has been B. F. Skinner, whose radical behaviorism has had a significant impact not only on behavior therapy (particularly applied behavior analysis) but also on psychology in general. Like Watson, Skinner insisted that overt behavior is the only acceptable subject of scientific investigation and rejected mentalistic concepts.

The second event was experimental research on the psychology of learning. In Russia, around the turn of the century, Ivan Pavlov, a Nobel Laureate in physiology, established the foundations of classical conditioning. About the same time in the United States,

pioneering research on animal learning by E. L. Thorndike showed the influence of consequences (rewarding and punishing events) on behavior. Beginning in the late 1930s, instrumental learning was elaborated upon by Skinner in his research on operant conditioning.

Research on conditioning and learning principles, conducted largely in the animal laboratory, became a dominant part of experimental psychology in the United States following World War II. Workers in this area, in the traditions of Pavlov and Skinner, were committed to the scientific analysis of behavior using the laboratory rat and pigeon as their prototypic subjects. Among the early applications of conditioning principles to the treatment of clinical problems were two particularly notable studies. In 1924, Mary Cover Jones described the use of different behavioral procedures for overcoming children's fears. Later, in 1938, O. Hobart Mowrer and E. Mowrer extended conditioning principles to the treatment of enuresis. The method that resulted from their work is now a demonstrably effective and widely used treatment (Ross, 1981). These isolated and sporadic efforts had scant impact on psychotherapy then, partly because conditioning principles, demonstrated with animals, were rejected as too simplistic and irrelevant to the treatment of complex human problems. Conditioning treatments were rejected as superficial, mechanistic, and naive. A schism existed between academic-experimental and clinical psychologists. The former were trained in scientific methods, with an emphasis on controlled experimentation and quantitative measurement. The latter concerned themselves with the "soft" side of psychology, including uncontrolled case studies, speculative hypotheses, and psychodynamic hypotheses about unconscious motivation. Some efforts were made to integrate conditioning principles with psychodynamic theories of abnormal behavior, but these eclectic formulations had little effect and only obscured crucial differences between the respective behavioral and psychodynamic approaches. Dollard and Miller (1950), for example, translated psychodynamic therapies into the language of Hullian learning theory but with little consequence for any clinical innovation because they were merely reinterpreting psychotherapy as it was, rather than advocating different concepts and procedures. The advent of behavior therapy was marked by its challenge of the status quo and the presentation of a systematic and explicitly formulated clinical alternative that attempted to bridge the gap between the laboratory and the clinic.

BEGINNINGS

The formal beginnings of behavior therapy can be traced to separate but related developments in the 1950s in three countries.

Joseph Wolpe (1958), in South Africa, presented procedural details and results of his application of learning principles to adult neurotic disorders. Wolpe introduced several therapeutic techniques based on Pavlov's conditioning principles, Hull's stimulus-response (S-R) learning theory, and his own experimental research on fear reduction in laboratory animals. Anxiety was regarded as the causal agent in all neurotic reactions. It was defined as a persistent response of the autonomic nervous system acquired through the process of classical conditioning. Wolpe developed specific techniques designed to extinguish these conditioned autonomic reactions, including systematic desensitization, one of the most widely used methods of behavior therapy. A particularly controversial statement found in Wolpe's book was his claim that 90 percent of his patients were either "cured" or "markedly improved." Moreover, this unprecedented success rate was apparently accomplished, not after years and years of therapy, as posited to be necessary by psychoanalysis, but within a few months, or even weeks. Wolpe influenced A. A. Lazarus and S. Rachman, both of whom became leading figures in the development of behavior therapy. Wolpe's pioneering use of different conditioning techniques in therapy was consistent with similar proposals that had been put forward by Andrew Salter (1949) in New York.

Another landmark in the development of behavior therapy as an alternative approach to the traditional psychoanalytic model was the research and writings of Hans J. Eysenck and his students at the Institute of Psychiatry of London University. In a seminal paper published in 1959, Eysenck defined behavior therapy as the application of modern learning theory to the treatment of behavioral and emotional disorders. Eysenck emphasized the principles and procedures of Pavlov and Hull, as well as learning theorists such as Mowrer (1947) and Miller (1948). In Eysenck's formulation, behavior therapy was an applied science, the defining feature of which was that it is testable and falsifiable. A testable theory can be specified with sufficient precision for experimental investigation. A falsifiable theory specifies experimental conditions that can result in the theory's being disproved or falsified. In 1963 Eysenck and Rachman established the first journal devoted exclusively to behavior therapy— *Behaviour Research and Therapy*. As a result of the continuing research and writings of Eysenck and Rachman and their colleagues at the Institute of Psychiatry of London, this institute has remained one of the foremost centers of behavior therapy in the world.

A major force in the emergence of behavior therapy was the growth of operant conditioning in the United States and the extension of operant conditioning principles to clinical problems. This development was spurred by the publication in 1953 of Skinner's book *Science and Human Behavior*, in which he criticized psychodynamic concepts and reformulated psychotherapy in behavioral terms. The most important initial clinical application of operant conditioning was with children, work carried out under the direction of Sidney Bijou at the University of Washington. The broad application of operant conditioning to the whole range of psychiatric disorders reached full expression in the publication of Leonard Ullmann and Leonard Krasner's influential *Case Studies in Behavior Modification* in 1965. This book presented contrasting descriptions of medical and psychological models of treatment and illustrated how learning principles, particularly operant conditioning, could be used to modify diverse clinical problems. In 1968, the *Journal of Applied Behavior Analysis* began publication, providing the premier outlet for research on the modification of socially significant problems through the use of operant conditioning procedures.

Toward the end of the 1960s the theoretical and research bases of behavior therapy began to be expanded by drawing more broadly upon areas of experimental research and psychological theory beyond classical and operant conditioning principles. Increasingly, behavior therapists turned to current developments in areas such as social, personality, and developmental psychology for different ways of conceptualizing their activities and as sources of innovative therapeutic strategies. Particularly noteworthy in this regard was Bandura's (1969) social learning theory, with its emphases on vicarious learning (modeling), symbolic processes, and self-regulatory mechanisms. The 1970s witnessed an increased emphasis on cognitive processes and procedures in behavior therapy, as noted in the preceding section.

The 1980s have been marked by an even broader focus on developments in other areas of psychology. Particular attention has been paid to the role of affect in therapeutic change. The experimental analysis of the complex interactions among cognition, affect, and behavior is one of the more important areas of theory and research in contemporary behavior therapy. There is also increasing recognition of the importance of biological factors in many of the disorders commonly treated with behavioral methods (e.g., anxiety disorders and obesity). The study of biobehavioral interactions is an increasingly significant part of behavior therapy (O'Leary & Wilson, 1987). (See Kazdin [1978a] for a detailed history of behavior therapy.)

CURRENT STATUS

Within the space of only two decades, behavior therapy has established itself as a major form of psychological therapy. It has helped to transform graduate training in clinical psychology in the United States. Several doctoral training programs are predominantly behavioral in orientation. Few training programs in clinical psychology have no behavioral training component. Counseling programs in schools of education and doctoral programs in schools of psychology also reflect the influence of behavior therapy. In a survey of a random sample of clinical and counseling psychologists, Smith concluded that "no single theme dominates the present development of professional psychotherapy. Our findings suggest, however, that cognitive-behavioral options represent one of the strongest, if not *the* strongest, theoretical emphases today" (1982, p. 808). The impact of behavior therapy on psychiatry has been less significant (Brady & Wienckowski, 1978), although the American Psychiatric Association issued a report concluding that "behavioral principles ... have reached a stage of development where they now unquestionably have much to offer informed clinicians in the service of modern clinical and social psychiatry" (Birk et al., 1973, p. 64).

The Association for Advancement of Behavior Therapy (AABT) is the major behavior therapy organization in North America. It is a professional, interdisciplinary organization with over 3,000 members. Membership is open to professionals and students in disciplines such as psychology, psychiatry, social work, medicine, nursing, dentistry, rehabilitation, and education, but the majority of members are clinical psychologists with doctoral degrees. Participation in AABT activities is open to qualified nonmembers. AABT does not certify or license be-havior therapists. AABT publishes a major journal, *Behavior Therapy*, produces a monthly newsletter called the *Behavior Therapist*, and holds annual conventions.

Behavior therapy is also well represented throughout Europe, particularly in Great Britain, the Netherlands, West Germany, and Scandinavia. The umbrella organization in Europe is the European Association of Behaviour Therapy. The British Association of Behaviour Therapy alone has over 1,100 members and publishes *Behavioural Psychotherapy*, an interdisciplinary international journal for the helping professions.

The practice of behavior therapy is developing in Latin America, with active organizations in Bolivia, Chile, Columbia, Mexico, Peru, and Venezuela, among other countries. The federated association representing Central and South America is the Latin American Association for the Analysis and Modification of Behavior (ALOMOC). Brownell (1981) provides an analysis of behavior therapy organizations around the world.

The explosion of literature on behavior therapy has been dramatic. At present there are at least nine journals devoted exclusively to behavior therapy: *Advances in Behaviour Research and Therapy, Behaviour Research and Therapy, Behavior Therapy, Behavioural Assessment, Behavioural Psychotherapy, Behavior Modification, Journal of Behavior Therapy and Experimental Psychiatry, Journal of Behavioral Assessment*, and *Journal of Applied Behavior Analysis. Cognitive Therapy and Research* is an outlet for the cognitive connection in cognitive behavior modification, while *Biofeedback and Self-Regulation* and *Journal of Behavioral Medicine* overlap greatly with traditional behavior therapy research and practice. Behavior therapists are also significant contributors to, and editorial board members of, journals such as *Journal of Consulting and Clinical Psychology*, the most widely distributed clinical journal in the United States. In 1973 C. M. Franks and G. T. Wilson edited the first volume of *Annual Review of Behavior Therapy: Theory and Practice*. Books abound in behavior therapy, to the point where Rachman and Wilson noted that it "is no exaggeration to say that a major text on the subject is published virtually every month" (1980, p. 3).

PERSONALITY

THEORY OF PERSONALITY

There are specific theoretical differences within the broad framework of contemporary behavior therapy. These differences are most noticeable in personality theories on which the respective approaches are based. Eysenck (1967) has developed an elaborate trait theory of personality. Briefly, Eysenck classifies people on two major personality dimensions. The first, introversion-extraversion, refers to characteristics normally associated with the words *introverted* and *extraverted*. The second dimension is neuroticism-emotional stability, ranging from moody and touchy at one extreme to stable and even-tempered at the other. These personality dimensions are believed by Eysenck to be genetically determined. According to Eysenck's theory, introverts are more responsive to conditioning procedures than extraverts, so that where a client is classified on this dimension predicts how he or she will respond to treatment. Aside from Eysenck's own work and that of some of his students, this personality theory appears to have had little impact on clinical behavior therapy. Classifying clients on introversion-extraversion and neuroticism-stability dimensions has not proved useful in designing therapeutic interventions or in predicting outcome. Behavior therapists in general have rejected trait theories of personality.

Applied behavior analysis, derived directly from Skinner's radical behaviorism, restricts itself to the study of overt behavior and environmental conditions that presumably regulate the behavior. Covert unobservable elements, such as needs, drives, motives, traits, and conflicts, are disregarded. Behaviorists criticize such typical personality concepts as being vague pseudo-explanations of behavior. Skinner's analyses of behavior are couched in terms of conditioning processes, such as reinforcement, discrimination, and generalization.

However, radical behaviorism, with its emphasis on the overriding importance of environmental control of behavior, has been criticized for losing sight of the importance of the person—and lacking a theory of personality. The objection from humanistic psychologists is that applied behavior analysts treat people as though they were externally controlled only by situational forces rather than being free, self-directed agents responsible for their own growth and actions. A solution to this clash between two extreme viewpoints is to recognize that the characteristics of the environment interact with the nature of the people in it, and both commonsense and experimental findings show how unwise it is to ignore either side of this crucial interaction. A social learning framework of personality development and change provides a detailed and sophisticated analysis of this interaction between person and situation (Bandura, 1969; Mischel, 1968, 1981).

Much debate has centered on the question of whether the person or the situation is more important in predicting behavior. This question is misguided and unanswerable. In terms of a social learning analysis, the relative importance of individual differences and situations will depend on the situation selected, the type of behavior assessed, the particular individual differences sampled, and the purposes of the assessment (Mischel, 1973).

Consider the varying influence of different situations on different behaviors. Evidence clearly shows that an individual's behavioral patterns are generally stable and consistent over time. Nevertheless, studies also reveal that behavioral patterns are not highly generalized in different situations. The specificity or discriminativeness of behavior in different situations poses a significant problem for trait theories of personality. The central assumption of such theories is that people possess stable and generalized personality traits which determine behavioral consistency across a wide variety of different situations. Yet as Mischel (1968) has pointed out, with the exception of activities closely related to intelligence and certain forms of problem solving, the correlations between different measures of the same trait are usually very low and there is little consistency in behavior patterns across different stimulus situations.

Some psychodynamic conceptualizations of personality assume that the underlying personality structure is stable irrespective of the situation. Apparent inconsistencies in behavior are explained away as the surface or symptomatic manifestations of the "real" underlying motives. Overt behavior is of interest only to the extent that the behavior provides signs of deep-seated, generalized personality traits. It is said that behavior cannot be taken at face value but must be interpreted symbolically because the personality's defense mechanisms disguise and distort the "real" motivations being expressed in observed behavior. This practice of disregarding the importance of the patient's behavior in real-life situations in favor of a search for hidden motivational states is defensible only if the underlying motives can be reliably inferred and then shown to be useful for selecting specific treatment techniques. However, "the accumulated findings give little support for the utility of clinical judgments. . . . Clinicians guided by concepts about underlying genotypic dispositions have not been able to predict behavior better than have the person's own direct self-report, simple indices of directly relevant past behavior, or demographic variables" (Mischel, 1973, p. 254).

Social learning theory readily accounts for the discriminativeness of human behavior. A person would be predicted to act consistently across situations only to the extent that similar behavior leads, or is expected to lead, to similar consequences across those conditions. Because it is rare to find the same behavior reinforced across situations, it is not surprising that people make subtle discriminations and behave differently in different settings. An illustration from Mischel will help clarify this key concept:

Consider a woman who seems hostile and fiercely independent some of the time but passive, dependent, and feminine on other occasions. What is she really like? Which one of these two patterns reflects the woman that she really is? Is one pattern in the service of the other, or might both be in the service of a third motive? Must she be a really aggressive person with a facade of passivity—or is she a warm, passive-dependent woman with a surface defense of aggressiveness? Social learning theory suggests that it is possible for her to be all of these—a hostile, fiercely independent, passive, dependent, feminine, aggressive, warm person all in one. Of course which of these she is at any particular moment would not be random and capricious; it would depend on discriminative stimuli —who she is with, when, how, and much, much more. But each of these aspects of herself may be a quite genuine and real aspect of her total being. (1976, p. 86)

The difference between the behavioral and psychodynamic approaches in explaining the development of abnormal behavior can be illustrated with reference to Freud's Little Hans. The child developed a phobia for horses, which Freud attributed to castration anxiety and oedipal conflict. In their reinterpretation of this case, Wolpe and Rachman (1960) point out that Little Hans had recently experienced four incidents in which horses were associated with frightening events that could have created a classically conditioned phobic reaction, the most striking being an accident in which he was terrified by seeing a horse drawing a loaded cart knocked down and apparently killed. From a psychodynamic viewpoint, these external stimuli (what Little Hans saw) had little effect on the phobia; the fear of horses per se was less significant than the underlying conflict. As Freud put it, "the anxiety originally had no reference to horses but was transposed onto them secondarily." This interpretation does not account for the discriminative pattern of the boy's reac-

tions. For example, he was fearful of a single horse pulling a loaded cart (viewed by Freud as a symbol of pregnancy) but not of two horses, of a large rather than a small horse, of rapidly moving horse-drawn carts more than slowly moving ones, and so on. How is this pattern predicted by a global, internal construct such as an Oedipus conflict? In the accident that the boy witnessed, a single, large horse, moving rapidly, was believed to have been killed. A conditioning explanation emphasizes that specific stimulus elements elicit particular responses and therefore accounts plausibly for the discriminative fear responses of Little Hans.

Trait theories emphasize differences among people on some dimension selected by the clinician. For some purposes, such as gross screening (e.g., administering an MMPI to a client to explore further the extent of his or her psychopathology) or group comparisons, a trait approach is useful. But it does not aid the therapist in making treatment decisions about a particular individual. Take the traits of introversion-extraversion. According to Eysenck's theory, particular treatments will have different effects on clients who vary along these dimensions. In a well-controlled study, Paul (1966) correlated performance on paper-and-pencil personality tests measuring extraversion, emotionality, and anxiety, among other traits, with the therapeutic success obtained by treating public speaking anxiety with systematic desensitization. His results revealed no relationship whatsoever between global personality measures and therapeutic outcome. This result is typical of other outcome studies.

VARIETY OF CONCEPTS

Learning Principles

The case of Little Hans, described on page 252, illustrates the role of classical conditioning. When a previously neutral stimulus is paired with a frightening event (the unconditioned stimulus, or US), it can become a conditioned stimulus (CS) that elicits a conditioned response (CR) such as anxiety. Current analyses of classical conditioning have moved away from the once popular notion that what was learned consisted of simple stimulus-response (S-R) bonds. Rather, learning of correlational or contingent relationships between the CS and US defines the conditioning process. Classical conditioning is no longer seen as the simple pairing of a single CS with a single US on the basis of temporal contiguity. Instead, correlations between entire classes of stimulus events can be learned. People may be exposed to traumatic events (contiguity) but not develop phobic reactions unless a correlational or contingent relationship is formed between the situation and the traumatic event.

Operant conditioning emphasizes that behavior is a function of its environmental consequences. Behavior is strengthened by positive and negative reinforcement; it is weakened by punishment. Positive reinforcement refers to an increase in the frequency of a response followed by a favorable event. Reinforcement involves a contingency between behavior and the reinforcing event. An example would be a teacher or parent praising a child for obtaining a good report card. Negative reinforcement refers to an increase in behavior as a result of avoiding or escaping from an aversive event that one would have expected to occur had the escape behavior not been emitted. For example,

an agoraphobic, fearing loss of control and panic in a crowded shopping mall, will escape this aversive prospect by staying at home. This individual now experiences relief from anxiety by having avoided this panic and thereby finds it increasingly difficult to leave the house.

In punishment, an aversive event is contingent on a response; the result is a decrease in the frequency of that response. If a child is criticized or punished by his parents for speaking up, he is likely to become an inhibited and unassertive adult. Extinction refers to the cessation or removal of a response. Thus the family of an obsessive-compulsive client might be instructed to ignore requests for reassurance from the client that he has not done something wrong. The reinforcer that is no longer presented is inappropriate attention.

Discrimination learning occurs when a response is rewarded (or punished) in one situation but not in another. Behavior is then under specific stimulus control. This process is particularly important in explaining the flexibility or discriminativeness of human behavior under different physical and social conditions. For example, an obese client who goes on eating binges may show good food self-control under some circumstances but lose control in predictable situations (e.g., when alone and feeling frustrated or depressed). Generalization refers to the occurrence of behavior in situations other than that in which it was acquired. A therapist might help a client to become more assertive and expressive during treatment sessions. But the goal of therapy is for the client to act more assertively in real-life situations—in other words, it is important for generalization to occur.

Social learning theory recognizes both the importance of awareness in learning and the person's active cognitive appraisal of environmental events. Learning is facilitated when people are aware of the rules and contingencies governing the consequences of their actions. Reinforcement does not involve an automatic strengthening of behavior. Learning from response consequences is attributable to the informative and incentive functions of rewards. By observing the consequences of behavior, the person learns what action is appropriate in what situation. By symbolic representation of anticipated future outcomes of behavior, the person helps to generate the motivation to initiate and sustain current actions (Bandura, 1977). Often, people's expectations and hypotheses about what is happening to them may affect their behavior more than the objective reality of the rules and contingencies associated with the behavior. Clinical practice provides numerous instances that our subjective perception of the external world rather than objective reality frequently determines behavior. Clinical problems often arise when a significant discrepancy between a person's perception of events and objective reality develops. This is one of the reasons for the growing importance of cognitive restructuring methods in behavior therapy.

The importance social learning theory attaches to *vicarious learning* (*modeling*) is consistent with its emphasis on cognitive processes. In this form of learning, people acquire new knowledge and behavior by observing other people and events without engaging in the behavior themselves and without any direct consequences to themselves. Vicarious learning may occur when people watch what others do or when they attend to the physical environment, to events, and to symbols such as words and pictures. The influence of vicarious learning on human behavior is pervasive, and this concept greatly expands the power of social learning theory.

Person Variables

People do not passively interact with situations with empty heads or an absence of feelings. Rather, they actively attend to environmental stimuli, interpret them, encode them, and selectively remember them. Mischel (1973) has spelled out a series of person variables that explain the interchange between person and situation. These person variables are the products of each person's social experience and cognitive development that, in turn, determine how future experiences influence him or her. Briefly, they include the individual's *competencies* to construct (generate) diverse behaviors under appropriate conditions. In addition, there is the person's *encoding* and *categorization* of events and people, including the self. To understand how and what a person will perform in particular situations also requires attention to his or her *expectancies*, the *subjective values* of any expected outcomes, and the individual's *self-regulatory systems and plans*.

A full discussion of these person variables is beyond the scope of the present chapter, but some illustrative examples may be given. Take the role of *personal constructs*. Common clinical phenomena are the clients who constantly "put themselves down," considering themselves incompetent even though it is clear to the objective onlooker that they are competent and that they are distorting reality. In cases like these, behavior is mainly under the control of internal stimuli rather than environmental events. Different people might respond differently to the same objective stimulus situation depending on how they subjectively perceive or interpret what is happening to them. Therapy concentrates on correcting such faulty cognitive perceptions. But the behavior therapist must also assess a client's cognitive and behavioral competencies to ascertain whether he or she really can engage in a particular response. A client may be depressed not because he misperceives the situation but because he actually lacks the appropriate skills and behavior necessary to secure rewards which are important to him. A case in point would be a shy, underassertive college freshman who is motivated to date girls but realizes that he does not have the social skills needed to meet and befriend members of the opposite sex. Therapy would be geared to overcoming his behavioral deficit, helping the freshman to acquire the requisite interpersonal skills.

Self-efficacy is assessed simply by asking the person to indicate the degree of confidence that he or she can do a particular task which is described in detail.

Such person variables differ from traits in that they do not assume broad cross-situational consistency. Instead, they depend on specific contexts. Constructs such as generalized expectancies have not proved fruitful in predicting behavior. However, specific evaluations of individuals' efficacy expectations with respect to particular tasks are useful.

Applied behavior analysts, given their rejection of cognitive mediating processes in assessment and modification of behavior, find little use for the person variables described so far. They agree that the environment interacts with the person but, as radical behaviorists, contend that the role of the person is best explained in terms of past history of reinforcement. To illustrate the differences between the social learning and the radical behaviorist positions, imagine a client who is phobic about flying. This client typically becomes highly anxious when he hears a sudden noise at takeoff due to the normal retracting of the plane's landing gear. A therapist with a cognitive social learning view might attribute this anxiety reaction to the client's perception that something is wrong. The radical behaviorist would suggest that the client is reacting, not only to the present environment (the sudden noise), but also to stories he has heard in the past about engines falling off and planes crashing. This example makes it clear that radical behaviorism is not free from inferential reasoning, as is commonly supposed. The question is not whether inferences will be made in trying to account for human behavior, but what sort of inference is the most useful. And there is now evidence to demonstrate that taking person variables into account improves prediction about behavior and enhances therapeutic efficacy (O'Leary & Wilson, 1987).

PSYCHOTHERAPY

THEORY OF PSYCHOTHERAPY

Learning

Behavior therapy emphasizes corrective learning experiences in which clients variously acquire new coping skills and improved communication competencies or learn how to break maladaptive habits and overcome self-defeating emotional conflicts. In contemporary behavior therapy these corrective learning experiences involve broad changes in cognitive, affective, and behavioral spheres of functioning; they are not limited to modifications of narrow response patterns in overt behavior. These corrective learning experiences are the product of a wide range of different strategies continually being modified and refined on the basis of research and clinical findings. These therapeutic strategies are implemented during and between formal treatment sessions.

The learning that characterizes behavior therapy is carefully structured. Perhaps more than any other form of treatment, behavior therapy involves asking a patient to do something such as practice relaxation training, self-monitor daily caloric intake, engage in assertive acts, confront anxiety-eliciting situations, and refrain from carrying out compulsive rituals. The high degree to which behavior therapists emphasize the client's activities in the real world between therapy sessions is one of the distinctive features of the behavioral approach. However, behavior therapy is not a one-sided influence process by the therapist to effect changes in a client's beliefs and behavior. It involves both dynamic interaction between therapist and client and directed work on the part of the client. A crucial factor in therapy is the client's motivation, the willingness to cooperate in the arduous and challenging task of making significant changes in real-life behavior. Resistance to change and lack of motivation are common reasons for treatment failures in behavior therapy. Much of the art in therapy involves coping with these issues (Lazarus & Fay, 1982).

The Therapeutic Relationship

Behavior therapy demands considerable therapist skill, sensitivity, and clinical acumen. Brady underscores the importance of the therapeutic relationship as follows.

There is no question that qualitative aspects of the therapist-patient relationship can greatly influence the course of therapy for good or bad. In general, if the patient's relationship to the therapist is characterized by belief in the therapist's competence (knowledge, sophistication, and training) and if the patient regards the therapist as an honest, trustworthy, and decent human being with good social and ethical values (in his own scheme of things), the patient is more apt to invest himself in the therapy. Equally important is the quality and tone of the relationship he has with the therapist. That is, if he feels trusting and warm toward the therapist, this generally will facilitate following the treatment regimen, will be associated with higher expectations of improvement, and other generally favorable factors. The feelings of the therapist toward the patient are also important. If the therapist feels that his patient is not a desirable person or a decent human being or simply does not like the patient for whatever reasons, he may not succeed in concealing these attitudes toward the patient, and in general they will have a deleterious effect. There are some exceptions to these generalizations, however. Some patients will feel frightened and vulnerable with a therapist toward whom they feel attracted, particularly if from past experience they perceive such relationships as dangerous (danger of being hurt emotionally). With such a patient, a somewhat more distant and impersonal relationship may be more desirable in that it will facilitate the patient's involvement in the treatment, following the treatment regimen, etc. (1980, pp. 285–86)

A survey of behavior practitioners indicated that among the treatment procedures most frequently reported were methods aimed at improving the therapeutic relationship (Swan & MacDonald, 1978). O'Leary, Turkewitz, and Tafel (1973) found that virtually all parents whose children were treated at a child-guidance clinic rated their behavior therapists as understanding, warm, sincere, and interested. Similarly, in a study of marital therapy by Turkewitz and O'Leary (1981), clients' ratings of their behavior therapists were very positive.

There are important theoretical and practical differences between behavior therapy and traditional psychotherapies in the way in which the relationship in psychotherapy is conceptualized. As opposed to the neutral and detached role that the psychoanalytically oriented therapist is taught to assume, the behavior therapist is more directive and more concerned—a problem solver and a coping model who tries to instigate behavioral change in the client's natural environment and who serves as a source of personal support. In their comparative study of behavior therapy and psychoanalytically oriented psychotherapy, Sloane, Staples, Cristol, Yorkston, and Whipple concluded:

Differences between behavior therapy and analytically-oriented psychotherapy ... involved the basic patterns of interactions between patient and therapist and the type of relationship formed. Behavior therapy is not psychotherapy with special "scientific techniques" superimposed on the traditional therapeutic paradigm; rather, the two appear to represent quite different styles of treatment although they share common elements. (1975, p. 1521)

The behavior therapists were rated as more directive, more open, more genuine, and more disclosing than their psychoanalytically oriented counterparts. An early criticism was that behavior therapy would result in "symptom substitution." However, careful treatment outcome research shows that symptom substitution does not occur (Kazdin & Wilson, 1978; Sloane et al., 1975). The latter investigators summarize their findings as follows:

Not a single patient whose original problems had substantially improved reported new symptoms cropping up. On the contrary, assessors had the informal impression that when a patient's primary symptoms improve, he often spontaneously reported improvement of other minor difficulty. (p. 100)

Both behavioral and psychodynamic treatments attempt to modify underlying causes of behavior. The difference is what proponents of each approach regard as causes. Behavior analysts look for current variables and conditions that control behavior. Some psychodynamic approaches (e.g., psychoanalysis) ask, "How did he become this kind of person?" Others (e.g., Adlerian psychotherapy) ask, "What is this person trying to achieve?" Behavioral approaches ask, "What is causing this person to behave in this way right now, and what can we do right now to change that behavior?"

Ethical Issues

In behavior therapy the client is encouraged to participate actively. Consider, for example, the important issue of who determines the goals of therapy. Because it is fundamental to behavior therapy that the client should have the major say in setting treatment goals, it is important that the client is fully informed and consents to and participates in setting goals. A distinction is drawn between how behavior is to be changed—in which the therapist is presumably expert—and the objectives of therapy. The latter must ultimately be determined by the client. The client controls *what*, we control *how*. The major contribution of the therapist in this regard is to assist clients by helping them to generate alternative courses of action and to analyze the consequences of pursuing various goals. Because this process involves an expression of the therapist's own values, the therapist should identify them and explain how they might affect his or her analysis of therapeutic goals.

Selecting goals is far more complicated in the case of disturbed clients (such as institutionalized psychotics) who are unable to participate meaningfully in deciding treatment objectives. To ensure that treatment is in the client's best interests, it is important to monitor program goals and procedures through conferences with other professionals (Risley & Sheldon-Wildgen, 1982).

All forms of therapy involve social influence. The critical ethical question is whether therapists are aware of this influence. Behavior therapy entails an explicit recognition of the influence process and emphasizes specific, client-oriented behavioral objectives. Behavior therapists have formulated procedures to guarantee protection of human rights and personal dignity of clients, including homosexuals, the retarded, mental hospital patients, and school children, among others (Stolz, 1978; Wilson & O'Leary, 1980).

PROCESS OF PSYCHOTHERAPY

Problem Identification and Assessment

The initial task of behavior therapists is to identify and understand the client's presenting problem(s). The therapist using behavioral theory seeks detailed information about the specific dimensions of problems, such as initial occurrence, severity, and frequency. What has the client done to cope with the problems? What does the client think about his or her problem and

any previous therapeutic contacts? Obtaining answers to such searching questions, which the client might find distressing or embarrassing, is facilitated by first building a relationship of trust and mutual understanding. To achieve this, the therapist is attentive, tries to be emotionally objective, and, ideally, is an empathic listener. The therapist then proceeds to make a functional analysis of the client's problem, attempting to identify specific environmental and person variables that are thought to be maintaining maladaptive thoughts, feelings, or behavior. The emphasis on variables currently maintaining the problem does not mean that the client's past history is ignored. However, past experiences at any time in life are important only to the degree that they are still active in directly contributing to the client's present distress.

Assessment Methods

In the behaviorally oriented interview the therapist seldom asks the client *why* questions; for example, "Why do you become anxious in crowded places?" Questions starting with *how*, *when*, *where*, and *what* are more useful in identifying relevant personal and situational variables currently maintaining the client's problems. The therapist does not necessarily take everything the client says at face value and is constantly looking for inconsistencies, evasiveness, or apparent distortions. Nevertheless, the therapist relies heavily on clients' self-reports, particularly in assessing thoughts, fantasies, and feelings. Self-report has often proved to be a superior predictor of behavior compared to clinicians' judgments or scores on personality tests (Mischel, 1981). Of course, therapists must ask the right questions if they are to get meaningful answers. Given the tendency of most people to describe themselves in terms of broad personality labels, therapists may have to guide clients in finding specific behavioral referents of global subjective impressions.

Guided Imagery

A useful method for assessing clients' reactions to particular situations is to have them symbolically recreate a problematic life situation. Instead of asking clients simply to talk about an event, the therapist has them imagine it actually happening to them. When clients have conjured up an image of a situation, they are then asked to verbalize any thoughts that come to mind, an especially useful way of uncovering the specific thoughts associated with particular events.

Roleplaying

Another alternative is to ask clients to roleplay a situation rather than to describe or imagine it. This method lends itself well to the assessment of interpersonal problems, with the therapist adopting the role of the person with whom the client reports problems. Roleplaying provides the therapist with a sample of the problem behavior, albeit under somewhat artificial circumstances. If the therapist is assessing a client couple, the two partners are asked to discuss chosen issues that enable the therapist to observe first-hand the nature of their interpersonal skills and ability to resolve conflict.

Physiological Recording

Technological progress in monitoring different psychophysiological reactions has opened up possibilities of objectively measuring a number of problems, although these sophisti-

cated resources are often available only in some clinics or hospital settings. Monitoring a client's sexual arousal in response to specific stimuli that cause changes in penile or vaginal blood flow (Rosen & Keefe, 1978) is an example of how physiological recording instruments can be used in behavioral assessment and treatment strategies.

Self-Monitoring

Clients are typically instructed to keep detailed, daily records of particular events or psychological reactions. Obese clients, for example, are asked to self-monitor daily caloric intake, the degree to which they engage in planned physical activities, the conditions under which they eat and overeat, and so on. In this way it is possible to detect behavioral patterns in clients' lives functionally related to their problems.

Behavioral Observation

Assessment of overt problem behavior, ideally, is based on actual observation of the client's behavior in the natural environment in which it occurs. Accordingly, behavior therapists have developed sophisticated behavioral observation rating procedures for measuring behavior directly. These procedures have most often been used with children either in the classroom or at home and with hospitalized patients. Parents, teachers, nurses, and hospital aides have been trained as behavioral observers. Once these individuals have learned to observe behavior they can then be taught how to make a behavioral analysis of the problem and then instructed in how to alter their own behavior in order to modify the problem behavior.

Psychological Tests and Questionnaires

In general, behavior therapists do not use standardized psychodiagnostic tests, which are often based on questionable assumptions of personality trait theory. Tests such as the MMPI may be useful for providing an overall picture of the client's personality profile, but they do not yield the kind of information necessary for a functional analysis or for the development of a strategy of therapeutic interventions. Projective tests are widely rejected in view of their assumptions of psychodynamic theory and the lack of acceptable evidence for their validity or utility (Mischel, 1968). Behavior therapists do use checklists and questionnaires, such as the Marks and Mathews Fear Questionnaire (1979), self-report scales of depression like the Beck Depression Inventory (Beck, Rush, Shaw & Emery, 1979), assertion inventories like the Rathus (1973) questionnaire, and paper-and-pencil measures of marital satisfaction such as the Locke and Wallace inventory of marital adjustment (1959). These assessment devices are not sufficient for carrying out a functional analysis of the determinants of the problem, but are useful in establishing the initial severity of the problem and for charting therapeutic efficacy over the course of treatment.

Treatment Techniques

Behavior therapy offers a wide range of different treatment methods. Rather than artificially molding the client's problems to suit the therapist's preconceived theoretical notions, behavior therapy attempts to tailor the principles of social learning theory to each individual's unique problem. Some techniques are more appropri-

ate with some problems and clients than with others. In selecting treatment techniques, the behavior therapist relies heavily on available empirical evidence about the efficacy of that technique applied to the particular problem. This information is frequently not sufficient for guiding therapeutic interventions, and in many cases the empirical evidence is unclear or largely nonexistent. Here the therapist is influenced by accepted clinical practice (the state of the art) and the basic logic and philosophy of a social learning approach to human behavior and its modification. In the process, the therapist must often use intuitive skill and clinical savvy in deciding not only on the appropriate treatment methods, but also the important matter of timing—when to use any specific technique. Both science and art enter into informed clinical practice, and the most effective therapists are those aware of the advantages and limitations of each.

The following are some selective illustrations of the varied methods the typical behavior therapist is likely to employ in clinical practice.

Imagery-Based Techniques

In systematic desensitization, after isolating specific events that trigger unrealistic anxiety, the therapist constructs a stimulus hierarchy in which different situations that the client fears are ordered along a continuum from mildly stressful to very threatening. The client is instructed to conjure a clear and vivid image of each item while he or she is deeply relaxed. Wolpe (1958) adapted from Jacobson (1938) the method of progressive relaxation training as a means of producing a response incompatible with anxiety. Briefly, this consists of training clients to concentrate on systematically relaxing the different muscle groups of the body, which results in lowered physiological arousal and a comfortable subjective feeling of calmness. In the event that any item produces much anxiety, the client is instructed to cease visualizing the particular item and to restore feelings of relaxation. The item is then repeated, or the hierarchy adjusted, until the client can visualize the scene without experiencing anxiety. Only then does the therapist present the next item of the hierarchy.

Symbolically generated aversive reactions are used to treat unwanted problems including alcoholism and sexual disorders such as exhibitionism. In this procedure the client is asked to imagine the aversive consequence. An alcoholic might be asked to imagine experiencing nausea at the thought of a drink. As illustrated in the "Case Example," an exhibitionist might be asked to imagine being apprehended by the police. This method is often referred to as covert sensitization (Cautela, 1967). A hierarchy of scenes that reliably elicit the problem urge or behavior is developed and each scene is systematically presented until the client gains control over the problem.

Cognitive Restructuring

The treatment methods in this category are based on the assumption that emotional disorders result from maladaptive thought patterns. The task of therapy is to alter these faulty cognitions. Ellis' (1962) RET may be viewed as a cognitive-behavioral approach to cognitive restructuring. Another widely used method is Meichenbaum's (1977) self-instructional training, which involves the following steps: (a) the client is trained to iden-

tify and become aware of maladaptive thoughts (self-statements); (b) the therapist models appropriate behavior while verbalizing effective action strategies; these verbalizations include an appraisal of task requirements, self-statements that stress personal adequacy and counteract worry over failure, and self-reinforcement for successful performance; (c) the client performs the target behavior first while verbalizing aloud the appropriate self-instructions and then by covertly rehearsing them. Beck's (1976) cognitive therapy is a particularly useful form of cognitive restructuring that combines cognitive with behavioral methods.

Assertiveness and Social Skills Training

A common clinical problem is presented by unassertive clients who are unable to express their emotional feelings and do not stand up for their legitimate rights. They are often exploited by others, feel anxious in social situations, and suffer from a low sense of self-esteem. In behavior rehearsal the therapist may model the appropriate assertive behavior and may ask the client to engage repeatedly in a graduated sequence of similar actions. Attention is focused on developing nonverbal as well as verbal features of expressive behavior (e.g., body posture, voice training, and eye contact). The therapist then encourages the client to carry out assertive actions in the real world to ensure generalization. Behavior therapy is frequently conducted in a group as well as on an individual basis (Upper & Ross, 1981). Behavior rehearsal for assertiveness training is well suited to group therapy, because group members can provide more varied sources of educational feedback than can a single therapist and can also offer a diversified range of modeling influences.

Aside from enhancing assertiveness, the instructional, modeling, and feedback components of behavior rehearsal facilitate a broader range of communication competencies, including active listening, giving personal feedback, and building trust through self-disclosure. These communication principles, drawn from nonbehavioral approaches to counseling but integrated within a behavioral framework, are an important ingredient of behavioral marital therapy (Jacobson & Margolin, 1979).

Self-Control Procedures

In behavioral treatment programs, both child and adult clients are taught that they must play an active part in determining their treatment goals and in implementing the treatment program. Behavior therapists use a number of self-control procedures (Bandura, 1977; Kanfer, 1977). Fundamental to successful self-regulation of behavior is self-monitoring, a process to make clients more aware of their specific problems and actions. The therapist helps the client to set goals or standards that guide behavior. In the treatment of obesity, for example, daily caloric goals are mutually selected. Behavioral research has identified certain properties of goals that increase the probability of successful self-control. For example, one should set highly specific, unambiguous, and short-term goals, such as consumption of no more than 1,200 calories each day. Compare this to the goal of "cutting back" on eating for the "next week." Failure to achieve such vague goals elicits negative self-evaluative reactions by clients, whereas successful accomplishment of goals produces self-

reinforcement that increases the likelihood that the self-regulatory behavior will be further maintained.

Self-instructional training, described above, is often used as a self-control method for coping with problems such as impulsivity, stress, excessive anger, and pain. Similarly, progressive relaxation training is widely applied as a self-control method for reducing different forms of stress, including insomnia, tension headaches, and hypertension (O'Leary & Wilson, 1987). Biofeedback methods used to treat a variety of psychophysiological disorders also fall under the category of self-control procedures (Yates, 1980).

Real-Life Performance-Based Techniques

The foregoing techniques are applied during treatment sessions, and most are routinely coupled with instructions to clients to complete homework assignments: namely, specific tasks carried out *between* therapy sessions in the real world. In addition, some treatment methods are to be implemented primarily in the client's natural environment. The behavioral treatment of agoraphobia is an example of a real-life performance-based technique.

The diversity of behavioral treatment methods, including radical departures from conventional practice, is seen in the application of operant conditioning principles in settings ranging from classrooms to institutions for the retarded and the mentally ill. An excellent illustration is the use of token economy. The main elements of a token reinforcement program can be summarized as follows: (a) carefully specified and operationally defined target behaviors, (b) backup reinforcers, the "good things in life" or what people are willing to work for, (c) tokens that represent the backup reinforcers, and (d) rules of exchange that specify the number of tokens required to obtain backup reinforcers.

A token economy in a classroom might consist of the teacher, at regular intervals, making ratings in special books on each child's desk indicating how well the student had behaved both academically and socially. At the end of the day the ratings would be exchangeable for various small prizes. These procedures reduce disruptive social behavior in the classroom and can improve academic performance (O'Leary & O'Leary, 1977). In the case of psychiatric inpatients the staff might make tokens contingent upon improvements in self-care activities, reductions in belligerent acts, and cooperative problem-solving behavior (Kazdin, 1977). The behavior therapist designs the token economy and monitors its implementation and efficacy. The procedures themselves are implemented in real-life settings by teachers, parents, nurses, and psychiatric aides—whoever has most direct contact with the patient. Ensuring that these psychological assistants are well trained and supervised is the responsibility of the behavior therapist.

Length of Treatment

Much of behavior therapy is short-term treatment, but therapy lasting from 25 to 50 sessions is commonplace, and still longer treatment is not unusual. Therapy in excess of 100 sessions, however, is relatively rare. There are no established guidelines for deciding on the length of therapy in any a priori fashion. The usual approach in clinical practice is to carry out a detailed behavioral assessment of the problem(s) and to embark upon interventions as rapidly as possible. Assessment is an ongoing process, as the consequences of initial treatment interventions are evaluated against therapeutic goals. Unless treatment time is explicitly limited from the start, the length of therapy and the scheduling of the treatment sessions are contingent upon the patient's progress.

Typically, a behavior therapist might contract with the patient to pursue a treatment plan for two to three months (approximately 8 to 12 sessions) and reevaluate progress at the end of this period. The relative absence of any discernible improvement is cause for the therapist to reevaluate whether he or she conceptualized the problem accurately, whether he or she is using the appropriate techniques or needs to switch tactics, whether there is some personal problem with him or her as the therapist, or whether a referral to another therapist or another form of treatment might be more helpful.

In terminating a successful case, the behavior therapist usually avoids abruptness. A typical procedure is to lengthen gradually the time between successive therapy sessions, from weekly to fortnightly to monthly and so on. These concluding sessions, which progressively phase out the therapist's active involvement, may be shorter than earlier ones, with occasional telephone contacts.

MECHANISMS OF PSYCHOTHERAPY

Research on behavior therapy has not only demonstrated that particular treatment methods are effective, but has also identified what components of multifaceted treatment methods and programs are responsible for therapeutic success. For example, empirical evidence has established that the changes produced by token reinforcement programs are due to the learning principles of operant conditioning on which they are based (Kazdin, 1977).

Learning Processes

A pioneering token reinforcement program with predominantly schizophrenic patients on a psychiatric hospital ward was reported by Ayllon and Azrin (1965). The target behaviors in this investigation were self-care and improved capacity for productive work. Rewards were made contingent on improvement in these two areas. The decisive role of the response-reinforcement contingency in producing significant increases in working habits was shown by using an ABA design in which each patient served as her own control. Following a period during which the job assignments of all 44 patients on the entire ward were rewarded contingently (phase A), tokens were administered on a noncontingent basis (phase B). In phase B, patients were given tokens each day regardless of their performance, which broke the contingency between reinforcer and response without eliminating the reinforcer completely. This ensured that the amount of social interaction between the attendants and ward staff who administered the tokens and the patients remained unchanged. Any deterioration in performance was then directly attributable to the precise functional relationship between behavior and reinforcement. In other words, any observed improvement in the patients' functioning during the reinforcement phase could not be attributed to increases in attention from the hospital staff or other uncontrolled factors. Phase C marked a return to contingent

reinforcement as in phase A. The results showed that "free" reinforcement (phase B) was totally ineffective in maintaining the work performance of the patients. Similarly, the complete withdrawal of all tokens resulted in their job performance decreasing to less than one-fourth the rate at which it had previously been maintained by contingently rewarding the patients with tokens.

The theoretical mechanisms that account for therapeutic success vary, depending on treatment methods and problems. No single, monolithic theory encompasses the diverse methods and applications of the different behavior therapies. Although operant conditioning principles explain the efficacy of a broad range of behavioral procedures, they do not account for the success of a number of other methods. Numerous studies using innovative methodological strategies have identified the critical element of this multicomponent technique in treating fears. Neither the therapist-patient relationship, the training in progressive relaxation, nor any other placebo value of the method is essential for success. The necessary (and usually sufficient) therapeutic component is repeated exposure to the fear-eliciting object or situation. Relaxation training and the use of a carefully graded hierarchy facilitate exposure and hence contribute indirectly to treatment success. Real-life exposure, where possible, is more powerful than imaginal processes.

Why does systematic, repeated exposure work? The answer to this question remains elusive. Originally, the explanation was based on Mowrer's (1947) two-factor theory of learning, according to which repeated exposure to anxiety-eliciting situations, as in systematic desensitization, resulted in the extinction of the classically conditioned anxiety that mediates phobic avoidance behavior. However, recent research (Bandura, 1977) casts doubt on the validity of this explanation.

Cognitive Mechanisms

In terms of social learning theory, exposure leads not to the extinction of any underlying anxiety drive state, but rather to modification of the client's expectations of self-efficacy (Bandura, 1982). Self-efficacy refers to clients' beliefs that they can cope with formerly feared situations. Self-efficacy itself is really a capsule summary construct comprising several specific cognitive processes, including the type of attributions the client makes. For efficacy expectations to change, the client must make a self-attribution of behavioral change. For example, it is not uncommon for an agoraphobic client to approach situations she has avoided without increases in self-efficacy or reductions in fear. The explanation seems to be that some clients do not credit themselves for the behavioral change. The agoraphobic might say that she was "lucky" that she did not have a panic attack or that she just happened to have one of those rare "good days." The therapist must anticipate this frequent occurrence and be prepared to help the client use cognitive methods to attribute changes to herself so that her sense of personal efficacy increases.

Initial studies with phobic subjects have generally provided empirical support for self-efficacy theory, although some of the findings are mixed (Rachman, 1978). Experiments by Bandura and his associates have shown that efficacy expectations accurately predicted reductions in phobic avoidance behavior regardless of whether they were created by in vivo exposure or symbolic modeling, covert modeling, or systematic desensitization. Moreover, measures of personal efficacy predicted differences in coping behavior by different individuals receiving the same treatment and even specific performance by subjects in different tasks. Consistent with the theory, participant modeling, a performance-based treatment, produced greater increases in level and strength of efficacy expectations and in related behavior change (Bandura, 1986).

APPLICATIONS

PROBLEMS

Behavior therapy is applicable to a full range of psychological disorders in different populations (Kazdin & Wilson, 1978). It also has broad applicability to problems in education, medicine, and community living (Franks et al., 1982; Kazdin, 1978a). The following are some selected examples of problems in different domains for which behavior therapy appears to be an effective treatment.

Anxiety Disorders

Evidence from controlled clinical investigations in a number of different countries has convincingly demonstrated the efficacy and efficiency of behavior therapy in the treatment of phobic disorders, and it can be argued that behavior therapy is the treatment of choice for phobias (Marks, 1981; Mathews et al., 1981). The main technique is systematic exposure, possibly supplemented with additional cognitive-behavioral strategies (e.g., cognitive restructuring, behavioral marital therapy, and so on) in the case of some agoraphobic disorders. This treatment is cost-effective. However, although the majority of clients are successfully treated, and this improvement is maintained in follow-ups five to nine years later, therapeutic failures (figures that range from roughly 10 percent to 40 percent with agoraphobics) remain a problem (Munby & Johnston, 1980).

Depression

Combined cognitive and behavioral treatment programs have shown promising results in the treatment of unipolar depression. In one study, A. T. Beck's cognitive-behavioral therapy produced greater improvement and fewer dropouts from treatment than did pharmacotherapy, which is widely regarded as the most powerful therapy for depression (Beck et al., 1979). The clients in this study were depressed outpatients between the ages of 18 and 65 years. On average, they had been chronically or intermittently depressed for about nine years, 75 percent reported suicidal ideas, and 12 percent had a history of previous suicide attempts. The majority had had previous psychotherapy without success, and 22 percent had been hospitalized as a result of their depression. MMPI profiles indicated that these subjects were severely disturbed. It is too soon to tell whether cognitive-behavioral therapy is more effective than pharmacotherapy in certain types of depression. It is not recommended for bipolar affective disorders. Nevertheless, current findings indicate that it is well suited for a large number of mildly to severely depressed outpatients.

Sexual Disorders

There is now consensus that behavior therapy is the preferred treatment for male and female sexual problems, such as impotence, premature ejaculation, orgasmic dysfunction, and vaginismus (LoPiccolo & LoPiccolo, 1978). Masters and Johnson's (1970, 1979) two-week rapid treatment program is the best-known example of short-term behavioral treatment of sexual dysfunction in heterosexual and homosexual men and women. Consistently successful results, comparable to those of Masters and Johnson, have been reported by other groups of investigators using these and other brief behavioral methods. In many cases of sexual dysfunction that are uncomplicated by interpersonal and communication problems, brief self-help behavioral programs, ranging from 6 to 15 sessions, have proved to be an efficient and cost-effective treatment strategy. In less straightforward cases requiring intensive behavioral marital therapy or other cognitive-behavioral interventions as a prelude to, or in addition to specific sex therapy, treatment may taken anywhere from 20 to 50 sessions.

A variety of other sexual disorders, the paraphilias, which include exhibitionism, transvestism, and sadomasochism, are commonly treated with different cognitive-behavioral methods.

Interpersonal and Marital Problems

Social skills training and assertiveness training are used to treat a broad range of interpersonal problems, ranging from limited social-behavioral repertoires to social anxiety. Behavioral marital therapy is a relatively recent development, the central focus of which is helping partners to learn more positive and productive means of achieving desired behavioral changes in one another (Jacobson & Margolin, 1979). As in the case of anxiety and sexual disorders, specialized behavior marital therapy clinics are now in operation. Behavior therapy has shown clear promise as an effective and efficient treatment for marital problems, but comprehensive investigations of severely distressed couples, with longer follow-ups, are necessary before definitive conclusions can be reached.

Chronic Mental Patients

Behavior therapy is not useful in treating acute psychotic reactions. Most behavior therapists favor pharmacotherapy as the treatment of choice for schizophrenic disorders. Yet behavioral programs are clearly indicated for treating the chronically mentally ill. Paul and Lentz (1977) studied chronic mental patients, all of whom were diagnosed as process schizophrenic, were of low socioeconomic status, had been confined to a mental hospital for an average of 17 years, and had been treated previously with drugs and other methods without success. Approximately 90 percent were being maintained on drugs at the onset of the study. Their level of self-care was too low and the severity of their bizarre behavior too great to permit community placement despite the best efforts of the hospital administrators. According to Paul and Lentz, these subjects were "the most severely debilitated chronically institutionalized adults ever subjected to systematic study" (p. v). In the most detailed, comprehensive, and well-controlled evaluation of the treatment of chronic, mental hospital patients ever conducted, Paul and Lentz produced a wealth of objective data, including evidence of cost effectiveness, showing that behavioral procedures (predominantly a sophisticated token reinforce-ment program) are the treatment of choice.

Childhood Disorders

Children with problems varying in type and severity have been treated from the earliest days of behavior therapy. Treatment programs have addressed problems ranging from circumscribed habit disorders in children whose behaviors are otherwise "normal" to multiple responses of children who suffer all-encompassing excesses, deficits, or bizarre behavior patterns. These problems include conduct disorders, aggression, and delinquency. Hyperactivity is widely treated by behavioral methods, such as token reinforcement programs. The documented success of the behavioral approach, particularly in improving the academic performance of these children, suggests that it be used to complement widespread use of medication for controlling hyperactivity, or even as an alternative to drug treatment in some cases (O'Leary, 1980).

Autism is a particularly severe early childhood disorder with a very poor prognosis. Traditional psychological and medical treatments have proved ineffective. Behavioral methods, however, have achieved notable success. Lovaas (1987) has recently reported that intensive, long-term behavioral treatment of autistic children resulted in 47 percent achieving normal intellectual and educational functioning. Another 40 percent were mildly retarded and assigned to special classes for the language delayed. Of a control group of autistic children, only 2 percent achieved normal functioning. These findings are the most positive ever obtained with autistic children and illustrate the efficacy of behavioral methods with even the most serious childhood disorders.

Childhood psychoses, characterized by such symptoms as lack of affect, performance of repetitive and self-stimulatory behavior, severe withdrawal, and muteness or echolalia, have also been treated with behavioral techniques. Self-stimulatory and self-destructive behavior such as biting and head banging have been eliminated with aversive procedures. Positive behaviors have been developed to improve language and speech, play, social interaction and responsiveness, and basic academic skills (O'Leary & Carr, 1982).

One of the most effectively treated childhood problems has been enuresis. The well-known bell-and-pad method has produced improvement rates greater than 80 percent in many reports. Toileting accidents have been effectively altered with other behavioral procedures (Ross, 1981).

Behavioral Medicine

Behavioral medicine, a recent but already influential development, has been defined as the "interdisciplinary field concerned with the development and integration of behavioral and biomedical science knowledge and techniques relevant to health and illness and the application of this knowledge and these techniques to prevention, diagnosis, treatment and rehabilitation" (Schwartz & Weiss, 1978, p. 250). Behavior therapy has helped to catalyze the rapid growth of this field, in which the procedures of behavior modification are used to treat illness-related behavior and to promote improved personal health care.

Prevention and Treatment of Cardiovascular Disease

Specific behavior patterns have been identified that appear to increase the risk of needless or premature cardio-vascular disease. Modification of these behavior patterns is likely to produce significant reductions in cardiovascular disease. Among the risk factors that have been the target of behavioral treatment programs are cigarette smoking, obesity, lack of exercise, stress, hypertension, and excessive alcohol consumption. Substance abuse is typically treated with a combination of the self-control procedures. Stress and hypertension have been successfully treated using methods such as relaxation training. Behavior intervention methods have been applied not only to identified clients in both individual and group therapy sessions, but also to essentially healthy individuals in the work place and the community in programs designed to prevent cardiovascular disease. An illustration of the latter is the Stanford Three Community Study (Maccoby, Farquhar, Wood & Alexander, 1977). A multimedia campaign was conducted for two years, in two Northern California communities, in one of which it was supplemented by an intensive instruction program for high-risk individuals. A third community served as a control. Results from a sample survey of the populations showed that both interventions produced substantial increases in knowledge about health care, alteration in unhealthy behavior patterns, and change in the estimated risk of cardiovascular disease.

Other Applications

Behavioral techniques have also been successfully applied to such diverse health-related problems as tension headaches, different forms of pain, eating disorders such as anorexia nervosa and bulimia, asthma, epilepsy, sleep disorders, nausea reactions in cancer patients (resulting from radiation therapy), and children's fears about being hospitalized and undergoing surgery (Melamed & Siegel, 1980). Finally, cognitive-behavioral principles show promise in increasing compliance with medical treatments.

EVALUATION

Evaluation of therapy outcome must be guided by the question "*What* treatment, by *whom*, is most effective for *this* individual with *that* specific problem and under *which* set of circumstances?" (Paul, 1967, p. 111). "On what measures" and "at what cost" round off this appeal to specificity of therapy outcome evaluation. The issue of "what problems" behavior therapy is appropriate for has been addressed in the immediately preceding section.

What Treatment Methods?

Behavior therapy consists of a broad range of different techniques, some of which are differentially effective for different problems. Hence it is difficult to evaluate some global entity called "behavior therapy." Instead, evaluation must be directed at specific methods applied to particular problems.

What Measures Should Be Used to Evaluate Therapy Outcome?

A major contribution of behavior therapy to the evaluation of therapy outcome has been the development of a wide range of measurement strategies for the assessment and modification of various disorders. Examples of these innovations in the objective measurement of psychological change include behavioral measures of phobic avoidance and compulsive rituals, coding systems for direct behavioral observation of diverse behaviors across different situations (for example, patients'

level of functioning on a hospital ward, unhappy spouses discussing a problem, or parents interacting with their child), and psychophysiological systems for anxiety and sexual disorders. Adequate assessment of treatment outcome will necessarily require multiple objective and subjective measures. In the treatment of anxiety-related disorders, for example, it is now clear that measures of three response systems—avoidance behavior, physiological arousal, and self-report—are necessary. The correlations among these systems are often low. Thus, by simply measuring one dimension, one might miss important changes in the other two. Moreover, there is evidence that these response systems may change at different speeds and be differentially reactive to different treatment methods.

Treatment at What Cost?

Behavior therapy can be a relatively cost-effective method. Paul and Lentz (1977) found that their behavioral treatment program was less expensive than either of the two alternative approaches with which it was compared: milieu therapy and traditional psychiatric care typical of state hospitals in the United States. This benefit, added to the significantly greater efficacy of the behavioral program, makes it the cost-effective choice. In England, Marks (1981) and his colleagues improved on the cost-effectiveness of the behavioral treatment of agoraphobics and obsessive-compulsives by using nurses as therapists instead of more highly trained clinical psycholo̶g̶i̶s̶t̶ and psychiatrists. N̶ was observed.

Evaluating Therapy

Behavior therapists ha̶ ious research strategi̶

different issues related to therapy outcome. Some brief examples can be mentioned. Single-case experimental designs are particularly important because they enable cause-effect relationships to be drawn between treatments and outcome in the individual case. There are several single-case experimental designs. The ABA, or reversal, design was illustrated in the Ayllon and Azrin study previously described. In the multiple-baseline design, different responses are continuously measured. Treatment is then applied successively to each response. If the desired behavior changes maximally only when treated, then a cause-effect relationship can be inferred. Among the advantages of single-case experimental designs are that individual clinical problems can be studied which are unsuitable for group designs and that innovative treatments can be developed efficiently before being tested in group outcome studies. Limitations of single-subject methodology include the inability to examine the interaction of subject variables with specific treatment effects and difficulty in generalizing findings to other cases.

Several different types of between-group designs are used in the evaluation of treatment outcome, each design having its particular advantages and limitations, depending on the question being asked. Laboratory-based studies permit the evaluation of specific techniques applied to particular problems under tightly controlled conditions; for example, evaluating fear reduction methods with snake-phobic subjects (Bandura, 1986). The advantages of this methodology include the use of multiple objective measures of outcome, the selection of homogeneous subject samples and herapists, and the freedom to assign

subjects to experimental and control groups. Limitations include the possibility that findings with only mildly disturbed subjects might not be generalizable to more severely disturbed clients.

The treatment package strategy evaluates the effect of a multifaceted treatment program. If the package proves to be successful, its effective components are analyzed in subsequent research. One way of doing this is to use the dismantling strategy, in which components of the treatment package are systematically eliminated and the associated decrement in treatment outcome is measured. The relative contributions of each component can then be evaluated.

The comparative research strategy is directed toward determining whether some therapeutic techniques are superior to others. Comparative studies are appropriate after specific techniques have been shown to be effective in single-subject or laboratory-based research and the parameters that maximize their efficacy are known. Different group designs require different control groups, depending on the research question addressed. The no-treatment control group controls for the possible therapeutic effects of assessment of outcome, maturation, and other changes in clients' behavior that occur independently of formal treatment. Attention-placebo control groups are used to parcel out the contribution to treatment effects of factors that are common to all forms of therapy. These factors include the relationship between therapist and client, expectations of therapeutic progress, suggestion, and others.

TREATMENT

Some clinical details of a cognitive-behavioral approach to therapy may be illustrated by the treatment of agoraphobia, a complex anxiety disorder. Initially, the therapist carries out a careful assessment of the nature of the problem and the variables that seem to be maintaining it. Subsequent treatment may vary, but it is probable that some form of in vivo exposure method will be a central part of therapy. Together, therapist and client work out a hierarchy of increasingly fear-eliciting situations that the client has been avoiding. The behavioral basis of the treatment is repeated and systematic exposure to these situations occurs until avoidance is eliminated and fear is decreased. Cognitive principles and procedures feature prominently in preparing the client for these corrective learning experiences.

Clients are given an explanation of the treatment procedures and their rationales, together with an interpretation of their problems as learned fear/avoidance reactions that can be overcome by guided relearning experiences. The therapist is careful to distinguish systematic exposure treatment from the unsystematic and ill-considered attempts clients have typically made to enter feared situations too quickly. Preparation for each exposure experience involves anticipating the inevitable fearful reactions and teaching clients appropriate coping skills. This includes recognizing and accepting feelings of fear, identifying cognitive distortions that elicit or exacerbate fear, and counteracting cognitive distortions. Instead of catastrophizing (e.g., "Oh, no! Here I go again. I'm really in trouble. I must get out of here fast!"), they learn coping self-instructions (e.g., "This anxiety is distressing but not dangerous." "It'll pass. Concentrate on what you need to do now." "One step at a time."). These preparatory coping responses are often rehearsed in imagery.

The therapist might accompany the client during in vivo exposure sessions, providing encouragement, support, and social reinforcement. Although empathic about the discomfort the agoraphobic might experience, the therapist remains firm about the necessity for systematic exposure. Once clients enter the feared situation, the golden rule is no leaving it until anxiety has decreased. Clients are allowed to withdraw if absolutely necessary, but in a manner mutually agreed upon in advance. First, abrupt withdrawal is strongly discouraged; clients are to try to remain in the situation as long as possible, even though they experience considerable discomfort. Second, if they cannot remain in the situation, they follow a preplanned withdrawal instead of fleeing the scene. If the situation is a supermarket, for example, they move to the least crowded area of the store and try to calm themselves. If that fails, they exit from the store, but instead of rushing to the car and going home to "safety," they try to reenter the supermarket as soon as possible.

Following the exposure, therapist and client analyze what happened. This provides the therapist an opportunity to see how the client interprets his or her experience and to uncover any faulty cognitive processing. For example, agoraphobics tend to discount positive accomplishments, do not always attribute success experiences to their own coping ability, and therefore do not develop greater self-efficacy.

Clients are given specific instructions about exposure homework assignments between therapy sessions and are asked to keep detailed daily records of what they attempted, how they felt, and what problems they encountered. These self-recordings are reviewed by the therapist at the beginning of the next session. In addition to providing the therapist with information on the clients' progress (or lack of progress), these daily records facilitate the process of changing clients' cognitive sets about their problems. For example, because of their negative thinking, clients often bemoan their perceived lack of improvement and dwell on the difficulties of completing exposure assignments. Usually the therapist can point to specific successes as indicated in the weekly behavioral recordings that these clients had not taken seriously enough. By directing their attention to the records of their own experience, the therapist helps clients to gain a more objective and balanced view of their problems and progress.

Homework assignments typically require the active cooperation of the client's spouse (or some other family member). The therapist invites the spouse to one or more therapy sessions to assess his or her willingness and ability to provide the necessary support and to explain what is required. Mathews et al. (1981) have developed treatment manuals for both the agoraphobic and the spouse in which they detail each step of in vivo exposure treatment and describe mutual responsibilities. In many cases, these manuals can greatly reduce the number of sessions the couple need spend with the therapist.

Not uncommonly agoraphobics fail to complete homework assignments.

There are several possible reasons for lack of compliance, ranging from poorly chosen homework assignments to resistance to change by the agoraphobic. All of these potential problems need to be considered as the therapist begins to analyze the causes of noncompliance. Another possibility is that the spouse is uncooperative or even tries to sabotage therapy. One of the advantages of including the spouse in treatment is that this resistance to progress is rapidly uncovered and can be directly addressed in the therapy sessions. Marital therapy might be necessary to resolve interpersonal conflict that may block the agoraphobic's progress.

Additional techniques might be needed to supplement in vivo exposure, as indicated above. These are usually in the service of helping clients cope more constructively with different sources of stress. Some clients for example, need assertiveness training to overcome the stress of interpersonal conflicts, whereas others need to acquire ways of coping with suppressed anger. Finally, before terminating successful treatment, the therapist works on relapse prevention training with clients. Briefly, clients are told that it is possible that they might experience an unexpected return of some fear at unpredictable points in the future. Using imagery to project ahead to such a recurrence of fear, clients learn to cope with their feelings by reinstituting previously successful coping responses. They are reassured that these feelings are quite normal and time-limited and do not necessarily signal a relapse. Clients learn that it is primarily the way they interpret these feelings that determines whether or not they experience a relapse. Specifically, the therapist tries to inoculate them against such anxiety-inducing cognitive errors as catastrophizing, selective focus on an isolated anxiety symptom, and so on.

MANAGEMENT

Behavior therapists work in a variety of settings—private clinical practice, clinics, mental health centers, hospitals, institutions for the retarded, schools, and even industry. In their typical practice, behavior therapists function quite similarly to other psychotherapists. For instance, they have emulated the treatment format and scheduling of the more traditional psychotherapies in sticking to the standard 50- to 60-minute session on a weekly basis. Occasionally, alternative treatment formats are used. For example, there is some tentative evidence that longer, more intensive sessions may be more effective with agoraphobic clients.

Behavior therapy sessions may often be different from psychotherapy, however. Thus the therapist might accompany the client on some in vivo assignment (e.g., going with an agoraphobic to a shopping mall). In some instances, particularly with children's problems, the therapist might go to the client's home or school to observe or intervene. Behavior therapists are actively concerned with what occurs between therapy sessions, and intermittent telephone contacts with clients and psychological assistants such as family members and teachers are common. Similarly, even after therapy has ended successfully, the therapist frequently keeps in touch with clients through the telephone or mail, a strategy designed to facilitate maintenance of improvement, particularly in problems with a high probability of relapse.

The clients that behavior therapists treat come from diverse sources. Many clients are referrals from the medical community or from other mental health professionals. Once the majority of clients seen by behavior therapists were failures of the then dominant psychoanalytically oriented psychotherapy. This still happens, but to a much lesser extent. Today a growing number of clients enter into behavioral treatment as their first therapy experience. Whereas most clients once consulted behavior therapists for treatment of specific problems (e.g., phobias or habit disorders), modern clientele suffer from the full range of problems, from the simple to the complex, including those that are well defined and those that are shadowy and ambiguous. Occasionally, clients who are in some form of long-term, psychoanalytically oriented psychotherapy consult a behavior therapist for concurrent help with a specific problem. In some cases these clients are referred by their psychotherapists. In other cases these clients initiate behavioral treatment themselves, with or without the knowledge of their psychotherapist. The feasibility of this sort of arrangement depends on the details of the individual client, the particular problem, and, of course, the attitudes of the therapists involved.

CASE EXAMPLE[1]

Mr. B was a 35-year-old man, married, with two sons aged eight and five, from a successful, middle-class family. He was a persistent exhibitionist whose

---

[1]This case example, with minor modifications, is taken from G. T. Wilson and K. D. O'Leary, *Principles of Behavior Therapy* (Englewood Cliffs, NJ: Prentice-Hall, 1980). Reprinted with permission.

pattern over the past 20 years had been to expose his genitals to unsuspecting adult women as often as five or six times a week. Fifteen years of intermittent psychoanalytic treatment, several hospitalizations at psychiatric institutions in the United States, and a six-year prison sentence for his deviant sexual behavior had failed to help Mr. B change his apparently uncontrollable behavior. He was currently under grand jury indictment for exposing himself to an adult woman in the presence of a group of young children. There was every prospect that he would receive a life sentence in view of his repeated offenses and numerous failures to show improvement in response to lengthy and costly psychiatric treatment. At least one psychiatrist had diagnosed him as untreatable and had advocated a lifelong removal from free society. Shortly before coming to trial, Mr. B's psychoanalyst referred him to a behavior therapist as a last resort to see if behavior therapy might succeed where traditional forms of treatment had failed.

Mr. B was hospitalized and treated on a daily basis for six weeks, a total of about 50 hours of direct therapist contact. After spending some time to develop a trusting personal relationship so that Mr. B would feel comfortable in disclosing intimate details about his problems, the therapist conducted a series of intensive interviews to ferret out the specific environmental circumstances and psychological factors that were maintaining Mr. B's deviant behavior. With his permission, his parents and wife were also interviewed to obtain more information and to corroborate aspects of his own description of the development and present status of the problem. To obtain a sample of his actual exhibitionist behavior, a situation was arranged in a hospital office that closely resembled the conditions under which Mr. B would normally expose himself in real life. Two attractive female professional colleagues of the therapist were seated in a simulated doctor's waiting room, reading magazines, and the patient was instructed to enter, sit across from them, and expose himself. Despite the artificial setting, he proceeded to expose himself, became highly aroused, and nearly masturbated to orgasm. This entire sequence was videotaped, and objective measures of his response to this scene as well as to various other adult sexual stimuli were obtained by recording the degree of penile erection he showed while observing the videotape and selected other erotic films.

On the basis of this behavioral assessment, a detailed picture was developed of the sequence of internal and external stimuli and responses that preceded his acts of exposure. For example, a woman standing alone at a bus stop as he drove past in his car often triggered a pattern of thoughts and images that caused him to circle the block and eventually expose himself. Alternatively, the anger he experienced after a heated argument with his father, which he could not handle, could also elicit the urge to expose himself. The more Mr. B thought about exposing himself, the more obsessed he became with a particular woman and her anticipated reactions. Because he tuned out everything except his immediate feelings and intentions, he became oblivious to the consequences of his actions. His behavior was out of control. Mr. B hoped that his victim would express some form of approval, either by smiling or making some sexually toned comment. Although this did happen periodically, most women ignored him, and some called the police.

Not atypically, Mr. B's idea about behavior therapy was that he would be passively "conditioned" so that his problem would disappear. The therapist systematically disabused him of this notion by explaining that success could be achieved only with his active cooperation in all phases of the treatment program. He was told that there was no automatic "cure" for his problem, but that he could learn new behavioral self-control strategies, which, if practiced conscientiously and applied at the right time, would enable him to avoid further deviant behavior.

As in most complex clinical cases, treatment was multifaceted, meaning that a number of different techniques were employed to modify different components of the disorder. His own beliefs about his problem were that he was suddenly seized by a desire, which he could not consciously control, and that his subsequent actions were "involuntary." Analysis of the sequence of events that always preceded exposure altered Mr. B's expectation that he was unable to control his behavior. He was shown how he himself was instrumental in transforming a relatively weak initial urge into an overpowering compulsion to expose because he attended to inappropriate thoughts and feelings and engaged in behaviors that increased, rather than decreased, the temptation. It was explained that the time to break this behavioral chain, to implement the self-control strategies he would acquire as a result of treatment, was at the beginning, when the urge was weakest. In order to do this, he would have to learn to be aware of his thoughts, feelings, and behavior and to recognize the early danger signals.

Specific tension states had often precipitated exposure. Accordingly, Mr. B was trained to reduce this tension through the procedure of progressive relaxation. Instead of exposing himself, he learned to relax, an activity incompatible with exposure behavior. Assertion training was used to help Mr. B cope constructively with feelings of anger and to express them appropriately, rather than to seek relief through deviant behavior. Using role-playing, the therapist modeled an appropriate reaction and then provided Mr. B with reinforcing feedback as he rehearsed progressively more effective ways of responding to anger-inducing events. In covert modeling Mr. B was taught to imagine himself in a range of situations that customarily had resulted in exposure and to see himself engaging in alternative responses to exposure; for example, relaxing away tension, expressing anger appropriately, reminding himself of the consequences of being caught, or simply walking away from a tempting situation.

Aversion conditioning was used to decrease the positive appeal exposure had for him. During repeated presentations of the videotape of his exposure scene, on an unpredictable schedule, a loud, subjectively aversive police siren was blared over earphones he was wearing. Whereas Mr. B initially found watching the videotape pleasurable and sexually arousing, he progressively lost all sexual interest in it. He reported that he experienced marked difficulty in concentrating on the scene because he began to anticipate the disruptive—and given his personal social learning history, understandably frightening—police siren in connection with thoughts of exposure. The siren was also paired systematically with a range of fantasies of different situations in which he would expose himself. In addition to the siren, Mr. B learned how to associate self-administered aversive cognitive events with deviant thoughts or images. For example, imagery of an aversive event, such as being apprehended by the police, was coupled with thoughts of exposure. Periodically, Mr. B's sexual arousal to the videotape was assessed directly by measuring penile erection to provide an evaluation of his progress.

Following every session with the therapist, Mr. B was given specific homework assignments to complete. These included self-monitoring and recording any urges to expose himself in order to ensure awareness about any signs of reverting back to old habits. Other assignments involved (a) practicing relaxation exercises and recording the degree to which the relaxation was associated with reduced tension; (b) rehearsing the association of aversive imagery with fantasies of exposure and recording the intensity of the aversive imagery and the clarity of the exposure fantasies on 10-point rating scales; and (c) engaging in assertive behavior, where appropriate, during interactions with other patients and staff on his assigned ward. Direct observation of his interpersonal behavior on the hospital ward provided an index of his utilization of assertive behavior.

Finally, after speaking with the therapist about cooperation and apparent progress in the treatment program, Mr. B's wife agreed to several joint therapy sessions that used behavioral methods for improving marital communication and interaction. Although the behavioral assessment had indicated that Mr. B's exhibitionist behavior was not directly caused by an unhappy marriage or lack of sexual satisfaction from his wife, the rationale was that improvement in these spheres of functioning would help consolidate and support his self-control over deviant sexual behavior acquired through the rest of the treatment program.

On leaving the hospital at the end of treatment, Mr. B continued to self-monitor any thoughts or feelings about exposing himself, relax systematically, assert himself, and rehearse the pairing of aversive imagery with thoughts of exposure. Every week he mailed these records to the therapist for analysis, a procedure designed to generalize treatment-produced improvement to the real world and to maintain self-control over time. Another facet of this maintenance strategy was a series of booster sessions scheduled approximately four months after therapy in which he returned to the hospital for a week of intensive treatment along the same lines as described above.

In large part owing to the therapist's strong recommendation, the court gave Mr. B a suspended sentence. A five-year follow-up showed that Mr. B had refrained from any exhibitionism, had experienced very few such desires, and felt confident in his newly found ability to control any urges that might arise.

SUMMARY

Behavior therapy is a young field that is still developing. The future will witness continued development and change in its theoretical foundations, research evidence, and practical applications. As the theoretical bases of behavior therapy are broadened, there will be renewed interest in identifying the commonalities among different therapies and in bringing about a rapprochement between behavior therapy and other forms of psychotherapy (Goldfried, 1980). Other behavior therapists contend that this proposal is premature (Wilson, 1982). Alternatively, behavior therapists might better devote their energies to developing replicable, testable, and effective methods of therapeutic change within the general social learning framework of behavior therapy and invite other theoretical orientations to do the same. There will be time enough to discuss common principles of change when different approaches can show convincing evidence of what they can and cannot accomplish.

The advent of behavior therapy has resulted in a dramatic increase in the quantity and quality of treatment research. Nevertheless, the preponderance of outcome studies has been with mildly disturbed subjects, usually in laboratory-based or analogue research. Controlled studies of patient populations with complex disorders have been underrepresented. Yet this sort of clinical research seems necessary if the gap between research and practice is to be closed. Confronted with substantial changes of obvious clinical relevance obtained with "real" patients, by using clearly described and replicable methods under realistic conditions of clinical practice, the practitioner is more likely to take notice. Happily, there are indications that clinical research in behavior therapy is increasing (Agras & Berkowitz, 1980).

Future developments in behavior therapy will have to be evaluated within the context of fundamental changes that are beginning to occur in the field of clinical psychology as a whole. In the United States the movement toward professionalism, for better or worse, is well under way. As the number of applicants to scientist-practitioner training programs appears to be decreasing, the applications to at least some of the new professional schools are increasing. Behavior therapy has always been rooted in the scientist-practitioner model of training, but, in principle, the practitioner model is not inconsistent with behavior therapy.

Another major challenge facing clinical psychology and psychiatry is the increasing demand for accountability and evidence of treatment efficacy by government, insurance companies, and the consumer movement. Some suggest that psychotherapy is facing a crisis, while others refer to an attack from outside the system. Behavior therapists, however, view this demand for accountability as an important opportunity to promote the use of empirically based treatments wherever possible. It can be argued that procedures that are grounded in empirical research are used sparingly, if at all, in general clinical practice, whereas unsupported and even discredited methods continue to flourish. The implications are obvious. To quote Liberman:

After almost 20 years of behavioral analysis and therapy, workers in the field must realize that political, personal, and social factors determine upwards of 90% of the success and survival of technical procedures. . . . Implementation, survival, and dissemination of empirically validated interventions require much more than data and journal publications. . . . If we want our work to live beyond a library bookshelf, we will have to jump into the political mainstream and get our feet wet as administrator researchers. (1980, pp. 370–71)

Ideally, in the near future, behavior therapists, possibly through the AABT, will join with other organizations in supporting reasonable legislation that seeks to make reimbursable only those mental health services that are safe and effective, and to guarantee the appropriate recognition of psychologists and other professionals as independent health providers.

ANNOTATED BIBLIOGRAPHY

Franks, C. M., Wilson, G. T., Kendall, P., & Brownell, K. D. (1984). *Annual review of behavior therapy: Theory and practice. (Vol. 10).* New York: Guilford Press.

The latest volume in this annual review series begun in 1973 offers broad coverage of virtually all aspects of theory, research, and application in behavior therapy, with critical commentary by the authors. This series provides perhaps the most up-to-date and comprehensive overview of the field on a year-to-year basis.

Goldstein, A., & Foa, E. (Eds.) (1980). *Handbook of behavioral interventions: A clinical guide.* New York: Wiley.

This edited volume presents chapters of specific behavioral techniques applied to anxiety and sexual disorders. By remaining close to the clinical data, including the generous use of transcripts from individual therapy sessions, the authors provide a flavor of the clinical practice of behavior therapy.

Kazdin, A. E. (1980). *Behavior modification in applied settings (rev. ed.).* Homewood, IL: Dorsey.

A clearly written, comprehensive review of primarily operant-conditioning principles and procedures in behavior modification, this book's focus is on application of learning principles in applied settings (e.g., classrooms and institutions for the retarded and psychiatric patients).

O'Leary, K. D., & Wilson, G. T. (1987). *Behavior therapy: Application and outcome (2nd ed.).* Englewood Cliffs, NJ: Prentice-Hall.

This book presents detailed description and evaluation of cognitive-behavior treatment of a wide range of childhood and adult disorders. Aside from traditional psychiatric disorders (e.g., anxiety, addictive, and schizophrenic disorders), areas covered include interpersonal and marital problems, behavioral medicine and preventive health care, and various educational and clinical problems in children.

Rhoades, L. J. (1981). *Treating and assessing the chronically ill: The pioneering research of Gordon L. Paul.* Rockville, MD: U.S. Department of Health and Human Services.

One of the *Science Reports* series published by the National Institute of Mental Health, this publication explains significant achievements in mental health services and is directed at the general scientific, academic, and professional communities. A clearly written, nontechnical summary account of the detailed Paul and Lentz (1977) book, it describes the treatment procedures and important findings of the most thorough study of chronic mental hospital patients ever conducted.

CASE READINGS

Bachrach, A. J., Erwin, W. J., & Mohr, J. P. (1965). The control of eating behavior in an anorexic by operant conditioning techniques. In L. P. Ullmann & L. Krasner (Eds.), *Case studies in behavior modification (pp. 153–163)*. New York: Holt, Rinehart and Winston.

This classic case study illustrates the application of operant conditioning principles to the life-threatening disorder of anorexia nervosa. This case helped shape the development of what is now a widely used method in the inpatient treatment of anorexia.

Melamed, B., & Siegel, L. (1975). Self-directed in vivo treatment of an obsessive-compulsive checking ritual. *Journal of Behavior Therapy and Experimental Psychiatry.* 6, 31–35.

This case illustrates the application of exposure and response prevention, among other techniques, in the treatment of compulsions. Subsequent research has documented the effectiveness of these methods. The case also describes the detailed, ongoing assessment of treatment progress characteristic of behavior therapy.

Novaco, R. (1977). Stress inoculation: A cognitive therapy for anger and its application to a case of depression. *Journal of Consulting and Clinical Psychology, 45,* 600–608.

This case illustrates the use of cognitive techniques within behavior therapy. It also shows how cognitive-behavioral methods are used to treat problems of anger, which, together with anxiety and depression, are the most common emotions encountered by clinicians.

Sajwaj, T., Libet, J., & Agras, S. (1974). Lemon-juice therapy: Control of life threatening rumination in a six-month-old infant. *Journal of Applied Behavior Analysis, 7,* 557–653. [Reprinted in D. Wedding & R. J. Corsini (Eds.) (1989). *Case studies in psychotherapy.* Itasca, IL: F. E. Peacock.]

This is a straightforward case reported in one of the leading behavioral journals. It is a good illustration of an ABAB design and operant technology; however, it is only one of potentially hundreds of cases which could have been selected to represent behavior therapy.

Wolf, M. M., Risley, T., & Mees, H. (1965). Application of operant conditioning procedures to the behavior problems of an autistic child. In L. P. Ullmann & L. Krasner (Eds.), *Case studies in behavior modification (pp. 138–145)*. New York: Holt, Rinehart and Winston.

Another classic case study, illustrating the application of operant principles and procedures to the treatment of an autistic child. The assessment and treatment approach described here provides a model for the use of behavioral methods with a wide range of problems among the developmentally disabled.

REFERENCES

Agras, W. S., & Berkowitz, R. (1980). Clinical research in behavior therapy: Halfway there? *Behavior Therapy, 11,* 472–487.

Andrews, G., & Harvey, R. (1981). Does psychotherapy benefit neurotic patients? *Archives of General Psychiatry, 38,* 1205–1208.

Ayllon, T., & Azrin, N. H. (1965). The measurement and reinforcement of behavior of psychotics. *Journal of the Experimental Analysis of Behavior, 8,* 357–383.

Bandura, A. (1969). *Principles of behavior modification.* New York: Holt, Rinehart and Winston.

Bandura, A. (1977). *Social learning theory.* Englewood Cliffs, N.J.: Prentice-Hall.

Bandura, A. (1982). Self-efficacy mechanism in human agency. *American Psychologist, 37,* 122–147.

Bandura, A. (1986). *Social foundations of thought and action: A social cognitive theory.* Englewood Cliffs, NJ: Prentice-Hall.

Beck, A. T. (1976). Cognitive therapy and the emotional disorders. New York: International Universities Press.

Beck, A. T., Rush, A. J., Shaw, B. F., & Emery, G. (1979). Cognitive therapy of depression. New York: Guilford Press.

Birk, L., Stolz, S. B., Brady, J. P., Brady, J. V., Lazarus, A. A., Lynch, J. J., Rosenthal, A. J., Skelton, W. D., Stevens, J. B., & Thomas. E. J. (1973). Behavior therapy in psychiatry. Washington, DC: American Psychiatric Association.

Brady, J. P., & Wienckowski, L. A. (1978). Update on the teaching of behavior therapy in medical student and psychiatric resident training. Journal of Behavior Therapy and Experimental Psychiatry, 9, 125–127.

Brady, J. P. (1980). In M. Goldfried (Ed.), Some views on effective principles of psychotherapy. Cognitive Therapy and Research, 4, 271–306.

Brownell, K. D. (1981). Report on international behavior therapy organizations. Behavior Therapist, 4, 9–14.

Cautela, J. (1967). Covert sensitization. Psychological Reports, 20, 459–468.

Dollard, J., & Miller, N. E. (1950). Personality and psychotherapy. New York: McGraw-Hill.

Ellis, A. (1962). Reason and emotion in psychotherapy. New York: Lyle Stuart.

Eysenck, H. J. (1959). Learning theory and behavior therapy. British Journal of Medical Science, 105, 61–75.

Eysenck, H. J. (1967). The biological basis of personality. Springfield, IL: Charles C Thomas.

Franks, C. M., & Wilson, G. T. (1973). Annual review of behavior therapy: Theory and practice (Vol. 1). New York: Brunner/Mazel.

Franks, C. M., Wilson, G. T., Kendall, P., & Brownell, K. (1982). Annual review of behavior therapy: Theory and practice (Vol. 8). New York: Guilford Press.

Gelder, M. G., Bancroft, J. H. J., Gath, D., Johnston, D. W., Matthews, A. M., & Shaw, P. M. (1973). Specific and nonspecific factors in behavior therapy. British Journal of Psychiatry, 123, 445–462.

Goldfried, M. R. (1980). Toward the delineation of therapeutic change principles. American Psychologist, 35, 991–999.

Jacobson, E. (1938). Progressive relaxation. Chicago: University of Chicago Press.

Jacobson, N., & Margolin, G. (1979). Marital therapy. New York: Brunner/Mazel.

Jones, M. C. (1924). The elimination of children's fears. Journal of Experimental Psychology, 7, 382–390.

Kanfer, F. H. (1977). The many faces of self-control, or behavior modification changes its focus. In R. B. Stuart (Ed.), Behavioral self-management. New York: Brunner/Mazel.

Kazdin, A. E. (1977). The token economy. New York: Plenum.

Kazdin, A. E. (1978a). The application of operant techniques in treatment, rehabilitation, and education. In S. L. Garfield & A. E. Bergin (Eds.), Handbook of psychotherapy and behavior change (2nd ed.). (pp. 549–590). New York: Wiley.

Kazdin, A. E. (1978b). History of behavior modification. Baltimore, MD: University Park Press.

Kazdin, A. E., & Wilson, G. T. (1978). Evaluation of behavior therapy: Issues, evidence and research strategies. Cambridge, MA: Ballinger.

Kendall, P., & Hollon, S. (Eds.) (1979). Cognitive-behavioral interventions: Theory, research, and procedures. New York: Guilford Press.

Knudson, R. M., Gurman, A. S., & Kniskern, D. P. (1979). Behavioral marriage therapy: A treatment in transition. In C. M. Franks & G. T. Wilson (Eds.), Annual review of behavior therapy: Theory and practice (Vol. 7). (pp. 543–574). New York: Brunner/Mazel.

Lang, P. J. (1979). A bio-informational theory of emotional imagery. Psychophysiology, 16, 495–512.

Lazarus, A. A. (1971). Behavior therapy and beyond. New York: McGraw-Hill.

Lazarus, A. A. (1981). The practice of multimodal therapy. New York: McGraw-Hill.

Lazarus, A. A., & Fay, A. (1982). Resistance or rationalization? A cognitive-behavioral perspective. In P. L.

Wachtel (Ed.), *Resistance: Psychodynamic and behavioral approaches.* (pp. 94–107). New York: Plenum.

Liberman, R. P. (1980). Review of *Psychosocial treatment for chronic mental patients* by Gordon L. Paul and Robert J. Lentz. *Journal of Applied Behavior Analysis, 13,* 367–372.

Locke, H. J., & Wallace, K. M. (1959). Short marital adjustment and prediction tests: Their reliability and validity. *Marriage and Family Living, 21,* 251–255.

LoPiccolo, J., & LoPiccolo, L. (Eds.) (1978). *Handbook of sex therapy.* New York: Plenum.

Lovaas, O. I. (1987). Behavioral treatment and normal educational and intellectual functioning in young autistic children. *Journal of Consulting and Clinical Psychology, 55,* 3–9.

Maccoby, N., Farquhar, J., Wood, P. D., & Alexander, J. (1977). Reducing the risk of cardiovascular disease: Effects of a community-based campaign on knowledge and behavior. *Journal of Community Health, 3,* 100–114.

Mahoney, M. J. (1980). Psychotherapy and the structure of personal revolutions. In M. J. Mahoney (Ed.), *Psychotherapy process.* (pp. 157–180). New York: Plenum.

Marks, I., & Mathews, A. (1979). Brief standard self-rating for phobic patients. *Behavior Research and Therapy, 17,* 263–267.

Marks, I. M. (1981). *Cure and care of the neuroses.* New York: Wiley.

Masters, W., & Johnson, V. (1970). *Human sexual inadequacy.* Boston: Little, Brown.

Masters, W., & Johnson, V. (1979). *Homosexuality in perspective.* Boston: Little, Brown.

Mathews, A. M., Gelder, M. G., & Johnston, D. W. (1981). *Agoraphobia: Nature and treatment.* New York: Guilford.

Meichenbaum, D. (1977). *Cognitive behavior modification.* New York: Plenum.

Meichenbaum, D., & Cameron, R. (1982). Cognitive behavior modification: Current issues. In G. T. Wilson & C. M. Franks (Eds.), *Contemporary behavior therapy: Conceptual and empirical foundations.* (pp. 310–338). New York: Guilford Press.

Melamed, B., & Siegel, L. (1980). *Behavioral medicine.* New York: Springer.

Miller, N. E. (1948). Studies of fear as an acquirable drive. I. Fear as motivation and fear reduction as reinforcement in the learning of new responses. *Journal of Experimental Psychology, 38,* 89–101.

Mischel, W. (1968). *Personality and assessment.* New York: Wiley.

Mischel, W. (1973). Toward a cognitive social learning reconceptualization of personality. *Psychological Review, 80,* 252–283.

Mischel, W. (1976). *Introduction to personality.* New York: Holt, Rinehart and Winston.

Mischel, W. (1981). A cognitive social learning approach to assessment. In T. V. Merluzzi, C. R. Glass, & M. Genest (Eds.), *Cognitive assessment.* (pp. 479–500). New York: Guilford Press.

Mowrer, O. H. (1947). On the dual nature of learning—A reinterpretation of "conditioning" and "problem solving." *Harvard Educational Review, 17,* 102–148.

Mowrer, O. H., & Mowrer, E. (1938). Enuresis: A method for its study and treatment. *American Journal of Orthopsychiatry, 4,* 436–459.

Munby, M., & Johnston, D. W. (1980). Agoraphobia: The long-term follow-up of behavioural treatment. *British Journal of Psychiatry, 137,* 418–427.

Nelson, R. O. (1981). Realistic dependent measures for clinical use. *Journal of Consulting and Clinical Psychology, 49,* 168.

O'Leary, K. D. (1980). Pills or skills for hyperactive children. *Journal of Applied Behavior Analysis, 13,* 191–204.

O'Leary, K. D., & Carr, E. G. (1982). Childhood disorders. In G. T. Wilson & C. M. Franks (Eds.), *Contemporary behavior therapy: Conceptual and empirical foundations.* (pp. 495–496). New York: Guilford.

O'Leary, K. D., & Wilson, G. T. (1987). *Behavior therapy: Application and outcome (2nd ed.).* Englewood Cliffs, NJ: Prentice-Hall.

O'Leary, K. D., & O'Leary, S. G. (1977). *Classroom management.* New York: Pergamon Press.

O'Leary, K. D., Turkewitz, H., & Tafel, S. (1973). Parent and therapist evaluation of behavior therapy in a child psychological clinic. *Journal of Consulting and Clinical Psychology, 41,* 289–293.

Paul, G. L. (1966). *Insight versus desensitization in psychotherapy.* Stanford: Stanford University Press.

Paul, G. L. (1967). Outcome research in psychotherapy. *Journal of Consulting Psychology, 31,* 109–188.

Paul, G. L., & Lentz, R. J. (1977). *Psychological treatment of chronic mental patients.* Cambridge, MA: Harvard University Press.

Rachlin, H. A. (1977). Review of *Cognition and Behavior Modification* by M. J. Mahoney. *Journal of Applied Behavior Analysis, 10,* 369–374.

Rachman, S. (Ed.) (1978). Perceived self-efficacy: Analyses of Bandura's theory of behavioural change. *Advances in Behavior Research and Therapy, 1,* 139–369.

Rachman, S., & Hodgson, R. (1980). *Obsessions and compulsions.* Englewood Cliffs, NJ: Prentice-Hall.

Rachman, S., & Wilson, G. T. (1980). *The effects of psychological therapy.* Oxford: Pergamon Press.

Rathus, S. A. (1973). A 30-item schedule for assessing assertive behavior. *Behavior Therapy, 4,* 398–406.

Risley, T., & Sheldon-Wildgen, J. (1982). Invited peer review: The AABT experience. *Professional Psychology, 13,* 125–131.

Rosen, R. C., & Keefe, F. J. (1978). The measurement of human penile tumescence. *Psychophysiology, 15,* 366–376.

Ross, A. (1981). *Child behavior therapy.* New York: Wiley.

Salter, A. (1949). *Conditioned reflex therapy.* New York: Farrar, Straus.

Schwartz, G. E., & Weiss, S. M. (1978). Behavioral medicine revisited: An amended definition. *Journal of Behavioral Medicine, 1,* 249–252.

Shapiro, D. A., & Shapiro, D. (1983). Meta-analysis of comparative therapy outcome research: A critical appraisal. *Behavioural Psychotherapy, 10,* 4–25.

Skinner, B. F. (1953). *Science and human behavior.* New York: Macmillan.

Sloane, R. B., Staples, F. R., Cristol, A. H., Yorkston, J. J., & Whipple, K. (1975). *Psychotherapy versus behavior therapy.* Cambridge, MA: Harvard University Press.

Smith, D. (1982). Trends in counseling and psychotherapy. *American Psychologist, 37,* 802–809.

Staples, F. R., Sloane, R. B., Whipple, K., Cristol, A. H., & Yorkston, N. (1975). Differences between behavior therapists and psychotherapists. *Archives of General Psychiatry, 32,* 1517–1522.

Stolz, S. G. (1978). *Ethical issues in behavior modification.* San Francisco: Jossey-Bass.

Swan, G. E., & MacDonald, M. D. (1978). Behavior therapy in practice: A national survey of behavior therapists. *Behavior Therapy, 9,* 799–807.

Turkewitz, H., & O'Leary, K. D. (1981). A comparative outcome study of behavioral marital and communication therapy. *Journal of Marital and Family Therapy, 7,* 159–169.

Ullmann, L. P., & Krasner, L. (1965). *Case studies in behavior modification.* New York: Holt, Rinehart and Winston.

Upper, D., & Ross, S. M. (Eds.) (1981). *Behavioral group therapy.* Champaign, IL: Research Press.

Wilson, G. T. (1982). Psychotherapy process and procedure: The behavioral mandate. *Behavior Therapy, 13,* 291–312.

Wilson, G. T., & Evans, I. M. (1977). The therapist-client relationship in behavior therapy. In R. S. Gurman & A. M. Razin (Eds.), *The therapist's contribution to effective psychotherapy: An empirical approach* (pp. 544–565). New York: Pergamon Press.

Wilson, G. T., & O'Leary, K. D. (1980). *Principles of behavior therapy.* Englewood Cliffs, NJ: Prentice-Hall.

Wolpe, J. (1958). *Psychotherapy by reciprocal inhibition.* Stanford: Stanford University Press.

Wolpe, J., & Rachman, S. (1960). Psychoanalytic evidence: A critique based on Freud's case of Little Hans. *Journal of Nervous and Mental Disorders, 131,* 135–145.

Yates, A. J. (1980). *Biofeedback and the modification of behavior.* New York: Plenum.

AARON T. BECK

8

Cognitive Therapy

AARON T. BECK and MARJORIE E. WEISHAAR

OVERVIEW

Cognitive therapy is based on a theory of personality which maintains that how one thinks largely determines how one feels and behaves. The therapy is a collaborative process of empirical investigation, reality testing, and problem solving between therapist and patient. The patient's maladaptive interpretations and conclusions are treated as testable hypotheses. Behavioral experiments and verbal procedures are used to examine alternative interpretations and to generate contradictory evidence that supports more adaptive beliefs and leads to therapeutic change.

BASIC CONCEPTS

Cognitive therapy can be thought of as a theory, a system of strategies, and a series of techniques. The theory is based on the conception that the processing of information is crucial for the survival of any organism. If we did not have a functional apparatus for taking in relevant information from the environment, synthesizing it, and formulating a plan of action on the basis of this synthesis, we would soon die or be killed.

In various psychopathological conditions, such as anxiety disorders, depressive disorders, mania, paranoid states, obsessive-compulsive neurosis, and others, a systematic bias is introduced into processing of information. A specific bias plays a central role in the symptomatology of the various psychological disturbances. Thus, an individual whose thinking selectively synthesizes themes of loss or defeat is likely to be depressed. Similarly, in anxiety there is a systematic shift toward selectively interpreting themes of danger, in paranoid conditions the dominant shift is toward indiscriminate attribution of abuse or interference, and in mania the shift is toward exaggerated interpretations of personal gain.

Contributing to these shifts are certain specific attitudes that predispose people under the influence of certain life situations to start interpreting their experiences in this biased way. For example, a person may have an attitude that any minor loss represents a major deprivation and may thus react catastrophically to even the smallest losses. A person who feels vulnerable to sudden death may, after exposure to a life-threatening episode, begin to interpret normal body sensations as signs of impending death and experience a panic attack. Other specific sets of beliefs and misinterpretations are characteristic of other psychological disorders.

Strategies

The overall strategies of cognitive therapy involve primarily a collaborative enterprise between the patient and the therapist to explore dysfunctional interpretations and try to modify them when the therapist finds them unrealistic or unreasonable. This collaborative empiricism views the patient as a practical scientist who lives by interpreting stimuli but who has been temporarily thwarted by his or her own information-gathering and integrating apparatus (cf., Kelly, 1955).

The second strategy, guided discovery, is directed toward discovering what threads run through the patient's present misperceptions and beliefs and linking them to analogous experiences in the past. Thus, the therapist and patient collaboratively weave a tapestry that tells the story of the development of the patient's disorder.

The therapy attempts to improve reality testing through continuous evaluation of personal conclusions. The immediate goal is to shift the information-processing apparatus to a more "neutral" condition so that events will be evaluated in a more balanced way.

The cognitive shift that occurs may be pictured as analogous to a computer program. Each disorder has a separate, specific program. The program dictates the kind of data admitted, decides the way data are integrated, and determines the resultant behavior. In anxiety disorder, for instance, a "survival program" has been activated: one selectively attends to "danger signals" and blocks out "safety signals." The resulting behavior will be consistent with how one integrates this information, dictating that one will overreact to relatively minor stimuli as though they are major threats, responding with avoidance or escape.

The program activated is responsible for the cognitive shift in information processing. The normal program of orderly selecting and interpreting data is dislocated by the anxiety program, panic program, depressive program, or some other program. When this occurs, the individual experiences the typical symptoms of anxiety, depression, or panic. The strategies and techniques of cognitive therapy are designed to deactivate such maladaptive programs, to shift the cognitive apparatus to a more neutral position. This shift to normal is accomplished by systematically checking and reversing misinterpretations. Corrective information is "fed back" into the system and catalyzes a readjustment.

Techniques

Techniques used in cognitive therapy are designed to shift information processing to a more functional position and to modify basic beliefs that make one more vulnerable to misinterpretation. A variety of techniques may be used consistent with the cognitive model. The purely cognitive techniques focus on the patient's misinterpretations and provide a mechanism for testing them, exploring their logical (or illogical) basis, and correcting them if they fail an empirical or logical test. In addition, the patient's imagery is used as a pictorial representation of his or her cognitive distortions. Imagery is subjected to the same type of evaluation and modification as cognitions.

Basic beliefs are explored in a somewhat similar manner and are tested for their accuracy and adaptiveness. The patient who discovers these beliefs are not accurate is encouraged to try out a different set of beliefs constructed with the therapist to determine if the new beliefs are more accurate and functional.

OTHER SYSTEMS

Procedures used in cognitive therapy, such as identifying common themes in a patient's emotional reactions, narratives, and imagery, are similar to the *psychoanalytic method*. However, in cognitive therapy the common thread is a meaning readily accessible to conscious interpretation, whereas in psychoanalysis the meaning is unconscious (or repressed) and must be inferred. Psychoanalysis, in its more recent phase, is based on a motivational model, whereas cognitive therapy derives from a cognitive model.

Both psychodynamic psychotherapy and cognitive therapy assume that behavior can be influenced by beliefs of which one is not immediately aware. However, cognitive therapy maintains that the thoughts contributing to a patient's distress are not deeply buried in the unconscious. Moreover, the cognitive therapist does not regard the patient's self-report as a screen for more deeply concealed ideas. Cognitive therapy focuses on

the linkages among symptoms, conscious beliefs, and current experiences. Psychoanalytic approaches are oriented toward repressed childhood memories and motivational constructs, such as libidinal needs and infantile sexuality.

Cognitive therapy is highly structured and short-term, lasting from 12 to 16 weeks. The therapist is actively engaged in collaboration with the patient. Psychoanalytic therapy is long-term and relatively unstructured. The analyst is largely passive. Cognitive therapy attempts to shift biased information processing through the application of logic to dysfunctional ideas and the use of behavioral experiments to test dysfunctional beliefs. Psychoanalysts rely on free association and depth interpretations to penetrate the encapsulated unconscious residue of unresolved childhood conflicts.

Cognitive therapy and *rational-emotive therapy* (RET) share emphases on the primary importance of cognition in psychological dysfunction, seeing the task of therapy as changing maladaptive assumptions and the stance of the therapist as active and directive. There are some differences, nevertheless, between these two approaches.

Cognitive therapy, using an information-processing model, is directed towards modifying the "cognitive shift" by addressing biased selection of information and distorted interpretations. The shift to normal cognitive processing is accomplished by testing the erroneous inferences that result from biased processing. Continual disconfirmation of cognitive errors, working as a feedback system, gradually restores more adaptive functioning. However, the dysfunctional beliefs that contributed to the unbalanced cognitive processing in the first place also require further testing and invalidation.

RET theory states that a distressed individual has irrational beliefs that contribute to irrational thoughts and that by modifying these through confrontation, they will disappear and the disorder will clear up. The cognitive therapist, operating from an inductive model, helps the patient translate interpretations and beliefs into hypotheses, which are then subjected to empirical testing. An RET therapist is more inclined to use a deductive model to point out irrational beliefs. The cognitive therapist eschews the word "irrational" in favor of "dysfunctional" because problematic beliefs are nonadaptive rather than irrational. They contribute to psychological disorders because they interfere with normal cognitive processing, not because they are irrational.

A profound difference between these two approaches is that cognitive therapy maintains that each disorder has its own typical cognitive content. The *cognitive profiles* of depression, anxiety, and panic disorder are significantly different and require substantially different approaches. RET, on the other hand, assumes that all psychopathology has a similar set of underlying irrational beliefs.

The cognitive therapy model emphasizes the impact of cognitive deficits in psychopathology. Some clients experience problems because their cognitive deficits do not let them foresee delayed or long-range negative consequences. Others have trouble with concentration, directed thinking, or recall. These difficulties occur in severe anxiety, depression, and panic attacks. Cognitive deficits produce perceptual errors as well as faulty interpretations. Further,

inadequate cognitive processing may interfere with use of coping abilities or techniques and with interpersonal problem solving, as occurs in suicidal people.

Finally, RET views patient's beliefs as philosophically incongruent with reality. Miechenbaum (1977) criticizes this perspective, stating that non-patients have irrational beliefs as well, but are able to cope with them. Cognitive therapy teaches patients to *self-correct* faulty cognitive processing and to bolster assumptions that allow them to cope. Thus, RET views the problem as philosophical; cognitive therapy views it as functional.

Cognitive therapy shares many similarities with some forms of *behavior therapy* but is quite different from others. Within behavior therapy are numerous approaches that vary in their emphasis on cognitive processes. At one end of the behavioral spectrum is applied behavioral analysis, an approach that ignores "internal events," such as interpretations and inferences, as much as possible. As one moves in the other direction, cognitive mediating processes are given increasing attention until one arrives at a variety of cognitive-behavioral approaches. At this point, the distinction between the purely cognitive and the distinctly behavioral becomes unclear.

Cognitive therapy and behavior therapy share some features: they are empirical, present-centered, problem-oriented, and require explicit identification of problems and the situations in which they occur as well as the consequences resulting from them. In contrast to radical behaviorism, cognitive therapy applies the same kind of functional analysis to internal experiences—to thoughts, attitudes, and images. Cognitions, like behaviors, can be modified by active collaboration between the patient and therapist and through behavioral experiments that foster new learning. Also, in contrast to behavioral approaches based on simple conditioning paradigms, cognitive therapy sees individuals as active participants in their environments, judging and evaluating stimuli, interpreting events and sensations, and judging their own responses.

Studies of some behavioral techniques, such as exposure methods for the treatment of phobias, demonstrate that cognitive and behavioral changes work together. For example, in agoraphobia, cognitive improvement has been concomitant with behavioral improvement (Williams & Rappoport, 1983). Simple exposure to agoraphobic situations while verbalizing negative automatic thoughts may lead to improvement on cognitive measures (Gournay, 1986). Bandura (1977) has demonstrated that one of the most effective ways to change cognitions is to change performance. In in vivo exposure, patients confront not only the threatening situations, but also their personal expectations of danger and their assumed inability to cope with their reactions. Because the experience itself is processed cognitively, exposure can be considered a cognitive procedure.

Cognitive therapy maintains that a comprehensive approach to the treatment of anxiety and other disorders includes targeting anxiety-provoking thoughts and images. Work with depressed patients (Beck, Rush, Shaw & Emery, 1979) demonstrates that desired cognitive changes do not necessarily follow from changes in behavior. For this reason, it is vital to know the patient's expectations, interpreta-tions, and reactions to events. Cognitive change must be demonstrated, not assumed.

Cognitive therapy has some similarities with *multimodal therapy* (MMT), a cognitive-behavioral approach to psychotherapy. Both approaches are empirically based, thoughts and images are assessed and are targets of intervention, and functional analyses are done of problem behaviors. Yet, cognitive therapy differs from MMT in several ways. Cognitive therapy stresses the primacy of cognition; it uses thoughts and images as the entry to the system of behavior, affect, relationships, and biology. Multimodal therapy gives equal coverage to all modalities. Further, the specific cognitive profile for each disorder guides the cognitive therapist in the selection of techniques and tactics. The multimodal therapist, in contrast, is required to approach each case without a superordinate theory to help organize the mass of available data.

Multimodal therapy does not maintain that borrowed techniques be theoretically uniform. In contrast, cognitive therapy uses techniques consistent with the cognitive theory of emotional disorders. Finally, while MMT claims to address many areas of the patient's functioning, Kwee & Lazarus (1986) state that only in the assessment phase is MMT "multi." In actual practice, treatment is usually bimodal or unimodal.

HISTORY

PRECURSORS

Cognitive therapy's theoretical underpinnings are derived from three main sources: (1) the phenomenological approach to psychology, (2) structural theory and depth psychology, and (3) cognitive psychology. The phenomenological approach posits that the individual's view of self and the personal world are central to behavior. This concept was originally founded in Greek Stoic philosophy and can be seen in Immanuel Kant's (1798) emphasis on conscious subjective experience. This approach is also evident in the writings of Adler (1936), Alexander (1950), Horney (1950), and Sullivan (1953).

The second major influence was the structural theory and depth psychology of Kant and Freud, particularly Freud's concept of the hierarchical structuring of cognition into primary and secondary processes.

Finally, more modern developments in cognitive psychology have had an impact. George Kelly (1955) is credited with being the first among contemporaries to describe the cognitive model through his use of "personal constructs" and his emphasis on the role of beliefs in behavior change. Cognitive theories of emotion, such as those of Magda Arnold (1960) and Richard Lazarus (1984), which give primacy to cognition in emotional and behavioral change, have also contributed to cognitive therapy.

BEGINNINGS

Cognitive therapy began in the early 1960s as the result of Aaron Beck's research on depression (Beck, 1963, 1964, 1967). Trained in psychoanalysis, Beck attempted to validate Freud's theory of depression as having at its core "anger turned on the self." To substantiate this formulation, Beck made clinical observations of depressed patients and investigated their treatment under traditional psychoanalysis. Rather than finding retroflected anger in their thoughts and dreams, Beck ob-

served a negative bias in their cognitive processing. With continued clinical observations and experimental testing, Beck developed his theory of emotional disorders and a cognitive model of depression.

The work of Albert Ellis (1962) gave major impetus to the development of cognitive-behavior therapies. Both Ellis and Beck believed that people can consciously adopt reason, and both view the patient's underlying assumptions as targets of intervention. Similarly, they both rejected their analytic training and replaced passive listening with active, direct dialogues with patients. While Ellis confronted and persuaded patients that the philosophies they lived by were unrealistic, Beck "turned the client into a colleague who researches verifiable reality" (Wessler, 1986, p. 5).

The work of a number of contemporary behaviorists influenced the development of cognitive therapy. Bandura's (1977) concepts of expectancy of reinforcement, self and outcome efficacies, the interaction between person and environment, modeling, and vicarious learning catalyzed a shift in behavior therapy toward the cognitive domain. Mahoney's (1974) early work on the cognitive control of behavior and his continuing theoretical contributions also influenced cognitive therapy. Along with cognitive therapy and rational-emotive therapy, Meichenbaum's (1977) cognitive-behavior modification is recognized as one of the three major self-control therapies (Mahoney & Arnkoff, 1978). Meichenbaum's combination of cognitive modification and skills training in a coping skills paradigm is particularly useful in treating anxiety, anger, and stress.

CURRENT STATUS

Research: Cognitive Model and Outcome Studies

The cognitive model of depression postulates three specific concepts (Beck, 1967; Beck et al., 1979): (1) the cognitive triad, (2) schemas, and (3) cognitive errors. Subsequent research provided empirical support for this model (summarized in Beck & Rush, 1978) and demonstrated the efficacy of cognitive therapy in the treatment of unipolar depression. For example, an unpublished study by Don Ernst (1987) indicated 86 of 99 studies supported specific hypotheses of the cognitive model of depression while 30 of 34 studies supported hypotheses of bias in information processing.

Studies from seven independent centers have compared the efficacy of cognitive therapy to antidepressant medication, a treatment of established efficacy. Comparisons of cognitive therapy alone to drugs alone have found cognitive therapy to be superior (Blackburn, Bishop, Glen, Whalley & Christie, 1981; Dunn, 1979; Maldonado, 1982; Rush, Beck, Kovacs & Hollon, 1977) or equal to antidepressant medication (Blackburn, Eunson & Bishop, 1986; Hollon, Evans & DeRubeis, 1983; Murphy, Simons, Wetzel & Lustman, 1983; Simons, Murphy, Levine & Wetzel, 1986).

Six studies compared drugs alone to the combination of cognitive therapy and medication. Four showed superiority of the combination (Blackburn et al., 1981; Blackburn et al., 1986; Maldonado, 1982; Teasdale, Fennell, Hibbert & Amies, 1984), and two showed drugs alone to be equivalent to the combined treatment (Murphy et al., 1983; Simons et al., 1986).

Follow-up studies, observing patients for three months to two years after treatment, indicate that cognitive therapy has greater long-term effects than drug therapy (Blackburn et al., 1986; Hollon et al., 1983; Kovacs et al., 1981; Maldonado, 1982). Thus, cognitive therapy has demonstrated efficacy alone and in combination with standard drug treatment. Of special significance is the evidence of greater sustained improvement over time with cognitive therapy.

Of six studies comparing cognitive therapy alone versus the combination of drugs and cognitive therapy, five found cognitive therapy to be equal to the combined treatment and one found the combination of cognitive therapy and medication superior to cognitive therapy alone.

Suicide Research

Beck has developed key theoretical concepts regarding suicide and its prevention. Chief among his findings about suicide risk is the notion of hopelessness. A 10-year longitudinal study of 207 depressed, suicidal patients found that 90 percent of patients high in hopelessness (as defined by a score of 9 or more on Beck's Hopelessness Scale) eventually killed themselves. Only one patient with a score less than 9 committed suicide (Beck, Steer, Kovacs & Garrison, 1985). Hopelessness as a predictor of eventual suicide has been confirmed in subsequent studies.

Assessment Scales

Beck's work has generated a number of assessment scales for depression and suicidality, most notably the Beck Depression Inventory (Beck, Ward, Mendelson, Mock & Erbaugh, 1961), the Scale for Suicide Ideation, (Beck,

Kovacs & Weissman, 1979), the Suicide Intent Scale (Beck, Schuyler & Herman, 1974), and the Hopelessness Scale (Beck, Weissman, Lester & Trexler, 1974). The Beck Depression Inventory is the best known of these. It has been used in hundreds of outcome studies and is routinely employed by psychologists, physicians, and social workers to monitor depression in their patients and clients.

Training

The Center for Cognitive Therapy at the University of Pennsylvania, affiliated with the University of Pennsylvania Medical School, provides outpatient services and trains pre- and postdoctoral psychologists and psychiatric residents in cognitive therapy. The center is also a research institute, integrating clinical observations with empirical findings to develop theory and further provide treatment to clinic patients. Each year, visiting scholars from diverse areas of the world participate in the research and clinical activities of the center, learning about cognitive therapy and then training therapists in their home sites. They also exchange information on the theory and practice of cognitive therapy.

There are currently 10 other training centers for cognitive therapy in the United States. Research and treatment efforts in cognitive therapy are being conducted in a number of universities and hospitals in the United States and Europe. The *International Cognitive Therapy Newsletter* began in 1985 for the exchange of information among cognitive therapists. Therapists from five continents participate in the newsletter network.

Cognitive therapists routinely contribute to behavior therapy journals as well as to psychiatric journals. The primary journals devoted to research in cognitive therapy are *Cognitive Therapy and Research* and the *Journal of Cognitive Psychotherapy: An International Quarterly.* Cognitive therapy is represented at the annual meetings of the American Psychological Association, the American Psychiatric Association, the American Orthopsychiatric Association, the Phobia Society of America, and others. It is a major force in the Association for the Advancement of Behavior Therapy. There have been two world congresses of the International Association of Cognitive Therapy, in Philadelphia in 1981 and in Umea, Sweden, in 1986. A congress will be held at Oxford University in 1989.

Because of its efficacy as a short-term form of psychotherapy, cognitive therapy is achieving wider use in settings that must demonstrate cost-effectiveness or that require short-term contact with patients, such as health maintenance organizations, community mental health centers, and acute care hospitals. It has applications in both inpatient and outpatient settings.

Many talented researchers and innovative therapists have contributed to the development of cognitive therapy. Controlled outcome studies comparing cognitive therapy with other forms of treatment are conducted with anxiety disorders, panic, drug abuse, anorexia and bulimia, geriatric depression, acute depression, and dysphoric disorder. Beck's students and associates do research on the nature and treatment of depression, anxiety, loneliness, marital conflict, eating disorders, agoraphobia, pain, and personality disorders.

As cognitive therapy has interacted with behavior therapy and other disciplines, new theories of cognitive processing have emerged, represented in the writings of Mahoney (1980) and Guidano and Liotti (1983), who combined the cognitive model with such fields as evolutionary epistemology and the philosophy of science to propose a theory of individual knowledge.

PERSONALITY

THEORY OF PERSONALITY

Cognitive therapy emphasizes the role of cognitive processing in emotion and behavior. An individual's emotional and behavioral responses to a situation are largely determined by how that individual perceives, interprets, and assigns meaning to that event.

Cognitive therapy views personality as shaped by central values, or superordinate schemas, and sees psychological distress as "caused" by a number of factors. While people may have biochemical predispositions to illness, they respond to specific stressors because of their learning history. The phenomena of psychopathology (but not necessarily the cause) are on the same continuum as normal emotional reactions, but they are manifested in exaggerated and persistent ways. In depression, for example, sadness and loss of interest are intensified and prolonged, in mania there is heightened investment in self-aggrandizement, and in anxiety there is an extreme sense of vulnerability and danger. The behavioral consequences of psychopathology will depend on the content of cognitive structuring.

Individuals experience psychological distress when they perceive a situation as threatening their vital interests. At such times, their perceptions and interpretations of events are highly selective, egocentric, and rigid. This results in a functional impairment of normal cognitive activity. There is a decreased ability to turn off idiosyncratic thinking, to concentrate, recall, or reason. Corrective functions, which allow reality testing and refinement of global conceptualizations, are attenuated.

Cognitive Vulnerability

Each individual has a set of idiosyncratic vulnerabilities and sensitivities that predispose him or her to psychological distress. These vulnerabilities appear related to personality structure. Personality is shaped by *schemas*, cognitive structures that consist of the individual's fundamental beliefs and assumptions, which develop early in life from personal experiences and identification with significant others. People form concepts about themselves, others, and how the world operates. These concepts are reinforced by further learning experiences and, in turn, influence the formation of other beliefs, values, and attitudes.

Schemas may be adaptive or dysfunctional. They may be general or specific in nature. A person may even have competing schemas. Schemas are enduring cognitive structures, latent during nonstressful periods, that become active when triggered by specific stimuli, stressors, or circumstances.

The basic nature of schemas can be unraveled by observing people whose cognitive structures are most accessible to exploration through introspection, such as patients with borderline personality disorders (Pretzer, 1983; Young, 1983). This disorder is characterized by intensity of emotion and reactivity to events, abrupt shifts in mood, particularly to anxious agitation or anger, impulsive and counterproductive behavior, and unstable relationships. Dichotomous (black-white) thinking (particularly seeing self or others as *all good* or *all bad*) and subjective reasoning (equating feelings with facts) are dominant cognitive distortions.

Young (1983) conceptualized the borderline patient as having early negative schemas. An early negative core belief is a basic assumption about oneself or the world central to one's psychological functioning. Examples of early negative schemas of the borderline patient include "There's something fundamentally wrong with me," "People should support me and should not criticize, abandon, disagree with, or misunderstand me," and "I am my feelings." With such beliefs about the self, the borderline patient's delicate emotional balance is easily upset, especially by perceived abandonment by others. The behavioral and emotional patterns that make up personality are derived from individual rules about life and beliefs about the self. Other disorders may be characterized by similar core beliefs but they are less strong or rigid.

Another ubiquitous belief has been labeled *conditional assumption*. Such assumptions or attitudes begin with an *if*. Two examples, frequently found in depression-prone patients, are "If I don't succeed at everything I do, nobody will respect me" and "If a person doesn't like me, it means I'm unlovable." Such individuals may function fairly well until they experience a series of defeats or rejections. At this point, they begin to believe that nobody respects them or that they are

unlovable. In most cases, such beliefs can be dispelled in brief therapy—however, if they constitute core beliefs, more protracted treatment is necessary.

Dimensions of Personality

The idea that certain clusters of personality attributes or cognitive structures are related to certain types of emotional response has been studied by Beck, Epstein, and Harrison (1983), who found two major personality dimensions relevant to depression and possibly other disorders: social dependence (sociotropy) and autonomy. Beck's research revealed that dependent individuals became depressed following disruption of relationships. Autonomous people became depressed after defeat or failure to attain a desired goal. The sociotropic dimension is organized around closeness, nurturance, and dependency; the autonomous dimension around independence, goal setting, self-determination, and self-imposed obligations.

Research has also established that while "pure" cases of sociotropy and autonomy do exist, most people display features of each, depending on the situation. Thus, sociotropy and autonomy are modes of behavior, not fixed personality structures. This position stands in marked contrast with psychodynamic theories of personality, which postulate fixed personality dimensions.

Thus, cognitive therapy views personality as reflecting the individual's cognitive organization and structure, which are both biologically and socially influenced. Within the constraints of one's neuroanatomy and biochemistry, personal learning experiences help determine how one develops and responds.

VARIETY OF CONCEPTS

Cognitive therapy emphasizes the individual's learning history, including the influence of significant life events, in the development of psychological disturbance. It is not a reductionistic model but recognizes that psychological distress is usually the result of many interacting factors.

Cognitive therapy's emphasis on the individual's learning history endorses social learning theory and the importance of reinforcement. The social learning perspective requires a thorough examination of the individual's developmental history and his or her own idiosyncratic meanings and interpretations of events. Cognitive therapy emphasizes the idiographic nature of cognition, for the same event may have very different meanings for two individuals.

The conceptualization of personality as reflective of schemas and underlying assumptions also relates to social learning theory. The way a person structures experience is based on consequences of past behavior, vicarious learning from significant others, and expectations about the future. Assumptions about the self have a great impact on one's interactions with the social and physical environments. Societal rules and norms may become internal standards, and even become absolute in their application. Consequences of early interactions may lead to assumptions of success or failure, encouraging or limiting future risk taking.

Theory of Causality

Psychological distress is ultimately caused by many innate, biological, developmental, and environmental factors interacting with one another, and so there is no single "cause" of psychopathology. Depression, for instance, is characterized by predisposing factors such as hereditary susceptibility, diseases that cause persistent neurochemical abnormalities, developmental traumas leading to specific cognitive vulnerabilities, inadequate personal experiences that fail to provide appropriate coping skills, and counterproductive cognitive patterns, such as unrealistic goals, assumptions, or imperatives. Physical disease, severe and acute stress, and chronic stress are also precipitating factors.

Cognitive Distortions

Systematic errors in reasoning called *cognitive distortions* are evident during psychological distress (Beck, 1967). These include:

Arbitrary inference: Drawing a specific conclusion without supporting evidence or even in the face of contradictory evidence. An example of this is the working mother who concludes after a particularly busy day, "I'm a terrible mother."

Selective abstraction: Conceptualizing a situation on the basis of a detail taken out of context, ignoring other information. An example is a man becomes jealous upon seeing his girlfriend tilt her head towards another man to hear him better at a noisy party.

Overgeneralization: Abstracting a general rule from one or a few isolated incidents and applying it too broadly and to unrelated situations. After a discouraging date, a woman concluded, "All men are alike. I'll always be rejected."

Magnification and minimization: Seeing something as far more significant or less significant than it actually is. A student catastrophized, "If I appear the least bit nervous in class it will mean disaster." Another person, rather than facing the fact that his mother is terminally ill, decides that she will soon recover from her "cold."

Personalization: Attributing external events to oneself without evidence supporting a causal connection. A man waved to an acquaintance across a busy street. After not getting a greeting in return, he concluded, "I must have done something to offend him."

Dichotomous thinking: Categorizing experiences in one of two extremes; for example, as complete success or total failure. A doctoral candidate stated, "Unless I write the best exam they've ever seen, I'm a failure as a student."

Systematic Bias in Psychological Disorders

A bias in information processing is a characteristic of most psychological disorders. This bias is generally applied to "external" information, such as communications or threats, and may start operating at early stages of information processing. The bias may be extended to misinterpretation of internal "messages" received within the body, as in panic attacks, hysteria, anorexia nervosa, and hypochondriasis. The kind of bias found in typical disorders is described in Table 8.1.

Cognitive Model of Depression

A *cognitive triad* characterizes depression (Beck, 1967). The depressed individual has a negative view of the self, the world, and the future, and perceives the self as inadequate, deserted, and worthless. A negative view is apparent in beliefs that enormous demands exist and that immense barriers block access to goals. The world

Table 8.1:
The Cognitive Profile of Neurotic Disorders

Disorder	Systematic Bias in Processing Information
Depression	Negative view of self, experience, and future
Hypomania	Inflated view of self and future
Anxiety Disorder	Physical or psychological danger
Panic Disorder	Catastrophic interpretation of bodily/mental experiences
Phobia	Danger in specific, avoidable situations
Paranoid State	Attribution of bias to others
Hysteria	Concept of motor or sensory abnormality
Obsession	Repeated warning or doubting about safety
Compulsion	Rituals to ward off threat
Suicidal Behavior	Hopelessness and deficiencies in problem solving
Anorexia Nervosa	Fear of being fat
Hypochondriasis	Attribution of serious medical disorder

seems devoid of pleasure or gratification. The depressed person's view of the future is pessimistic, reflecting the belief that current troubles will not improve. This hopelessness may lead to suicidal ideation.

Motivational, behavioral, and physical symptoms of depression stem from these cognitive patterns. *Paralysis of will* is due to the belief that one lacks the ability to cope or control an event's outcome. Consequently, there is a reluctance to commit oneself to a goal. Suicidal wishes often reflect a desire to escape from unbearable problems.

The increased dependency often observed in depressed patients reflects the view of self as incompetent, an overestimation of the difficulty of normal life tasks, the expectation of failure, and the desire for someone more capable to take over. Indecisiveness similarly reflects the belief that one is incapable of making correct decisions. The physical symptoms of depression —low energy, fatigue, and inertia— are also related to negative expectations. Work with depressed patients indicates that initiating activity actually reduces inertia and fatigue. Moreover, refuting negative expectations and demonstrating motor ability play important roles in recovery.

Cognitive Model of Anxiety Disorders

Anxiety disorders are conceptualized as excessive functioning or malfunctioning of normal survival mechanisms. Thus, the basic mechanisms for coping with threat are the same for both normal and anxious people: physiological responses prepare the body for escape or self-defense. The same physiological responses occur in the face of psychosocial threats as in the case of physical dangers. The anxious person's perception of danger is either incorrectly based on false assumptions or excessive, while the normal response is based on a more accurate assessment of risk and the magnitude of danger. In addition, normal individuals can correct their misperceptions using logic and evidence. Anxious individuals have difficulty recognizing cues of safety and other evidence that would reduce the threat of danger. Thus, in cases of anxiety, cognitive content revolves around themes of danger, and the individual tends to maximize the likelihood of harm and minimize his or her ability to cope.

Mania

The manic patient's biased thinking is the reverse of the depressive's. Such individuals selectively perceive significant gains in each life experience, blocking out negative experiences or reinterpreting them as positive, and unrealistically expecting favorable results from various enterprises. Exaggerated concepts of abilities, worth, and accomplishments lead to feelings of euphoria. The continued stimulation from inflated self-evaluations and overly optimistic expectations provide vast sources of energy and drive the manic individual into continuous goal-directed activity.

Panic Disorder

Patients with panic disorder are prone to regard any unexplained symptom or sensation as a sign of some impending catastrophe. Their cognitive processing system focuses their attention on bodily or psychological experiences and shapes these sources of internal information into a belief of impending disaster. Each patient has a specific "equation." For one, distress in the chest or stomach equals heart attack; for another, shortness of breath means the cessation of all breathing; and for another, lightheadedness is a sign of imminent unconsciousness.

Some patients regard a sudden surge of anger as a sign that they will lose control and injure somebody. Others interpret a mental lapse, momentary confusion, or mild disorientation as a sign they are losing their mind. A crucial characteristic of people having panic attacks is the conclusion that vital systems (cardiovascular, respiratory, or central nervous system) will collapse. Because of their fear, they tend to be overly vigilant towards internal sensations and thus detect and magnify sensations that pass unnoticed in other people.

Patients with panic disorder show a specific *cognitive deficit*—an inability to view their symptoms and catastrophic interpretations realistically.

Agoraphobia

Patients who have had one or more panic attacks in a particular situation tend to avoid that situation. For example, people who have had panic attacks in supermarkets will avoid going there. If they push themselves to go, they become increasingly vigilant toward their sensations and begin to anticipate having another panic attack.

The anticipation of such an attack triggers a variety of autonomic symptoms that are then misinterpreted as signs of an impending disaster (e.g., heart attack, loss of consciousness, suffocation), which can lead to a full-blown panic attack. Patients with a panic disorder that goes untreated frequently develop agoraphobia. They may eventually become housebound or so restricted in their activities that they cannot travel far from home and require a companion to venture any distance.

Phobia

In phobias, there is anticipation of physical or psychological harm in specific situations. As long as the patients can avoid these situations, they do not feel threatened and may be relatively comfortable. When they enter into these situations, they experience the typical subjective and physiological symptoms of severe anxiety. As a result of this unpleasant reaction, their tendency to avoid the situation in the future is reinforced.

In *evaluation phobias*, there is fear of disparagement or failure in social situations, examinations, and public speaking. The behavioral and physio-logical reactions to the potential "danger" (rejection, devaluation, failure) may interfere with the patient's functioning to the degree that these responses can produce just what the patient fears will happen.

Paranoid States

The paranoid individual is biased toward attributing prejudice to other people in their dealings with him or her. The paranoid persists in assuming that other people are deliberately abusive, interfering, or critical. In contrast to depressed patients, who believe that supposed insults or rejections are justified, paranoid patients persevere in thinking others treat them unjustly.

Unlike depressed patients, paranoid patients do not experience low self-esteem. They are more concerned with the *injustice* of the presumed attacks, thwarting, or intrusions than with the actual loss, and they rail against the presumed prejudice and malicious intent of others.

Obsessions and Compulsions

Patients with obsessions introduce uncertainty into the appraisal of situations that most people would consider safe. The uncertainty is generally attached to circumstances that are potentially unsafe and is manifested by continual doubts—even though there is no evidence of danger.

Obsessives continually doubt whether they have performed an act necessary for safety (for example, turning off a gas oven or locking the door at night). They may fear contamination by germs, and no amount of reassurance can alleviate the fear. A key characteristic of obsessives is this *sense of responsibility* and the belief that they are accountable for having taken an action—or having failed to take an action—that could harm them or their family.

Compulsions are attempts to reduce excessive doubts by performing rituals designed to neutralize the anticipated disaster. A hand-washing compulsion, for instance, is based on the patients' belief that they have not removed all the dirt or contaminants from parts of their body. Some patients regard dirt as a source of danger, either as a cause of physical disease or as a source of offensive, unpleasant odors, and they are compelled to remove this source of physical or social danger.

Suicidal Behavior

The cognitive processing in suicidal individuals has two features. First, there is a high degree of hopelessness. The greater the hopelessness, the more the likelihood of suicide increases (Beck, Steer, Kovacs & Garrison, 1985). A second feature is a cognitive deficit—a difficulty in solving problems with other people or at work or school. Although the hopelessness accentuates poor problem solving and vice versa, the difficulties in coping with life situations can, by themselves, contribute to the suicidal potential.

Anorexia Nervosa

Anorexia nervosa and bulimia represent a constellation of maladaptive beliefs that revolve around one central assumption: "My body weight and shape determine my worth and/or my social acceptability." Centered around this assumption are such beliefs as "I will look ugly if I gain much more weight," "The only thing in my life that I can control is my weight," and "If I don't starve myself, I will let go completely and become enormous."

Anorexics show typical distortions in information processing. They mis-

interpret symptoms of fullness after meals as signs they are getting fat. And they misperceive their image in a mirror or photograph as much fatter than it actually is.

PSYCHOTHERAPY

THEORY OF PSYCHOTHERAPY

The goals of cognitive therapy are to correct faulty information processing and to help patients modify assumptions that maintain maladaptive behaviors and emotions. Cognitive and behavioral methods are used to challenge dysfunctional beliefs and to promote more realistic adaptive thinking. Cognitive therapy initially addresses symptom relief, including problem behaviors and distortions in logic, but its ultimate goal is to remove systematic biases in thinking.

Cognitive therapy fosters change in patients' beliefs by treating beliefs as testable hypotheses to be examined through behavioral experiments jointly agreed upon by patient and therapist. The cognitive therapist does not tell the client that the beliefs are irrational or wrong or that the beliefs of the therapist should be adopted. Instead, the therapist asks questions to elicit the meaning, function, usefulness, and consequences of the patient's beliefs. The patient ultimately decides whether to reject, modify, or maintain all personal beliefs, being well aware of their emotional and behavioral consequences.

Cognitive therapy is not the substitution of positive beliefs for negative ones. It is based in reality, not in wishful thinking. Similarly, cognitive therapy does not maintain that people's problems are imaginary. Patients may have serious social, financial, or health problems as well as functional deficits. In addition to reality problems, however, they have biased views of themselves, their situations, and their resources that limit their range of responses and prevent them from generating solutions.

Cognitive change can promote behavioral change by allowing the patient to take risks. In turn, experience in applying new behaviors can validate the new perspective. Emotions can be moderated by considering evidence and facts and by enlarging perspectives to include alternative interpretations of events. Emotions play a role in cognitive change, for learning is enhanced when emotions are triggered. Thus, the cognitive, behavioral, and emotional channels interact in therapeutic change, but cognitive therapy emphasizes the primacy of cognition in promoting and maintaining therapeutic change.

Cognitive change occurs at several levels: in voluntary thoughts, in continuous or automatic thoughts, and in assumptions. According to the cognitive model, cognitions are organized in a hierarchy, with each level differing from the next in its accessibility and stability. The most accessible and least stable cognitions are voluntary thoughts, for one can summon them at will and they are temporary. At the next level are automatic thoughts, which come to mind spontaneously when triggered by circumstances. They are the thoughts that intercede between an event or stimulus and the individual's emotional and behavioral reactions.

An example of an automatic thought is "Everyone will see I'm nervous," experienced by a socially anxious person before going to a party. Automatic thoughts are accompanied by emotions and at the time they are experienced seem plausible, are highly salient, and are internally consistent with individual logic. They are given credibility without ever being challenged. Though automatic thoughts are more stable and less accessible than voluntary thoughts, patients can be taught to recognize and monitor them. Cognitive distortions are evident in automatic thoughts. In the early sessions of cognitive therapy, much attention is given to the role of automatic thoughts in behavior and emotion.

Automatic thoughts are generated from underlying assumptions. For example, the belief "I am responsible for other people's happiness" produces numerous negative automatic thoughts in people who perceive themselves as causing distress to others. Assumptions shape perceptions into cognitions, determine goals, and provide interpretations and meanings to events. They may be quite stable and outside the patient's awareness.

Core beliefs are called *schemas*. Therapy aims at identifying these assumptions and counteracting their effects. If the assumptions themselves can be changed, the patient is less vulnerable to future distress.

The Therapeutic Relationship

The therapeutic relationship is collaborative. The therapist assesses sources of distress and dysfunction and helps the patient clarify goals. In cases of severe depression or anxiety, patients may need the therapist to take a directive role in helping them organize their thoughts and wishes. In other instances, patients may take the lead in determining goals for therapy. As part of the collaboration, the patient provides the thoughts, images, and beliefs that occur in various situations as well as the emotions and behaviors that accompany the thoughts. The patient also shares responsibility by helping to set the agenda for each session and by doing homework between sessions. Homework helps therapy to proceed more quickly and gives the patient an opportunity to practice newly learned skills and perspectives.

The therapist functions as a guide who helps the patient understand how beliefs and attitudes influence affect and behavior. The therapist is also a catalyst who promotes corrective experiences that lead to cognitive change and skills acquisition. Thus, cognitive therapy employs a learning model of psychotherapy. The therapist has expertise in examining and modifying beliefs and behavior but does not adopt the role of a passive expert.

Cognitive therapists actively pursue the patient's point of view. By using warmth, accurate empathy, and genuineness (see Rogers, 1951), the cognitive therapist appreciates the patient's personal world view. However, these qualities alone are not sufficient for therapeutic change. The cognitive therapist specifies problems, focuses on important areas, and teaches specific cognitive and behavioral techniques.

Along with having good interpersonal skills, cognitive therapists are flexible. They are sensitive to the patient's level of comfort and use self-disclosure judiciously. They provide supportive contact, when necessary, and operate within the goals and agenda of the cognitive approach. Flexibility in the use of therapeutic techniques depends on the targeted symptoms. For example, the inertia of

depression responds best to behavioral interventions, while the suicidal ideation and pessimism of depression respond best to cognitive techniques. A good cognitive therapist does not use techniques arbitrarily or mechanically, but with sound rationale and skill, and with an understanding of each individual's needs.

To maintain collaboration, the therapist elicits feedback from the patient, usually at the end of each session. Feedback focuses on what the patient found helpful or not helpful, whether the patient has concerns about the therapist, and whether the patient has questions. The therapist may summarize the session or ask the patient to do so. Another way the therapist encourages collaboration is by providing the patient with a rationale for each procedure used. This demystifies the therapy process, increases patients' participation, and reinforces a learning paradigm in which patients gradually assume more responsibility for therapeutic change.

Definitions

Three fundamental concepts in cognitive therapy are: *collaborative empiricism*, *Socratic dialogue*, and *guided discovery*.

Collaborative empiricism. The therapeutic relationship is collaborative and requires jointly determining the goals for treatment, eliciting and providing feedback, thereby demystifying how therapeutic change occurs. The therapist and patient become co-investigators, examining the evidence to support or reject the patient's cognitions. As in scientific inquiry, interpretations or assumptions are treated as testable hypotheses.

Empirical evidence is used to determine whether particular cognitions serve any useful purpose. Prior conclusions are subjected to logical analysis. Biased thinking is exposed as the patient becomes aware of alternative sources of information. This process is conducted as a partnership between patient and therapist, with either taking a more active role as needed.

Socratic dialogue. Questioning is a major therapeutic device in cognitive therapy (Beck & Young, 1985) and Socratic dialogue is the preferred method. The therapist carefully designs a series of questions to promote new learning. The purposes of the therapist's questions are generally to (1) clarify or define problems, (2) assist in the identification of thoughts, images, and assumptions, (3) examine the meanings of events for the patient, and (4) assess the consequences of maintaining maladaptive thoughts and behaviors.

Socratic dialogue implies that the patient arrives at logical conclusions based on the questions posed by the therapist. Questions are not used to "trap" patients, lead them to inevitable conclusions, or attack them. Questions enable the therapist to understand the patient's point of view and are posed with sensitivity so that patients may look at their assumptions objectively and nondefensively.

Beck and Young describe how questions change throughout the course of therapy:

In the beginning of therapy, questions are employed to obtain a full and detailed picture of the patient's particular difficulties. They are used to obtain background and diagnostic data; to evaluate the patient's stress tolerance, capacity for introspection, coping methods and so on; to obtain information about the patient's external situation and interpersonal context; and to modify vague complaints by working with the patient to arrive at specific target problems to work on.

As therapy progresses, the therapist uses questioning to explore approaches to problems, to help the patient weigh advantages and disadvantages of possible solutions, to examine the consequences of staying with particular maladaptive behaviors, to elicit automatic thoughts, and to demonstrate maladaptive assumptions and their consequences. In short, the therapist uses questioning in most cognitive therapeutic techniques. (1985, p. 223)

Guided discovery. Through guided discovery the patient modifies maladaptive beliefs and assumptions. The therapist serves as a "guide" who elucidates problem behaviors and errors in logic by designing new experiences (*behavioral experiments*) that lead to the acquisition of new skills and perspectives. Through both cognitive and behavioral methods, the patient discovers more adaptive ways of thinking and behaving. The patient learns how to correct faulty cognitive processing so that it is eventually no longer necessary to depend on a therapist. Guided discovery implies that the therapist does not exhort or cajole the patient to adopt a new set of beliefs. Rather, the therapist encourages the patient's use of information, facts, and probabilities to obtain a realistic perspective.

PROCESS OF PSYCHOTHERAPY

Initial Sessions

The goals of the first interview are to initiate a relationship with the patient, to elicit essential information, and to produce symptom relief. Building a relationship with the patient may begin with questions about feelings and thoughts about beginning therapy. Discussing the patient's expectations helps put the patient at ease, provides information to the therapist regarding the patient's expectations, and presents an opportunity to demonstrate the relationship between cognition and affect (Beck, Rush, et al., 1979). The therapist also uses the initial sessions to socialize the patient to cognitive therapy, establish a collaborative framework, and deal with any misconceptions about therapy. The types of information the therapist seeks in the initial session regard diagnosis, past history, present life situation, psychological problems, attitudes about treatment, and motivation for treatment.

Problem definition and symptom relief begin in the first session. Although problem definition and background may take several sessions, it is often critical to focus on a very specific problem and provide rapid relief in the first session. For example, a suicidal patient needs direct intervention to undermine hopelessness immediately. Symptom relief can come from several sources: specific problem solving, clarifying vague or general complaints into workable goals, or gaining objectivity about a disorder (e.g., that a patient's symptoms represent anxiety, and nothing worse, or that difficulty concentrating is a symptom of depression and not a sign of brain disease).

Problem definition entails both functional and cognitive analyses of the problem. A functional analysis identifies elements of the problem: how it is manifested; situations in which it occurs; its frequency, intensity, and duration; and its consequences. A cognitive analysis of the problem identifies the thoughts and images a person has when emotion is triggered. It also includes investigation of the extent to which the person feels in control of thoughts and images, what the person imagines will happen in a distressing situation, and the probability of such an outcome actually occurring.

In the early sessions, the cognitive therapist plays a more active role than does the patient. The therapist gathers information, conceptualizes the patient's problems, socializes the patient to cognitive therapy, and actively intervenes to provide symptom relief. The patient is assigned homework beginning at the first session.

Homework, at this early stage, is usually directed at recognizing the connections between affect and behavior. Some patients might be asked to record their automatic thoughts when distressed. Others might practice recognizing thoughts by counting them, as they occur, on a wrist counter. Thus, the patient is trained from the outset to self-monitor thoughts and behaviors. In later sessions, the patient plays an increasingly active role in determining homework, and assignments focus on testing very specific assumptions.

During the initial sessions, a problem list is generated. A problem list may include specific symptoms, behaviors, or pervasive problems. These problems are assigned priorities as targets for intervention. Priorities are based on the relative magnitude of distress, the likelihood of making progress, the severity of symptoms, and the pervasiveness of a particular theme or topic.

If the therapist can help the patient solve a problem early in treatment, this success can motivate the patient to make further changes. As each problem is approached, the therapist chooses the appropriate cognitive or behavioral technique to apply and provides the patient with a rationale for the technique. Throughout therapy, the therapist elicits the patient's reactions to various techniques to ascertain whether they are being applied correctly, whether they are successful, and how they can be incorporated into homework or practical experience outside the session.

Middle and Later Sessions

As cognitive therapy proceeds, the emphasis shifts from the patient's symptoms to the patient's patterns of thinking. The connections among thoughts, emotions, and behavior are chiefly demonstrated through the examination of automatic thoughts. Automatic thoughts are relatively accessible and constant and provide ample opportunity to practice more logical thinking. Once the patient can challenge thoughts that interfere with functioning, he or she can consider the underlying assumptions that generate such thoughts.

There is usually a greater emphasis on cognitive rather than behavioral techniques in later sessions, which focus on complex problems that involve several dysfunctional thoughts. Often these thoughts are more amenable to logical analysis than to behavioral experimentation. For example, the prophecy "I'll never get what I want in life" is not easily tested. However, one can question the logic of this generalization and look at the advantages and disadvantages of maintaining it as a belief.

Often such assumptions outside the patient's awareness are discovered as themes of automatic thoughts. By observing automatic thoughts over time and across situations, assumptions appear or can be inferred. Once these assumptions and their power have been recognized, therapy aims at modifying them by examining their validity, adaptiveness, and utility for the patient.

In later sessions, the patient assumes more responsibility for identifying problems and solutions and for creating homework assignments. The therapist serves the role of advisor rather than teacher as the patient becomes more able to use cognitive techniques to solve problems. The frequency of sessions decreases as the patient becomes more self-sufficient. Therapy is terminated when goals have been reached and the patient feels able to practice his or her new skills and perspectives.

Ending Treatment

Length of treatment depends primarily on the severity of the client's problems. The usual length for unipolar depression is 15 to 25 sessions at weekly intervals (Beck, Rush, et al., 1979). Moderately to severely depressed patients usually require sessions twice a week for 4 to 5 weeks and then require weekly sessions for 10 to 15 weeks. Most cases of anxiety are treated within a comparable period of time.

Some patients find it extremely difficult to tolerate the anxiety involved in giving up old ways of thinking. For them, therapy may last for several months. Still others experience early symptom relief and leave therapy early. In these cases, little structural change has occurred and problems are likely to recur.

From the outset, the therapist and patient share the expectation that therapy is time-limited. Because cognitive therapy is present-centered and time-limited, there tend to be fewer problems with termination than in longer forms of therapy. As the patient develops self-reliance through graded tasks of increasing difficulty or in mastering the skills of challenging distorted thoughts, therapy becomes less frequent.

Termination is planned for, even in the first session as the rationale for cognitive therapy is presented. Patients are told that a goal of the therapy is for them to learn to be their own therapists. The problem list makes explicit what is to be accomplished in treatment. Behavioral observation, self-monitoring, self-report, and sometimes questionnaires (e.g., the Beck Depression Inventory), measure progress towards the goals on the problem list. Feedback from the patient aids the therapist in designing experiences to foster cognitive change and requires that the patient assess personal therapeutic change.

Some patients have concerns about relapse or about functioning autonomously. Some of these concerns include cognitive distortions, such as dichotomous thinking ("I'm either sick or 100 percent cured") or negative prediction ("I'll get depressed again and won't be able to help myself"). It may be necessary to review the goal of therapy: to teach the patient ways to handle problems more effectively, not to produce a "cure" or restructure core personality (Beck, Rush, et al., 1979). Education about psychological disorders, such as the possibility of recurrent depression, is done throughout treatment so that the patient has a realistic perspective on prognosis.

During the usual course of therapy, the patient experiences both successes and setbacks. Such problems give the patient the opportunity to practice new skills. As termination approaches, the patient can be reminded that setbacks are normal and have been handled before. The therapist might ask the patient to describe how prior specific problems were handled during treatment. Therapists can also use cognitive rehearsal prior to termination by having patients imagine future difficulties and report how they would deal with them.

Termination is usually followed by one or two booster sessions, usually one and two months after termination. Such sessions consolidate gains and assist the patient in employing new skills.

MECHANISMS OF PSYCHOTHERAPY

Several common denominators cut across effective treatments. Three mechanisms of change common to all successful forms of psychotherapy are (1) a comprehensible framework, (2) the patient's emotional engagement in the problem situation, and (3) reality testing in that situation.

Cognitive therapy maintains that the modification of dysfunctional assumptions leads to effective cognitive, emotional, and behavioral change. Patients change by recognizing automatic thoughts, questioning the evidence used to support them, and modifying cognitions to more closely fit the available data. Next, the patient behaves in ways congruent with new, more adaptive ways of thinking. Thus, the patient experiences a new way of processing information and the consequences stemming from it.

Change can occur only if the patient experiences a problematic situation as a real threat. According to cognitive therapy, thoughts underlie emotions, and with *affective arousal*, thoughts become accessible and modifiable. In the language of cognitive therapy, these thoughts are "hot cognitions." One mechanism of change, then, centers on making accessible those cognitive constellations that produced the maladaptive behavior or symptomatology. This mechanism is analogous to what psychoanalysts call "making the unconscious conscious."

Simply arousing emotions and the accompanying cognitions is not sufficient to cause lasting change. People express emotion, sometimes explosively, throughout their lives without benefit. However, the therapeutic milieu allows the patient to simultaneously experience emotional arousal and reality testing. For a variety of psychotherapies, what is therapeutic is the patient's ability to be engaged in a problem situation and yet respond to it objectively. In terms of cognitive therapy, this means to experience the hot cognitions and to test them within the therapeutic framework. An examination of evidence and personal logic allows the patient to recognize that the situation has been misconstrued.

APPLICATIONS

PROBLEMS

Cognitive therapy is a present-centered, directive, active, problem-oriented approach best suited for cases in which problems can be delineated and cognitive distortions are apparent. It is not designed for "personal growth" or as a way to understand one's past. It has wide-ranging applications to a variety of clinical problems. While originally used in individual psychotherapy, it is now used with couples, families, and groups as well. It can be applied alone or in conjunction with pharmacotherapy in inpatient and outpatient settings.

Cognitive therapy is widely recognized as an effective treatment for unipolar depression. Beck, Rush, Shaw, and Emery (1979, p. 27) list criteria for using cognitive therapy alone or in combination with medication. It is the treatment of choice in cases in which the patient refuses medication, prefers a psychological treatment, has unacceptable side effects to antidepressant medication, has a medical condition that precludes the use of antidepressants, or has proven to be refractory to adequate trials of antidepressants.

Cognitive therapy is not recommended as the exclusive treatment in cases of bipolar affective disorder or psychotic depression. It is also not used alone for the treatment of other psychoses, such as schizophrenia. While some patients with anxiety may begin treatment on medication, cognitive therapy teaches them to function without relying on medication.

Cognitive therapy produces the best results with patients who have adequate reality testing (i.e., no hallucinations or delusions), good concentration, and sufficient memory functions. It is ideally suited to patients who can focus on their automatic thoughts, accept the therapist-patient roles, are willing to tolerate anxiety in order to do experiments, can alter assumptions permanently, will take responsibility for their problems, and are willing to postpone gratification in order to complete therapy. Although these ideals are not always met, this therapy can proceed with some adjustment of outcome expectations and flexibility of structure. For example, therapy may not permanently alter schemas but may improve the patient's daily functioning.

Cognitive therapy works best with psychologically sophisticated patients. Lower-social-class and psychologically naive patients can also benefit after appropriate preparation for therapy. As long as the patient can recognize the relationships among thoughts, feelings, and behavior and takes some responsibility for self-help, cognitive therapy can be beneficial.

EVALUATION

Therapists

Therapists who are beginning training at the Center for Cognitive Therapy are evaluated prior to training through live observation and videotaped roleplaying. A confederate plays the role of the patient, and raters, using the Competency Checklist for Cognitive Therapists (Beck, Young, and El Shamma, 1979), observe the roleplay through a one-way mirror as the session is videotaped. At the end of a year's training, another roleplay interview is done and the therapist's progress is assessed. The Competency Checklist for Cognitive Therapists is divided into three parts. Part One, General Interview Procedures, assesses collaboration and mutual understanding. Part Two evaluates the use of specific cognitive and behavioral techniques. Part Three assesses the personal and professional characteristics of the therapist.

Therapists in training are supervised by experienced therapists. Supervision consists of weekly meetings during which trainees and supervisors review videotapes, audiotapes, or notes of cases in progress.

Patients

Patients' presenting problems are evaluated by clinical interviews and psychological tests. The intake interview at the Center for Cognitive Therapy is part of a three-hour protocol during which patients also complete psychological tests and question-naires. The clinical interview contributes to a diagnosis and provides a thorough description of the background factors contributing to the patient's distress. Current level of functioning, prominent symptoms, and expectations for therapy are also explored.

The psychological tests most frequently used are the Beck Depression Inventory (BDI) (Beck et al., 1961), the Scale for Suicide Ideation (SSI) (Beck et al., 1979), the Anxiety Checklist (Beck, 1978), the Young Loneliness Inventory (Young, 1979), and the Dysfunctional Attitudes Scale (Weissman, 1979). These self-report inventories increase the efficiency of therapy by quickly providing the therapist with information that would otherwise have to be elicited in interview. Questionnaires like the BDI and the SSI may also alert a therapist to suicidal risk. These questionnaires are not projective tests and their purposes are obvious to the patient. Cognitive therapists do not generally use standard personality tests but may use the Sociotropy and Autonomy Scale (Beck, Epstein & Harrison, 1983) to determine how best to work with the patient's style of interaction.

Progress in Therapy

Progress evaluation depends on the goals of therapy. In general, relief from symptoms is indicated by changes in scores on standardized inventories such as the BDI, changes in behavior as indicated through self-monitoring and observation by others, and changes in thinking as evident in such measures as the Daily Record of Dysfunctional Thoughts. Because patients have weekly homework designed for their particular goals, progress can be assessed by the outcome of the homework assignments. Progress in therapy is apparent in the relative ease with which a patient challenges automatic thoughts, the decrease in frequency of maladaptive cognitions and behaviors, the increase in ability to generate solutions to problems, and improved mood.

If there are problems in the progress of therapy, several factors must be considered: the patient may have dysfunctional beliefs about therapy or the therapist; the therapist may lack rapport or may have failed to provide a rationale for a procedure; an assignment may be too difficult for the patient or the patient may have higher order anxieties; or there may be a lack of consensus on the aims and goals of therapy (see Beck, Rush, et al., 1979, and Golden, 1983). Feedback during each session is designed to clarify misunderstandings and increase collaboration, thereby reducing the likelihood of problems in the progress of therapy.

TREATMENT

Cognitive therapy consists of highly specific learning experiences designed to teach patients (1) to monitor their negative, automatic thoughts (cognitions), (2) to recognize the connections between cognition, affect, and behavior, (3) to examine the evidence for and against distorted automatic thoughts, (4) to substitute more reality-oriented interpretations for these biased cognitions, and (5) to learn to identify and alter the beliefs that predispose them to distort their experiences (Beck, Rush, et al., 1979).

Both cognitive and behavioral techniques are used in cognitive therapy to reach these goals. The technique used at any given time depends on the patient's level of functioning and the particular symptoms and problems presented.

Cognitive Techniques

Verbal techniques are used to elicit the patient's automatic thoughts, analyze the logic behind the thoughts, identify maladaptive assumptions, and examine the validity of those assumptions. Automatic thoughts are elicited by questioning the patient about those thoughts that occur during upsetting situations. If the patient has difficulty recalling thoughts, imagery or role-playing can be used. Automatic thoughts are most accurately reported when they occur in the real-life situation rather than in the therapist's office. Such hot cognitions are accessible, powerful, and habitual. The patient is taught to recognize and identify thoughts and to record them when upset.

Cognitive therapists do not interpret patients' automatic thoughts, but explore their meanings, particularly when a patient reports fairly neutral thoughts yet displays strong emotions. In such cases, the therapist asks what those thoughts mean to the patient. For example, after an initial visit, an anxious patient called his therapist in great distress. He had just read an article about drug treatments for anxiety. His automatic thought was, "Drug therapy is helpful for anxiety." The meaning he ascribed to this was, "Cognitive therapy can't possibly help me. I am doomed to failure again."

Automatic thoughts are tested by direct evidence or by logical analysis. Evidence can be derived from past and present circumstances, but true to scientific inquiry, it must be as close to the facts as possible. Data can also be gathered in behavioral experiments. Such experiments give the patient the opportunity to try a new skill or challenge a belief firsthand. For example, if a man believes he cannot conduct a conversation, he might try to initiate brief exchanges with three people. The empirical nature of behavioral experiments allows patients to think in a more objective way.

Examination of the patient's thoughts can also lead to cognitive change. Questioning may uncover logical inconsistencies, contradictions, and other errors in thinking. Identifying and labeling cognitive distortions is in itself helpful, for patients then have specific errors to correct.

Maladaptive assumptions are usually much less accessible to patients than are automatic thoughts. While some patients are able to articulate their assumptions, most find it difficult. Assumptions appear as themes in automatic thoughts. The therapist may ask the patient to abstract rules underlying specific thoughts. The therapist might also make assumptions from these data and present these assumptions to the patient for verification. A patient who had trouble identifying her assumptions broke into tears upon reading an assumption inferred by her therapist, an indication of the salience of that assumption. Patients always have the right to disagree with the therapist and find more accurate statements of their beliefs.

Once an assumption has been identified, it is open to modification. This can occur in several ways: by asking the patient if the assumption seems reasonable, by having the patient generate reasons for and against maintaining the assumption, and by presenting evidence contrary to the assumption. While a particular assumption may seem reasonable in a specific situation, it may appear dysfunctional when universally applied. For example, being highly productive at work is generally reasonable. To be highly productive during recreational time may be unreasonable. A physician who believed he should work to his top capacity throughout his career may not have considered the prospect of early burnout. Thus, what may have made him successful in the short run could lead to problems in the long run. Specific cognitive techniques include decatastrophizing, reattribution, redefining, and decentering.

Decatastrophizing, also known as the "what if" technique (Beck and Emery, 1979), helps patients prepare for feared consequences. This is helpful in decreasing avoidance, particularly when combined with coping plans (Beck and Emery, 1985). If anticipated consequences are likely to happen, these techniques help to identify problem-solving strategies. Decatastrophizing is often used with a time-projection technique to widen the range of information and broaden the patient's time perspective.

Reattribution techniques test automatic thoughts and assumptions by considering alternative causes of events. This is especially helpful when patients personalize or perceive themselves as the cause of events. It is unreasonable to conclude, in the absence of evidence, that another person or single factor is the sole cause of an event. Reattribution techniques encourage reality testing and appropriate assignment of responsibility by requiring examination of all the factors that impinge on a situation.

Redefining is a way to mobilize a patient who believes a problem to be beyond personal control. Burns (1985) recommends that lonely people who think, "Nobody pays any attention to me," redefine the problem as, "I need to reach out to other people and be caring." Redefining a problem may include making it more concrete and specific and stating it in terms of the patient's own behavior.

Decentering is used primarily in treating anxious patients who wrongly believe they are the focus of everyone's attention. After examining the logic behind why others would stare at them and be able to read their minds, behavioral experiments are designed to test these particular beliefs. For example, one student who was reluctant to speak in class believed his classmates watched him constantly and noticed his anxiety. By observing them instead of focusing on his own discomfort, he saw some students taking notes, some looking at the professor, and some daydreaming. He concluded his classmates had other concerns.

The cognitive domain comprises thoughts and images. For some patients, pictorial images are more accessible and easier to report than thoughts. This is often the case with anxious patients. Ninety percent of anxious patients in one study reported visual images before and during episodes of anxiety (Beck, Laude and Bohnert, 1974). Gathering information about imagery, then, is another way to understand conceptual systems. Spontaneous images provide data on the patient's perceptions and interpretations of events. Induced imagery, long used by behavior therapists in relaxation and skills training, is finding new use in dream restructuring (Freeman, 1981). Other specific imaginal procedures used to modify distorted cognitions are discussed by Beck and Emery (1979, 1985).

Behavioral Techniques

Cognitive therapy uses behavioral techniques to modify automatic thoughts and assumptions. It employs behavioral experiments designed to challenge specific maladaptive beliefs and promote new learning. In a behavioral experiment, for example, a patient may predict an outcome based on personal automatic thoughts, carry out the agreed-upon behavior, and then evaluate the evidence in light of the new experience.

Behavioral techniques are also used to expand patients' response repertoires (skills training), to relax them (progressive relaxation) or make them active (activity scheduling), to prepare them for avoided situations (behavioral rehearsal), or to expose them to feared stimuli (exposure therapy). Because behavioral techniques are used to foster cognitive change, it is crucial to know the patient's perceptions, thoughts, and conclusions after each behavioral experiment.

Homework gives patients the opportunity to apply cognitive principles between sessions. Typical homework assignments focus on self-observation and self-monitoring, structuring time effectively, and implementing procedures for dealing with concrete situations. Self-monitoring is applied to the patient's automatic thoughts and reactions in various situations. New skills, such as challenging automatic thoughts, are also practiced as homework.

Hypothesis testing has both cognitive and behavioral components. In framing a "hypothesis" it is necessary to make it specific and concrete. Global labels, vague terms, and generalities need to be operationally defined using specific criteria. A resident who insisted, "I am not a good doctor," was asked to list what was needed to arrive at that conclusion. The therapist contributed other criteria as well, for the physician had overlooked such factors as rapport with patients and the ability to make decisions under pressure. The resident then monitored his behavior and sought feedback from colleagues and supervisors to test his hypothesis, coming to the conclusion, "I am a good doctor after all."

Exposure therapy serves to provide data on the thoughts, images, physiological symptoms, and self-reported level of tension experienced by the anxious patient. Specific thoughts and images can be examined for distortions and specific coping skills can be taught. By dealing directly with a patient's idiosyncratic thoughts, cognitive therapy is able to focus on that patient's particular needs. Patients learn that their predictions are not always accurate and they then have data to challenge anxious thoughts in the future.

Behavioral rehearsal and *roleplaying* are used to practice skills or techniques that are later applied in vivo. Modeling is also used in skills training. Often roleplaying is videotaped so that an objective source of information is available with which to evaluate performance.

Diversion techniques, which are used to reduce strong emotions and to decrease negative thinking, include physical activity, social contact, work, play, and visual imagery.

Activity scheduling provides structure and encourages involvement. By rating the degree of mastery and pleasure (using a scale of 0 to 10) experienced during each activity of the day, several goals are accomplished: patients who believe their depression is at a constant level see mood fluctuations; those who believe they cannot accomplish or enjoy anything are con-

tradicted by the evidence; and those who believe they are inactive because of an inherent defect are shown that activity involves some planning and is reinforcing in itself.

Graded task assignment calls for the patient to initiate an activity at a nonthreatening level while the therapist gradually increases the difficulty of assigned tasks. For example, someone who has difficulty socializing might begin interacting with one other person or a small group of acquaintances, or might socialize with people for just a brief period of time. Step-by-step, the patient comes to increase the time spent with others.

MANAGEMENT

Cognitive therapists work in a variety of settings, including hospitals, outpatient clinics, and private practices. Patients are referred by physicians, schools and universities, and other therapists who believe that cognitive therapy would be especially helpful to a patient. Many patients are self-referred. The Center for Cognitive Therapy maintains an international referral list of therapists.

Cognitive therapists generally adhere to 45-minute sessions. Because of the structure of cognitive therapy, much can be accomplished in this time. Patients are frequently asked to complete questionnaires, such as the Beck Depression Inventory, prior to the start of each session. Most sessions take place in the therapist's office. However, in vivo work with anxious patients occurs outside the therapist's office. A therapist might travel on public transportation with an agoraphobic, go to a pet store with a rodent phobic, or fly in an airplane with someone afraid of flying.

Confidentiality is always maintained and the therapist obtains informed consent for audiotaping and videotaping. Such recording is used in skills training or as a way to present evidence contradicting the patient's assumptions. For example, a patient who believes she looks nervous whenever she converses might be videotaped in conversation to test her assumption. Her appearance on camera may convince her that her assumption was in error or help her to identify specific behaviors to improve. Occasionally, patients take home audiotaped sessions to review content material between sessions.

Sessions are usually conducted on a weekly basis, with severely disturbed patients seen more frequently in the initial sessions. Cognitive therapists give their patients their home phone numbers in case of emergency.

Whenever possible, and with the patient's permission, significant others, such as friends and family members, are included in a therapy session to review the treatment goals and to explore ways in which the significant others might be helpful. This is especially important when family members misunderstand the nature of the illness, are overly solicitous, or are behaving in counterproductive ways. Significant others can be of great assistance in therapy, helping to sustain behavioral improvements by encouraging homework and assisting the patient with reality testing.

Problems may arise in the practice of cognitive therapy. For example, patients may misunderstand what the therapist says, resulting in anger, dissatisfaction, or hopelessness. When the therapist perceives such a reaction, he or she elicits the patient's thoughts, as with any other automatic thoughts. Together the therapist and client look for alternative interpretations. The therapist who has made an error accepts responsibility and corrects the mistake.

Problems sometimes result from unrealistic expectations about how quickly behaviors should change, from the incorrect or inflexible application of a technique, or from lack of attention to central issues. Problems in therapy require that the therapist attend to his or her own automatic thoughts and look for distortions in logic that create strong affect or prevent adequate problem solving.

Beck et al. (1979) provide guidelines for working with difficult patients and those who have histories of unsuccessful therapy: (1) avoid stereotyping the patient as *being* the problem rather than *having* the problem; (2) remain optimistic; (3) identify and deal with your own dysfunctional cognitions; (4) remain focused on the task instead of blaming the patient; and (5) maintain a problem-solving attitude. By following these guidelines, the therapist is able to be more resourceful with difficult patients. The therapist also can serve as a model for the patient, demonstrating that frustration does not automatically lead to anger and despair.

CASE EXAMPLE

This case example of the course of treatment for an anxious patient illustrates the use of both behavioral and cognitive techniques.

PRESENTING PROBLEM

The patient was a 21-year-old male college student who complained of sleep onset insomnia and frequent awakenings, halting speech and stuttering, shakiness, feelings of nervousness, dizziness, and worrying. His sleep difficulties were particularly acute prior to exams or athletic competitions. He explained his speech problems as due to his search for the "perfect word."

The patient was raised in a family that valued competition. His parents encouraged competitiveness in the patient and his siblings. As the eldest child, he was expected to win all the contests. His parents were determined that their children should surpass them in achievements and successes. They so strongly identified with the patient's achievements that he believed, "My success is their success."

The patient was taught to compete with other children outside the family as well. His father reminded him, "Never let anyone get the best of you." As a consequence of viewing others as adversaries, he developed few friends. Feeling lonely, he tried desperately to attract friends by becoming a prankster and by telling lies to enhance his image and make his family appear more attractive. Although he had acquaintances in college, he had few friends, for he was unable to self-disclose, fearing that others would discover he was not all that he would like to be.

EARLY SESSIONS

After gathering initial data regarding diagnosis, context, and history, the therapist attempted to define how the patient's cognitions contributed to his distress.

Therapist: What types of situations are most upsetting to you?
Patient: When I do poorly in sports, particularly swimming. I'm on the swim team. Also, if I make a mistake, even when I play cards with my roommates. I feel really upset if I get rejected by a girl.

Therapist: What thoughts go through your mind, let's say, when you don't do so well at swimming?
Patient: I think people think much less of me if I'm not on top, a winner.
Therapist: And how about if you make a mistake playing cards?
Patient: I doubt my own intelligence.
Therapist: And if a girl rejects you?
Patient: It means I'm not special. I lose value as a person.
Therapist: Do you see any connections here, among these thoughts?
Patient: Well, I guess my mood depends on what other people think of me. But that's important. I don't want to be lonely.
Therapist: What would that mean to you, to be lonely?
Patient: It would mean there's something wrong with me, that I'm a loser.

At this point, the therapist began to hypothesize about the patient's organizing beliefs: that his worth is determined by others, that he is unattractive because there is something inherently wrong with him, that he is a loser. The therapist looked for evidence to support the centrality of these beliefs and remained open to other possibilities.

The therapist assisted the patient in generating a list of goals to work on in therapy that included (1) decreasing perfectionism, (2) decreasing anxiety symptoms, (3) decreasing sleep difficulties, (4) increasing closeness in friendships, and (5) developing his own values apart from those of his parents. The first problem addressed was anxiety. An upcoming exam was chosen as a target situation. This student typically studied far beyond what was necessary, went to bed worried, finally fell asleep, woke during the night thinking about details or possible consequences of his performance, and went to exams exhausted. To reduce ruminations about his performance, the therapist asked him to name the advantages of dwelling on thoughts of the exam.

Patient: Well, if I don't think about the exam all the time I might forget something. If I think about the exam constantly, I think I'll do better. I'll be more prepared.

Therapist: Have you ever gone into a situation "less prepared"?

Patient: Not an exam, but once I was in a big swim meet and the night before I went out with friends and didn't think about it. I came home, went to sleep, got up, and swam.

Therapist: And how did it work out?

Patient: Fine. I felt great and swam pretty well.

Therapist: Based on that experience, do you think there's any reason to try to worry less about your performance?

Patient: I guess so. It didn't hurt me not to worry. Actually, worrying can be pretty distracting. I end up focusing more on how I'm doing than what I'm doing.

The patient came up with his own rationale for decreasing his ruminations. He was then ready to consider giving up his maladaptive behavior and risk trying something new. The therapist taught the patient progressive relaxation and the patient began to use physical exercise as a way to relieve anxiety.

The patient was also instructed in how cognitions affect behavior and mood. Picking up on the patient's statement that worries can be distracting, the therapist proceeded:

Therapist: You mentioned that when you worry about your exams you feel anxious. What I'd like to do now is imagine lying in your bed the night before an exam.

Patient: Okay, I can picture it.

Therapist: Imagine that you are thinking about the exam and you decide that you haven't done enough to prepare.

Patient: Yeah, OK.

Therapist: How are you feeling?

Patient: I'm feeling nervous. My heart is beginning to race. I think I need to get up and study some more.

Therapist: Good. When you think you're not prepared, you get anxious and want to get up out of bed. Now I want you to imagine that you are in bed the night before the exam. You have prepared in your usual way and are ready. You remind yourself of what you have done. You think that you are prepared and know the material.

Patient: OK. Now I feel confident.

Therapist: Can you see how your thoughts affect your feelings of anxiety?

The patient was instructed to record automatic thoughts, recognize cognitive distortions, and respond to them. For homework, he was asked to record his automatic thoughts if he had trouble falling asleep before an exam. One automatic thought he had while lying in bed was, "I should be thinking about the exam." His response was, "Thinking about the exam is not going to make a difference at this point. I did study." Another thought was, "I must go to sleep now! I must get eight hours of sleep!" His response was, "I have left leeway, so I have time. Sleep is not so crucial that I have to worry about it." He was able to shift his thinking to a positive image of himself floating in clear blue water.

By observing his automatic thoughts across a variety of situations—academic, athletic, and social—the patient identified dichotomous thinking (e.g., "I'm either a winner or a loser") as a frequent cognitive distortion. Perceiving the consequences of his behavior as either totally good or completely bad resulted in major shifts in mood. It also gave him a false sense of himself, for if he was good, then others should be attracted to him. The fact that not everyone was attracted to him was interpreted as evidence that he was bad and a loser. Two techniques that helped with his dichotomous thinking were reframing the problem and building a continuum between his dichotomous categories.

Here the problem is reframed:

Therapist: Can you think of reasons for someone not to respond to you other than because you're a loser?

Patient: No. Unless I really convince them I'm great, they won't be attracted.

Therapist: How would you convince them of that?

Patient: To tell you the truth, I'd exaggerate what I've done. I'd lie about my grade point average or tell someone I placed first in a race.

Therapist: How does that work out?

Patient: Actually, not too well. I get uncomfortable and they get confused by my stories. Sometimes they don't seem to care. Other times they walk away after I've been talking a lot about myself.

Therapist: So in some cases, they don't respond to you when you focus the conversation on yourself.

Patient: Right.

Therapist: Does this have anything to do with whether you're a winner or a loser?

Patient: No, they don't even know who I am deep down. They're just turned off because I talk too much.

Therapist: Right. It sounds like they're responding to your conversational style.

The therapist reframed the problem from a situation in which something was inherently wrong with the patient to one characterized by a problem of social skills. Moreover, the theme "I am a loser" appeared so powerful to the patient that he labeled it as his "main belief." This assumption was traced historically to the constant criticism from his parents for mistakes and perceived shortcomings. By reviewing his history, he was able to see that his lies prevented people from getting closer, reinforcing his belief that they didn't want to be close. In addition, he believed that his parents made him whatever success he was and that no achievement was his alone. This had made him angry and lacking in self-confidence.

LATER SESSIONS

As therapy progressed, the patient's homework increasingly focused on social interaction. He practiced initiating conversations and asking questions in order to learn more about other people. He also practiced "biting his tongue" instead of telling small lies about himself. He monitored people's reactions to him and saw that they were varied, but generally positive. By listening to others, he found that he admired people who could openly admit shortcomings and joke about their mistakes. This experience helped him understand that it was useless to categorize people, including himself, as winners and losers.

In later sessions, the patient described his belief that his behavior reflected on his parents and vice versa. He said, "If they look good, it says something about me and if I look good, they get the credit." One assignment required him to list the ways in which he was different from his parents. He remarked, "Realizing that my parents and I are separate made me realize I could stop telling lies." Recognizing how he was different from his parents freed him from their absolute standards and allowed him to be less self-conscious when interacting with others.

Subsequently, the patient was able to pursue interests and hobbies that had nothing to do with achievement. He was able to set moderate and realistic goals for schoolwork, and he began to date.

SUMMARY

Although a relative newcomer to the field of psychotherapy, cognitive therapy has enjoyed an enormous increase in popularity. A system of psychotherapy borrowing some of its concepts from psychodynamic therapy and a number of techniques from behavior therapy and client-oriented psychotherapy, cognitive therapy consists of a broad theoretical structure of personality and psychopathology, a set of well-defined therapeutic strategies, and a wide variety of therapeutic techniques. Similar in many ways to rational-emotive therapy, which preceded but developed in parallel to cognitive therapy, this new system of psychotherapy has acquired strong empirical support for its theoretical foundations. A number of outcome studies have demonstrated its efficacy, especially in the treatment of depression. The related theoretical formulations of depression have been supported by over 100 empirical studies. Other concepts, such as the cognitive triad in depression, the concept of specific cognitive profiles for specific disorders, cognitive processing, and the relationship of hopelessness to suicide, have also received strong support.

Outcome studies have investigated cognitive therapy with major depressive disorders, generalized anxiety disorder, dysthymic disorder, drug abuse, alcoholism, panic disorder, anorexia, and bulimia. In addition, cognitive therapy has been applied successfully to the treatment of obsessive-compulsive disorder, hypochondriasis, and various personality disorders. In conjunction with psychotropic medication it has been used for the treatment of delusional disorders and manic-depressive disorder.

Much of the popularity of cognitive therapy is due to the strong empirical support for its theoretical framework and the large number of outcome studies with clinical populations. In addi-

tion, there is no doubt that the zeitgeist represented by the "cognitive revolution" has made the field of psychotherapy more receptive to this new therapy. A further attractive feature of cognitive therapy is the fact that it is not only testable, but is readily teachable. The various therapeutic strategies and techniques have been described and defined in such a way that one year's training is usually sufficient for a psychotherapist to attain a reasonable level of competence as a cognitive therapist.

Although cognitive therapy focuses on understanding the patient's problems and applying appropriate techniques, it also attends to the nonspecific therapeutic characteristics of the therapist. Consequently, the basic qualities of empathy, acceptance, and personal regard are highly valued.

Because therapy is not conducted in a vacuum, cognitive therapists pay close attention to patients' interpersonal relations and confront patients continuously with problems they may be avoiding. Further, therapeutic change can only take place when patients are emotionally engaged with their problems. Therefore, the experience of emotion during therapy is a crucial feature. The patient's reactions to the therapist, and vice versa, are also important. Excessive and distorted responses to the therapist are elicited and evaluated just like any other type of ideational material. The role of the corrective emotional experience, by which patients are able to correct, in the presence of the therapist, their misconceptions, often derived from early experiences, is an integral part of the treatment process.

Cognitive therapy may offer an opportunity for a rapprochement between psychodynamic therapy and behavior therapy. In many ways it provides a common ground for these two disciplines. At the present time, the number of cognitive therapists within the behavior therapy movement is growing. In fact, many behavior therapists view themselves as cognitive-behavior therapists.

In view of the ongoing research into cognition and affect, it is anticipated that there will be a gradual expansion of the boundaries of the theoretical background of cognitive therapy that will encompass or penetrate the fields of cognitive psychology and social psychology. There is already an enormous amount of interest in social psychology, which provides the theoretical background of cognitive therapy.

In this era of cost containment this short-term approach will prove to be increasingly attractive to third-party payers as well as to patients. Future empirical studies of its processes and effectiveness will undoubtedly be conducted to determine if cognitive therapy can fulfill its promise.

ANNOTATED BIBLIOGRAPHY

Beck, A. T., Rush, A. J., Shaw, B. F., & Emery, G. (1979). *Cognitive therapy of depression*. New York: Guilford Press.

This book presents the cognitive theory of depression and actual techniques used with depressed patients. This comprehensive description of cognitive techniques makes a theoretical contribution and serves as a clinical handbook as well.

Beck, A. T., & Emery, G. (1985). *Anxiety disorders and phobias: A cognitive perspective*. New York: Basic Books.

The first half of this book, written by Beck, presents the cognitive theory and model of anxiety disorders, including agoraphobia and panic. The second half of the book, written by Emery, is devoted to clinical techniques used with anxious patients.

Emery, G., Hollon, S., & Bedrosian, R. C. (Eds.) (1981). *New directions in cognitive therapy*. New York: Guilford Press.

This edited volume contains cases presented by major cognitive therapists. It focuses on the application of cognitive therapy to a wide range of presenting problems (e.g., loneliness and agoraphobia) and diverse populations (adolescents, the elderly, the psychologically naive).

CASE READINGS

Abrams, J. L. (1983). Cognitive-behavioral strategies to induce and enhance a collaborative set in distressed couples. In A. Freeman (Ed.), *Cognitive therapy with couples and groups* (pp. 125–155). New York: Plenum.

Two cases of married couples demonstrate the importance of including cognitive interventions with traditional behavioral approaches to marital therapy. The dysfunctional attitudes and expectations that these couples bring to their marriages are explored.

Beck, A. T., Rush, J., Shaw, B., & Emery, G. (1979). Interview with a depressed suicidal patient. In *Cognitive therapy of depression* (pp. 225–243). New York: Guilford Press. [Reprinted in D. Wedding & R. J. Corsini (Eds.) (1988). *Case studies in psychotherapy*. Itasca, IL: F. E. Peacock.]

This interview with a suicidal patient features an outline of the types of assessments and interventions made by cognitive therapists in an initial session. Substantial change occurs in one session, as demonstrated in the verbatim transcript of the interview.

Beck, A. T., & Young, J. E. (1985). Cognitive therapy of depression. In D. Barlow (Ed.), *Clinical handbook of psychological disorders: A step-by-step treatment manual* (pp. 206–244). New York: Guilford Press.

This case of a depressed young woman demonstrates how a therapist elicits and challenges maladaptive thoughts and assumptions throughout the course of treatment.

Young, J. E. (1981). Cognitive therapy and loneliness. In G. Emery, S. Hollon & R. C. Bedrosian (Eds.), *New directions in cognitive therapy.* (pp. 139–159). New York: Guilford Press.

The treatment of a lonely college student demonstrates both the cognitive and the behavioral techniques that are used to help the patient initiate and deepen relationships.

REFERENCES

Adler, A. (1936). The neurotic's picture of the world. *International Journal of Individual Psychology, 2*, 3–10.

Alexander, F. (1950). *Psychosomatic medicine: Its principles and applications.* New York: Norton.

Arnold, M. (1960). *Emotion and personality* (Vol. 1). New York: Columbia University Press.

Bandura, A. (1977). *Social learning theory.* Englewood Cliffs, NJ: Prentice Hall.

Beck, A. T. (1963). Thinking and depression. 1. Idiosyncratic content and cognitive distortions. *Archives of General Psychiatry, 9*, 324–333.

Beck, A. T. (1964). Thinking and depression. 2. Theory and therapy. *Archives of General Psychiatry, 10*, 561–571.

Beck, A. T. (1967). *Depression: Clinical, experimental, and theoretical aspects.* New York: Hoeber. (Republished as *Depression: Causes and treatment.* Philadelphia: University of Pennsylvania Press, 1972.)

Beck, A. T. (1976). *Cognitive therapy and the emotional disorders.* New York: International Universities Press.

Beck, A. T. (1978). *Anxiety checklist.* Philadelphia: Center for Cognitive Therapy.

Beck, A. T. (1986). Cognitive therapy: A sign of retrogression or progress? *The Behavior Therapist, 9*, 2–3.

Beck, A. T., & Emery, G. (1979). *Cognitive therapy of anxiety and phobic disorders.* Philadelphia: Center for Cognitive Therapy.

Beck, A. T., & Emery, G. (1985). *Anxiety disorders and phobias: A cognitive perspective.* New York: Basic Books.

Beck, A. T., Epstein, N., & Harrison, R. (1983). Cognitions, attitudes and personality dimensions in depression. *British Journal of Cognitive Psychotherapy, 1*(1), 1–16.

Beck, A. T., Kovacs, M., & Weissman, A. (1979). Assessment of suicidal intention: The scale for suicidal ideation. *Journal of Consulting and Clinical Psychology, 47*, 343–352.

Beck, A. T., Laude, R., & Bohnert, M. (1974). Ideational components of anxiety neurosis. *Archives of General Psychiatry, 31*, 319–325.

Beck, A. T., & Rush, A. J. (1978). Cognitive approaches to depression and suicide. In G. Serban (Ed.), *Cognitive defects in the development of mental illness.* (pp.

235–257). New York: Bruner/Mazel.

Beck, A. T., Rush, A. J., Shaw, B. F., & Emery, G. (1979). Cognitive therapy of depression. New York: Guilford Press.

Beck, A. T., Schuyler, D., & Herman, I. (1974). Development of the suicidal intent scales. In A. T. Beck, H. L. P. Resnik, & D. J. Lettieri (Eds.), The prediction of suicide (pp. 45–56). Bowie, MD: Charles Press.

Beck, A. T., Steer, R. A., Kovacs, M., & Garrison, B. (1985). Hopelessness and eventual suicide: A 10-year study of patients hospitalized with suicidal ideation. American Journal of Psychiatry, 142, 559–563.

Beck, A. T., Ward, C. H., Mendelson, M., Mock, J. E., & Erbaugh, J. K. (1961). An inventory for measuring depression. Archives of General Psychiatry, 4, 561–571.

Beck, A. T., Weissman, A., Lester, D., & Trexler, L. (1974). The measurement of pessimism: The hopelessness scale. Journal of Consulting and Clinical Psychology, 42, 861–865.

Beck, A. T., & Young, J. E. (1985). Cognitive therapy of depression. In D. Barlow (Ed.), Clinical handbook of psychological disorders: A step-by-step treatment manual (pp. 206–244). New York: Guilford Press.

Beck, A. T., Young, J. E., & El Shamma, K. (1979). Competency checklist for cognitive therapists. Philadelphia: Center for Cognitive Therapy.

Blackburn, I. M., Bishop, S., Glen, A. I. M., Whalley, L. J., & Christie, J. E. (1981). The efficacy of cognitive therapy in depression: A treatment trial using cognitive therapy and pharmacotherapy, each alone and in combination. British Journal of Psychiatry, 139, 181–189.

Blackburn, I. M., Eunson, K. M., & Bishop, S. (1986). A two-year naturalistic follow-up of depressed patients treated with cognitive therapy, pharmacotherapy, and a combination of both. Unpublished manuscript. Royal Edinburgh Hospital, Scotland.

Burns, D. D. (1985). Intimate connections. New York: Morrow.

Dunn, R. J. (1979). Cognitive modification with depression-prone psychiatric patients. Cognitive Therapy and Research 3, 307–317.

Ellis, A. (1962). Reason and emotion in psychotherapy. New York: Lyle Stuart.

Ellis, A. (1976). The biological basis of human irrationality. Journal of Individual Psychology, 32, 145–168.

Ernst, D. (1987). A review of systematic studies of the cognitive model of depression. Unpublished manuscript. Center for Cognitive Therapy, Philadelphia, PA.

Freeman, A. (1981). Dreams and images in cognitive therapy. In G. Emery, S. Hollon, & R. C. Bedrosian (Eds.), New directions in cognitive therapy (pp. 224–238). New York: Guilford Press.

Golden, W. L. (1983). Resistance in cognitive-behavior therapy. British Journal of Cognitive Psychotherapy, 1(2), 33–42.

Gournay, K. (1986). Cognitive change during the behavioral treatment of agoraphobia. Paper presented at Congress of European Association for Behavior Therapy, Lucerne, Switzerland.

Guidano, V. P., & Liotti, G. (1983). Cognitive processes and emotional disorders. New York: Guilford Press.

Hollon, S. D., Evans, M. D., & DeRubeis, R. (1983). The cognitive-pharmacotherapy project: Study design, outcome, and clinical follow-up. Paper presented at the World Congress of Behavior Therapy, Washington, DC.

Horney, K. (1950). Neurosis and human growth: The struggle toward self-realization. New York: Norton.

Kant, I. (1798). The classification of mental disorders. Konigsberg, Germany: Nicolovius.

Kelly, G. (1955). The psychology of personal constructs. New York: Norton.

Kovacs, M., Rush, A. J., Beck, A. T., & Hollon, S. D. (1981). Depressed outpatients treated with cognitive therapy or pharmacotherapy. Archives of General Psychiatry, 38, 33–39.

Kwee, M. G. T., & Lazarus, A. A. (1986). Multimodal therapy: The cognitive-behavioural tradition and beyond. In W. Dryden & W. Golden (Eds.), Cognitive-behavioral approaches to psychotherapy (pp. 320–355). London: Harper & Row.

Lazarus, A. (1976). Multimodal behavior therapy. New York: Springer.

Lazarus, R. (1984). On the primacy of cognition. *American Psychologist, 39,* 124–129.

Mahoney, M. J. (1974). *Cognition and behavior modification.* Cambridge, MA: Ballinger.

Mahoney, M. J. (1980). Psychotherapy and the structure of personal revolutions. In M. J. Mahoney (Ed.), *Psychotherapy process* (pp. 157–180). New York: Plenum.

Mahoney, M. J., & Arnkoff, D. (1978). Cognitive and self-control therapies. In S. L. Garfield & A. E. Bergin (Eds.), *Handbook of psychotherapy and behavior change: An empirical analysis* (pp. 689–722). New York: Wiley.

Maldonado, A. (1982). Terapía de conducta y depresión: Un análisis experimental de los modelos conductal y cognitivo [Cognitive and behavioral therapy for depression. Its efficacy and interaction with pharmacological treatment]. *Revista de psicología general y aplicada, 37*(1), 31–56.

Meichenbaum, D. (1977). *Cognitive-behavior modification: An integrative approach.* New York: Plenum.

Murphy, G. E., Simons, A. D., Wetzel, R. D., & Lustman, P. J. (1983). Cognitive therapy and pharmacotherapy: Singly and together in the treatment of depression. *Archives of General Psychiatry, 41,* 33–41.

Pretzer, J. L. (1983). *Borderline-personality disorder: Too complex for cognitive therapy?* Paper presented at the annual meeting of the American Psychological Association, Anaheim, CA.

Rogers, C. (1951). *Client-centered therapy.* Boston: Houghton Mifflin.

Rush, A. J., Beck, A. T., Kovacs, M., & Hollon, S. (1977). Comparative efficacy of cognitive therapy and imipramine in the treatment of depressed outpatients. *Cognitive Therapy and Research, 1,* 17–37.

Simons, A. D., Murphy, G. E., Levine, J. L., & Wetzel, R. D. (1986). Cognitive therapy and pharmacotherapy: Sustained improvement over one year. *Archives of General Psychiatry, 43,* 43–48.

Sullivan, H. S. (1953). *The interpersonal theory of psychiatry.* New York: Norton.

Teasdale, J. D., Fennell, M. J. V., Hibbert, G. A., & Amies, P. L. (1984). Cognitive therapy for major depressive disorder in primary care. *British Journal of Psychiatry, 144,* 400–406.

Weissman, A. (1979). *The dysfunctional attitudes scale.* Philadelphia: Center for Cognitive Therapy.

Wessler, R. L. (1986). Conceptualizing cognitions in the cognitive-behavioural therapies. In W. Dryden & W. Golden (Eds.), *Cognitive-behavioural approaches to psychotherapy* (pp. 1–30). London: Harper & Row.

Williams, S. L., & Rappoport, A. (1983). Cognitive treatment in the natural environment for agoraphobics. *Behavior Therapy, 14,* 299–313.

Young, J. E. (1979). *An instrument for measuring loneliness.* Paper presented at the annual meeting of the American Psychological Association, New York.

Young, J. E. (1983). *Borderline personality: Cognitive theory and treatment.* Paper presented at the annual meeting of the American Psychological Association, Anaheim, CA.

FREDRICK S. PERLS, 1893–1970

9

Gestalt Therapy

GARY M. YONTEF and JAMES S. SIMKIN

OVERVIEW

Gestalt therapy is a phenomenological-existential therapy founded
by Frederick (Fritz) and Laura Perls in
the 1940s. It teaches therapists and patients the phenomenological method
of awareness, in which perceiving,
feeling, and acting are distinguished
from interpreting and reshuffling preexisting attitudes. Explanations and
interpretations are considered less reliable than what is directly perceived
and felt. Patients and therapists in Gestalt therapy dialogue, i.e., communicate their phenomenological perspectives. Differences in perspectives become the focus of experimentation
and continued dialogue. The goal is for
clients to become aware of what they
are doing, how they are doing it, and
how they can change themselves, and,
at the same time, to learn to accept and
value themselves.

Gestalt therapy focuses more on
process (what is happening) than content (what is being discussed). The emphasis is on what is being done,
thought, and felt at the moment rather

than on what was, might be, could be,
or should be.

BASIC CONCEPTS

The Phenomenological Perspective

Phenomenology is a discipline that
helps people stand aside from their
usual way of thinking so that they can
tell the difference between what is actually being perceived and felt in the current situation and what is residue from
the past (Idhe, 1977). A Gestalt exploration respects, uses, and clarifies immediate, "naive" perception "unde-
bauched by learning" (Wertheimer,
1945, p. 331). Gestalt therapy treats
what is "subjectively" felt in the present, as well as what is "objectively" observed, as real and important data. This
contrasts with approaches that treat
what the patient experiences as "mere
appearances" and uses interpretation to
find "real meaning."

The goal of Gestalt phenomenological exploration is awareness, or insight. "Insight is a patterning of the
perceptual field in such a way that the
significant realities are apparent; it is

the formation of a gestalt in which the relevant factors fall into place with respect to the whole" (Heidbreder, 1933, p. 355). In Gestalt therapy insight is clear understanding of the structure of the situation being studied.

Awareness without systematic exploration is not ordinarily sufficient to develop insight. Therefore, Gestalt therapy uses focused awareness and experimentation to achieve insight. How one becomes aware is crucial to any phenomenological investigation. The phenomenologist studies not only personal awareness but also the awareness process itself. The patient is to learn how to become aware of awareness. How the therapist and the patient experience their relationship is of special concern in Gestalt therapy (Yontef, 1976, 1982, 1983).

The Field Theory Perspective

The scientific world view that underlies the Gestalt phenomenological perspective is field theory. Field theory is a method of exploring that describes the whole field of which the event is currently a part rather than analyzing the event in terms of a class to which it belongs by its "nature" (e.g., Aristotelian classification) or a unilinear, historical, cause-effect sequence (e.g., Newtonian mechanics).

The field is a whole in which the parts are in immediate relationship and responsive to each other and no part is uninfluenced by what goes on elsewhere in the field. The field replaces the notion of discrete, isolated particles. The person in his or her life space constitutes a field.

In field theory no action is at a distance; that is, what has effect must touch that which is affected in time and space. Gestalt therapists work in the here and now and are sensitive to how the here and now includes residues of the past, such as body posture, habits, and beliefs.

The phenomenological field is defined by the observer and is meaningful only when one knows the frame of reference of the observer. The observer is necessary because what one sees is somewhat a function of how and when one looks.

Field approaches are descriptive rather than speculative, interpretive, or classificatory. The emphasis is on observing, describing, and explicating the exact structure of whatever is being studied. In Gestalt therapy, data unavailable to direct observation by the therapist are studied by phenomenological focusing, experimenting, reporting of participants, and dialogue (Yontef, 1982, 1983).

The Existential Perspective

Existentialism is based on the phenomenological method. Existential phenomenologists focus on people's existence, relations with each other, joys and suffering, etc., as directly experienced.

Most people operate in an unstated context of conventional thought that obscures or avoids acknowledging how the world is. This is especially true of one's relations in the world and one's choices. Self-deception is the basis of inauthenticity: living that is not based on the truth of oneself in the world leads to feelings of dread, guilt, and anxiety. Gestalt therapy provides a way of being authentic and meaningfully responsible for oneself. By becoming aware, one becomes able to choose and/or organize one's own existence in a meaningful manner (Jacobs, 1978; Yontef, 1982, 1983).

The existential view holds that people are endlessly remaking or discovering themselves. There is no essence of human nature to be discovered "once and for all." There are always new horizons, new problems, and new opportunities.

Dialogue

The relationship between the therapist and the client is the most important aspect of psychotherapy. Existential dialogue is an essential part of Gestalt therapy's methodology and is a manifestation of the existential perspective on relationship.

Relationship grows out of contact. Through contact people grow and form identities. Contact is the experience of boundary between "me" and "not-me." It is the experience of interacting with the not-me while maintaining a self-identity separate from the not-me. Martin Buber states that the person ("I") has meaning only in relation to others, in the I-Thou dialogue or in I-It manipulative contact. Gestalt therapists prefer experiencing the patient in dialogue to using therapeutic manipulation (I-It).

Gestalt therapy helps clients develop their own support for desired contact or withdrawal (L. Perls, 1976, 1978). Support refers to anything that makes contact or withdrawal possible: energy, body support, breathing, information, concern for others, language, and so forth. Support mobilizes resources for contact or withdrawal. For example, to support the excitement accompanying contact, a person must take in enough oxygen.

The Gestalt therapist works by engaging in dialogue rather than by manipulating the patient toward some therapeutic goal. Such contact is marked by straightforward caring, warmth, acceptance, and self-responsibility. When therapists move pa-

tients toward some goal, the patients cannot be in charge of their own growth and self-support. Dialogue is based on experiencing the other person as he or she really is and showing the true self, sharing phenomenological awareness. The Gestalt therapist says what he or she means and means what he or she says and encourages the patient to do the same. Gestalt dialogue embodies authenticity and responsibility.

The therapeutic relationship in Gestalt therapy emphasizes four characteristics of dialogue:

1. *Inclusion.* This is putting oneself as fully as possible into the experience of the other without judging, analyzing, or interpreting while simultaneously retaining a sense of one's separate, autonomous presence. This is an existential and interpersonal application of the phenomenological trust in immediate experience. Inclusion provides an environment of safety for the patient's phenomenological work and, by communicating an understanding of the patient's experience, helps sharpen the patient's self-awareness.

2. *Presence.* The Gestalt therapist expresses herself to the patient. Regularly, judiciously, and with discrimination she expresses observations, preferences, feelings, personal experience, and thoughts. Thus, the therapist shares her perspective by modeling phenomenological reporting, which aids the patient's learning about trust and use of immediate experience to raise awareness. If the therapist relies on theory-derived interpretation, rather than personal presence, she leads the patient into relying on phenomena not in his own immediate experience as the tool for raising awareness. In Gestalt therapy the therapist does not use presence to

manipulate the patient to conform to pre-established goals, but rather encourages patients to regulate themselves autonomously.

3. *Commitment to dialogue.* Contact is more than something two people do to each other. Contact is something that happens between people, something that arises from the interaction between them. The Gestalt therapist surrenders herself to this interpersonal process. This is *allowing* contact to happen rather than manipulating, *making* contact, and controlling the outcome.

4. *Dialogue is lived.* Dialogue is something done rather than talked about. "Lived" emphasizes the excitement and immediacy of doing. The mode of dialogue can be dancing, song, words, or any modality that expresses and moves the energy between or among the participants. An important contribution of Gestalt therapy to phenomenological experimentation is enlarging the parameters to include explication of experience by nonverbal expressions. However, the interaction is limited by ethics, appropriateness, therapeutic task, and so on.

OTHER SYSTEMS

Yontef notes that:

The theoretical distinction between Gestalt Therapy, behavior modification and psychoanalysis is clear. In behavior modification, the patient's behavior is directly changed by the therapist's manipulation of environmental stimuli. In psychoanalytic theory, behavior is caused by unconscious motivation which becomes manifest in the transference relationship. By analyzing the transference the repression is lifted, the unconscious becomes conscious. In Gestalt Therapy the patient learns to fully use his internal and external senses so he can be self-responsible and self-supportive. Gestalt Therapy helps the patient regain the key to this state, the awareness of the process of awareness. Behavior modification conditions [by] using stimulus control, psychoanalysis cures by talking about and discovering the cause of mental illness [The Problem], and Gestalt Therapy brings self-realization through Here-and-Now experiments in directed awareness. (1969, pp. 33–34)

Behavior modification and other therapies that primarily try for direct control over symptoms (for example, chemotherapy, ECT, hypnosis, etc.) contrast with both Gestalt therapy and psychodynamic therapies in that the latter systems foster change primarily by the patient's learning to understand him- or herself in the world through insight.

The methodology of Gestalt and psychodynamic therapy uses an accepting relationship and a technology to help the patient change via emotional and cognitive self-understanding. In psychoanalysis the basic patient behavior is free association; the chief tool of the analyst is interpretation. To encourage transference, the analyst withholds any direct expression of personhood (no "I" statements) and practices the "Rule of Abstinence"; that is, the therapist does not gratify any of the patient's wishes. This approach is true of all psychodynamic schools: classical, object relations, ego psychological, Kohutian, Jungian. The psychodynamic therapist isolates his or her person in order to encourage a relationship based explicitly on transference (rather than contact).

Gestalt therapy works for understanding by using the active, healing presence of the therapist *and the patient* in a relationship based on true contact. Transference, explored and worked through as it arises, is not encouraged by the Gestalt therapist

(Polster, 1968). Characterological issues are *explicitly dealt with in Gestalt therapy* via the dialogic and phenomenological method.

In Gestalt therapy the immediate experience of the patient is actively used. Rather than free associate while passively awaiting the therapist's interpretation and subsequent change, the patient is seen as a collaborator who is to learn how to self-heal. The patient "works" rather than free associates. "What can I do to work on this?" is a frequent question in Gestalt therapy and frequently there is an answer. For example, a couple with sexual difficulties might be asked to practice sensate focusing.

More than any other therapy, Gestalt therapy emphasizes that whatever exists is here and now and that experience is more reliable than interpretation. The patient is taught the difference between *talking about* what occurred five minutes ago (or last night or 20 years ago) and *experiencing* what is now.

Applebaum, a psychoanalyst, observes that:

In Gestalt Therapy the patient quickly learns to make the discrimination between ideas and ideation, between wellworn obsessional pathways and new thoughts, between a statement of experience and a statement of a statement. The Gestalt goal of pursuing experience and not explanations, based on the belief that insight which emerges as the Gestalt emerges is more potent than insight given by the therapist, does help the patient and the therapist draw and maintain these important distinctions. (1976, p. 757)

Therapies such as behavior modification, reality therapy, and rational emotive therapy do not work with the *patient's* experience enough to do this. In Rogerian therapy the passivity imposed on the therapist severely narrows the range or power of the therapy to teach these distinctions.

The practice of most therapy systems encourages intellectualizing: talking about the irrationality of patient beliefs, talking about behavior changes the therapist believes that the patient should make, and so forth. The Gestalt therapy methodology utilizes active techniques that clarify experience. Gestalt therapists will often experiment by trying something new in the therapy hour. Unlike most other therapies, in Gestalt therapy the *process* of discovery through experimentation is the end point rather than the feeling or idea or content.

The psychoanalyst can only use interpretation. The Rogerian can only reflect and clarify. Gestalt therapists may use any techniques or methods as long as (a) they are aimed toward increasing awareness, (b) they emerge out of dialogue and phenomenologic work, and (c) they are within the parameters of ethical practice.

The power and responsibility for the present are in the hands of the patient. In the past the patient was psychologically in mutual interaction with the environment and not a passive recipient of trauma. Thus the patient may have received shaming messages from his parents, but swallowing the message and coping by self-blame were his own, as was the continuation of the shaming internally from then until now. This point of view is at variance with psychodynamic attitudes, but consonant with Adler's and Ellis' views.

This viewpoint enables patients to be more responsible for their own existence, including their therapy. When the therapist believes that the past causes the present and that patients are controlled by unconscious motivation not readily available to them, they are encouraged to rely on the therapist's interpretations rather than their own autonomy.

In therapies in which the therapist undertakes to directly modify the patient's behavior, the immediate experience of the patient and therapist are not honored. This separates Gestalt therapy from most other therapies. A resentful patient may increase awareness by expressing resentment. If the therapist suggests this as a means of catharsis, it is not the phenomenological focusing of Gestalt therapy.

In Gestalt therapy there are no "shoulds." Instead of emphasizing what should be, Gestalt therapy stresses awareness of what is. *What is, is.* This contrasts with any therapist who "knows" what the patient "should" do. For example, cognitive behavior modification, rational-emotive therapy, and reality therapy all try to modify patient attitudes the therapist judges to be irrational, irresponsible, or unreal.

Even though Gestalt therapy discourages interrupting the organismic assimilating process by focusing on cognitive explanatory intellectualizations, Gestalt therapists do work with belief systems. Clarifying thinking, explicating beliefs, and mutually deciding what fits for the patient are all part of Gestalt therapy. Gestalt therapy deemphasizes thinking that avoids experience (obsessing) and encourages thinking that supports experience. Gestalt therapy excludes the therapist's narcissistically teaching the patient rather than being contactful and expediting the patient's self-discovery.

Many persons claim they practice "TA [transactional analysis] and Gestalt." Usually these people use the TA *theory* and some Gestalt therapy *techniques.* Techniques are not the impor-

tant aspect of Gestalt therapy. When used in an analytic, cognitive style, these techniques are not Gestalt therapy! Such a combination often aborts, prevents, or neutralizes the organismic awareness work of the phenomenological-existential method. A better combination would be integrating concepts of TA into a Gestalt framework. Thus the parent, adult, and child ego states, crossed transactions, and life scripts can be translated into Gestalt process language and worked with experimentally and dialogically.

Another difference from other therapies is Gestalt therapy's genuine regard for holism and multidimensionality. People manifest their distress in how they behave, think, and feel. "Gestalt therapy views the entire biopsychosocial field, including organism/environment, as important. Gestalt therapy actively uses physiological, sociological, cognitive, motivational variables. No relevant dimension is excluded in the basic theory" (Yontef, 1969, pp. 33–34).

HISTORY

PRECURSORS

The history of Gestalt therapy starts with the professional development of Fritz Perls and the zeitgeist in which he lived. After acquiring the M.D. degree, Perls went to Frankfurt-am-Main in 1926 as an assistant to Kurt Goldstein at the Institute for Brain Damaged Soldiers. Here he was exposed to Professors Goldstein and Adhemar Gelb and he met his future wife, Laura. At that time Frankfurt-am-Main was a center of intellectual ferment and Perls was directly and indirectly exposed to leading Gestalt psychologists, existential philosophers, and psychoanalysts.

Fritz Perls became a psychoanalyst. He was influenced directly by Karen Horney and Wilheim Reich, and indirectly by Otto Rank and others. Perls was especially influenced by Wilheim Reich, who was Perls' analyst in the early 1930s, and "who first directed my attention to a most important aspect of psychosomatic medicine—to the function of the motoric system as an armour" (F. Perls, 1947, p. 3).

Three influences on Perls' intellectual development should be noted. One was the philosopher, Sigmund Friedlander, from whose philosophy Perls incorporated the concepts of differential thinking and creative indifference, spelled out in Perls' first book, *Ego, Hunger and Aggression* (1947). Perls was also influenced by Jan Smuts, the prime minister of South Africa when Perls moved there with his family (having first escaped from Nazi Germany and then Nazi-occupied Holland). Before becoming prime minister, Smuts had written a major book on holism and evolution that, in effect, examined the broader ecological world from a Gestalt perspective. Smuts coined the word *holism*. Third, Alfred Korzybski, the semanticist, was an influence on Perls' intellectual development.

Laura Posner Perls was a co-founder of Gestalt therapy. Her influence on Perls was generally known, and she wrote several chapters of *Ego, Hunger and Aggression*. She was a psychology student at the time she met Perls, receiving the D.Sc. degree from the University of Frankfurt in 1932. She had contact with and was influenced by the existentialist theologians Martin Buber and Paul Tillich. Much of the Gestalt, phenomenological and existential influences in Gestalt therapy are through her, although credit and influence were limited by how little she wrote (under her name) (Rosenfeld, 1978).

Although Perls was a training psychoanalyst, he was among those who chafed under the dogmatism of classical Freudian psychoanalysis. The 1920s, 1930s, and 1940s were periods of great ferment and rebellion against Newtonian positivism. This was true in science (for example, Einstein's field theory), theater and dance, philosophy, art, architecture, and existentialism. Both Laura and Fritz lived in a zeitgeist permeated by a phenomenological-existentialist influence that later became integrated into Gestalt therapy (Kogan, 1976). Among these were acknowledgment of responsibility and choice in creating one's personal existence, the primacy of existence over essence, and the existential dialogue.

Gestalt psychology provided Perls with the organizing principle for Gestalt therapy as an integrating framework. Gestalt refers to the configuration or pattern of a set of elements. Gestalt psychologists believe that organisms instinctively perceive whole patterns and not bits and pieces. Whole patterns have characteristics that cannot be gleaned by analyzing parts. Perception is an active process and not a result of passively received stimulation of sense organs. All situations are believed to possess inherent organization. Organisms have the capacity for accurate perception when they use their native ability of immediate experience in the here and now. The task of phenomenological research and therapy is to utilize this capacity to gain insight into the structure of that which is being studied. Because people naturally perceive whole patterns as they occur, actual awareness can be trusted more than interpretation and dogma.

BEGINNINGS

Perls' *Ego, Hunger and Aggression* was written in 1941–42. In its first publication in South Africa in 1946, it was subtitled *A Revision of Freud's Theory and Method*. The subtitle of the book when it appeared in 1966 was changed to *The Beginning of Gestalt Therapy*. The term *Gestalt therapy* was first used as the title of a book written by Fritz Perls, Ralph Hefferline, and Paul Goodman (1951). Shortly after, the New York Institute for Gestalt Therapy was organized, headquartered in the apartment of Fritz and Laura Perls in New York City. This apartment was used for seminars, workshops, and groups. Among those who studied with Perls at that time were Paul Weisz, Lotte Weidenfeld, Buck Eastman, Paul Goodman, Isadore From, Elliot Shapiro, Leo Chalfen, Iris Sanguilano, James Simkin, and Kenneth A. Fisher.

During the 1950s, intensive workshops and study groups were established throughout the country. Before the American Psychological Association Convention held in New York City in 1954, a special intensive workshop limited to 15 qualified psychologists was given over a three-day period. Similar workshops were held in Cleveland, Miami, and Los Angeles. In 1955 the Cleveland study group formed the Gestalt Institute of Cleveland.

Fritz Perls moved to the West Coast in 1960, at which time Simkin arranged a Gestalt therapy workshop for him. Perls, Walter Kempler, and James Simkin offered the first Gestalt therapy training workshops at the Esalen Institute during the summer of 1964. These training workshops continued under the leadership of Perls and Simkin through 1968. After Perls moved to Canada, Simkin, along with Irma Shepherd, Robert W. Resnick, Robert L. Martin, Jack Downing, and John Enright, continued to offer Gestalt therapy training at Esalen through 1970.

During this beginning period, Gestalt therapy pioneered many ideas subsequently accepted into eclectic psychotherapy practice. The excitement of direct contact between therapist and patient, the emphasis on direct experience, the use of active experimentation, the emphasis on the here and now, the responsibility of the patient for him- or herself, the awareness principle, the trust in organismic self-regulation, the ecological interdependence of person and environment, the principle of assimilation, and other such concepts were new, exciting, and shocking to a conservative establishment. In this period the practice of psychotherapy was dichotomized between the older, traditional approach of psychoanalytic drive theory and the ideas pioneered largely by Gestalt therapy. This was a period of expansion, with integration of the principles with each other and the elucidation and enucleation of the principles left for the future. Thus, for example, Gestalt therapy pioneered the use of the active presence of the therapist in a contactful relationship but did not consider in detail what constituted a healing dialogic presence.

CURRENT STATUS

There are at least 62 Gestalt Therapy institutes throughout the world, and the list continues to grow. Virtually every major city in the United States has at least one Gestalt institute.

No national organization has been established. As a result, there are no established standards for institutes, trainers, and trainees. Each institute has its own criteria for training, membership, selection, and so on. Attempts in the recent past to organize a nationwide conference for establishing standards for trainers have not been successful. There are no agreed-upon standards for what constitutes good Gestalt therapy or a good Gestalt therapist. Therefore, it is incumbent on Gestalt therapy consumers to carefully evaluate the educational, clinical, and training background of people who call themselves Gestalt therapists or give training in Gestalt therapy (see Yontef, 1981a, 1981b).

The *Gestalt Journal* is devoted primarily to articles on Gestalt therapy. *Gestalt Theory* publishes articles on Gestalt psychology, including some on Gestalt therapy. Bibliographic information can be obtained from Kogan (1980), Rosenfeld (1981), and Wysong (1986).

As experience in doing Gestalt therapy has grown, earlier therapeutic practices have been altered. For example, earlier Gestalt therapy practice often stressed the clinical use of frustration, a confusion of self-sufficiency with self-support, and an abrasive attitude if the patient was interpreted by the therapist as manipulative. This approach tended to enhance the shame of shame-oriented patients. There has been a movement toward more softness in Gestalt therapy practice, more direct self-expression by the therapist, more of a dialogic emphasis, decreased use of stereotypic techniques, increased emphasis on description of character structure (with utilization of psychoanalytic formulations), and increased use of group process.

Thus a patient is more likely to encounter, among Gestalt therapists who are involved in the newer mode, an emphasis on self-acceptance, a softer demeanor by the therapist, more trust of the patient's phenomenology, and more explicit work with psychodynamic themes. There has also been an increase in emphasis on group process, including relation between group members, and a decrease in formal, one-to-one work in groups. There is also an increased attention to theoretical instruction, theoretical exposition, and work with cognition in general.

PERSONALITY

THEORY OF PERSONALITY

Ecological Interdependence: The Organism/Environment Field

A person exists by differentiating self from other and by connecting self and other. These are the two functions of a boundary. To make good contact with one's world, it is necessary to risk reaching out and discovering one's own boundaries. Effective self-regulation includes contact in which one is aware of novelty in the environment that is potentially nourishing or toxic. That which is nourishing is assimilated and all else is rejected. This kind of differentiated contact inevitably leads to growth (Polster & Polster, 1973, p. 101).

Mental Metabolism

In Gestalt therapy, metabolism is used as a metaphor for psychological functioning. People grow through biting off an appropriate-sized piece (be this food or ideas or relationships), chewing it (considering), and discovering whether it is nourishing or toxic. If nourishing, the organism assimilates it and makes it part of itself. If toxic, the organism spits it out (rejects it). This requires people to be willing to trust their taste and judgment. Discrimination requires *actively* sensing outside

stimuli and processing these extero-
ceptive stimuli along with interocep-
tive data.

Regulation of the Boundary

The boundary between self and environment must be kept permeable to
allow exchanges and firm enough for
autonomy. The environment includes
toxins to be screened out. Even what is
nourishing needs to be discriminated
according to the dominant needs. Metabolic processes are governed by the
laws of homeostasis. Ideally, the most
urgent need energizes the organism
until it is met or is superseded by a
more vital need. Living is a progression of needs, met and unmet, achieving homeostatic balance and going on
to the next moment and new need.

Disturbances of the
Contact Boundary

When the boundary between self and
other becomes unclear, lost, or impermeable, this results in a disturbance of
the distinction between self and other,
a disturbance of both contact and
awareness (see Perls, 1973; Polster &
Polster, 1973). In good boundary functioning, people alternate between connecting and separating, between being
in contact with the current environment and withdrawal of attention
from the environment. The contact
boundary is lost in polar opposite ways
in confluence and isolation. In *confluence* (fusion), the separation and distinction between self and other becomes so unclear that the boundary is
lost. In *isolation*, the boundary becomes so impermeable that connect-
edness is lost, i.e., the importance of
others for the self is lost from awareness.

Retroflection is a split within the
self, a resisting of aspects of the self by

the self. This substitutes self for environment, as in doing to self what one
wants to do to someone else or doing
for self what one wants someone to do
for self. This mechanism leads to isolation. The illusion of self-sufficiency is
one example of retroflection as it substitutes self for environment. Although one can do one's own breathing and chewing, the air and food must
come from the environment. Introspection is a form of retroflection
which can be pathological or healthy.
For example, resisting the impulse to
express anger may serve to cope with a
dangerous environment. In such a
situation, biting one's lip may be more
functional than saying something
biting.

Through *introjection*, foreign material is absorbed without discriminating or assimilating. Swallowing whole
creates an "as if" personality and rigid
character. Introjected values and behavior are imposed on self. As in all
contact boundary disturbances, swallowing whole can be healthy or pathological, depending on the circumstances and degree of awareness. For
example, students taking a lecture
course may, with full awareness that
they are doing so, copy, memorize, and
regurgitate material without full "di-
gestion."

Projection is a confusion of self and
other that results from attributing to
the outside something that is truly self.
An example of healthy projection is
art. Pathological projection results
from not being aware of and accepting
responsibility for that which is projected.

Deflection is the avoidance of contact or of awareness by turning aside,
as when one is polite instead of direct.
Deflection can be accomplished by not
expressing directly or by not receiv-

ing. In the latter case, the person usually feels "untouched"; in the former case, the person is often ineffective and baffled about not getting what is wanted. Deflection can be useful where, with awareness, it meets the needs of the situation (e.g., where the situation needs cooling down). Other examples of deflection include not looking at a person, verbosity, vagueness, understating, and talking *about* rather than *to* (Polster & Polster, 1973, pp. 89–92).

Organismic Self-Regulation

Human regulation is to varying degrees either (a) organismic, that is, based on a relatively full and accurate acknowledgment of *what is*, or (b) "shouldistic," based on the arbitrary imposition of what some controller thinks should or should not be. This applies to intrapsychic regulation, to the regulation of interpersonal relations, and to the regulation of social groups.

"There is only one thing that should control: the *situation*. If you understand the situation you are in and let the situation you are in control your actions, then you learn to cope with life" (F. Perls, 1976, p. 35). Perls explicated the above with an example of driving a car. Instead of a preplanned program, "I want to drive 65 miles per hour," a person cognizant of the situation will drive a different speed at night or differently when in traffic, or still differently when tired, and so on. Here Perls makes it clear that "let the situation control" means regulating through awareness of the contemporary context, including one's wants, rather than through what was thought "should" happen.

In organismic self-regulation, choosing and learning happen holistically,

with a natural integration of mind and body, thought and feeling, spontaneity and deliberateness. In shouldistic regulation, cognition reigns and there is no felt, holistic sense.

Obviously, everything relevant to boundary regulation cannot be in full awareness. Most transactions are handled by automatic, habitual modes, with minimal awareness. Organismic self-regulation requires that the habitual becomes fully aware as needed. When awareness does not emerge as needed and/or does not organize the necessary motor activity, psychotherapy is a method of increasing awareness and gaining meaningful choice and responsibility.

Awareness

Awareness and dialogue are the two primary therapeutic tools in Gestalt therapy. Awareness is a form of experience that may be loosely defined as being in touch with one's own existence, with *what is*.

Laura Perls states:

The aim of Gestalt Therapy is the *awareness continuum*, the freely ongoing Gestalt formation where what is of greatest concern and interest to the organism, the relationship, the group or society becomes Gestalt, comes into the foreground where it can be fully experienced and coped with (acknowledged, worked through, sorted out, changed, disposed of, etc.) so that then it can melt into the background (be forgotten or assimilated and integrated) and leave the foreground free for the next relevant Gestalt. (1973, p. 2)

Full awareness is the process of being in vigilant contact with the most important events in the individual/environment field with full sensorimotor, emotional, cognitive, and energetic support. Insight, a form of awareness, is an immediate grasp of the obvious unity of disparate elements in the field. Aware contact creates new, meaningful wholes and thus is in itself an integration of a problem.

Effective awareness is grounded in and energized by the dominant present need of the organism. It involves not only self-knowledge, but a direct knowing of the current situation and how the self is in that situation. Any denial of the situation and its demands or of one's wants and chosen response is a disturbance of awareness. Meaningful awareness is of self in the world, in dialogue with the world, and with awareness of Other—it is not an inwardly focused introspection. Awareness is accompanied by *owning*, that is, the process of knowing one's control over, choice of, and responsibility for one's own behavior and feelings. Without this, the person may be vigilant to experience and life space, but not to what power he or she has and does not have. Awareness is cognitive, sensory, and affective. The person who verbally acknowledges his situation but does not really *see* it, *know* it, *react* to it and *feel* in response to it is not fully aware and is not in full contact. The person who is aware knows *what* he does, *how* he does it, that he has alternatives, and that he *chooses* to be as he is.

The act of awareness is always here and now, although the content of awareness may be distant. The act of remembering is now; what is remembered is not now. When the situation calls for an awareness of the past or anticipation of the future, effective awareness takes this into account. For example:

P: [Looking more tense than usual.] I don't know what to work on.
T: What are you aware of right now?
P: I am glad to see you, but I'm tense

about a meeting tonight with my boss. I have rehearsed and prepared and I've tried to support myself as I wait.
T: What do you need right now?
P: I thought of putting her in the empty chair and talking to her. But I am so tense I need to do something more physical—I need to move, breathe, make noise.
T: [Looks but remains silent.]
P: It's up to me, huh? [Pause. Patient gets up, starts stretching, yawning. The movements and sounds become more vigorous. After a few minutes he sits down, looking more soft and alive.] Now I'm ready.
T: You look more alive.
P: Now I am ready to explore what had me so uptight about tonight.

Self-rejection and full awareness are mutually exclusive. Rejection of self is a distortion of awareness because it is a denial of who one is. Self-rejection is simultaneously a confusion of who "I am" and a self-deception, or "bad faith" attitude of being above that which is ostensibly being acknowledged (Sartre, 1966). Saying "I am" as if it were an observation of another person, or as if the "I" were not chosen, or without knowing how one creates and perpetuates that "I am" is bad faith rather than insightful awareness.

Responsibility

People, according to Gestalt therapy, are responsible (response-able); that is, they are the primary agents in determining their own behavior. When people confuse responsibility with blaming and shoulds, they pressure and manipulate themselves; they "try" and are not integrated and spontaneous. In such instances their true wants, needs, and responses to the environment and choices in the situation are ignored and they overcomply or rebel against shoulds.

Gestalt therapists believe in the importance of a clear distinction between what one chooses and what is given. People are responsible for what they choose to do. For example, people are responsible for their action on behalf of the environment. Blaming outside forces (e.g., genetics or parents) for what one chooses is self-deception. Taking responsibility for what one did not choose, a typical shame reaction, is also a deception.

People are responsible for moral choices. Gestalt therapy helps patients discover what is moral according to their own choice and values. Far from advocating "anything goes," Gestalt therapy places a most serious obligation on each person: choosing and valuing.

VARIETY OF CONCEPTS

Gestalt therapy personality theory has evolved primarily out of clinical experience. The focus has been a theory of personality that supports our task as psychotherapists rather than an overall theory of personality. The constructs of Gestalt therapy theory are field theoretical rather than genetic and phenomenological rather than conceptual.

Although Gestalt therapy is phenomenological, it also deals with the unconscious, that is, with what does not enter into awareness when needed. In Gestalt therapy, awareness is conceived of as being in touch and unawareness as being out of touch. Unawareness can be explained by a variety of phenomena, including learning what to attend to, repression, cognitive set, character, and style. Simkin (1976) compared personality to a floating ball—at any given moment only a portion is exposed while the rest is submerged. Unawareness is the result of the organism's not being in touch with

its external environment due to its being mostly submerged in its own internal environment or fantasies, or not being in touch with its inner life due to fixation on the external.

Gestalt Therapy Theory of Change

Children swallow whole (introject) ideals and behavior. This results in an enforced morality rather than an organismically compatible morality. As a result, people frequently feel guilt when they behave in accordance with their wants as opposed to their shoulds. Some people invest an enormous amount of energy in maintaining the split between shoulds and wants—the resolution of which requires a recognition of their own morality as opposed to an introjected one. Shoulds sabotage such people, and the more they push to be what they are not, the more resistance is set up, and no change occurs.

Beisser advanced the theory that change does not happen through a "coercive attempt by the individual or by another person to change him," but does happen if the person puts in the time and effort to be "what he is," "to be fully in his current position" (1970, p. 70). When the therapist rejects the change agent role, change that is orderly and also meaningful is possible.

The Gestalt therapy notion is that awareness (including owning, choice, and responsibility) and contact bring natural and spontaneous change. Forced change is an attempt to actualize an image rather than to actualize the self. With awareness, self-acceptance, and the right to exist as is, the organism can grow. Forced intervention retards this process.

The Gestalt psychology principle of Prägnanz states that the field will form itself into the best Gestalt that global conditions will allow. So, too, Gestalt therapists believe that people have an innate drive to health. This propensity is found in nature, and people are part of nature. Awareness of the obvious, the awareness continuum, is a tool that a person can deliberately use to channel this spontaneous drive for health.

Differentiation of the Field: Polarities versus Dichotomies

A dichotomy is a split whereby the field is considered not as a whole differentiated into different and interlocking parts, but rather as an assortment of competing (either/or) and unrelated forces. Dichotomous thinking interferes with organismic self-regulation. Dichotomous thinking tends to be intolerant of diversity among persons and paradoxical truths about a single person.

Organismic self-regulation leads to integrating parts with each other and into a whole that encompasses the parts. The field is often differentiated into *polarities*: parts that are opposites that complement or explicate each other. The positive and negative poles of an electrical field are the prototypical mode for this differentiation in a field theoretical way. The concept of polarities treats opposites as part of one whole, as *yin* and *yang*.

With this polar view of the field, differences are accepted and integrated. Lack of genuine integration creates splits, such as body-mind, self-external, infantile-mature, biological-cultural, and unconscious-conscious. Through dialogue there can be an integration of parts, into a new whole in which there is a differentiated unity. Dichotomies such as the self-ideal and the needy self, thought and impulse, and social requirements and personal

needs can be healed by integrating into a whole differentiated into natural polarities (Perls, 1947).

Definition of Health I: The Good Gestalt as Polarity

The *good Gestalt* describes a perceptual field organized with clarity and good form. A well-formed figure clearly stands out against a broader and less distinct background. The relation between that which stands out (figure) and the context (ground) is meaning. In the good Gestalt the meaning is clear. The good Gestalt gives a content-free definition of health.

In health, the figure changes as needed; that is, it shifts to another focus when the need is met or superseded by a more urgent need. It does not change so rapidly as to prevent satisfaction (as in hysteria) or so slowly that new figures have no room to assume organismic dominance (as in compulsivity). When figure and ground are dichotomized, one is left with a figure out of context or a context without focus (F. Perls et al., 1951). In health, awareness accurately represents the dominant need of the whole field. Need is a function of external factors (physical structure of the field, political activity, acts of nature, and so on) and internal factors (hunger, fatigue, interest, past experience, and so forth).

Definition of Health II: The Polarity of Creative Adjustment

The Gestalt therapy concept of healthy functioning includes *creative adjustment*. A psychotherapy that only helps patients adjust creates conformity and stereotypy. A psychotherapy that only led people to impose themselves on the world without considering others would engender pathological narcissism and a world-denying realization of self isolated from the world.

A person who shows creative interaction takes responsibility for the ecological balance between self and surroundings.

This is the theoretical context (F. Perls et al., 1951) within which some seemingly individualistic and even anarchistic statements of Gestalt therapy are most accurately considered. The individual and environment form a polarity. The choice is not between the individual and society, but between organismic and arbitrary regulation.

Resistance is part of a polarity consisting of an impulse and resistance to that impulse. Seen as a dichotomy, resistance is often treated as "bad" and, in such a context, often turns out to be nothing more than the patient's following personal dictates rather than the therapist's. Seen as a polarity, resistance is as integral to health as the trait's being resisted.

Gestalt therapists attend to both the working process of consciousness and the resistance process of consciousness. Many Gestalt therapists avoid the word *resistance* because of its pejorative dichotomized connotation, which frames the process as a power battle between therapist and patient rather than as the self-conflict of the patient that needs to be integrated into a harmoniously differentiated self.

Impasse

An *impasse* is a situation in which external support is not forthcoming and the person believes he cannot support himself. The latter is due in large part to the person's strength being divided between impulse and resistance. The most frequent method of coping with this is to manipulate others.

An organismically self-regulating person takes responsibility for what is done for self, what is done by others for self, and what is done for others by self. The person exchanges with the environment, but the basic support for regulation of one's existence is by self. When the individual does not know this, external support becomes a replacement for self-support rather than a source of nourishment for the self.

In most psychotherapy the impasse is circumvented by external support by the therapist, and the patient does not find that self-support is sufficient. In Gestalt therapy, patients can get through the impasse because of the emphasis on loving contact without doing the patient's work, that is, without *rescuing* or infantilizing.

PSYCHOTHERAPY

THEORY OF PSYCHOTHERAPY

Goal of Therapy

In Gestalt therapy, the only goal is awareness. This includes greater awareness in a particular area and also greater ability for the patient to bring automatic habits into awareness as needed. In the former sense awareness is a content, in the latter sense it is a process. Both awareness as content and awareness as process progress to deeper levels as the therapy proceeds. Awareness includes knowing the environment, responsibility for choices, self-knowledge, and self-acceptance, and the ability to contact.

Beginning patients are chiefly concerned with the solution of problems. The issue for the Gestalt therapist is how patients support themselves in solving problems. Gestalt therapy facilitates problem solving through increased self-regulation and self-support by the patient. As therapy goes on, the patient and the therapist turn more attention to general personality issues. By the end of successful therapy the patient directs much of the work and is able to integrate problem solving, characterological themes, relationship issues with the therapist, and means of regulating his or her own awareness.

Gestalt therapy is most useful for patients open to working on self-awareness and for those who want natural mastery of their awareness process. Although some people claim they are interested in changing their behavior, most people seeking psychotherapy mainly want relief from discomfort. Their complaint may be generalized malaise, specific discomforts, or dissatisfaction in relationships. Patients often expect that relief will result from their therapist's doing the work rather than from their own efforts.

Psychotherapy is most appropriate for persons who create anxiety, depression, and so forth by rejecting themselves, alienating aspects of themselves, and deceiving themselves. In short, people who do not know how they further their own unhappiness are prime candidates, providing they are open to awareness work, especially awareness of self-regulation. Gestalt therapy is especially appropriate for those who know intellectually about themselves and yet don't grow.

Those who want symptom relief without doing awareness work may be better candidates for behavior modification, medication, biofeedback, and so on. The direct methods of Gestalt therapy facilitate patients' making this choice early in the therapy. However, patients' difficulty in doing the con-

tact or awareness work should not automatically be interpreted as meaning that they do not want to work. Respect for the total person enables a Gestalt therapist to help the patients become clear about the differences between "can't" and "won't" and to know how internal barriers or resistance, such as prior learning, anxiety, shame, and sensitivity to narcissistic injury, inhibit awareness work.

No Shoulds

There are no shoulds in Gestalt therapy. In Gestalt therapy a higher value is placed on the autonomy and the self-determination of the patient than on other values. This is not a "should," but a preference. The "no-should" ethic takes precedence over the therapist's goals for the patient and leaves the responsibility and sanctioning of the patient's behavior to the patient (of course, the injunctions and requirements of society are not suspended just because the patient is in Gestalt therapy).

How Is the Therapy Done?

Gestalt therapy is an exploration rather than a direct modification of behavior. The goal is growth and autonomy through an increase in consciousness. Rather than maintaining distance and interpreting, the Gestalt therapist meets patients and guides active awareness work. The therapist's active presence is alive and excited (hence warm), honest, and direct. Patients can see, hear, and be told how they are experienced, what is seen, how the therapist feels, what the therapist is like as a person. Growth occurs from real contact between real people. Patients learn how they are seen and how their awareness process is limited, not primarily from talking about their problems, but from how they and the therapist engage each other.

Focusing runs the range from simple inclusion or empathy to exercises arising mostly from the therapist's phenomenology while with the patient. Everything is secondary to the direct experience of both participants.

The general approach of Gestalt therapy is to facilitate exploring in ways that maximize what continues to develop after the session and without the therapist. The patient is often left unfinished but thoughtful or "opened up," or with an assignment. This is like a roast that continues to cook after being removed from the oven. This is in part how Gestalt therapy can be so intensive on fewer sessions per week. We cooperate with growth occurring without us; we initiate where needed. We give the degree of facilitation necessary to foster patient self-improvement. We facilitate growth rather than complete a cure process.

Perls believed that the ultimate goal of psychotherapy was the achievement of "that amount of integration which facilitates its own development" (1948). An example of this kind of facilitation is the analogy of a small hole cut into an accumulation of snow. Once the draining process begins, the base that began as a small hole enlarges by itself.

Successful psychotherapy achieves *integration*. Integration requires identification with *all* vital functions—not with only *some* of the patient's ideas, emotions, and actions. Any rejection of one's own ideas, emotions, or actions results in alienation. Reowning allows the person to be whole. The task, then, in therapy is to have the person become aware of previously alienated parts and taste them, con-

sider them, and assimilate them if they are ego-syntonic or reject them if they prove to be ego-alien. Simkin (1968) has used the simile of a cake in encouraging patients to reown the parts of themselves that they have considered noxious or otherwise unacceptable: although the oil, or flour, or baking powder by themselves can be distasteful, they are indispensable to the success of the whole cake.

The I-Thou Relation

Gestalt therapy focuses on the patient, as any therapy does. However, the relationship is horizontal, thus differing from the traditional therapy relationship. In Gestalt therapy the therapist and patient speak the same language, the language of present centeredness, emphasizing direct experience of both participants. Therapists as well as patients in Gestalt therapy show their full presence.

Since its beginning, Gestalt therapy has emphasized the patient's experience as well as the therapist's *observation* of what is not in the patient's awareness. This allows the patient to act as an equal who has full access to the data of his own experience so he can directly experience from inside what is *observed* by the therapist from outside. In an interpretive system the patient is an amateur and does not have the theoretical foundation for the interpretation. It is assumed that the important internal data are unconscious and not experienced.

An important aspect of the Gestalt therapy relationship is the question of responsibility. Gestalt therapy emphasizes that both the therapist and the patient are self-responsible. When therapists regard themselves as responsible for patients, they collude with patients' not feeling self-responsible and thereby reinforce the necessity for manipulation due to the belief that patients are unable to support and regulate themselves. However, it is *not enough for the therapist to be responsible for self and for the patient to be responsible for self*—there is also an alliance of patient and therapist that must be carefully, constantly, and competently attended to.

Therapists are responsible for the quality and quantity of their presence, for knowledge about themselves and the patient, for maintaining a nondefensive posture, and for keeping their awareness and contact processes clear and matched to the patient. They are responsible for the consequences of their own behavior and for establishing and maintaining the therapeutic atmosphere.

The Awareness of What and How

In Gestalt therapy there is a constant and careful emphasis on *what* the patient does and *how* it is done. What does the patient face? How does the patient make choices? Does the patient self-support or resist? Direct experience is the tool, and it is expanded beyond what is at first experienced by continuing to focus deeper and broader. *The techniques of Gestalt therapy are experimental tasks. They are a means of expanding direct experience. These are not designed to get the patient somewhere, to change the patient's feelings, to recondition, or to foster catharsis.*

Here and Now

In a phenomenological therapy "now" starts with the present awareness of the patient. What happens first is not childhood, but what is experienced *now.* Awareness takes place *now.* Prior events may be the object of present awareness, but the awareness process (e.g., remembering) is *now.*

Now I can contact the world around me, or *now* I can contact memories or expectations. Not knowing the present, not remembering, or not anticipating are all disturbances. The present is an ever-moving transition between the past and future. Frequently patients do not know their current behavior. In some cases patients live in the present as if they had no past. Most patients live in the future as if it were now. All these are disturbances of time awareness.

"Now" refers to *this moment.* In the therapy hour, when the patients refer to their lives out of the hour, or earlier in the hour, that is *not* now. In Gestalt therapy we orient more to the now than in any other form of psychotherapy. Experiences of the past few minutes, days, years, or decades that are of present importance are dealt with. We attempt to move from talking about to directly experiencing. For example, talking *to* a person who is not physically present rather than talking *about* that person mobilizes more direct experience of feelings.

In Gestalt therapy this I and Thou, what and how, here and now methodology is frequently used to work on characterological and developmental psychodynamics.

For example, a 30-year-old female patient is in group therapy. She is in the middle phase of therapy. She says she is very angry at a man in the group. One legitimate and frequent Gestalt approach is "Say it to him." Instead, the therapist takes a different tack:

T: You sound not only angry but something more.
P: [Looks interested.]
T: You sound and look like you are enraged.
P: I am, I would like to kill him.
T: You seem to feel impotent.
P: I am.

T: Impotence usually accompanies rage. What are you impotent about?

P: I can't get him to acknowledge me.

T: [The therapist's observations of her previous encounters with the man agree with that statement.] And you don't accept that.

P: No.

T: And there is an intensity to your rage that seems to be greater than the situation calls for.

P: [Nods and pauses.]

T: What are you experiencing?

P: A lot of men in my life who have been like that.

T: Like your father? [This comes from prior work with patient and isn't a shot in the dark. The work proceeds into a reexperiencing the narcissistic injury from her father, who was never responsive to her.]

PROCESS OF PSYCHOTHERAPY

Gestalt therapy probably has a greater range of styles and modalities than any other system. It is practiced in individual therapy, groups, workshops, couples, families, and with children. It is practiced in clinics, family service agencies, hospitals, private practices, growth centers, and so on. The styles in each modality vary drastically on many dimensions: degree and type of structure; quantity and quality of techniques used; frequency of sessions; abrasiveness-ease of relating; focus on body, cognition, feelings, interpersonal contact; knowledge of and work with psychodynamic themes; degree of personal encountering, and so forth.

All styles and modalities of Gestalt therapy have in common the general principles we have been discussing: emphasis on direct experience and experimenting (phenomenology), use of direct contact and personal presence (dialogic existentialism), and emphasis on the field concepts of what and how and here and now. Within these parameters, interventions are patterned according to the context and the personalities of the therapist and the patient.

At the heart of the methodology is the emphasis on the difference between "work" and other activities, especially "talking about." Work has two meanings. First, it refers to a deliberate, voluntary, and disciplined commitment to use phenomenologically focused awareness to increase the scope and clarity of one's experience and achieve greater awareness of one's life. When one moves from talking about a problem or being with someone in a general way to studying what one is doing, especially being aware of how one is aware, one is working. Second, in a group, work means being the primary focus of the therapist's and/or the group's attention.

Differences in techniques are not important, although the quality and type of therapeutic contact and a fit between the attitude and emphasis of the therapist and the patient's needs are important. Techniques are just techniques: the overall method, relationship, and attitude are the vital aspects.

Nevertheless a discussion of some techniques or tactics might elucidate the overall methodology. These are only illustrative of what is possible.

Techniques of Patient Focusing

All techniques of patient focusing are elaborations of the question, "What are you aware of (experiencing) now?" and the instruction, "Try this experiment and see what you become aware of (experience or learn)." Many interventions are as simple as asking what the patient is aware of, or more narrowly, "What are you feeling?" or "What are you thinking?"

"Stay with it." A frequent technique

is to follow an awareness report with the instruction: "Stay with it," or "Feel it out."

"Stay with it," encourages the patient to continue with the feeling that is being reported, which builds the patient's capacity to deepen and work a feeling through to completion. For example:

P: [Looks sad.]
T: What are you aware of?
P: I am sad.
T: Stay with it.
P: [Tears well up. Then the patient tightens and looks away and starts to look thoughtful.]
T: I see you are tightening. What are you aware of?
P: I don't want to stay with the sadness.
T: Stay with the not wanting to. Put words to the not wanting to. [This intervention is likely to bring awareness of the patient's resistance to melting. The patient might respond: "I won't cry here—I don't trust you," or "I am ashamed," or "I am angry and don't want to admit I miss him."]

Enactment. Here the patient is asked to put feelings or thoughts into action. For example, the therapist may encourage the patient to "say it to the person" (if present) or use some kind of roleplaying (such as speaking to an empty chair if the person is not present). "Put words to it" is another example. The patient with tears in his eyes might be asked to "put words to it." Enactment is intended as a way of increasing awareness, not as a form of catharsis. It is not a universal remedy.

Exaggeration is a special form of enactment. A person is asked to exaggerate some feeling, thought, movement, etc., in order to feel the more intense (albeit artificial) enacted or fantasied vision. Enactment into movement, sound, art, poetry, etc., can both stimulate creativity and be therapeutic.

For instance, a man who had been talking about his mother without showing any special emotion was asked to describe her. Out of this description came the suggestion to move like her. As the patient adopted her posture and movement, intense feelings came back into his awareness.

Guided fantasy. Sometimes a patient can bring an experience into the here and now more efficiently by visualizing than by enacting:

P: I was with my girlfriend last night. I don't know how it happened but I was impotent. [Patient gives more detail and some history.]
T: Close your eyes. Imagine it is last night and you are with your girlfriend. Say out loud what you experience at each moment.
P: I am sitting on the couch. My friend sits next to me and I get excited. Then I go soft.
T: Let's go through that again in slow motion, in more detail. Be sensitive to every thought or sense impression.
P: I am sitting on the couch. She comes over and sits next to me. She touches my neck. It feels so warm and soft, I get excited—you know, hard. She strokes my arm, and I love it. [Pause, looks startled.] Then I thought, I had such a tense day, maybe I won't be able to get it up.

This patient became aware of how he created his own anxiety and impotence. This fantasy was recreating an event that happened in order to get in better touch with it. The fantasy could be of an expected event, a metaphorical event, and so forth.

In another case, a patient working on shame and self-rejection is asked to imagine a mother who says and means "I love you just the way you are." As the fantasy is given detail, the patient attends to her experience. This fantasy helps the patient become aware of the possibility of good self-mothering and can serve as a transition to integrate good self-parenting. The image can be used to work between sessions or as a meditation. It also raises feelings about experiences with abandonment, loss, and bad parenting.

Loosening and integrating techniques. Often the patient is so fettered by the bonds of the usual ways of thinking that alternative possibilities are not allowed into awareness. This includes traditional mechanisms, such as denial or repression, but also cultural and learning factors affecting the patient's way of thinking. One technique is just to ask the patient to imagine the opposite of whatever is believed to be true.

Integrating techniques bring together processes the patient doesn't bring together or actively keeps apart (splitting). The patient might be asked to put words to a negative process, such as tensing, crying, or twitching. Or when the patient verbally reports a feeling, that is, an emotion, she might be asked to locate it in her body. Another example is asking a patient to express positive *and* negative feelings about the same person.

Body techniques. These include any technique that brings patients' awareness to their body functioning or helps them to be aware of how they can use their bodies to support excitement, awareness and contact. For example:

P: [Is tearful and clamping jaw tight.]
T: Would you be willing to try an experiment?
P: [Patient nods.]
T: Take some deep, deep breaths, and each time you exhale, let your jaw loosely move down.
P: [Breathes deeply, lets jaw drop on the exhale.]
T: Stay with it.
P: [Starts melting, crying, then sobbing.]

Therapist Disclosures

The Gestalt therapist is encouraged to make "I" statements. Such statements facilitate both the therapeutic contact and the patient's focusing and are to be made discriminately and judiciously. Using the "I" to facilitate therapeutic work requires technical skill, personal wisdom, and self-awareness on the therapist's part. Therapists may share what they see, hear, or smell. They can share how they are affected. Facts of which the therapist is aware and the patient is not are shared, especially if the information is unlikely to be spontaneously discovered in the phenomenological work during the hour, yet is believed to be important to the patient.

MECHANISMS OF PSYCHOTHERAPY

Old Deficits, New Strengths

The child needs a parental relationship with a nurturant, organismic/environmental, ecological balance. For example, a mother must see that a child's needs are met and that the development of its potentialities are facilitated. A child needs this warm, nurturing kind of mirroring. And a child also needs room to struggle, to be frustrated, and to fail. A child also needs limits to experience the consequences of behavior. When parents cannot meet these needs because they need a dependent child or lack sufficient inner resources, the child develops distorted contact boundaries, awareness and lowered self-esteem.

Unfortunately, children are often shaped to meet the approval of parents and society, without equal emphasis on their own needs. As a result, the spontaneous personality is superseded by an artificial one. Other children come to believe they can have their own needs met by others without consideration for the autonomy of others. This results in the formation of impulsivity rather than spontaneity.

Patients need a therapist who will relate in a healthy, contactful manner, neither losing self by indulging the patient at the expense of exploration and working through nor creating excessive anxiety, shame, and frustration by not being respectful, warm, receptive, direct, and honest.

Patients who enter psychotherapy with decreased awareness of their needs and strengths, resisting rather than supporting their organismic self, are in pain. They try to get the therapist to do for them what they believe they cannot do for themselves. When therapists go along with this, patients do not reown and integrate their lost or never developed potential. Therefore they still cannot operate with organismic self-regulation, being responsible for themselves. They do not find out if they have the strength to exist autonomously because the therapist meets their needs without strengthening their awareness and ego boundaries (see Resnick, 1970).

As Gestalt therapy proceeds and patients learn to be aware and responsible and contactful, their ego functioning improves. As a result, they gain tools for deeper exploration. The childhood experiences of the formative years can then be explored without the regression and overdependency necessary in regressive treatment and without the temporary loss of competence that a transference neurosis entails. Childhood experiences are brought into present awareness without the assumption that patients are determined by past events. Patients actively project transference material on the Gestalt thera-

pist, thereby giving opportunities for deeper exploration.

The following two examples show patients with different defenses, needing different treatment, but with similar underlying issues.

Tom was a 45-year-old man proud of his intelligence, self-sufficiency, and independence. He was not aware that he had unmet dependency needs and resentment. This affected his marriage in that his wife felt unneeded and inferior because she was in touch with needing and showed it. This man's self-sufficiency required respect—it met a need, was in part constructive, and was the basis of his self-esteem.

P: [With pride.] When I was a little kid my mom was so busy I just had to learn to rely on myself.
T: I appreciate your strength, and when I think of you as such a self-reliant kid I want to stroke you and give you some parenting.
P: [Tearing a little.] No one has been able to do that for me.
T: You seem sad.
P: I am remembering when I was a kid. . . .
[Exploration led to awareness of a shame reaction to unavailable parents and a compensatory self-reliance.]

Bob was a 45-year-old man who felt shame and isolated himself in reaction to any interaction that was not totally positive. He was consistently reluctant to experiment with self-nourishment.

P: [Whiny voice.] I don't know what to do today.
T: [Looks and does not talk.]
P: I could talk about my week. [Looks questioningly at therapist.]
T: I feel pulled on by you right now. I imagine you want me to direct you.
P: Yes. What's wrong with that?
T: Nothing. I prefer not to direct you right now.
P: Why not?
T: You can direct yourself. I believe you are directing us away from your inner self

right now. I don't want to cooperate with that. [Silence.]

P: I feel lost.

T: [Looks and does not talk.]

P: You are not going to direct me, are you?

T: No.

P: Well, let's work on my believing I can't take care of myself. [Patient directs a fruitful piece of work that leads to awareness of abandonment anxiety and feelings of shame in response to unavailable parents.]

Frustration and Support

Gestalt therapy balances frustration and support. The therapist explores rather than gratifies the patient's wishes—and this is frustrating for the patient. Providing contact is supportive, although honest contact frustrates manipulation. The Gestalt therapist expresses self and emphasizes exploring, including exploring desire, frustration, and indulgence. The therapist responds to manipulations by the patient *without reinforcing them*, without judging, and without being purposely frustrating. A balance of warmth and firmness is important.

The Paradoxical Theory of Change

The paradox is that the more one tries to be who one is not, the more one stays the same (Beisser, 1970). Many patients focus on what they "should be" and at the same time resist these shoulds.

The Gestalt therapist attempts to work toward integration by asking the client to identify with each conflicting role. The client is asked what he or she experiences at each moment. When the client can be aware of both roles, integrating techniques are used to transcend the dichotomy.

There are two axioms in Gestalt therapy: "What is, is," and "One thing leads to another" (Polster and Polster, 1973). The medium of change is a relationship with a therapist who makes contact based on showing who he or she truly is and who understands and accepts the patient.

Awareness of "what is" leads to spontaneous change. When the person manipulating for support finds a therapist who is contactful and accepting and who does not collude with the manipulation, he may become aware of what he is doing. This *Aha!* is a new gestalt, a new outlook, a taste of a new possibility: "I can be with someone and not manipulate or be manipulated." When such a person meets "therapeutic" collusion, derision, mind games, game busting, and so on, this increase in awareness is unlikely to happen.

At each and every point along the way this new *Aha!* can occur. As long as the therapist or the patient can see new possibilities and the patient wants to learn, new *Aha!*'s are possible and with them, growth. Awareness work can start anywhere the patient is willing, if the therapist is aware and connects it to the whole. The ensuing process in Gestalt therapy leads to changes everywhere in the field. The more thorough the investigation, the more intense the reorganization. Some changes can only be appreciated years later.

Patients in Gestalt therapy are in charge of their lives. The therapist facilitates attention to opening restricted awareness and areas of constricted contact boundaries; the therapist brings firmness and limits to areas with poor boundaries. As sensing increases in accuracy and vividness, as breathing becomes fuller and more relaxed, and as patients make better contact, they bring the skills of therapy into their lives. Sometimes intimacy and job improvements follow Gestalt work like an act of grace, without the patient's connecting the increase to the work done in therapy. But the organism does grow with awareness and contact. One thing does lead to another.

APPLICATIONS

PROBLEMS

Gestalt therapy can be used effectively with any patient population that the therapist understands and feels comfortable with. If the therapist can relate to the patient, the Gestalt therapy principles of dialogue and direct experiencing can be applied. With each patient, *general principles must be adapted to the particular clinical situation.* If the patient's treatment is made to conform to "Gestalt therapy," it can be ineffective or harmful. A schizophrenic, a sociopath, a borderline, and an obsessive-compulsive neurotic may all need different approaches. Thus, *the competent practice of Gestalt therapy requires a background in more than Gestalt therapy.* A knowledge of diagnosis, personality theory, and psychodynamic theory is also needed.

The individual clinician has a great deal of discretion in Gestalt therapy. Modifications are made by the individual therapist according to therapeutic style, personality, diagnostic considerations, and so on. This encourages and requires individual responsibility by the therapist. Gestalt therapists are encouraged to have a firm grounding in personality theory, psychopathology, and theories and applications of psychotherapy, as well as adequate clinical experience. Participants in the therapeutic encounter are encouraged to experiment with new behavior and then share cognitively and emotionally what the experience was like.

Gestalt therapy has traditionally been considered most effective with "overly socialized, restrained, constricted individuals" (e.g., anxious, perfectionistic, phobic, and depressed clients), whose inconsistent or restricted functioning is primarily a result of "internal restrictions" (Shepherd, 1970, pp. 234–35). Such individuals usually show only a minimal enjoyment of living.

Although Shepherd's statement accurately delineates a population Gestalt therapy is effective with, current clinical practice of Gestalt therapy includes treatment of a much wider range of problems.

Gestalt therapy in the "Perlsian" workshop style is of more limited application than Gestalt therapy in general (Dolliver, 1981; Dublin, 1976). In Shepherd's discussion of limitations and cautions, she notes restrictions that apply to any therapist but should especially be noted in a workshop setting, as well as by therapists not well trained or experienced with disturbed patient populations.

Work with psychotic, disorganized, or otherwise severely disturbed people is more difficult and calls for "caution, sensitivity, and patience." Shepherd advises against doing such work where it is not feasible to make a "long-term commitment" to the patient. Disturbed patients need support from the therapist and at least a minimal amount of faith in their own natural healing capacity before they can explore deeply and experience intensely the "overwhelming pain, hurt, rage, and despair" that underlie the psychological processes of disturbed patients (Shepherd, 1970, pp. 234–35).

Working with more disturbed populations requires clinical knowledge of how to balance support and frustration, knowledge of character dynamics, need for auxiliary support (such as day treatment and medication) and so forth. Some statements which seem to make sense in a workshop encounter are obvious nonsense when applied in a broader context. Consider for example, "do your own thing" in the context of treatment with acting out patients!

A perusal of the Gestalt therapy literature such as *Gestalt Therapy Now* (Fagan & Shepherd, 1970), *The Growing Edge of Gestalt Therapy* (Smith, 1976), and the *Gestalt Journal*, will show Gestalt therapy is used for crisis intervention, ghetto adults in a poverty program (Barnwell, 1968), interaction groups, psychotics, and almost any group imaginable. Unfortunately the literature provides examples (and a small number at that) without sufficient explication of necessary alterations in focus and without discussing negative results.

Gestalt therapy has been successfully employed in the treatment of a wide range of "psychosomatic" disorders including migraine, ulcerative colitis, and spastic neck and back. Gestalt therapists have successfully worked with couples, with individuals having difficulties coping with authority figures, and with a wide range of intrapsychic conflicts. Gestalt therapy has been effectively employed with psychotics and severe character disorders.

Because of the impact of Gestalt therapy and the ease with which strong, frequently buried affective reactions can be reached, it is necessary to establish "safety islands" to which both the therapist and patient can comfortably return. It is also imperative for the therapist to stay with the patient until he or she is ready to return to these "safety islands." For example, after an especially emotional laden experience, the patient may be encouraged to make visual, tactile, or other contact with the therapist or with one or more group members and report the experience. Another "safety" technique is to have the patient shuttle back and forth between making contact in the *now* with the therapist or group members and with the emotionally laden unfinished situation that the patient was experiencing *then* until all of the affect has been discharged and the unfinished situation worked through.

The Gestalt therapy emphasis on personal responsibility, interpersonal contact, and increased clarity of awareness of what is, could be of great value in meeting the problems of the present. One example is application of Gestalt therapy in schools (Brown, 1970; Lederman, 1970).

EVALUATION

Gestalt therapists are singularly unimpressed with formal psychodiagnostic evaluation and nomothetic research methodology. No statistical approach can tell the individual patient or therapist what works for him or her. What is shown to work for most does not always work for a particular individual. This does not mean that Gestalt therapists are not in favor of research; in fact, the Gestalt Therapy Institute of Los Angeles has offered grants to subsidize research. Perls offered no quantified, statistical evidence that Gestalt therapy works. He did say, "we present nothing that you cannot verify for yourself in terms of your own behavior" (F. Perls et al., 1951, p. 7). In the publication *Gestalt Therapy*, a series of experiments are provided that can be used to test for oneself the validity of Gestalt therapy.

Each session is seen as an experiment, an existential encounter in which both the therapist and the patient engage in calculated risk taking (experiments) involving exploration of heretofore unknown or forbidden territories. The patient is aided in using phenomenological focusing skills and dialogic contact to evaluate what is and is not working. Thus, constant idiographic research takes place. Gestalt therapy has "sacrificed exact verification for the value in ideographic experimental psychotherapy" (Yontef, 1969, p. 27).

Harman (1984) reviewed Gestalt research literature and found quality research on Gestalt therapy sparse. He did find studies that showed increased self-actualization and positive self-concept following Gestalt therapy groups (Guinan & Foulds, 1970; Foulds & Hannigan, 1976).

A series of studies conducted by Leslie Greenberg and associates (Greenberg, 1986) addressed the lack of attention to context in psychotherapy research and the unfortunate separation of process and outcome studies. The Greenberg studies related specific acts and change processes in therapy with particular outcomes. Their research distinguished three types of outcome (immediate, intermediate, and final) and three levels of process (speech act, episode, and relationship). They studied speech in the context of the type of episodes in which it appears, and they studied the episodes in the context of the relationships in which they occur.

In one study Greenberg examined the use of the two-chair technique to resolve splits. He defined a split as "a verbal performance pattern in which a client reports a division of the self process into two partial aspects of the

self or tendencies." He concludes that "two-chair operations conducted according to the principles [of his study] have been found to facilitate an increase in the Depth of Experiencing and index of productive psychotherapy ... and to lead to resolutions of splits with populations seeking counseling" (1979, p. 323).

A study called the "Effects of Two-Chair Dialogues and Focusing on Conflict Resolution" by L. S. Greenberg and H. M. Higgins found that "Two-chair dialogue appeared to produce a more direct experience of conflict [split] and encouraged the client in a form of self-confrontation that helped create a resolution to the conflict" (1980, p. 224).

Harman (1984) found a number of studies that compared the behavior of Gestalt therapists with that of other therapists. Brunnink and Schroeder compared expert psychoanalysts, behavior therapists, and Gestalt therapists and found the Gestalt therapists "provided more direct guidance, less verbal facilitation, less focus on the client, more self-disclosure, greater initiative and less emotional support." They also found that the "interview content of Gestalt therapists tended to reflect a more experiential or subjective approach to therapy" (1979, p. 572).

No claim is made in the Gestalt therapy literature that Gestalt therapy is demonstrated to be the "best." There is theoretically no reason why Gestalt therapy should be more generally effective than therapies under other names that follow the principles of good psychotherapy. General outcome research may yield less useful results than process research looking at behavior, attitudes, and consequences. An example of this is Simkin's assessment of the effectiveness of Gestalt therapy in workshops ("massed learning") as contrasted with "spaced" weekly therapy sessions. He found evidence for the superiority of massed learning (Simkin, 1976).

Some Gestalt therapy viewpoints on what constitutes good therapy are supported by general research. The research on experiencing within the Rogerian tradition demonstrated the effectiveness of an emphasis on direct experience by any therapist. In Gestalt therapy there is also an emphasis on personal relating, presence, and experience. Unfortunately, some therapists regularly and blatantly violate the principles of good psychotherapy according to the Gestalt therapy model, but still call themselves Gestalt therapists (Lieberman, Yalom & Miles, 1973).

TREATMENT

Ongoing Individual Gestalt Therapy

Although Gestalt therapy has acquired a reputation for being primarily applicable to groups, its mainstay is actually individual treatment. Several examples can be found in *Gestalt Therapy Now* (Fagan & Shepherd, 1970). An annotated bibliography of case readings can be found in Simkin (1979, p. 299).

Gestalt therapy begins with the first contact. Ordinarily, assessment and screening are done as a part of the ongoing relationship rather than in a separate period of diagnostic testing and social history taking. The data for the assessment are obtained by beginning the work, for example, by therapeutic encounter. This assessment includes the patient's willingness and support for work within the Gestalt therapy framework, the match of patient and therapist, the usual professional diagnostic and characterological discriminations, decisions on frequency of sessions, the need for adjunctive treatment and the need for medical consultation.

An average frequency for sessions is once per week. Using the Gestalt methodology, an intensity equivalent to psychoanalysis can often be achieved at this frequency. Often individual therapy is combined with group therapy, workshops, conjoint or family therapy, movement therapy, meditation, or biofeedback training. Sometimes patients can utilize more frequent sessions, but often they need the interval to digest material, and more frequent sessions may result in overreliance on the therapist. Frequency of sessions also depends on how long the patient can go between sessions without loss of continuity, decompensation, or lesser forms of relapse. Frequency of sessions varies from five times per week to every other week. Meeting less frequently than every week obviously diminishes intensity unless the patient attends a weekly group with the same therapist. More than twice a week is ordinarily not indicated, except with psychotics, and is definitely contraindicated with borderline personality disorders.

All through the therapy patients are encouraged and aided in doing the decision making for themselves. When to start and stop, whether to do an exercise, what adjunctive therapies to use, and the like are all discussed with the therapist, but the competence and ultimate necessity for the patient to make these choices is supported.

Group Models

Gestalt therapy groups vary from one and one-half to three hours in length, with an average length of two hours. A typical two-hour group has up to 10 participants. Gestalt therapists usually experience maximal involvement with heterogeneous groups, with a balance of men and women. Participants need to be screened. Any age is appropriate for Gestalt therapy, but an ongoing private practice group would typically range from ages 20 to 65, with the average between 30 and 50.

Some Gestalt therapists follow Perls' lead in doing one-on-one therapy in the group setting and use the "hot seat" structure. "According to this method, an individual expresses to the therapist his interest in dealing with a particular problem. The focus is then on the extended interaction between patient and group leader (I and Thou)" (Levitsky & Simkin, 1972, p. 240). One-on-one episodes average 20 minutes, but range from a couple of minutes to 45 minutes. During the one-on-one work, the other members remain silent. After the work, they give feedback on how they were affected, what they observed, and how their own experiences are similar to those the patient worked on. In recent years the one-on-one work has been expanded to include awareness work that is not focused around a particular "problem."

In the early 1960s Perls wrote a paper in which he said:

Lately, however, I have eliminated individual sessions altogether except for emergency cases. As a matter of fact, I have come to consider that all individual therapy is obsolete and should be replaced by workshops in Gestalt Therapy. In my workshops I now integrate individual and group work. (1967, p. 306)

This opinion was not then shared by most Gestalt therapists, and is not currently recognized Gestalt theory or practice.

Some observers have described the Gestalt therapist's style of group work as doing individual therapy in a group setting. This statement is valid for those Gestalt therapists who use the model just discussed and do not emphasize or deal with group dynamics or strive for group cohesiveness. However, this is only one style of Gestalt therapy—many Gestalt therapists do emphasize group dynamics.

Greater use of the group is certainly within the Gestalt methodology and is increasingly used in Gestalt therapy (Enright, 1975; Feder & Ronall, 1980; Zinker, 1977). This includes greater involvement of group members when an individual is doing one-to-one work, working on individual themes by everyone in the group, emphasis on interrelationships (contact) in the group, and working with group processes per se. The varied degree and type of structure provided by the leader include structured group exercises or no structured group exercises, observing the group's evolving to its own structure, encouraging one-on-one work, and so on. Often Gestalt groups begin with some exercise to help participants make the transition into working by sharing here-and-now experience.

A frequently used model is one that encourages both increased awareness through focus on contact between group members and one-on-one work in the group (with other members encouraged to participate during the work). This encourages greater fluidity and flexibility.

Workshop Style

Some Gestalt therapy and a good deal of training in Gestalt therapy is conducted in workshops, which are scheduled for a finite period, some for as short as one day. Weekend workshops may range from 10 to 20 or more hours. Longer workshops range from a week through several months in duration. A typical weekend workshop membership consists of one Gestalt therapist and 12 to 16 people. Given longer periods (ranging from one week up to a month or longer), as many as 20 people can be seen by one therapist. Usually if the group is larger than 16 participants, co-therapists are used.

Because workshops have a finite life and because just so many hours are available to the participants, there is usually high motivation to "work." Sometimes, rules are established so that no one can work a second time until every other participant has had an opportunity to work once. At other times, no such rules are set. Thus, depending on their willingness, audacity, and drive, some people may get intense therapeutic attention several times during a workshop.

Although some workshops are arranged with established groups, most assemble people for the first time. As in ongoing groups, the ideal practice is to screen patients before the workshop. An unscreened workshop requires a clinician experienced with the range of severe pathology and careful protection for possibly vulnerable group members. Confrontive or charismatic Gestalt styles are particularly likely to exacerbate existing mental illness in some participants (Lieberman et al., 1973).

Other Treatment Modalities

The application of Gestalt therapy to working with families has been most extensively elaborated by Walter Kempler (1973, pp. 251–86). The most complete description of Kempler's work appears in his *Principles of Gestalt Family Therapy* (1974).

Gestalt therapy has also been used in short-term crisis intervention (O'Connell, 1970), as an adjunct treatment for visual problems (Rosanes-Berret, 1970), for awareness training of mental health professionals (Enright, 1970), for children with behavior problems, (Lederman, 1970), to train staff for a day-care center (Ennis & Mitchell, 1970), to teach creativity to teachers and others (Brown, 1970), with a dying person (Zinker & Fink, 1966), and in organization development (Herman, 1972).

MANAGEMENT

Case management by a Gestalt therapist tends to be quite practical and guided by the goal of supporting the person-to-person relationship. Appointments are usually arranged over the telephone by the therapist. Office decor reflects the personality and style of the therapist and is not purposely neutral. The offices are designed and furnished to be comfortable and to avoid a desk or table between therapist and patient. Typically the physical arrangement leaves room for movement and experimentation. The therapist's dress and manner are usually quite informal.

Arrangement of fees varies with the individual, and there is no particular Gestalt style, except straightforwardness. Fees are discussed directly with the patient and usually collected by the therapist.

Clarity of boundaries is stressed, with both the patient and the therapist responsible for attending to the task at hand. The "work," or therapy, starts from the first moment. No notes are taken during the session because it interferes with contact. The therapist takes personal responsibility for note taking after the session, if needed, and for safeguarding notes, video or tape recordings, and other clinical material. The therapist sets down conditions of payment, cancellation policy, and so forth. Violations or objections are directly discussed. Decisions are made together and agreements are expected to be kept by both. The therapist arranges the office to protect it from invasion and, where possible, soundproofs the office.

The evaluation process occurs as part of the therapy and is mutual. Some of the considerations involved in the evaluation process include deciding on individual and/or group therapy, estimating the therapist's capacity to establish a trusting, caring relationship, and letting the patient decide after an adequate sample if the therapist and the therapy are suitable.

Problems arising in the relationship are discussed directly, both in terms of dealing with the concrete problem and in terms of exploring any related characterological life-styles or relationship processes that would be fruitful for the patient to explore. Always the needs, wishes, and direct experience of both participants guide the exploration and problem solving.

CASE EXAMPLE

Peg was originally seen in a Gestalt training workshop, where she worked on the grief and anger she felt toward her husband, who had committed suicide. His death left her with the full responsibility of raising their children and beginning a career outside the home to support herself and her family. She was in her late 30s at the time.

With considerable courage and initiative, Peg had organized a crisis clinic sponsored by a prominent serv-ice organization in the large Southern California city in which she resided. She was one of 11 people who participated in making a Gestalt therapy training film with Simkin (1969). The following is excerpted from the film, *In the Now:*

Peg: I have a . . . recurring dream. I'm standing on the ground, up by Camp Pendleton. There's an open, rolling countryside. Wide dirt roads crisscrossing all over it. A series of hills and valleys and hills and valleys. . . . And off to my right I see a tank, like in the army—marine tanks with the big tracks . . . and there's a series of them and they're all closed tight and they're rumbling over these hills and valleys in a line, all closed up. And I'm standing beside this road and I'm holding a platter of Tollhouse cookies. And they're hot cookies. And they are just on the platter— I'm just standing there, and I see these tanks coming by one at a time. And as the tanks come past, I stand there and I watch the tanks. And as I look to my right I see one—and there's a pair of shiny black shoes, running along between the treads of the tank as it comes over the hill. And just as it gets in front of me . . . the man bends down and the tank goes on, and he comes over toward me and it's my best friend's husband. And I always wake up. I always stop my dream . . . and I laughed. It doesn't seem so funny anymore.

Jim: True. What are you doing?

Peg: Trying to stop my teeth from chattering.

Jim: What's your objection?

Peg: I don't like the feeling of anxiety and fear I have now.

Jim: What do you imagine?

Peg: Ridicule.

Jim: Okay. Start ridiculing.

Peg: Peg, you're ridiculous. You're fat . . . you're lazy. You're just comic. You're pretending to be grown up and you're not. Everybody looking knows that you're a kid inside, masquerading as a 39-year-old woman and . . . it's a ridiculous disguise. You haven't any business being 39. A ridiculous age. You're comic. You have a job you don't have the remotest idea how to do. You're making all kinds of grandiose plans that you haven't brains enough to carry through and people are going to be laughing at you.

Jim: Okay, now please look around and note how people are laughing at you.

Peg: I'm scared to. [Looks around, slowly.] They appear to be taking me quite seriously.

Jim: So who is laughing at you?

Peg: I guess . . . only my fantasy . . . my . . .

Jim: Who creates your fantasy?

Peg: I do.

Jim: So who's laughing at you?

Peg: Yeah. That's so. I . . . I'm really laughing at what's not funny. I'm not so damned incompetent. [Pause.]

Jim: What are you really good at?

Peg: I'm good with people. I'm not judgmental. I'm good at keeping house. I'm a good seamstress, good baker, I . . .

Jim: Maybe you'll make somebody a good wife.

Peg: I did.

Jim: Maybe you'll make somebody a good wife again.

Peg: I don't know.

Jim: So say that sentence. "I don't know if I'll ever make somebody a good wife again."

Peg: I don't know if I'll ever make someone a good wife again.

Jim: Say that to every man here.

Peg: I don't know if I'll make someone a good wife again. . . . [Repeats the sentence five more times.]

Jim: What do you experience?

Peg: Surprise. Boy . . . I assumed I would never make anybody a good wife again.

Jim: Right.

Jim: What do you experience right now?

Peg: Satisfaction. Pleasure. I feel good. I feel done.

Although Peg's "ticket of admission" was a dream, what became foreground was her anxiety and fantasies of being ridiculed. The dream served as a vehicle for starting and, as is frequently the case, the work led to a most unpredictable outcome.

At the weekend workshop during which the training film was made, Peg met a man to whom she was attracted and who, in turn, was attracted to her. They began to date and within a few months they married.

A second sample of Gestalt therapy follows, selectively excerpted from a book to illustrate some techniques (Simkin, 1976, pp. 103–18). It is a condensed transcript of a workshop with six volunteers. The morning session included a lecture-demonstration and film.

Jim: I'd like to start with saying where I am and what I'm experiencing at this moment. This seems very artificial to me, all of these lights and the cameras and the people around. I feel breathless and burdened by the technical material, the equipment, etc., and I'm much more interested in getting away from the lights and the cameras and getting more in touch with you. [Inquires as to the names of participants of the group and introduces himself.]

I am assuming that all of you saw the film and the demonstration, and my preference would be to work with you as you feel ready to work. I'll reiterate our contract, or agreement. In Gestalt therapy the essence of the contract is to say where you are, what you are experiencing at any given moment, and, if you can, to stay in the continuum of awareness, to report where you are focusing, what you are aware of.

* * * * * *

I'd like to start first with having you say who you are and if you have any programs or expectations.

Tom: Right now I'm a little tense, not particularly because of the technical equipment because I'm kind of used to that. I feel a little strange about being in a situation with you. This morning I was pretty upset because I didn't agree with a lot of the things you were talking about, and I felt pretty hostile to you. Now I more or less accept you as another person.

Jim: I'm paying attention to your foot now. I'm wondering if you could give your foot a voice.

Tom: My foot a voice? You mean how is my foot feeling? What's it going to say?

Jim: Just keep doing that, and see if you have something to say, as your foot.

Tom: I don't understand.

Jim: As you were telling me about feeling hostile this morning, you began to kick and I'm imagining that you still have some kick coming.

Tom: Uh, yeah. I guess maybe I do have some kick left, but I really don't get the feeling that that's appropriate.

* * * * * *

Lavonne: Right now I'm feeling tense.

Jim: Who are you talking to, Lavonne?

Lavonne: I was just thinking about this morning, I was feeling very hostile. I still think I am somewhat hostile.

Jim: I am aware that you are avoiding looking at me.

Lavonne: Yes, because I feel that you are very arrogant.

Jim: That's true.

Lavonne: And as if I might get into a struggle with you.

Jim: You might.

Lavonne: So the avoidance of eye contact is sort of a put-off of the struggle. I have some things that I'd like to work on. I don't know whether they can be resolved.

Jim: Would you be willing to tell me what your objections are to my arrogance?

Lavonne: Well, it's not very comforting. If I have a problem and I talk to you about it and you're arrogant, then that only makes me arrogant.

Jim: You respond in kind is what you are saying. Your experience is you respond that way.

Lavonne: Yes. Right on. Then at this university I feel that I must be arrogant and I must be defensive at all times. Because I'm black, people react to me in different ways ... different people ... and I feel that I have to be on my toes most of the time. . . .

* * * * * *

Mary: I want to work on my feelings for my older son and the struggle that I have with him—only, I suspect it is really a struggle I'm having with myself.

Jim: Can you say this to him? Give him a name and say this to him.

Mary: All right. His name is Paul.

Jim: Put Paul here [empty chair] and say this to Paul.

Mary: Paul, we have a lot of friction. Every time you go out of the drive on your own, independent, I hate you for it. But. . . .

Jim: Just a moment. Say the same sentence to Mary. Mary, each time you go out the drive, independent, I hate you for it.

Mary: That fits. Mary, each time you go out the drive, independent, I hate you for it, because you are not being a good mother.

Jim: I don't know about your because.

Mary: No. That's my rationale. That's the same I do to myself doing yoga.

Jim: You sound identified with Paul.

Mary: I am. I know this. I envy his freedom, even from the time he was a little kid and went to the woods. I envied his ability to go to the woods.

Jim: Tell Paul.

Mary: Paul, even when you were a little boy and you would go for all day Saturday, and not tell me where you were going but just go, I envied you for it. I envied you very much, and I felt hurt because I couldn't do it too.

Jim: You couldn't, or you wouldn't?

Mary: I would not do it. I wanted to, but I would not do it.

Jim: Yeah. For me to have somebody around that keeps reminding me of what I can do and don't really pisses me off.

Mary: This is what I do to myself. I keep reminding myself of what I can do and won't do. And then I don't do anything. I'm at a standstill. Firmly planted.

Jim: I'd like you to get in touch with your spitefulness. Put your spitefulness out here and talk to Mary's saboteur.

Mary: You idiot. You've got the time to do your work. You also have the energy to do your work ... which you dissipate. You get involved in umpteen dozen things so you will have an excuse not to do your work, or to do anything else ... [Pause.] You just spend time making yourself miserable and complicating your life.

Jim: What's going on here? [Points to Mary's hand.]

Mary: Yes. Tight-fisted ... won't do.

Jim: Are you tight-fisted?

Mary: Yes, I think I am.

Jim: OK. Can you get in touch with the other part of you—your generous self?

Mary: I don't really know my generous self very well.

Jim: Be your tight-fisted self just saying, "Generous self, I have no contact with you, I don't know you, etc."

Mary: Generous self, I don't know very much of you. I think you try every now and then when you give presents to people instead of giving yourself. You withhold an awful lot that you could give.

Jim: What just happened?

Mary: I rehearsed. I just wasn't talking to my generous self. I was talking to . . . you primarily. I was withholding part.

Jim: I have difficulty imagining you as a withholding person. You came on in the beginning as very vibrant and alive . . . to me, very giving.

Mary: I don't know whether I really am giving or not.

Jim: Say that again, please.

Mary: I don't know whether I really am giving or not. Sometimes I feel like I do give and what I give is not accepted as a gift. And sometimes I want to give and I can't. And I feel sometimes I have given too much and I shouldn't have.

Jim: Yeah. This is what I'm beginning to sense. Some hurt. You look like you've been hurt—in the past. That you've been vulnerable and somehow hurt in the process.

Mary: To some degree I'm hurting.

Jim: To me you look like you're hurting now, especially around your eyes.

Mary: I know that, and I don't want to do that . . . I don't want to show that.

Jim: OK. Would you be willing to block?

Mary: [Covering her eyes.] When I do that, I can't see you.

Jim: That's true.

Mary: When I do that, I can't see anyone.

Jim: Very true. When I block my hurt, no one exists for me. This is my choice.

Mary: I made it my choice too.

Jim: I am enjoying looking at you. To me, you are very generous at this moment.

Mary: You are very generous to me. I feel that you are. I hear you respond to me and I feel that I'm responding to you . . .

Jim: I'm curious if you can come back to Paul for a moment now. Encounter him and explore what happens.

Mary: Paul, I want to be warm to you, and I want to be generous to you, and I think I might hurt you by being so. You're six feet tall now and sometimes I very much want to come up to you and just give you a kiss goodnight or just put my arms around you and I can't do it anymore.

Jim: You can't?

Mary: I won't. I won't, because, uh . . . I've been shoved away.

Jim: You've been hurt.

Mary: Yeah, I've been hurt. Paul, I think it's your own business if you want to shove me away, but that doesn't stop me from being hurt.

Jim: I like what, I believe, Nietzsche once said to the sun, "It's none of your business that you shine at me."

Mary: I keep hoping that, Paul, when you're 25 or if you go to the Army or whatever . . . that I can kiss you good-bye. [Pause.] I'll try to remember what Nietzsche said to the sun.

Jim: OK. I enjoyed working with you.

Mary: Thank you.

SUMMARY

Fritz Perls prophesied three decades ago that Gestalt therapy would come into its own during the 1960s and become a significant force in psychotherapy during the 1970s. His prophecy has been more than fulfilled.

In 1952, there were perhaps a dozen people seriously involved in the movement. In 1987 there were scores of training institutes, hundreds of psychotherapists who had been trained in Gestalt therapy, and many hundreds of nontrained or poorly trained persons who called themselves "Gestaltists." Thousands of people have experienced Gestalt therapy—many with quite favorable results—others with questionable or poor outcomes.

Because of the unwillingness of Gestalt therapists to set rigid standards, there is a wide range of criteria for the selection and training of Gestalt therapists. Some people, having experienced a weekend workshop, consider themselves amply equipped to do Gestalt therapy. Other psychotherapists spend months and years in training as Gestalt therapists and have an enormous respect for the simplicity and infinite innovativeness and creativity that Gestalt therapy requires and engenders.

Despite the fact that Gestalt therapy attracts some people who are looking for shortcuts, it also has attracted a substantial number of solid, experienced clinicians who have found in Gestalt therapy not only a powerful psychotherapy but also a viable life philosophy.

Those looking for quick solutions and shortcuts will go on to greener pastures. Gestalt therapy will take its place along with other substantive psychotherapies in the next several decades. It should continue to attract creative, experimentally oriented psychotherapists for many years to come.

Gestalt therapy has pioneered many useful and creative innovations in psychotherapy theory and practice. These have been incorporated into general practice, usually without credit. Now Gestalt therapy is moving into further elaboration and refinement of these principles. Regardless of label, the principles of existential dia-

logue, the use of the direct phenomenological experience of patient and therapist, the trust of organismic self-regulation, the emphasis on experimentation and awareness, the "no should" attitude by the therapist, and the responsibility of the patient and therapist for their own choices all form a model of good psychotherapy that will continue to be used by Gestalt therapists and others.

To summarize, a quote from Levitsky and Simkin (1972, pp. 251–252) seems appropriate:

If we were to choose one key idea to stand as a symbol for the Gestalt approach, it might well be the concept of authenticity, the quest for authenticity... If we regard therapy and the therapist in the pitiless light of authenticity, it becomes apparent that the therapist cannot teach what he does not know.... A therapist with some experience really knows within himself that he is communicating to his patient his [the therapist's] own fears as well as his courage, his defensiveness as well as his openness, his confusion as well as his clarity. The therapist's awareness, acceptance, and sharing of these truths can be a highly persuasive demonstration of his own authenticity. Obviously such a position is not acquired overnight. It is to be learned and relearned ever more deeply not only throughout one's career but throughout one's entire life.

ANNOTATED BIBLIOGRAPHY

Fagan, J., & Shepherd, I. L. (Eds.). (1970). *Gestalt therapy now*. Palo Alto, CA: Science and Behavior Books. (Paperback edition, New York: Harper & Row, 1971.)

This classic collection of articles on the theory, techniques, and applications of Gestalt therapy incorporates original articles by F. S. Perls, Erving Polster, Walter Kempler, James Simkin, I. L. Shepherd, Abraham Levitsky, and other leading Gestalt therapists. Each section has an introduction by the authors, and the appendix has a bibliography of books, articles, tape recordings, and films that were available in 1970, when the book was first published. A more recent collection of articles is *The Growing Edge of Gestalt Therapy*, E. W. L. Smith (Ed.) (1976). New York: Brunner/Mazel. Note especially articles by Smith, L. Perls, Shepherd, and Dublin.

Hatcher, C., & Himelstein, P. (Eds.) (1976). *The handbook of Gestalt therapy.* New York: Jason Aronson.

Some of the articles in this collection appear here for the first time. Others have appeared in other sources. Although this volume is marred by a number of typographical errors and several poor selections, it contains the most up-to-date bibliography in existence (chapter 32) as of 1976 and several outstanding contributions, such as Appelbaum's "A Psychoanalyst Looks at Gestalt Therapy," Gerald Kogan's "The Genesis of Gestalt Therapy," and Miriam Polster's "Women in Therapy: A Gestalt Therapist's View." It also contains the first section of *Gestalt Therapy Verbatim* (Moab, Utah: Real People Press, 1969). This section deals primarily with the theory of Gestalt therapy in a seminar style with interspersed questions from participants. The bulk of *Gestalt Therapy Verbatim* is not included in the *Handbook* and consists of specific verbatim transcripts of Perls' Gestalt therapy work with people who attend a weekend dreamwork seminar and excerpts from audio tapes of a four-week, intensive workshop.

Perls, F. S. (1969). *In and out of the garbage pail.* Moab, UT: Real People Press. (Paperback edition, New York: Bantam, 1971.)

This is Fritz Perls' autobiography, written over a period of three months in 1969, about one year before he died. It has a wide-ranging, free-floating style that includes poetry and prose, tragedy and humor, seriousness and lightness, and a host of other polarities that characterized the primary founder of Gestalt therapy. For individuals who never had the opportunity to meet Perls in person, this book is the next best thing.

Perls, F. (1973). *The Gestalt approach.* Palo Alto: Science & Behavior Books. (Paperback edition, New York: Bantam, 1976.)

This, Perls' last and clearest general statement on Gestalt therapy, is especially good on contact boundaries.

Perls, F., Hefferline, R., & Goodman, P. (1951). *Gestalt therapy.* New York: Dell Books.

This book has two parts. Volume 1 contains an important introduction, a series of 18 graduated experiments (phenomenological exploration exercises), and the comments of students taking the experiments. Many find these exercises useful in self-exploration. The second volume is a major theoretical source in Gestalt therapy. Unfortunately, it is very difficult reading. Essential for the serious scholar or therapist, this is not an easy introduction to Gestalt therapy.

Polster, E., & Polster, M. (1973). *Gestalt therapy integrated: Contours of theory and practice.* New York: Brunner/Mazel.

This is a scholarly, penetrating, and well-written book. It covers topics such as the now ethos, figure and ground, resistance, contact-boundary, contact functions and contact episodes, awareness, and experiment, and a description of working with a variety of groups in a section labeled "Beyond One to One." The chapters on contact (chapters 4 to 6) are especially noteworthy.

Simkin, J. S. (1976). *Gestalt therapy mini-lectures.* Millbrae, CA: Celestial Arts.

The first section contains an introductory chapter on Gestalt therapy in groups. The second section— "Theoretical and Practical Issues"— consists of short mini-lectures covering a range of concepts and constructs popular in Gestalt therapy. The third section deals with techniques. Section 4 is an extensive example of working with a dream in Gestalt therapy, and the fifth section—"Clinical Work" is the condensed transcript of a two-hour workshop.

CASE READINGS

Fagan, J. (1947). Three sessions with Iris. *The Counseling Psychologist, 4,* 42–59. [Also in C. Hatcher, & P. Himelstein, (Eds.) (1976). *The handbook of Gestalt therapy* (pp. 673–721). New York: Jason Aronson.]

Dr. Fagan describes her work with Iris as "an example of good, hard, routine work with a resistant patient in individual therapy in a heavily Gestalt style" (1976, p. 674). The patient was a volunteer for a doctoral dissertation. She had agreed to be videotaped and had no previous experience with Gestalt therapy.

Perls, F. S. (1969). Jane's three dreams. In *Gestalt therapy verbatim* (pp. 251–272). Moab, UT: Real People Press.

Three dreams, labeled "Jane I," "Jane II," and "Jane III," are presented verbatim. In the section called "Jane III," Jane continues to work on an unfinished part of the dream she worked on in "Jane II." [Portions of this material are also found in D. Wedding, & R. J. Corsini, (Eds.) (1989). *Case studies in psychotherapy.* Itasca, IL: F. E. Peacock.]

Perls, L. P. (1956). Two instances of Gestalt therapy. In P. D. Pursglove (Ed.) (1968), *Recognition in Gestalt therapy* (pp. 42–68). New York: Funk & Wagnalls.

Laura Perls presents the case of Claudia, a 25-year-old black woman who comes from a lower-middle-class West Indian background, and the case of Walter, a 47-year-old Central European Jewish refugee.

Simkin, J. S. (1967). *Individual Gestalt therapy.* Orlando, Florida: American Academy of Psychotherapists tape library (50 minutes).

In this tape of the eleventh hour of therapy with a 34-year-old actor, emphasis is on the present, nonverbal communications leading to production of genetic material. The use of fantasy dialogue is also illustrated.

Simkin, J. S. (1972). The use of dreams in Gestalt therapy. In C. J. Sager & H. S. Kaplan (Eds.), *Progress in group and family therapy* (pp. 95–104). New York: Brunner/Mazel.

In a verbatim transcript, a patient works on a dream about his youngest daughter.

REFERENCES

Appelbaum, S. A. (1976). A psychoanalyst looks at Gestalt therapy. In C. Hatcher & P. Himelstein (Eds.), *The handbook of Gestalt therapy* (pp. 753–778). New York: Jason Aronson.

Barnwell, J. E. (1968). Gestalt methods and techniques in a poverty program. In J.

S. Simkin (Ed.), *Festschrift for Fritz Perls.* Los Angeles, CA: Author.

Beisser, A. R. (1970). The paradoxical theory of change. In J. Fagan & I. L. Shepherd (Eds.), *Gestalt therapy now.* Palo Alto, CA: Science and Behavior Books.

Brown, G. I. (1970). Teaching creativity to teachers and others. *Journal of*

Teacher Education, 21, 210–216.

Brunnink, S., & Schroeder, H. (1979). Verbal therapeutic behavior of expert psychoanalytically oriented, Gestalt and behavior therapists. *Journal of Consulting and Clinical Psychology, 47,* 567–574.

Dolliver, R. (1981). Some limitations in Perls' Gestalt therapy. *Psychotherapy, Research and Practice, 8,* 38–45.

Dublin, J. (1976). Gestalt therapy. Existential-Gestalt therapy and/versus "Perls-ism." In E. Smith (Ed.), *The growing edge of Gestalt therapy* (pp. 124–150). New York: Brunner/Mazel.

Ennis, K., & Mitchell, S. (1970). *Staff training for a day care center.* In J. Fagan & I. L. Shepherd (Eds.), *Gestalt therapy now* (pp. 295–300). Palo Alto, CA: Science and Behavior Books.

Enright, J. B. (1970). Awareness training in the mental health professions. In J. Fagan & I. L. Shepherd (Eds.), *Gestalt therapy now* (pp. 263–273). Palo Alto, CA: Science and Behavior Books.

Enright, J. B. (1975). Gestalt therapy in interactive groups. In F. D. Stephenson (Ed.), *Gestalt therapy primer: Introductory readings in Gestalt therapy* (pp. 127–141). Springfield, IL: Charles C Thomas.

Fagan, J. (1970). Gestalt techniques with a woman with expressive difficulties. In J. Fagan & I. L. Shepherd (Eds.), *Gestalt therapy now* (pp. 169–193). Palo Alto, CA: Science and Behavior Books.

Fagan, J. (1974). Personality theory and psychotherapy. *Counseling Psychologist, 4,* 4–7.

Fagan, J., & Shepherd, I. L. (Eds.) (1970). *Gestalt therapy now.* Palo Alto, CA: Science and Behavior Books.

Feder, B., & Ronall, R. (Eds.) (1980). *Beyond the hot seat.* New York: Brunner/Mazel.

Foulds, M., & Hannigan, P. (1976). Effects of a Gestalt marathon workshop on measured self-actualization: A replication and follow-up study. *Journal of Consulting Psychology, 23,* 60–65.

Greenberg, L. S. (1979). Resolving splits: Use of the two-chair technique. *Psychotherapy: Theory, Research and Practice, 16,* 316–324.

Greenberg, L. S. (1986). Charge process research. *Journal of Consulting and Clinical Psychology, 54,* 4–9.

Greenberg, L. S., & Higgins, H. M. (1980). Effects of two-chair dialogues and focusing on conflict resolution. *Journal of Counseling Psychology, 27,* 221–224.

Guinan, J., & Foulds, M. (1970). Marathon groups: Facilitator of personal growth? *Journal of Consulting Psychology, 17,* 145–149.

Harman, R. (1984). Gestalt therapy research. *The Gestalt Journal, 7,* 61–69.

Hatcher, C., & Himelstein, P. (Eds.) (1976). *The handbook of Gestalt therapy.* New York: Jason Aronson.

Heidbreder, E. (1933). *Seven psychologies.* New York: Century.

Herman, S. N. (1972). The Gestalt orientation to organizational development. In *Contemporary organization development.* Bethel, ME: National Institute of Applied Behavioral Science.

Idhe, D. (1977). *Experimental phenomenology.* New York: G. P. Putnam & Sons, Capricorn Books.

Jacobs, L. (1978). I-thou relations in Gestalt therapy. Unpublished doctoral dissertation. California School of Professional Psychology, Los Angeles.

Kempler, W. (1973). Gestalt therapy. In R. J. Corsini (Ed.), *Current psychotherapies* (pp. 251–286). Itasca, IL: F. E. Peacock.

Kempler, W. (1974). *Principles of Gestalt family therapy.* Costa Mesa, CA: Kempler Institute.

Kogan, G. (1976). The genesis of Gestalt therapy. In C. Hatcher & P. Himelstein (Eds.), *The handbook of Gestalt therapy* (pp. 235–258). New York: Jason Aronson.

Kogan, J. (1980). *Gestalt therapy resources* (3rd ed.). Berkeley, CA: Transformation Press.

Lederman, J. (1970). Anger and the rocking chair. In J. Fagan & I. L. Shepherd (Eds.). *Gestalt therapy now* (pp. 274–284). Palo Alto, CA: Science and Behavior Books.

Levitsky, A., & Simkin, J. S. (1972). Gestalt therapy. In L. N. Solomon & B. Berzon (Eds.), *New perspectives on encounter groups* (pp. 245–253). San Francisco: Jossey-Bass.

Lieberman, M., Yalom, I., & Miles, M. (1973). *Encounter group: First facts.* New York: Basic Books.

O'Connell, V. F. (1970). Crisis psychotherapy: Person, dialogue and the organismic approach. In J. Fagin & I. L. Shepherd (Eds.), *Gestalt therapy now* (pp. 274–284). Palo Alto, CA: Science and Behavior Books.

Perls, F. S. (1947). *Ego, hunger and aggression.* London: Allen & Unwin. (Paperback edition, New York: Vintage, 1969).

Perls, F. S. (1948). Theory and technique of personality integration. *American Journal of Psychotherapy, 2,* 572–573.

Perls, F. S. (1967). Group vs. individual therapy. *ETC, 24,* 306–312.

Perls, F. S. (1969). *Gestalt therapy verbatim.* Moab, UT: Real People Press.

Perls, F. S. (1973). *The Gestalt approach.* Palo Alto: Science and Behavior Books. (Paperback edition, New York: Bantam, 1976).

Perls, F. S. (1975). Resolution. In J. O. Stevens (Ed.), *Gestalt is* (pp. 69–74). Moab, UT: People Press.

Perls, F. S. (1976). Gestalt therapy verbatim: Introduction. In C. Hatcher & P. Himelstein (Eds.), *The handbook of Gestalt therapy* (pp. 21–80). New York: Jason Aronson.

Perls, F. S., Hefferline, R. F., & Goodman, P. (1951). *Gestalt therapy.* New York: Julian Press.

Perls, L. (1973). Some aspects of Gestalt therapy. Annual Meeting of the Orthopsychiatric Association.

Perls, L. (1976). Comments on the new directions. In E. Smith (ed.), *The growing edge of Gestalt therapy* (pp. 221–226). New York: Brunner/Mazel.

Perls. L. (1978). Conceptions and misconceptions of Gestalt therapy. *Voices 14,* 31–36.

Polster, E. A. (1968). A contemporary psychotherapy. In P. D. Pursglove (Ed.), *Recognitions in Gestalt therapy* (pp. 3–19). New York: Funk & Wagnalls.

Polster, E., & Polster, M. (1973). *Gestalt therapy integrated.* New York: Brunner/Mazel.

Resnick, R. (1970). Chicken soup is poison. *Voices, 6,* 75–78. [Also in Stephenson, F. D. (Ed.) (1975). *Gestalt therapy primer* (pp. 142–146). Springfield, IL: Charles C Thomas.]

Rosanes-Berret, M.D. (1970). Gestalt therapy as an adjunct treatment for some visual problems. In J. Fagan & I. L. Shepherd (Eds.), *Gestalt therapy now* (pp. 257–262). Palo Alto, CA: Science and Behavior Books.

Rosenfeld, E. (1978). An oral history of Gestalt therapy. Part I: A conversation with Laura Perls. *The Gestalt Journal, 1* (1), 8–31.

Rosenfeld, E. (1981). The Gestalt bibliography. *The Gestalt Journal, 4,* (1), 8–31.

Sartre, J. P. (1966). *Being and nothingness.* New York: Washington Square Press.

Shepherd, I. L. (1970). Limitations and cautions in the Gestalt approach. In J. Fagan & I. L. Shepherd (Eds.), *Gestalt therapy now* (pp. 234–238). Palo Alto, CA: Science and Behavior Books.

Simkin, J. S. (Ed.) (1968). *Festschrift for Fritz Perls.* Los Angeles, CA: Author.

Simkin, J. S. (1969). *In the now.* A training film. Beverly Hills, CA.

Simkin, J. S. (1970). Mary: A session with a passive patient. In J. Fagan & I. L. Shepherd (Eds.), *Gestalt therapy now* (pp. 162–168). Palo Alto, CA: Science and Behavior Books.

Simkin, J. S. (1976). *Gestalt therapy minilectures.* Millbrae, CA: Celestial Arts.

Simkin, J. S. (1979). Gestalt therapy. In R. J. Corsini (Ed.), *Current psychotherapies (2nd ed.)* (pp. 273–301). Itasca, IL: F. E. Peacock.

Smith, E. (1976). *The growing edge of Gestalt therapy.* New York: Brunner/Mazel.

Wertheimer, M. (1945). *Productive thinking.* New York: Harper & Brothers.

Wysong, J. (1986). *Gestalt bibliography.* New York: The Center for Gestalt Development.

Yontef, G. (1969). *A review of the practice of Gestalt therapy.* Los Angeles, CA: Trident Books. [Also in Stephenson, F. D. (Ed.). *Gestalt therapy primer* (pp. 161–208). Springfield, IL: Charles C Thomas.]

Yontef, G. (1976). Gestalt therapy: Clinical phenomenology. In V. Binder, A. Binder & R. Rimland (Eds.), *Modern therapies* (pp. 65–79). New York: Prentice-Hall. [Also in *The Gestalt Journal,* 1979, 1, (1979), 27–45.]

Yontef, G. (1981a). The future of Gestalt therapy: A symposium with L. Perls,

M. Polster, J. Zinker, & M. V. Miller. *The Gestalt Journal, 4,* 7–11.

Yontef, G. (1981b). Mediocrity and excellence: An identity crisis in Gestalt therapy. *ERIC/CAPS,* University of Michigan, *214,* 062.

Yontef, G. (1982). Gestalt therapy: Its inheritance from Gestalt psychology. *Gestalt Theory, 4,* 23–39.

Yontef, G. (1983). Gestalt therapie als dialogische Methode. *Integrative Therapie, 9,* 98–130.

Zinker, J. C. (1977). *Creative process in Gestalt therapy.* New York: Brunner/ Mazel.

Zinker, J. D., & Fink, S. L. (1966). The possibility for psychological growth in a dying person. *Journal of General Psychology, 74,* 185–189.

ROLLO MAY

10

Existential Psychotherapy

ROLLO MAY and IRVIN YALOM

OVERVIEW

Existential psychotherapy arose spontaneously in the minds and works of a number of psychologists and psychiatrists in Europe in the 1940s and 1950s who were concerned with finding a way of understanding human beings that was more reliable and more basic than the then current psychotherapies. The "existential orientation in psychiatry," wrote Ludwig Binswanger, one of its spokesmen, "arose from dissatisfaction with the prevailing efforts to gain scientific understanding in psychiatry" (1956, p. 144). These existential therapists believed drives in Freudian psychology, conditioning in behaviorism, and archetypes in Jungianism all had their own significance. But where was the actual, *immediate person* to whom these things were happening? How can we be sure that we are seeing patients as they really are, or are we simply seeing a projection of our own theories *about* them?

These therapists were keenly aware that we are living in an age of transition, when almost every human being feels alienated from fellow humans, threatened by nuclear war and economic upsets, perplexed by the radical changes in marriage and almost all other mores in our culture—in short, almost everyone is beset by anxiety.

Existential psychotherapy is not a specific technical approach that presents a new set of rules for therapy. It asks deep questions about the nature of the human being and the nature of anxiety, despair, grief, loneliness, isolation, and anomie. It also deals centrally with the questions of creativity and love. Out of the understanding of the meaning of these human experiences, existential psychotherapists have devised methods of therapy that do not fall into the common error of distorting human beings in the very effort of trying to help them.

BASIC CONCEPTS

The "I-Am" Experience

The realization of one's being—"I am now living and I could take my life"—can have a salutary effect on a patient. "The idea of suicide has saved many lives," said Nietzsche. The human being will be victimized by circumstances and other people until he or she is able to realize, "I am the one living, experiencing. I choose my own being."

It is not easy to define *being* because in our society we often subordinate the sense of being to our economic status or the external type of life that we lead. A person is known (and knows self) not as a being or a self, but as a ticket seller in the subway, a grocer, a professor, a vice president of AT&T, or as whatever his or her economic function may be. This loss of the sense of being is related to mass collectivist trends and widespread conformist tendencies in our culture. The French existentialist Gabriel Marcel (May, Angel & Ellenberger, 1958, p. 40), makes this trenchant challenge: "Indeed I wonder if a psychoanalytic method, deeper and more discerning than any that has been evolved until now, would not reveal the morbid effects of the repression of this sense [of being] and of the ignoring of this need."

Existential therapy endeavors to be this "deeper and more discerning" type of therapy.

A patient, the daughter of a prostitute, had been an illegitimate child and had been brought up by relatives. She said:

I remember walking that day under the elevated tracks in a slum area, feeling the thought, *I am an illegitimate child.* I recall the sweat pouring forth in my anguish in trying to accept that fact. Then I understood what it must feel like to accept "I am a Negro in the midst of privileged whites," or "I am blind in the midst of people who see." Later on that night I woke up and it came to me this way, "I accept the fact that I am an illegitimate child." But "I am not a child anymore." So it is "I am illegitimate." That is not so either. "I was born illegitimate." Then what is left? What is left is

this, "I Am." This act of contact and acceptance with "I am," once gotten hold of, gave me (what I think was for me the first time) the experience "Since I Am, I have the right to be." (May et al., 1958)

This "I-Am" experience is not in itself a solution to an individual's problems. It is, rather, the *precondition* for the solution. The patient in the preceding example spent some two years thereafter working through specific psychological problems, which she was then able to do on the basis of her experience of being.

This experience of being points also to the experience of *not being*, or nothingness. Nonbeing is illustrated in the threat of death, or destructive hostility, severe incapacitating anxiety, critical sickness, and so on. The threat of nonbeing is present in greater or lesser intensity at all times. When we cross the street while looking both ways to guard against being struck by an automobile, when someone makes a remark that disparages us, or when we go into an examination ill-prepared— all of these represent the threat of nonbeing.

The "I-Am" experience, or the experience of being, is known in existential therapy as an *ontological* experience. This word comes from two Greek words, *ontos* meaning "to be" and *logical* meaning "the science of." Thus it is the "science of being." The term *ontological* is valuable in existential psychotherapy, as we shall see in the following discussion of anxiety.

Normal and Neurotic Anxiety

Existential therapists define anxiety more broadly than other psychotherapeutic groups. *Anxiety arises from our personal need to survive, to preserve our being, and to assert our being.* Anxiety shows itself physically in the faster beat of the heart, in the rising of blood pressure, the preparing of the skeletal muscles for fighting or fleeing, and, most painful of all, the sense of apprehension within ourselves. Rollo May defines anxiety as, "the threat to our existence or to values we identify with our existence" (1977, p. 205).

Anxiety is more basic than fear. In psychotherapy, one of our aims is to help the patient confront anxiety as fully as possible, thus reducing anxiety to fears, which are then objective and can be dealt with. But the main therapeutic function is to help the patient confront the normal anxiety that is an unavoidable part of the human condition.

Normal anxiety has three characteristics. First, it is proportionate to the situation confronted. Second, normal anxiety does not require repression: we can come to terms with it, as we come to terms with the fact that we all face eventual death. Third, such anxiety can be used creatively, for example, as a stimulus to help identify and confront the dilemma out of which the anxiety arose.

Neurotic anxiety, on the other hand, is not appropriate to the situation. For example, parents may be so anxious that their child will be hit by a car that they never let the child leave the house. Second, it is repressed, in the way most of us repress the fear of nuclear war. Third, neurotic anxiety is destructive, not constructive. Neurotic anxiety tends to paralyze the individual rather than stimulate creativity.

The function of therapy is *not* to do away with all anxiety. No person could survive completely without anxiety. The cliché that mental health consists of living without anxiety is absurd. Mental health is living as much as possible without *neurotic* anxiety, but *with* the ability to tolerate the unavoidable existential anxiety of living.

Guilt and Guilt Feelings

The experience of guilt has special meaning for the existential therapist. Guilt can, like anxiety, take both normal and neurotic forms. Neurotic guilt feelings (generally called *guilt*) often arise out of fantasized transgressions. Other forms of guilt, which we call *normal guilt*, sensitize us to the ethical aspects of our behavior.

Still another form is guilt toward ourselves for failure to live up to our potentialities, for "forgetting being" as Medard Boss puts it. The attitude toward such guilt in existential therapy is well illustrated in a case Medard Boss (1957b) cites of a severe obsessional-compulsive whom he treated. This patient, a physician suffering from hand-washing compulsions, had gone through both Freudian and Jungian analyses. He had had for some time a recurrent dream involving church steeples, interpreted in the Freudian analysis in terms of phallic symbols and in the Jungian in terms of religious archetypal symbols. The patient could discuss these interpretations intelligently and at length, but his neurotic compulsive behavior, after temporary abeyance, continued as crippling as ever. During the first months of his analysis with Boss, the patient reported a recurrent dream in which he would approach a lavatory door that would always be locked. Boss confined himself only to asking each time why the door needed to be locked—to "rattling the doorknob," as Boss put it. Finally the patient had a dream in which he opened the door and found himself inside a church. He was waist deep in feces and was tugged by a rope wrapped around his waist and leading up to the bell tower. The patient was suspended in such tension that he thought he would be pulled to pieces. He then went through a psychotic episode of four days, during which Boss remained by his bedside and after which the analysis continued with an eventual successful outcome.

Boss (1957b) points out that the patient was guilty because he had locked up some essential potentialities in himself. *Therefore* he had guilt feelings. "If you lock up potentialities, you are guilty . . . (or indebted to) . . . what is given you in your origin, in your 'core.' In this . . . condition of being indebted and being guilty are founded all guilt feelings, in whatever thousand and one concrete forms and malformations they may appear in actuality." This patient had locked up both the bodily and the spiritual possibilities of experience (what had been called the "drive" aspect and the "god" aspect, as Boss also phrases it). The patient had previously accepted the libido and archetype explanations and knew them all too well; but that is a good way, says Boss, to escape the whole thing. Because the patient did not accept and take into his existence these two aspects, he was guilty, indebted to himself. This was the origin of his neurosis and psychosis.

The Three Forms of World

Another basic concept in existential psychotherapy is called being-in-the-world. This is to say that we must understand the phenomenological world in which the patient exists and participates.

A person's world cannot be comprehended by describing the environment, no matter how complex the description. The environment is only one mode of world. The biologist J. von Uexküll argues that one is justified in assuming as many environments as there are animals, depending on how the ant or the elephant or the fox participates in this environment. "There is not one space and time only," he goes on to say, "but as many spaces and times as there are subjects" (von Uexküll, cited in May et al., 1958). How much more is it true that the human being also has his or her own world? This confronts us with no easy problem: for we cannot describe world in purely objective terms, nor is world to be limited to our subjective, imaginative participation in the structure around us, although that too is part of being-in-the-world.

The human world is the structure of meaningful relationships in which a person exists and in the design of which, generally without realizing it, he or she participates. That is, the same past or present circumstances can mean very different things to different people. Thus, world includes the past events that condition one's existence and all the vast variety of deterministic influences that operate upon one. But it is these *as one relates to them*, as one is aware of them, molds, and constantly reforms them. For to be aware of one's world means at the same time to be designing it, *constituting* one's world.

From the point of view of existential psychotherapy, there are three modes of world. The first is *Umwelt*, meaning "world around," the biological world, what is generally called the environment. The second is *Mitwelt*, literally the "with-world," the world of one's fellow human beings, one's community. The third is *Eigenwelt*, the "own-world," the relationship to one's self.

The first, *Umwelt*, is the world of objects about us, the natural world. All organisms have an *Umwelt*. For animals and human beings the *Umwelt* includes biological needs, drives, instincts—the world we would exist in if we had no self-awareness. It is the world of natural law and natural cycles, of sleep and awakeness, of being born and dying, of desire and relief, the world of finiteness and biological determinism to which each of us must in some way adjust. Existential analysts accept the reality of the natural world. "The natural law is as valid as ever," as Kierkegaard put it.

Strictly speaking, animals have an environment but human beings have a world, for world includes the structure of meaning designed by the inter-relationship of the persons in it.

The *Eigenwelt*, or "own-world," has been least adequately dealt with or understood in modern psychology and depth-psychology. Own-world presupposes self-awareness and self-relatedness and is uniquely present in human beings. It is a grasping of what something in the world—this bouquet of flowers, this other person—personally means to the individual observer. D. T. Suzuki has remarked that in Eastern languages, such as Japanese, adjectives always include the implication of "for-me-ness." That is to say, "This flower is beautiful" means "For me, this flower is beautiful."

One implication of this analysis of the modes of being-in-the-world is that it gives us a basis for understanding love. The human experience of love obviously cannot be adequately described within the confines of *Umwelt*. We can never accurately speak of human beings as "sexual objects," because once a person is a sexual object, we are not talking about a person anymore. The interpersonal schools of personality theory have dealt with love as an interpersonal relationship, particularly in Harry Stack Sullivan's concept of the meaning of the word *chum* and in Erich Fromm's analysis of the difficulties of love in contemporary estranged society. But there is reason for doubting whether a theoretical foundation for going further is yet present in these or other schools. Without an adequate concept of *Umwelt*, love becomes empty of vitality, and without *Eigenwelt*, it lacks power and the capacity to fructify itself. The importance of *Eigenwelt* was stressed by Friedrich Nietzsche and Søren Kierkegaard, who continually insisted that to love presupposes that one must already have become the "true individual," the "Solitary One," the one who "has comprehended the deep secret that also in loving another person one must be sufficient unto oneself."

The Significance of Time

Existential psychotherapists are struck by the fact that the most profound human experiences, such as anxiety, depression, and joy, occur more in the dimension of time than in space. Eugene Minkowski, a psychiatrist in Paris, has presented a case study that illustrates the time dimension. In his study of a depressed schizophrenic suffering under the delusion that he would be executed, Minkowski points out that the patient could not relate to time—that is, could not hope for the future—that every day was a separate island with no past and no future. The patient could not sense any continuity with tomorrow. Traditionally a psychiatrist would reason simply that this patient cannot relate to the future, cannot "temporize," *because* he has his delusion that he is going to be executed. Minkowski proposes the exact opposite. "Could we not," he asks, "on the contrary suppose *the more basic disorder is the distorted attitude toward the future,* while the delusion is only one of its manifestations?" (Minkowski, cited in May et al., 1958, p. 66).

Minkowski goes on to consider this possibility in his case study. His original approach throws a beam of illumination on these dark, unexplored areas of time and introduces a new freedom from the limits and shackles of clinical thought, in which time is bound only to the traditional conceptions. O. Hobart Mowrer (1950) held that "Time binding is the distinctive characteristic of human personality. That is, the capacity to bring the past into the present as part of the total causal nexus in which living organisms act and react, together with the capacity to act in the light of the long-term future—is 'the essence of mind and personality alike.' "

Existential therapists agree with Henri Bergson that "time is the heart of existence" and that our error in the modern day has been to think of ourselves primarily in terms of space, as though we were objects which could be located like substances at this spot or that. By this distortion we lose our genuine existential relation with ourselves, and indeed also with other persons around us. As a consequence of this overemphasis on spatial thinking, says Bergson, "the moments when we grasp ourselves are rare, and consequently we are seldom free" (Bergson, cited in May et al., 1958, p. 56).

But in the with-world, the mode of personal relations and love, we can see particularly that quantitative time has much less to do with the significance of an occurrence. The nature or degree of one's love, for example, can never be measured by the number of years one has known the loved one. It is true, of course, that clock time has much to do with *Mitwelt:* many people sell their time on an hourly basis and daily life runs on schedules. We are referring rather to the inner meaning of the events. "No clock strikes for the happy one," says a German proverb. Indeed, the most significant events in a person's psychological existence are likely to be precisely the ones which are "immediate," breaking through the usual steady progression of time, like a sudden insight or a view of beauty that one sees in an instant, but which may remain in one's memory for days and months.

Finally, the *Eigenwelt,* the world of self-relatedness, self-awareness, and insight into the meaning of an event for one's self, has practically nothing whatever to do with clock time, in which one hour routinely follows another. The essence of self-awareness and insight is that they are *there*— instantaneous and immediate—and the moment of awareness has its significance for all time. One can see this easily by noting what happens in oneself at the instant of an insight. The instant occurs with suddenness; it is born whole, so to speak. One will discover that, though meditating on an insight for an hour or so may reveal many of its further implications, the insight is not clearer—and disconcertingly enough, often not as clear—at the end of the hour as it was at the beginning.

Whether or not a patient can even recall the significant events of the past depends upon his or her decision with regard to the future. Every therapist knows that patients may bring up past memories ad nauseam without any memory ever moving them, the whole recital being flat, inconsequential, and tedious. From an existential point of view, the problem is not that these patients endured impoverished pasts; it is rather that they cannot or do not commit themselves to the present and future. Their past does not become alive because nothing matters enough to them in the future. Some hope and commitment to work toward changing something in the immediate future, be it overcoming anxiety or other painful symptoms or integrating the self for further creativity, are necessary before a patient's uncovering of the past will have reality.

Our Human Capacity to Transcend the Immediate Situation

If we are to understand a given person as existing, dynamic, at every moment becoming, we cannot avoid the dimension of transcendence. Existing involves a continual emerging, in the sense of emergent evolution, a transcending of one's past and present in order to reach the future. Thus *transcendere*—literally "to climb over and beyond"—describes what every human being is engaged in doing every moment when not seriously ill or temporarily blocked by despair or anxiety. One can, of course, see emergent evolution in all life processes. Neitzsche has his old Zarathustra proclaim, "And this secret spake Life herself to me. 'Behold' said she, 'I am that which must ever surpass itself'" (cited in May et al., 1958, p. 72).

The neurobiological base for this capacity is classically described by Kurt Goldstein (cited in May et al., 1958, p. 72). He found that brain-injured patients—chiefly soldiers with portions of the frontal cortex shot away—

had specifically lost the ability to abstract, to think in terms of the possible. They were tied to any immediate concrete situation in which they happened to be. When their closets happened to be in disarray, they were thrown into profound anxiety and disordered behavior. They exhibited compulsive orderliness—which is a way of holding oneself at every moment rigidly to the concrete situation. When asked to write their names on a sheet of paper, they would typically write in the very corner, any venture out from the specific boundaries of the edges of the paper representing too great a threat. Goldstein held that the distinctive capacity of the normal human being is precisely this capacity to abstract, to use symbols, to orient oneself beyond the immediate limits of the given time and space, to think, in terms of "the possible." The injured, or "ill," patients were characterized by loss of range of possibility. Their world space was shrunk, their time curtailed, and they suffered a consequent radical loss of freedom.

We human beings possess the ability to transcend time and space by transporting ourselves back 2,000 years to ancient Greece, and we can watch the drama of Oedipus being performed in ancient Athens. We can instantaneously transport ourselves to the future, conceiving what life will be like in, say, the year 2500. These forms of transcendence are part and parcel of human consciousness. This capacity is exemplified in the human being's unique capacity to think and talk in symbols. Thus, to make promises presupposes conscious self-relatedness and is a very different thing from simple conditioned social behavior, acting in terms of the requirements of the group or herd or hive. Jean-Paul Sartre writes that dishonesty is a uniquely human form of behavior. "The lie is a behavior of transcendence," because to lie we must at the same moment *know* we are departing from the truth.

This capacity to transcend the immediate situation is not a "faculty" to be listed along with other faculties. It is rather given in the ontological nature of being human. To abstract, to objectivate, are evidences of it, but as Martin Heidegger puts it, "transcendence does not consist of objectivation, but objectivation presupposes transcendence" (cited in May et al., 1958, p. 75). The fact that human beings can be self-related gives them, as one manifestation, the capacity to objectify their world, to think and talk in symbols and so forth. This is Kierkegaard's point when he reminds us that to understand the self we must see clearly that "imagination is not one faculty on a par with others, but, if one would so speak, it is the faculty *instar omnium* (for all faculties). What feeling, knowledge, or will a man has depends in the last resort upon what imagination he has, that is to say, upon how these things are reflected. Imagination is the possibility of all reflection, and the intensity of this medium is the possibility of the intensity of the self" (Kierkegaard, 1954, p. 163).

OTHER SYSTEMS

Behaviorism

First we shall consider the differences between existential theory and the theory of *behaviorism*. This radical distinction can be seen when we note the chasm between abstract truth and existential reality.

Kenneth W. Spence (1956), leader of one wing of behavior theory, wrote: "The question of whether any particular realm of behavior phenomena is more real or closer to real life and hence should be given priority in investigation does not, or at least should not, arise for the psychologist as scientist." That is to say, it does not primarily matter whether what is being studied is real or not.

What realms, then, should be selected for study? Spence gives priority to phenomena that lend themselves "to the degrees of control and analysis necessary for the formulation of abstract laws." Nowhere has this point been put more unabashedly and clearly than by Spence—what can be reduced to abstract laws is selected, and whether what is studied has *reality* or not is irrelevant to this goal. Many an impressive system in psychology has been erected, with abstraction piled high upon abstraction —the authors succumbing, as intellectuals are wont, to their "edifice complex" until an admirable and imposing structure is built. The only trouble is that the edifice has often been separated from reality in its very foundations.

Psychiatrists and psychologists in the existential psychotherapy movement insist that it is necessary and possible to have a science which studies human beings in their reality.

Orthodox Freudianism

Ludwig Binswanger and some other existential therapists differed from Freud in several important respects, including rejection of the concept of the patient propelled by instincts and drives. As Sartre put it, Freudians have lost the human being *to whom* these things happen.

The existentialists also question the view of the unconscious as a reservoir of tendencies, desires, and drives from which the motivation for behavior arises. This "cellar" view of the unconscious leads patients in therapy to avoid responsibility for their actions by such phrases as, "My unconscious did it, not I." Existentialists always insist that the patient in therapy accept responsibility by asking such questions as, "Whose unconscious is it?"

The differences between existentialism and Freudianism are also seen in the modes of the world. The genius and the value of Freud's work lie in uncovering the mode of instincts, drives, contingency, and biological determinism. But traditional Freudianism has only a shadowy concept of the interrelation of persons as *subjects*.

The Interpersonal School of Psychotherapy

A consideration of the three modes of world discloses the differences between existential therapy and the interpersonal school, such as seen in the writings of Erich Fromm and H. S. Sullivan. Interpersonal schools do have a theoretical basis for dealing directly with *Mitwelt*. This is shown, to take only one example, in Sullivan's theory. Though they should not be considered identical, *Mitwelt* and interpersonal theory have a great deal in common. The danger of this point, however, is that if *Eigenwelt*, one's own-world is omitted, interpersonal relations tend to become hollow and sterile. Sullivan argued against the concept of individual personality and went to great efforts to define the self in terms of "reflected appraisal" and social categories—that is, the roles the person plays in the interpersonal world. Theoretically, this suffers from considerable logical inconsistency and indeed goes directly against other con-

tributions of Sullivan. Practically, it tends to make the self a mirror of the group around one, to empty the self of vitality and originality, and to reduce the interpersonal world to mere "social relations." It opens the way to a tendency directly opposed to the goals of Sullivan and other interpersonal thinkers: namely, social conformity.

Jungian Psychology

There are similarities between Jungian and existential therapy. Medard Boss was a member for several years of the seminar that Jung called together in regular meetings at his house. But the main criticism existentialists make is that Jungians too quickly avoid the immediate existential crises of patients by leaping into theory. This is illustrated in Boss' case related in the section "Guilt and Guilt Feelings." A patient who was afraid to go out of the house alone was analyzed by a Jungian therapist for six years, in the course of which the therapist interpreted several dreams as indicating that "God is speaking to you." The patient was flattered, but still couldn't go out of her house alone. She later was enabled to get over her crippling neurosis by an existential therapist who insisted that she could overcome her problem only if she actively *wanted* to, which was a way of insisting that she, not God, needed to take responsibility for her problem.

Client-Centered Approach

The difference between existentialism and Rogerian therapy is seen in statements made by Rollo May when he was acting as a judge of client-centered therapy in the client-centered experiment at the University of Wisconsin. Twelve outside experts were sent tapes of the therapy to judge. Rollo May (1982) as one of the outside experts, reported that he often felt that there were not two distinct people in the room. When the therapist only reflects the patient's words, there transpires "only an amorphous kind of identity rather than two subjects interacting *in a world in which both participate, and in which love and hate, trust and doubt, conflicts and dependence, come out and can be understood and assimilated*" (p. 16). May was concerned that the therapist's overidentification with the patient could "take away the patient's opportunity to experience himself as a subject in his own right or to take a stand against the therapist, to experience being in an interpersonal world" (p. 16).

In spite of the fact that client-centered therapists, both individually and collectively, have advocated openness and freedom in the therapeutic relationship, the outside judges in the Wisconsin study concluded that "the therapist's rigid and controlling nature closed him off to many of his own as well as to the patient's experiences" (p. 16).

One of the Rogerian therapists, after experience as an independent therapist, wrote this criticism:

I used the early concept of the client-centered therapist to bolster the inhibition of my anger, my aggression, etc. I got some feedback at that time that it was difficult for people, because I was so nice, to tell me things that were *not* nice, and that it was hard for people to get angry at *me*. (Raskin, 1978, p. 367)

In other words, client-centered therapy is not fully existential in that it does not confront the patient directly and firmly.

HISTORY

PRECURSORS

There are two streams in the history of human thought. One is of *essences*, seen most clearly in Plato's belief that there are perfect forms of everything and that things such as a specific chair are imperfect copies. These essences are clearest if we imagine mathematics: a perfect circle and a perfect square exist in heaven, of which our human circles and squares are imperfect copies. This requires an abstraction that leaves the *existence* of the individual thing out of the picture. For example, we can demonstrate simply that three apples added to three makes six. But this would be just as true if we substituted unicorns for apples. It makes no difference to mathematical truth whether unicorns actually exist. A proposition can be true without being real. Perhaps just because this approach has worked so magnificently in certain areas of science, we tend to forget that it omits *the living individual*.

But there is another stream of thought coming down through history: namely, *existence*. This viewpoint holds that truth depends upon the existing person, existing in a given situation (world) at that *time*. Hence the term *existential*. This is what Sartre meant in his famous statement, "Existence precedes essence." The human being's awareness (i.e., his existence) precedes everything he has to say about the world around him.

Down through history, the existential tradition is exemplified by many thinkers. These include Augustine, who held that "Truth dwells in the inner man"; Duns Scotus, who argued against Thomas Aquinas' rational essences and insisted that human *will* must be taken as basic to any statement; and Blaise Pascal, as in his famous statement, "The heart has its reasons which reason knows nothing of."

There remains in our day the chasm

between truth and reality. And the crucial question that confronts us in psychology and other aspects of the science of man is precisely this chasm between what is abstractly true and what is existentially real for the given living person.

BEGINNINGS

Kierkegaard, Nietzsche, and those existentialists who followed them foresaw this growing split between truth and reality in Western culture, and they opposed the delusion that reality can be comprehended in an abstracted, detached way. Though they protested vehemently against arid intellectualism, they were by no means simple activists, nor were they antirational. Anti-intellectualism and other movements that make thinking subordinate to feeling must not be confused with existentialism. Either alternative—making a human being entirely subject or object—results in *losing the living, existing person*. Kierkegaard and the existential thinkers appealed to a reality underlying *both* subjectivity and objectivity. We must not only study a person's experience as such, they held, but even more, we must study the one who is doing the experiencing.

It is by no means accidental that the greatest existentialists in the nineteenth century, Kierkegaard and Nietzsche, happen also to be among the most remarkable psychologists of all time. A contemporary leader of existential philosophy, Karl Jaspers, originally a psychiatrist, wrote a notable text on psychopathology. When one reads Kierkegaard's profound analyses of anxiety and despair or Nietzsche's amazingly acute insights into the dynamics of resentment and the guilt and hostility that accompany repressed emotional powers, it is difficult to realize that one is reading works written 75 and 100 years ago and not a contemporary psychological analysis.

Existential therapists are centrally concerned with rediscovering the living person amid the dehumanization of modern culture, and in order to do this they engage in depth psychological analysis. Their concern is not with isolated psychological reactions in themselves but rather with the psychological being of the living person doing the experiencing. They use psychological terms with an ontological meaning.

The existential philosophers included Martin Heidegger and Karl Jaspers in Germany; Jean-Paul Sartre, Gabriel Marcel, and Nicolas Berdyaev in France; and José Ortega y Gasset and Miguel de Unamuno y Jugo in Spain. Paul Tillich shows the existential approach in his work, and in many ways his book *The Courage to Be* (1952) is the best and most cogent presentation of existential philosophy.

Existential therapy sprang up spontaneously in different parts of Europe and among different schools, and has a diverse body of researchers and creative thinkers.[1] There were

---

[1]In this orientation section we note the relation between existentialism and oriental thought as shown in the writings of Lao-tzu and Zen Buddhism. The similarities are striking. One sees this immediately in glancing at some quotations from Lao-tzu's *The Way of Life* (Bynner, 1946): "Existence is beyond the power of words to define: terms may be used but none of them is absolute." "Existence, by nothing bred, breeds everything, parent of the universe." "Existence is infinite, not to be defined; and though it seem but a bit of wood in your hand, to carve as you please, it is not to be lightly played with and laid down." "The way to do is to be." "Rather abide at the center of your being; for the more you leave it, the less you learn."

psychiatrists—Eugene Minkowski in Paris, Erwin Straus in Germany and then in America, V. E. von Gebsattel in Germany—who represent chiefly the first, phenomenological stage of this movement. Ludwig Binswanger, A. Storch, Medard Boss, G. Bally, Roland Kuhn in Switzerland, and J. H. Van Den Berg and F. J. Buytendijk in Holland represented the second, or existential, stage.

CURRENT STATUS

Existential psychotherapy was introduced to the United States in 1958 with the publication of *Existence: A New Dimension in Psychiatry and Psychology*, edited by Rollo May, Ernest Angel, and Henri Ellenberger. The main presentation and summary of existential therapy was in the first two chapters, written by May: "The Origins of the Existential Movement in Psychology" and the "Contributions of Existential Psychology." The remainder of the book is made up of essays and case studies by Henri Ellenberger, Eugene Minkowski, Erwin Straus, V. E. von Gebsattel, Ludwig Binswanger, and Ronald Kuhn. The first comprehensive textbook in existential psychiatry was by Irwin Yalom (1981) and entitled *Existential Psychotherapy*.

The spirit of existential psychotherapy has never supported the formation of specific institutes because it deals with the *presuppositions underlying therapy of any kind*. Its concern was with concepts about human beings and not with specific techniques. This leads to the dilemma that existential therapy has been quite influential, but there are very few adequate training courses in this kind of therapy simply because it is not a specific training in technique.

The founders of the existential movement always stated that specific training in techniques of therapy could be obtained at any number of schools of therapy, and that the student was responsible for molding his or her own presuppositions in existential form.

Rollo May, an existentialist before he knew the word, found that the existing person was the important consideration, and not a theory *about* this person. He had argued in his Ph.D. dissertation, published under the title *The Meaning of Anxiety* in 1950, for a concept of normal anxiety as the basis for a theory of human beings. He had already, before his training in the William Alanson White Institute, experienced the futility of going to analysis five times a week for two years. He was trained as a psychoanalyst in the William Alanson White Institute, the neo-Freudian institute in New York, and was already a practicing analyst when he read in the early 1950s about existential therapies in Europe. He felt these new concepts in existential psychology were the ones he needed but had never been able to formulate.

The theme of the International Congress of Psychotherapy in 1958 in Barcelona, Spain, was "Existential Psychotherapy." Five hundred therapists, including such prominent psychiatrists as Medard Boss and Jacques Lacan, and a hundred therapists from the United States, attended this conference. Some present followed Freud, some Jung, some were from the William Alanson White Institute, but all paid tribute to the value of the insights and concepts of existential therapy.

The belief of the founders of existential psychotherapy is that its contributions will be absorbed into other schools. Fritz Perls, in the foreword of *Gestalt Therapy Verbatim* (1969), states quite accurately that Gestalt therapy is a form of existential psychotherapy. Therapists trained in different schools can legitimately call themselves existential if their assumptions are similar to those described in this chapter. Irvin Yalom was trained in the neo-Freudian tradition. Even such an erstwhile behavior therapist as Arnold Lazarus uses some existential presuppositions in his multimodal psychotherapy. All of this is possible because existential psychotherapy is a way of conceiving the human being. It goes deeper than the other forms of psychotherapy to emphasize the assumptions underlying all systems of psychotherapy.

Major works include May's *The Meaning of Anxiety* (1977), *Man's Search for Himself* (1953), and *Existential Psychology* (1961). Others are James Bugental's *The Search for Existential Identity* (1976), Medard Boss' *The Analysis of Dreams* (1957a) and *Psychoanalysis and Daseinanalysis (1982)*, and Viktor Frankl's *Man's Search for Meaning* (1963). Helmut Kaiser has written valuably on existential therapy in his *Effective Psychotherapy* (1965). Leslie Farber (1966, 1976), Avery Weisman (1965), and Lester Havens (1974) have also contributed significantly to the existential literature.

PERSONALITY

THEORY OF PERSONALITY

Existential psychotherapy is a form of *dynamic psychotherapy* that posits a dynamic model of personality structure. *Dynamic* is a commonly used term in psychology and psychotherapy. We often, for example, speak of the patient's "psychodynamics," or a "dynamic" approach to therapy. *Dynamic* has both lay and technical meanings, and it is necessary to be precise about its meaning in the context of personality theory. In its lay meaning *dynamic* has the connotation of vitality; the word evokes such associations as dynamo, dynamite, a dynamic football player, or a dynamic political leader.

The technical meaning of *dynamic* relevant to personality theory refers to the concept of *force*. Its use in personality theory was first invoked by Freud, who viewed the personality as a system consisting of forces in conflict with one another. The result of this conflict is the constellation of emotions and behavior (both adaptive and pathological) that constitute personality. Furthermore (and this is an essential part of the definition), these forces in conflict *exist at different levels of awareness*. Indeed, some of the forces are entirely out of awareness and exist on an unconscious plane.

Thus, when we speak of the "psychodynamics" of an individual, we refer to that individual's conflicting, conscious and unconscious forces, motives, and fears. "Dynamic psychotherapy" is psychotherapy based upon this dynamic model of personality structure.

There are many dynamic models of personality. To differentiate these various models and to define the existential model of personality structure, we must ask: What is the *content* of the internal, conscious, and unconscious struggle? Forces, motives, and fears conflict with one another within the personality. But which forces? Which motives? Which fears?

The existential view of the internal struggle can be made clearer by contrasting it with two other common dynamic views of personality: the Freudian model and the interpersonal (neo-Freudian) model.

The Freudian Model of Psychodynamics

The Freudian model posits that the individual is governed by innate instinctual forces that, like a fern frond, inexorably unfurl throughout the psychosexual developmental cycle. Freud postulated conflicts on several fronts: dual instincts collide with one another (ego instincts versus libido instincts in Freud's first theory or, in the second theory, Eros versus Thanatos); the instincts also collide with the demands of the environment, and later the instincts collide with the superego (the internalized environment).

We can summarize the nature of the conflict in the Freudian dynamic model by stating that an instinctually driven being is at war with a world that prevents the satisfaction of these innate aggressive and sexual drives.

The Interpersonal (Neo-Freudian) Model of Psychodynamics

In the interpersonal model of personality (posited by such theorists as Harry Stack Sullivan, Karen Horney, and Erich Fromm), the individual is not instinct guided and preprogrammed, but is instead almost entirely shaped by the cultural and interpersonal environment. The child desperately requires acceptance and approval by important survival figures. But the child also has an inner press toward growth, mastery, and autonomy, and these tendencies are not always compatible with the demands of significant adults in the child's life. If the child is unlucky enough to have parents who are too caught up in their own neurotic struggles to provide the

child security and encourage the child's autonomous development, then a conflict develops between the child's need for security and natural growth inclinations. In such a struggle, growth is always compromised for the sake of security.

Existential Psychodynamics

The existential model of personality rests on a different view of inner conflict. It postulates that the basic conflict is not with suppressed instinctual drives or with the significant adults in the individual's early life; instead the conflict is between the individual and the "givens" of existence.

What are these "givens"? The reflective individual can discover them without a great deal of effort. If we "bracket" the outside world, if we put aside the everyday concerns with which we ordinarily fill our lives and reflect deeply upon our situation in the world, then we must confront certain "ultimate concerns" (to use Tillich's phrase) that are an inescapable part of the human being's existence in the world.

Yalom (1981) identifies four ultimate concerns that have considerable relevance for psychotherapy: *death, freedom, isolation,* and *meaninglessness.* The individual's confrontation with each of these constitutes the content of the inner conflict from the existential frame of reference.

Death. Death is the most obvious ultimate concern. It is apparent to all that death will come and that there is no escape. It is a terrible truth, and at the deepest levels we respond to it with mortal terror. "Everything," as Spinoza states, "wishes to persist in its own being" (1954, p. 6). From the existential point of view a core inner conflict is between awareness of inevitable death and the simultaneous wish to continue to live.

Death plays a major role in one's internal experience. It haunts the individual as nothing else. It rumbles continuously under the membrane of life. The child at an early age is pervasively concerned with death, and one of the child's major developmental tasks is to deal with the terror of obliteration.

To cope with this terror, we erect defenses against death awareness. These defenses are denial-based; they shape character structure and, if maladaptive, result in clinical maladjustment. Psychopathology, to a very great extent, is the result of failed death transcendence; that is, symptoms and maladaptive character structure have their origin in the individual terror of death.

Freedom. Ordinarily we do not think of freedom as a source of anxiety. Quite the contrary, freedom is generally viewed as an unequivocally positive concept. The history of Western civilization is punctuated by a yearning and striving toward freedom. Yet freedom in the existential frame of reference has a technical meaning—one that is riveted to dread.

In the existential frame of reference, freedom means that, contrary to everyday experience, the human being does not enter and ultimately exit from a structured universe with a coherent, grand design. Freedom refers to the fact that the human being is responsible for and the author of his or her own world, own life design, own choices and actions. The human being, as Sartre puts it, is "condemned to freedom" (1956, p. 631). Rollo May (1981) holds that freedom, in order to be authentic, requires the individual to confront the limits of his or her destiny.

The existential position that the human being constitutes a personal world has been germinating for a long time in philosophic thought. The heart of Kant's revolution in philosophy was his postulate that human consciousness, the nature of the human being's mental structures, provides the external form of reality. Kant stated that even space "is not something objective and real but something subjective and ideal; it is, as it were, a schema issuing by a constant law from the nature of the mind for the coordinating of all outer sensa" (1954, p. 308).

This existential view of freedom has terrifying implications. If it is true, as philosophers such as Heidegger and Sartre argue, that we create our own selves and our own world, then it also means that there is no ground beneath us: there is only an abyss, a void, nothingness.

An important internal dynamic conflict emanates from our confrontation with freedom: conflict issues from our awareness of freedom and groundlessness on the one hand and, on the other hand, our deep need and wish for ground and structure.

The concept of freedom encompasses many themes that have profound implications for psychotherapy. The most apparent is *responsibility*. Individuals differ enormously in the degree of responsibility they are willing to accept for their life situation and in their modes of denying responsibility. For example, some individuals displace responsibility for their situation onto other people, onto life circumstances, onto bosses and spouses, and, when they enter treatment, they transfer responsibility for their therapy to their psychotherapist. Other individuals deny responsibility by experiencing themselves as "innocent victims" who suffer from external events (and remain unaware that they themselves have set these events into motion). Still others shuck responsibility by temporarily being "out of their minds"—they enter a temporary irrational state in which they are not accountable even to themselves for their behavior.

Another aspect of freedom is *willing*. To be aware of responsibility for one's situation is to enter the vestibule of action or, in a therapy situation, of change. Willing represents the passage from responsibility to action. Willing, as May (1969) points out, consists first of wishing and then of deciding. Many individuals have enormous difficulties in experiencing or expressing a wish. Wishing is closely aligned to feeling, and affect-blocked individuals cannot act spontaneously because they cannot feel and thus cannot wish. *Impulsivity* avoids wishing by failing to discriminate among wishes. Instead, individuals act impulsively and promptly on all wishes. *Compulsivity,* another disorder of wishing, is characterized by individuals not pro-acting, but instead being driven by ego-alien inner demands that often run counter to their consciously held desires.

Once an individual fully experiences a wish, he or she is faced with decision. Many individuals can be extremely clear about what they wish but still not be able to decide or to choose. Often they experience a decisional panic; they may attempt to delegate the decision to someone else, or they act in such a way that the decision is made for them by circumstances that they, unconsciously, have brought to pass.

Isolation. A third ultimate concern is isolation. It is important to differentiate *existential isolation* from other types of isolation. *Interpersonal isolation* refers to the gulf that exists between oneself and other people—a gulf that results from deficient social skills and psychopathology in the sphere of intimacy. *Intrapersonal isolation,* a term first introduced by Freud, refers to the fact that we are isolated from parts of ourselves. Enclaves of self (of experience, affect, desire) are dissociated out of awareness, and the goal of psychotherapy is to help the individual reclaim these split-off parts of self.

Existential isolation cuts beneath other forms of isolation. No matter how closely we relate to another individual, there remains a final unbridgeable gap. Each of us enters existence alone and must depart from it alone. Each individual in the dawn of consciousness created a primary self *(transcendental ego)* by permitting consciousness to curl back upon itself and to differentiate a self from the remainder of the world. Only after that does the individual, now "self-conscious," begin to constitute other selves. Beneath this act, as Mijuskovic (1979) notes, there is a fundamental loneliness; the individual cannot escape the knowledge that (1) he constitutes others and (2) he can never fully share his consciousness with others.

There is no stronger reminder of existential isolation than a confrontation with death. The individual who faces death invariably becomes acutely aware of isolation. Such a sequence is the theme of the medieval morality play *Everyman.* Everyman is visited by the angel of death, who informs him that he must take his final pilgrimage to God. Everyman pleads for more time, but to no avail. Death informs him that he must make himself ready for the journey. Everyman then asks to be permitted to take companions on his trip. Death grants him that wish, and the remainder of the play portrays Everyman's attempt to persuade others to accompany him on his journey. He appeals to a number of allegorical characters: fellowship, worldly goods, kindred, and knowledge. All refuse to accompany him, and Everyman faces the terror of existential isolation. (Ultimately Everyman finds one companion, good deeds, who is willing to take the journey with him. That is indeed the moral of the morality play: good works within the context of Christian faith provide a buttress against ultimate isolation.)

The third dynamic conflict, thus, is between the awareness of our fundamental isolation and the wish to be protected, to merge and to be part of a larger whole.

Fear of existential isolation (and the defenses against it) underlie a great deal of interpersonal psychopathology. This dynamic offers a powerful, parsimonious explanatory system for understanding many miscarried interpersonal relationships in which one uses another for some function rather than relates to the other out of caring for that person's being.

Although no relationship can eliminate isolation, it can be shared with another in such a way that the pain of isolation is assuaged. If one acknowledges one's isolated situation in existence and confronts it with resoluteness, one will be able to turn lovingly toward others. If, on the other hand, one is overcome with dread in the face of isolation, one will not be able to turn toward others but instead will use others as a shield against isolation. In such instances relationships will be out-of-joint miscarriages and distortions of what might have been authentic relationships.

Some individuals (and this is particularly true of individuals with a borderline personality disturbance) experience panic when alone that emanates from a dissolution of ego boundaries. These individuals begin to doubt their own existence and believe that they exist only in the presence of another, that they exist only so long as they are responded to or are thought about by another individual.

Many attempt to deal with isolation through fusion: they soften their ego boundaries and become part of another individual. They avoid personal growth and the sense of isolation that accompanies growth. Fusion underlies the experience of being in love. The wonderful thing about romantic love is that the lonely "I" disappears into the "we." Others may fuse with a group, a cause, a country, a project. To be like everyone else—to conform in dress, speech, and customs, to have no thoughts or feelings that are different —saves one from the isolation of the lonely self.

Compulsive sexuality is also a common response to terrifying isolation. Promiscuous sexual coupling offers a powerful but temporary respite for the lonely individual. It is temporary because it is only a caricature of a relationship. The sexually compulsive individual does not relate to the whole being of the other but relates only to the part of that individual that meets his or her need. Sexually compulsive individuals do not know their partners; they show and see only those parts that facilitate seduction and the sexual act.

Meaninglessness. The fourth ultimate concern is meaninglessness. If each person must die, and if each person constitutes his or her own world, and if each is alone in an indifferent universe, then what possible meaning can life have? Why do we live? How shall we live? If there is no preordained design in life, then we must construct our own meaning in life. The fundamental question then becomes, "Is it possible that a self-created life meaning is sturdy enough to bear one's life?"

The human being appears to require meaning. Our perceptual neuropsychological organization is such that we instantaneously pattern random stimuli. We organize them automatically into figure and ground. When confronted with a broken circle, we automatically perceive it as complete. When any situation or set of stimuli defies patterning, we experience dysphoria, which persists until we fit the situation into a recognizable pattern. In the same way individuals organize random stimuli so too do they face existential situations: in an unpatterned world an individual is acutely unsettled and searches for a pattern, an explanation, a meaning of existence.

A sense of meaning in life is necessary for still another reason: from a meaning schema we generate a hierarchy of values. Values provide us with a blueprint for life conduct; values tell us not only *why* we live but *how* to live.

The fourth internal conflict stems from this dilemma: *How does a being who requires meaning find meaning in a universe that has no meaning?*

VARIETY OF CONCEPTS

The content of the internal conflict from the existential frame of reference consists of ultimate concerns and the conscious and unconscious fears and motives spawned by them. The dynamic existential approach retains Freud's basic dynamic *structure* but has a radically different *content*. The old Freudian formula of

DRIVE → ANXIETY → DEFENSE
MECHANISM

is replaced in the existential system by

AWARENESS OF ULTIMATE
CONCERN → ANXIETY →
DEFENSE MECHANISM[2]

Both psychoanalysis and the existential system place anxiety at the center of the dynamic structure. Anxiety fuels psychopathology: conscious and unconscious psychic operations (i.e., defense mechanisms) are generated to deal with anxiety. These psychic operations constitute psychopathology: they provide safety, but they also restrict growth.

An important difference is that Freud's sequence begins with drive, whereas an existential framework begins with awareness. The existential frame of reference views the individual primarily as fearful and suffering rather than as driven.

To an existential therapist, anxiety springs from confrontation with death, groundlessness (freedom), isolation, and meaninglessness. The individual uses two types of defense mechanisms to cope with anxiety. The first, the conventional mechanisms of

---

[2]To Freud, anxiety is a signal of danger (i.e., if instinctual drives are permitted expression, the organism becomes endangered; either the ego is overwhelmed or retaliation by the environment is inevitable). The defense mechanisms restrict direct expression of drives but provide indirect expression—that is, in displaced, sublimated, or symbolic form.

defense, thoroughly described by Sigmund Freud, Anna Freud, and Harry Stack Sullivan, defend the individual against anxiety regardless of source. The second are specific defenses that serve to cope with specific primary existential fears.

For example, consider the individual's defense mechanism for dealing with the anxiety emerging from awareness of death. Yalom (1981, p. 115) describes two major, specific intrapsychic defenses: an irrational belief in personal "specialness" and an irrational belief in the existence of an "ultimate rescuer." These defenses resemble delusions in that they are fixed, false beliefs. However, they are not delusions in the clinical sense, but are universally held irrational beliefs.

Specialness

Individuals have deep, powerful beliefs in personal inviolability, invulnerability, and immortality. Although, at a rational level, we recognize the foolishness of these beliefs, nonetheless, at a deeply unconscious level, we believe that the ordinary laws of biology do not apply to us.

No one has ever described this deep irrational belief in personal specialness more powerfully than Tolstoy who, through the lips of Ivan Illych, says:

In the depth of his heart he knew he was dying, but not only was he not accustomed to the thought, he simply did not and could not grasp it.

The syllogism he had learnt from Kiezewetter's *Logic*: "Caius is a man, men are mortal, therefore, Caius is mortal," had always seemed to him correct as applied to Caius, but certainly not as applied to himself. That Caius—man in the abstract—was mortal, was perfectly correct, but he was not Caius, not an abstract man, but a creature quite, quite separate from all others. He had been little Vanya, with a mamma and a papa, with Mitya and Volodya, with the toys, a coachman and a nurse, afterwards with Katenka and with all the joys, griefs, and delights of childhood, boyhood, and youth. What did Caius know of the smell of that striped leather ball Vanya had been so fond of? Had Caius kissed his mother's hand like that, and did the silk of her dress rustle so for Caius? Had he rioted like that at school when the pastry was bad? Had Caius been in love like that? Could Caius preside at a session as he did? "Caius really was mortal, and it was right for him to die; but for me, little Vanya, Ivan Ilych, with all my thoughts and emotions, it's altogether a different matter. It cannot be that I ought to die. That would be too terrible" (1960, p. 131).

If this defense is weak or absent, then the individual manifests one of a number of clinical syndromes: for example, the narcissistic character, the compulsive workaholic consumed by a search for glory, the self-aggrandizing, paranoid individual. The crisis in the lives of these individuals occurs when their belief system is shattered and a sense of unprotected ordinariness intrudes. They frequently seek therapy when the defense of specialness is no longer able to ward off anxiety—for example, at times of severe illness or at the interruption of what had always appeared to be an eternal, upward spiral.

The Belief in the Existence of an Ultimate Rescuer

The other major mechanism of defense that serves to block death awareness is our belief in a personal omnipotent servant who eternally guards and protects our welfare, who may let us get to the edge of the abyss but who will always bring us back. A hypertrophy of this particular defense mechanism results in a character structure displaying passivity, dependency, and obsequiousness. Often such individuals dedicate their lives to locating and appeasing an ultimate rescuer. In Silvano Arieti's terms, they live for the "dominant other" (1977, p. 864)—a life ideology that precedes and prepares the ground for clinical depression. These individuals may adapt well to life while basking in the presence of the dominant other, but they decompensate and experience extraordinary distress at the loss of this dominant other.

Another major difference between the existential dynamic approach and other dynamic approaches lies in temporal orientation. The existential therapist works in the present tense. The individual is to be understood and helped to understand himself from the perspective of a here-and-now *cross-section*, not from the perspective of a historical *longitudinal section*. Consider the use of the word *deep*. Freud defined *deep* as "early," and so the deepest conflict meant the earliest conflict in the individual's life. Freud's psychodynamics are developmentally based. *Fundamental* and *primary* are to be grasped chronologically: each is synonymous with "first." Thus the fundamental sources of anxiety, for example, are considered to be the earliest calamities: separation and castration.

From the existential perspective, *deep* means the most fundamental concerns facing the individual at that moment. The past (i.e., one's memory of the past) is important only insofar as it is part of one's current existence and has contributed to one's current mode of facing ultimate concerns. The immediate, currently existing ground beneath all other ground is important from the existential perspective. Thus the existential conception of personality is in the awareness of the depths of one's immediate experiences. Exis-

tential therapy does not attempt to excavate and understand the past; instead it is directed toward the future's becoming the present and explores the past only as it throws light on the present. The therapist must continually keep in mind that we create our past and that our present mode of existence dictates what we choose to remember of the past.

PSYCHOTHERAPY

THEORY OF PSYCHOTHERAPY

A substantial proportion of practicing psychotherapists consider themselves existentially (or "humanistically") oriented. Yet few, if any, have received any systematic training in existential therapy. One can be reasonably certain of this because there are few comprehensive training programs in existential therapy. Although many excellent books illuminate some aspect of the existential frame of reference (Becker, 1973; Bugental, 1956; Koestenbaum, 1978; May, 1953, 1977; May et al., 1958), Yalom's book (1981) is the first to present a systematic, comprehensive view of the existential therapeutic approach.

When one asks existentially oriented therapists to describe their reasons for so labeling themselves, they describe not a system of psychotherapy but rather a mode of viewing the human being. Existential therapy is *not* a comprehensive psychotherapeutic system; it is a frame of reference—a paradigm in which one views and understands a patient's suffering in a particular manner.

Existential therapists begin with presuppositions about the sources of a patient's anguish and views the patient in human rather than behavioral or mechanistic terms. They may employ any of a large variety of techniques used in other approaches insofar as they are consistent with basic existential presuppositions and a human, authentic therapist-patient encounter.

The vast majority of experienced therapists, regardless of adherence to some particular ideological school, employ many existential insights and approaches. All competent therapists realize, for example, that an apprehension of one's finiteness can often catalyze a major inner shift of perspective, that it is the relationship that heals, that patients are tormented by choice, that a therapist must catalyze a patient's "will" to act, and that the majority of patients are bedeviled by a lack of meaning in their lives.

It is also true that the therapist's belief system determines the type of clinical data which he or she encounters. Therapists subtly or unconsciously cue patients to provide them with certain material. Jungian patients have Jungian dreams. Freudian patients discover themes of castration, anxiety, and penis envy. The therapist's perceptual system is affected by her ideological system. She "tunes in" to the material that she wishes to obtain. So too with the existential approach. If the therapist tunes her mental apparatus to the right channel, it is astounding how frequently patients discuss concerns emanating from existential conflicts.

The basic approach in existential therapy is strategically similar to other dynamic therapies. The therapist assumes that the patient experiences anxiety which issues from some existential conflict that is at least partially unconscious. The patient handles anxiety by a number of ineffective, maladaptive defense mechanisms that may provide temporary respite from anxiety but ultimately so cripple the individual's ability to live fully and creatively that these defenses merely result in still further secondary anxiety. The therapist assists the patient to embark on a course of self-investigation in which the goals are to understand the unconscious conflict, to identify the maladaptive defense mechanisms, to discover their destructive influence, to diminish secondary anxiety by correcting these heretofore restrictive modes of dealing with self and others, and to develop other ways of coping with primary anxiety.

Although the basic strategy in existential therapy is similar to other dynamic therapies, the content is radically different. In many respects, the process differs as well; the existential therapist's different mode of understanding the patient's basic dilemma results in many differences in the strategy of psychotherapy. For example, because the existential view of personality structure emphasizes the depth of experience at any given moment, the existential therapist does not spend a great deal of time helping the patient to recover the past. The existential therapist strives for an understanding of the patient's *current* life situation and *current* enveloping unconscious fears. The existential therapist believes, as do other dynamic therapists, that the nature of the therapist-client relationship is fundamental in good psychotherapeutic work. However, the accent is not upon transference but instead upon the relationship as fundamentally important in itself.

PROCESS OF PSYCHOTHERAPY

Each of these ultimate concerns (death, freedom, isolation, and meaninglessness) has implications for the process of therapy. Let us examine the practical, therapeutic implications of the ultimate concern of freedom. A major component of freedom is *responsibility*—a concept that deeply influences the existential therapist's therapeutic approach.

Sartre equates responsibility to authorship: to be responsible means to be the author of one's own life design. The existential therapist continually focuses upon each patient's responsibility for his or her own distress. Bad genes or bad luck do not cause a patient to be lonely or chronically abused or neglected by others. Until patients realize that they are responsible for their own conditions, there is little motivation to change.

The therapist must identify methods and instances of responsibility avoidance and then make these known to the patient. Therapists may use a wide variety of techniques to focus the patient's attention on responsibility. Many therapists interrupt the patient whenever they hear the patient avoiding responsibility. When patients say they "can't" do something, the therapist immediately comments, "You mean you 'won't' do it." As long as one believes in "can't," one remains unaware of one's active contribution to one's situation. Such therapists encourage patients to *own* their feelings and statements and actions. If a patient comments that he did something "unconsciously," the therapist might inquire, "Whose unconscious is it?" The general principle is obvious: whenever the patient laments about his or her life situation, the therapist inquires how the patient created that situation.

Often it is helpful to keep the patient's initial complaint in mind and then, at appropriate points in therapy, juxtapose these initial complaints with the patient's in-therapy behavior. For example, consider a patient who sought therapy because of feelings of isolation and loneliness. During the course of therapy the patient expressed at great length his sense of superiority and his scorn and disdain of others. These attitudes were rigidly maintained; the patient manifested great resistance to examining, much less changing, these opinions. The therapist helped this patient to understand his responsibility for his personal predicament by reminding the patient, whenever he discussed his scorn of others, "And you are lonely."

Responsibility is one component of freedom. Earlier we described another, *willing*, which may be further subdivided into *wishing* and *deciding*. Consider the role of *wishing*. How often does the therapist participate with a patient in some such sequence as this:

"What shall I do? What shall I do?"

"What is it that stops you from doing what you want to do?"

"But I don't *know* what I want to do! If I knew that, I wouldn't need to see you!"

These patients actually know what they should do, ought to do, or must do, but they do not experience what they *want* to do. Many therapists, in working with patients who have a profound incapacity to wish, have shared May's inclination to shout "Don't you ever *want* anything?" (1969, p. 165). These patients have enormous social difficulties because they have no opinions, no inclinations, and no desires of their own.

Often the inability to wish is imbedded in a more global disorder— the inability to feel. In many cases, the bulk of psychotherapy consists of helping patients to dissolve their affect blocks. This therapy is slow and grinding. Above all, the therapist must persevere and, time after time, must continue to press the patient with, "What do you feel?" "What do you want?" Repeatedly the therapist will need to explore the source and nature of the block and of the stifled feelings behind it.

Some therapists attempt to dynamite the affect block with dramatic breakthrough efforts (for example, emotional flooding, primal scream, implosion therapy, intense feeling therapy, Gestalt therapy). The inability to feel and to wish is a pervasive characterological trait, and considerable time and therapeutic perseverance are required to effect enduring change.

There are other modes of avoiding wishing in addition to blocking of affect. Some individuals avoid wishing by not discriminating among wishes, by acting impulsively on all wishes. In such instances, the therapist must help the patient to make some internal discrimination among wishes and assign priorities to each. The patient must learn that two wishes which are mutually exclusive demand that one be relinquished. If, for example, a meaningful, loving relationship is a wish, then a host of conflicting interpersonal wishes—such as the wish for conquest or power or seduction or subjugation—must be denied.

Decision is the bridge between wishing and action. Some patients, even though they are able to wish, are still unable to act because they cannot *decide*. One of the more common reasons that deciding is difficult is that every yes involves a no. Renunciation invariably accompanies decision, and a decision requires a relinquishment of other options—often options that may never come again. There are other patients who cannot decide because a major decision makes them more aware of the degree to which they constitute their own lives. Thus a major irreversible decision is a boundary situation in the same way that awareness of death may be a boundary situation.

The therapist must help patients make choices. A useful strategy is to help patients consider the options available to them. The therapist must help patients recognize that they themselves, not the therapist, must generate and choose among options. In helping patients to communicate effectively, therapists teach that one must *own* one's feelings. It is equally important that one owns one's decisions. Some patients are panicked by the various implications of each decision. The "what ifs" torment them. *What if I leave my job and can't find another? What if I leave my children alone and they get hurt?* It is often useful to ask the patient to consider the entire scenario of each "what if" in turn, to fantasize it happening with all the possible ramifications, and then to experience and analyze emerging feelings.

A general posture toward decision making is to assume that the therapist's task is not to *create* will but instead to *disencumber* it. The therapist cannot flick the decision switch or inspirit the patient with resoluteness. But the therapist can influence the factors that influence willing. After all, no one has a congenital inability to decide. Decision making is blocked by obstacles, and it is the therapist's task to help remove obstacles. Once that is done, the individual will naturally move into a more autonomous position in just the way, Karen Horney (1950) put it, an acorn develops into an oak tree.

The therapist must help patients understand that decisions are unavoidable. One makes decisions all the time and often conceals from oneself that one is deciding. It is important to help patients understand the inevitability of decisions and to identify how they make decisions. Many patients decide *passively* by, for example, letting another person decide for them. They may terminate an unsatisfactory relationship by unconsciously acting in such a way that the partner makes the decision to leave. In such instances the final outcome (i.e., the dissolution of the relationship) is achieved, but the patient may be left with many negative repercussions. The patient's sense of powerlessness is merely reinforced and he continues to experience himself as one to whom things happen rather than as the author of his own life situation. The *way* one makes a decision is often as important as the content of the decision. An active decision reinforces the individual's active acceptance of his own power and resources.

MECHANISMS OF PSYCHOTHERAPY

We can best understand the mechanisms of the existential approach by considering the therapeutic leverage inherent in some of the ultimate concerns.

Death and Psychotherapy

There are two distinct ways in which the concept of death plays an impor-

tant role in psychotherapy. First, an increased awareness of one's finiteness stemming from a personal confrontation with death may cause a radical shift in life perspective and lead to personal change. Second, the concept that death is a primary source of anxiety has many important implications for therapy.

Death as a boundary situation. A *boundary situation* is a type of urgent experience that propels the individual into a confrontation with an existential situation. The most powerful boundary situation is confrontation with one's personal death. Such a confrontation has the power to provide a massive shift in the way that one lives in the world. There are innumerable examples both from great literature and from clinical work with dying patients that illustrate this principle (Yalom, 1981, p. 160).

Yalom reports a number of important personal changes that have occurred to cancer patients who confront their own deaths (1981, p. 161). Some patients report that they learn simply that "existence cannot be postponed." They no longer postpone living until some time in the future; they realize that one can really live only in the present. The neurotic individual rarely lives in the present but is either continuously obsessed with events from the past or fearful of anticipated events in the future.

A confrontation with a boundary situation persuades individuals to count their blessings, to become aware of their natural surroundings: the elemental facts of life, changing seasons, seeing, listening, touching, and loving. Ordinarily what we *can* experience is diminished by petty concerns, by thoughts of what we cannot do or what we lack, or by threats to our prestige.

Many terminally ill patients, when reporting personal growth emanating from their confrontation with death, have lamented, "What a tragedy that we had to wait till now, till our bodies were riddled with cancer, to learn these truths." This is an exceedingly important message for therapists. The therapist can obtain considerable leverage to help "everyday" patients (i.e., patients who are not physically ill) increase their awareness of death earlier in their life cycle. With this aim in mind, some therapists have employed structured exercises to confront the individual with personal death. Many death awareness workshops are reported in the literature (Yalom, 1981, p. 174). Some group leaders begin a brief group experience by asking members to write their own epitaph or obituary, or they provide guided fantasies in which group members imagine their own death and funeral. The National Training Laboratory has offered a life cycle group experience in which participants spend time living, talking, and dressing like old people. They visit a local cemetery. They imagine their own dying, death, and funeral.

Many existential therapists do not believe that artificially introduced death confrontations are necessary or advisable. Instead they attempt to help the patient recognize the signs of mortality that are part of the fabric of everyday life. If the therapist and the patient are "tuned-in," there is considerable evidence of death anxiety in every psychotherapy. Every patient suffers losses through death of parents, friends, and associates. Dreams are haunted with death anxiety. Every nightmare is a dream of raw death anxiety. Everywhere around us are reminders of aging: our bones begin to creak, senile plaques appear on our skin, we go to reunions and note with dismay how everyone *else* has aged. Our children grow up. The cycle of life envelops us.

An important opportunity for confrontation with death arises when patients experience the death of someone close to them. The traditional literature on grief primarily focuses on two aspects of grief work: loss and the resolution of ambivalence that so strongly accentuates the dysphoria of grief. But a third dimension must be considered: the death of someone close to us confronts us with our own death. This is of course the point that John Donne made in the well-known lines: "and therefore never send to know for whom the bell tolls. It tolls for thee" (Donne, 1952, p. 332).

Often grief has a very different tone, depending upon the individual's relationship with the person who has died. The loss of a parent confronts us with our vulnerability: if our parents could not save themselves, who will save us? When parents die, nothing remains between ourselves and the grave. At the moment of our parents' death, we ourselves constitute the barrier between our children and their death.

The death of a spouse often evokes the fear of existential isolation. The loss of the significant other increases our awareness that, try as hard as we can to go through the world two by two, there is nonetheless a basic aloneness we must bear. Yalom reports a patient's dream the night after learning that his wife had inoperable cancer.

I was living in my old house in _____ [a house that had been in the family for three generations]. A Frankenstein monster was chasing me through the house. I was terrified. The house was deteriorating, decaying. The tiles were crumbling and the roof leaking. Water leaked all over my mother. [His mother had died six months ago.] I fought with him. I had a choice of weapons. One had a curved blade with a handle, like a scythe. I slashed him and tossed him off the roof. He lay stretched out on the pavement below. But he got up and once again started chasing me through the house. (1981, p. 168)

The patient's first association to this dream was "I know I've got a hundred thousand miles on me." Obviously his wife's impending death reminded him that his life and his body (symbolized in the dream by the deteriorating house) were also finite. As a child this patient was often haunted by the monster who returned in this nightmare.

Children try many methods of dealing with death anxiety. One of the most common is the personification of death—the imagining of death as some finite creature, a monster, a sandman, a bogeyman, and so on. This is very frightening to children but nonetheless far less frightening than the truth—that they carry the spores of their own death within them. If , death is "out there" in some physical form, then possibly it may be eluded, tricked, or pacified.

Milestones provide another opportunity for the therapist to focus the patient on existential facts of life. Even simple milestones, such as birthdays and anniversaries, are useful levers. These signs of passage are often capable of eliciting pain (consequently, we often deal with such milestones by reaction formation, in the form of a joyous celebration).

Major life events, such as a threat to one's career, a severe illness, retirement, commitment to a relationship, and separation from a relationship, are important boundary situations and offer opportunities for an increased awareness of death anxiety. Often these experiences are painful, and therapists feel compelled to focus entirely on pain alleviation. In so doing, however, they miss rich opportunities for deep therapeutic work that reveal themselves at those moments.

Death as a primary source of anxiety. The fear of death constitutes a primary fount of anxiety: it is present early in life, it is instrumental in shaping character structure, and it continues throughout life to generate anxiety that results in manifest distress and the erection of psychological defenses. However, it is important to keep in mind that death anxiety, despite the fact that it is ubiquitous and has pervasive ramifications, exists at the very deepest levels of being, is heavily repressed, and is rarely experienced in its full sense. Often death anxiety per se is not easily visible in the clinical picture. It often does not become an explicit theme in therapy, especially in brief therapy. There are other patients, however, who are suffused with overt death anxiety at the very onset of therapy. There are often life situations in which the patient has such a rush of death anxiety that the therapist cannot evade the issue. In long-term, intensive therapy, explicit death anxiety is always to be found and must be considered in the therapeutic work.

In the existential framework, anxiety is so riveted to existence that it has a different connotation from the way that anxiety is regarded in other frames of reference. The existential therapist hopes to alleviate crippling levels of anxiety but not to eliminate it. Life cannot be lived (nor can death be faced) without anxiety. The therapist's task, as May reminds us (1977, p. 374), is to reduce anxiety to tolerable levels and then to use the anxiety constructively: as a guide and as a mode of increasing a patient's awareness and vitality.

It is important to keep in mind that, even though death anxiety may not explicitly enter the therapeutic dialogue, a theory of anxiety based on death awareness may provide therapists with a frame of reference, an explanatory system, that greatly enhances their effectiveness. Therapists, as well as patients, seek to order events into some coherent sequence. Once that is done the therapist begins to experience a sense of control and mastery that allows organization of clinical material. The therapist's self-confidence and sense of mastery will help patients develop trust and confidence in the therapy process—an essential condition of therapy. Furthermore, the therapist's belief system often serves to keep the patient and therapist cemented to one another while the real agent of change, the therapeutic relationship, germinates and matures.

The therapist's belief system provides a certain consistency. It permits the therapist to know what to explore so that the patient does not become confused. Although the therapist may not make full, explicit interpretations of the unconscious roots of a patient's problem, the therapist may, with subtlety and good timing, make comments that at an unspoken level click with the patient's unconscious and allow the patient to feel understood.

Existential Isolation and Psychotherapy

Patients discover in therapy that interpersonal relationships may temper isolation but cannot eliminate it. Patients who grow in psychotherapy learn not only the rewards of intimacy but also its limits: they learn what they *cannot* get from others. An important step in treatment consists of helping patients address existential isolation directly, to plunge into feelings of lostness and loneliness. Those who lack sufficient experiences of closeness and true relatedness in their lives are particularly incapable of tolerating isolation. Otto Will[3] made the point that adolescents from loving, supportive families are able to grow away from their families with relative ease and to tolerate the separation and loneliness of young adulthood. On the other hand those who grow up in tormented, highly conflicted families find it extremely difficult to leave the family. One might expect these individuals would kick up their heels with joy at the prospect of dancing away from such a family, but the opposite occurs. The more disturbed the family, the harder it is for children to leave—they are ill equipped to separate and therefore cling to the family for shelter against isolation and anxiety.

Many patients have enormous difficulty spending time alone. Consequently they construct their lives in such a way that they eliminate alone time. One of the major problems that ensues from this is the desperation with which they seek certain kinds of relationships. In one way or another they do not relate to or love another person but instead use others to avoid some of the pain accompanying isolation. The therapist must find a way to help the patient confront isolation in a dosage and with a support system suited to that patient. Some therapists,

---

[3]Oral communication. Child psychiatry grand rounds. Stanford University, Department of Psychiatry, 1978.

at an advanced stage of therapy, advise or prescribe periods of self-enforced isolation during which the patient is asked to monitor and record thoughts and feelings.

Meaninglessness and Psychotherapy

To deal effectively with meaninglessness, therapists must first increase their sensitivity to the topic, listen differently, and become aware of the importance of meaning in the lives of individuals. For some patients the issue is not crucial, but for others the sense of meaninglessness is profound and pervasive. Carl Jung once estimated that over 30 percent of his patients sought therapy because of a sense of personal meaninglessness (1966, p. 83).

The therapist must be attuned to the overall focus and direction of the patient's life. Is the patient reaching beyond himself or herself? Or is he or she entirely immersed in the daily routine of staying alive? Yalom (1981) reports that he has treated many young adults who are immersed in a California singles' life-style, characterized to a large extent by sensuality, sexual clamor, and pursuit of prestige and materialistic goals. He noted that his therapy was rarely successful unless he was able to help patients focus on something beyond these pursuits. Simply by increasing the sensitivity of patients to these issues the therapist can help them focus on values outside of themselves. Therapists, for example, can begin to wonder about the patient's belief systems, inquire deeply into the loving of another, ask about long-range hopes and goals, and explore creative interests and pursuits.

Viktor Frankl, who placed great emphasis on the importance of meaninglessness in contemporary psychopathology, stated that "happiness cannot be pursued, it can only ensue" (1969, p. 165).

The more we deliberately search for self-satisfaction, the more it eludes us, whereas the more we fulfill some self-transcendent meaning, the more happiness will ensue. Frankl suggested that this means that some patients must be helped to take their gaze off themselves; that is, some patients must be helped in the process of "dereflection."

Therapists must find a way to help such patients develop curiosity and concern for others. The therapy group is especially well suited for this endeavor: the pattern in which self-absorbed, narcissistic patients take without giving often becomes highly evident in the therapy group. In such instances therapists may attempt to increase an individual's ability and inclination to empathize with others by requesting, periodically, that patients guess how others are feeling at various junctures of the group.

But the major solution to the problem of meaninglessness is engagement. Wholehearted engagement in any of the infinite array of life's activities enhances the possibility of one's patterning the events of one's life in some coherent fashion. To find a home, to care about other individuals, about ideas or projects, to search, to create, to build—these and all other forms of engagement are twice rewarding: they are intrinsically enriching, and they alleviate the dysphoria that stems from being bombarded with the unassembled brute data of existence.

The therapist must approach engagement with the same attitudinal set used with wishing. The therapist cannot create engagement or inspirit the patient with engagement. That is not necessary: the desire to engage life is always there with the patient, and therefore the therapist's activity should be directed toward the removal of obstacles in the patient's way. The therapist begins to explore what prevents the patient from loving another individual. Why is there so little satisfaction from his or her relationship with others? Why is there so little satisfaction from work? What blocks the patient from finding work commensurate with his or her talents and interests or finding some pleasurable aspects of current work? Why has the patient neglected creative or religious or self-transcendent strivings?

APPLICATIONS

PROBLEMS

The clinical setting often determines the applicability of the existential approach. In each course of therapy the therapist must consider the goals appropriate to the clinical setting. To take one example, in an acute inpatient setting where the patient will be hospitalized for approximately one to two weeks, the goal of therapy is crisis intervention. The therapist hopes to alleviate symptoms and to restore the patient to a precrisis level of functioning. Deeper, more ambitious goals (including the goal of increasing the patient's awareness of existential conflicts) are unrealistic and inappropriate to that situation.

In situations where patients desire not only symptomatic relief but also hope to attain greater personal growth, the existential approach is generally useful. A thorough existential approach with ambitious goals is most appropriate in long-term therapy, but even in briefer approaches some as-

pect of the existential mode (e.g., an emphasis on responsibility, deciding, an authentic therapist-patient encounter, grief work, and so on) is often incorporated into the therapy.

An existential approach to therapy is much more obviously appropriate with patients who confront some boundary situation—that is, a confrontation with death, the facing of some important irreversible decision, a sudden thrust into isolation, milestones that mark passages from one life era into another (e.g., children leaving home, retirement, career failure, marital separation and divorce, major physical illness). But therapy need not be limited to these more explicit existential crises. In every course of therapy, as we have indicated earlier, there is abundant evidence of patients' anguish stemming from existential conflicts. The availability of this data is entirely a function of the therapist's attitudinal set and perceptivity. The decision to work on these levels should be a joint patient-therapist decision.

EVALUATION

Psychotherapy evaluation is always a difficult task. As a general rule, the more focused and specific the approach and the goals, the easier it is to measure outcome. Symptomatic relief or behavioral change may be quantified with reasonable precision. But more ambitious therapies, which seek to affect deeper layers of the individual's mode of being in the world, defy quantification. These problems of evaluation are illustrated by the following vignettes reported by Yalom (1981, p. 336).

A 46-year-old mother accompanied the youngest of her four children to the airport, from where he departed for college. She had spent the last 26 years rearing her children and longing for this day. No more impositions, no more incessantly living for others, no more cooking dinners, and picking up clothes. Finally she was free.

Yet as she said good-bye she unexpectedly began sobbing loudly, and on the way home from the airport a deep shudder passed through her body. "It is only natural," she thought. It was only the sadness of saying good-bye to someone she loved very much. But it was much more than that, and the shudder soon turned into raw anxiety. The therapist whom she consulted identified it as a common problem: the empty-nest syndrome. Of course she was anxious. How could it be otherwise? For years she had based her self-esteem on her performance as a mother and suddenly she found no way to validate herself. The whole routine and structure of her life had been altered. Gradually, with the help of Valium, supportive psychotherapy, an assertiveness training group, several adult education courses, a lover or two, and a part-time volunteer job, the shudder shrunk to a tremble and then vanished. She returned to her premorbid level of comfort and adaptation.

This patient happened to be part of a psychotherapy research project and there were outcome measures of her psychotherapy. Her treatment results could be described as excellent on each of the measures used—symptom checklists, target problem evaluation, self-esteem. Obviously she had made considerable improvement. Yet, despite this, it is entirely possible to consider this case as one of missed therapeutic opportunities.

Consider another patient in almost precisely the same life situation. In the treatment of this second patient the therapist, who was existentially oriented, attempted to nurse the shudder rather than to anesthetize it. This patient experienced what Kierkegaard called "creative anxiety." The therapist and the patient allowed the anxiety to lead them into important areas for investigation. True, this patient suffered from the empty-nest syndrome; she had problems of self-esteem; she loved her child but also envied him for the chances in life she had never had; and, of course, she felt guilty because of these "ignoble" sentiments.

The therapist did not simply allow her to find ways to help her fill her time but plunged into an exploration of the *meaning* of the fear of the empty nest. She had always desired freedom but now seemed terrified of it. Why?

A dream illuminated the meaning of the shudder. The dream consisted simply of herself holding in her hand a 35-mm photographic slide of her son juggling and tumbling. The slide was peculiar, however, in that it showed movement; she saw her son in a multitude of positions all at the same time. In the analysis of the dream her associations revolved around the theme of time. The slide captured and framed time and movement. It kept everything alive but made everything stand still. It froze life. "Time moves on," she said, "and there's no way I can stop it. I didn't want John to grow up ... whether I like it or not time moves on. It moves on for John and it moves on for me as well."

This dream brought her own finiteness into clear focus and, rather than rush to fill time in with various distractions, she learned to appreciate time in richer ways than previously.

She moved into the realm that Heidegger described as authentic being: she wondered not so much at the *way* things are but *that* things are. Although one could argue that therapy helped the second patient more than the first it would not be possible to demonstrate this conclusion on any standard outcome measures. In fact, the second patient probably continued to experience more anxiety than the first did; but anxiety is a part of existence and no individual who continues to grow and create will ever be free of it.

TREATMENT

Existential therapy has its primary applications in an individual therapy setting. However, various existential themes and insights may be successfully applied in a variety of other settings including group therapy, family therapy, couples therapy, and so forth.

The concept of responsibility has particularly widespread applicability. It is a keystone of the group therapeutic process. Group therapy is primarily based on interpersonal therapy; the group therapeutic format is an ideal arena to examine and correct maladaptive interpersonal modes of behavior. However, the theme of responsibility underlies much interpersonal work. Consider, for example, the following sequence through which group therapists, explicitly or inplicitly, attempt to guide their patients:

1. *Patients learn how their behavior is viewed by others.* (Through feedback from other group members patients learn to see themselves through others' eyes.)
2. *Patients learn how their behavior makes others feel.* (Through members sharing their personal affective responses to one another.)
3. *Patients learn how their behavior creates the opinions others have of them.* (By sharing here-and-now feelings, members learn that, as a result of their behavior, others develop certain opinions and views of them.)
4. *Patients learn how their behavior influences their opinions of themselves.* (The information gathered in the first three steps leads to the patient formulating certain kinds of self-evaluations.)

Each of these four steps begins with the patients' own behavior, which underscores their role in shaping interpersonal relations. The end point of this sequence is that group members begin to understand that they are responsible for how others treat them and that furthermore they are responsible for the way in which they regard themselves.

This is one of the most fascinating aspects of group therapy: all members are "born" simultaneously. Each starts out on an equal footing. Each gradually scoops out and shapes a particular life space in the group. Thus each person is responsible for the interpersonal position he scoops out for himself in the group (and, by analogy, in life as well). The therapeutic work in the group then not only allows individuals to change their way of relating to one another but also brings home to them in a powerful way the extent to which they have created their own life predicament—clearly an existential therapeutic mechanism.

Often the therapist uses his or her own feelings to identify the patient's contribution to his or her life predicament. For example, a depressed 48-year-old woman complained bitterly about the way her children treated her: they dismissed her opinions, were impatient with her, and, when some serious issue was at stake, addressed their comments to their father. When the therapist tuned in to his feelings about this patient, he became aware of a whining quality in her voice that tempted *him* not to take her seriously and to regard her somewhat as a child. He shared his feelings with the patient, and it proved enormously useful to her. She became aware of her child-like behavior in many areas and began to realize that her children treated her precisely as she "asked" to be treated (i.e., asked nonverbally through whining, her excuses based on weakness, and her depression and posture of helplessness).

Not infrequently therapists must treat patients who are panicked by a decisional crisis. Yalom (1981) describes one therapeutic approach in such a situation. The therapist's basic strategy consisted of helping the patient uncover and appreciate the existential implications of the decision. The patient was a 66-year-old widow who sought therapy because of her anguish about a decision to sell a summer home. The house (approximately 150 miles from her permanent residence) required constant attention to gardening, maintenance, and protection, and seemed a considerable burden to a frail elderly woman in poor health. Finances affected the decision as well, and she asked many financial and realty consultants to assist her in making the decision.

The therapist and the patient explored many factors involved in the decision and then gradually began to explore more deeply. Soon a number of painful issues emerged. For example, her husband had died a year ago and she mourned him yet. The house was still rich with his presence, and drawers and closets brimmed with his personal effects. A decision to sell the house also required a decision to come to terms with the fact that her husband would never return. Another fact was the entertainment value of the home. She often referred to the house as her "hotel" because she had always entertained large numbers of people there. She considered her house as her "drawing card" and harbored serious doubts whether anyone would visit her without the enticement of her lovely estate. Thus a decision to sell the house meant testing the loyalty of her friends and risking loneliness and isolation. Yet another reason centered on the great tragedy of her life—her childlessness. She had always envisioned the estate passing on to her children and to her children's children. But she was the last leaf; the line ended with her. The decision to sell the house thus was a decision to acknowledge the failure of her major symbolic immortality project. The therapist used the house-selling decision as a springboard to these deeper issues and eventually helped the patient mourn her husband, herself, and her unborn children.

Once the deeper meanings of a decision are worked through, the decision generally glides easily into place, and after approximately a dozen sessions the patient effortlessly made the decision to sell the house.

MANAGEMENT

Existential psychotherapy is a paradigm, a frame of reference; it is not an organization with well-delineated rules. Hence everyday arrangements of practice cannot be satisfactorily described: they vary widely, depending upon the therapist's organizational and ideological affiliation.

Existentially oriented therapists strive toward honest, mutually open relationships with their patients; consequently they arrange the therapeutic setting accordingly. No desks are placed between patient and therapist. No walls are covered with authority-inspiring diplomas. Therapist and patient address one another equally, generally both on a first-name basis. The therapist strives toward demystification of the therapy process, answering questions openly and fully—not remaining impassive in an effort to evoke transferential distortions.

The patient-therapist relationship serves many central functions in therapy. It helps the patient clarify other relationships. Patients almost invariably distort some aspect of their relationship to the therapist. The therapist, drawing from self-knowledge and experience of how others view him or her, is able to help the patient distinguish distortion from reality.

There is also potential benefit in the patient's developing a real (as opposed to a transferential) relationship to the therapist. Once a patient is able to relate deeply to a therapist, then the patient has changed. The patient learns that the potential for love exists within him- or herself and experiences feelings that have lain dormant. No matter that the patient's relationship to the therapist is temporary, the *experience* of intimacy is permanent and can never be taken away. It exists in the patient's inner world as a permanent reference point: a reminder of the patient's potential for intimacy.

The experience of an intimate encounter with a therapist has implications that extend beyond relationships with other people. For one thing, the therapist is generally someone whom the patient particularly respects. But even more important, the therapist is someone, often the only one, who *really* knows the patient. To tell someone else all one's darkest secrets, all one's illicit thoughts, sorrows, vanities, and passions, and still to be fully accepted by that person is enormously affirmative.

There is much controversy over the nature of the ideal therapist-patient relationship. There is an inescapable dissonance in the world of the therapist: concepts like "50-minute sessions," "$X an hour," and "third-party payments" do not fit comfortably with what we ordinarily think of as a genuine, caring relationship. Furthermore there is little or no reciprocity in the therapist-patient relationship. The patient comes to the therapist for help, but the therapist does not come to the patient.

Existential thinkers such as Erich Fromm, Abraham Maslow, and Martin Buber all stress that true caring for another means to care about the other's growth and to want to bring something to life in the other. The therapist's raison d'être is to be midwife to the birth of the patient's yet unlived life. Buber uses the term *unfolding*, which he suggests should be the way of the educator and the therapist. That means that one uncovers what was there all along. The term *unfolding* has rich connotations and stands in sharp contrast to the goals of the therapist in other therapeutic systems (for example, reconstruction, deconditioning, behavioral shaping, reparenting). One helps the patient unfold by *meeting*, by existential communication. The therapist is not a shaper or a director but is instead, in Sequin's terms, a "possibilitator" (1965, p. 123).

Perhaps the most important concept of all in describing the patient-therapist relationship is what Rollo May et al. term *presence* (1958, p. 80). The therapist must be present with the patient, must strive for an authentic encounter with the patient. Even though the therapist has spent only one hour a week with the patient, it is of vital importance that the therapist *be there* with the patient for that hour, that the therapist be fully present and be intensely involved. If the therapist feels bored, irritated, or removed from the patient, if the therapist is impatient for the end of the hour, then to that extent the therapist is failing to provide the relationship the patient so urgently requires.

CASE EXAMPLE

A SIMPLE CASE OF DIVORCE

A 50-year-old scientist, whom we will call David, had been married for 27 years and had recently decided to separate from his wife. He applied for therapy because of the degree of anxiety he was experiencing in anticipation of confronting his wife with his decision.

The situation was in many ways a typical midlife scenario. The patient has two children; the youngest had just graduated from college. In David's mind the children had always been the main element binding him and his wife together. Now that the children were self-supporting and fully adult, David felt there was no reasonable point in continuing the marriage. He reported that he had been dissatisfied with his marriage for many years and on three previous occasions separated from his wife, but, after only a few days, became anxious and returned, crestfallen, to his home. Bad as the marriage was, David concluded that it was less unsatisfactory than the loneliness of being single.

The reason for his dissatisfaction with his marriage was primarily boredom. He met his wife when he was 17, a time when he had been extremely insecure, especially in his relationship with women. She was the first woman who had ever expressed interest in him. David (as well as his wife) came from a blue-collar family. He was exceptionally intellectually gifted and was the first member of his family to attend college. He won a scholarship to an ivy league school, obtained two graduate degrees, and embarked upon an outstanding academic research career. His wife was not gifted intellectually, chose not go to to college, and during the early years of their marriage worked to support David in graduate school.

For most of their married life his wife immersed herself in the task of caring for the children while David ferociously pursued his professional career. He had always experienced his relationship to his wife as empty and had always felt bored with her company. In his view she had an extremely mediocre mind and was so restricted characterologically that he found it constraining to be alone with her and embarrassing to share her with friends. He experienced himself as continually changing and growing, whereas his wife, in his opinion, had become increasingly rigid and unreceptive to new ideas.

The prototypic scenario of the male in midlife crisis seeking a divorce was made complete by the presence of the "other woman"—an intelligent, vivacious, attractive woman 15 years younger than himself.

David's therapy was long and complex, and several existential themes emerged during the course of therapy.

Responsibility was an important issue in his decision to leave his wife. First, there is the moral sense of responsibility. After all, his wife gave birth to and raised his children and had supported him through graduate school. He and his wife were at an age where he was far more "marketable" than she; that is, he had significantly higher earning power and was biologically able to father children. What moral responsibility, then, did he have to his wife?

David had a high moral sense and would, for the rest of his life, torment himself with this question. It had to be explored in therapy, and, consequently, the therapist confronted him explicitly with the issue of moral responsibility during David's decision-making process. The most effective mode of dealing with this anticipatory dysphoria was to leave no stone unturned in his effort to improve and, thus, to save the marriage.

The existential concept of responsibility interdigitated with this process of trying to improve the marriage. The therapist helped David examine the question of his responsibility for the failure of the marriage. To what degree was he responsible for his wife's mode of being with him? For example, the therapist noted that he himself felt somewhat intimidated by David's quick, facile mind: the therapist also was aware of a concern about being criticized or judged by David. How judgmental was David? Was it not possible that he squelched his wife, that he might have helped his wife to develop greater flexibility, spontaneity, and self-awareness?

The therapist also helped David ex-

plore another major issue. Was his marriage merely a symbol for another source of dysphoria in his life? Was he displacing onto the marriage dissatisfaction that belonged elsewhere in his life? An exploration of this issue soon led him into the middle of the typical dynamics of the midlife crisis. A dream pointed the way toward some important dynamics:

I had a problem with liquefication of earth near my pool. John [a friend who was dying from cancer] sinks into the ground. It was like quicksand. I used a giant power auger to drill down into the quicksand. I expect to find some kind of void under the ground but instead I found a concrete slab five to six feet down. On the slab I found a receipt of money someone had paid me for $501. I was very anxious in the dream about that receipt since it was greater than it should have been.

One of the major themes of this dream had to do with death and aging. First, there was the theme of his friend who had cancer. David attempted to find his friend by using a giant auger. In the dream, David experienced a great sense of mastery and power during the drilling. The symbol of the auger seemed clearly phallic and initiated a profitable exploration of sexuality— David had always been sexually driven and the dream illuminated how he used sex (and especially sex with a young woman) as a mode of gaining mastery over aging and death. Finally, he is surprised to find a concrete slab (which elicited associations of morgues, tombs, and tombstones).

He was intrigued by the numerical figures in the dream (the slab was "five to six feet" down and the receipt was for precisely $501). In his associations David made the interesting observation that he was 50 years old and the night of the dream was his 51st birthday. Though he did not consciously dwell on his age, the dream made it clear that at an unconscious level he had considerable concern about being over 50. Along with the slab that was between five and six feet deep and the receipt that was just over $500, there was his considerable concern in the dream about the amount cited in the receipt being too great. On a conscious level he denied his aging. His major attitude was that he was growing and expanding very rapidly. He was more physically fit than he had been for most of his life and recently had been running 10 miles a day. In his career, as well, he considered himself in a phase of rapid growth and saw himself on the verge of making an important scientific breakthrough.

If David's major distress stemmed from his growing awareness of his aging and diminishment, then a precipitous separation from his wife might have represented an attempt to solve the wrong problem. Consequently, the therapist helped David plunge into a thorough exploration of his feelings about his aging and his mortality. The therapist's view was that only by fully dealing with these issues would he be more able to ascertain the true extent of the marital difficulties. The therapist and David explored these issues over several months. He attempted to deal more honestly with his wife than before, and soon he and his wife made arrangements to see a marital therapist for several months.

After these steps were taken, David and his wife decided that there was nothing salvageable in the marriage and they separated. The months following his separation were exceedingly difficult. The therapist, of course, provided support during this time but did not try to help David elim-inate his anxiety; instead he attempted to help David use his anxiety in a constructive fashion. David's inclination was to rush into an immediate second marriage, whereas the therapist persistently urged him to look at the fear of isolation that on each previous separation had sent him back to his wife. It was important now to be certain that fear did not propel him into an immediate second marriage.

David found it difficult to heed this advice because he felt so much in love with the new woman in his life. The state of being "in love" is one of the great experiences in life. In therapy, however, being in love raises many problems; the pull of romantic love is so great that it engulfs even the most well-directed therapeutic endeavors. David found his new partner to be the ideal woman, no other woman existed for him, and he attempted to spend all his time with her. When with her he experienced a state of continual bliss: all aspects of the lonely "I" vanished, leaving only a very blissful state of "we-ness."

What finally made it possible for David to work in therapy was that his new friend became somewhat frightened by the power of his embrace. Only then was he willing to look at his extreme fear of being alone and his reflex desire to merge with a woman. Gradually he became desensitized to being alone. He observed his feelings, kept a journal of them, and worked hard on them in therapy. He noted, for example, that Sundays were the very worst time. He had an extremely demanding professional schedule and had no difficulties during the week. Sundays were times of extreme anxiety. He became aware that part of that anxiety was that he had to take care of himself on Sunday. If he wanted to do something, he himself had to schedule the activity. He could no longer rely on that being done for him by his wife. He discovered that an important function of ritual in culture and the heavy scheduling in his own life was to conceal the void, the total lack of structure beneath him.

These observations led him, in therapy, to face his need to be cared for and shielded. The fears of isolation and freedom buffeted him for several months, but gradually he learned how to be alone in the world and what it meant to be responsible for his own being. In short, he learned how to be his own mother and father—always a major therapeutic objective of psychotherapy.

SUMMARY

Existential psychotherapy perceives the patient as an existing, immediate person, not as a composite of drives, archetypes, or conditioning. Instinctual drives and history are obviously present, but they come into existential therapy only as parts of the living, struggling, feeling, thinking human being in unique conflicts and with hopes, fears, and relationships. Existential therapy emphasizes that normal anxiety and guilt are present in all of life and that only the neurotic forms of these need to be changed in therapy. The person can be freed from neurotic anxiety and guilt only as he or she recognizes normal anxiety and guilt at the same time.

The original criticism of existential therapy as "too philosophical" has lessened as people recognize that all effective psychotherapy has philosophical implications.

Existential therapy is concerned with the "I Am" (being) experience, the culture (world) in which a patient lives, the significance of time, and the aspect of consciousness called transcendence.

The significance of the therapist's presence and encounter, both central existential emphases, are shown in the movie *Ordinary People*. Here the therapist's chief characteristic was availability for an adolescent's aggression.

Karl Jaspers, who was a psychiatrist and later became an existential philosopher, put his finger on this harmfulness of lack of presence and of its importance: "What we are missing! What opportunities of understanding we let pass by because at a single, decisive moment we were, with all our knowledge, lacking in the simple virtue of a *full human presence!*" It is this presence that existential therapy seeks to cultivate.

The central aim of the founders of existential psychotherapy was that its emphases would influence therapy of all schools. That this has been occurring is quite clear.

The depth of existential ideas is shown in what is called the existential neurosis. This refers to the condition of the person who feels life is meaningless. This neurosis is seen increasingly in patients in all schools. Freud in his formative years saw hysterical cases almost entirely. Now, all schools of therapy report that their patients are rarely hysterics but are much more frequently afflicted with what are called "character neuroses," which is another description of existential neurosis.

Existential therapy always sees the patient in the center of his or her own culture. Most people's problems are now loneliness, isolation, and alienation.

Our present age is one of disintegration of cultural and historical mores, of love and marriage, the family, the inherited religions, and so forth. This disintegration is the reason that psychotherapy of all sorts has burgeoned in the twentieth century; people cried for help for their multitudinous problems. Thus the existential emphasis on different aspects of the world (environment, social world, and subjective world) will, in all likelihood, become increasingly important. It is predicted that the existential approach in therapy will then become more widely used.

ANNOTATED BIBLIOGRAPHY

May, R. (1977). *The meaning of anxiety* *(rev. ed.)*. New York: (Norton. First edition published in 1950.)

A discussion of the prevalence of anxiety in the twentieth century and its roots in philosophy, biology, psychology, and modern culture, this is the first book written in America on the central theme of anxiety and the third book in history on this topic. The others were written by Sigmund Freud and Søren Kierkegaard. *The Meaning of Anxiety* was the first firm presentation of anxiety as a normal as well as a neurotic condition, and it argues that normal anxiety has constructive uses in human survival and human creativity.

May, R. (1981). *Freedom and destiny*. New York: Norton.

This is a presentation of the basic existential concept that our human freedom is always in juxtaposition with destiny, the latter defined as the givens of life, such as death, our biological inheritance, and our culture, as well as the sheer circumstances of existence. We are free to the extent that we acknowledge, confront, and struggle with our destiny. Creativity is the outcome of this confrontation.

May, R., Angel, E., & Ellenberger, H. (1958). *Existence: A new dimension in psychology and psychiatry*. New York: Basic Books. [Paperback by Simon & Schuster.]

This volume contains the two essays on existential psychotherapy, "The Origins of Existential Movement in Psychology" and "Contributions of Existential Psychology," that introduced this form of therapy to America. The rest of the book consists of essays and case studies by Henri Ellenberger, Eugene Minkowski, Erwin Straus, V. E. von Gebsattel, Ludwig Binwanger, and Ronald Kuhn. Though these last articles may be difficult for the student, the first two essays are very readable. The book was described by Abraham Maslow as "Easily the best introduction available for Americans. . . . A strong antidote against triviality and superficiality in psychology."

Yalom, I. D. (1980). *Existential psychotherapy*. New York: Basic Books.

This volume offers a comprehensive clinical overview of the field of existential psychotherapy. A major task of the book is to build a bridge between theory and clinical application. It posits that psychopathology issues from the individual's confrontation with the ultimate concerns of death, freedom, isolation, and meaninglessness and explores the implications of each ultimate concern for the practice of psychotherapy.

CASE READINGS

Binswanger, L. (1958). The case of Ellen West. In R. May, E. Angel & H. Ellenberger (Eds.), *Existence: A new dimension in psychology and psychiatry* (pp. 237–364). New York: Basic Books.

This is a classic case of considerable historical importance. It should be read by all serious students of psychotherapy.

Holt, H. (1966). The case of Father M: A segment of an existential analysis. *Journal of Existentialism, 6,* 369–495. [Also in Wedding, D. & Corsini, R. J. (Eds.) (1979). *Great cases in psychotherapy.* Itasca, IL: F. E. Peacock.]

This is a well written case study which offers insight into the manner in which an existential analysis might unfold.

May, R. (1973). Black and impotent: The life of Mercedes. In *Power and Innocence* (pp. 81–97). New York: Norton. [Reprinted in Wedding, D., & Corsini, R. J. (Eds.) (1988). *Case Studies in Psychotherapy.* Itasca, IL: F. E. Peacock.]

This brief case history illustrates the existential treatment by Rollo May of a young black woman dealing with core issues of power and self esteem. We believe this case provides an excellent example of many of the fundamental points made in the current chapter.

REFERENCES

Arieti, S. (1977). Psychotherapy of severe depression. *American Journal of Psychiatry, 134,* 864–68.

Becker, E. (1973). *Denial of Death.* New York: Free Press.

Binswanger, L. (1956). Existential analysis and psychotherapy. In E. Fromm-Reichmann and J. L. Moreno (Eds.), *Progress in psychotherapy* (pp. 144–168) New York: Grune & Stratton.

Boss, M. (1957a). *The analysis of dreams.* London: Rider & Co.

Boss, M. (1957b). Psychoanalyse und Daseinsanalytik. Bern & Stuttgart: Verlag Hans Huber.

Boss, M. (1982). *Psychoanalysis and daseinanalysis.* New York: Simon & Schuster.

Bugental, J. (1976). *The search for existential identity.* San Francisco: Jossey-Bass.

Bugental, J. (1956). *The search for authenticity.* New York: Holt, Rinehart and Winston.

Bynner, W. (Ed.) (1946). *The way of life, according to Lao tzu (An American version).* New York: John Day.

Donne, J. (1952). *Complete poetry and selected prose.* New York: Modern Library.

Farber, L. (1966). *The ways of the will: Essays toward a psychology and psychopathology of will.* New York: Basic Books.

Farber, L. (1976). *Lying, despair, jealousy, envy, sex, suicide, drugs, and the good life.* New York: Basic Books.

Frankl, V. (1963). *Man's search for meaning: An introduction to logotherapy.* New York: Pocket Books.

Frankl, V. (1969). *Will to meaning.* New York: World Publishing.

Havens, L. (1974). The existential use of the self. *American Journal of Psychiatry, 131.*

Heidegger, M. (1962). *Being and time.* New York: Harper & Row.

Horney, K. (1950). *Neurosis and human growth*. New York: Norton.

Jung, C. G. (1966). *Collected works: The practice of psychotherapy (Vol. 16)*. New York: Pantheon, Bollingen Series.

Kaiser, H. (1950). *Learning theory and personality dynamics*. New York: Ronald Press.

Kaiser, H. (1965). *Effective psychotherapy*. New York: Free Press.

Kant, I. (1954). *The encyclopedia of philosophy* (Vol. 4). P. Edwards (Ed.). New York: Macmillan and Free Press.

Kierkegaard, S. (1954). *Fear and trembling and the sickness unto death*. Garden City, NY: Doubleday.

Koestenbaum, P. (1978). *The new image of man*. Westport, CT: Greenwood Press.

Lasch, C. (1979). *The culture of narcissism*. New York: Norton.

May, R. (1953). *Man's search for himself*. New York: Norton.

May, R. (1961). *Existential psychology*. New York: Random House.

May R. (1969). *Love and will*. New York: Norton.

May, R. (1977). *The meaning of anxiety (rev. ed.)*. New York: Norton.

May, R. (1981). *Freedom and destiny*. New York: Norton.

May, R. (1982). The problem of evil: An open letter to Carl Rogers. *Journal of Humanistic Psychology, 3*, 16.

May, R., Angel, E., & Ellenberger, H. (Eds.) (1958). *Existence: A new dimension in psychiatry and psychology*. New York: Basic Books.

Mijuskovic, B. (1979). *Loneliness in philosophy, psychology and literature*. The Netherlands: Van Gorcum.

Mowrer, O. H. (1950). Time as a determinant in integrative learning. In O. H. Mowrer (Ed.), (pp. 418–454). *Learning theory and personality dynamics*. New York: Ronald Press.

Mowrer, O. H., & Ullman, A. D. (1952). Time as a determinant in integrative learning. *Psychological Review*, 61–90.

Perls, F. (1969). *Gestalt therapy verbatim*. Moab, UT: Real People Press.

Raskin, N. (1978). Becoming—A therapist, a person, a partner, and a parent. *Psychotherapy: Theory, Research and Practice, 4*, 15.

Sartre, J. P. (1956). *Being and nothingness*. New York: Philosophical Library.

Sequin, C. (1965). *Love and psychotherapy*. New York: Libar Publishers.

Spence, K. (1956). *Behavior therapy and conditioning*. New Haven, CT: Yale University.

Spinoza, B. (1954). Cited by M. De Unamuno in *The tragic sense of life* (E. Flitch, Trans). New York: Dover.

Tillich, P. (1952). *The courage to be*. New Haven, CT: Yale University Press.

Tolstoy, L. (1960). *The death of Ivan Illych and other stories*. New York: Signet.

Van Kaam, A. (1966). *Existential foundations of psychology*. Pittsburgh: Duquesne University Press.

Weisman, A. (1965). *Existential core of psychoanalysis: Reality sense and responsibility*. Boston: Little, Brown.

Yalom, I. (1981). *Existential psychotherapy*. New York: Basic Books.

ERIC BERNE, 1910–1970

11

Transactional Analysis

JOHN M. DUSAY and

KATHERINE MULHOLLAND DUSAY

OVERVIEW

Transactional analysis (TA), originated by Dr. Eric Berne in the 1950s, is a complete theory of personality. TA also uses a wide variety of related treatment techniques specifically designed to meet the needs and goals of clients. TA adheres to the presence of three active, dynamic, and observable ego states labeled the Parent, the Adult, and the Child, each of which exists and operates in any individual. Each person has a basic innate need for *strokes* (recognition) and will design a *life script* (plan), formed during childhood, based upon early beliefs about oneself and others. These existential beliefs are reinforced by repetitive, stereotyped *games* (unstraight social interactions) with others. The dynamic representation of any individual's psychological energy forces (Critical Parent, Nurturing Parent, Adult, Free Child, and Adapted Child) may be graphically portrayed on the person's *egogram* (a bar graph of one's personality portrait). One's egogram energy balance will remain "fixed" unless one actively decides to change one's behavior. An effective TA therapist is a potent catalyst who facilitates change and growth in clients.

BASIC CONCEPTS

TA therapists share certain challenges and basic questions with all other psychotherapists: Why are people the way they are? What are the basic human commonalities? How and why do individuals differ from one another? Why do they develop and retain negative patterns of thinking, feeling, and behaving even when doing so hurts them? Why do people resist changing even when a therapist offers them a vehicle for change? TA offers both answers and effective directions to such questions through its theoretical concepts and systematic approach. TA's simple vocabulary (Berne, 1964a;

Harris, 1969; James & Jongeward, 1971) is intentionally designed to enable clients to demystify the esoteric jargon of traditional therapies. Some basic terms used in TA are: Parent, Adult, and Child *ego states; transactions; games; strokes; scripts;* and *egograms.* An important TA attitude will be noted throughout this work: Concepts are not only expressed verbally, but also have accompanying symbols—circles, arrows, triangles, and bar graphs—that increase clarity and understanding, as well as represent a commitment by the therapist to explain his or her viewpoint. The therapist and client both share these mutual "tools" and simple vocabularies, and while this tends to eliminate some of the therapist's magic, the client is facilitated to "own" his appropriate share of responsibility for treatment.

Ego States

Eric Berne discovered that clients were at times thinking, feeling, and behaving like children and at other times like rational adults. He differentiated between two distinct ego states: the Child and the Adult. The *Child* ego state within each of us is sometimes creative, intuitive, and pleasure seeking and other times rebellious or conforming. Originally Berne labeled the Child ego state the *archaeopsyche,* which connoted the developmentally archaic, regressive ego state (Berne, 1961). The *Adult* ego state, which is the realistic, logical part of us, he termed the *neopsyche,* which referred to computing and data processing. Each ego state has its own observable mannerisms, a special repertoire of words, thoughts, emotions, body postures, gestures, voice tones, and expressions. The Child ego state behaves and

sounds like an actual child, regardless of the person's biological age. The Adult ego state resembles a computer in that it takes in, stores, retrieves, and processes information about self and environment. The Adult deals exclusively with facts and logical data in a nonemotional way.

Soon, another basic aspect of human behavior became evident—the *Parent,* or *exteropsyche*—both an introjection from and an identification with one's actual biological parents. The Parent ego state expresses one's value systems, morals, and beliefs. These attitudes may take the form of promoting growth in others as well as being critical and controlling. The Parent may portray traits and mannerisms of one's actual mother, father, and other parenting figures. The Parent in a person may be judgmental and opinionated, as well as nurturing and protective. One's Parent ego state is frequently familial and cultural in origin, often passed down from parents to their children, who in turn pass it down to their children. (The three ego states are capitalized as Parent, Adult, and Child to distinguish them from the biological entities of parents, adults, and children.)

The completed tripartite system of one's personality structure is symbolized by three connected, distinct circles to represent that they are unique, separate, and independent entities. Each ego state functions independently from the others and has separate boundaries, wherein it contains specific properties (see Figure 11.1). The three ego states are dynamic and observable. They are unlike Freud's personality structure of id, ego, and superego, which are hypothetical concepts and not observable phenomena.

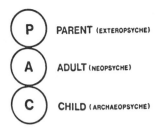

EGO-STATE DIAGRAM

FIGURE 11.1

Transactions

Social action begins when two (or more) people get together. Psychologically speaking, two people in a room means there are actually six structured ego states present, and these ego states may transact and communicate with one another. A transaction is a unit of human communication. A *transaction* is defined as a stimulus and a related response between two persons' ego states; the word *transaction* is preferred over the more general term *communication* for clarity and precision. There are two basic levels of transactions: the *social level*, which is overt or manifest, and the *psychological level*, which is covert or latent. These two levels of transactions are visually symbolized by arrows: the socially stated, overt transaction is represented by a solid-line arrow, and the psychologically stated, covert transaction is symbolized by a dotted-line arrow.

Games

When these two levels (psychological and social) are actively operating at the same time, a game is usually taking place. A *game* is defined as an orderly series of ulterior transactions (with both an overt and a covert level), which results in "payoffs" with spe-

cific bad feelings for both game players. The overt series of transactions is straightforward and in this particular example is an Adult-to-Adult transaction: The boss asks his secretary, "What time is it?" She answers, "Three o'clock." However, his covert nonverbal message (represented by the dotted lines of his Parent to her Child) is, "You're always late." Her hidden nonverbal response (dotted lines of her Child to his Parent) is, "You're always criticizing me." Even though neither the boss nor his secretary expresses these hidden sentiments out loud, each is fully aware of the hidden messages and each will receive a personal payoff of bad feelings. The boss is playing his part in the game colloquially known as *Now I Got You, You SOB*, and he feels angry and self-righteous. His secretary is playing *Kick Me* and feels bad and picked on (see Figure 11.2). People transact in certain stereotyped ways that are predictable and unique for each person, and these are called games. Each of the players ends up with "bad feelings" called *rackets*. After several repeated episodes of these games with themselves and with other players, the secretary will have collected enough psychological trading *stamps* to cash in and will entitle

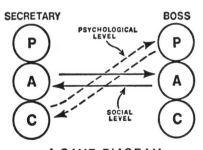

A GAME DIAGRAM

FIGURE 11.2

herself to a "free" depression, while the boss will entitle himself to a "free" rampage and perhaps fire her.

Strokes

The basic motivation for any human social interaction is based on people's ongoing needs for strokes (human contact and recognition). When straightforward, positive strokes are not available, people will employ ulterior methods and use games to receive strokes. Although positive strokes feel better than negative strokes, negative strokes are better than no strokes at all! Specific patterns of giving and receiving strokes are learned, and they are unique to each family. The ways that people give and get strokes serve to shape each individual's personality. During infancy and early childhood, positive "strokes" are given and received by actual touching, holding, and cuddling. This touching is necessary for the healthy survival of any newborn human infant (Spitz, 1945). Somewhere between the ages of two and four, the stroking tends to become less physical and more verbal, although actual physical stroking remains important throughout life, from infancy to old age. Stroking can be positive (caring and approving) or negative (damaging and disapproving). Because strokes are essential to each person's survival, negative strokes are sought if positive strokes are not available.

Scripts

Through early interactions with parents and others, a pattern of stroking develops, which may be either supportive or attacking (Berne, 1972). From this stroking pattern, the child at some point early in life makes a basic existential decision about himself, essentially that he is either OK as a person or not OK. This basic decision is then re-

inforced by continuing messages, both verbal and nonverbal, the person receives throughout life. The developing child not only makes these crucial decisions about himself, but also develops a viewpoint about what other people are like. The child decides either that other people are OK and to be trusted or that they are not OK (Berne, 1964b; Harris, 1969). This process of deciding about both oneself and others becomes one's basic belief system.

Through the script matrix (Steiner, 1971a), we can note the Parent ego states of both mother and father supply (1) their values, morals, opinions, and prejudices to the developing Parent ego state of their child. The Child ego states of both mother and father provide (2) the injunctions or the negative messages to the Child ego state of their child. On the basis of these early verbal (solid line) and nonverbal (dotted line) messages (which are frequently incongruent and incompatible), the Child ego state of the young child will decide what life will be like. The Adult ego states of the opposite-sex parent of the child usually provide (3) the here's how message of how to make it through life (see Figure 11.3).

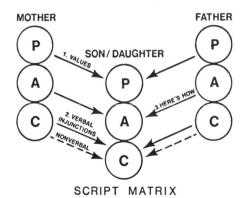

SCRIPT MATRIX

FIGURE 11.3

One's script or life course is based upon one's early existential decisions. Scripts incorporate specific elements from myths, fairy tales, and theatrical dramas in that they include a wide variety of characters, along with the elements of suspense, surprise, triumph, tragedy, anger, scare, joy, and other emotions. One's life script may be either winning or losing, hamartic (tragic) or banal, and each script includes specific roles. Some people approach life as heroes and heroines (K. Dusay, 1975), and others operate as rescuers, persecutors, and victims (Karpman, 1968). After the child incorporates early messages from the parents, a script develops into a strong belief system, so when the client arrives at the psychotherapist's office years later, the basic life script is both apparent and staunchly defended.

Egograms

Although TA's structure of personality is symbolized by the three circles of ego states, the function and amount of energy placed within these ego states is symbolized by the egogram (J. Dusay, 1972). The circles illustrate which ego states are involved in the transactions, and the egogram exemplifies, in bar graph form, how much energy exists in the five functional ego states of any person. The Parent is divided into its functional aspects of both Critical Parent (CP) and Nurturing Parent (NP); the Adult (A) is not divided because it is unemotional and functions solely as a computer; and the Child is divided into its Free Child (FC) functions, which are natural and uninhibited, and its Adapted Child (AC) functions, which are compliant or rebellious. These basic psychological energies are present in each person in varying amounts.

Because each person has a distinct and unique personality, these five psychological forces are aligned in different amounts and balances in each individual. An egogram is constructed on a five-position bar graph that represents CP, NP, A, FC, and AC. The higher columns signify the greater amounts of time and energy expended in these ego states, and the smaller columns portray lesser degrees of time and energy. The egogram operates with a constancy hypothesis in that when one raises the time and energy in one ego state, another ego state will lose energy. This is a simple illustration of the growth model. A person's egogram will remain fixed and not change unless the person actively decides to change the energy balances in his or her ego states (see Figure 11.4). The Critical Parent is the part of one's personality that criticizes or finds fault. The CP is also assertive, directing, and limiting; makes rules; enforces one's value system; and stands up for one's rights. (Too much CP is dictatorial.) The Nurturing Parent in a person is empathetic and promotes growth. (Too much NP is smothering.) The Adult's function is clear, rational thinking. The Adult is factual, precise, accurate, nonemotional, and nonjudgmental. (Too much Adult is boring.) The Free Child is spontaneous, curious, playful, fun, free, eager, and intuitive. (Too much FC is seen as being out of control.) The Adapted Child is conforming, compromising, adapting, easy to get along with, and compliant. The Adapted Child may also manifest itself as a pseudorebel that does the opposite of everything that is expected. (Too much AC will manifest itself in many ways, including being guilty, depressed, or robotlike, or throwing temper tantrums reminiscent of small children.)

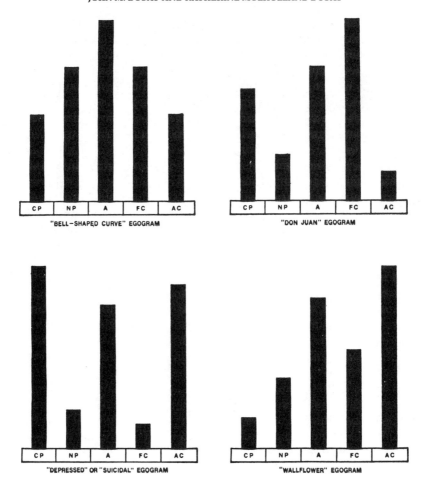

EXAMPLES OF EGOGRAMS

FIGURE 11.4

Because each person has a psychological energy portrait (or egogram) of personality, the complexities and changes of the human personality can be described through this system. There are neither "good" nor "bad" egograms per se, but generalizations may be formed about certain egogram balances. A *bell-shaped egogram* implies that the personality has a well-balanced energy system with psychological energy fairly evenly distrib- uted. A *Don Juan* will have a high Free Child (interested in fun and sexual trysts), a high Critical Parent (knows how to tell women to get lost), a low Nurturing Parent (does not care about their feelings), a medium-high Adult (logically knows how to find women), and a low Adapted Child (feels little guilt and will not compromise). A *Wallflower* by contrast is highest in Adapted Child (is worried about what others will think), low in Free Child (is seldom playful or fun), and low in Critical Parent (will seldom assert self or stand up for own rights). A depressed or suicidal person will be quite low on Nurturing Parent (both to self and others), and also low on Free Child (feels little zest for life and happiness).

OTHER SYSTEMS

TA differs from other systems of personality in that explanations about human behavior are viewed on the basis of Parent, Adult, and Child ego states. Human behavior not explained in terms of these ego states is not TA, although statements from other fields may sound similar to TA statements. Freud once remarked that it is one thing to flirt with an idea and another thing to be married to it. The transactional analyst is married to the concept of ego states.

A major difference between psychoanalysis and TA is that TA does not rely upon a theory of the unconscious. Although Berne himself never denied this theory, he and his followers find that the concept of a dynamic unconscious is unnecessary for the practice of TA. A basic difference between TA and Freudian theory is that while the id, ego, and superego are *hypothetical* constructs, the Parent, Adult, and Child ego states are *observable* phenomena. Ego-state recognition and the alignment of these states on an egogram enable one to restructure behavior by making *new* decisions about self and life.

Many TA therapists incorporate versions of Gestalt techniques that were practiced by Fritz Perls (1969). TA encourages a person's intellectual cognition (which was discounted by Perls) and also supports a client's emotional expressions. TA's use of cognitive

models is evident in its clearly stated theory of personality. By comparison, Perls left little in the way of a clear record or system for his later theories and techniques. The major difference between TA and Gestalt is TA's use of a therapeutic treatment contract. TA therapists and their clients use specific, oral, measurable goals by which both the therapist and the client are mutually involved and directed.

As far as actual living in the world is concerned, TA shares with existential analysis a high esteem for personal qualities of honesty, integrity, autonomy, and authenticity. However, TA places importance on personality structure and views the problem of "self" to be a balance of ego-state structure and function.

Beck's cognitive therapy and TA have much in common. However, cognitive therapy does not use the same colloquial terms as TA. Both therapies accept the concept that the patient has the power to grow and change and needs to operate in an authentic reality rather than the "reality" he or she learned as a child.

Similarities exist between encounter and TA in that both are practiced in groups, workshops, and marathons. Many techniques used by encounter leaders are also used by TA therapists; however, TA therapists use specific techniques tailor-made for each individual to raise low energies in deficient ego states. No particular type of encounter maneuver is thought by the TA analyst to be appropriate for everyone. Rather, each technique is geared and designed for each individual's unique personality egogram. Pillow pounding, rage, and anger expressions are beneficial only for those people who have a poorly developed Critical Parent; they are *not* indicated for those who already have too much anger! Likewise, exercises in expressing feelings are necessary only for those who have too much Adult and have limited their emotional and social responses; these techniques are not as beneficial for those who are already uninhibited and open with their feelings.

Therapists who call themselves eclectic may or may not use certain ideas in common with TA. Eclectics frequently mix bits and pieces from other theoretical approaches. They may also jump back and forth from one framework to another in theory, and thereby may confuse structures, function, behavior, phenomenology, history, and social systems with one another. This resembles mixing apples with oranges, and frequently, a clear path or a defined strategy may be missing.

HISTORY

TA was evolved by Eric Berne in the mid-1950s, at a time when psychoanalysis was the primary psychotherapy, communication theory was being applied to emotional problems, and group therapy was emerging as an important modality. The literature and impact of these three influences were especially important to the development of TA.

PRECURSORS

Ego-State Precursors

Wilder Penfield's research (1952) at McGill Medical School, where Berne was a medical student, deserves special mention. Penfield reported that the memories of epileptics are retained and replayed in their natural form:

The subject feels again the emotions which the situation originally produced in him, and he is aware of the same interpretation, true or false, which he himself gave to the experience in the first place. This evoked recollection is not the exact photographic reproduction of past scenes and events. It is a reproduction of what the patient saw and heard and felt and understood. (p. 178)

Penfield's remarkable neurosurgical experiments demonstrated that different ego states (Penfield did not use the term *ego state*) are reexperienced under direct electrical stimulation of the brain and that one experiences a complete revival in the present of both the experience and the memories along with the corresponding feelings of a past situation (Penfield & Roberts, 1959). Berne, a psychiatrist, was especially interested in ego psychology, then an important topic in the New York Psychoanalytic Institute circles because of the influence of Heinz Hartmann, Ernst Kris, and others. Berne was impressed with the apparent intact structure of the past states of the ego.

Pharmacological studies in the early work with LSD-25 by Chandler and Hartman (1960) describe the reactivation of the archaic states, and they discuss the employing of two simultaneous states: one oriented to current external and psychological reality, and the other reliving (not merely recalling) scenes dating back to the first year of life. These scenes are accompanied by vivid color, detail, and a feeling of actual experience with all of the original intensity.

Paul Federn (1952), Berne's analyst, first expressed in the psychiatric field what Penfield and the drug experimenters later proved: the complete states of the ego are permanently retained and may be reactivated. Federn used the term *ego state* and this met resistance from those more accustomed to thinking in orthodox conceptual terms. Eduardo Weiss (1950), Federn's exponent, described ego states as one's actually experienced reality, with the complete contents that one relived from a past period. Weiss reiterated what Penfield proved: the ego states of former age levels are maintained in a potential existence within the personality, and they may be evoked under special conditions—hypnosis, dreams, and psychosis.

Before Berne's elucidation of the structure of the three basic ego states, ego psychologists described, and anatomists and pharmacologists proved, the general existence of intact ego states.

Games and Transactions Precursors

General communication theorists such as Alfred Korzybski and Norbert Wiener were studied by Berne and other early TA theorists. The application of communication-system theory to psychological issues by Gregory Bateson and Jurgen Ruesch (1951) and their Palo Alto associates in the Bay Area of San Francisco, where TA was concomitantly developing, became a direct influence. Bateson (Bateson, Jackson, Haley & Weakland, 1956) espoused the double-bind theory of schizophrenia, a communication model which essentially postulates that there are two different and incompatible levels of communication between a schizophrenogenic mother and her child. As each level is incompatible with the other, the dependent child has no easy escape except for psychosis. Berne independently specified these two types of levels (overt and covert), and from this he developed rules for games (the corresponding game for a double bind is Corner).

Years before, Karl Abraham (1948) had described various character types and related these personality characteristics and behaviors to specific fixations that occurred at various stages of psychosexual development. He labeled these character types according to specific orifices—oral, anal, urethral, and genital. Berne later compared Abraham's analyses of character types with specific game patterns: oral types play Do Me Something, anal types play Schlemiel or Now I Got You, You SOB, urethral types play Kick Me, and genital types may play Rapo. Berne was quite impressed by Abraham's work, and he presented a panel entitled "Character Types and Game Analysis" at the American Psychiatric Association meeting in 1969.

René Spitz's work (1945) emphasized the importance of both the quantity and quality of early mother-to-child transactions. This research is frequently quoted by TA writers and became the inspiration for the term strokes (see p. 408).

Script Precursors

The notion of scripts is not new; many allusions in classical and modern literature are made to the fact that the world is a stage and all the people on it are players. Joseph Campbell (1949), the mythologist, takes the view that human lives follow the similar patterns of myths. His works are influential to TA script theorists. In fact, Berne once remarked that Campbell's The Hero with a Thousand Faces is the best textbook for script analysis. Much of Campbell's thinking is based on Jung's and Freud's ideas. Jung's notion of archetypes (which correspond to Berne's magic figure in a script) and the persona (the style in which a script is played) were useful to Berne, who, although he admired Jung's focus of attention on myths and fairy tales, found that mythical discussions were difficult to understand and relate to real people without elaborate training. Freud directly related many aspects of human living to a single drama: Oedipus. Berne, a serious student of psychoanalysis for three decades, initially accepted and later rejected the notion that each patient is an Oedipus who exhibits the same reactions and drama within his or her head. Instead, Berne viewed Oedipus as a single possibility of the many that may take place in a patient's life.

Adler (1963) was interested in an individual's goal, which he likened to a secret life plan. Goals, types of scripts, and therapeutic contracts became an important influence to Berne.

Action and Energy Precursors

Abraham Maslow (self-actualization), Will Schutz (encounter), Fritz Perls (Gestalt), and other growth therapists had a profound effect upon the present practice of TA. More direct theoretical applications have been employed by Berne's followers since his death in 1970. Berne occasionally went to Esalen Institute, the influential growth center on the Big Sur Coast of California, and met with Fritz Perls (Gestalt), Will Schutz (encounter), Virginia Satir (family dynamics), Michael Murphy (human growth), and others involved in the human-potential movement. Robert Goulding, John Dusay, and other TA teachers conducted Esalen workshops, and Berne's followers became directly exposed to growth psychologies that appeared simultaneously with TA's development in northern California. Indeed, many encounter, marathon, and Gestalt leaders embraced TA's theories, as they would enrich TA with their human experiential techniques.

BEGINNINGS

Like many psychiatric innovators, Eric Berne was formally trained in classical psychoanalysis. However, in the mid-1950s, he amiably parted from the psychoanalytical school of thought in favor of employing more rapidly effective techniques to cure patients. TA's history until Berne's death in 1970 is the history of his theory and techniques (J. Dusay, 1975). Berne began doing group therapy when he was an army major in World War II. Following his discharge, he began unique experiments on the nature of intuition, and he published six articles on this subject between 1949 and 1962, published posthumously in 1977 (Berne, 1949, 1977). The intuition articles reflect the evolution of TA and trace Berne's development as the leader of an innovative approach.

The most important discovery for TA was the dynamic nature of three distinct ego states, which occurred in 1955, when Berne worked in a group with Belle, a 40-year-old disturbed housewife who was discharged from a state hospital and behaved in two distinct ways toward the men in her life:

Belle would subtly mock and jeer at men whom she considered weak and tease and torment those men whom she felt were strong. She was continually intrigued and confused as to whether the therapist was weak or strong, and she confessed her fantasy that she could see the conformation of his genitals and then attempted to determine if his penis were flabby or erect. She remembered doing the same with her father. Her husband reminded her of a strong man implacable as stone, whose tremendous erections frightened her.... She became ... nauseated when her husband had an erection and could not bear to fantasize about it.... She became ... indisposed when her husband told her a graphic joke about an erection.... She could intellectually discuss the vagina but could not bear thinking of it as actually pictured, "a raw, red slimy gash." The image terrified her and she desperately avoided it. . . . Smells also played a significant part in this type of imagery with her. (Berne, 1955, pp. 634–58)

Berne called these images Belle experienced *primal images.* They gave rise to the primal judgments she made about men in her life: "This man is flaccid" and "This man is virile." Berne observed these same types of primal judgments occurring in everyday life: "He's an asshole (prick, stinker, jerk, pushover, fart, bleeding heart)." Primal judgments were also seen to be zonal and connected to oral, gastrointestinal, anal, genital, and excretory functions. People relate to others according to their primal images and judgments. Berne noted that the "bleeding heart" and the "jerk" were prone to find each other.

The first phase of TA began with Berne's discovery and delineation of ego states (J. Dusay, 1977a), which are a coherent system of thinking, feeling, and behaving. Berne elucidated his discovery of ego states:

An 8-year-old boy vacationing at a dude ranch in his cowboy suit helped the hired man unsaddle a horse. When they were finished, the hired man said, "Thanks, Cowpoke." The "assistant" replied, "I'm not really a cowpoke. I'm just a little boy." The patient went on to remark, "That's just the way I feel. Sometimes I feel that I'm not really a lawyer. I'm just a little boy."

This story illustrates the separation of two ways of feeling, thinking, and behaving in this particular patient; everything that was said was heard by two different people, one an adult lawyer and the other an inner little boy. This particular patient was in treatment for a compulsive gambling habit. Sometimes he used a rational, logical gambling system, which was occasionally successful, but more often he governed his behavior with superstitious and little-boy ways of explaining his losses. . . .

It became apparent that there were two types of arithmetic employed. (Berne, 1957, p. 611)

Both systems were conscious, deliberate, visible, and active parts of the patient's ego system.

Berne emphasized that the archaic intuitive faculty of the Child could be cultivated by the therapist. Dynamically, intuition works best when the Child predominates, the Adult monitors, and the Parent reduces its influence. To Berne, creativity was the Child knowing and the Adult confirming.

TA moved into its second phase (1958–65) with Berne's attention to the *transaction,* which is a stimulus from one person's ego state and the corresponding response from another person's ego state. Berne's interest in communications theory enabled him to recognize that there were often two different types of messages emanating from one source. For instance, a radio would emit a meaningful message, "It's raining in California," and another simultaneous type of communication would be pops, whirrs, and radio static. With these two types of communication in mind, Berne observed what happens when people get together, and he formulated a specific, concise definition of communication, along with the corresponding three rules (see p. 420). By observing both the overt and the covert levels of transacting individuals, Berne began to classify games.

Human behavior that involves two levels of communication with predictable, stereotyped, and destructive actions that are motivated by hidden desires and lead to specific *payoffs* (bad feelings) were labeled games. The first game Berne analyzed was *Why Don't*

You . . . ? Yes, But . . . , which occurred during one of his therapy groups:

Patient S: I wish I could fix the leak in our roof.
Respondent 1: Why don't you ask your friend to do it?
Patient S: That's a good idea, but my friend has to work this weekend.
Respondent 2: Why don't you do it yourself?
Patient S: I would, but I don't have any tools.
Respondent 3: Why don't you get some tools?
Patient S: Yes, but I overspent my budget this month.
Respondent 4: Why don't you . . . ?
Patient S: Yes, but . . . yes, but . . .

On the overt social level, Patient S provides an Adult stimulus by requesting help for the specific problem, and the respondents reciprocate with straightforward Adult advice. On the covert psychological level, Patient S is transacting on a Child-Parent level and secretly implying, "Just you try to suggest something I haven't already thought of, hee-hee." The group members try and try, with the result that they become frustrated and S maintains a triumphant, coy smile.

An entire classification of psychological games has been elucidated in *Games People Play* (Berne, 1964b). People are inclined to have a specific repertoire of favorite games they play, and they base their entire social relationships upon finding suitable partners to play the corresponding opposite roles. Berne and members of the original San Francisco TA seminar were pursuing the question, "Why do different people play the same games over and over?" Freud's repetition compulsion was an appealing, yet obscure, notion that did not satisfactorily answer this question. Because plausible explanations were sought, TA historically moved into its third phase (1960–70), which resulted in script the-

ory. A *script* is "a life plan based on a decision made in childhood, reinforced by the parents, justified by subsequent events, and culminating in a chosen alternative" (Berne, 1972, p. 162). The direct script message transmissions from parents to their children became symbolized by Claude Steiner (1971a) with the script matrix (see Figure 11.3).

As TA theorists began to delve into folk and fairy tales, they found various life-styles were based on specific characters with whom patients and their relatives identified. These could be traced back to ancient myths, with their victims, persecutors, and rescuers (Karpman, 1968), and the more popular heroines and heroes who starred in popular folktales, dramas, movies, novels, and television shows (K. Dusay, 1976). One's script became written and fixed in the Child (p. 39) and reinforced through fantasies, dreams, and, later, "reality."

Berne was a prolific writer who published 64 articles and 8 books. He originated the TA Bulletin, which later emerged as a quarterly, *Transactional Analysis Journal*. Berne was at the height of his creativity, insight, and power when he died of a coronary infarction in the summer of 1970.

CURRENT STATUS

Since Berne's death, a fourth phase of TA has emerged: energy transfers, distribution, and action. The *egogram* (J. Dusay, 1972) symbolizes the amount of time and energy any person exudes in his or her ego states. The energy system of an egogram remains constant, unless a person actively changes his or her balance and relationship to others through direct energy transfers (raising weak, underused ego states). Since 1970, TA practitioners have developed many suitable techniques for raising energy levels in the various ego states.

The clinical use of TA will relate to one of the four phases of TA's development: (1) ego states, (2) transactions and games, (3) script analysis and redecision, and (4) egogram energy shift.

The San Francisco TA Seminar was formerly called the San Francisco Social Psychiatry Seminar (founded by Berne in 1958) and is now known as the Eric Berne Seminar of San Francisco. This is the world's longest ongoing weekly seminar for group therapy. From the original eight members who met in Berne's office in the 1950s, the International Transactional Analysis Association (ITAA) presently includes over 10,000 members in the United States and throughout the world. The ITAA is experiencing rapid growth in Europe, South America, India, and the Pacific Rim countries of Japan, Australia, and Malaysia.

Berne maintained that trying to "look professional" was not as important as curing patients. He willingly taught his system to all interested persons in the helping professions. Through the ITAA, an advanced, rigorous training program is available for members to train formally for a period of two to five years to attain clinical competency and certification as TA therapists and teachers. Two distinct lines of advanced training have evolved and presently exist: advanced clinical training (for mental health professionals) and special fields training (for teachers and business-oriented people).

In 1971, the editorial board of the *Transactional Analysis Journal* instituted the Eric Berne Memorial Scientific Awards for outstanding contributions to TA theory and practice. Each year, TA persons are nominated who have devised original and applicable concepts to Berne's goal of "curing patients faster," and the winner is chosen by the advanced members' votes of the ITAA.

PERSONALITY

THEORY OF PERSONALITY

The basic motivating factor for all human social behavior is a lifelong need for human recognition, which TA therapists term *strokes*. Strokes may be either physical (a hug) or verbal ("You're nice"). René Spitz (1945), a child psychoanalyst, studied the mortality rate of infants in two types of orphanages in England. He found that the extent to which the children were physically stroked and handled had a profound effect upon their survival.

TA analysts maintain that continual strokes are necessary throughout one's life, and a lack of strokes has a deleterious and long-lasting effect, both physically and emotionally.

Habitual criminals with high recidivism rates illustrate that negative strokes are better than no strokes at all. The primate studies of Harry Harlow (1958) demonstrate that both isolated baby monkeys reared without mother monkeys and those "fed" by surrogate wire monkeys become emotionally disturbed and exhibit abnormal behaviors. Sensory-deprivation experiments with normal adults at Harvard (Vernon, 1961) illustrate that both cognitive and motor functioning will rapidly deteriorate and deficits will persist for days, even after the persons go back into a normal environment. Illusions and hallucinations can be produced by a temporary lack of sensory stimuli. More than 700 TA articles and descriptions of strokes have appeared in scientific journals and related literature since 1957 (Blair & McGahey, 1974, 1975).

Human children growing up begin to look for ways to get both verbal and symbolic strokes from others when physical strokes are not forthcoming (K. Dusay, 1988). Although spoken words may become the major sources of strokes for people in later life, it is doubtful whether words alone can ever completely replace actual physical touching. In *Having A Baby* (1984), K. Dusay states that many mothers actually stroke their bellies throughout pregnancy; this becomes the infants' earliest strokes.

Specific stroking patterns develop that may be more clearly understood by attention to both the structural and the functional analyses of ego states, transactions, psychological games, egograms, and scripts.

Structural Analysis

Ego states are defined as a consistent pattern of feelings and experiences directly related to a corresponding pattern of behavior. A distinct tripartite system of Parent, Adult, and Child, which are separate entities, has been described and is the subject of struc-

tural analysis. Although most of the salient features of ego states have been presented in the "History" section, it is important to reemphasize that ego states are a phenomenological system based upon here-and-now observable data, in contrast to psychoanalytic concepts that primarily emphasize developmental stages and view pathology as resulting from fixations in development.

Ego states are not related to chronological age, except developmentally during early childhood, when an individual's Adult and Parent are not yet fully developed. A teenager may have a staunch moral and value system (P); an 8-year-old boy may look to the right and left for oncoming cars before crossing the street (A); and a 65-year-old chairman of the board will gleefully chase his young, sexy secretary around the conference table (C).

Certain pathologies in personalities can be structurally understood with the three ego states (see Figures 11.5, 11.6, 11.7, and 11.8). Figure 11.5 illustrates a normal personality structure, in which each ego state has a distinct and separate boundary. Figure 11.6 is the structure of a delusion. In this instance, there is a Child-Adult delusion in that the separating boundaries have

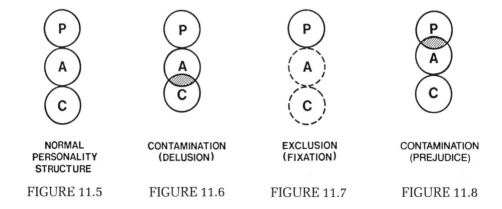

NORMAL PERSONALITY STRUCTURE	CONTAMINATION (DELUSION)	EXCLUSION (FIXATION)	CONTAMINATION (PREJUDICE)
FIGURE 11.5	FIGURE 11.6	FIGURE 11.7	FIGURE 11.8

broken down. The Child's fantasies and dreams are inappropriately mixed in with Adult reality and logic testing. This person might say, "The TV is giving me special instructions." His Adult accurately believes there is a TV transmitting information. The Child ego has regarded itself as the center of the TV's attention, thereby causing a break in the boundaries between the Adult and the Child. Figure 11.7 illustrates the structure of an exclusion. The Parent is represented by a heavy, dark, solid circle, while the Adult and the Child have only dotted lines. This strong boundary ensures that the Parent is in charge and that the Adult and Child are excluded. A fundamentalist country preacher who is obsessed with finding sins is operating from an excluding Parent ego state. Figure 11.8 is a diagram of contamination. The Parent and Adult egostates have broken down boundaries and mix into each other. When one speaks from a contamination, the statement might be something like "Boys are smarter than girls."

The Functional Aspects of Personality

The structural description of ego states with their circles and boundaries indicates the "what and where" of the personality. The concept of "how much energy" of the five ego-state forces (Critical Parent—CP, Nurturing Parent—NP, Adult—A, Free Child—FC, and Adapted Child—AC) is answered by the functional approach of the egogram.

Any group of trained ego-state observers can readily identify these five basic forces within people, and each will construct similar egograms of the same person. They will consensually agree on the personality-force bal-

ance, or imbalance, as depicted on the subject's egogram. These same egograms can be drawn accurately week after week by different trained observers. The ego states will line up differently on each person's egogram and correspond directly to the specific complaints and problems these people express. An egogram with an excessively high CP, a high A, a high AC, a low NP, and a low FC is characteristically associated with a person who is self-destructive (see Figure 11.9). Other consistent findings reveal that when a very high AC is combined with a very low NP, the common complaint will be of loneliness and lack of friends (see Figure 11.10). A certain type of obesity, colloquially labeled "Big Mama," is correlated with a very high NP, a high AC, a low CP, and a very low FC. This Big Mama egogram is common among overweight people in the helping professions: social workers, nurses, dieticians, and those who live with demanding spouses and children who seem to require an abundance of nurturing and strokes. These persons spend most of their energies giving to

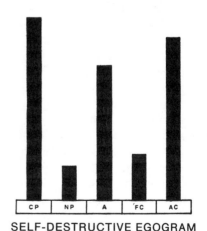

SELF-DESTRUCTIVE EGOGRAM

FIGURE 11.9

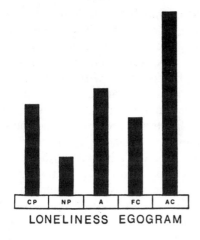

LONELINESS EGOGRAM

FIGURE 11.10

others and unfortunately get very little back for their FC in the way of strokes. People who are too low in CP are exploited and pushed around. People who are quite low in NP are lonely, depressed, and ungiving. Those low in A have difficulty concentrating and problem solving. Those low in FC have lost their creativity, intuition, and the zest of life. And people who are low in AC do not compromise or conform and are difficult to get along with.

An egogram reflects the type of person one is, one's probable types of problems, and the strengths and weaknesses within one's personality. The egogram also provides a personal map for growth and change. Although there is no ideal egogram, people experience difficulties when one ego state is extremely low and another is disproportionately high. Relative to that, a harmonious egogram becomes a matter of balance in the relationship between the ego states. A creative artist needs a high FC, a successful district attorney needs a high CP, an accountant needs a strong A, a diplomat needs lots of AC, and a therapist needs a well-developed NP.

Transactions and the Three Rules of Communication

TA focuses keen attention upon how different individuals tend to communicate with one another. A *transaction* is defined as a stimulus and a related response between various ego states of two or more people, and, graphically, they are symbolized by arrows. The two primary types of transactions are the *social* overt and easily observed level, represented by a solid arrow, and the *psychological* covert, body-language level, represented by a dotted arrow.

Three specific types of transactions, with their three corresponding rules of communication, have been delineated in Figures 11.11, 11.12, and 11.13. In Figure 11.11, entitled Complementary Transaction, the arrows are parallel. The boss (A) asks the secretary (A), "What time is it?" He gets a complementary straightforward, overt response (A to A), "It's 3 o'clock." The first rule of communication involves a complementary transaction: *whenever the arrows are parallel, communication can proceed indefinitely.* Communication may be A-A, P-P, C-C, P-C, C-P, C-A, A-P, P-A, or the reverse. In Figure 11.12, there is a crossed transaction, so the arrows are crossed. The boss asks (A-A), "What time is it?" and the secretary angrily answers (P-C), "Look at your own watch!" This crossed transaction effectively stops the communication about "time" between them. Therefore, the corresponding second rule of communication is: *Whenever the arrows cross, communication on the specific subject ceases immediately.* This second rule of communication clarifies the phenomenon of *transference* as described in psychoanalytic literature. The therapist says, "You seem to be late for your

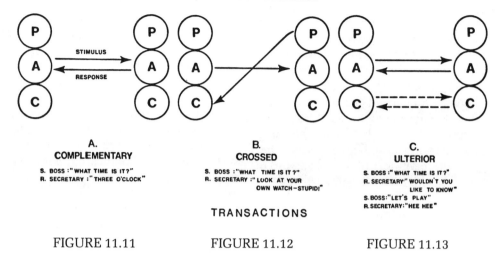

A.
COMPLEMENTARY

S. BOSS : " WHAT TIME IS IT ? "
R. SECRETARY : " THREE O'CLOCK "

B.
CROSSED

S. BOSS : " WHAT TIME IS IT ? "
R. SECRETARY : " LOOK AT YOUR
OWN WATCH — STUPID! "

C.
ULTERIOR

S. BOSS : " WHAT TIME IS IT ? "
R. SECRETARY· " WOULDN'T YOU
LIKE TO KNOW "
S. BOSS : " LET'S PLAY "
R. SECRETARY : " HEE HEE "

TRANSACTIONS

FIGURE 11.11   FIGURE 11.12   FIGURE 11.13

Friday appointment" (A-A), and the client reports, "You're always criticizing me for being late—just like my father" (C-P). A *countertransference* occurs when a therapist crosses a complementary transaction; that is, the client says, "How long do you think my treatment will be? (A-A), and the therapist replies, "You shouldn't ask questions like that" (P-C). Figure 11.13 illustrates an ulterior transaction with dual levels (the social and the psychological) occurring simultaneously. The boss again asks the secretary the time (A-A social level and C-C hidden psychological level). She gives him the time (A-A social level and C-C playful psychological level). A dual-level transaction with an ulterior message is necessary for a psychological game. This leads to the third rule of communication: *Behavior cannot be predicted by attention to the social level alone; the psychological message is the key to predicting behavior and understanding the meaning.* The first game ever discovered, *Why don't you . . . Yes, but . . .* , is one in which the client enticed the group to "try" to help her solve her problem. After continuing to try, they became frustrated and finally gave up, while the client coyly smiled and triumphantly exulted that no one could solve her problem (hee-hee). Analyzing and identifying the ulterior transactions are necessary to understanding psychological games.

Psychological Games

A *game* is played between two or more people, and each game has certain traits in common. The players transact on an *open* (overt) level and at the same time transmit a *hidden* agenda (covert level). Consider Fanny, who complained that she was unable to hold a job, having been fired 20 times in 10 years. She stated she wanted a solid, long-term working relationship with an employer (she also wanted a long-term, social relationship in her life). Her therapist agreed with her goal and contracted to work with her to achieve it. During their initial interview, Fanny started by criticizing the therapist's necktie; then she began to rearrange her chair and the rest of the office furniture; and finally, she "accidentally" knocked over the therapist's favorite lamp. As Fanny was apologizing and bending over to reposition the lamp, she placed the distinctive target of her posterior near the therapist's foot, which he instantly considered kicking. Suddenly, with an intuitive laugh, he checked his anger and his foot. Fanny turned to face him with a knowing look, and she, too, began to laugh as they both became aware that she was playing a physical version of her favorite *Kick Me* game (see Figure 11.2).

On the obvious social level (solid lines), Fanny said to the therapist (A-A), "Please help me with my problem." The therapist responded (A-A), "Your problem seems psychological. Let's work it out." On the surface, their conversation sounded A-A; however, on the hidden psychological level (broken lines), Fanny's C was inviting the therapist's P to kick her as she insulted his clothing, rearranged his furniture, and knocked over his favorite lamp. This same pattern of interaction, occurring in the therapist's office, directly corresponded with her past history of repeated rejections and was reflected in her chief complaint. In Fanny's case, an unknowing therapist may have actually responded by playing her game, by kicking her out of treatment as an inappropriate candidate for psychotherapy, and by thinking, "Some patients just mess up the office and don't get any better, no matter what you do." Fanny's payoff could have been, "Why do rejections always happen to me?"

A TA analyst understands personality by first observing the "here-and-now" transactional sequences between him- or herself and the client. Games conform to a general, yet specific game formula, as shown in Figure 11.14): C + G = R → S → X → P. The initial Con (C) is the "bait" in which

$$C + G = R \dashrightarrow S \dashrightarrow X \dashrightarrow P$$

GAME FORMULA

FIGURE 11.14

client (Fanny) transacts on an ulterior level from her C to the therapist's P. On the surface, her transaction looks like a straightforward request for help, yet underneath, she is secretly asking for a rejection as she "hooks" the therapist's feeling of omnipotence, which is seen as the Gimmick (G). His response (R) is initially accepting and forgiving, as he continues to overlook her critique of his necktie and her rearrangement of his furniture. Fanny continues to annoy him, yet the therapist remains composed until the final Switch (S) of feelings. The therapist and client both feel a Cross-up (X), which quickly leads to the final Payoff (P) for both. Had the therapist not stopped the game, his Payoff would have entitled him to feel angry at his ungrateful client, and Fanny's Payoff would have entitled her to another desired rejection as well as potential banishment.

Certain symptoms and syndromes of psychopathology can be understood by analyzing the final payoffs of games. By playing their favorite games, people will repetitively collect payoff *trading stamps*, which are those specific treasured feelings about themselves and others. For example, Fanny received "black and blue" trading stamps each time she was kicked out and fired. After she collected enough stamps, she would entitle herself to a "free depression" and perhaps end up in the hospital. Although some psychotherapists will observe the precipitating event, the TA analyst will look at the entire system of events for each interactional pattern. These continuing repetitive patterns of payoffs and their corresponding negative feelings are seen as *racket feelings*. These are common feelings that persons have chosen to use, since a young age, whenever they are in stressful situations. Persons will commonly choose racket feelings of sadness, fear, or anger. A racket feeling is the same feeling used repeatedly, regardless of whether it is appropriate. Game sequences and rackets are important to the therapist in understanding a client's present behavior and personality, as well as for anticipating probable future behavior. A person who commits suicide has a long history of collecting rejections and playing self-negating games. Therefore, by correctly diagnosing and interrupting games, rather than unknowingly entering into them, the therapist can thwart a client's entire payoff system.

Berne referred to the first-, the second-, and the third-degree states of games (1964b). A *first-degree game* is considered socially acceptable in that no one gets physically hurt, although one may be admonished or yelled at. A *second-degree game* is more serious, in that there is frequently a punch in the nose or a face slap. A *third-degree game* is deadly serious and may be "played for keeps." The payoffs are frequently ostracism, a messy divorce, or a trip to the court room or the morgue. Game switches are characteristically sudden, abrupt, and dramatic—particularly in second- and third-degree games.

Game players operate from three distinct roles—the victim, the persecutor, and the rescuer—and they make switches between these roles. The role switches are illustrated on a drama triangle (Karpman, 1968). Each role is interchangeable and persons frequently

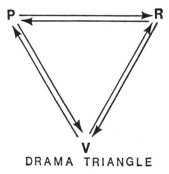

DRAMA TRIANGLE

FIGURE 11.15

switch back and forth during the course of the game (see Figure 11.15). Fanny entered treatment as a *victim*, complaining of being fired and of having a miserable childhood. The unwitting therapist commenced as a *rescuer*. Fanny then switched into a *persecutor* by criticizing the therapist's necktie, rearranging his furniture, and knocking over his lamp, while the therapist became a *victim* of her persecutions. Quickly, he switched into a *persecutor* as his anger mounted, while Fanny quickly switched back into her familiar *victim* role and positioned her bottom by his foot. Role switches occur quickly and dramatically. They have been the backbone of drama and theater throughout the centuries. Role switches also occur throughout mythology, fairy tales, literature, and even in everyday TV soap operas (K. Dusay, 1976).

Scripts

The important question for understanding personality is, why do different individuals choose specific games? The answer is found by analyzing the crucial transactions between parents and their children during the early development years. This system is illustrated on a script matrix (Steiner, 1971a; Figure 11.3). Fanny was given a typical Standard Success Story (SSS) by her parents: "Go to college, make money, get married, and have children." These *values* (Arrow 1) were introjected from the P ego states of her parents to her developing P ego state. Fanny accepted her parents' values and eventually made them her own. The *injunctions* (Arrow 2) are usually unspoken and delivered as a "curse" from a parent's C to the child's C (technically the Adapted Child—not the autonomous Free Child). Injunctions are usually delivered from the parent of the opposite sex, and they are frequently symbolized by a dotted line, in that they are seldom discussed or stated out loud. Fanny's father had difficulty in being close and intimate, and he would insinuate "get lost" messages. Because he nonverbally ignored her with his scowl and frowns, Fanny began to decide she was not a worthwhile person and could not make it ("don't be" and "don't make it"). The *values* from her father ("be a success") directly contradicted his injunctions ("don't be" and "don't make it"). Confronted with the dilemma of these incongruent messages, Fanny looked to her mother to tell her how to get along in a family like this. As a child, Fanny noted that her mother pestered and irritated her father for attention—her *technique* (Arrow 3). After her father mentally and physically assaulted her mother, the mother would sulk into her separate bedroom. Fanny's mother thus "showed" Fanny specific techniques of how to be a pest and get rejected, the *here's how* (Arrow 3), which was her personal version of the *Kick Me* game. Values, injunctions, and techniques constitute the elements of one's script. The values are also called the *counterscripts* or *counterinjunctions*. When Fanny was not getting "kicked," she was being a success-oriented, well-behaved person.

TA analysts have written and theorized about scripts throughout the last decade. Berne's views about script formation are found in *What Do You Say After You Say Hello?* (1972). Berne classified specific types of scripts: an *over and over* script corresponds to the myth of Sisyphus; an *always* script relates to persons who perpetually suffer; an *until* script ensures that the individual will be unhappy until a significant event happens; a *never* script forbids happiness and love; an *after* script requires that the person complete many things first and then have enjoyment after; and *open-ended* scripts ensure that persons will lose their vitality and enthusiasm as they drift into old age. To Berne the five requirements of a script are (1) directives from parents, (2) a corresponding personality development, (3) a confirming childhood decision about oneself and life, (4) a penchant for either success or failure, and (5) a convincing way of behaving.

Berne believed the patient's script and corresponding myths and fairy tales would be evident in the therapist's office. As was Berne's style, he would begin with the presenting problem and then take it back into the past. A client wearing a bright red, hooded cape came into his office complaining that her wolfish boyfriend had just jilted her, and she sighed, "Why does this always happen to me? Wolves seem to prey on me." Not surprisingly, her favorite fairy tale was Little Red Riding Hood, frequently told to her by her mother when she went to bed at night. The Child part of her mother would emphasize that wolves prey on helpless victims. Berne traced the genesis of this human script back to the tale of Europa, who was kidnapped by Zeus disguised as a bull. Berne's impression was that the mythologies in fairy tales show up in modern living. Steiner's book *Scripts People Live* (1971) distinguishes between banal scripts and *hamartic* (tragic) scripts. K. Dusay (1975) has made an analysis of the recurrence of fairy tales and myths in the therapist's office by analyzing the scripts and egograms of classical heroes and heroines throughout history.

VARIETY OF CONCEPTS

Although TA therapists work with the psychology of ego states, there are divergencies and different focuses, depending upon the various problems encountered.

Decision-Redecision Methods

Robert and Mary Goulding, the co-directors of the Western Institute for Group and Family Therapy, provided an important redecision model used by many TA therapists, especially in the treatment of nonpsychotic individuals. They emphasize early childhood decisions wherein a young child decides to be an "OK" or "not-OK" person, based upon parental injunctions. The Gouldings have identified and classified the types of childhood decisions that result from injunctions such as "don't be you," "don't think," "don't feel," "don't be a child," "don't grow up," and "don't be." Because one's basic life decision has survival value in early childhood, the individual develops racket feelings that are the same habitual, stereotyped, emotional responses to each situation. Early decisions and racket feelings are carried throughout life, and a client will protect them in therapy through impasses (Goulding & Goulding, 1976).

In redecision work, a milieu for change is created, the individual reexperiences decision moments, and then chooses to redecide by self-confrontation.

Reparenting

The cathexis approach to TA (or Schiff family method) was founded by Jacqui Lee Schiff. Both her theoretical model and her treatment are focused upon seriously disturbed persons who have generally been diagnosed as schizophrenic. Although the common end point of therapy is autonomy, initially the client is passive, dependent, and accepts no responsibility for his or her behavior. Four passivity behaviors have been identified by Jacqui and Aaron Schiff (1971): (1) doing nothing, (2) overadaptation, (3) agitation, and (4) incapacitation or violence. These behaviors are attempts to reestablish or maintain a symbiotic relationship (see Figure 11.16).

In a *symbiotic* relationship, a mother and her child become intimately linked in a mutually dependent way, and they behave as a *single* individual. Usually the mother functions as the operating Parent and Adult, and her offspring maintains only the Child ego state. In other words, two persons are operating as one complete individual

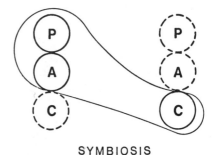

SYMBIOSIS

FIGURE 11.16

in a symbiotic relationship. Symbiosis is normal during early infancy, but later it is seen as pathological. A *discount* is an internal mechanism whereby a person will deny self and others as responsible or capable. Jacqui and Aaron Schiff have identified the four principal discounts that maintain a symbiosis and "entitle" the person to remain passive. One can discount: (1) the existence of a problem ("The fire in the house is not a problem"), (2) the significance of the problem ("Well, the house is on fire but it isn't important"), (3) the solution to the problem ("Well, the house is on fire, but there's nothing that can be done about it"), and (4) oneself and others ("Yes, the house is on fire, and it possibly could be changed, but I cannot do anything about it and neither can you"). By employing these discounts, a person effectively removes his or her responsibility to solve problems. *Grandiosity* is another mechanism defined by the Schiffs that involves either a maximized or minimized exaggeration about a person, problem, or event, in which a person entitles him- or herself to stay the same and thus justify the symbiosis ("I am too scared to think"). The Schiff's employ unique, and frequently controversial, treatment methods (J. Schiff, 1975).

TA and Variations from Other Theories

TA theory is based upon here-and-now social interactions and does not adhere to a theory of the dynamic unconscious. Drives are viewed as script-determined and programmed by early parental messages rather than as drives and instincts. Transference and countertransference phenomena are seen as two specific types of transactions. *Homeostasis* is considered from an energy system on the egogram. *Resistances* to growth and change in psychotherapy are viewed functionally as a stronger ego-state force holding down a lower force. A highly critical individual (high CP, low FC, and low NP) was being seen in a TA group because he had few friends. His case illustrates the principles of resistance. When the TA therapist asked the group members to take off their shoes and sit on the floor, this "true grit" person stood up, banged his fist, and roared, "I won't take off my shoes—that's stupid! I came here to get friends—not to take off my shoes!" His resistance was seen as protecting the homeostasis of his personality (his CP holding down his FC).

Rebellion to a TA analyst is a type of conformity to a script injunction and is seen as a pseudorebellion. Authentic rebellion is breaking away from the script.

PSYCHOTHERAPY

THEORY OF PSYCHOTHERAPY

Transactional analysts focus upon three primary areas for psychotherapy: egogram balances, game interruptions, and script redecisions. A client's change in one area will facilitate a corresponding change in other areas. *Balance* is a key word in personality change, and although a TA therapist does not expect clients to be *homogenized* (all with the same egogram), efforts are made to ensure that no one ego-state force is gravely under-energized. Awareness of the specific games one plays will lead to a position of choice for interrupting these stereotyped, habitual patterns. A game-free individual is frequently rewarded both with interpersonal and social intimacy, which is not possible through game playing. A person's script redecision will facilitate living an autonomous life, free from the influences of parental injunctions.

Although a TA therapist becomes a catalyzer of change, there is a basic underlying TA assumption that the client alone is responsible for basic survival in the unique family environment. A person's negative existential life decisions (I'm not OK, or you're not OK) about self and others do not need to be dragged around throughout life like a bag of dirty laundry. Instead, people have the ability to review their negative childhood decisions and thereby change their minds, personalities, and life-styles. Unfortunately, many people give up their recognition of personal power and actively deny and defend their lack of responsibility.

A few TA approaches have unique views of the individual's responsibility. Steiner's "radical" therapy focuses upon oppressive social institutions and emphasizes positive social action in addition to personal psychotherapy. The Schiff family techniques are designed for psychotic clients who may initially regress to a dependent child state and are then reparented and reraised with new OK messages. Eventually these clients establish a personal responsibility for their lives.

PROCESS OF PSYCHOTHERAPY

To facilitate a client's personal responsibility, a TA therapist will use a simple, common vocabulary, will enter into a contractual treatment goal, and will then use specific techniques designed to enhance each individual's power and responsibility. These three methods are used by all TA therapists.

Simple Language

The simple vocabulary of TA, ego states (Parent, Adult and Child), games (colloquially expressed, for example, *Now I Got You, You SOB*), scripts, and strokes are easily learned and have also been successfully taught to mentally retarded people. Family members (parents and their children) are on an equal vocabulary footing, and even well-educated professionals are encouraged to talk straight and not hide behind complex jargon. The time and energy a client spends in treatment are directed toward getting better—not toward defining and redefining.

Unfortunately, naive critics of TA sometimes focus exclusively upon its colloquialisms in an attempt to discount the scientific profundity of the theory. A popular joke in TA circles concerns a TA therapist who sat next to an astronomer on an airplane flight. The astronomer asked what she did for a living and the TA therapist replied: Transactional Analysis. The astronomer then exclaimed, "Oh, I know all about that— 'I'm OK, You're OK!' " The TA therapist politely smiled, then asked, "What do you do for a living?" and the response was "I'm an astronomer." The TA therapist smiled and quipped back, "Oh, I know all about that—'Twinkle, Twinkle, Little Star!' "

Contractual Therapy

A key question in contractual therapy is, "How will both you and I know when you get what you came for?" This statement immediately clarifies that the client and the therapist are mutual allies working to accomplish a mutual goal. Throughout the therapy contract, each will be defining their mutual responsibilities in achieving the goal. The therapist will not enter in a passive spectator position and the client will not sit back waiting for the therapist to perform a miracle (seen as the game of *Do Me Something*). A TA treatment contract has the four major components of a legal contract:

1. *Mutual assent.* A simply stated contract *goal* between the Adult ego states of both the therapist and the client is made; both persons become Adult ego-state allies. Examples of contracts include statements such as "I will have sex again" from an impotent man; "I will hold a job for at least one year" from a habitually fired person; and "I will not kill myself accidentally or on purpose" from a suicidal person. Contracts are also stated by specific egogram changes: "I'll be satisfied when the group constructs my egogram with my Free Child greater than my Adapted Child." Therapy contracts are frequently reviewed, updated, and changed. Mini or weekly contracts may also lead to a more profound change. For example, "I will speak to three people this week" would be a step toward a long-term goal of having an intimate social relationship.

Initial difficulties in making contracts may take the form of games. Clients may pay substantial fees to the therapist and continue to say that they do not know what they want to change about themselves. A TA therapist may then ask, "What does your Parent say you *should* get out of treatment? What *fantasies* does your Child have? What will your Adult *decide* to be a worthwhile goal?" Unless a therapist and client have mutual assent about a common goal, the therapist may become a nontherapeutic, rescuing advice giver, and not a catalytic mutual ally of the client.

2. *Competency.* The TA therapist will agree to provide only those services he or she can *competently* deliver. The therapist will also actively confront the client's misperceptions and fantasies about the assumed "magical" powers of the therapist. A competent therapist would not contract with a 55-year-old man to become the world's champion in the 100-yard dash. However, the therapist may contract to help the client exercise and become healthy. A client also needs to be competent in achieving the goals of the contract. If the client is still legally or financially dependent upon parents, they need to be included in the treatment contract.

3. *Legal object.* The contract must have a *legal* aim or objective. "Provide me with mind-altering drugs, Doctor, so I can become more aware of myself" is not a legal contract. On the other hand, "I want to graduate from college with a B average" may be an acceptable contract.

4. *Consideration.* Usually the *consideration* is the therapist's fee the client agrees to pay. The therapist will provide expertise and time. TA therapists who treat clients either in social agencies or under circumstances where the client is not expected personally to pay for therapy will encourage the client to offer a type of consideration, perhaps in the form of a service, a painting, a poem, or some other product that represents the client's commitment to therapy.

Specific Techniques to Enhance Personal Responsibility

People who experience themselves as powerless to change continue to reinforce this position by habitually broadcasting their plight. The TA therapist will confront this observation to create an awareness of self-power in the individual. When a client says, "I *can't* think," the TA therapist will confront with, "I *won't* think!" When a client says, "She *makes* me feel bad," the therapist will correct with, "*I choose to feel* bad in response to her." Persons who continually say "you know" and other cliches are confronted and shown why others do not take them seriously. *Gallows humor* is inappropriate smiling, laughing, and inviting others to laugh at one's tragic situation. A client with a serious drinking problem who says, "I just had one little drink . . . hee-hee," is confronted with the fact that drinking himself to death is not funny. J. McNeel (1975) has elaborated specific, commonly used TA techniques and attitudes that clients use to rob themselves of power.

Blackboards are commonplace in TA groups so clients can visually represent their explanations in clear ways. Chalk is frequently handed to clients who play the game of *Stupid* to provide them with permission to problem solve. TA emphasizes symbols and simple diagrams so both the therapist and the client can clearly delineate their ideas.

Although TA therapists use simple vocabularies, treatment contracts, and specific pertinent techniques to restore the client's power, the types of therapy may differ widely. Originally, Berne designed TA as an adjunct to psychoanalysis, to be practiced in small groups with seven or eight clients that meet for two hours weekly. Now people are seen individually, in families, as couples, in marathons, in inpatient and outpatient wards, in prisons, and in business and industry settings. Each modality has certain ad-vantages and disadvantages. What can typically be seen and heard by TA practitioners varies widely beyond the previously described general processes, depending upon the types of problems, the treatment settings, and the styles of the therapists. Therapists are encouraged to use their personal attributes and not fit into a TA mold. Some common processes are discussed in the following pages, and although attention to games, scripts, and ego-state structure and function does not follow a particular order in treatment, the descriptions provide the historical development of these processes.

Game Analysis by Confrontation

During the initial interview, the therapist observes the usual social amenities, like saying hello, and neither uses gimmicks to increase stress nor leans over backward to provide comfort. The business of establishing a treatment contract, deciding on whether the therapist and client are able to work together, and choosing a proper treatment setting (individual, group, family, etc.) are the usual topics.

Because games are habitual, stereotyped patterns of transacting, they will usually begin to manifest in the initial interview, and the therapist is keenly interested in picking up game clues, such as a person's telling a sad history of failure and then subtly smiling. This tips off the therapist that two levels of transactions are occurring, and as soon as the therapist is aware of a game's occurrence, the decision to intervene is made (see "Applications," page 435, for a description of intervention).

In addition to observing the client's dual levels of transacting, the communication pattern between therapist and client is also observed. Eric Berne called himself a "Martian" in therapy.

This implied that the therapist transcended the setting and observed how the therapist and the client transacted with each other, that is, "When the therapist offers a suggestion, the client says, 'Yes . . . but. . . ,' and the therapist looks disgruntled." The therapist observes the process as well as the client. This is reminiscent of Theodore Reik's (1948) "Listening with the Third Ear" and Harry Stack Sullivan's concept of observing the interpersonal processes.

More important than the therapist's knowing what is happening is the awareness of the client and the *interruption* of the patterns. Groups are often useful because of the increased transactional possibilities. In addition, other clients may pick up blind spots of the therapist. Verbal interruptions are extremely important for counteracting games. For instance, the therapist may quickly say, "But . . . ," just before the client says it himself. Or when a young female *Rapo* player is complaining that men are just interested in her body, as her skirt slips slowly up her thighs, the therapist acknowledges the seductive moves and says, "I think I know why!"

In addition to verbal interruption, the therapist may stand up and ask the client to do likewise. They then both comment on what is going on between the two of them. Like Berne's "Martian" observers, they have an Adult-to-Adult ego-state conversation. Occasionally an empty chair is offered and the client is asked to sit in it and describe the ongoing interaction.

Game Interruption by Psychodrama

When a client enters into a game with either the therapist or another group member, or even when the client talks about a game he played with someone outside of the group ("My wife and I had another *Uproar*"), the TA therapist may structure a psychodrama. The client becomes the director and is asked to stand up (a client-empowering technique) and then choose two people in the group to play his and his wife's roles in the game in the identical ways they play *Uproar*.

The therapist encourages the client-director to think, direct, and plot out the important game moves that will lead to the usual conclusion or the negative payoff feelings that both players receive. The client-director may actually reexperience his or her own feelings while directing the psychodrama, which will provide clarity and even release of affect. By using this type of psychodrama, the client is able to step outside a personal game system and can view, think, and direct his or her own part in the game. This client-director role is seen as the "Martian" position in that the client can be an interested observer, rather than a habitual participant. Through these maneuvers, the client will gain a new awareness and experiment with corrective procedures.

Script Treatment

An individual will gain social control by an intact, aware Adult, yet many individuals need also to direct their energies into reversing their basic life scripts.

Fanny, the woman who was repeatedly fired from her jobs, was able to catch herself and stop playing *Kick Me* when she used her Adult. She also decided to continue her therapy to make a script change. Fanny remembered being kicked out of many groups while she was growing up—the Brownies' summer camp, various grade school classes, high school classes, a social club, her college sorority—in addition to being fired from each job she held. Her earliest memories included banishment and punishments for her behavior by her impatient parents. She developed negative stroking patterns that became the foundation of her script. Her early injunctions were "Get lost, you bother me." After receiving a bombardment of these injunctions, Fanny decided to live her life getting put down and kicked, as this was how she got "strokes" and survived in her family. Through therapy and script redecisions, Fanny was able to change her script and stop her negative patterns.

Script Reversal

Berne devised the original script-change technique in the 1960s. He believed in a mutual, trusting relationship between the client and the therapist, which would facilitate the client's receiving a potent *counter-injunction* (the opposite of what mother or father said to the client), thereby removing the negative influences. Berne, after attaining a suicidal client's trust, would state decisively, *"Do not kill yourself."* Many suicidal clients responded to him that *no one* ever said that to them before.

Eric Berne, Claude Steiner, Stephen Karpman, Muriel James, Joe Concannon, Vi Callahan, Ken Everts, Frank Ernst, John Dusay, and other participants in the early San Francisco seminars considered the script injunction to be like an electrode lodged in the Child. The term *electrode* is appropriate because scripted individuals habitually and automatically react in predictable, destructive manners under a wide variety of circumstances. Therefore, Berne's powerfully potent, curative, counterscript mes-

sage, delivered at the proper time, enabled persons to revise their scripts.

Reparenting

Another form of script intervention is the *reparenting* technique developed by Jacqui Schiff and others. Reparenting was developed for severely disturbed and psychotic patients. Severely disturbed individuals have a natural tendency to regress and relive early childhood experiences. Reparenting is done in a therapeutic, residential treatment center, and the clients are "rereared" by positive parenting. This treatment may take many years, and there is a direct, active commitment by the therapist, who performs the functions of the new parents. Although reparenting is viewed as controversial, it has been found to be effective in work with "untreatable" schizophrenics (J. Schiff, 1970; J. Schiff, 1975).

Redecision

A popular and effective technique to bring about script change is *redecision therapy* in a TA framework using Gestalt techniques, formulated by Fritz Perls. By the use of double chairs, Perls had the client separate the negative and the positive parts of self to oppose one another. Robert and Mary Goulding took this further by combining Perls' techniques and Berne's theories to create an environment for a client's growth and change (Goulding, 1972, 1974). They are chiefly credited for the development of redecision work.

Ego-State Oppositions

People can change their weaknesses into their strengths and redecide about their life scripts by transferring their ego-state energies to lesser-used ego states (J. Dusay, 1972), as illustrated in Figure 11.17).

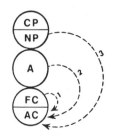

EGO-STATE
OPPOSITION

FIGURE 11.17

Script decisions commonly take three general forms: (1) "I'm sad," a person who has decided he or she is not OK in relation to others; (2) "I'm mad," a person who has decided to be OK, but the cost is that other people are seen as not OK; and (3) "I'm scared," a person who has decided he or she is not OK and neither are the other people. Individuals coming into treatment will, during times of stress, revert into their habitual stereotyped patterns of thinking, feeling, and behaving. A person who has decided to be not OK will look, think, feel, and behave depressed. The same will occur with a person who has decided to be scared or one who has decided to become mad. A trained TA therapist will watch for these habitual script patterns to occur and then will move into an ego-state opposition process and employ the techniques described by John Dusay in his *TA Treatment-Training Manual* (1978). The process goes this way:

1. The client is encouraged to enhance the here-and-now expression of the racket feelings. The therapist may recognize telltale signs and symptoms of the client's racket behavior, such as tense muscles, and will instruct the client to become temporarily more tense. This facilitates the client's reexperiencing of negative feelings so that he or she can move from the here-and-now back to earlier decisive moments of childhood.

2. The individual is asked via a regressive technique, such as hypnosis or guided fantasy, to close his or her eyes and trace the same feeling back to the earliest recollection. Breuer and Freud (1962) termed these early feelings *hyperesthetic memories*.

3. When a person has gone back to an early moment of making a script decision, the therapist encourages the client to *oppose* that decision with another growth ego state. For instance, depressed people will oppose their scripted Adapted Child ego states with their underused Free Child states by being directed to switch between them using empty double chairs (Arrow 1). A "mad" person who is frequently paranoid will be encouraged to oppose the Adapted Child with the Adult to distinguish clearly which people are friends and which are not (Arrow 2). A scared person will be encouraged to oppose that part with the Nurturing Parent for reassurance (Arrow 3). This process hastens the transfer of psychological energy and begins the road toward a script redecision. The client, not the therapist, uses and summons his or her own psychological strengths to oppose these stubbornly held viewpoints of self.

4. Resistances commonly arise when the client slips out of the "curative" ego state and back into the "stuck" scripted state. An adroit TA therapist will quickly confront this behavior so the resistant person will not reinforce the stuck pathology.

There are several advantages to doing script redecision work in a group setting. Other members are inspired and can reflect on their own situation, the therapist is aided as other members confront resistances, other group members can correct blind spots that occasionally occur in one-to-one therapy, and the client is both congratulated and stroked for positive work.

Egogram Transfer of Energy

When one shifts energies from an overused ego state to a low-power ego state, the experience is exhilarating and becomes self-reinforcing. Fanny usually behaved as a "naughty little pest" intent on provoking negative responses from others. The initial scripting she accepted dictated that this behavior was her most profitable method of getting strokes. Her *Kick Me* game behavior was functionally part of her Adapted Child ego state, and it was this part of her personality that overwhelmed other people (see Figure 11.18).

The delightful and creative side of Fanny's Child ego state, her Free Child, was barely functioning, as she experienced little fun, creativity, or sexual enjoyment. It was as if her an-

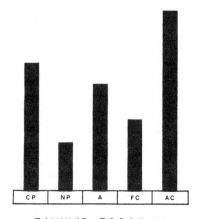

FANNY'S EGOGRAM

FIGURE 11.18

noying, pesty part, the Adapted Child, had most of the power and drained it away from the fresh and creative side. Her Adult was solid; she was bright and a good thinker. However, she seldom had any spare energy to help or console others, and this was reflected in her relatively low-functioning Nurturing Parent. Fanny copied her father's temper and judgmental nature when she criticized and found fault with others. This was reflected in the high amount of energy in her Critical Parent.

For Fanny functionally to approach the world in a different and more constructive way, a shift is necessary (Figure 11.18). Her Free Child and her Nurturing Parent need enhancement and greater energy investment, and this is one of the reasons the group-therapy milieu may be superior to individual psychotherapy. In a group, exercises can be repeated and practiced with others to raise a low-energy ego state. For example, nurturing can be developed by hugging, or the exercise of giving authentic positive comments to other people can be practiced. Fanny at first resisted doing this, but she started out slowly and persisted until she raised and became conditioned in her low ego states. After nurturing others, she was better able to nurture herself. Many encounter-group techniques are useful in raising low-energy ego states in people. Free Child, important for Fanny, is elicited by humor.

Each person has different ego-state imbalances and needs to raise, energize, and strengthen lower, weaker ego states. Briefly, those who are low in the Critical Parent aspect are encouraged to use assertiveness techniques; those low in Nurturing Parent will need empathy and caring-for-others techniques; persons low in Adult are given thinking exercises; those who do not have enough Free Child are invited to be spontaneous and participate in creative, intuitive activities; and those low in Adapted Child are encouraged to practice the art of compromise and getting-along-with-others exercises. An important concern in shifting psychological energies is that individuals practice *raising what is low for them* and that they do not take what is a useful technique for others and indiscriminately apply it to themselves.

To facilitate a script redecision, a client is encouraged to go back in time to an early feeling and decisive moment. The client is then directed to oppose a well-established ego-state force, which becomes a major problem for the client in that his or her personality is already low in the very force that is needed to bring about a cure. For example, Fanny was depressed, and to overcome depression, she needed to oppose and raise her Free Child in relation to her Adapted Child. Her greatest problem was that her Free Child was low and her Adapted Child was high (see Figure 11.18). It took many weeks of Free-Child-raising techniques for her to be able to confront her own Adapted Child self to a significant degree. A person's weak ego states need strengthening because they are the very personality forces needed to make a redecision and change the balance of the egogram. Lonely persons, chronically anxious people, and those with severe dependency needs who fear abandonment need to nurture themselves and others; however, the Nurturing Parent is the lowest force on their egograms. By analyzing someone's egogram, one can predict the curative oppositional force for that particular individual. Like-

wise, a low Adult force is prevalent for distrustful paranoid problems (a low Nurturing Parent and a low Adult are evident in severe examples). Suicidal, depressed, and lethargic persons manifest a low Free Child.

A growth-oriented opposing force needs to be sufficiently developed to reverse a lifelong (early childhood decision) pattern that shows up in one's here-and-now manifestation of personality.

Various settings provide an effective milieu for change. These retreats come in various forms, such as Esalen Institute, the Western Institute for Group and Family Therapy, and other therapeutic centers where persons may reside for several weeks or months in a strong Nurturing Parent, Adult, and Free Child atmosphere to undergo personal, lasting changes. TA groups provide a similar safe atmosphere where both growth and change are stroked and reinforced.

In summary, the major ways that people change are through their own efforts by stopping games, redeciding scripts, and redistributing the energy balances on their egograms.

MECHANISMS OF PSYCHOTHERAPY

Basic mechanisms include game interruption, script redecision, and ego-state energy shift. A game is a habit with stereotyped thinking that justifies behavior. Even the accompanying affect is habitual. When a client is asked, "Have you ever felt this way before?" the answer is usually, "Always." Game interruption brings to awareness the client's involvement with different ego states and establishes the Adult as the executive. With the Adult in control, the client can choose. Berne said that treatment was at a terminal phase when choice was available: "At this juncture, transactional analysis has completed its task with or without interpretation in the area under consideration. TA does not try to 'make the patient better' but to bring him into a position where he can exercise an Adult option to get better" (1966, p. 245). The therapist is, in an existential sense at least, indifferent about which choice the patient makes. All one can do is make it possible for the patient to choose. There is, however, no use in trying to conceal from the patient the fact that the therapist is biased by personal prejudices in favor of health and sanity.

When games are successfully interrupted, the client has social control. Although clients may substitute other games, equally destructive, they also have an excellent chance of developing positive new ways of relating.

Script redecision is usually accomplished concomitantly with game therapy, by overcoming early childhood decisions and by applying an opposing force against stubbornly held decisions. A chief reason for using a psychoregressive technique is to lay bare the earlier moments before the client added years of justification (by game playing) and reinforced his or her script decision. Although the TA therapist may use double chairs to separate ego states and allow for their external replay, the same forces are occurring in the client's head. Although feelings and affect are primary in script redecision work, they are usually followed by Adult cognitive confirmation and discussion.

Ego-state energy shift is necessary to build up weak areas on an egogram to oppose the adapted, script-bearing part. Most TA groups use humor and encourage the airing of hunches and

intuition to develop the Free Child. Nurturing behavior such as touching, hugging, and giving authentic positive strokes is encouraged, and away from the treatment setting, the client prescribes corrective nurturing behavior for him- or herself—for example, taking an orphan to the zoo.

Just when a person actually strengthens a weaker ego-state force is difficult to ascertain, but an analogy with the physical conditioning of a jogger seems appropriate. The unconditioned runner does not feel like jogging; to him it is a burden. However, if he persists and overcomes the "this just isn't the real me" resistance and keeps on practicing, he changes. The first time his change is noticeable is when he has no time to run on a given day and he feels uncomfortable and sluggish because he has not run! He is now a conditioned runner and he feels different. People become psychologically conditioned by exercising previously weak areas.

APPLICATIONS

PROBLEMS

Because TA begins with the observation of what goes on between human beings, theoretically, all problems can be analyzed. Being a contractual treatment, TA requires the cooperation and willingness of the client to seek and participate in treatment. A distinction is made between what is primarily a "caring" relationship between therapist and client and what is an actual "curing" TA treatment. In "caring" the client receives support and nurturing from the therapist as the major activity. The therapist is a primary source of strokes and the relationship is not working toward the attainment of an ultimate goal.

In contrast, TA treatment, although

emphasizing the importance of the nurturing and caring personality of the therapist, primarily focuses on change as defined by the treatment contract based on an Adult-to-Adult agreement between the therapist and the client about what will be the process and the desired goal. Rather than being a primary source of strokes, except temporarily, the TA therapist is a catalyst for the client's own efforts.

TA is devised for those who will exert enough responsibility to undertake a contract. However, TA has been applied to severely disturbed individuals who are not able to make an Adult contract at the onset of treatment. Jacqui and Aaron Schiff (J. Schiff, 1969) represent a special group of TA therapists who have developed an alternative, yet compatible, theory with specific techniques that encourage clients to regress to earlier infantlike states, which may be preverbal. Although the client is expected to be as responsible as possible, the expectation during this phase of treatment is different from expectations for chronologically mature, nonregressed individuals. The approach is controversial, is not accepted by all TA therapists, and is considered an offshoot of TA.

TA is effectively used with both couples and family relationships in that TA's game theory focuses on the common, predictable, destructive game patterns of behavior that occur among individuals. These patterns can be easily recognized, dealt with, and ultimately changed to strengthen the relationship. Berne chose the game *If It Weren't for You* to illustrate game principles in his work *Games People Play* (1964b), and stated that this is the most commonly occurring game among married couples. By the maneuvers in the game, the wife complains that "If it weren't for my husband, I would be a princess . . ." and so on.

Difficulties with authority figures are frequently encountered in TA. Fanny, previously mentioned, is a classical example of a person with authority conflicts. The same patterns that occur with the boss, school authorities, and others also tend to occur with the therapist or other group members.

The problem of self-concept has two special considerations. First, clients may not actually see themselves the way others do, being psychologically blind. When an entire TA group constructs an egogram and they agree, this is potent feedback about how one appears to others. By increasing perception and sharpening intuition about others, self-perception tends to become more acute. The second problem of self-concept is resistance to change even if people do not like what they see in themselves. Basic script redecisions and game interruptions are employed to improve self-concept.

Fears of a crippling or phobic nature may be treated at the level of personality identity, as portrayed by the egogram, by exercising and strengthening underdeveloped ego states. People who fear abandonment cling to others and even to the therapist by playing *Do Me Something* (a game by which the client offers the therapist some bait in the nature of a potentially resolvable problem, such as insomnia, then says, "That's not good enough," after the therapist tries drugs, interpretations, or other maneuvers). By structuring time and performing exercises such as nurturing or assertive exercises, the client takes on more Parent energy and is therefore not as frightened.

The client fearing abandonment is asked to join a TA group, not to talk about self, but to focus on the needs of others, encouraging nurturing. When this force develops, it is easier to nurture oneself and decrease the fear. Script redecision may also be used in overcoming fears—for instance, when the client has decided at an early age that life is scary.

Maladjustments occur as a result of psychological blindness. For example, a high Free Child, low Adapted Child person may, in good spirits, take a job as an accountant, which requires lower Free Child (unless the corporation wants a creative accountant) and high Adapted Child, which encourages conformity. Recognizing strengths and weaknesses of personality forces allows one to choose jobs and relationships that are most compatible.

So-called *perversions* can best be understood at the script level. An individual may be told to be "normal" on the value level, but at the injunction level the message is, "You are different." Even though this message may be nonverbal and hidden, if the child accepts this injunction, *perverse* behavior later in life is seen as conformity not to values, but to injunctions. Social difficulties, such as teenage drug problems and what is commonly called rebellious behavior, which may best be called pseudorebellion, is actually viewed as conformity to script (J. Dusay, 1977a).

Personality trait problems are best understood by considering the egogram. Assertiveness is too much Critical Parent, while too little Critical Parent corresponds with the passive acceptance of oppression—getting psychologically pushed around by others. Too much Nurturing Parent is overbearing and actually inhibits the inde-

pendent growth of children; too little Nurturing Parent makes one inconsiderate; and a low Nurturing Parent corresponds with loneliness. High Adult is technical but perhaps boring, while someone with a low Adult lacks logic and orderly causal thinking and finds problem solving difficult. Someone with too high a Free Child, although creative and zesty, may fail to pay the rent; low Free Child is associated with depression. People who are too high in the Adapted Child trait overconform and are too accepting or compromising, but with too little, the problem is the opposite—too little compromise in human relationships (K. Dusay, 1985). Personality trait disturbances are seen by looking not at one specific trait on the egogram but by looking at the balance or imbalance of the total mosaic. One's specific problems, trait disturbances, and specific egogram imbalances are directly related to one's early script decisions as well as to the specific games the person developed to reinforce this script.

Delusions are structurally seen as a contaminated ego state where the boundaries between Adult and Child are broken down (Figure 11.6). The subject of psychosis is quite involved, and the controversy that rages between different academicians and therapists of many persuasions also occurs within the TA family. Some mention that the basic lesion is genetic or biochemical and that psychotherapy should be directed toward better social adjustment. Others vigorously pursue the developmental motive of psychosis, structure a long-term live-in environment, encourage regression in severe psychosis, and basically start over.

Most of what was previously called neurosis is redefined by TA practitioners into more useful theory-related terms. The depressive neurotic, for example, would be seen as a person who made an existential life decision of I'm Not OK—You Are OK in response to an injunction script message of "Get lost" (or some specific variation). This was followed by a long string of games such as Kick Me or Reject Me. Personality developed as a high Adapted Child and a low Free Child. A TA diagnosis will commonly state that the client has too much AC, too little A, too much CP, too little NP, and so on. This is more effective terminology than diagnosing "neurosis" or "psychosis" because the TA diagnosis immediately suggests the treatment for the person's problems. Cures are accomplished when the clients strengthen and build up their underdeveloped ego states to achieve harmonious balances on their egograms.

EVALUATION

TA, like most psychotherapies, was developed outside the university setting and early in its history reported mainly anecdotal individual case histories. Although these early reports were enthusiastic, they lacked controls or comparison to other methods, a basic problem in most psychotherapy outcome research. The culmination of this type of reporting occurred in 1968, when Berne, Dusay, and Poindexter reviewed their record of success and presented the results to the San Francisco TA Seminar. They found that 80 percent of the clients stated they got what they came for and their therapists agreed.

Following the first decade of TA, independent investigators began to review the outcome of TA treatment. One of the most important outcome studies was a comparison of TA and behavior modification (McCormick, 1973). Behavior modification is generally also a contractual therapy based on research data. The project studied the effects of treatment on hard data changes in a population of 904 young men aged 15, 16, and 17 who were in two schools of the California Youth Authority. Almost all of the subjects had serious arrest records, most failed as probationers in the home community, and all had serious emotional or behavioral problems. More than 60 percent had used drugs (a third were heroin or LSD users).

There was random assignment to TA methods (460) and behavior modification (444). Although both TA and behavior modification showed significant academic improvement and fewer parole violations relative to controls, the TA population was treated for 7.6 months, at which time the TA program was completed (as defined by the goals of the therapists). To achieve similar improvement, the behavior modification subjects were treated for 8.7 months. TA achieved similar results in significantly less time.

The foundation of TA, the ego state, has been subjected to several investigations. George Thomson (1972) established that ego states are observable, that trained TA experts have a high inter-rater agreement about which ego state is in operation in a given subject, and that naive observers can be trained to correctly (in agreement with experts) identify ego states. Thomson used a tape recorder to preserve nine hours of group-therapy sessions. From these tapes, he extracted a research tape whereby each participant was heard to say a couple of words or phrases for a few seconds. When played back, there were varied words, tones, and inflections on each segment. These were presented to a panel of TA experts, who were asked to judge between Parent, Adult, and Child. The experts had a 95 percent consensual agreement about the ego-state classification. Naive listeners from various backgrounds were then presented the research tape and were found to do poorly, but after a week's training, their proficiency at identifying ego states improved markedly. Thomson proved what Berne and early transactional analysts claimed: that ego states are observable and that people can spot ego states, classify them, mimic them, and actually improve upon their ability to do so by study and observation.

Five advanced members of the weekly San Francisco TA Seminars (now known as the Eric Berne Seminar of San Francisco) volunteered themselves as egogram subjects in 1971. Their egograms were drawn by 15 other seminar members who had known them for varying lengths of time. While the 15 persons drew each subject's personality profile privately, the subjects also drew their own. The result was 100 percent agreement on both the high and low columns of the five-ego-state graph.

John Kendra (1973) viewed a sample of Rorschach reports of various psychiatric patients. He constructed egograms from these projective tests and was able to distinguish a group of egograms different from the others that were characteristically low in Nurturing Parent and Free Child, while the Critical Parent, Adult, and Adapted Child were markedly high (the Adult slightly lower). These turned out to be the profiles of patients who had committed suicide (Figure 11.9).

While Kendra used intuition to construct his suicide egogram, Robert Heyer (1979) began to develop a concept-oriented written test. Heyer's ego-state profile questionnaire consists of 49 researched items that the subject rank orders (Heyer, 1979). Egogram profiles have now been constructed for various populations, such as San Quentin prisoners, clients of outpatient clinics, alcoholics, attendees at weekend growth-encounter groups, students, and government employees.

Ego states and egograms especially lend themselves to research. With the development of a standard hard data test, research possibilities are expanding.

TREATMENT

TA historically and traditionally has been practiced in groups, although since its beginnings in the late 1950s, TA has been diversely applied by therapists from different backgrounds, with varying levels of professional education and training, who have approached the entire gamut of psychological problems and challenges. Therefore, TA has been successfully practiced in almost all settings. The earlier observations in groups tend to hold up in dyadic, family, marathon, and other settings.

Berne (1966) distinguished between six possible ways that people spend their time with each other, in ascending order of stroke potential. The six time-structuring ways are withdrawal, rituals, pastimes, work, games, and intimacy. These methods will be defined as they relate to therapy.

Withdrawal

Occasionally, people *withdraw* in the presence of others, either by fantasy or by delusion. The therapist discourages withdrawal by stroking and encouraging conversation.

Ritual

There are formal and informal *rituals*. Formal rituals are culturally determined and of little concern for psychotherapy; however, informal rituals are encouraged as a warm-up. The greeting ritual of saying hello followed by a hello response is an example. This gives a stroke and also illustrates the almost syllable-for-syllable (stroke-for-stroke) quality. If one person says, "Hello, how are you? Haven't seen you in weeks," and gets a simple "Hello" in response, a game is developing. Overresponding likewise becomes a game; for example, one person says, "How are you?" The respondent replies, "I'm glad you asked. My hemorrhoids ache. I can't sleep," and so on. Again a game is started. Informal rituals are mainly social courtesies, not encouraged beyond a warm-up and good-bye. However, the breaking of a mundane ritual is seen as a takeoff for possible game behavior.

Pastimes

These are an orderly series of transactions designed simply to while away the time in a socially acceptable, but nonmeaningful, manner. Unlike games, there is no distinct payoff of negative feelings. A popular *pastime* is called *General Motors*, whereby one player says, "I like Chevy, Plymouth, Ford (choose one), better than Chevy, Plymouth, Ford because . . . (fill in with 25 words or less)." There is a tendency for therapy groups to play pastimes, sometimes for an entire session, to avoid more meaningful activity. This is called playing *Psychiatry*. The therapist breaks up pastimes to get to more meaningful work.

Work

This is goal-directed activity to solve problems or expand potentials. Much TA is at this level.

Games

Clients frequently slip into *games* to reinforce their basic script decisions and, by doing so, avoid work and prevent intimacy. This is counteracted by the TA therapist.

Intimacy

This is a straightforward human interaction and is none of the above. Intimacy is a desired goal in human relationships and is encouraged in TA treatment.

TA therapists as group leaders pay attention to all six ways of spending time, encouraging work and intimacy, interrupting games, and avoiding meaningless pastimes.

Beyond attention to group functioning, Berne, in observing himself and his trainees, delineated eight specific therapeutic interventions (1966):

Interrogation

A TA therapist *interrogates* to document specific points that may be clinically useful in the future. "Did you actually hit her?" is directed to the client's Adult. Overinterrogation is to be avoided or the client will be prone to play *Psychiatric History*.

Specification

This is a declaration by the therapist that categorizes certain information. "So you have always viewed yourself as having an excessive temper" is intended to *specifically* fix certain information about the client so it can be referred to later in therapy.

Confrontation

A TA therapist will use information previously elicited to disconcert the patient's Parent, Child, or contaminated Adult by pointing out incongruencies. For example, if the client says, "I can't stop smoking," the therapist counters with, "Will you say, 'I *won't* stop smoking'?" This *confrontation* is intended to disturb the client's egogram energy balance and cause a redistribution of energies. The client may insightfully say, "There I go giving away my power again," which indicates a switch from Child to Adult.

Explanation

The therapist will encourage clear explanations to strengthen the client's Adult. The therapist may say, "Sometimes your Child becomes overactive and that's when your Adult fades out. Quite possibly you reach for a cigarette without thinking."

Interrogation, specification, confrontation, and explanation are *interventions*. The next operations are more than that. They are *interpositions* that are an attempt by the therapist to interpose something between the patient's Adult and other ego states to stabilize the Adult and make it more difficult to slide into Parent or Child activity.

Illustration

This is an anecdote or comparison that follows a successful confrontation; its purpose is to reinforce the confrontation and avoid possibly undesirable effects. The therapist may interpose by saying, "You are saying *can't* just like Gladys does," as Gladys is listening. Some illustrations are remote, yet provide humor or meaning to the Child. "Your going to the party is similar to Little Red Riding Hood's going to the woods—they both have a lot of wolves."

Illustration is an artful form of psychotherapy that may be effectively used with a client when both the Adult is listening and the Free Child is finding it humorous. When working with a self-righteous, literal Parent (as with many paranoids), the therapist may be chided for "making fun of me" if an illustration is attempted.

Confirmation

The interposition of a *confirmation* by the therapist is to stabilize the patient's Adult. The therapist encourages the client to offer further material to confirm the confrontation and this will reinforce the ego boundaries and the Adult functioning. If the client says, "I just can't do this—Oops, I mean, I *won't* do it," the therapist will immediately confirm and acknowledge the client's awareness.

Each of these operations is designed to activate the client's functional Adult. The client will then possess a clear, defined, competent, uncontaminated Adult. When the Adult is in control, the client is filled with positive choices and options for growth.

Interpretation

Interpretations are not necessary for treatment to be successful; in fact, occasionally the reverse is true. Overzealous therapists may interpret games and symbols for their clients and receive passive acceptance, but the messages are frequently forgotten. Each of the operations before this is employed to strengthen the client's Adult so a clear interpretation will be assimilated by an informed Adult. Little benefit accrues just from telling a person what is going on.

Crystallization

TA's technical aim is to facilitate the client's acceptance of an effective crystallization statement from the therapist. This takes the form of an

Adult-to-Adult statement: "So now you're in a position to stop playing that game if you choose."

Often the client will incorporate the statement, which may represent readiness to terminate and begin an autonomous, choice-making existence. Berne himself would emphasize the importance of strengthening the client's Adult, which would enable the person to make better choices. Berne would interrupt the client's habitual patterns by directly confronting and intervening; rather than by remaining passive and anonymous, and he became an active therapist. Berne's active techniques of the mid-1960s are still used today; however, TA has developed into an even more active and dynamic system of psychotherapy.

The following additional techniques and attitudes are commonly employed by many TA therapists:

Emphasis on the Client's Personal Power and Responsibility

People are responsible for their lives. Clients may feel they are victims of events or circumstances, and confrontations will reinforce their feelings of responsibility. A client who says, "You make me feel . . ." will be confronted because this is a common ploy to deny responsibility for one's own feelings. A person who habitually says "I can't" will be confronted and encouraged to substitute "I won't," which illustrates that the person is making a choice not to do something.

Developing a Nurturing Environment

Nonjudgmental nurturing is an effective milieu, and persons are warmly stroked for taking personal responsibility for their actions and feelings. Likewise, the use of humor is preva-lent, although there is an avoidance of laughing at gallows humor, which is encouraging others to laugh at pathological behavior (drinking, overeating, etc.).

Separating Myth from Reality

Many clients cherish myths about themselves, and the effective confrontation is, "Do you really believe that?" Clients then receive permission to question and discard their myths.

Confrontation of Incongruity

When a client offers two incongruent communications at the same time (verbal and nonverbal), the therapist needs to recognize that both forms of communication are important. A "no" head shake that accompanies a "yes" verbal response and smiling during a tragic story are examples of the incongruous behaviors that therapists will interrupt.

Specific Techniques

Analysis is used to raise a deficient Adult. Double-chair techniques aid participants to own all of their psychological parts and reach the emotions of the Child ego state. Verbally saying good-bye to the past is also important in that people will drag their negative past experiences around with them, like a ball and chain. Techniques may involve roleplaying a deceased parent and then saying good-bye. Fantasy techniques are used to raise the Free Child. Parent ego-state interviews in which the therapist interviews the client's Parent projections are also useful.

Procedural Rules

During therapy, there is no small talk or gossip. An actual time limit is put on each client's work so it will not go on indefinitely. In effective therapy, there are specific rules, such as no violence or threats of violence, sex only with attending partners at weekend functions, and no use of alcohol or mind-altering drugs. People also make a commitment to remain in therapy for a specific period.

Such procedures are used by leading TA therapists to create a milieu conducive to redecision and change.

MANAGEMENT

The Setting

TA therapy may effectively take place in a wide variety of settings. Certain TA therapists prefer a homelike atmosphere, comparable to a living room, with the accompanying furniture, books, plants, and artwork. Some like a more traditional office setting, while others enjoy conducting therapy outdoors in retreat settings and at resorts. While some therapists utilize traditional couches and chairs, others prefer to conduct therapy on the floor or on cushions. An important commonality with TA therapists is that no tables or desks are used that could block the participants' full view of one another. Because body language, postures, and other nonverbal clues to personality are important in doing TA therapy, there must be good lighting as well as nonobstructive seating arrangements.

The majority of TA treatment environments include the customary blackboards and giant paper pads that can be used by both the therapists and their clients to draw pictures, elucidate games and transactions, construct egograms, and engage in Adult ego-state clarifications. Some therapists may employ audiovisual aids to facilitate client feedback, awareness, and understanding. Because of the wide and diverse backgrounds of professionally trained TA therapists (from office-practicing psychiatrists to inmates working within the confines of a prison), it becomes impossible to generalize about a typical TA therapeutic setting.

Relationships

TA therapists provide a supportive, nurturing environment conducive to growth and change. An agreement of confidentiality is respected by both the therapist and the clients. The therapist provides permission for the client to maintain an active role in therapy. The client is also given protection and encouragement from the therapist as he or she begins to change and validate a new way of thinking, feeling, and behaving. For the therapist's permission and protection to be effective, the therapist must be potent, well-trained, and competent to be in this role. Authentic TA therapists undergo years of required training, schooling, and clinical experience under authorized clinical teaching members of the ITAA before they are endorsed as certified TA therapists. TA therapists may work independently or in co-therapy teams. They conduct therapy with individuals, couples, families, and group members according to the specific needs of the client.

The simple vocabulary of TA and commonly understood words are used in therapeutic sessions so that time isn't wasted with unclear verbiage or confusing concepts. The client is viewed as an equal partner in the therapeutic process. The common goal of each TA therapist is to catalyze a cure—defined as reaching therapy goals—and to do so as quickly as possible. A TA therapist is generally an active participant in the client's process and will frequently operate on intuitive perceptions and will invite clients to be open and intuitive as well.

Client Problems

Whenever there is a break from the agreed-upon course of action—for instance, nonpayment of the therapist's fee or missing scheduled appointments —the therapist will view these transactions as psychological games and will provide therapy from this standpoint. The simplest to the most severe human psychological problems have been successfully resolved through TA therapy.

CASE EXAMPLE

Judd had been diagnosed as a hypochondriac by many physicians. He complained about fatigue, weariness, headaches, and anxiety as he displayed his collection of pills and remedies. Judd's belief that he was sick was seen to reach far back into his past, as he nostalgically reminisced about his family's medicine cabinet and remembered his mother's taking his temperature, giving him pills, and stroking him for being a weak, sickly child. He was able to repeat his early life-style with his wife, whose attitude toward Judd was similar to his mother's. Both wife and mother were high in Nurturing Parent and in Adapted Child on their own egograms.

At Judd's first TA group session, the other members drew his egogram (Figure 11.19), and he established a treatment contract: to experience a full month without having a noticeable headache.

In a subsequent session, Judd was habitually complaining of feeling "sick," and another group member, Wayne, who in contrast to Judd had a critical personality (high CP), told him

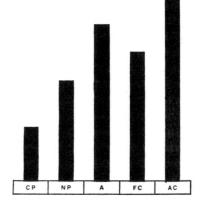

JUDD'S EGOGRAM (BEFORE TA)

FIGURE 11.19

to "stand up for yourself." Judd appeared especially frightened and the therapist, noticing this, asked him if he wanted to work on his feelings. Judd nodded affirmatively.

Knowing that this feeling was a repetitive racket, the therapist did not comfort Judd; rather, the negative feelings were enhanced by instructing Judd to exaggerate his tight jaw and tense wrinkled brow. When Judd was in obvious pain, the therapist asked him to close his eyes to enable him to leave the here-and-now of the group setting and begin to trace his racket feeling back to a childhood prototype episode of his script decision.

After pausing briefly at the reexperience of his wedding ceremony, then later at school episodes, Judd began to quiver and said, "I'm five years old, and I want my Mommie to come to nursery school with me, but she won't. Please, Mommie, I'm not big enough. I'm scared . . . I'm sick!"

Beads of perspiration formed on his forehead and he rubbed his stomach. He was instructed to place his fantasized "Mommie" in the empty chair and tell her what he was feeling. The roleplaying served to enhance his emotional state.

Judd [age five]: I'm scared. My tummy aches and my head aches, and I want to stay home with you.

Mommie [played by Judd]: I know you don't feel very good, so let me give you some medicine for your head and tummy and then you can go to school.

Judd: I feel so sick. I don't think the medicine will help.

Mommie: Well, then, I'll put you back to bed now, and I'll give you some pills, and by tomorrow you'll feel good enough to go to school.

Judd [very relieved]: Okay. If I'm sick and stay home, at least I won't be so scared.

"What are you deciding about yourself now?" the therapist asked.

"I'm scared of people," Judd replied. "I'm scared of going to school and being with the other little boys. If I stay sick, I won't have to face them."

Judd's biological mother, for her own psychological reasons, probably was nervous about having a healthy child who would someday leave her. She passed her anxiety and scared feelings on to Judd by the usual scripting process (see Figure 11.20). From her Parent, she sent him the life value, "Go to school." (Later in life, this ex-

MOTHER

JUDD'S SCRIPT MATRIX

FIGURE 11.20

pressed itself as "Be a man," and so on.) But her Child ego state sent him the incompatible injunction, "Don't leave me!" Eventually Judd's Adapted Child made his decision, "I'm scared and sick. I won't leave you." This basic childhood decision carried through his life. In treatment Judd was encouraged to reexperience his "little boy" ego-state feeling and express it fully. By surfacing his early feelings and thoughts, he was able to view the original scene that set the tone for his life.

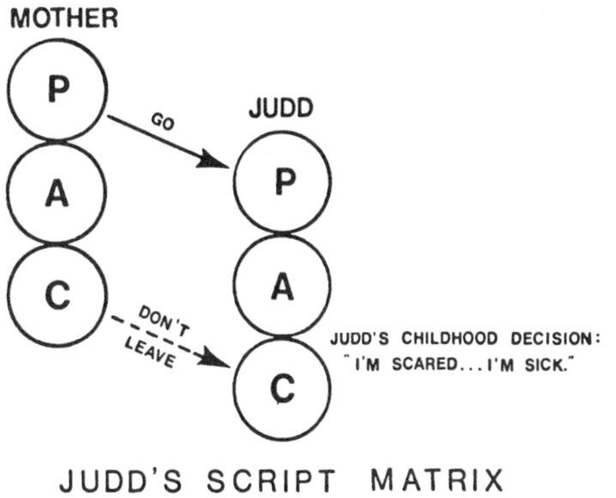

To change, one must redecide. Judd was soon reintroduced to his other powers by focusing on the other forces in his egogram. His Adult was chosen to oppose his scripted Adapted Child because this logical force was quite strong in him, and although his Nurturing Parent force would also be helpful, a conversation between his weak, conforming Adapted Child and his scientific, rational Adult was structured. As before, he switched chairs as he switched ego states:

Judd [AC]: I feel sick and I'm scared to go to school by myself.

Judd [A]: Why are you scared?

Judd [AC]: Because I'm afraid I'll get lost and I can't take care of myself.

Judd [A]: Little five-year-olds can't take care of themselves!

Judd [AC]: I know! I'm so scared and I think my stomach hurts.

Judd [A]: You said you *think* your stomach hurts?

Judd [AC]: Well, it kind of hurts, and my mother thinks it hurts.

Judd [A]: Do you think you might have talked yourself into this?

Judd [AC]: Yes, I think so. My stomach doesn't hurt me any more than anyone else's stomach hurts, but it helps me forget about my scare.

Judd [A]: How long do you want to keep scaring yourself and have stomachaches?

Judd [AC]: No longer. I don't have anything to be scared of. I can take care of myself now. I'm not so little anymore.

The conversation was stopped and Judd said he felt great, as if he were healthy for the first time in his life. He no longer was dominated by the little boy in his head. Others in the group were happy for him and freely gave him hugs and congratulations. Judd, with tears in his eyes, spontaneously said, "There is one more thing I'm going to say to that little boy in me." He then went to another chair and said in a nurturing voice, "You're really an OK person."

Judd decided he would be OK, not scared, and thought that getting into good physical shape would be helpful in reinforcing outside of the group what he had redecided in therapy. He committed himself to jogging even though it did not feel right at first. He soon worked up to running at least two miles a day and exercised at the local gym. His legs and lungs felt better and he soon lost his craving for cigarettes. He chose a new set of friends at the office who shared his new interest in exercise and nourishing foods. The structures in his life supported his new healthy view of himself.

Unfortunately, when the redecision process is not successful, it is due to a resistance. The intrapsychic resistance occurs, in Judd's case, when he slips from his Adult or Nurturing Parent, into his Adapted Child. In this instance, he would be switching back and forth from chair to chair, commiserating with his Adapted Child. This occurs as follows:

Judd [AC]: I feel bad.
Judd [A becoming AC]: Gulp! I feel bad, too.

When this occurs, the therapist quickly introduces a third observer chair to combat the slippage. The chair is placed perpendicular to the ongoing dialogue chair and Judd is asked to switch and describe what he is observing. Usually this successfully allows Judd to confront his own resistance. If not, he is probably not ready for redecision and needs to have more group experience to strengthen his Adult and/or other curative ego-state forces that are low on his egogram. Then he will reapproach the problem with increased strength.

In addition to his own internal resistance, Judd challenged the subtle resistances from outside himself: socially at home, institutionally at work, and even culturally in the rest of his environment. When Judd announced to his wife he was going to start jogging and was not going to have headaches anymore, she was outwardly full of joy but somehow did not seem to know what to do with herself. She was used to the old Judd, whom she greeted every day with, "How are you feeling today?" His typical response had been, "Not so good." When he overcame his script injunction, his answer became, "Oh, I feel fine." This was met by a sickening smile from his wife and she would plead, "Are you sure?" The first few times this happened, Judd replied, "Well, now that you mention it, I think I do have a little ache in my neck." Temporarily he succumbed to this volley of social resistances from his wife. Soon he increased his awareness of these day-to-day hindrances and gathered support from those who had no vested interest in his being sick (the group members). As he insisted on being treated as a healthy person, his wife became more and more frantic. "It's about time to go to the doctor and get your prescription filled," she said. Judd's response was, "I don't need medicine anymore." It can be predicted in advance that close social contacts will resist the change at least as hard as the person undergoing it. Game analysis and group support were aids at this level.

Cultural resistances to personal change are subtle, ever present, and strongly influential. One of Western civilization's "cultural truths" is that if you are feeling bad, the remedy is to open your mouth and put in some magic elixir, as did the Greek deity Bacchus. Television advertising abounds with graphically suffering men and women who are dramatically "cured" by ingesting the right product. Fairy tales passed from generation to generation reinforce the belief in the power of magic potions to influence life. Just as Ponce de León wandered in search of the fountain of youth, Judd sought the elixir for "relief from his chronic pain and discomfort" and for everlasting health and vigor. Judd's mother also bought this mythology, as evidenced by her intriguing medicine cabinet. The commonly shared myths made it easy and culturally acceptable for Judd to avoid facing his real problems.

Judd's egogram, constructed again after more than a year of rigorous attention to change via diagnosis of weak areas, surfacing inner conflicts, confronting resistance, redeciding, practicing, exercising both psychologically and physically, and overcoming resistances, showed his Critical Parent gained power as he was able to say no to harmful outside influences and stop being a social patsy (see Figure 11.21). His Adult gained particularly in his ability to see himself more accurately. Also, he laughed more as his Free Child grew. The most dramatic change was the decrease in his Adapted Child as he lived his life with personal strength and freedom.

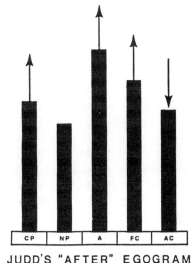

JUDD'S "AFTER" EGOGRAM

FIGURE 11.21

SUMMARY

TA is an interactive, complete theory of psychotherapy that consists of many phases and continues to evolve. The first phase, ego states (1955–62), focused upon Eric Berne's discovery that the dynamic personality can be observed by paying attention to here-and-now phenomena. The therapist and client are able to predict future problems as well as infer past history by attention to present attitude, gestures, voice, vocabulary, social response, and other observable criteria. Eric Berne at that time used these findings about ego states in group psychotherapy as an adjunct for his psychoanalytic approach, but it soon became clear that the concept of the dynamic unconscious was not necessary for clients to gain insight and social control.

The second phase of transactional analysis focused on transactions and games (1962–66) and stressed the delineation of games. Transactional analysis during this period was basically an intellectual approach, still imbued with the idea that insight, or catching onto what is happening, would be curative. This, of course, was true for many individuals, but certainly not for the majority. It was during this phase that TA became popular, because it was based on forthright and simple vocabulary and because people could readily identify their game patterns. The third phase, script analysis (1966–70), encouraged strong emotional reexperience in the practice of transactional analysis. Clients not only analyzed but also relived those decisive moments in their lives with the emotions that accompanied childhood decisions. Transactional analysts then began to incorporate other systems, especially Robert Goulding's combination of Gestalt techniques with TA. The fourth phase (1970 onward) was stimulated by the action techniques of the human-potential movement, Gestalt, psychodrama, encounter, and many of the other explosive, energy-liberating systems. The new model, the egogram, was developed to bridge the gap between the more structural definitions and theories of early transactional analysis and to provide a model for the otherwise haphazard explosive action techniques.

TA has had a rather full history in a short time and has a remarkable amount of clinical and theoretical research for such a young psychotherapy movement (Blair & McGahey, 1974, 1975). Because of its easily understood vocabulary and because of the willingness of therapists to share ideas with clients, TA rapidly became a popular psychotherapy. As such, TA has been used not only by psychiatrists, psychologists, social workers, and other traditional therapists, but also by paraprofessionals, who found the theoretical aspects of TA were easy to learn and had direct applicability to their concerns. Indeed, street workers and prison inmates have become outstanding TA therapists. Effort for the TA therapist is in practical applications rather than in decoding mystical jargon.

The history of TA is characterized by rapid change to new and more effective techniques rather than adherence to earlier models. The structural concepts of ego states, the transaction (the unit of social action), and the script or games theory will not be discarded; however, the techniques employed to bring about change have and will be distinctly shifted from major reliance upon understanding and insight (which is still thought to be important) to an approach that is more experiential and emotive.

ANNOTATED BIBLIOGRAPHY

Berne, E. (1964). *Games people play.* New York: Grove Press.

Written as a handbook for transactional group therapists, this book, because of its readability and forthright vocabulary, became a best-seller in 1965. This book summarizes the early phases of TA: ego states, transactions, and games. The theory of games opened an entirely new psychology of human relationships.

Berne, E. (1966). *Principles of group treatment.* New York: Oxford University Press.

In this widely used textbook on group interaction and treatment of individuals in a group setting, Berne provides an excellent comparative approach and a workable model for group structure and process.

Berne, E. (1972). *What do you say after you say hello?* New York: Grove Press.

This is Berne's final statement, published posthumously. It outlines the total theory of personality that evolved after 15 years of TA. The occurrence of scripts is the major focus.

Dusay, J. (1977). Egograms: *How I see you and you see me.* New York: Harper & Row.

An expansion of TA via a functional and energy model is presented for the first time. Egograms represent a specific growth model that departs from a theory of a dynamic unconscious.

Steiner, C. (1974). *Scripts people live.* New York: Grove Press.

A comprehensive discussion of script theory by the creator of the script matrix. There is a special focus on political and social institutions.

CASE READINGS

Berne, E. (1961). A terminated case with follow-up. In *Transactional analysis in psychotherapy.* New York: Grove Press. (Reprint in D. Wedding & R. J. Corsini (Eds.) (1989). *Case studies in psychotherapy.* Itasca, IL: F. E. Peacock.)

This case illustrates six months of TA treatment in a woman with multiple medical and psychiatric problems. The case is an excellent initial introduction to TA.

Berne, E. (1961). The case of Mr. Sequndo. In *Transactional analysis in psychotherapy.* New York: Grove Press.

The case of Sequndo, a lawyer who thought, felt, and acted like a little boy, stimulated the evolution of structured analysis and the study of ego states, which are building blocks of Transactional Analysis.

Berne, E. (1964). A typical game. In *Games people play* (pp. 50–58). New York: Grove Press.

Berne presented the phenomenology of games and chose the game colloquially called, "If It Weren't For You," which is the most common game played between spouses to illustrate the character of

games in general. While psychological games are now well accepted and have become incorporated into everyday problems, the profoundity and complexity of this class of behavior are most succinctly presented here.

Berne, E. (1966). The case of Rita. *Principles of group treatment* (pp. 264–272). New York: Oxford University Press.

The case of Rita was used to illustrate the script decision. Attention to these negative childhood decisions gave rise to the redecision work that has been the predominant treatment in Transactional Analysis from the mid-1970's until the present.

Dusay, J. (1978). *Egograms.* New York: Harper & Row.

This book illustrates the functional aspects of egostates and presents many case examples of how energy imbalance in personalities is treated by redecision and exercises. Especially important is the section on conflicts in coupling. See "Big Mama" and "Mama's Boy."

Goulding, R. E., & Goulding, M. (1978). The case of Tim. *The power is in the patient: A Transactional Analysis/ Gestalt approach to psychotherapy* (pp. 43–55). San Francisco: TA Press.

The case of Tim, taken from a transcript of a group therapy weekend marathon, demonstrates in detail the application of the combination of Transactional Analysis and Gestalt, a common current practice.

REFERENCES

Abraham, K. (1948). *Selected papers.* London: Hogarth Press.

Adler, A. (1963). Individual psychology. In G. B. Levitas (Ed.), *The world of psychology.* New York: Brazille.

Babcock, D., & Keepers, T. (1976). *Raising kids OK.* New York: Grove Press.

Barnes, G. (Ed.) (1977). *Transactional analysis after Eric Berne.* New York: Harper College Press.

Bateson, G., & Ruesch, J. (1951). *Communication.* New York: Norton.

Bateson, G., Jackson, D., Haley, J., & Weakland, J. (1956). Toward a communication theory of schizophrenia. *Behavior Science, 1,* 251–264. [Reprinted in D. Jackson (Ed.), *Communication, family and marriage (Vol. 1).* Palo Alto, CA: Science & Behavior Books.]

Beck, A. T. (1976). *Cognitive therapy and the emotional disorders.* New York: International University Press.

Belkin, G. S. (1984). *Introduction to counseling* (2nd ed.). Dubuque, IA: William C. Brown.

Berne, E. (1949). The nature of intuition. *Psychiatric Quarterly, 23,* 203–226.

Berne, E. (1951). Intuition v. the ego image. *Psychiatric Quarterly, 31,* 611–627.

Berne, E. (1952). Concerning the nature of diagnosis. *International Review of Medicine, 165,* 283–292.

Berne, E. (1953). Concerning the nature of communication. *Psychiatric Quarterly, 27,* 185–198.

Berne, E. (1955). Intuition IV. Primal images and primal judgment. *Psychiatric Quarterly, 29,* 634–658.

Berne, E. (1957). *A layman's guide to psychiatry and psychoanalysis.* New York: Simon & Schuster.

Berne, E. (1957). Ego states in psychotherapy. *American Journal of Psychotherapy, 11,* 293–309.

Berne, E. (1958). Transactional analysis: A new and effective method of psychotherapy. *American Journal of Psychotherapy, 12,* 735–743.

Berne, E. (1961). *Transactional analysis in psychotherapy.* New York: Grove Press.

Berne, E. (1962). Intuition VI: The psychodynamics of intuition. *Psychiatric Quarterly, 36,* 294–300.

Berne, E. (1963). *Structure and dynamics of groups and organizations.* Philadelphia: Lippincott.

Berne, E. (1964a). Trading stamps. *Transactional Bulletin, 3,* 10–12.

Berne, E. (1964b). *Games people play.* New York: Grove Press.

Berne, E. (1966). *Principles of group treatment.* New York: Oxford University Press.

Berne, E. (1970). *Sex in human loving.* New York: Simon & Schuster.

Berne, E. (1971a). Away from a theory of the impact of interpersonal interaction on non-verbal participation. *Transactional Analysis Journal, 1,* 23–29.

Berne, E. (1971b). Annotated bibliography. *Transactional Analysis Journal, 1,* 33–39.

Berne, E. (1971c). *The happy valley.* New York: Grove Press.

Berne, E. (1972). *What do you say after you say hello?* New York: Grove Press.

Berne, E. (1975). *Intuition and ego states.* San Francisco: TA Press.

Berne, E. (1976). *Beyond games and scripts.* New York: Ballantine Books.

Berne, E. (1977). *Intuition and ego states.* San Francisco: Harper & Row.

Battaenfly, L. V. (1950). An outline of general systems theory. *British Journal for Philosophy of Science, 1,* 139–164.

Blair, M., & McGahey, C. (1974, 1975). *Transactional analysis research index (Vols. 1 & 2).* Tallahassee: Florida Institute for Transactional Analysis.

Boyce, M. (1980). Before, during and after Berne. *Transactional Analysis Journal, 2,* 33–34.

Boyd, H., & Boyd, L. (1980). Going crazy. *Transactional Analysis Journal, 4,* 317–319.

Breuer, J., & Freud, S. (1962). On the physical mechanism of hysterical phenomena. In J. Strachey (Ed.), *Standard edition of the complete psychological works of Sigmund Freud (Vol. 3).* London: Hogarth Press. (Originally published 1893.)

Campbell, J. (1949). *The hero with a thousand faces.* New York: Pantheon Books.

Chandler, A., & Hartman, J. (1960). Lysergic acid diethylamid (LSD-25) as a facilitating agent in psychotherapy. *Archives of General Psychiatry, 2,* 286–299.

Cheney, W. (1971). Eric Berne: Biographical Sketch. *Transactional Analysis Journal, 1,* 14–22.

Corey, G. (1986a). *Case approach to counseling and psychotherapy (2nd ed.).* Monterey, CA: Brooks/Cole.

Corey, G. (1986b). *Theory and practice of counseling and psychotherapy (3rd ed.).* Monterey, CA: Brooks/Cole.

Crossman, P. (1966). Permission, protection and potency. *Transactional Analysis Bulletin, 5,* 152–153.

Dusay, J. (1971). Eric Berne's studies of intuition, 1949–1962. *Transactional Analysis Journal, 1,* 34–44.

Dusay, J. (1972). Egograms and the constancy hypothesis. *Transactional Analysis Journal, 2,* 37–41.

Dusay, J. (1975). Eric Berne. In A. Freedman, H. Kaplan, & B. Sadock (Eds.), *Comprehensive Textbook of Psychiatry* (pp. 95–101). Baltimore: Williams & Wilkins.

Dusay, J. (1977a). Four phases of TA. In G. Barnes (Ed.), *Transactional analysis for Eric Berne* (pp. 45–72). New York: Harper College Press.

Dusay, J. (1977b). *Egograms: How I see you and you see me.* New York: Harper & Row.

Dusay, J. (1978). *TA treatment-training manual.* Unpublished manuscript.

Dusay, J. (1981). Eric Berne: Contributions and limitations. *Transactional Analysis Journal, 2,* 41–45.

Dusay, K. (1975). *The hero in your head: An analysis of the hero.* Master's thesis, Lone Mountain College, San Francisco.

Dusay, K. (1976). Recurring themes throughout world literature: Persecutors, rescuers and victims. Master's thesis, San Francisco State University.

Dusay, K. (1985). *Egostate imbalance: An indicator of marital dissatisfaction* Doctoral dissertation, California Coast University, Santa Ana, CA.

Dusay, K., Bert, D., Haydock, A., Keel, S., Oei, M., Steel-Traina, D., & Yanehiro, J. (1984). *Having a baby.* New York: Dell/Delacourt.

Dusay, K., Bert, D., Keel, S; Oei, M. & Yanehiro, J (1988). *After having a baby.* New York: Dell Publishing.

English, F. (1962). Episcript and the hot potato game. *Transactional Analysis Bulletin, 8,* 77–82.

English, F. (1971). The substitution factor: Rackets and real feelings. Part I. *Transactional Analysis Bulletin, 1,* 340–343.

English, F. (1972). The substitution factor: Rackets and real feelings. Part II. *Transactional Analysis Bulletin, 2,* 421–424.

Ernst, F. (1971). The OK Corral: The grid for get-on-with-it. *Transactional Analysis Bulletin, 1,* 337–339.

Erskine, R. G. (1982). Transactional analysis and family therapy. In A. M. Horne and M. M. Olhsen (Eds.), *Family Counseling and Therapy* (pp. 63–72). Itasca, IL: F. E. Peacock.

Erskine, R., & Zaleman, M. (1979). The racket system: A model for racket analysis. *Transactional Analysis Bulletin, 9,* 1–7.

Federn, P. (1952). *Ego psychology and the psychoses.* New York: Basic Books.

Forman, L. H., & Ramsburg, J. S. (1978). *Hello, Sigmund. This is Eric.* Kansas City: Sheed, Andrews and McMeel.

Glasser, W., & Zunin, L. (1973). Reality therapy. In R. J. Corsini (Ed.), *Current psychotherapies* (pp. 287–316). Itasca, IL: F. E. Peacock.

Goulding, M., & Goulding, R. (1978). *The power is in the patient: A TA/Gestalt approach to psychotherapy.* San Francisco: TA Press.

Goulding, M., & Goulding, R. (1979). *Changing lives through redecision therapy.* New York: Brunner-Mazel.

Goulding, R. (1972). New directions in transactional analysis: Creating an environment for redecision and change. In C. Sager and H. Kaplan (Eds.), Progress in group and family therapy (pp. 85–98). New York: Brunner-Mazel.

Goulding, R. (1974). Thinking and feeling in psychotherapy (three impasses). Voices, 10, 11–13.

Goulding, R., & Goulding, M. (1976). Injunctions, decisions, and redecisions. Transactional Analysis Journal, 6, 41–48.

Hansen, J., Stevic, R., & Warner, R. (1977). Counseling: Theory and Process (2nd ed.). Boston: Allyn & Bacon.

Harlow, H. (1958). The nature of love. American Psychologist, 13, 673–685.

Harris, T. (1969). I'm OK, you're OK. New York: Harper & Row.

Heyer, R. (1979). Development of a questionnaire to measure ego states with some applications to social and comparative psychiatry. Transactional Analysis Journal, 9, 379–384.

Heyer, R. (1987). Empirical research on ego state theory. Transactional Analysis Journal, 17, 286–294.

Hurley, J., & Porter, H. (1967). Child ego state in the college classroom. Transactional Analysis Bulletin, 6, 28–29.

James, M., & Jongeward, D. (1971). Born to win. Reading, MA: Addison-Wesley.

James, M. (1974). Self-reparenting. Transactional Analysis Journal, 4, 3–7.

James, M., & Scott, D. (1976). Women as winners: Transactional analysis for personal growth. Reading, MA: Addison-Wesley.

James, M. (1977). Principles of TA. In M. James (Ed.), Techniques in Transactional Analysis for Psychotherapists and Counselors (pp. 15–46). Reading, MA: Addison-Wesley.

James, M. (1979). Marriage is for loving. Reading, MA: Addison-Wesley.

Kahler, T. (1975). Scripts: Process and content. Transactional Analysis Journal, 5, 277–279.

Kapur, R., & Miller, K. (1987). A comparison between therapeutic factors in TA and psychodynamic therapy groups. Transactional Analysis Journal, 17, 294–300.

Karpman, S. (1968). Script drama analysis. Transactional Analysis Bulletin, 26, 16–22.

Karpman, S. (1971). Options. Transactional Analysis Journal, 1, 294–298.

Kendra, J. (1973). Research presentation at ITAA Conference. In J. Dusay, Egograms: How I see you and you see me (pp. 56–57). San Francisco: Harper & Row.

Klein, M. (1980). Lives people live: A textbook of transactional analysis. London: Wiley.

Levin, P. (1974). Becoming the way we are. San Francisco: Trans Publications.

McCormick, P. (1971). Guide for use of a life script questionnaire in transactional analysis. Transactional Analysis Journal, 2, 32–46.

McCormick, P. (1973). TA and behavior modification: A comparison study. Transactional Analysis Journal, 3, 10–14.

McNeel, J. (1975). Redecisions in psychotherapy: A study of the effects of an intensive weekend group workshop. Unpublished doctoral dissertation, California School of Professional Psychology, San Francisco.

McNeel, J. (1976). The parent interview. Transactional Analysis Journal, 6, 33–39.

Mellor, K., & Sigmend, E. (1973a). Discounting. Transactional Analysis Journal, 5, 3–9.

Mellor, K., & Sigmend, E. (1973b). Redefining. Transactional Analysis Journal, 5, 13–17.

Patterson, C. H. (1980). Theories of counseling and psychotherapy (3rd ed.). New York: Harper & Row.

Penfield, W. (1952). Memory mechanisms. Archives of Neurology and Psychiatry, 67, 178–198.

Penfield, W., & Roberts, L. (1959). Speech and brain mechanisms. Princeton: Princeton University Press.

Perls, F. (1969). Gestalt therapy verbatim. Lafayette, CA: Real People Press.

Prochaska, J. O. (1984). Systems of psychotherapy: A transtheoretical analysis (2nd ed.). Homewood, IL: Dorsey Press.

Reik, T. (1948). Listening with the third ear. New York: Farrar, Strauss.

Schiff, E., & Mellor, K. (1975). Discounting. Transactional Analysis Journal, 5, 303–311.

Schiff, J. (1969). Reparenting schizophrenics. *Transactional Analysis Bulletin, 8*, 158–164.

Schiff, J. (1970). *All my children.* New York: Evans.

Schiff, J. (1975). *The cathexis reader.* New York: Harper & Row.

Schiff, J., & Schiff, A. (1971). Passivity. *Transactional Analysis Journal, 1*, 71–78.

Shilling, L. E. (1984). *Perspectives on counseling theories.* Englewood Cliffs, NJ: Prentice-Hall.

Spitz, R. (1945). Hospitalism: Genesis of psychiatric conditions in early childhood. *Psychoanalytic Study of the Child, 1*, 53–57.

Steiner, C. (1964). A script checklist. *Transactional Analysis Bulletin, 6*, 38–39.

Steiner, C. (1970). *Games alcoholics play.* New York: Grove Press.

Steiner, C. (1971a). *Scripts people live.* New York: Grove Press.

Steiner, C. (1971b). The stroke economy. *Transactional Analysis Journal, 1*, 3–6.

Steiner, C. (1981). *The other side of power.* New York: Grove Press.

Thomson, G. (1972). The identification of ego states. *Transactional Analysis Journal, 2*, 196–211.

Vernon, J., et al. (1961). The effect of human isolation upon some perceptual and motor skills. In S. Solomon, (Ed.), *Sensory deprivation* (pp. 27–43). Cambridge, MA: Harvard University Press.

Wagner, J. (1979). Despooking: The understanding and treatment of anxiety. *Transactional Analysis Journal, 9*, 268–273.

Watzlawick, P. (1974). *Change: Principles of problem formation and problem resolution.* New York: W. W. Norton.

Weiss, E. (1950). *Principles of psychodynamics.* New York: Grune & Stratton.

Wolpe, J. (1961). The systematic desensitization treatment. *Journal of Nervous and Mental Diseases, 132*, 189–195.

Woolams, S., & Brown, M. (1978). *Transactional analysis: A modern and comprehensive text of TA theory and practice.* Dexter, MI: Huron Valley Institute Press.

Woolams, S., & Brown, M. (1979). *TA: The total handbook of transactional analysis.* Englewood Cliffs, NJ: Prentice-Hall.

Yalom, I. (1975). *The theory and practice of group psychotherapy.* New York: Basic Books.

MURRAY BOWEN

NATHAN ACKERMAN
1908–1971

SALVADOR MINUCHIN

CARL WHITAKER

12

Family Therapy

VINCENT D. FOLEY

OVERVIEW

The focus of family therapy is not on an individual patient, but rather on the family as a whole. The basic argument for this form of treatment is that it is more logical, faster, more satisfactory, and more economical to treat all members of a family than to concentrate on a person who is supposed to be in need of treatment. The task of the family therapist is to change relationships between members of the troubled family so that symptomatic behavior disappears. To accomplish this, family therapists have developed a variety of different strategies and techniques, based on somewhat different theories, for the ultimate goals of realigning relationships to achieve better adjustment of all individuals in the family, including the so-called identified patient.

BASIC CONCEPTS

Family therapy may be defined broadly as an attempt to modify the relationships in a family to achieve harmony. A family is seen as an open system, created by interlocking triangles, maintained or changed by means of feedback. There are three basic concepts in family therapy: *system, triangles,* and *feedback.*

A *paradigm* (Kuhn, 1962) is a way of looking at scientific data and is the critical dimension in how one goes about investigating evidence. Family therapy offers a paradigm that brings with it new concepts and new ways of making interventions (Haley & Hoffman, 1967; Levenson, 1972). Family therapy is therefore a quantum leap from (a) the prior paradigm of viewing people as individuals apart from one another to (b) seeing them in relationships with others. As a result, the locus of pathology is shifted from the *individual* to the *system.* The attention of the therapist shifts from the "disturbed" individual to the dysfunctional system. In family therapy, the "identified patient" is seen as but a symptom, and the system itself (the family) is viewed as the client.

Concept of System

A *system* (Buckley, 1967) is made up of sets of different parts with two things in common: (a) the parts are interconnected and interdependent with mutual causality each affecting the other, and (b) each part is related to the other in a stable manner over time. A heating unit in a house is a system, whereas people traveling to work on a bus are not. If a system has a continuous flow of elements entering and leaving, it is an *open system*. If it lacks such a flow, as in the case of a heating system, it is a *closed system* (Von Bertalanffy, 1974). An open system, such as a family, has three important properties: *wholeness, relationship,* and *equifinality.*

Wholeness means the system is not just the sum of its parts taken separately, but also includes their interaction. It follows from this that one cannot understand a given part unless one understands its connection to the other parts. Therapeutically, this means that clients must be seen in the context of their lives, especially their relationship to their family. Wholeness, therefore, refers to the interdependence among the parts of the system. Wholeness represents a Gestalt conception because the whole is more than and different from the sum of its parts; the family consists of the people in it *and* the relationships between the individuals.

Relationship considers what is happening between the parts and examines interactions. It puts an emphasis on *what* is happening rather than *why* it is happening. This shift results from the use of a paradigm based on the system concept rather than on a collection of separated and separable individuals. *What* becomes more important than *why.* The family therapist asks, "*What* is the family doing?" rather than, "*Why* is the family doing this?" If the ongoing patterns of interaction can be discovered, the therapist believes an ameliorative change can be made in the system without uncovering the *why* of the pattern. We shift our attention from what is going on *inside* family members to what is going on *between* them.

Equifinality, or self-perpetuation of structures, means that if interventions are made here and now, changes can be produced because open systems are not governed by their initial conditions. A system has no memory. This concept has enormous importance for family therapy because it justifies concentrating on the here and now. Regardless of the origin of a problem, any difficulty can be removed if a change is made at any point in time in the system. Silvano Arieti (1969) suggests that avoiding getting involved in the past, what he calls the "genetic fallacy," might be the most important contribution system thinking has made to therapy. Almost all other therapeutic systems concentrate on the past, seeking underlying causes, making interpretations about past events, implying that the "real problem" is in the past. The family therapist does not deny the importance of the past, but emphasizes that what perpetuates the problem is the current interaction within the system. For example, say that a man began heavy drinking 20 years ago because he had unresolved problems with his mother, but if he drinks now, it may be because of the present relationship with his wife. If the interaction between husband and wife can be altered, the drinking may be changed without ever getting involved in the why or in the past. Equifinality has many practical ramifications in the way in which a therapist will make interventions into a family system.

Interlocking Triangles

A series of *interlocking triangles* are the basic building blocks of the family relationship system (Bowen, 1971). An emotional network such as a family is composed of a series of interlocking triangles that lend stability to the system. They are a means of reducing or increasing the emotional intensity of a system. One can formulate an axiom as follows: *Whenever the emotional balance between two people becomes too intense or too distant, a third person or thing can be introduced to restore equilibrium to the system and give it stability.* This is why marriages in trouble frequently have presenting problems such as husbands having affairs or becoming "workaholics" or alcoholics and wives becoming overinvolved with children, clubs, or family. These troubling behaviors can be viewed either (a) as the result of problems of the individuals or (b) as tactics for gaining closeness or distance within the context of the marriage or the family. Family therapy takes this latter view.

Analyzing the various triangles in a system and making interventions to change the system are the primary tasks of the family therapist. Murray Bowen and proponents of *family systems theory* (see Liebman et al., 1976) are particularly concerned with triangles over three generations involving grandparents, parents, and children. Salvador Minuchin (1974) and *structuralists* in general are more concerned with triangles in the nuclear family of father, mother, and child. Both, however, work on the triangles as a way of producing change and not with individuals in the system.

Feedback

In system theory, *feedback* refers to the process through which a system adjusts itself. *Negative feedback* is the process through which the deviation in a system is corrected and previous equilibrium is restored. *Positive feedback* destroys a system by forcing it to change, not allowing it to return to its former state.

A frequently observed clinical pattern illustrating the concept of negative feedback would be the following. John's parents ask for help with their son, who is labeled "school phobic." The therapist views John's problem as a response to the family system; he is overclose with his mother and too distant from his father. He sees John, the identified patient, as a cover-up for parental problems. The counselor works with the parents and their marriage. John is thereby relieved and begins to go to school. The marriage, however, worsens as more and more problems between husband and wife are uncovered. John senses their worsening relationship and begins to become phobic again. The parents now unite and stay together "for the sake of the child." John's school phobia can be labeled as "negative feedback" needed to maintain the old system.

Positive feedback has been aptly described by Carl Whitaker (1975) as the "leaning tower of Pisa" approach. A therapist, instead of correcting a symptom, pushes the problem in the other direction so the system falls of its own weight. This approach uses the absurdity of a symptom, and instead of restoring balance, moves it into further chaos to its ultimate destruction. The most recent and creative use of positive feedback can be found in the writings of Mara Palazzoli and her associates in Milan, Italy (1978). Originally trained as a child analyst, she came under the influence of Gregory Bateson by way of the Palo Alto group (Mental Research Institute) and incorporated their ideas into her work with anorexic children.

OTHER SYSTEMS

Many early pioneers in family therapy, such as Murray Bowen and Nathan Ackerman, were trained as psychoanalysts and, consequently, there are similarities between their ideas and those of psychoanalysis. There are many interfaces between family therapy and psychoanalytic thinking, and some family therapists, such as Ivan Boszormenyi-Nagy and Geraldine Spark (1973), and Helm Stierlin (1974) in particular, work on these. A major difference between psychoanalysis and family therapy is that in psychoanalysis, parental involvement is excluded as a hindrance to the development of the transference neurosis, which is seen as necessary to successful therapy, whereas in family therapy, all members of the family are brought into the therapy sessions.

Adlerian psychotherapeutic theory shares much with family therapy. Its emphasis on the family constellation is a major concept borrowed by family therapists. Adler's approach was holistic, as is family therapy. The use of paradox, a major weapon in family therapy, has its roots in Alfred Adler (Mozdzierz, Macchitelli & Lisiecki, 1976). Likewise, an emphasis on the conscious and the present are Adlerian concepts. The freedom to improvise is a feature of family therapy and it, too, has its roots in Adler. Adler died in 1937 before the full impact of system thinking, so although he took the family system into account in ther-

apy, he did not give it the same importance as do family therapists. The basic concepts of family therapy are found in a latent state in Adler's thinking (Christensen, 1971).

Client-centered therapy, similarly to family therapy, stresses the here and now, puts responsibility for behavior on the person, and views human beings holistically. However, client-centered therapy does not use system thinking. Its basic model is alien to the family therapist.

Rational-emotive therapy (RET), too, uses a different model. The similarities between it and family therapy are superficial: sharing here-and-now emphasis and taking responsibility. Its differences are major. RET stresses rugged individualism and overemphasizes the cognitive, whereas family therapy strives to strike a balance between being an independent self and relating to others in the family.

Behavior therapy has been used by several family therapists (Engeln, Knutson, Laughy & Garlington, 1976; Liberman, 1976; Liberman, Wheeler, De Visser, Kuehnel & Kuehnel, 1980). The frequently used technique known as "prescribing the symptom" is behavioral. However, there is a critical difference between behavior therapy and family therapy. Behavior therapy regards the "problem" as the symptomatic client; family therapy sees the "problem" as a response to a system, as a notice that something is wrong in the system. Behavior therapy puts the burden of change on the individual, family therapy on the system.

Gestalt therapy clearly shares a common base with family therapy. Its concern for the present and its emphasis on behavior and active participation by the therapist are common to both approaches. However, with families, Gestalt gives more importance to feelings and confrontation than do most family therapists (Kempler, 1974).

Transactional analysis (TA) uses an interpersonal model and tends to emphasize the "why" rather than the "what," as in family therapy. TA recognizes the importance of triangles in its concept of games (Berne, 1964) and shares the belief that symptoms are strategies to control the behavior of others, especially in alcoholics (Steiner, 1971). Nevertheless, TA rarely uses the family as the unit of treatment, preferring to deal with the individuals either alone or in therapeutic groups.

Psychodrama is the basis for a technique known as *family sculpting,* widely used in family therapy, in which a family member recreates his or her family of origin in space and position. For example, does Mr. Jones place his mother next to his father or at his feet looking up at him? Does he put his sister equidistant between them or close to his father? Where does John himself fit in the family? Sculpting is a way of visualizing the closeness or distance experienced in a family. The difference between sculpting and psychodrama, however, is that the latter is used to relive and resolve a traumatic event, whereas sculpting is more concerned with closeness and space as a means of understanding emotional involvement (see Papp, Silverstein & Carter, 1973).

Group therapy bears some resemblance to family therapy in that it takes into account the importance of others, but there are two major differences. First, the group does not have a history. It has no past and no future. The family has both. Second, the agent of the change is the group, with the therapist in the role of facilitator

(Yalom, 1985). The family therapist, on the other hand, serves more as model or teacher than facilitator.

In summary, family therapy has similarities to most active therapies and borrows techniques liberally from many. The critical difference between family therapy and other approaches is the role given to the family system. Other therapies deal either with the individual, the dyadic unit, or the group, but only family therapy sees the family system as the "client." The family is treated, not the individuals. Family therapy is concerned with *how* family members interact and not with *why* they so act. It is a therapy of the family as a system of relationships and not the treatment of maladjusted persons as individuals. We may even say it is concerned with the "spaces" between people—their relationships—rather than with individual processes. As such, it has much in common with Asian personality theory (Pedersen, 1977).

HISTORY

PRECURSORS

A humanistic approach to the alleviation of suffering due to relationship problems began with the psychological discoveries of Freud. In addition, with reference to the precursors of family therapy as we know it today, two other therapists were important: Alfred Adler and Harry Stack Sullivan.

Sigmund Freud

There are two discernible threads in the thinking of Freud. The first, coming from his early training in the biological sciences, is his theory of instincts. The second, going beyond instinct to a more psychological explanation, culminated in the theory of the Oedipus complex.

Most of Freud's life was spent in examining instincts; it was left to others, especially Sullivan and other object relational thinkers or ego analysts such as Melanie Klein, Ronald Fairbairn, and Heinz Hartmann, to elaborate on the more purely psychological aspects (Guntrip, 1971).

As early as 1909, Freud (1964) saw the connection between a young boy's phobic symptoms and his relationship with his father. Nevertheless, Freud chose to treat young Hans independently of the father, and this choice was to influence therapists for decades.

Alfred Adler

Adler has had an important but indirect influence on family therapy in a number of ways. The most influential of the so-called social thinkers in therapy, Adler saw context and environment as essential. A human was not primarily an instinctual being but rather a social, purposeful being motivated not by drives but by goals. An individual was, in brief, a responsible agent able to make choices. Change in the here and now, despite one's past, was not only possible but attainable. Virginia Satir says it simply, "All of the ingredients in a family that count are changeable and correctable" (1972, p. XI).

Second, Adler stressed the importance of the family constellation. It was not just a case of looking at the interaction of child and parent—the concept had to be widened to include siblings and their relationships. Adler's emphasis on sibling position has become one of the essential concepts in the thinking of a school of family therapy associated with Murray Bowen (1971).

Adler emphasized the conscious, the positive, and the ability to change. This typifies family therapy. Family therapists are less concerned with the past than with the present. They look at the positive in family relations, members' communication, and the "growing edge" of the family, as well as at dysfunction. Oscar Christensen, an Adlerian family therapist, says, "Adler would view behavior as movement, communication, movement toward others, and the desire to belong—the desire to be part of" (1971, p. 49). This is a description of family therapy.

Harry Stack Sullivan

Sullivan's contribution to family therapy lies in his investigation of schizophrenia. Sullivan moved away from a biological explanation and toward a psychological one, sensing that the primitive relationship between mother and child was critical in schizophrenia. Sullivan's thinking shifted the focus of therapy from purely intrapsychic to the interpersonal. Therapy was moving toward a system concept.

Sullivan's thinking entered family therapy through Don Jackson, who was influenced by Sullivan's disciple, Frieda Fromm-Reichmann. Jackson later began a school of family therapy that stressed the importance of communication and the use of paradox.

BEGINNINGS

The beginnings of the modern family-therapy movement started in the mid-1950s and focused largely on research in schizophrenia. This produced a series of concepts that became the core ideas in family therapy. The following are some major concepts.

The Double Bind

In 1956, a paper on communication, "Toward a Theory of Schizophrenia," combined the thinking of Gregory Bateson, Don Jackson, Jay Haley, and John Weakland. They discovered that in schizophrenic families *double binding* occurred regularly. This means a person is put into a situation in which whatever choice he makes is unacceptable. "He is damned if he does and damned if he doesn't" because, in fact, no good choice is possible. The "victim" in a double bind, however, is not aware of his dilemma. A child, for example, is told, "Mommy loves you." On the verbal level, such a message shows love and concern. However, in a double-bind situation, the message is delivered in a cold, distant manner. Consequently, he is told (verbally), "I love you," and is informed (non-verbally), "I don't love you." If the child cannot deal with the two contradictory messages, he cannot deal effectively with this problem. The authors of the paper suggested that such double binding is frequently found in the communication of schizophrenic families. Repeated episodes of double binding produce bewilderment and ultimately withdrawal. Such behavior is then labeled "abnormal" and the person in question is "put away."

Fusion

Bowen (1971) used the term *fusion* to describe a process he observed in schizophrenic families. By this he meant that various family members relate to each other in such a way that none of them has a true sense of self as an independent individual. The family forms into an amorphous mass without distinguishing characteristics. Family members can neither gain true intimacy nor separate and become persons. *Fusion* gives them no freedom or option to move closer or to get away.

Schism and Skew

Theodore Lidz, Alice Cornelison, Stephen Fleck, and Dorothy Terry (1957) at Yale observed two processes in particular in families. One pattern involved a dominant spouse who took control of the relationship. This pattern was labeled *marital skew*, meaning the marital relationship was not an equal partnership. Another pattern involved a marriage in which the husband and wife could not attain role reciprocity or in which there was an overattachment to the parental home of one of the spouses. This pattern, called *marital schism*, was particularly evident in marriages in which there was a schizophrenic member. The primary alliance that should exist between a husband and wife in their role as parents was noticeably absent, and in its place was a violation of the boundaries between husband and wife brought about by an alliance between one parent and that parent's parent.

Pseudomutuality

Lyman Wynne, Irving Ryckoff, Juliana Day, and Stanley Hirsch coined the phrase *pseudomutuality* to describe a false kind of closeness in schizophrenic families, defined as "a predominant absorption in fitting together at the expense of the differentiation of the identities of the persons in the relations" (1958, p. 207). To be in such a family is to lose one's boundaries, to become disoriented. The consequence of this process of confusion is a state of dependency on the family. Family members are caught and cannot leave. There is no true intimacy or closeness, only a pseudo-love or caring. The family becomes all not by choice but by necessity.

Mystification

R. D. Laing in England, in doing research with the families of hospitalized schizophrenic teenage girls, noted a process of confusion and obfuscation that he called *mystification,* a process in which "One person (p) seeks to induce in the other some change necessary for his (p's) security" (1956, p. 349). This process in popular language might be called double-talk, a blatant form of manipulation. Laing came to the conclusion that such girls, identified as patients by their parents and others, were often, in fact, the healthiest members of the family.

Interlocking Pathologies

Nathan Ackerman began his career as an orthodox child psychiatrist who did not see parents of patients. In time, however, he realized it was impossible to understand children without getting some idea of the family environment and dynamics. His book *The Psychodynamics of Family Life* (1958) was the first major work in the field in which the relationships between an individual and his or her family were investigated. Ackerman (1956) referred to the difficulties in a family as *interlocking pathologies* in that the problems of one member could not be understood apart from those of other family members.

His contribution to family therapies is special for two reasons. First, he did not work with schizophrenic families exclusively and thus considered relationship processes in less disturbed families. Second, he brought family therapy to the attention of a largely hostile community of psychodynamically oriented therapists and acted as a go-between for many years between the more traditional approach and that of family therapy.

These various ideas and concepts began to jell into a more coherent form when in 1962 Ackerman and Don Jackson united to found *Family Process,* a journal dedicated to examining family research and treatment. The family-therapy movement now had a vehicle through which ideas could be filtered and concepts developed.

CURRENT STATUS

We can identify four schools of family therapy in terms of the emphasis given to various aspects of the treatment process (Foley, 1986).

Object Relations

This viewpoint has close connections with the theory of *object relations* as articulated by Ronald Fairbairn (Guntrip, 1971). Whereas Freud maintained that instinctual gratification was the fundamental need, others, such as Melanie Klein and Ronald Fairbairn, opted for a satisfying object relationship as more basic. The word *object* in this connection refers to people. The inability of a person to work out such a relationship with the family of origin carries over and "contaminates" the new family system in relation to mate and children. Boszormenyi-Nagy states that family pathology is "a specialized multiperson organization of shared fantasies and complementary need gratification patterns, maintained for the purpose of handling past object loss experience" (1965, p. 310). Others who use this kind of framework include James Framo (1970, 1982), Gerald Zuk (1975), and Norman and Betty Paul (1975). In an object relations approach, the identified patient is often seen as the carrier of the split-off and unacceptable impulses of other family members (Stewart, Peters, Marsh & Peters, 1975). In therapy much time will be spent on working with these prior relationships for those who use an object relations theoretical viewpoint.

Family Systems

This school is linked to the work of Murray Bowen and his associates (Bowen, 1978; Kerr, 1981). Bowen began his work in family therapy in the 1950s, when he first developed the idea of the triangle as a way people handled conflict. Since that time he has evolved a theory made up of eight concepts (Bowen, 1978). They are as follows:

1. Triangles
2. Differentiation of self (which measures the amount of fusion between people)
3. The nuclear family emotional system (how a given generation patterns itself)
4. The family projection process (how a family selects a member to be the identified patient)
5. Emotional cut-off (the extent to which a family member relates to a member of his family of origin)
6. Multigenerational transmission (how pathology is passed from one generation to another)
7. Sibling position (this determines one's existential view of the world)
8. Societal regression (patterns found in a family occur in a similar fashion in society) (Kerr, 1981, pp. 241–52).

Bowen maintains that people are born into complex family systems and destined for certain roles in the system. Fusion is a common problem in families, and the goal of family therapy is to teach people to *respond* and not to *react* to their system. Reacting means to act on the basis of feeling alone, not taking into account what the individual wants. Responding, on the other hand, means taking into account the needs of others but still making a rational choice rather than an emotional one.

In the Bowen system, one does not make an either-or choice of self or system. The goal is to stay in touch with the system while, at the same time, maintaining an "I" position. An individual has to learn to be both a self and a member of a system because both are necessary to healthy functioning.

Learning to become a self is a process developed over a period of time and is ongoing. The struggle for balance is always an issue and can never be regarded as over. In the course of therapy one learns to become less reactive and eventually to develop a solid self—that is, one is able to take "I" positions.

Structural Family Therapy

Salvador Minuchin (Minuchin et al., 1967; Minuchin, 1974) has taken the concepts of "alignments" and "splits" of Lyman Wynne (1961) and developed a theory of family process that sees pathology as being either "enmeshed" or "disengaged." The structural family therapist works on either loosening the boundaries or establishing them, depending on the amount of closeness or distance in the family structure. Here, as in Bowen's theory, triangles are important. Minuchin, however, focuses attention on the parent-child relationship rather than the three-generational analysis of Bowen (1976).

The most recent work by Minuchin and his associates has been in the area of psychosomatic medicine (1978, 1981). The relationship of the symptom to the family system is most clearly set forth in an interview with an anorexic girl (Aponte & Hoffman, 1973). In the article the process of realignment is made clear as the therapist restructures the family system without getting into family history. A detailed analysis of the structural approach can be found in Umbarger (1983). After outlining the theoretical base of this school, Umbarger presents a step-by-step procedure, from the initial contact through the final phases, showing how one does structural family therapy.

The main center for structural family therapy is the Philadelphia Child Guidance Clinic.

Strategic Intervention

This school grows out of the ideas generated by Don Jackson and Jay Haley, two of the pioneers in the family therapy field. It is perhaps the most exciting approach in family therapy currently in vogue and has established centers in Palo Alto, Milan, and New York City.

The term *strategic intervention* comes from Jay Haley (1973). Haley sees therapy as a power struggle between client and therapist. The critical issue is one of control. In a family system the identified patient is in control, making others feel helpless. It is the role of the therapist to reestablish family boundaries and to restructure the system (Haley, 1980). To do so the therapist must devise strategies or ways of changing the power balance (Haley, 1977), hence the term *strategic intervention*.

Strategic therapists at the Mental Research Institute in Palo Alto are almost exclusively concerned with the "symptom" as the problem and not the structure of the family. Briefly stated, the MRI approach involves the following beliefs: (a) the symptom *is* the problem; (b) these problems arise because the system cannot handle change, for example, birth, death, and adolescence; (c) attempted solutions fail because "they are more of the same"; (d) intensifying the problem (i.e., by prescribing the symptom) is often the solution (Weakland, Fisch, Watzlawick & Bodin, 1974).

A group of therapists based in Milan, Italy, has taken the basic thinking of Jackson and the MRI and developed it into a theoretical approach called the *systemic model* (Palazzoli, Boscolo, Cecchin & Prata, 1978). The theory states that the problem in families is *hubris,* the Greek word for "overweening pride." In their view, everyone wants to control the family without openly declaring this. In fact, however, all members are involved in the process because family causality is *circular* and not *linear.* The Milan group has added the need to devise strategies that involve all the family members and give each person's motivation a positive connotation. They emphasize the need to find tasks for the family that will force it into change. *Paradox and Counterparadox,* by Palazzoli, Boscolo, Cecchin, and Prata (1978), is a clear statement of both theory and practice.

Another center using this approach is the Nathan W. Ackerman Institute in New York. Their thinking has been greatly influenced by the Milan group (Hoffman, 1981).

It should be noted that the strategic approach, especially in the Milan model, is not just a technique of change but a method tied intimately to a theory of family process.

The issue in family therapy for the coming decade is the relationship of epistemology, or theory, to its art and practice. The interface between the two is the growing edge of family therapy (Keeney & Sprenkle, 1982).

Psychoanalysis   Systems

←————————————————————————————→

(1)	(2)	(3)	(4)
Object	Family		Strategic
Relations	Systems	Structural	Intervention

FIGURE 12.1
Four schools of family therapy schematized in
terms of continuum ranging from the ego psychology of psychoanalysis to the objective theory of
strategic intervention

Summary. The four schools mentioned share things in common, yet
each has different approaches to time,
level, and intensity of treatment. All
agree that troubling, symptomatic behavior is the result of dysfunctional interaction in the family system. Schools
1 and 2 believe that more time and energy have to be spent on clarifying relationships from the past, and schools
3 and 4 (see Figure 12.1) take more literally the concept of equifinality and
stress that if the present system can be
changed, the past need not be an issue.
The schools presented have the same
basic concept of the family—a commonality of thought and approach that
unites them—but at the same time,
each school differentiates itself from
the others in terms of its special viewpoints.

PERSONALITY

Family therapy implies a unique theory of personality. This is true of any
approach to therapy because underlying any treatment approach is a concept of what human nature is, what
health is, what sickness is, and what a
therapist can do to intervene.

THEORY OF PERSONALITY

Family personality theory states that
the psychological development of any

person results from the family system.
The family is the basic source of health
or sickness. Family theory focuses on
the family system more than other
psychotherapeutic systems because,
all things being equal, the major force
in the development of an individual is
the family. In terms of time and emotional force, the family is dominant.
Neither the school nor the church nor
any other group has as much effect on
a young person as the primary family.

Murray Bowen noted that an identified patient who functioned adequately in the hospital would often regress when sent back into the family.
Bowen discovered that family forces
often opposed the interventions of the
therapist. The emotional pull of forces
exerted by the family was extremely
powerful and potent.

There can be little argument that
the family is the most critical factor in
the determination of personality.
What we are genetically and how we
look, think, feel, and act are all influenced by the family into which we are
born.

Family therapy views people in a
holistic manner and in relation to their
environment. Although it affirms the
importance of heredity, it stresses
more the importance of environment.
A person is the net result of social interactions, and foremost among these

is *family of origin*. Therefore, the explanation of the development of an individual's personality will be found by examining the family. From this arises the notion that making interventions that restructure the system is the method of choice in the therapy of people in families.

In family therapy, when one talks about personality theory, one is talking about the family nexus. Three issues must be discussed: (a) What is a family? (b) What is a "dysfunctional" family? (c) Why must a family change?

What Is a Family?

Each individual has basic needs: some physical, some emotional. The physical ones are easily recognized; the emotional ones are less obvious. Emotional needs can be reduced to three dimensions: *intimacy, power,* and *meaning.* People need to be close to others, to belong. They also need to express themselves, to be unique. Finally, there must be meaning or purpose in their lives. For most people, the dimension of intimacy involves a heterosexual relationship, the dimension of power involves work, and the dimension of meaning involves having children.

Although it can be argued that the family unit is not necessary to fulfill these goals, nevertheless, it is rarely possible to achieve these three needs without a family. A family is the social unit in which people by mutual choice attempt to attain their needs for these three dimensions.

People usually marry because they find that marriage is the most satisfactory way of getting the things they need emotionally. The way in which they negotiate differences determines the success or failure of the marriage. *Can I be close to you and still remain*

myself? Can I avoid being swallowed up by you? Does our relationship make sense in my life? The process of marriage answers these questions.

What Is a "Dysfunctional Family"?

Family therapists prefer talking about *dysfunction* rather than sickness because this states more clearly what they see as the fundamental problem —the inability of family members to attain the desired goals of closeness, self-expression, and meaning. When these goals cannot be attained, symptomatic behavior takes place. For example, the husband gets involved in an affair, the wife becomes depressed, the child becomes a school phobic.

The difference between seeing symptoms as system-oriented or as the property of an individual is not merely semantic. The therapist believes the other members of the system are critically important if change is to be made in the identified patient. In the more traditional approach, family members are likely to be seen as obstacles to treatment who interfere with the transference process. In a family system concept, however, the other members are an essential part of the therapeutic process.

In *functional families* the needs of various family members are met. In a *dysfunctional family* such needs are not being met and therefore symptomatic behavior occurs. The important difference between a functional family system and a dysfunctional one is not the presence or absence of conflict, but rather the attainment of need satisfaction. In either case, there will be *conflict* in the family. Such conflict should be expected because the goals of various people or subsystems in the family rarely coincide.

For example, the father of a family

may want his children at home on Christmas Eve with his wife and himself, feeling this will foster his goal of closeness for the family. His son, however, wants to be with his friends at a basketball game. His daughters, who form a family subsystem based on a common interest in ice skating, want to practice. The mother sides with the girls, pointing out to the father that they have spent the day decorating the tree and deserve some time to themselves. Clearly the goals of the father, mother, son, and daughters are in conflict. Their ability to solve such differences will answer the question regarding the functioning of the family. A functioning family will make compromises; a dysfunctional one will not.

In this example, the issues that ultimately are critical are closeness, self-expression, and meaning—especially meaning.

Why Must a Family Change?

Just as an individual passes through a series of stages, so does the family. In the beginning of the family, the husband and wife need to unite into a functional system. They must form a functional "we" in addition to their own personalities.

The next step is opening the system, allowing others to enter: specifically, children (Entwistle & Doering, 1981). This critical step presents the couple with a crisis situation. The presence of a third party means the possibility of alignments and splits. Husband and wife must assume a new role, that of parents. This is a much different role from that of spouse. The anxiety level of many people is aroused by becoming a parent, but society tends to emphasize the positive aspect of parenthood, playing down the doubt and anxiety of the new parent.

System thinking explains the difference and the difficulty in parenthood by the concept of feedback. If a husband displeases his wife, feedback can be instant and immediate correction can be made. This is not true in the role of parent. The parent must wonder about what he or she is doing. *Am I too strict? Am I too easy?* The answer will not be known for many years. Feedback is not immediate.

The birth of subsequent children likewise creates a change in the family system. A second child is not simply an addition but rather a change in the family system. In a system concept, one plus one does not equal two. An additional family member means the system is restructured.

A new stage in family process is introduced when children go to school. The family system must again open, this time to outsiders. This may prove traumatic in many instances. The phenomenon of school phobia is seen as the inability of the system to make a proper adjustment, to widen its boundaries, and not just as the inability of a child to leave his mother. It can be seen that a new paradigm leads to a new way of conceptualizing a problem and a new way of approaching treatment. The family therapist asks, "What is going on in the *family* that produces school phobia in this child?"

Adolescence brings a need for further freedom for children. Overcloseness between a parent and a child may result in symptomatic behavior in one of the family members. A mother, for example, may not be able to allow a child freedom because it means a loss of meaning in her life.

The separation of children and parents through marriage creates a crisis situation for the parents. It means, frequently, a loss of meaning in life, the so-called empty-nest syndrome. The unresolved problems of the beginning of marriage may now surface as children move away, creating the possibility of marital difficulties.

The stages of the family and their relationship to therapy are described at length in Carter and McGoldrick (1980). The changes brought about by developmental issues are also central to Palazzoli (1978) and Haley (1977, 1980). See also Palazzoli, Boscolo, Cecchin, and Prata (1978).

VARIETY OF CONCEPTS

In family therapy, an individual personality—how one thinks, feels, and acts—is seen as the result of myriad, complex relationships that go on in the family. What has been traditionally called intrapsychic, the depth dimension of personality, is the result of the process of the family system. Harry Stack Sullivan recognized this by emphasizing the importance of others, especially the mother, in personality development. Alfred Adler, likewise, gave the family constellation an important place in his thinking. He thought one's personality is affected by one's ordinal position in the family. Thus, older children tend to be more responsible as adults, more traditionally minded, middle children are more likely to be difficult and moody, while younger children, who came into the family system late, tend to be spoiled and remain relatively incapable as adults (Adler, 1949). Family therapy has taken these insights and emphasized three dimensions: (1) the marital subsystem, (2) the sibling subsystem, and (3) homeostasis.

Marital Subsystem

Family therapists vary widely in their approach to both theory and practice, but all are agreed on the above three dimensions. The beginning of a family system starts with the couple. They form a oneness that places them squarely on one side of the fence, apart from others. The violation of generational boundaries in particular is the beginning of family dysfunction. The process of differentiation is one that must be made by both an individual and a couple. Fusion, or enmeshment, is the result of an inability to separate from a family of origin with a concomitant overcloseness to a parent, spouse, or child. The boundaries are violated to the detriment of all.

Symbolically, the ability to "close a door," to shut out others, is vital for a healthy marriage. Husband and wife ought to have secrets from their parents and children. There should be an intimacy between them that maintains their privacy. Early researchers in schizophrenia noted the obtrusiveness of parents into their children's lives and vice versa.

Another way of saying this is that in a good marriage the spouse is first and any others are second. Children-oriented marriages are always dysfunctional. Children ought to add meaning to a marriage and express the creativity and warmth of the parents, but they must always be subservient to the marital relationship. A man should always be a husband first and then a father, and a woman a wife first and then a mother.

Perhaps, paradoxically, the most successful parents are those in which each partner is spouse first and parent second. The reason seems to be that a normal married person does not need the child for fulfillment or to give life or the marriage meaning. Being satisfied in himself or herself and with the marriage, the spouse can give children freedom of choice. Children are not caught in the bind of conforming to the parent and being angry—or of "doing their own thing" and feeling guilty.

The triangle that exists among husband, wife, and child is kept less activated when the spouses are united. If they have a coalition, this prevents the child from forming a permanent alliance with one of the parents. It requires the child to seek a relationship with others of his or her own generation, especially with brothers and sisters.

Sibling Subsystem

A natural consequence of the parental coalition is the formation of a sibling subsystem that affords each child a chance to build a closeness with brothers and sisters. Family therapists insist that children should have secrets from parents: matters that pertain to their private lives. Each subsystem, like each person, should have appropriate boundaries. A rule for determining dysfunction in families is to look at the presence or absence of discernible boundaries. Are parents clearly separated from children? Are children differentiated among themselves? Older children should be treated differently from younger children. If given more responsibility, they should be given more privileges.

As children grow, individual differences should be respected. Privacy is important for the development of personality. Reading mail addressed to others and not knocking before entering another's room are not merely signs of discourtesy but represent essential issues in a family. How much freedom will be given to children in a family is determined by two factors: maturity and culture.

Children do not grow at the same speed physically or intellectually or emotionally. The pace will be unique in each case. Consequently, one cannot say that because A was given a privilege, B should get the same privilege at the same time. Obviously, this can become an area of difficulty. It certainly will be one of conflict. The willingness to discuss differences and to compromise is a sign of a functional family system. The issue is one of negotiation and the ability to bring harmony among conflicting goals in the family.

Perhaps the most neglected area in family therapy is the impact of culture. The concepts of the spouse subsystem and the sibling subsystem find general agreement among family therapists. How they will be worked out concretely, however, will differ from culture to culture. How affection is expressed, money used, time spent with others, and so on are issues that vary greatly (Papajohn & Spiegel, 1975).

The relationship of cultural norms to family therapy is found in *Ethnicity and Family Therapy* (McGoldrick, Pearce & Giordano, 1982), which examines major ethnic groups in the United States. Some family therapists have suggested that a particular approach to a family may be more effective by reason of the cultural dimension. For example, a Bowenian approach emphasizing the individual seems best suited to Irish families, whereas a paradoxical one might be more effective with an Italian one because of its attitude toward authority (McGoldrick & Pearce, 1981). The study of the relationship between cultural norms and family therapy is just in its beginning phase.

Culture determines the kind of relationship the nuclear family has with the extended family. In traditional rural settings, this has been very close;

in modern, urban ones, it is more diffuse. Which is more effective is open to dispute. How spouses should relate to each other is similarly a cultural issue. Until recently, the man has been considered to be the instrumental leader and the woman the affectional-expressive one. Social changes currently in progress seem to be destructive to this way of thinking. Although there may be a greater exchange of roles between husband and wife in the future, there will be no exchange of basic dependency between parent and child, and generational boundaries will probably remain intact.

Homeostasis

How the marital and the sibling subsystems interact results in what family therapists call the *homeostasis*, or balance, in a family. Any system operates within given limits, and when these are transgressed, the system experiences difficulty. If that difficulty cannot be corrected, the system will eventually disintegrate.

The family system operates within limits determined in part by its members and in part by its culture. Families coming to a new culture frequently encounter cultural shock, which destroys the family balance if the changes dictated by the new culture cannot be absorbed into the old system.

In family therapy, one looks at the behavior patterns in the family as balance mechanisms of the system more than as individual properties of family members. An alcoholic, for example, in a family concept is seen differently than in other approaches. Traditionally, therapists have regarded such behavior as bad or destructive and have attempted to deal with the alcoholic and his or her drinking in that light. In family therapy, however, the therapist regards alcoholism as a property of the system that performs a *positive* role in the family by maintaining its homeostasis. Rather than deal with the alcoholic as an individual, the family therapist prefers looking at the system to understand better its need for this behavior.

The goal of family therapy is change in the system: the creation of a new homeostasis, a new way of relating. If *therapy* is defined as the process of working through resistance, *family therapy* means working through the resistance to creating new ways of interacting. The key issue in the conflict is homeostasis, with the family fighting to hold on to its old way of relating and the therapist trying to produce a new one. Sometimes the battle is overt, but more often it will be covert. In either case, there will be a conflict if the therapy is to be effective. Conflict cannot be avoided because the family will define the issue as this or that member's bad behavior, and the therapist will see it as involving the entire family. The ability to move the family from its prior point of view to the new one—the view of the therapist—is the measure of the therapist's skill and the success of the therapeutic process.

Several family therapists believe that the concept of homeostasis fails to account adequately for all the data (Dell, 1982; Hoffman, 1981). Paul Dell states that the term *homeostasis* is superfluous because an interactional system is a result of the individuals who compose it and not because of any "homeostatic mechanism" or "family rules" (1982, p. 37). He suggests the term *coherence* as a more accurate one.

A family therapist is most concerned with the process by which the family system operates: How does a family maintain itself? Specifically, this is done by examining the marital subsystem and the sibling subsystem within the context of a given culture. How one will go about this, the process itself, will vary among therapists, depending on the weight given to issues of power, communication, and meaning.

PSYCHOTHERAPY

Family therapy is essentially a unique way of viewing pathology that sees problems within the context of the family system. Historically, it is a development of a process that began with concentration on an individual, emphasizing intrapsychic aspects, and then moved to individuals as family members, emphasizing interpersonal relationships and communication modalities. Family therapy focuses on the way a system is organized and structured. Pathology is viewed as the result of the incorrect way in which the system is organized. The system of relationships is to be changed to achieve desirable changes in individuals and not the intrapersonal aspects of the identified client. Or more exactly, it is the person who is to be changed—but indirectly through changing the structure and texture of family relationships.

THEORY OF PSYCHOTHERAPY

The heart of therapy is change in behavior. Philosophers have broken down human behavior into three areas: the emotional, the cognitive, and the volitional. Therapists, following this pattern, talk about feeling, thinking, and action. These divisions are arbitrary because a human being cannot be divided into sections but must be regarded as an indivisible entity. Nevertheless, in individuals or groups, one of these modes tends to dominate. Change in family therapy is ultimately change in behavior, change in interaction. What one feels and how one thinks are important, but unless these get put into action, nothing really changes. A primary goal in family therapy is producing overt behavior change, even if the family members are unaware of what is happening. Therapists who use paradox, in particular, are concerned mostly with altering the family behavioral system. If this can best be done apart from the family's awareness of the process, that goal takes precedence.

Insight is not important in family therapy. Getting the family to see what it is doing and why members are acting as they do is not a goal for most family therapists. Insight is considered an intellectual game that prevents real change from taking place. It is not important for the family to understand the way it is structured; this is only important for the therapist. Jay Haley (1963) represents a large number of family therapists in maintaining that getting the family aware of its interaction is actually antitherapeutic because real change occurs in behavior and not just in thinking.

Family therapists see different dimensions of therapy as having varying degrees of importance.

History

Object relations theory and family systems theory regard a knowledge of the family's history as important for understanding the present structure of the family. The present family system is seen as a reflection of past structures, and a transferencelike process operates in the here and now. For family systems therapists, the triangles that constitute the system extend over several generations and must be examined.

Structural family and strategic intervention therapists are less interested in family history because they believe the important dimension is the current structure, and this can be changed without an involved analysis of the family history. How things got the way they are is relatively unimportant. What to do about things the way they are now is what is important. The analogy is of a broken leg. Does it really matter to the doctor how it snapped? It is broken—and the issue is how to fix it. Setting the bone will be the same whether the bone was broken from a fall or a kick or a blow.

Diagnosis

Traditional therapy pays much attention to getting a correct diagnosis. It is considered important to know if a client is neurotic, has a character disorder, or is psychotic. In family therapy, there is less concern for diagnosis. In part, this is due to a paucity of ways of measuring family dysfunction as it pertains to a system. One can talk about the specific feelings of a family member or the role one member plays in the pathology of another, but an adequate nomenclature or classification system has not yet been developed. While some work has been done on how people solve problems in families or how they cooperate in performing a task, there has been a general resistance to diagnosis because many feel it better serves the needs of the therapist than the needs of the client or family.

Affect

Feelings are thought by family therapists to be the result of behavior and therefore are not considered to be of primary importance. Apart from Virginia Satir, and to a lesser degree Salvador Minuchin, most family therapists would not use family feelings to any great extent. This is one of the neglected aspects in family therapy due to an overwhelming emphasis on the concept of system, which tends to minimize the role and importance of emotion. This will probably change as more work is done with cultural dimensions.

Minuchin (Minuchin, 1974; Minuchin & Fishman, 1981) uses feelings, but more by employing them to change the family interaction than by addressing himself to the feelings themselves. For example, he will become angry with a father who allows his son to make fun of him to get the father to make some changes in his relationship to the son. He will not concentrate on the lack of feeling that the father is experiencing as such, but rather on the way in which that lack can be used to move the system in another direction.

The Role of Learning

To some extent, all therapies use learning. The issue usually is how to make the client or family aware of the learning process. Object relations therapists spend time analyzing past relationships and discussing how they influence the present. Teaching the family members new ways of relating will be a goal for object relations therapists. The learning process, furthermore, tends to be conscious and deliberate. Likewise, family systems therapists, who regard themselves as teachers of self-differentiation, underline the importance of learning new and effective ways of interacting. The other family therapists tend to play down the conscious aspect of learning, believing that an emphasis on this cognitive process slows the rate of change.

Transference and the Unconscious

In the psychodynamic model, the locus of pathology is thought to be deep in the client. The process of cure is said to depend on the development of a *transference* neurosis, which most analysts maintain is the critical step in therapy (Greenson, 1967). In family therapy, however, the locus of the pathology is the very structure itself and the critical step is restructuring the system. Transferencelike phenomena do occur between the therapist and the family, but no true transference is developed because the medium of therapy is not their relationship but the impact of the therapist's interventions, the force of the feedback into the system. Murray Bowen (1971) and Don Jackson and Jay Haley (1968) insisted that transference was not a necessary part of family therapy. This might be of some concern for those therapists in the object relations group because they are generally concerned with the role of the *unconscious* on family process. Transference and countertransference have a unique role in the thinking of Carl Whitaker (Whitaker & Keith, 1981). Whitaker uses his own feelings and reactions to help move the family system, seeing therapy as a growth process both for himself and the family. This is why he calls his approach an experiential one. This issue of transference is not of great importance for other family therapists.

Therapist as Teacher and Model

Family therapists generally agree that the medium of change is the therapist not as an object of transference but as a model or teacher. What is taught is communication or individuation. The family learns new ways of solving problems and of avoiding dead-end discussions. Behavior is analyzed and relabeled and seen in a new light. For example, a mother complains that her son is "impossible," by which she means that he has some problem inside of him that causes him to act in a certain manner. The therapist listens to her, patiently examines her interaction with the boy, and later is able to relabel the behavior from another point of view, such as the mother's inability to communicate with the child.

In the practice of family therapy, despite differences in approach, all therapists are active and not passive. They are not nondirective, reflecting feelings, but rather make interventions according to certain guidelines. In no way are they blank screens upon which projections are made. There is an attempt to be themselves and not to assume a role. This accounts for the wide divergence of therapeutic styles observed among family therapists. Beneath these differences, however, is the striving to teach or to model behavior for the family.

PROCESS OF PSYCHOTHERAPY

The course of family therapy varies widely with the goals of the therapist. It can range from several sessions to several years, depending on a number of interconnected issues.

Families being treated by object relations and family systems therapists will tend to be seen over a longer period than will families seen by structural or strategic intervention therapists. This is due to a difference in goals. In the first group, deep changes in interactional patterns will be the goals; in the latter, the problem is more symptom-oriented and treatment time will be shorter. This illustrates how the way a problem is posed influences the treatment process.

Initial Interview

This is a most important session because it sets the tone for the therapy. Specifically, it will determine who will control the process. There are two goals in this interview: first, to relabel the presenting problem, and second, to engage the family.

Phases

The therapist, let us presume, has gathered all the family members for the initial session. He or she proceeds in a series of phases or stages in the treatment process.

Warm-up. The therapist generally allows the family members who enter the room to sit where they choose. There should be more chairs present than people, giving family members a freedom of placement. This is the therapist's first live contact with the family, and how they arrange themselves tells much about how they relate to one another, how they feel about the therapist in relation to the family, and how successful therapy will be.

How does the family distribute itself? Do the parents sit next to each other? Does a child sit between them? Does a family member pull his or her chair back from the others? Do the girls sit close to each other? Do the boys sit far apart? Frequently, the way such sitting occurs gives the family therapist a clue to the underlying problems and to the alliances and splits in the family.

Typically, one of the children will be presented by a parent as the "problem." He or she is therefore the identified patient. It is best for the therapist to begin the session by saying something like, "Before we talk about some of the problems in the family, I'd like to say hello to each of you and to find out something about you." The therapist should then address the parent who made the initial contact, saying something like, "It's nice to meet you in person, Mrs. Jones," and then address the other parent. In this way one recognizes the existence and importance of the marital subsystem. The therapist can then turn to the other members of the family. It is helpful to follow some sequence based on age. In this way, the sibling subsystem is acknowledged, as is the fact that there are differences among the children. This first meeting is a *warm-up* phase. It is important for two reasons. First, it shows the family the therapist's personality, which is something each of them has only been able to fantasize, and diminishes the "therapeutic mystique" by mitigating the transference phenomenon. Second, it says indirectly that the "family problem" is not the only issue in the family.

This simple first phase is important because the therapist is an outsider whose worthiness to be allowed inside the family boundaries is being judged by the family. Accommodating oneself to the family enables one to join the system, and anything one can do to accomplish this is important. One shows oneself to the family before asking them to expose themselves.

Relabeling the "problem." Phase two begins after all the family members have been met. The therapist initiates it by saying to the parent who made the contact, "I'm wondering, Mrs. Jones, if you would tell me what brings you to see me," or "Could you tell me in what way you think I can help you?"

These simple questions communicate certain important attitudes to the family. Asking Mrs. Jones to state her reason for seeking help makes her put her request into the specific form of defining a person or a feeling or a behavior as the family problem. For example, it is certain that other family members will not agree with the mother's formulation of the problem. Instead of making this obvious comment, the therapist can conclude this phase of the process by noting, "It seems that some of you have different ideas about what the problem is in this family." This second phase relabels or redefines the problem. By proceeding in this way, the therapist avoids painful hassles with family members about the "real" problem.

Spreading the problem. Phase three heightens the conflict in the family by pointing out the different ways in which the problem may be defined. The therapist, having listened to the parents and their formulation of the problem, and perhaps having also listened to the children's comments or objections, may simply reformulate the problem quite differently as a kind of hypothesis, getting all to think differently about the "real" issues. This is also a way of pointing out the family's need for outside help. It tends to reduce guilt and enhance hope. Comments on the pain in the family, its frustration, unhappiness, and so on are useful in emphasizing the impotence of the family system to solve its own problems.

Need for change. Phase four begins when the therapist asks the family what solutions they have tried in the past for dealing with their pain. The issue is getting the family to focus on change. The therapist may ask, "What have you done about this

problem?" or "Have you done anything about this problem?" These statements are made (1) to reinforce awareness of the inability of the family to find successful techniques for dealing with the problem, or (2) to point out that nothing constructive has been done about the problem so far. It stresses the need for new attempts to solve the problem or for the development of new techniques. In either case, the emphasis is on *change* among all family members. The therapist focuses on behavioral change and the family's inability to make those changes up to this point. This narrows down the problem to behavior and keeps it within the boundaries of the family.

Changing pathways. Phase five begins when the therapist begins to make interventions into the family by means of suggestions. For example, the therapist may request that an uninvolved parent take charge of a child's behavior, thus building an alliance between that parent and the child while putting some distance between the child and the overinvolved parent. The therapist may ask the uninvolved parent to plan a day of fun with the child and not to tell the other parent about it. Or the therapist may ask a parent to teach the child how to light matches with the help of another child (Minuchin, 1974). The possibilities are endless.

These suggestions for the initial interview follow most closely the procedures of the structural school but are similar for the other family approaches as well. More family background information, or more concentration on family of origin, or more use of specific tactics such as paradoxical injunctions might be featured by other schools of family therapy. However, in all schools, the therapist informs the family that each member is part of the process, that no problem is ever to be seen as the personal property of one person but always involves two or more family members, and that the behavior of the family in the here and now is either creating or perpetuating the problem.

The first interview is important in family therapy as in other approaches because it concerns the issue of the therapeutic contract. It should state in a clear manner what family therapy is. In addition to these theoretical goals, it should begin the process, if possible, in the session itself by not only talking about the process but reenacting it.

Use of Techniques

Some techniques employed by family therapists include the following.

1. Reenactment. If a presenting problem is the inability of a father and son to talk to each other, instead of asking for an example, the therapist might request that the two talk to each other in the session. If the father complains that when he tries to talk to his son, his wife interferes, the therapist might ask them to begin talking and then have her intrude into their conversation. If a problem can be reenacted in the therapy session, this is frequently done. The obvious advantage of this approach is that the therapist can personally see what is happening in the family and does not have to rely on reports. This is an effective technique, what Moreno called "psychodrama in situ," because so many complaints relate to the inability of two people to talk with each other. Communication problems can become the major substance of the sessions.

2. Homework. As the name indicates, this refers to actions the therapist asks family members to perform between sessions. It has the value of making the therapy sessions places where solutions to problems are found and not just where talking takes place. In addition, it accustoms family members to understand that if they change their behavior, they can change how they feel and think as well. The homework assignments restructure family pathways by building coalitions and changing the intimacy-distance lines between members.

3. Family sculpting. This is the process by which the dimensions of closeness and power within the family are examined in a nonverbal manner. For example, a father is asked to describe his parents and his place in the family not by using words but by using space. Family sculpting has the advantage of making feelings about family structures visible. It also explains to current family members why the parents may act in a certain way, as one of the concepts underlying family sculpting is that people tend to repeat earlier patterns (Papp, Silverstein & Carter, 1973).

4. Genograms. Family system theorists, in particular, are interested in the emotional climate of a family and how this influences the relationships within the family system. Boundaries within the family, boundaries between the family and the outside world, and membership within the family are some of the more pertinent issues that some believe can best be handled by using this approach. A genogram is "a structural diagram of a family's three-generational relation-

Genogram

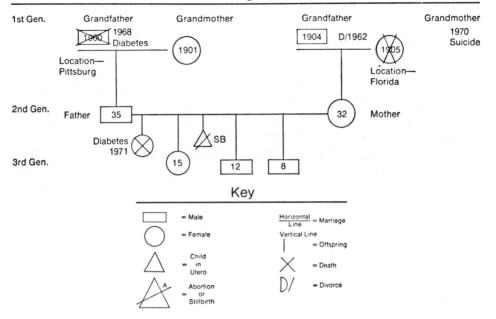

FIGURE 12.2

ship system. This diagram is a road map of the family relationship system" (Guerin & Pendagast, 1976, p. 452). It is a means of getting at significant issues in a more graphic manner than by simply talking about them. It is widely used by followers of Bowen's system although other schools of thought employ genograms also (see Figure 12.2).

5. Behavior modification techniques. This area of rapid growth in the field is closely tied to research. The underlying concepts are derived from social psychology (Thibaut & Kelly, 1959), in which reward is maximized and cost is minimized. Complete studies of this approach can be found in Liberman, Wheeler, De Visser, Kuehnel, and Kuehnel (1980) and Jacobson and Margolin (1979). Another brief but clear treatment of behavioral marital

therapy (BMT) is also presented by Jacobson (1981).

There are similarities between the techniques of BMT and the strategic approach, but the former derives its epistemology from behavior modification and the latter from Gregory Bateson. Although there is some question about the effectiveness of BMT with more serious problems (Gurman & Kniskern, 1981a), nevertheless, it is an approach that is of wide interest and whose results are well researched (Jacobson & Weiss, 1978).

6. Multiple family therapy. This technique, which involves seeing several families at the same time, has a long history in the field of family therapy (Laqueur, 1973). It has two advantages. First, it offers family members a glimpse of other families and allows them to see firsthand that there are similarities in problems, thus enabling family members to identify with others. Second, by permitting others to participate in a quasi-therapist role, it tends to lesson the authority of the therapist, which at times may be most advantageous. Foley (1975), for example, found that with black, disadvantaged families, multiple-family therapy helps hasten the therapeutic alliance by breaking down the family's hostile feelings for a white therapist.

The techniques mentioned above are only illustrative. Because family therapy is based on a model that sees pathology as the result of dysfunctional relationships, it is freer than other approaches in adopting techniques to help change the interactional system. Family therapy is open to any number of techniques as long as they serve to change family process.

Length of Treatment

Family therapy treatment can last from a few sessions to a period of years. Structural and strategic interventions tend to be briefer than those of object relationists and family system therapists. Gerald Zuk (1975) sees the length of treatment as dependent on the goals presented by the family. If its main goal is to reduce tension, there will tend to be 1 to 6 interviews. If symptom reduction is the aim, it more likely will take 10 to 15 sessions. If better communication is sought, 25 to 30 sessions over a 6- to 8-month period are necessary. If a restructuring of the family with better differentiation of family members is considered, the length will tend to be 40 or more sessions over an extended period. James Trotzer (1982) has elaborated on Zuk's categories as an indication of the outcome of therapy and suggests the longer the better.

Indications and Contraindications

Lyman Wynne (1965) suggested that interlocking problems, those one family member believes cannot be solved without the cooperation of another, were good indicators of the need for family therapy. In general, problems of paranoia and sexual acting out in the family are considered poor indicators for this kind of treatment.

It is difficult to make absolute statements about what problems are suitable for family therapy other than to say that therapists who incline more toward a system concept would tend to see most psychological adjustment problems as amenable to family therapy while those coming from a more traditional psychoanalytic background are inclined to be less certain.

MECHANISMS OF PSYCHOTHERAPY

Despite all the theoretical concepts any system uses to justify its existence, ultimately one question matters: How does change take place? Within that question, one finds related ones, such as: Can the process that one describes be analyzed into its component parts? Is it measurable? Is it teachable? In the final analysis, is it beyond articulation? Is it an art or a science?

At this point in family therapy, there is more speculation than hard data. Most therapists do not take pretests and posttests either in individual or in family therapy. Most of the data gathered are self-reports of the families. Unfortunately, self-reports can be unreliable. With these observations in mind, let us now proceed with some tentative answers.

Family therapists concentrate on changes in behavior as evidence of progress. Changes in feelings and thinking are considered less important. How is behavior change accomplished? There is a growing belief among family therapists that therapy is a power struggle between the therapist and the client. It is a battle of wills in which the stronger one prevails.

Jay Haley (1963) drew an analogy between the therapist and the hypnotist in that both seem to ask for change while at the same time denying it. Haley took the position that the therapist has the responsibility for change and that failure in therapy can always be attributed to the therapist who has the responsibility to analyze problems correctly and to devise tactics that lead people into change. Feelings do not produce change, nor does thinking. Empathy, although important for engaging the family, is not corrective. Insight is even less helpful because it can provide a convenient way of avoiding change, giving the family intellectual games to play. The name of the game is power. The therapist must create situations that force the family into a bind. Either it continues its behavior, but does so under the command of the therapist, or it rebels, thus producing the desired change. In either case, the family system is under assault.

Most family therapists, although perhaps not taking as extreme a position as Haley, would tend to accept his thinking, seeing all family therapy as a power struggle. Family therapists tend to be more open about the power element in therapy. Giving directives or telling people what to do can be either overt or covert. In either case, it is at the heart of therapy. The nondirective therapist, for example, is covertly giving directives by picking up on the client's comments about feelings. He is teaching that a response is given when the client approaches things in that manner. The cues are reinforced by other nonverbal comments, such as nods of the head and smiles.

Some family therapists might object to the emphasis Haley gives to the power struggle, but at some level, all will likely agree with the notion of relabeling as a critical step in the change process. To accept this concept is to agree with the idea of power as the main ingredient in change. To illustrate, suppose that a family comes for help with a child who will not go to school. A long story of the family's failure to be effective in dealing with this problem is recounted. Kindness has been tried and found wanting, punishment has followed and has not worked, and now the child is labeled as "sick." He is labeled a problem to the family and has become an outcast. The therapist, however, may see the school phobia as the child's response to difficulties between husband and wife. This becomes clearer as the parents talk about the problem, illustrating that the mother is overinvolved with the child and the father underinvolved. The therapist may suggest that the father spend more time with the child and that he should take command of the problem.

The therapist may have relabeled the problem as a conflict between husband and wife that they are not dealing with overtly in their roles as father and mother. Instead of bringing this redefinition or relabeling into the open, where it can be denied, the therapist may shift the family balance, in effect neutralizing the mother's power. This shift can be made even more effective if he then instructs the wife that she is to keep after the husband to make sure he carries out his job of being a good father.

Once the child's behavior has

changed as a result of this power change, the covert conflict of husband and wife will surface as that of husband-and-wife rather than father-and-mother. At this point, the child might be dismissed from the sessions and work might be done with just the couple. Changes have been accomplished not by interpretation or by insight or by improving communication but by making structural variations in the way in which the family operates. Thus, the therapist who covertly reinterprets the family's problem relabels the pathology and suggests changes without giving explanations, leading to new behaviors and affecting family relationships.

At this point, a therapist might want to work with issues of closeness or meaning with the couple or investigate areas of differentiation of self.

This example of a school phobia taken from a structural family model illustrates the process of relabeling, but similar examples could be given from any of the other schools as well. Change in family therapy begins with a shift from the way the family sees the problem to the way the therapist sees it. This is best done by maneuvers that realign the family rather than by cognitive measures—by action, not by talk.

Change in family therapy is accomplished by modifying the structures of the system. This means working on the triangles that compose it and producing new alignments. This in turn produces changes in behavior that influence feelings. Devising techniques that change existing structure is the major goal of psychotherapy for family therapy. Change in how the system operates produces change in individual members of the system.

APPLICATIONS

PROBLEMS

Family Problems

Problems labeled "family ones" by the family itself are most amenable to treatment. However, such presenting problems are rarely encountered. People with a disturbed member in their family rarely think the essential cause is that the family itself is in need of treatment. This should not be surprising given that the idea of thinking in terms of systems—field psychology— has not filtered down to the public, and indeed the concept of restructuring the field is still a minority concept with psychotherapists. The general tendency in families and also among therapists is to locate and deal with the so-called identified patient, who from the point of view of a family therapist is in reality the scapegoat for the family.

Marital Problems—Both Partners

Frequently family problems are labeled "marital problems" rather than "family problems." Marriage counseling is well known to most people, and columns on such problems are a staple in most magazines. Newspapers, too, carry columns such as "Ann Landers" and "Dear Abby," and a large percent of their questions concern marriage. However, even though a client may call and state, "We are having some problems with our marriage," it is soon evident that one of the partners to the marriage believes the problem is the exclusive domain of the other. In an initial interview of a couple, the caller will often begin with, "My husband drinks too much," or "My wife is depressed," or "I know I'm not perfect, but my wife/husband *really* has problems." The clear implication is that the other one is the so-called identified patient.

Individual Problems

One rarely encounters the isolated individual who is truly alone, not part of any family system. Most people in our society are married and have families. A spouse, children, parents, and siblings are relationships that are deepest and most lasting. Literally, we never get over them. They should be the context within which therapy takes place. Individual problems may be seen either as the exclusive property of one person or as a response to the context of a family. Family therapy clearly opts for the latter.

Other Relationships

It should be clear that system thinking applies to any system, not just the family. This means that difficulties in meetings, PTA groups, and other social systems may be analyzed as individual problems or as system difficulties. When seen in the former way, one concludes that some people are "difficult" or "destructive." If seen in the latter way, one looks at the process of the system as the cause of the behavior. The staff member who "messes up" and forgets can be considered as "dumb" or as responding to the system in a hostile, nonverbal manner.

Family therapists state that all systems are built from interlocking triangles, not just family systems. Analyzing the structure of such triangles and learning how to deal with them by responding instead of reacting is a possibility open to all. Family therapy is system thinking that involves a search to find ways to change the system. The first step is to analyze the structure of the system; the second, to see one's role in it; and the third, to change one's behavior in that system. These con-

cepts can be applied to any human relations system, whether it be a club, a factory, a team, a military unit, a congregation, a union, or a partnership.

EVALUATION

Evaluation can be divided into two sections: (a) *process research* and (b) *outcome research.* The former refers to the interaction between the family and the therapist, and the latter refers to the results obtained after treatment. An excellent summary of process research is given by Pinsof (1981), and a definitive chapter by Gurman and Kniskern (1981a) summarizes outcome research.

1. Process Research

Self-report and direct observation have been the usual means of doing process research. Under the heading of self-report, the studies of Hollis (1967a, 1967b, 1968a, 1968b), Shapiro and Budman (1973), and Rice (Rice, Fey & Kepecs, 1972; Rice, Gurman & Razin, 1974; Rice, Razin & Gurman, 1976) are noteworthy.

Hollis developed her research originally in individual casework but later (1968b) applied it to marital counseling, comparing individual sessions with conjoint ones, using the process notes of the therapist. The weakness in her study is the fact that process notes do not necessarily reflect what occurs in the sessions.

The Shapiro and Budman study (1973) shifts the emphasis from the therapist to the family and indicates that the activity of the therapist is critical in determining the continuation or termination of the family's treatment. The research finding matches the theoretical constructs of many theorists in the field (Haley, 1980; Minuchin, 1974).

The Rice et al. studies (1972, 1974, 1976) have produced a valuable questionnaire on the behavior of the therapist. Despite overlapping samples and some lack of specificity (i.e., it is not aimed exclusively at family therapists), it is labeled by Pinsof as research that "generates reliable, accurate and valid data" (1981, p. 705).

Direct observation has been more widely used in process research. Direct observation of the therapist was used twice by Sigal et al. (Sigal, Lasry, Guttman, Chagoya & Pilon, 1977; Sigal, Presser, Woodward, Santa-Barbara, Epstein & Levin, 1979). In the 1977 study Sigal et al. compared simulated and real responses in therapy, and in 1979 they examined the relationship between the responses of family therapy trainees and the outcome of therapy for families they had treated. The results were mixed. However, out of these studies done at the Jewish General Hospital in Montreal has come a research tool called the Family Therapy Intervention Scale (FTIS-1) that has been used in several other studies (Sigal et al., 1979). Its weakness is its reliance on the response of the therapist.

Pinsof (1979a) at Northwestern University developed the Family Therapist Behavior Scale (FTBS) that differentiates 19 specific kinds of verbal intervention. Pinsof (1979b) also developed another coding system known as the family therapist coding system (FTCS), a more sophisticated tool aimed at identifying and differentiating the verbal behaviors of therapists with different orientations. This instrument is currently being tested for reliability and validity (Pinsof, 1981) and is clearly the most developed research instrument in this area.

Coming from an Adlerian frame-work, Allred and Kersey (1977) have developed a system for analyzing the verbal behavior of counselors and clients in marriage and family sessions called the Allred Interaction Analysis for Counselors (AIAC). This system shows considerable promise. Emilia Dowling (1979) in Wales has also developed a family therapist coding device of interest because of its cross-cultural dimension. In particular, she notes that self-report measures are of doubtful use because in her findings even experienced therapists are poor evaluators of their own behavior.

Direct observation of the family has a long and significant history in family therapy. In an early study Zuk et al. (Zuk, Boszormenyi-Nagy & Heiman, 1963) postulated that laughter during sessions disguised anxiety. Although there are flaws in the study, it indicated the potential for direct observation.

Lyman Wynne and Margaret Singer (1963) did research on the role of the identified patient in a schizophrenic family demonstrating that the patient's behavior was merely a reflection of a larger disturbance in the family unit.

Another study was done in Montreal as a complement to the therapist coding system in which Guttman et al. (Guttman, Spector, Sigal, Epstein & Rakoff, 1972) measured the underlying affective content of the family as expressed verbally. Allred and Kersey (1977) also devised two categories in their instrument (AIAC) assessing the verbal behavior of clients, but further testing is needed to establish its usefulness.

De Chenne (1973) used the widely recognized Experiencing Scale (EXP) in conjoint marital therapy. The instrument has been shown to have predictive and discriminant validity (Kiesler, 1973), and De Chenne demonstrated that the EXP scale was valid for measuring client progress in therapy.

Winer (1971) attempted to measure Murray Bowen's basic concept "differentiation of self," by developing the Change (c) Ratio, which purported to measure the number of "I" statements made during therapy. Her study is indicative of the attempt in the field to operationalize basic concepts as a way of giving some support to theoretical concepts.

Summary. The area of process research is just beginning. Pinsof says it exactly: "The field of family process research has just been born" (1981, p. 700). There are numerous reasons for this. Foremost among them is the inherent difficulty in developing an instrument. Family therapy involves a number of people and thereby increases the variables to be controlled. A second factor is the lack of replication. At this point there is more need for work on the various instruments that have been used. Finally, there is a great need to make constructs more precise and distinctive so that categories do not overlap.

2. Outcome Research

This area is more developed than that of process research due largely to the work of Alan Gurman (1973, 1975, 1978) in collaboration with David Kniskern (Gurman & Kniskern, 1978, 1981a, 1981b).

Wells et al. (Wells, Dilkes & Trivelli, 1972) identified only 13 studies they thought were relevant to outcome in family therapy. Six years later Gurman and Kniskern (1978) found a total of 200 relevant outcome studies. An extensive review of the field can be found in Gurman (1978) and Gurman and Kniskern (1981a). A brief summary of their findings is available (1981b).

The value in the work of Gurman and Kniskern is that outcomes from all perspectives have been studied and evaluated with reasonable objectivity but with some disagreement (Jacobson & Weiss, 1978). This lends added importance to their conclusions. Gurman and Kniskern (1981b) reach 19 conclusions vis-à-vis family therapy. Among the more significant ones are: (a) nonbehavioral marital therapies are of benefit in about two-thirds of the cases; (b) therapy with both spouses is more effective than therapy with only one; (c) length of treatment does not correlate with effectiveness; (d) at times family therapy makes relationships worse; (e) this seems related to the inactivity of the therapist; (f) individual therapy is ineffective with marital problems; (g) conjoint therapy is most effective; (h) behavioral family therapy seems more effective with less distressed families; (i) co-therapy does not enhance effectiveness; and (j) the severity of a problem is not a determining factor in outcome.

Gurman and Kniskern (1981a) elaborate on those family therapies that are most effective. They cite Minuchin's work with psychosomatic families (structural family therapy), Stanton and Todd's (1979) work with drug-addicted families (structural family therapy), operantly oriented behavioral family therapy in changing intrafamilial childhood behaviors (Patterson, 1971), and the functional family therapy of Alexander (Barton & Alexander, 1981) combining social learning and family systems with adolescents. These systems have received the most support in outcome research.

This is not to say that other approaches are not effective but only that they have not been as well researched. It should be clear that this is a sensitive area in which the adherents of one school sometimes suggest their approach is more effective than another. In the absence of comparative research, such claims are invalid.

Summary. The infancy stage of outcome research is over. If the field is to continue to be fruitful and grow, it needs to attend to several issues regarding the family and the therapist. In regard to the family, focus must be given to such factors as what constitutes change, duration of "cure," number of family members present, and the effectiveness of various methods with specific disorders.

In regard to the therapist, focus must be given to such factors as the need to know (or not to know) individual dynamics, the need for the therapist to have undergone personal therapy, and the relevance of a co-therapist or co-therapists.

In brief, it is clear that family therapy has demonstrated its power to produce change, but it is not clear *how* that is accomplished or *why* one approach seems more effective with a given population. It is the task of researchers to devise studies making both the process and the outcome of family therapy more specific.

TREATMENT

In family therapy, methods of treatment will vary among therapists according to their theoretical orientations and/or differences in personality. Therapy is always a blend of three factors that interact: (a) the theoretical stance of the therapist, (b) the personal style of the therapist, and (c) the type

of family, its current state of functioning, and where it is developmentally.

Theoretical Stance

Therapists of the object relations and family system schools are concerned with issues that deal with generational conflict, intimacy or distance, and unresolved problems of the past—in particular, grief. Therapists who are more system-oriented, those of the structural and the strategic intervention schools, will be more symptom-oriented and concerned with how the system boundaries are structured and what techniques may prove helpful in getting change to occur. If a therapist believes issues of the past are important, the therapy will tend to resemble a more traditional approach and be of a longer duration. If the therapist is governed more by the notion of equifinality, therapy will tend to be more situational and of shorter duration.

Personal Style

Personal style varies widely among family therapists. There are some basic concepts that one must accept to be classified as a family therapist, but the manner in which one works will be highly individualized. Unlike some other training approaches, family therapy is not rigidly structured. Some therapists are warm and empathetic, while others tend to be more distant and cognitive. Some follow a particular system closely, while others use an idiosyncratic approach. What binds them together as family therapists is the way in which they conceptualize family interaction, not the way in which they operationalize it. Family therapy has long regarded this as its strength. Because it allows the therapist's personality to shine through, the individual can be authentic and not play a role called "therapist." This is also why family therapy has not been controlled by the single group in the field of mental health but has been open to people from varied backgrounds.

Type of Family

The family the therapist meets also can be classified according to (a) the relationship's closeness or distance, (b) its current state of functioning, and (c) where it is developmentally.

Whether a family can be classified as enmeshed-disengaged or open-closed will be important to the therapist's evaluation. These classifications enable the family therapist to know how much the family will open to admit an outsider or close to keep others out. More importantly, it will indicate the flexibility of the system and how much stress it can handle. This in turn will govern the tactics used to change the structure.

Current state of functioning refers to the amount of stress that presently exists. Is this a family under unusual pressure and about to fall apart, or is it reporting minor chronic problems? The therapist is interested in finding out what therapeutic leverage is possible. Families in crisis are generally more open to outside intervention than those that are not in crisis. There is less resistance to the therapist. Some family therapists, such as Minuchin and Barcai (1969), argue for the occasional need to create a disturbance in the system if one is not present. The issue is one of homeostasis. The family frequently wants to maintain or reestablish the old balance and cannot accomplish this. They then call in a professional, one with expertise, to produce calm again. This situation often occurs in rigid families facing the problem of adolescence.

Developmental issues, too, cause constant family tensions (Carter & McGoldrick, 1980). People are always undergoing change because of the need to adapt to ever-changing circumstances. Intimacy wanes between a husband and wife, economic changes affect the marriage, and, above all, children grow into adolescents. Parents who tend to be overprotective and all-knowing often have problems with their growing children. The need of the family to open and allow the children to move out is absent and conflict develops between the generations. The behavior of such children is labeled as "bad" or "sick," and finally a therapist is summoned. The therapist must identify the developmental issues in the family. Some recent research indicates that such families are intrusive, overresponsive to each other, intolerant of change, and tend to produce family members who suffer psychosomatic symptoms, especially abdominal pain (Liebman et al., 1976). The therapist will seek to alleviate the presenting problems, but, more importantly, will strive to restructure the system to eliminate the need for such behavior.

Family therapy is a blend of theory, style, and family structure. It will be approached in line with the style of the therapist. The depth of the problems will be determined in part by closeness or distance, acuteness of the problem, and stage of family development.

Taking into account the three factors of therapy, the therapist then decides how to proceed, acting like the director of a drama. One might well liken family therapy to the theater, in particular Brechtian theater, with its use of paradox as a means of dramatizing family issues. The comparison is in line with what family therapists would consider the proper relationship of the therapist to the client family.

Therapy is a drama—a tension-filled process that takes place between a therapist and traditionally one person or, more recently, a couple or a family. The focus may be on the past, present, or future, but in any event, the process of change, whether of feeling, thinking, or doing, is always in the present. Therapy means a change of one or all of these ways of speaking about human beings. How is it accomplished?

It is evident that therapy is a power struggle. Family therapists explain the struggle in terms of communication theory, which says that every communication is both a report and a command that attempts to define the relationship. For example, if I talk about trivia, I am telling the other person I am not interested in getting serious about our relationship. If, however, he asks, "Why don't you ever say anything about how you feel?" he is attempting to change the relationship and move it to a more intense level.

This shift can be overt or covert. It is overt when the other says so in words; it is covert when it is more subtle, when done behaviorally. This method, in fact, is a very powerful one because it is usually followed by the comment, "I can't help it." The person is saying that such behavior is involuntary. The child who "throws up," the wife who has "blinding headaches," and the husband who "forgets" can be viewed as having problems in themselves but also as covertly commenting on the relationships within their family system. These behaviors or symptoms can be considered as tactics in the struggle to deal with the relationship.

In family therapy, the therapist sees symptoms as control tactics, but instead of pointing to them and analyzing their purpose, will often say, "Of course you can't help it," and then tell the person to continue doing voluntarily what he or she claims is involuntary. The therapist thereby creates a benign "double bind," in which the person is faced with either (a) stopping the behavior or (b) continuing the behavior but now doing it under control of the therapist. In either case, it is voluntary. Frankl (1960) calls this process paradoxical intention.

The family therapist may attempt to change the context of the system so the previous undesired behavior is no longer possible. The literature abounds with examples of how this can be done (Bowen, 1971; Haley, 1963; Minuchin, 1974; Watzlawick, Weakland & Fisch, 1974). In more technical terms, changing the context means producing not just a substitution of one thing for another (first-order change) but a change of the structure (second-order change) (Watzlawick, Weakland & Fisch, 1974). One effective way of doing this is the aforementioned "prescribing the symptom," telling people to continue doing what they have been doing. For example, a therapist may demand that an overinvolved woman become even more concerned about her children and even set aside a special hour each day for "worrying." This use of paradox is an example of how one might prescribe a symptom to produce a second-order change (Palazzoli, 1978).

MANAGEMENT

The Setting

Family therapists function in all traditional settings and add the possibility of working in the home and the probability of making at least one home visit during treatment. This, of course, is understandable in light of the emphasis given to the context in which treatment takes place. Some would go so far as to say, "The beginning family therapist should require [home visits] of himself routinely, and *without exception*" (Bloch, 1973, p. 44).

Seeing people in their ordinary home conditions has two distinct advantages: (a) people tend to be more relaxed and open, in their homes and (b) the important issue of nurturance is more easily observed in the home. *To whom does a child go for attention? How is the request handled? What kinds of interaction go on between the parents in relation to the children's immediate needs? With what warmth or lack of it are they nurtured?* Observing these things in an office or clinic setting is sometimes impossible and usually unsatisfactory.

How Patients Come

Most referrals for family therapy come from mothers looking for help in dealing with either (a) adjustment problems in school for children making the transition from home to school, or (b) adolescent conflicts centering about how much freedom to give the growing child. Experience has shown that the most effective way of dealing with such referrals is to ask the whole family to come in initially for three sessions as a way of getting to know each other. This is normally sufficient time to redefine the problem in terms of other family members. Objections to bringing in other family members can be handled by saying, "Of course he's got a problem, but I can't do much about it without your help." Because most people like to think of themselves as being helpful, this usually will bring them into a session. The therapist who

can get other family members physically present can involve them in treatment.

Confidentiality

Murray Bowen (1975) believes the issue of confidentiality must be reevaluated in the light of family therapy. This does not mean that family therapists become indiscriminate gossips, but that they use their knowledge for the good of the system. The shift in perspective from seeing the individual as the client to seeing the family as the client necessitates a shift from viewing the relationship of an individual to a therapist to one in which the family is the center. How therapists accomplish their role in regard to confidentiality takes much sophistication and clinical skill. The family members are trying to set up an alliance between themselves and the therapist by including him or her in a relationship. This must be avoided. The therapist must create a new context in which behavior will change, and this cannot be done by a therapist who gets pulled into the ways in which the family normally interacts.

There are several ways of handling confidentiality. One is to announce at the first session that the therapist is relating to the family as a whole and therefore will not see individuals alone, and that any attempts at violating this rule, such as telephone calls, will be reported to the rest of the family. If it becomes necessary to see parts of the family alone, say, only the parents or only the children, the therapist should inform all concerned that he or she will make the choice of sharing or not sharing what is found.

A second way of handling requests for secrets is to ask how others feel about the alliance between the therapist and a family member who asks for a private interview. For example, a husband asks to see the therapist alone. Before granting the request, the therapist inquires about how other family members feel. "Mrs. Jones, your husband wants to tell me something that he doesn't want you to know. Do you think that's helpful to you or to the family?" Such a question focuses on the value of secrets to the family process.

In family therapy, raising the question of confidentiality is a ploy to control the system. It is a way of tying the hands of the therapist and setting up an alliance between the therapist and another family member. These "secret" sessions are to be discouraged. This does not mean that each and every issue in a family should be talked about in front of all other members. Family therapy is particularly concerned about boundaries between the generations. The sexual life of the husband and wife is a private matter and need not be discussed in the presence of the children. Similarly, the privacy of a child must be preserved in enmeshed and intrusive families.

Family structure can be destroyed by collusion between a member of one generation and a member of another. The family therapist must not become part of this destructive process by entering into separate secret pacts with some family members in the name of confidentiality. The most effective way for a therapist to avoid the problem is to make clear from the beginning that such alliances will not be tolerated. If that is clear, the problem will rarely arise.

Recordings

Most therapies are arcane; the outsider has little knowledge of how sessions are conducted. This is not true in family therapy. Recordings, both video and audio, are common. The use of one-way mirrors is increasing. Live supervision, where the supervisor watches the session in progress and calls in observations on a phone, or even enters the therapy session, is also used. Of course, for all of these observations, permission must be given by the family.

Recordings are invaluable for family therapy. They serve a double purpose. First, they preserve the process of the family therapy sessions and can be used for teaching purposes, and second, the material used with one family can be shared with another. For example, the Browns may have a problem similar to that of the Smiths. Showing them a videotape of the Smiths may provide the kind of feedback necessary for them to change. Showing the family themselves at earlier points can also be an enlightening experience. In particular, videotape is invaluable for getting at nonverbal communications that take place among the family members (Alger, 1973).

Family therapy has the most complete collection of films and videotapes of any therapeutic approach. Those offering material include the Eastern Pennsylvania Psychiatric Institute and the Family Psychiatry Department, Philadelphia, Pennsylvania; the Mental Research Institute, Palo Alto, California; the Nathan W. Ackerman Family Institute, New York, New York; and the Philadelphia Child Guidance Clinic, Philadelphia, Pennsylvania.

CASE EXAMPLE

BACKGROUND

Mr. Jones had been referred by a local minister who had seen him previously for a problem with drinking. The man subsequently quit drinking and joined AA. Shortly thereafter his wife became depressed, and following that his son was arrested for stealing. The man called the minister, saying, "My son is in trouble." Sensing that the issue involved all the family members, the minister referred the man to a therapist who dealt with "family problems."

The family therapist on the telephone asked Mr. Jones to bring his wife and son to the initial session. After a brief introduction, Mr. Jones began by saying that about a year ago he decided, at the urging of his boss, to give up drinking, and he also stated that he began drinking 19 years previously, shortly after the birth of his son. As a first corrective step, he had gone to his minister, who had urged him to join AA and become active in the church. He continued seeing the minister for about three months. About that time, his wife complained of feeling "down." She went to a family doctor and was given medication. She became worse and was sent to a psychiatrist, who suggested that at age 45 she was beginning to experience a change of life and a loss of feeling sexually attractive to her husband. She began seeing the psychiatrist weekly for private sessions. During this period, their son, who had been considered by all as a "model child," became more overtly hostile in his comments, careless about his appearance, and indifferent in his schoolwork. Finally, he was arrested for stealing an automobile but was told he would not be charged with the crime if he got "help." The father sent him to the psychiatrist, who referred him to a psychologist whose field of expertise was adolescent problems. The psychologist agreed to see the boy privately on a weekly basis.

The father stated in family therapy that he did not see any change in either his wife or his son and was becoming more upset himself. The wife said she was not being helped but would continue in treatment; the son said his sessions were a waste of time and he wanted to quit. The father said he was tempted to return to drinking, and this fear finally drove him again to call his minister.

In retelling the story, the father mentioned his fear of "falling off the wagon," and the son, quiet until then, commented, "At least then we'd know what to do with you." When the therapist asked the son to elaborate on the comment, he said that since sobriety his father had become a "pompous ass." The mother smiled at this comment as she looked at the son approvingly.

The therapist then asked the wife to "tell me something about yourself." She began by mentioning the difference between life before and life after her husband stopped drinking. It was clear that she had more roles while her husband was drinking and also more gratification. When the father was drinking, the son acted in the role of surrogate husband and had a closeness with the mother, which was inappropriate—a violation of the generational boundary.

The therapist began his first intervention by asking the son, John, to change places with him so the son could sit next to his father. The therapist then sat between the father and mother so the boundary between them might be visibly established. In moving his position, he commented to the mother, "As a good mother, Mrs. Jones, I'm sure you'd like to see your husband and son get along better." "Of course," she responded, although her face indicated otherwise. The therapist then asked the father and son to talk about interests they had in common.

PROBLEM

The case is typical of many in that a number of different analyses can be given. For example, the father can be considered an orally dependent man, as evidenced by his drinking. He could be seen alone in treatment. The drinking of the father and the depression of the mother can be viewed from a communication point of view as signs of their inability to express themselves in words. If this is the formulation of the problem, the therapist can work on their communication. Or the therapist can see the behavior of all three as related to each other and, more importantly, as contributing to the dysfunction in the here and now. From this viewpoint, one would want to work with all three members of the system. This last viewpoint is known as *field thinking* and represents family therapy concepts in that each person is viewed in the context of the system.

Two observations may be made about the minister's role in Mr. Jones' sobriety. First, he failed to take into account the *positive* role of alcohol in the family system. Simply put, the drinking served a homeostatic function in the family. Mr. Jones was taken care of, Mrs. Jones had a meaning and purpose, and John received special attention from his mother. When Mr. Jones stopped drinking, the position of everyone changed. Second, the initiative for change came less from Mr. Jones than from his boss, who had promised him a substantial raise. The minister reinforced the passivity by being so active in moving Mr. Jones toward involvement in AA and the church. Mr. Jones went from a dependency on his wife to a dependency on the minister and then on AA.

The problem in this case is to understand how each of the family members is entangled in the system and to observe the ongoing patterns of interaction that keep the system dysfunctional. It is the role of the family therapist to see this interaction and to make interventions that will restructure the system.

One could analyze the family in terms of dysfunctional triangles. By her overcloseness to the son, the wife prevented her husband from getting close. The husband in turn triangled in a "bottle." Having gotten rid of the bottle, he then triangled in work and the church. The son's growing up and wanting more distance from the mother, combined with the husband's distancing, produced depression in the wife because she was still isolated from her husband even when he was sober. She got depressed as a way of gaining recognition. This produced some sign of caring by the husband and guilt-induced caring by the son. However, the constant demands of his mother made the son angry, and he expressed this in his sullenness and eventually by stealing. The symptomatic response of all the family members can be regarded as tactics for survival and control of the system as well as properties of each person within it.

The therapist made the choice of intervening between father and son because he thought the best way of changing the system would be to get an alliance between them. At the same time, he put the mother in a bind by saying she should support such an alliance. Had he attacked the overcloseness by suggesting that the mother-son coalition was unhealthy, he probably would have met massive resistance. Rather than attacking, he felt a more effective strategy would be to create more closeness between father and son. This alliance, it is true, would produce more isolation for the mother, but instead of falling into a further depression, she could now bring this to the therapist, who in turn could reintroduce it into the system.

At the initial session, father and son had agreed to go fishing, an activity they both enjoyed. It also gave them a time and place for talking. Predictably, such activity caused the wife to become upset. After several fishing weekends, the wife called the therapist to say that she was very happy about how things were going between her husband and son, but that she now felt isolated. The therapist commented that he chose this alliance knowing it might cause her problems but did so because he knew she had great strength. He agreed, however, that it might be best to bring this problem up in the next session and further suggested that they leave John out of that session.

Mr. and Mrs. Jones came alone to the next session. Instead of dealing symptomatically with her isolation, Mrs. Jones was able to verbalize it. Mr. Jones at first was angry at his wife when she told him of her isolation. She responded to his anger by crying and saying, "It's no use." The therapist commended Mr. Jones for his anger, interpreting it as a way of showing concern, but pointed out that it was ineffective because it turned off his wife. The therapist then asked Mr. Jones if he wanted to take responsibility for moving toward his wife. The therapist continued probing the husband, trying to find out how much commitment he wanted to make to the relationship and how much energy he wanted to invest. The delicate and tedious task of rebuilding the marital relationship was under way.

TREATMENT

In family therapy, as in other therapeutic approaches, one can discern various phases or stages. Three phases can be distinguished: (a) observation, (b) intervention, and (c) consolidation.

The initial interviews focus on observing patterns of interaction. What kinds of information are exchanged? By whom? And how? Can certain sequences be observed? What are the alliances and splits?

Although one can make interventions from the beginning, as noted in the case given, most family therapists try out hypotheses before making interventions. These would be done to change the interaction of the system and constitute a second phase of treatment. Controlling the presence and absence of members at sessions, requesting people to dialogue with each other, and finding issues around which to build closeness are ways of intervening.

Consolidation is the last phase of treatment and the most important. The presence of the therapist creates a new system; absence may allow the old one to return. It is necessary, therefore, that one be sure interventions are of such magnitude that they last after removal of the therapist from the system. Termination must be a process and not a sudden withdrawal from the family. The possibilities for growth and decline must be discussed and examined.

In the case of the Jones family, it was decided that the husband and wife would be seen twice a month, Mr. Jones and his son once a month, and the three together once a month. In this way, the marital subsystem, the father-son subsystem, and the family system itself would receive attention. The husband's tentative moves toward his wife diminished her feelings of isolation and, at the same time, made her less demanding of her son's attention. This removal of pressure enabled John to feel better toward his mother, which showed itself in his willingness to drive her to the store and give other assistance. His father's attempts at moving closer made him feel more confidence in the father and his ability to take care of the needs of the mother. John then was able to move outside appropriately toward peers without either anger or guilt. Mr. Jones began to spend more time with his wife because she was more responsive. His involvement in outside activities continued but in a more controlled way.

RESOLUTION

In any family, there are individual problems usually seen in symptomatic ways, for example, feelings of depression; interpersonal problems seen in behavioral ways, such as a husband overinvolved at work; and family problems seen in the inability of family members to solve problems or get closure on important issues.

The resolution of the Jones family meant restructuring the system so each member would have options other than the stereotyped ones they had shown. This was accomplished over a period of 24 sessions without getting involved in issues of why and when and staying with those of what and how.

FOLLOW-UP

After 24 sessions, the family was seen twice a month for a period of three months and then once a month for six months, at which time, on the basis of mutual consent, therapy was discontinued. In all, 36 sessions were held over a period of one and one-half years. Since that time (1972), no further help has been requested, and no symptomatic expressions of depression, drinking, or antisocial behavior have been reported.

Each family case is unique and has its own specifics. Treatment will be governed in part by the theories of the therapist and in part by the family. Some therapists would work more on intergenerational issues and some more on symptoms. Some would hold fewer sessions, and some would hold more. In all cases, however, the focus would be on the system as the client and not on any single member.

SUMMARY

Family therapy started in about the middle 1950s. Its future looks bright for several reasons. First, the whole movement in therapy is away from a focus on the individual and toward the context in which one lives. Humans are social creatures, and the more one is isolated from others, the less social and the more like animals one becomes. Second, there is growing interest in family, in one's "roots." Interest in communal living is further evidence that if one cannot relate in the context into which one is born, one seeks a substitute family. These reasons give support to the feeling that family therapy will continue to grow in importance.

Family therapy is concerned with the most basic relationships in life, those of the family. Instead of dealing with the ghosts from the past, it brings them into the session itself. It teaches a person to be a self while remaining in touch with others. It strikes a balance between the self and the family because mental health requires a development of the self together with a meaningful relationship with others.

George Mora, a historian of psychiatry, notes, "Within the limits of psychiatry proper, there is no question that the field of family psychiatry will continue to develop, at the expense not only of individual psychotherapy but also of child and adolescent psychotherapy" (1974, p. 71). This is due to the introduction of context into the process of therapy. No longer can the therapist hide out in a room and shut out the world. Change comes about from bringing significant others into the therapy.

The history of therapy in the movement from Freud to the present has gone from the individual to the interpersonal to the system. If therapy is to be viable in the future, it must become ecological, given that ecology studies organisms in relation to their environment, and family therapy is the most ecological of all therapies because it always looks at a person in relation to the environment. Health and sickness are not attributes of an individual alone but are produced by the world in which we live. Change is contained within the system in which an individual lives. This power has only begun to be tapped, and those therapies that hope to survive must soon either learn to use the context of a client's life or cease to be effective.

ANNOTATED BIBLIOGRAPHY

Bowen, M., (1978). *Family therapy in clinical practice*. New York: Jason Aronson.

This is the definitive statement of *family systems theory* by its founder and major theorist. The articles represent a lifetime of thought and, although at times repetitious, they also document the genesis of a major theory in the field. Of special value is the article "Towards a Differentiation of Self in One's Own Family," which is a step-by-step process of how Bowen became differentiated in his family of origin.

Foley, D. (1986). *An introduction to family therapy, (2nd ed.)*. New York: Grune & Stratton.

This book is a primer meant for the beginning student in the field at a master's level. Designed to be used for a one-semester course in family therapy, it is divided into four sections. Part 1 deals with the seminal ideas in the field: the double bind, pseudomutuality, schism and skew, mystification, and general system theory. Part 2 treats the major historical figures: Nathan Ackerman, Virginia Satir, Don Jackson, Jay Haley, and Murray Bowen. Part 3 notes the similarities and differences in their concepts. Part 4 looks at the current state in the field and makes suggestions about the future.

This book establishes a structure

within which the reader can understand the evolution of thinking in family therapy from its beginnings to the present. It will provide a foundation that will allow for reading the works below with more understanding.

Framo, J. (1982). *Exploration in marital and family therapy: Selected papers of James L. Framo.* New York: Springer.

This work offers a good explanation of the *object relations* approach to family therapy. Framo writes clearly about the relationship between the intrapsychic and the interpersonal and represents the best model of one who is an integrationist working at the interface between the two systems. The evolution of Framo's thought can be found in these papers.

Gurman, A., & Kniskern, D. (1981). *Handbook of family therapy.* New York: Brunner/Mazel.

Nearly 800 pages of double columns, this book has everything in it: theory, practice, and research. All the major thinkers are here, following a general outline of the editors that makes comparison easier. At times it is overpowering and is best used with a knowledgeable guide.

Hoffman, L. (1981). *Foundations of family therapy.* New York: Basic Books.

This is a book that begins with Gregory Bateson and ends with a discussion of epistemology and its role in family therapy. It is both a history of family therapy and an elaboration of a theory based on an evolutionary paradigm, elaborating on the seminal thinking of Bateson. Although free of jargon and tersely written, it requires a sophisticated knowledge of the field to be fully appreciated.

Minuchin, S. (1974). *Families and family therapy.* Cambridge: Harvard University Press.

This is the best explanation of the theory of the structural position by its major exponent. Most of the book is taken up with examples of how the *structural approach* is used with functional and dysfunctional families at various points in the developmental process.

Watzlawick, P., Weakland, J., & Fisch, R. (1974). *Change: Principles of problem formation and problem resolution.* New York: Norton.

This book contains a complete explanation of the *strategic intervention approach* to therapy. It gives philosophical concepts together with excellent and detailed examples of how these concepts are applied. It explains the difference between first- and second-order change and the function of paradox in reframing messages.

CASE READINGS

Family therapy has an extensive amount of material on videotape, on audiotape, and in case studies. Two works in particular are devoted to cases. *Techniques of Family Therapy* (J. Haley & L. Hoffman [Eds.] [1967]. New York: Basic Books) gives the transcripts of initial interviews with 5 family therapists and their comments. *Family Therapy: Full Length Case Studies* (P. Papp [Ed.] [1977]. New York: Gardner Press) presents 12 therapists with varying approaches and their work with families in treatment.

Of special interest are two cases by Nathan Ackerman and Don Jackson, because many of the current techniques in family therapy have their roots in their work.

Ackerman, N. (1966). Rescuing the scapegoat. In N. Ackerman (Ed.), Treating the troubled family. New York: Basic Books.

This case presents a good example of Ackerman's style, which he called "tickling the defenses." Ackerman redefines the family conflict, thus shifting the focus from the identified patient to the family system itself. This shift enables him to unearth the reason for the father's role as family martyr, namely, his way of dealing with the memory of his own father, who was an irresponsible gambler. The roots of the current object relations approach can be seen in this case.

Aponte, H., & Hoffman, L. (1973). The open door: A structural approach to a family with an anorectic child. Family Process, 12, 1–44.

This article is a commentary on a videotape of an initial family interview conducted by Drs. Salvador Minuchin and Marriano Barragan with a family whose presenting problem is a 14-year-old girl diagnosed as anorexic. It is of special value because it can be read in conjunction with viewing the tape so one can get a clearer notion of the relationship of theory and practice in structural family therapy.

Fisch, R. (1977). Sometimes it's better for the right hand not to know what the left hand is doing. In P. Papp (Ed.), Family therapy: Full-length case studies (pp. 199–210). New York: Gardner Press.

This case study is a good example of the brief therapy practiced by the Palo Alto school. It is an extension and development of the ideas of Don Jackson. The therapist defines an issue as the problem as a first, critical step. He then uses paradox, prescribing the symptom, and therapeutic double binding as means of resolving the problem in a time-limited setting.

Foley, V. (1977). Alcoholism and couple counseling. In R. Stahmann & W. Hiebert (Eds.), Counseling in marital and sexual problems (pp. 146–159). Baltimore: Williams & Wilkins.

This is an analysis of a case in which a system approach to the role of alcohol in the family is examined. Drinking is seen as a homeostatic balance in the family and not just as a dysfunction of the identified client. In addition, the manipulation of the therapist by the client is analyzed. Finally, three stages of treatment—observation, intervention, and consolidation—are suggested. The case illustrates a structural approach with emphasis on what is happening in the system rather than why it is happening.

Framo, J. (1977). In-laws and out-laws. A marital case of kinship confusion. In P. Papp (Ed.), Family therapy: Full length case studies (pp. 167–181). New York: Gardner Press.

This case offers a good example of an object relations approach to family therapy. Framo gives a clear demonstration of the connection between current family difficulties and unresolved issues of the past. He shows how a skilled clinician can use history in a way that makes it relevant in defining current family problems and in finding solutions for them.

Guerin, P. (1976). The use of the arts in family therapy: I never sang for my father. In P. Guerin (Ed.), Family therapy: Theory and practice (pp. 480–500). New York: Gardner Press.

This brief article examines the well-known play and movie I Never Sang for My Father, by Robert Anderson, from the point of view of a therapist trained by Murray Bowen. The Garrison family becomes a case study for the therapist, who examines the script in terms of interlocking triangles, the possibility of relationships, the conflictual issues in the system, and the critical incidents that might have moved the system in a more healthy and differentiated direction.

Jackson, D. (1967). The eternal triangle. In J. Haley & L. Hoffman (Eds.), Techniques of family therapy (pp. 176–264). New York: Basic Books.

This is a classic case in which Jackson demonstrates his ability to relabel a problem in terms of the family interaction rather than as that of the identified patient. He accomplishes this by prescribing the symptom rather than by working toward insight.

Papp, P. (1983). Case presentation: The daughter who said no. In P. Papp, The *process of change* (pp. 67–103). New York: Guilford. [Reprinted in D. Wedding & R. J. Corsini (Eds.) (1989). *Case studies in psychotherapy*. Itasca, IL: F. E. Peacock].

This case illustrates strategic psychotherapy applied to a 23 year old anorexic woman and her family. It provides good examples of enmeshment, covert alliances, and power struggles within the family unit and it richly illustrates many of the practices and problems described in the current chapter.

Umbarger, C., & Hare, R. (1973). Disen-

gagement from a schizophrenic family. *American Journal of Psychiatry, 27*, 274–284. [Reprinted in D. Wedding & R. J. Corsini (Eds.) (1979). *Great cases in psychotherapy*. Itasca, IL: F. E. Peacock.)

This article describes the process of individuation within a family structure. The approach is an illustration of structural family therapy and is important because the family has been labeled as schizophrenic and many critics of structural family therapy say it is of value only with less serious family problems.

REFERENCES

Ackerman, N. (1956). Interlocking pathologies in family relationships. In S. Rado & G. Daniels (Eds.), *Changing concepts in psychoanalytic medicine* (pp. 135–150). New York: Grune & Stratton.

Ackerman, N. (1958). *The psychodynamics of family life*. New York: Basic Books.

Ackerman, N. (1966). *Treating the troubled family*. New York: Basic Books.

Adler, A. (1949). *Understanding human nature*. New York: Permabooks. (Original published 1918.)

Alger, I. (1973). Audio-visual techniques in family therapy. In D. Bloch (Ed.), *Techniques of family psychotherapy* (pp. 65–73). New York: Grune & Stratton.

Allred, G., & Kersey, F. (1977). The AIAC, a design for systematically analyzing marriage and family counseling: A progress report. *Journal of Marriage and Family Counseling, 3*, 17–25.

Aponte, H., & Hoffman, L. (1973). The open door: A structural approach to a family with an anoretic child. *Family Process, 12*, 1–44.

Arieti, S. (1969). General systems theory and psychiatry—An overview. In W. Gray, F. Duhl, & N. Rizzo (Eds.), *General systems theory and psychiatry* (pp. 33–50). Boston: Little, Brown.

Barton, C., & Alexander, J. (1981). Functional family therapy. In A. Gurman &

D. Kniskern (Eds.), *Handbook of family therapy* (pp. 403–443). New York: Brunner/Mazel.

Bateson, G., Jackson, D., Haley, J., & Weakland, J. (1956). Towards a theory of schizophrenia. *Behavioral Science, 1*, 251–264.

Berne, E. (1964). *Games people play*. New York: Grove Press.

Bloch, D. (1973). The clinical home visit. In D. Bloch (Ed.), *Techniques of family psychotherapy* (pp. 39–45). New York: Grune & Stratton.

Boszormenyi-Nagy, I. (1965). The concept of change in conjoint family therapy. In A. Friedman (Ed.), *Psychotherapy for the whole family* (pp. 305–319). New York: Springer.

Boszormenyi-Nagy, I., & Spark, G. (1973). *Invisible loyalties*. New York: Harper & Row.

Bowen, M. (1971). The use of family theory in clinical practice. In J. Haley (Ed.), *Changing families* (pp. 159–192). New York: Grune & Stratton.

Bowen, M. (1975). Family therapy after twenty years. In D. Friedman & K. Juzrud (Eds.), *American handbook of psychiatry (Vol. 5)*. New York: Basic Books.

Bowen, M. (1976). Theory in the practice of psychotherapy. In P. Guerin (Ed.), *Family therapy* (pp. 42–89). New York: Gardner Press.

Bowen, M. (1978). *Family therapy in clinical practice*. New York: Jason Aronson.

Buckley, W. (1967). *Sociology and modern systems theory.* Englewood Cliffs, NJ: Prentice-Hall.

Carter, E., & McGoldrick, M. (Eds.) (1980). *The family life cycle: A framework for family therapy.* New York: Gardner Press.

Christensen, O. (1971). Family counseling: An Adlerian orientation. In G. Gazda (Ed.), *Proceedings of a symposium of family counseling and therapy* (pp. 40–91). Athens, GA: University of Georgia Press.

De Chenne, T. (1973). Experiential facilitation in conjoint-marriage counseling. *Psychotherapy: Theory, research and practice, 10,* 212–214.

Dell, P. (1982). Beyond homeostasis: Toward a concept of coherence. *Family Process, 21,* 21–41.

Dowling, E. (1979). Co-therapy: A clinical searcher's view. In S. Walrond-Skinner (Ed.), *Family and marital therapy.* (pp. 188–194). London: Routledge & Kegan Paul.

Engeln, R., Knutson, J., Laughy, L., & Garlington, W. (1976). Behavior modification techniques applied to a family unit—A case study. In G. Erickson & T. Hogan (Eds.), *Family therapy: An introduction to theory and technique.* (pp. 316–324). New York: Jason Aronson.

Entwistle, D., & Doering, S. (1981). *The first birth: A family turning point.* Baltimore: Johns Hopkins Press.

Foley, V. (1986). *An introduction to family therapy (2nd ed.).* New York: Grune & Stratton.

Foley, V. (1975). Family therapy with black, disadvantaged families: Some observations on roles, communication and techniques. *Journal of Marriage and Family Counseling, 1,* 29–38.

Framo, J. (1970). Symptoms from a family transactional viewpoint. In N. Ackerman, J. Lieb & J. Pearce (Eds.), *Family therapy in transition* (pp. 125–171). Boston: Little, Brown.

Framo, J. (1982). *Family interaction: A dialogue between family therapists and family researchers.* New York: Springer.

Frankl, V. (1960). Paradoxical intention: A logo-therapeutic technique. *American Journal of Psychotherapy, 14,* 520–535.

Freud, S. (1964). Analysis of phobia in a five-year-old boy. In J. Strachey (Ed.), *The complete works of Sigmund Freud (Vol. 10)* (pp. 5–148). London: Hogarth Press.

Greenson, R. (1967). *The technique and practice of psychoanalysis.* New York: International University Press.

Guerin, P. (Ed.) (1976). *Family therapy.* New York: Gardner Press.

Guerin, P., & Pendagast, E. (1976). Evaluation of family system and genogram. In P. Guerin (Ed.), *Family therapy* (pp. 450–464). New York: Gardner Press.

Guntrip, H. (1971). *Psychoanalytic theory, therapy and the self.* New York: Basic Books.

Gurman, A. (1973). The effects and the effectiveness of marital therapy: A review of outcome research. *Family Process, 12,* 145–170.

Gurman, A. (1975). Couples' facilitative communication skill as a dimension of marital therapy outcome. *Journal of Marriage and Family Counseling, 1,* 163–174.

Gurman, A. (1978). Contemporary marital therapies: A critique and comparative analysis of psychoanalytic, behavioral and systems theory approaches. In T. Paolino & B. McCrady (Eds.), *Marriage and marital therapy* (pp. 445–566). New York: Brunner/Mazel.

Gurman, A., & Kniskern, D. (1978). Research on marital and family therapy: Progress, perspective and prospect. In S. Garfield & A. Bergin (Eds.), *Handbook of psychotherapy and behavior change (2nd ed.)* (pp. 817–901). New York: Wiley.

Gurman, A., & Kniskern, D. (1981a). Family therapy outcome research: Knowns and unknowns. *Handbook of family therapy.* New York: Brunner/Mazel.

Gurman, A., & Kniskern, D. (1981b). The outcomes of family therapy: Implications for practice and training. In G. Berenson & H. White (Eds.), *Annual review of family therapy (Vol. 1)* (pp. 507–519). New York: Human Sciences Press.

Guttman, H., Spector, R., Sigal, J., Epstein, N., & Rakoff, V. (1972). Coding of affective expression in conjoint family therapy. *American Journal of Psychotherapy, 26,* 185–194.

Haley, J. (1963). *Strategies of psychotherapy*. New York: Grune & Stratton.

Haley, J. (1973). *Uncommon therapy: The psychiatric techniques of Milton Erickson, M.D.* New York: Norton.

Haley, J. (1977). *Problem-solving therapy*. San Francisco: Jossey-Bass.

Haley, J. (1980). *Leaving home*. New York: McGraw-Hill.

Haley, J., & Hoffman, L. (1967). *Techniques of family therapy*. New York: Basic Books.

Hoffman, L. (1981). *Foundations of family therapy*. New York: Basic Books.

Hollis, F. (1967a). Explorations in the development of a typology of casework treatment. *Social Casework, 48,* 335–341.

Hollis, F. (1967b). The coding and application of a typology of casework treatment. *Social Casework, 48,* 489–497.

Hollis, F. (1968a). A profile of early interviews in marital counseling. *Social Casework, 49,* 35–43.

Hollis, F. (1968b). Continuance and discontinuance in marital counseling and some observations on joint interviews. *Social Casework, 49,* 167–174.

Jackson, D., & Haley, J. (1968). Transference revisited. In D. Jackson (Ed.), *Therapy, communication and change* (pp. 115–128). Palo Alto: Science and Behavior Books.

Jacobson, N. (1981). Behavioral marital therapy. In A. Gurman & D. Kniskern (Eds.), *Handbook of family therapy* (pp. 556–591). New York: Brunner/Mazel.

Jacobson, N., & Margolin, G. (1979). *Marital therapy: Strategies based on social learning and behavior exchange principles*. New York: Brunner/Mazel.

Jacobson, N., & Weiss, R. (1978). Behavioral marriage therapy. III. The contents of Gurman et al. may be hazardous to our health. *Family Process, 17,* 149–164.

Keeney, B., & Sprenkle, D. (1982). Ecosystemic epistemology: Critical implications for the aesthetics and pragmatics of family therapy. *Family Process, 21,* 1–19.

Kempler, W. (1974). *Principles of Gestalt family therapy*. Salt Lake City: Desert Press.

Kerr, M. (1981). Family systems theory and therapy. In A. Gurman & D. Kniskern (Eds.), *Handbook of family therapy* (pp. 226–264). New York: Brunner/Mazel.

Kiesler, D. (1973). *The process of psychotherapy: Empirical foundations and systems of analysis*. Chicago: Aldine.

Kuhn, T. (1962). *The structure of scientific revolutions*. Chicago: University of Chicago Press.

Laing, R. D. (1956). Mystification, confusion and conflict. In I. Boszormenyi-Nagy & J. Framo (Eds.), *Intensive family therapy* (pp. 343–363). New York: Harper & Row.

Laqueur, P. (1973). Multiple family therapy: Questions and answers. In D. Bloch (Ed.), *Techniques of family psychotherapy* (pp. 75–85). New York: Grune & Stratton.

Levenson, E. (1972). *The fallacy of understanding*. New York: Basic Books.

Liberman, R., Wheeler, E., De Visser, L., Kuehnel, J., & Kuehnel, T. (1980). *Handbook of marital therapy: A positive approach to helping troubled relationships*. New York: Plenum.

Liberman, R. (1976). Behavioral approaches to family and couple therapy. In G. Erickson & T. Hogan (Eds.), *Family therapy: An introduction to theory and technique* (pp. 120–134). New York: Jason Aronson.

Liebman, R., et al. (1976). An integrated treatment program for psychogenic pain. *Family Process, 15,* 397–405.

Lidz, T., Cornelison, A., Fleck, S., & Terry, D. (1957). The intrafamilial environment of schizophrenic patients. II. Marital schism and marital skew. *American Journal of Psychiatry, 114,* 241–248.

McGoldrick, M., & Pearce, J. (1981). Family therapy with Irish-Americans. *Family Process, 20,* 233–241.

McGoldrick, M., Pearce, J., & Giordano, J. (1982). *Ethnicity and family therapy*. New York: Guilford Press.

Minuchin, S. (1974). *Families and family therapy*. Cambridge, MA: Harvard University Press.

Minuchin, S., & Barcai, A. (1969). Therapeutically induced family crisis. In J. Masserman (Ed.), *Science and psychoanalysis* (Vol. 14) (pp. 199–205). New York: Grune & Stratton.

Minuchin, S., & Fishman, H. (1981). *Family therapy techniques*. Cambridge, MA: Harvard University Press.

Minuchin, S., Rosman, B., & Baker, L. (1978). *Psychosomatic families' anorexia nervosa in context*. Cambridge, MA: Harvard University Press.

Minuchin, S., Montalvo, B., Guerney, B., Rosman, B., & Schumer, F. (1967). *Families of the slum*. New York: Basic Books.

Mora, G. (1974). Recent psychiatric developments (since 1939). In S. Arieti (Ed.), *American handbook of psychiatry (Vol. 1)* (pp. 43–114). New York: Basic Books.

Mozdzierz, G. J., Macchitelli, F. J., & Lisiecki, J. (1976). The paradox in psychotherapy: An Adlerian perspective. *Journal of Individual Psychology, 32*, 169–184.

Olson, D., & Dahl, N. (1975). *Inventory of marriage and family literature (Vol. 3, 1973–1974)*. Minneapolis: University of Minnesota Press.

Palazzoli, M. (1978). *Self-starvation*. New York: Jason Aronson.

Palazzoli, M., Boscolo, L., Cecchin, G., & Prata, G. (1978). *Paradox and counterparadox*. New York: Jason Aronson.

Papajohn, J., & Spiegel, J. (1975). *Transactions in families*. San Francisco: Jossey-Bass.

Papp, P., Silverstein, O., & Carter, E. (1973). Family sculpting in preventive work with "well families." *Family Process, 12*, 197–212.

Patterson, G. (1971). Behavioral interventions procedures in the classroom and in the home. In A. Bergin & S. Garfield (Eds.), *Handbook of psychotherapy and behavior change* (pp. 751–775). New York: Wiley.

Paul, N., & Paul, B. (1975). *A marital puzzle*. New York: Norton.

Pedersen, P. B. (1977). Asian personality theories. In R. J. Corsini (Ed.), *Current personality theories* (pp. 367–397). Itasca, IL: F. E. Peacock.

Pinsof, W. (1979a). The family therapist behavior scale (FTBS): Development and evaluation of a coding system. *Family Process, 18*, 451–461.

Pinsof, W. (1979b). The family therapist coding system (FTCS) coding manual. Chicago: Center for Family Studies,

Department of Psychiatry, Northwestern University Medical School.

Pinsof, W. (1981). Family therapy process research. In A. Gurman & D. Kniskern (Eds.), *Handbook of family therapy* (pp. 699–741). New York: Brunner/Mazel.

Rice, D., Fey, W., & Kepecs, J. (1972). Therapist experience and "style" in cotherapy. *Family Process, 11*, 1–12.

Rice, D., Gurman, A., & Razin, A. (1974). Therapist sex, style and theoretical orientation. *Journal of Nervous and Mental Diseases, 159*, 413–421.

Rice, D., Razin, A., & Gurman, A. (1976). Spouses as co-therapists: Variables and implications for patient-therapist matching. *Journal of Marriage and Family Counseling, 2*, 55–62.

Satir, V. (1972). *Peoplemaking*. Palo Alto: Science and Behavior Books.

Shapiro, R., & Budman, S. (1973). Defection, continuation and termination in family and individual therapy. *Family Process, 12*, 55–67.

Sigal, J., Lasry, J., Guttman, H., Chagoya, L., & Pilon, R. (1977). Some stable characteristics of family therapists' interventions in real and simulated therapy sessions. *Journal of Consulting and Clinical Psychology, 45*, 23–26.

Sigal, J., Presser, B., Woodward, C., Santa-Barbara, J., Epstein, N., & Levin, S. (1979). Therapists' interventions in a simulated family as predictors of outcome in family therapy. Unpublished Manuscript, Institute of Community and Family Psychiatry, Jewish General Hospital, Montreal.

Stanton, M., & Todd, T. (1979). Structural family therapy with drug addicts. In E. Kaufman & P. Kaufmann (Eds.), *Family therapy of drug and alcohol abuse* (pp. 55–69). New York: Gardner Press.

Steiner, C. (1971). *Games alcoholics play*. New York: Ballantine Books.

Stewart, R., Peters, T., Marsh, S., & Peters, M. (1975). An object-relations approach to psychotherapy with marital couples, families and children. *Family Process, 14*, 161–177.

Stierlin, H. (1974). *Separating parents and adolescents*. New York: Quadrangle.

Thibaut, J., & Kelly, H. (1959). *The social*

psychology of groups. New York: Wiley.

Trotzer, J. (1982). Engaging families in therapy: A pilot study. *International Journal of Family Therapy, 4*, 4–19.

Umbarger, C. (1983). *Structural family therapy*. New York: Grune & Stratton.

Von Bertalanffy, L. (1974). General system theory and psychiatry. In S. Arieti (Ed.), *American handbook of psychiatry (Vol. 1)* (pp. 1095–1117). New York: Basic Books.

Watzlawick, P., Weakland, J., & Fisch, R. (1974). *Change: Principles of problem formation and problem resolution*. New York: Norton.

Weakland, J., Fisch, R., Watzlawick, P., & Bodin, A. (1974). Brief therapy: Focused problem resolution. *Family Process, 13*, 141–168.

Wells, R. (1982). Discussion: Engaging families in therapy: A pilot study. *International Journal of Family Therapy, 4*, 20–22.

Wells, R., Dilkes, T., & Trivelli, N. (1972). The results of family therapy: A critical review of the literature. *Family Process, 7*, 189–207.

Whitaker, C. (1975). Psychotherapy of the absurd: With a special emphasis on the psychotherapy of aggression. *Family Process, 14*, 1–16.

Whitaker, C., & Keith, D. (1981). Symbolic-experimental therapy. In A. Gurman & D. Kniskern (Eds.), *Handbook of family therapy* (pp. 187–225). New York: Brunner/Mazel.

Winer, L. (1971). The qualified pronoun count as a measure of change in family psychotherapy. *Family Process, 10*, 243–248.

Wynne, L. (1961). The study of intrafamilial alignments and splits in exploratory family therapy. In N. Ackerman, F. Beatman & S. Sherman (Eds.), *Exploring the base for family therapy* (pp. 95–115). New York: Family Service Association.

Wynne, L. (1965). Some indications and contraindications for exploratory family therapy. In I. Boszormenyi-Nagy & J. Framo (Eds.), *Intensive family therapy* (pp. 289–322). New York: Harper & Row.

Wynne, L., Ryckoff, I., Day, J., & Hirsch, S. (1958). Pseudomutuality in the family relations of schizophrenics. *Psychiatry, 21*, 205–220.

Wynne, L., & Singer, M. (1963). Thought disorder and family relations of schizophrenics. I. Research strategy. *Archives of General Psychiatry, 9*, 191–198.

Yalom, I. (1985). *The theory and practice of group psychotherapy (3rd ed)*. New York: Basic Books.

Zuk, G. (1975). *Process and practice in family therapy*. Haverford, PA: Psychiatry and Behavioral Science Books.

Zuk, G., Boszormenyi-Nagy, I., & Heiman, E. (1963). Some dynamics of laughter during family therapy. *Family Process, 2*, 302–314.

ARNOLD A. LAZARUS

13

Multimodal Therapy

ARNOLD A. LAZARUS

OVERVIEW

Multimodal therapy is a systematic and comprehensive psychotherapeutic approach developed by Arnold Lazarus, a clinical psychologist. While respecting the assumption that clinical practice should adhere firmly to the principles, procedures, and findings of psychology as an experimental science, the multimodal orientation transcends the behavioral tradition by adding unique assessment procedures and by dealing in great depth and detail with sensory, imagery, cognitive, and interpersonal factors and their interactive effects. A basic premise is that patients are usually troubled by a multitude of specific problems that should be dealt with by a similar multitude of specific treatments. A multimodal assessment examines each area of a person's BASIC I.D.:

B = Behavior
A = Affect
S = Sensation
I = Imagery
C = Cognition
I. = Interpersonal relationships
D. = Drugs/Biology

It provides an operational way of answering the question, What works, for whom, and under which conditions?

BASIC CONCEPTS

Multimodal therapy is personalistic and individualistic. A diligent scrutiny for individual exceptions to general rules and principles characterizes the approach; the search is for appropriate interventions for each person. Clinical effectiveness is predicated on the therapist's flexibility, versatility, and *technical* eclecticism. The *theoretical* eclectic tends to draw from diverse systems that may be epistemologically incompatible, whereas the technical eclectic uses procedures drawn from different sources without necessarily subscribing to the theories or disciplines that spawned them. The upshot is a consistent, systematic, and testable set of beliefs and assumptions about human beings and their problems, and an armamentarium of effective therapeutic strategies for remedying their afflictions.

While remaining technically eclectic, multimodal therapy rests primarily on the theoretical base of *social learning theory* (Bandura, 1969, 1977, 1986) while also drawing from *general system theory* (Bertalanffy, 1974; Buckley, 1967) and *group and communications theory* (Watzlawick, Weakland & Fisch, 1974). There seem to be no postulates or paradigms in these theoretical systems that are mutually contradictory or incompatible—they blend harmoniously into a congruent framework.

Most of our experiences comprise moving, feeling, sensing, imagining, thinking, and relating to one another. In the final analysis, we are biochemical-neurophysiological entities. Human life and conduct are products of ongoing behaviors, affective processes, sensations, images, cognitions, interpersonal relationships, and biological functions. BASIC IB is derived from the first letters of each of these modalities, but by referring to the biological modality as "Drugs/Biology" (because one of the most common biological interventions is the use of psychotropic medication), we have the more compelling acronym BASIC ID, or the preferred BASIC I.D. (I.D. as in *identity*). It is crucial to remember that D stands not only for drugs, medication, or pharmacological intervention, but also includes nutrition, hygiene, exercise, and all basic physiological and pathological inputs.

The BASIC I.D. is presumed to comprise human temperament and personality, and it is assumed that everything from anger, disappointment, disgust, greed, fear, grief, awe, contempt, and boredom to love, hope, faith, ecstasy, optimism, and joy can be accounted for by examining components and interactions within a person's BASIC I.D. It is also essential to recognize and include factors that fall outside the BASIC I.D., such as sociocultural, political, and other macroenvironmental events. While external realities are not part of temperament and personality, "psychopathology and society are inextricably bound together" (Nathan & Harris, 1980, p. xvii). There are obviously crucial differences in adaptive interpersonal styles between people raised and living in New York and New Guinea, but regardless of an individual's background, detailed descriptions of salient behaviors, affective responses, sensory reactions, images, cognitions, interpersonal dealings, and biological propensities, will provide the principal ingredients of his or her psychological makeup. To appreciate further the interactions among the various modalities—for example, how certain behaviors influence and are influenced by affects, sensations, images, cognitions, and significant relationships—is to know a great deal about individuals and their social networks.

While multimodal therapy draws heavily from several systems (especially behavior therapy, rational-emotive therapy, and cognitive therapy), there are six distinctive features that set MMT apart from all other approaches:

1. The specific and comprehensive attention given to the entire BASIC I.D.
2. The use of *second-order* BASIC I.D. assessments
3. The use of *modality profiles*
4. The use of *structural profiles*
5. Deliberate *bridging* procedures
6. *Tracking* the modality firing order

Each of these tactics and procedures will be discussed in this chapter.

The term *bespoke therapy* has been used to describe the multimodal orientation (see Zilbergeld, 1982) and aptly conveys the custom-made, personalistic emphasis. The form, style, and cadence of therapy are fitted, whenever possible, to each client's perceived requirements. The basic question is, *Who or what is best for this particular individual?* Some clients respond best to therapists who are warm and empathic; others are apt to progress by more distant and formal relationships. Quiet, passive, reflective listeners are especially suited to some clients; others want therapists who are active, directive, and bluntly outspoken. The same client may respond favorably to various therapeutic styles at different times. How is the therapist to gauge whether pensive reflection is more likely to succeed than direct disputation? The answer can be found largely by noting the client's implicit and explicit expectations and by observing the impact of applying various tactics (cf., Howard, Nance & Myers, 1987). Even effective therapists will make mistakes in gauging clients' expectations and in tactics applied, but capable therapists, on noticing these errors, will usually make adjustments to change the course of therapy. The choice of a particular therapeutic style and the selection of techniques are not capricious affairs. After drawing up a detailed modality profile (a chart depicting excesses and deficits across the client's BASIC I.D.), the multimodal therapist resorts to two main procedures—bridging and tracking.

Bridging

Bridging refers to a procedure in which the therapist deliberately tunes into the client's preferred modality before branching off into other dimensions that seem likely to be more productive. For example, instead of challenging a client or even pointing out that he or she tends to eschew the expression of feelings by erecting intellectual barriers, we find it better first to enter into the client's domain and then gently lead him or her into other (potentially more meaningful) channels. Here is an example:

Client: I think that Molly resorts to what I call a three-down maneuver when we disagree about virtually anything. In other words, I am not placed in a one-down position, but I am seen as the lowest man on the totem pole.

Therapist: How does that make you feel?

Client: I realize why she does it. It is exactly what her mother does to her father, and Molly is very much like her mother in many ways.

Therapist: [Going along with client's cognitive leanings.] So Molly has imitated her mother and uses her tactics. What are some of the other things she does that remind you of her mother?

Client: Well, there are a couple of things that come to mind immediately. First ... [Client intellectualizes about the alleged similarities between Molly and her mother.]

Therapist: [Bridging] When you think about all these ties that Molly has to her mother and the way she puts you down, are you aware of any feelings or sensations in your body?

Client: Right now I've got a knot in my stomach.

Therapist: Can you concentrate fully on that stomach tension? Can you focus on that knot?

Client: It feels like a vise is gripping it.

Therapist: Do you feel tension anywhere else in your body?

Client: My jaws feel tight.

Therapist: Will you concentrate on the tension in your jaws and your stomach and tell me what feelings or mental pictures come to mind?

Client: I feel sad. I think it gets down to the fact that I am afraid that my relationship with Molly will be a carbon copy of her parents' marriage.

Therapist: Let's hear more about your fears and your feelings of sadness.

The therapist wanted to move into affective areas right from the start but instead went along with the client's apparent desire to dwell on cognitive components. Shortly thereafter, when the therapist again inquired about affective and sensory responses, the client was willing to reveal his sensations and then to verbalize his feelings. Failure to tune into the client's presenting modality often leads to feelings of alienation—the client feels misunderstood or may conclude that the therapist does not speak his or her language. Thus, multimodal therapists *start where the client is* and then bridge into more productive areas of discourse.

Tracking

Tracking refers to a careful examination of the "firing order" of the different modalities. For example, some clients tend to generate negative emotions by dwelling first on sensations (S) (e.g., a slight dizziness accompanied by mild heart palpitations), to which they attach negative cognitions (C) (e.g., ideas of illness and death), immediately followed by aversive images (I) (e.g., pictures of hospitals and catastrophic disease), culminating in maladaptive behavior (B) (e.g., unnecessary avoidance or extreme withdrawal). Other people tend to experience a different firing order. Rather than a sensory-cognitive-imagery-behavioral sequence as just outlined, they may display a CISB pattern (cognitive-imagery-sensory-behavior), an I.BSCA order (interpersonal-behavior-sensory-cognitive-affective), or any other combination. An example of an I.BSCA firing order can be seen at a social gathering where a man insults one of his friends (I.) and walks out of the room (B). He starts feeling hot and shaky and develops a severe tension headache (S). He then regrets having acted aggres-sively and impulsively, but starts rationalizing his conduct (C). Nonetheless, he concludes that he is a stupid and unbalanced person. Soon he begins to feel depressed (A).

In studying panic disorders, Margraf, Ehlers, and Roth (1986) identified positive feedback loops in which unpleasant body sensations are followed by "catastrophizing cognitions," resulting in full-blown panic attacks. Clark (1986) also discusses trigger stimuli (excitement, anger), followed by bodily sensations (dizziness, breathlessness), followed by cognitive appraisals, culminating in a panic attack.

Firing orders are not fixed tendencies. A person may generate negative affect through a particular sequence on some occasions and follow a different pattern at other times. Different emotions may follow distinct firing orders. Thus, a client, when anxious, found that a CISB sequence was operative, but when depressed, an IBI.S order was established. Most people, however, report a reasonably stable proclivity toward a particular firing order much of the time. By tracking the precise sequence of events that results in the affective disturbance, the therapist enables the client to gain insight into the antecedent events and also enables him or her to intercede appropriately. The therapist may elect to track the I.BSCA order more closely. Thus, questions might be asked to determine what thoughts or feelings had led the client to insult his friend in the first place, thereby uncovering additional antecedent factors. Such precise information permits intervention at any of several entry points in the sequence.

Tracking also enables one to select the most appropriate intervention techniques. An agoraphobic woman complained of panic and anxiety. Medication helped to control her outbreaks of panic, but when she exposed herself to feared situations (such as shopping in a supermarket), she nevertheless experienced considerable anxiety. When asked to take particular note of how these anxious feelings arose, she observed a cognitive-imagery-sensory-affective sequence (CISA). First, she tended to *think* about the probability of becoming anxious, and this, in turn, led to other negative self-statements such as, "What if I pass out?" "What if I start feeling weak and dizzy?" Soon, she formed mental *images* of these unpleasant events—in her mind's eye she would see herself hyperventilating and fainting. As these thoughts and images grew stronger, she would notice a *sensation* of lightheadedness, and her palms would become sweaty. She would immediately feel tense and anxious. Following her firing order, she was first given *self-instructional training* (Meichenbaum, 1977) in which her irrational, self-defeating thoughts were replaced with self-statements that tend to mitigate anxiety. ("I will handle the situation." "I will remain in control." "I will stay cool, calm, and collected.") Next, she was taught *coping imagery* (Lazarus, 1978, 1982), which involves picturing oneself coping, vividly imagining oneself remaining calm and in control. In the sensory modality, she was taught slow abdominal breathing and differential muscle relaxation. While shopping in the supermarket, she was to follow a specified sequence— first to use positive self-instructions, then to add positive mental imagery, and then to employ breathing while deliberately relaxing those muscles she was not using at the time.

If the client had reported a different firing order, say sensory-imagery-cognitive-affect (SICA), she would have been advised to commence with slow abdominal breathing and differential relaxation and follow with coping images. The positive self-statements would have been her third line of defense. Our clinical observations suggest that when one selects techniques that follow the client's habitual sequence, the positive impact is greater. While this finding awaits experimental verification or disproof, clinically, it appears that if a client has, for example, a CIS sequence and is treated first with sensory procedures, followed by imagery techniques, and then with cognitive methods (i.e., an SIC treatment order) the results are less impressive than outcomes that adhere to the client's firing order.

OTHER SYSTEMS

It has often been pointed out that most approaches to psychotherapy share common features. A bond or a therapeutic relationship usually develops in psychotherapy, and most systems advocate a stance of mutual respect and regard for the other person(s). Therapists generally serve as facilitators who provide direct or indirect guidance with the intention of helping their clients. It is widely agreed that it is often necessary to alter clients' self-perceptions as well as the ways in which they perceive the world. These and many other commonalities can be delineated, but upon close scrutiny, these similarities are more specious than real.

For example, both multimodal therapy and psychoanalysis regard "conflict resolution" as necessary for successful treatment outcomes. Upon closer scrutiny, these phenotypical similarities reflect vast genotypical differences. The meaning of "conflict," its origins, functions, effects, and overall impact, as well as the best ways of dealing with or resolving conflicts, are all quite different according to psychoanalytic and multimodal tenets (Lazarus, 1981). It is a serious error to emphasize insignificant similarities at the expense of significant differences.

There are literally hundreds of different schools of psychological thought and practice (e.g., Corsini, 1981; Herink, 1980). When examining the claims and counterclaims of their proponents, one discerns a number of trends or clusters. There are those who advocate particular techniques or procedures and tout them as virtual panaceas. Thus, one finds relaxation pundits, meditation gurus, scream advocates, and promulgators of megavitamins, hypnosis, psychodrama, rebirthing, or some other unimodal intervention. These one-track procedures are the antithesis of multimodal therapy, which views human disquietude as multilayerd and multileveled and calls for the correction of deviant behaviors, unpleasant feelings, negative sensations, intrusive images, irrational beliefs, stressful relationships, and physiological difficulties. Yet multimodal therapy is equally opposed to those theoretical eclectics who endeavor to unite the morass of competing systems, models, vocabularies, and personal idiosyncrasies into a unified whole, thus ending up with an agglomerate of incompatible and contradictory notions (which may be called *multimuddle therapy*).

Each system can be evaluated on the extent to which it assesses and treats, or ignores, each modality of the BASIC I.D. For example, it is evident that Gestalt therapy tends to neglect the cognitive domain in favor of "gut reactions" and lacks precise and disciplined behavioral retraining procedures. Cognitive-behavior therapy does not delve as thoroughly into sensory and imagery modalities as we advocate, nor are behavior therapists sufficiently sensitive to systems networks (interpersonal factors) or certain unexpressed emotions (affective reactions). Beck's cognitive therapy places heavy emphasis on dysfunctional thoughts and on reparative behaviors, but from a multimodal perspective, pays insufficient attention to specific sensory components, the rich array of imagery procedures, and the client's interpersonal networks. (See Zilbergeld & Lazarus, 1988, for a detailed account of the synergistic properties of mental imagery and muscular relaxation.) The best-known clinician whose orientation is perhaps the polar opposite of the multimodal approach is Carl Rogers. His person-centered approach offers the therapist's genuineness, empathy, and unpossessive caring to all clients and regards these "facilitative conditions" as necessary and sufficient for therapeutic growth and change. The multimodal position emphasizes that people have diverse needs and expectancies, come from very different molds, and require a wide range of stylistic, tactical, and strategic maneuvers from the therapist. Furthermore, no amount of empathy, genuineness, or unpossessive caring is likely to fill the gaps left by impoverished learning histories (behavioral and attitudinal deficits). These require teaching, coaching, training, modeling, shaping, and directing.

Nevertheless, when a multimodal therapist is consulted by a client who requires no more (and no less) than a genuine, empathic, and unpossessive listener, there is nothing to prevent the multimodalist from adopting a Rogerian stance (or referring the client to a person-centered colleague if he or she is unable or unwilling to adopt this therapeutic posture). Multimodal therapists constantly ask, "What works, for whom, and under which particular circumstances?" Thus, they take care not to attempt to fit the client to a predetermined treatment. With most practitioners, the client seems to get only what the therapist practices— which may not necessarily be what is best for the client. In multimodal therapy, there is a deliberate attempt to determine precisely what type of relationship, what type of interactive posture, each particular client will respond to. The multimodal orientation emphasizes therapeutic flexibility and versatility above all else. There is no unitary way to approach peoples' problems. To exude empathy and warmth to a client who prefers distant, formal people's businesslike interactions is likely to impede treatment. In some cases, instead of attempting to match the client to the therapy and therapist, the multimodal therapist may prescribe no therapy. For example, we were consulted by a middle-aged woman who had been seeing therapists on and off for years. She complained of vague anxiety, depression, tension, and general dissatisfaction with her life. After conducting a BASIC I.D. assessment we gave the following advice: "Use that money that you would spend on therapy to have someone clean your house once a week, to visit the beauty parlor once a week, and to have a tennis lesson once a week. You will still have some change left over to meet a friend for coffee or a snack. Be sure to engage in these activities on four different days each week, and after doing this for two months, please call and let us know if you are enjoying life more, if you feel less tense, less anxious and less depressed." This no-treatment prescription appeared to result in a distinct amelioration of her problems.

Many therapists express the need for flexibility. Thus, Haley (1976) stated, "A skillful therapist will approach each new person with the idea that a unique procedure might be necessary for this particular person and social situation" (p. 10). Nevertheless, he then goes on to say, "Today it is assumed that to begin therapy by interviewing one person is to begin with a handicap" (p. 10). Haley then stresses that "at every stage of the interview all family members should be involved in the action, and particularly during the greeting stage" (p. 15). We have seen several clients at the various Multimodal Therapy Institutes who were greatly put off by family therapists' insistence that significant others had to be present at initial meetings. After working with these individuals and gaining their trust and confidence, we were then able to get them to bring family members into the treatment (if and when indicated). The multimodal therapist will shift the focus of attention back and forth from the individual and his or her parts to the individual in his or her social setting.

Multimodal clinicians may draw on Haley's strategic therapy, Beck's cognitive therapy, Skinner's operant conditioning, or any other school without being locked into that system. Whereas Beck employs a Socratic method of asking questions, multimodal therapists are apt to be more didactic because a directive stance is thought to be more rapid and effective; it exemplifies the psychoeducational thrust of MMT. For a detailed discussion of the differences between rational-emotive therapy and multimodal therapy, see Lazarus (1988).

Were an observer able to watch a multimodal therapist in action, he or she might see this therapist acting rather cold and austere with one client on a particular day, but being warm and effusive with the same client (or with someone else) at a different time. Yet another client might be exposed to a question-and-answer session. The next one might be treated in a directive, demanding manner, whereas a different client would receive a very soft, warm, and accepting mode. Multimodal therapists constantly adjust to the client in terms of that mode of interaction most likely to achieve the desired aims of the therapy.

Zilbergeld summarized the multimodal position succinctly and accurately:

The aim of MMT is to come up with the best methods for each client rather than force all clients to fit the same therapy. . . . Three depressed clients might be given very different treatments depending on their therapists' assessments and the methods they prefer. . . . The only goal is helping clients make desired changes as rapidly as possible; everything else, even MMT, can be sacrificed. (1982, p. 85)

Given that the BASIC I.D. is presumed to represent the pillars of human temperament and personality, any system that glosses over one or more of these seven dimensions during assessment or therapy is bound to be incomplete. The reader should have no difficulty, when reading the other chapters in this book, in determining which systems deal *explicitly* with maladaptive behaviors + affective disorders + negative sensations + intrusive images + faulty cognitions + interpersonal difficulties + biological factors. It seems to us that most systems are based on unimodal, bimodal, or at best, trimodal conceptions of human functioning—stressing affect, behavior, and cognition.

HISTORY

PRECURSORS

Hippocrates (c. 400 B.C.) was aware that human personality is multilayered. He underscored the need for eliciting a complete life history of all patients and he recognized the importance of relationship factors in therapy. Galen, in the second century; the 19th-century Swiss psychiatrist, Paul Dubois; and certainly, W. H. Burnham's *The Normal Mind* (1924) foreshadowed many of the best tactics advocated by multimodal therapists. One may also note many similarities between present-day multimodal conceptions and early or more recent writings. Thus, in 1874, Franz Brentano's *Psychologiei vom Empirischen Standpunkte* underscored the importance of acts (including ideation), together with feeling states and "sensory judgments." There is considerable overlap between multimodal eclecticism and the theory of functionalism put forth by William James (1890).

The direct precursors date back to the 1950s, when Lazarus was a student at the University of the Witwatersrand in Johannesburg, South Africa, where the psychotherapeutic climate was predominantly Freudian and Rogerian. There were some followers of Melanie Klein, Harry Stack Sullivan, and Carl Jung. Two behavioristic faculty members—C. A. L. Warffemius and Alma Hannon—underscored the internal inconsistencies in psychoanalytic theory and emphasized the untestable nature of most Freudian postulates. The contributions of the late James Taylor of the University of Cape Town and visiting lectures by Joseph Wolpe, a general medical practitioner, who was applying "conditioning methods" to his patients, led to the formation of a coterie of "neobehaviorists." The members of this group embraced animal analogues, extrapolated from infrahuman to human levels of functioning, and focused heavily on classical conditioning paradigms.

Clinically, it became apparent that performance-based methods were usually better than purely verbal and cognitive approaches at effecting change. Whereas the psychotherapeutic establishment viewed behavior as the outward manifestation of more fundamental psychic processes, the neobehaviorists stressed that behavior per se is often clinically significant. It became clear that people could acquire insight or alter significant beliefs and still engage in self-destructive behavior. Yet, after behaving differently, it was evident that people were inclined to feel and think differently. Nevertheless, most professionals still viewed overt behavior as the tip of the iceberg, as symptomatic of an underlying disease, as symbolic of unconscious complexes. To legitimize behavioral intervention as an essential part of effective clinical practice, Lazarus (1958) introduced the terms *behavior therapy* and *behavior therapist* into the scientific and professional literature. The observation and quantification of significant actions became firmly established as a crucial starting point for effective clinical interventions. Coupled with the search for rel-

evant antecedents as well as maintaining variables, the focus on maladaptive behaviors and their remediation resulted in positive outcomes. But when follow-up studies revealed a disappointingly high relapse rate for people who were exposed to behavioral methods alone, it became necessary to employ techniques that were considered outside the boundaries of traditional behavior therapy.

BEGINNINGS

In 1965 Lazarus wrote a paper on the need to treat alcoholism from a multidimensional perspective. The main components involved:

1. Medical care to return the patient to physical well-being

2. Aversion therapy and anxiety-relief conditioning to mitigate the patient's uncontrolled drinking

3. A thorough assessment to identify "specific stimulus antecedents of anxiety" in the patient's environment

4. The use of additional techniques, including systematic desensitization, assertiveness training, behavior rehearsal, and hypnosis

5. The development of a cooperative relationship with the patient's spouse

This was foreshadowed by Lazarus' (1956) statement that "the emphasis in psychological rehabilitation must be on a *synthesis* which would embrace a diverse range of effective therapeutic techniques, as well as innumerable adjunctive measures, to form part of a wide and all-embracing re-educative programme."

These earlier publications reveal a definite penchant for broad-based, or comprehensive, psychotherapeutic procedures. By 1966 Lazarus had become suspicious of what he subsequently termed *narrow band behavior therapy* and published "Broad-Spectrum Behavior Therapy and the Treatment of Agoraphobia" (Lazarus, 1966). This article not only challenged narrow stimulus-response formulations, but also elaborated on the notion that dyadic transactions, or interpersonal systems, are an integral part of the genesis and maintenance of agoraphobia. The durability of narrow-band behavior therapy was seriously questioned, and in *Behavior Therapy and Beyond* (Lazarus, 1971), a "broad-spectrum" approach was advocated. The work of Salter (1949) and Ellis (1962) had an enduring impact on underscoring the crucial significance of emotional freedom and rational thinking as integral elements of the broad-spectrum therapy.

While A. A. Lazarus was gathering outcome and follow-up data, a number of questions arose repeatedly. When do behavior therapy techniques suffice? What sorts of people with what types of problems seem to require more than behavior therapy? When the clinician steps outside the bounds of behavior therapy, which effective nonbehavioral methods are best incorporated into what types of specific treatment programs for which particular problems, under what set of circumstances, and with which individuals (cf., Paul, 1967)? The careful scrutiny of case notes revealed that positive results were obtained by individuals with situational crises, circumscribed phobias, specific adjustment problems, transient or relatively mild sexual inadequacies, stress and tension-related difficulties, and some psychobiological disorders. Enduring benefits seemed to accrue to those who needed support over a trying period or reassurance about difficult life decisions and to those who lacked assertion and other social skills. Less impressive results were obtained with obsessive-compulsive individuals (despite the use of flooding and response prevention procedures), in cases with self-destructive tendencies, with addicts (be they addicted to drugs, food, or alcohol), and with highly anxious individuals who were prone to panic attacks.

The search for additional systematic interventions led to an awareness that cognitive restructuring often called for more than the correction of misconceptions or the straightforward alteration of negative self-talk. For example, when intrusive images conjure up a gloomy and troubled future, no amount of rational self-talk seems to alter the depressive affect—it is necessary to change the negative imagery itself. Thus, a wide range of specific imagery techniques was added to the clinical armamentarium—goal rehearsal, time projection, coping imagery, and many others (see Lazarus, 1978, 1982). Similarly, people with sensory complaints (e.g., tension headaches, muscle spasms, bruxism) required specific sensory techniques (e.g., deep muscle relaxation, biofeedback, muscle-toning exercises) in addition to behavioral change, cognitive shifts, affective expression, and attention to other aspects of functioning. It seemed important to separate affect from sensation as well as imagery from cognition. The importance of overt behavior was well documented in the writings and practices of behavior therapists, but they seemed to gloss over crucial interpersonal factors. A comprehensive appraisal of human interactions called for an examination of Behavior, Affect, Sensation, Imagery, Cognition, and Interpersonal relationships (the first letters of which form the acronym BASIC I.). To ignore the physical-medical aspects would obviously bypass the fundamental realities of the neurophysiological-biochemical elements that contribute to human personality and temperament. Hence the D. modality was added to the BASIC I. (It should be emphasized again that the D. stands for Drugs/Biology and represents far more than an awareness that some people require medication. It deals with all aspects of physical well-being—diet, exercise, sleep habits—and all aspects of psychophysiology, such as CNS pathology, endocrinopathy, metabolic disorders, and recreational and therapeutic drugs that impinge on psychological processes.)

Initially (Lazarus, 1973, 1976) the term *multimodal behavior therapy* was used to describe BASIC I.D. assessment and treatment, but because emphasis is on comprehensive coverage of *all* the modalities, it was misleading to single out one particular dimension (the approach could just as well be regarded as "multimodal cognitive therapy"). While multimodal therapy is essentially behavioral (i.e., it places great value on meticulous observation, careful testing of hypotheses, and continual self-correction on the basis of empirically derived data), it has evolved into an approach that employs additional (extrabehavioral) assessment and treatment procedures and strategies. Kwee, in a critical review of multimodal therapy, underscores its historical development from narrowband via broad-spectrum behavior therapy and concludes that "whether or not multimodal therapy can be classified as behavior therapy is less important than the method itself" (1981, p. 65).

CURRENT STATUS

Since the appearance of the first presentation of multimodal therapy as a distinctive orientation (Lazarus, 1973), a considerable number of clinicians have been using the BASIC I.D. framework in assessment and therapy. The first book on multimodal procedures had 11 contributors (Lazarus, 1976). One issue of the *Journal of Humanistic Education and Development* (1985, Volume 23) and two entire issues of *Elementary School Guidance and Counseling* (Volume 13, 1978, and Volume 16, 1982) were devoted to multimodal approaches. Nieves (1978a) has provided a multimodal self-assessment procedure in a manual dealing with self-control systems for minority college students, and in a related publication (Nieves, 1978b) has described a multimodal self-help program for college achievement. Detailed accounts of multimodal assessment and therapy have been presented in several recent textbooks (Dryden & Golden, 1986; Jacobson, 1987; Norcross, 1986). Numerous articles in professional journals have focused on the BASIC I.D. format. Books, articles, and chapters on multimodal therapy have been written or translated into several languages—German, Italian, Portuguese, Spanish, and Dutch. In Holland, Kwee (1978, 1979, 1981, 1984; Kwee & Roborgh, 1987) has been most prolific. There are, at present, five books on multimodal therapy (Brunell & Young, 1982; Keat, 1979; Lazarus, 1976, 1981, 1985). Multimodal therapy has proved effective beyond the confines of private practices and has been applied in such diverse environments as mental hospitals, residential facilities, day hospitals, and other complete care systems (e.g., Brunell & Young,

1982; O'Keefe & Castaldo, 1981a; Roberts et al., 1980).

Training in multimodal therapy has been a formal aspect of the clinical doctoral program at Rutgers University, New Jersey, since 1972, and a number of former students now teach multimodal therapy at various universities and centers throughout the United States. Several unpublished doctoral dissertations have focused on specific aspects of the approach. (e.g., Aigen, 1980; Ferrise, 1978; Lawler, 1985; Mann, 1985; Olson, 1979; Rosenblad, 1985). There are several additional doctoral dissertations in progress.

There are, as of 1988, eight multimodal therapy institutes in the United States.

PERSONALITY

THEORY OF PERSONALITY

We are products of the interplay among our genetic endowment, our physical environment, and our social learning history. American psychologists have tended to be environmentalists, but as geneticists have shed more light on the impact of DNA on various behaviors, the crucial relevance of our genetic heritage has grudgingly been brought back into the picture. It seems foolhardy to deny the biological substrate or the physiological basis of temperament and personality.

At the physiological level, the concept of *thresholds* is most compelling. People have different pain-tolerance thresholds, different frustration-tolerance thresholds, different stress-tolerance thresholds. The foregoing are largely innate, as are the wide range of capacities for withstanding anything from environmental pollution to the rigors of direct sunlight.

While psychological interventions can undoubtedly modify various thresholds, the genetic diathesis will usually prevail in the final analysis. Thus, a person with extremely low pain-tolerance thresholds may, through hypnosis and other psychological means, be brought to a level of withstanding pain at somewhat higher intensities, but a penchant for overreacting to pain stimuli will nevertheless remain omnipresent. Expressed somewhat differently, individuals are inclined to react to a variety of arousing stimuli with a distinctive pattern of autonomic nervous system activity. The person whose autonomic nervous system is *stable* will have a different "personality" from someone with *labile* autonomic reactions. The latter are anxiety-prone and are apt to become pathologically anxious under stressful conditions (Tyrer, 1982).

While the importance of relatively fixed thresholds over a wide variety of reactions is noted, the concept of traits is not held in high esteem. The specificity of behavior is emphasized, so that exposure to different people and different situations at various times evinces varied reactions, rather than fixed, predictable global dispositions. Nonetheless, people tend to favor some BASIC I.D. modalities more than others. Thus, we may speak of a "sensory reactor" or an "imagery reactor" or a "cognitive reactor." This does not imply that a person will always favor or react in a given modality, but over time, a tendency to value certain response patterns can be noted. Thus, when a person's most highly valued representational system is visual, he or she is inclined to respond to the world and organize it in terms of mental images. As Bandler and Grinder (1976) point out, visualizers tend to

1. *Behavior:* How active are you? How much of a doer are you? Do you like to keep busy?

   Rating: 6 5 4 3 2 1 0

2. *Affect:* How emotional are you? How deeply do you feel things? Are you inclined to impassioned or soul-stirring inner reactions?

   Rating: 6 5 4 3 2 1 0

3. *Sensation:* How much do you focus on the pleasures and pains derived from your senses? How tuned in are you to your bodily sensations—to sex, food, music, art?

   Rating: 6 5 4 3 2 1 0

4. *Imagery:* Do you have a vivid imagination? Do you engage in fantasy and daydreaming? Do you think in pictures?

   Rating: 6 5 4 3 2 1 0

5. *Cognition:* How much of a thinker are you? Do you like to analyze things, make plans, reason things through?

   Rating: 6 5 4 3 2 1 0

6. *Interpersonal:* How much a social being are you? How important are other people to you? Do you gravitate to people? Do you desire intimacy with others?

   Rating: 6 5 4 3 2 1 0

7. *Drugs/Biology:* Are you healthy and health conscious? Do you take good care of your body and physical health? Do you avoid overeating, ingestion of unnecessary drugs, excessive amounts of alcohol, and exposure to other substances that may be harmful?

   Rating: 6 5 4 3 2 1 0

"make pictures" out of what they hear. In terms of split-brain research (Galin, 1974; Kimura, 1979; Sperry, Gazzaniga & Bogen, 1969), imagery reactors are probably right-hemispheric dominant, whereas cognitive reactors are perhaps left-hemispheric dominant. Then there are sensory reactors who may be further subdivided into each of the five basic senses. Imagery reactors tend to be predominately *auditory* or *visual*. These proclivities appear to be evident within the first decade of life.

A person with a high frustration tolerance, but a low pain tolerance, someone who is extremely active and whose mental imagery is penetratingly clear, is bound to have a very different "personality" from someone who succumbs easily to frustration, who is at best moderately active, deeply analytical (cognitive), and incapable of forming more than fleeting visual images. *Structural profiles*[1] may readily be drawn up from the following instructions: "Here are seven rating scales that pertain to various tendencies that people have. Using a scale of 0 to 6 (6 is high—it characterizes you, or you rely on it greatly; 0 means that it does not describe you, or you rarely rely on it) please rate yourself in each of the seven areas."

These subjective ratings are easily

---

1. These differ from "modality profiles" that list problems and proposed treatments across the BASIC I.D.

depicted on a graph. (At the time of writing, a 35-item questionnaire is being factor analyzed with a view to developing a valid and reliable instrument for obtaining structural profiles.)

In couples' therapy, it can prove illuminating for partners to compare their structural profiles and also to anticipate what ratings their mates will give them in each modality (see Lazarus, 1981). Despite the arbitrary and subjective nature of these ratings, useful clinical information is often derived. When the therapist asks the client about the meaning and relevance of each rating, important insights are often gained. In addition to global self-ratings, structural profiles may be obtained for specific areas of functioning. For example, in the realm of *sexuality*, the degree of activity, emotionality, sensuality, imagery, or fantasy may be rated on separate scales, together with questions about how highly valued sexual participation is (cognition), its specific interpersonal importance, and the rater's overall biological adequacy.

Having described the importance of thresholds and specific BASIC I.D. tendencies in determining the tone and quality of personality functioning, let us now address the main factors responsible for the content of personality. How, when, where, and why are certain behaviors, outlooks, ideas, fantasies, and interpersonal patterns acquired?

It is well documented that *association* plays a key role in all learning processes. Events that occur simultaneously or in close succession are more likely to be connected. Two stimuli that occur frequently in close temporal proximity are likely to become associated. An association may be said

to exist when responses evoked by one stimulus are predictably and reliably similar to those provoked by another stimulus. Without becoming embroiled in the controversies and intricacies of learning theory in general, or classical and operant conditioning in particular, it may be emphasized that a good deal of human thoughts, feelings, and behaviors are due to conditioning. Many aversions appear to result from *classical conditioning*. A client stated: "After undergoing surgery a few years ago, I experienced postoperative nausea for two days, during which time the man in the next bed kept playing a cassette recording of Beethoven's *Moonlight Sonata*. Now every time I hear any part of that composition, I feel sick to my stomach!"

Operant conditioning is based on the observation that behavior is frequently a function of its consequences. Another client stated, "I now realize that my headaches were in large part due to the fact that the only time my husband showed me any real caring was when I was in pain." In therapy, one endeavors to overcome classically conditioned problems by the deliberate introduction of new associations (as in desensitization techniques that help the client replace anxiety with coping images and feelings of serenity. Difficulties engendered by operant conditioning call for a reorganization of consequential behaviors.

Besides association or conditioning, how else do we acquire the totality of habits that make up our personalities? If we had to rely solely on conditioning for all our learned responses, errors made during the acquisition phase of various skills would prove hazardous. It would probably prove fatal to rely on trial and error or successive approximation methods when learning to swim or to drive a car. In mastering these tasks and many complex occupational and social requirements, success often depends on imitation, observational learning, and identification, which Bandura (1969, 1977) subsumes under *modeling and vicarious processes*. Human personality (if not survival) is strongly determined by our ability to acquire new responses by watching someone else performing an activity and then doing it ourselves. We tend to learn what to do and what not to do by observing positive and negative consequences experienced by others.

To Reiterate

Our personalities stem from the interplay among our genetic endowment, our physical environment, and our social learning history. The basic social learning triad—classical (respondent) conditioning, operant (instrumental) conditioning, and modeling and vicarious processes—does not account for the fact that people are capable of overriding the best-laid plans of contiguity, reinforcements, and example by their idiosyncratic perceptions. People do not respond to some *real* environment but rather to their *perceived* environment. This includes the personalistic use of language, semantics, expectancies, encoding and selective attention, problem-solving competencies, goals, and performance standards and the impact of numerous values, attitudes, and beliefs. As Bandura's (1978) principle of reciprocal determinism underscores, people do not react automatically to external stimuli. Their *thoughts* about those stimuli will determine which stimuli are noticed, how they are noticed, how much

they are valued, and how long they are remembered.

This brief outline of the structure and content of personality from the multimodal perspective has not addressed the specific ways in which mental and emotional disorders arise. The role of genetics in the schizophrenic disorders and major affective disorders is more than suggestive. The median risk of developing schizophrenia where both parents are schizophrenic is about 40 percent (Rosenthal, 1974). In bipolar depressive disorders, a review of six twin studies indicated a concordance rate of 74 percent for monozygotic twins, and a 19 percent rate for dizygotic twins, even when the monozygotic twins were reared apart (Mendels, 1974). These are only the more striking and better documented examples of the importance of biological determinants in mental and emotional disorders, but the role of *learning* may be no less compelling.

As we have emphasized, the main learning factors are our conditioned associations (respondent and operant responses) and the models with whom we identified and whom we imitated —deliberately or inadvertently. During the course of exposure to these inputs, we may have acquired conflicting information, faulty cognitions, and a variety of inhibitions and needless defenses.

Emotional problems and disorders also arise from inadequate or insufficient (as opposed to faulty) learning. Here the problems do *not* arise from conflicts, traumatic events, impositions from significant others, or false ideas. Rather, gaps in people's repertoires—they were never given necessary information and essential coping processes—render them ill-equipped to deal with societal demands.

The multimodal view emphasizes that most clients suffer from conflicts, the aftermaths of unfortunate experiences, *and* various deficits in their social and personal repertoires. Hence unimodal remedies are bound to leave significant areas untouched.

VARIETY OF CONCEPTS

What concepts are necessary for the full understanding of human personality? Can we do without instincts, racial unconscious, oedipal desires, archetypes, organ inferiority, psychic energy, the soul, and scores of other notions that are employed to account for the intricacies of human interaction? Psychotherapists could communicate their ideas with greater precision if they used everyday language instead of esoteric jargon. It could be argued that certain technical terms are useful for rapid and shorthand communication, but couldn't we keep these to the bare minimum? Moreover, if we heed Occam's razor (which holds that explanatory principles should not be needlessly multiplied), we can avoid much of the psychobabble that has arisen in psychotherapy (Rosen, 1977).

In accounting for the structure and content of human personality, the previous section underscored the role of the biological substrate and the impact of learning (classical and operant conditioning, modeling, vicarious processes, and private events—thoughts, feelings, images, and sensations). Given that much of our learning is neither conscious nor deliberate (Shevrin & Dickman, 1980), is it not essential to include the unconscious in our compendium of basic concepts? Unfortunately, the unconscious has become a reified entity, and we prefer the term *nonconscious processes*. This merely acknowledges (1) that people have different degrees and levels of self-awareness, and (2) that despite a lack of awareness or conscious comprehension, unrecognized (subliminal) stimuli can nevertheless influence conscious thoughts, feelings, and behaviors. This completely bypasses the psychoanalytic notions of the unconscious, with its topographical boundaries, putative complexes, and intrapsychic functions, all tied into the intricate mosaic of elaborate inferences about state, stage, and trait theories of personality development.

Similarly, psychodynamic theory views the defense mechanisms as perceptual, attitudinal, or attentional shifts that aid the ego in neutralizing overbearing id impulses. In the multimodal orientation these convoluted theories are not necessary to account for the fact that people are capable of truncating their awareness, beguiling themselves, mislabeling their feelings, and losing touch with themselves (and others) in various ways. We are apt to defend against or avoid pain, discomfort, or negative emotions such as anxiety, depression, guilt, and shame. The term *defensive reactions* avoids the surplus meanings that psychodynamic theory attaches to the mechanisms of defense. Empirically, it is clear that one may overintellectualize and rationalize. While attempting to reduce dissonance, we may deny the obvious or falsely attribute our own feelings to others (projection). We can readily displace our aggressions onto other people, animals, or things.

The addition of *nonconscious processes* and *defensive reactions* to our assemblage of basic concepts should not be misconstrued as falling into the quagmire of Freudian constructs. But it is not possible to have a comprehensive understanding of human personality without addressing the fact that people are capable of disowning, denying, displacing, and projecting numerous thoughts, feelings, wishes, and impulses. Furthermore, it has been demonstrated time and again that during altered states of consciousness one may have access to memories and skills that are not amenable to conscious recall. Nevertheless, when acknowledging and accounting for these important reactions, it is not necessary to resort to psychoanalytic hypotheses. It cannot be overstated that multimodal therapy is not a conglomeration of psychoanalysis, behavior therapy, and many other systems. While effective techniques may be drawn from many available sources, one need not subscribe to any of their underlying theories. The differences between technical eclecticism and theoretical eclecticism have already been stated.

As we enter the interpersonal modality and examine various dyadic and more complex interactions, communication breaks down (literally and figuratively) unless we add another explanatory concept. People not only communicate, they also *metacommunicate* (i.e., communicate about their communications). The use of *paradox* in therapy draws its impetus from the process of metacommunication (e.g., Fay, 1978; Frankl, 1960, 1978; Haley, 1973; Rabkin, 1977; Watzlawick, Weakland & Fisch, 1974; Weeks & L'Abate, 1982; Zeig, 1982). Effective communication requires one to step back, as it were, and examine the content and process of patterns of communication in ongoing relationships.

PSYCHOTHERAPY

THEORY OF PSYCHOTHERAPY

A fundamental premise of the multimodal approach is that clients are usually troubled by a multitude of specific problems that should be dealt with by a multitude of specific treatments. Multimodal therapy is very different from those systems that cluster presenting problems into ill-defined constructs and then direct one or two treatment procedures at these constructs. The basic assumption of the multimodal approach is that durability of results is a function of the amount of effort expended by client and therapist across the seven dimensions of personality (BASIC I.D.). The more adaptive and coping responses clients learn in therapy, the less likely they are to relapse afterward. Lasting change at the very least seems to depend upon combinations of techniques, strategies, and modalities. This outlook vitiates the search for a panacea, or a single therapeutic modality.

Multimodal therapy (MMT) overlaps cognitive behavior therapy (CBT) and rational-emotive therapy (RET) in many important respects. Some of the major points MMT, CBT, and RET have in common are:

1. Most problems are presumed to arise from deficient or faulty social learning processes.

2. The therapist-client relationship is more that of a trainer and trainee than that of a doctor treating a sick patient.

3. Transfer of learning (generalization) from therapy to the client's everyday environment is not considered automatic but is deliberately fostered by means of homework and other *in vivo* assignments.

4. Labels, fixed diagnostic categories, traits, and global descriptions are avoided in favor of behavioral and operational definitions.

There are also important differences between MMT and other cognitive and behavioral orientations. The personalistic emphasis of MMT goes beyond the lip service often paid to tailoring treatment procedures to different problems in different people. The *goodness of fit* in terms of clients expectancies, therapist-client compatibility, matching, and the selection of techniques is examined in great detail by multimodal therapists. Moreover, the scope of assessment and specific information obtained when examining sensory, imagery, cognitive, and interpersonal factors, and their interactive effects, goes beyond the confines of the usual stimulus and functional analyses conducted by behavior therapists. As will be *italicized* in subsequent sections of this chapter, significant *procedural* differences set MMT apart from CBT and RET.

Another fundamental assumption is that without new experiences there can be no change. In multimodal therapy clients are inspired and encouraged to do different things and to do things differently. Therapeutic change usually follows methods that are *performance based*; purely cognitive or verbal methods are often less effective. Yet before certain clients can take effective action, they require help in eliminating barriers in their interpersonal domain, in their sensory reactions, mental images, and cognitive processing. Indeed, from the multimodal perspective, some of the most important *insights* are gained when clients develop an awareness and under-

standing of content areas and interactive relationships within their BASIC I.D. patterns. As one client put it:

I never realized what an impact my mother and her older sister had on my life—how I let them shape my attitudes, how I treated my husband and children the way they treated my father, my uncle, my cousins, and me. Now I see that I even copied *their* aches and pains. . . . When I get a mental image I see their faces and hear their words. . . . Now I'm rewriting my BASIC I.D. the way *I* want to be. I'm tuning into *my* thoughts, *my* feelings, *my* images. . . . I've also learned to change my CISB pattern. If I catch myself thinking the way they think, I crowd out their ideas with my ideas, and then I picture myself coping, I see myself succeeding. This has ended my tensions, my headaches, and all the neurotic cop-outs.

MMT strongly differs with those who believe that as long as the client-therapist relationship is good, techniques are of little concern. Certainly, it is necessary for the therapist to be respected by clients and to establish sufficient trust for them to confide personal and emotionally significant material. Without the attainment of rapport, there will be little inclination for people to disclose distressing, embarrassing, and anxiety-provoking information. Woody stressed that an effective therapist "must be more than a 'nice guy' who can exude prescribed interpersonal conditions—he must have an armamentarium of scientifically derived skills and techniques to supplement his effective interpersonal relations" (1971, p. 8). In keeping with the pluralistic philosophy of the multimodal tradition, we see the client-therapist relationship on a continuum extending from a rather formal, businesslike investment at the one end to a very close-knit, dependent bonding at the other. In multimodal therapy, the client-therapist relationship is examined or discussed only when there is reason to suspect that it is impeding therapeutic progress. When therapy is proceeding well, why waste time analyzing the interpersonal feelings between the client and therapist? (See Lazarus, 1981.)

Multimodal therapy is predicated on the assumption that the more disturbed the client is, the greater the specific excesses and deficits will be throughout the BASIC I.D. The model employed may be viewed as based on actualization and self-determination rather than on pathology. Everyone can benefit from a change in behavior that eliminates unwanted or surplus reactions while increasing the frequency, intensity, and duration of creative, fulfilling responses. Likewise, the control or elimination of unpleasant emotions and the augmentation of positive feelings are worthy goals. In the sensory modality, it is eminently worthwhile to extinguish negative sensations, coupled with the benefits of deriving more pleasure and meaning from each of our five basic senses. Our mental imagery—those mental pictures that ultimately coalesce in a series of self-images—has a direct impact on the tone and cadence of our actions and feelings. Thus, we would do well to focus heavily on various coping images and try to keep them overridingly positive. Faulty assumptions, misconceptions, and irrational cognitions clearly undermine effective living. They are best replaced with as many reality-oriented, factual, and rational assumptions as can be mustered. Everyone would do well to cultivate the specific skills and prosocial interactions that produce good, close, and rewarding interpersonal relationships.

PROCESS OF PSYCHOTHERAPY

Multimodal therapy places primary emphasis on the uniqueness of each and every person. Hence, there is no typical treatment format. When tuning into the expectancies and demand characteristics of one client, the therapist may adopt a passive-reflective stance. At other times, or with someone else, the same therapist may be extremely active, directive, and confrontative. Bearing in mind that fundamental question—who or what is best for this individual—the first issue is whether or not the therapist will work with the client or refer him or her to someone else. If clients display grossly bizarre or inappropriate behaviors, delusions, thought disorders, and other signs of "psychosis," nonmedical therapists refer them to a psychiatrist or a psychiatric facility. Similarly, evidence of strong homicidal or suicidal tendencies often requires medical and custodial intervention.

In general, the initial interview focuses on presenting complaints and their main precipitants. Antecedent events are carefully assessed, as are those factors that appear to be maintaining the client's maladaptive behaviors. One endeavors to ascertain what the client wishes to derive from therapy. It is also useful to elucidate the client's strengths and positive attributes. Overriding each of these specific details is the question of adequate client-therapist compatibility. The therapist also tries to determine whether there are any clear indications or contraindications for the adoption of particular therapeutic styles (e.g., directive or nondirective postures).

The initial meeting may be with an individual, a couple, or a family. To put the client(s) at ease, a therapist may begin the first session with small talk, noting formal details, such as name, address, phone numbers, marital status, and occupation. This gives the client an opportunity to adjust to the environment of the consulting room, to experience a verbal interchange, and to be primed for the detailed inquiry that soon follows. After taking down formal details, the therapist may simply say, "What seems to be troubling you?" As various complaints are mentioned, the therapist pays particular attention to which modality of the BASIC I.D. they apply to, and two additional interlocking factors are carefully noted: (1) What has led to the current situation? and (2) Who or what is maintaining it?

In multimodal therapy, it is not uncommon for specific interventions to be made during the initial interview. One does not wait until the full assessment procedures are completed before commencing to alleviate distress, or to correct misconceptions, or to redefine the presenting complaint. Here is an example from the initial interview with a 38-year-old man:

Therapist: What seems to be troubling you?

Client: Well, according to my wife, I'm a premature ejaculator.

Therapist: Exactly what does that mean?

Client: I was married before for 10 years. I got married because she was pregnant, but we really never should have gotten together because we just were too different and never got along. I met my present wife about a year ago, and we've been married almost three months. She's a psychiatric social worker.

Therapist: Just how rapidly do you ejaculate? Do you last 2 seconds, 30 seconds, 60 seconds?

Client: Well, I can go for about, um, 10 vigorous thrusts. If I go slower, I can last longer. I've tried adding numbers in my

head, pinching my thigh, thinking of work, wearing two condoms . . .

Therapist: Do these things help?

Client: To some extent, but it sure takes most of the pleasure away.

Therapist: Have you ever ejaculated before entering your wife, or immediately after penetration?

Client: No. Like I said, if I do it vigorously, I come on the stroke of 10. [Laughs.]

Therapist: At which point you turn into a pumpkin.

Client: I become a jerk. My wife says I need help, so here I am!

Therapist: Is your pattern the same with other women? For example, were you the same with your first wife?

Client: Pretty much, but it never seemed to bother her or any of the others. If I wait 15 or 20 minutes and do it a second time, I can last almost indefinitely.

Therapist: Even with vigorous movements?

Client: That's right. If I feel myself getting too excited, I just stop for a few moments and then I can keep going.

Therapist: Well, from what you've told me, you are not a "premature ejaculator." You come fairly rapidly the first time, but after a rest pause you have excellent control. Do you usually want intercourse a second time, or after the first orgasm are you fully satisfied and maybe drop off to sleep?

Client: Let's put it this way. If the woman remains interested, I'm always willing and ready to give it a second go round. But I'm really happy to hear you say that I'm not a sexual cripple.

Therapist: Have you ever masturbated before having sex with your wife so that you will last longer right from the start of intercourse?

Client: Yes, but my wife says I shouldn't have to resort to that.

Therapist: If I may put it bluntly, I think your wife has several false ideas and you are a victim of her irrational shoulds.

Client: Her what?

Therapist: Shoulds. That you should do this and shouldn't do that. That this is a must. That everything is black or white.

Client: That's her alright! You've hit the nail on the head.

Therapist: I have the feeling that you take all this crap, that you allow yourself to be la-

beled, put down, and led by the nose. And my guess is that you endured a different type of abuse from your first wife until you reached a breaking point and got a divorce.

Client: I've always put women on a pedestal.

Therapist: What does that imply? That you treat women as your superiors, that you look up to them, that you do not see men and women as equal but different?

Client: [±30 second silence.] I can't really say for sure. I know this sounds awfully Freudian, but my mother has always been sort of scary. [He appears to be deep in thought.]

Therapist: Well, if I can sum up my impressions, it seems to me that your problem is not premature ejaculation but lack of assertiveness, plus some subtle attitudes and values that are tied into this whole perception. What do you think?

Client: I think you're right. I know you're right. A long time ago one of my buddies—he's a psychologist with Bell Labs—said I seem to be attracted to castrating bitches. You seem to be saying the same thing.

Therapist: Well, I wouldn't put it that way. Frankly, my guess is that you bring out the worst in women by the way you react to them. At any rate, I feel you and I have a few things to sort out, and maybe, a bit later, you and your wife might meet with me so that we can perhaps establish better communication and upgrade your marriage.

[The course of treatment was neither simple nor straightforward. As the multimodal assessment continued, several additional inadequacies were brought to light that called for extensive attention to his behavioral, cognitive, imagery, and interpersonal domains. The wife, a woman apparently riddled with many problems of her own, elected to see a female therapist and refused marital therapy. After about 15 months the couple met with the therapist for an evaluation session, and both claimed that individually and maritally, things were decidedly better.]

At the end of the initial interview, the usual adult outpatient is given a Multimodal Life History Questionnaire, a 12-page printed booklet that asks a myriad of crucial questions about antecedent events, ongoing problems, and maintaining factors (Lazarus, 1981). The answers are divided into BASIC I.D. categories. The client is asked to bring the completed questionnaire to the second session. (Obviously, young children and many mental hospital patients are incapable of filling out questionnaires. Keat [1979] has addressed the multimodal treatment of children, and Brunell and Young [1982] have provided a multimodal handbook for mental hospitals.)

By the start of the third session, the therapist usually has gleaned sufficient information from the first two meetings and the life history questionnaire to construct a preliminary modality profile (i.e., a list of specific problems in each area of the client's BASIC I.D.). Typically, the client is invited to scrutinize the profile and to comment upon or modify specific items. Client and therapist then discuss the particular strategies and techniques that may be applied, and a general treatment plan is instituted.

A 33-year-old client with the presenting complaint of "depression" agreed that the following modality profile summed up her main problems:

Behavior:	Withdrawal, avoidance, inactivity
Affect:	Depression, guilt, self-recrimination
Sensation:	Heavy, sluggish, enervated
Imagery:	Death images, visions of family rejection

Cognition: Monologue about past failures, self-statements about personal worthlessness

Interpersonal: Unassertive, passive

Drugs/Biologicals: After being on a tricyclic antidepressant for three months, the medication was changed to an MAO inhibitor about four weeks ago.

The interview with the client went as follows:

Therapist: Is there anything else we should add to the list?

Client: I don't know. The medicine helps me sleep better and I'm eating more, but I still don't *feel* any better.

Therapist: Well three things stand out for me. First, regardless of how you feel, we've got to get you to *do* more things, to get out, to stop hiding from the world.

Client: [Shakes her head negatively.]

Therapist: It's tough but necessary. The two other things are your negative images and all that nonsense you tell yourself about being utterly worthless. That needs to be changed.

Client: [On the verge of tears.] My brother was right. He said to me, "You're nothing!" God how that hurt. I always heard that from my father. Us girls were nothing. But I looked up to my brother, and coming from him . . . [Cries.]

Therapist: It seems that you desperately want approval from your father, your brother, perhaps all the men in the world before you will feel adequate. Can you close your eyes and picture saying to your father and to your brother, "I don't need your approval!"

Client: I wish I could say that and mean it.

Therapist: Shall we try some role-playing? I'll be your brother. "You're nothing! You are just a complete zero!" Now will you challenge that?

[Roleplaying, with considerable role reversal, in which the therapist modeled assertive answers, ensued for about 20 minutes.]

Client: I can say the right words but the wrong feelings are still there.

Therapist: As long as you start with the right words and use them in the right places and to the relevant people, the feelings will soon start to change.

* * * * *

Client: I just have these awful ideas about death. I dream about being at funerals, or getting lost in a cemetery. . . . And my mind often goes back to my cousin's death, and how my brother cried for him, all these horrible thoughts.

Therapist: Let's deal with that, but first, I'd like to review the treatment plan. First, I want to be sure that you will increase your activity level, go out and do things. I want you to keep notes of the things you do, of the activities you wanted to avoid but did not avoid. Second, I want to be sure that you will express your feelings and not be passive, especially with your husband and your brother. No matter how miserable you feel, can you promise me that you will do these two things this week?

Client: I'll try.

Therapist: Promise me you'll do it.

Client: [Cries.]

Therapist: If I'm coming on too strong, tell me to back off.

Client: I realize it's for my own good.

Therapist: So can I count on you?

Client: I'll do my best.

Therapist: Good. Now let's delve into those death images. Why don't we start with your dream about being lost in the cemetery? Close your eyes. Settle back and relax. You're in your dream, lost in the cemetery. Tell me what happens.

Client: [±30-second pause.] I feel awfully afraid. The ground is soggy as if it just rained. I see the tombstones but I can't make out the names. . . . There's someone else there. [Pause.] I'm frightened. [Pause.] I've seen him before, but his features are indistinct, he's too far from me to make out who it is.

Therapist: You have binoculars or a zoom lens. Look through the eyepiece. Who is it?

Client: It's . . . no it's not. It looked like my cousin for a moment. He went away.

Therapist: Let's bring your cousin into the dream so that he can talk to you. Can you bring him into the picture?

Client: [Pause.] Peculiar! He's dressed like a funeral director in a black suit.

[Over several sessions, guided imagery was used to conjure up encounters with several of her deceased relatives—her cousin, maternal grandmother, and several paternal aunts and uncles. A theme emerged. She had been close to all of her deceased relatives for the first 12 to 20 years of her life and had what Gestalt therapists call unfinished business with each of them. Imaginary dialogues with every one in turn, with the therapist encouraging her to assume an assertive position throughout, seemed to serve an important function. The problems in the other BASIC I.D. areas received equal attention. She was constantly encouraged to increase her activity level and to express her feelings, and her cognitive errors were corrected by emphasizing their irrational underpinnings.]

When treatment impasses arise, it is often helpful to introduce a *second-order BASIC I.D.* assessment. This consists of subjecting a problematic item on the initial modality profile to more detailed inquiry in terms of behavior, affect, sensation, imagery, cognition, interpersonal factors, and drugs or biological considerations. For example, the aforementioned woman remained extremely resistant to implementing assertive behaviors. While she acknowledged feeling less depressed and stated that her images and cognitions were more positive and rational, she remained interpersonally passive and unassertive. When asked for her BASIC I.D. associations to the concept of assertiveness, the following emerged:

Behavior:	Attacking
Affect:	Angry
Sensation:	Tension
Imagery:	Bombs bursting
Cognition:	Get even
Interpersonal:	Hurting
Drugs/ Biologicals:	High blood pressure

She had been told, and paid lip serv-ice to understanding, the essential differences between assertion and aggression. Nevertheless, the second-order BASIC I.D. indicated that in her mind, an assertive response was tantamount to a vicious attack. This alerted the therapist to model, explain, rehearse, and define assertive behaviors in much greater detail.

Again, it must be understood that what has been outlined is by no means a "typical" multimodal treatment of depression. With a different depressed individual, the treatment, while addressing all BASIC I.D. problem areas, might be quite dissimilar (Fay & Lazarus, 1981).

MECHANISMS OF PSYCHOTHERAPY

Consonant with the pluralistic outlook of the multimodal tradition, different mechanisms are responsible for positive change in different people. Thus, for some, the mere nonjudgmental acceptance of a highly respected outsider is sufficient to offset faulty attitudes and behaviors. For others, the main mechanism is largely didactic—they have learned more effective ways of processing information, of responding to significant others, of coping with the exigencies of life. The primary factors responsible for therapeutic change may be outlined by reference to the BASIC I.D.

Some of the main mechanisms and ingredients of psychotherapeutic change and the modalities to which they apply are:

Behavior

Extinction (e.g., when applying methods such as massed practice, response prevention, and flooding). *Counterconditioning* (e.g., when using incompatible response techniques such as graded exposure and desensitization). *Positive reinforcement, negative reinforcement, and punishment* (e.g., when using operant procedures such as token economies, contingent praise, time-out, and aversion therapy).

Affect

Abreaction (e.g., when reliving and recounting painful emotions in the presence of a supportive, trusted ally). *Owning and accepting feelings* (e.g., when therapy permits the client to acknowledge affect-laden materials that were nonconscious).

Sensation

Tension release (e.g., through biofeedback, relaxation, or physical exercise). *Sensory pleasuring* (e.g., the acquisition of positive tactile sensations during sexual retraining).

Imagery

Changes in self-image (e.g., when success in any modality is sustained). *Coping images* (e.g., when able to picture self-control or self-achievement in situations where these images had been impossible to evoke).

Cognition

Cognitive restructuring (e.g., changes in dichotomous reasoning, self-downing, overgeneralization, categorical imperatives, non sequiturs, and excessive desires for approval). *Awareness* (e.g., awareness of antecedents and their relation to ongoing behaviors, appreciation of how specific firing orders culminate in various affective reactions).

Interpersonal

Modeling (e.g., the therapist as role model through selective self-disclosure and deliberate modeling as during role-reversal exercises). *Dispersing unhealthy collusions* (e.g., when treating a family and changing counterproductive alliances). *Paradoxical maneuvers* (e.g., when countering double-binding responses with metacommunications). *Nonjudgmental acceptance* (e.g., when clients realize that in therapy they are offered desiderata not usually available in most social relationships).

Drugs/Biologicals

In addition to medical examinations and interventions when warranted, the implementation of better exercise and nutrition, and substance-abuse cessation, the use of psychotropic medication is sometimes essential—particularly in the treatment of schizophrenia, affective disorders, and some anxiety states.

In the broadest terms, psychological problems may be due to *learning* and/or *lesions*. The latter falls into the D modality; learning is exemplified by the BASIC I. Full understanding of the exact mechanisms of change in any modality is yet to be achieved. Indeed, even in the D modality, while new knowledge about receptor sites, neurotransmitters, biological markers, and other biochemical parameters have emerged, much remains unknown. Perusal of the psychotropic drugs listed in the *Physicians' Desk Reference* reveals that most of the descriptions under "Clinical Pharmacology" state that "The mechanism of action of . . . is not definitely known." In the psychological sphere, the exact and precise "mechanisms of action" are even less well elucidated.

APPLICATIONS

PROBLEMS

The multimodal orientation has implications for both prevention and treatment. Its purview extends from individuals, couples, families, and groups to broader community and organizational settings. Thus, some multimodal therapists have special expertise in dealing with children (Keat, 1979), applying multimodal methods in classroom settings (Gerler, 1979), in a child care agency (O'Keefe & Castaldo, 1980), in multimodal parent training (Judah, 1978), in mental retardation (Pearl & Guarnaccia, 1976), in management (O'Keefe & Castaldo, 1981), and in institutional settings (Roberts, Jackson & Phelps, 1980). Brunell and Young's (1982) edited volume *Multimodal Handbook for a Mental Hospital* shows the versatility of the multimodal framework in a variety of inpatient problem areas. The multimodal framework was even shown to have relevance when dealing with a community disaster (Sank, 1979), and when confronted by a nondisclosing black client (Ridley, 1984). Ponterotto & Zander (1984) have applied the multimodal approach to counselor supervision, Greenburg (1982) found multimodal methods especially helpful in counselor education, Edwards and Kleine (1986) used it as a model for working with gifted adolescents, and Ponterotto found it "a culturally sensitive and relevant therapeutic framework for nonminority and minority counselors working with clients of Mexican-American heritage" (1987, p. 308). Eimer (1988) described the application of multimodal assessment and therapy to the chronic pain patient.

Two distinct questions may be posed regarding the types of individuals and the variety of problems that may be dealt with multimodally: (1) Who can be helped by a multimodal practitioner? and (2) Who can be helped by multimodal therapy?

Multimodal therapists are drawn from the full range of health service providers. Psychiatrists, psychologists, social workers, psychiatric nurses, pastoral counselors, and other mental health workers each have members within their disciplines who are well versed in, and employ, multimodal methods. The therapist's professional background and personal qualities will equip him or her with special skills, talents, and knowledge to handle certain problems and particular individuals, and to function in specific settings. Thus, some multimodal therapists are highly skilled at using biofeedback, others have a strong background in behavioral medicine, and there are those who are especially gifted and clinically adept with substance-abuse disorders, sexual offenders, school-related problems, and so forth. A multimodal psychiatrist, when prescribing medication to control psychotic behaviors (addressing the D modality), is not practicing multimodal therapy. However, when the psychotic symptoms are in remission, the multimodal psychiatrist will systematically deal with the other six modalities (the BASIC I.). When specific clients require services that lie outside the realm of the given multimodal therapist's compass of skills, referral to an individual or agency better equipped to deal with the situation is a standard procedure. Surely this is true for every responsible clinician? Unfortunately not. While nearly everyone agrees, in principle, that it is undesirable to fit the client into one's system, and widespread lip service is paid to avoiding procrustean maneuvers by carefully tailoring treatment to the needs of the consumer, in practice the client is apt to receive what the therapist employs, whether or not this is what he or she needs (see Lazarus, 1981, pp. 1–5).

Multimodal practitioners constantly inquire *who or what is best for this individual (or couple, or family, or group)*. Referral to appropriate personnel is considered a most important technique. Thus, if the therapist is not equipped herself or himself to manage the client's problems, the multimodal practitioner, if true to the canons of this tradition, will not continue seeing the client (even if he or she is attractive, pleasant, and affluent). Nor is it sufficient for a multimodal therapist simply to inform the client that his or her clinical problems call for skills that the therapist does not possess—it is the clinician's duty to try to effect a judicious referral.

All therapists encounter clients who are so marginally adjusted that they require long-term supportive therapy —the development of a stable relationship with a caring person. A well-trained multimodal therapist is oriented and equipped to do more than offer concern and empathy. Within the context of a supportive therapeutic relationship, specific attention to critical BASIC I.D. excesses and deficits can transform a holding pattern into a framework where constructive learning takes place. Thus, when the mesh and artistry between client and therapist were such that thorough coverage of the BASIC I.D. was accomplished, successful outcomes were obtained even with floridly psychotic individuals, entrenched substance abusers, and vegetatively depressed persons who had failed to respond to years of chemotherapy and other psychiatric interventions. Nevertheless, it is obviously easier to achieve noteworthy gains with clients whose excesses and deficits across the BASIC I.D. are not especially rigid, encrusted, or pervasive.

Discussions with colleagues at the various Multimodal Therapy Institutes reveal consistent positive outcomes and follow-ups with marriage and family problems, sexual difficulties, childhood disorders, inadequate social skills, smoking, fears and phobias, anxiety states, obesity, psychosomatic complaints, and depression. Some of our colleagues also report impressive results with certain obsessive-compulsive problems.

EVALUATION

In multimodal therapy, the evaluation of treatment outcomes is usually straightforward. Since modality profiles are routinely constructed (i.e., lists of specific excesses and deficits throughout the client's BASIC I.D.), ongoing treatment evaluations are an integral part of the client-therapist interaction. Thus, instead of assuming that some ill-defined entity such as "emotional maturity" has evolved, the multimodal therapist specifies particular gains and achievements in each modality:

Behavior:	Less withdrawn; less compulsive; more outspoken
Affect:	More warm, less hostile; less depressed
Sensation:	Enjoys more pleasures; less tense, more relaxed
Imagery:	Fewer nightmares; better self-image
Cognition:	Less self-downing; more positive self-statements
Interpersonal:	Goes out on dates; expresses wishes and desires
Drugs/ Biologicals:	Stopped smoking; sleeps well; exercises regularly

Structural profiles, before and after multimodal therapy, tend to reflect only minor changes in most instances; that is, doers are still doers and thinkers are still thinkers. People who are active, tuned into sensory pleasures, imaginative, and social before therapy will usually show the same tendencies after therapy. If a high score on the interpersonal scale reflected an overly dependent penchant, this may decrease a few points after therapy. Conversely, if a low score on the interpersonal scale before treatment was a function of shyness and withdrawal, the posttherapeutic score will usually show an increase of several points. Depressed people are inclined to show the greatest pre- and posttreatment differences. While depressed, they usually show a low activity level, few or no feelings apart from sadness, a conspicuous absence of sensory pleasures, and decreased social participation. They may rate themselves fairly high on imagery and cognition because of visions of doom, loneliness, illness, and failure, and because of high self-blame and pervasive ideas of self-worthlessness (Fay & Lazarus, 1981). When therapy is successful, structural profiles do tend to depict significant changes in terms of greater activity, positive affect, sensory joys, and social participation.

In evaluating marital therapy, the use of a 12-term marital satisfaction questionnaire (Lazarus, 1981) has been useful. The questionnaire pinpoints the most important areas of personal and familial distress, and quantitative changes in this pencil-and-paper test usually reflect significant improvements in marital happiness.

A three-year follow-up evaluation of 20 complex cases who had completed a course of multimodal therapy (e.g., people suffering from obsessive-compulsive rituals, extreme agoraphobia, pervasive anxiety and panic, depression, alcohol addiction, or enmeshed family and marital problems) showed that 14 maintained their gains or had made additional progress without further therapy; 2 felt the need for medication from time to time, for which they had consulted their family physicians (1 person had suffered from extreme panic attacks; the other was prone to bouts of recurring depression); 1 man considered himself "pretty good," although his wife revealed that he was still "too compulsive"; and 3 other cases (an anorexic woman and 2 patients with chronic alcohol abuse) had failed to maintain their initial gains. A 70 percent successful follow-up with a sample of complex and difficult cases, some of whom were seemingly intractable, is most encouraging. Over the past seven years we have consistently found that treatment goals were achieved with more than 75 percent of the people who consulted us. Follow-ups reveal a relapse rate of less than 5 percent.

Kwee (1984) conducted a controlled outcome study using multimodal therapy with 44 severe obsessive-compulsive patients and 40 extremely phobic individuals in a general psychiatric hospital. Of these patients, 90 percent had previously undergone psychiatric treatment without success and 70 percent had suffered from their disorders for more than 4 years. Various process measures were administered at intake, on admission, after 12 weeks, at discharge, and at follow-up 9 months later. The follow-up data showed that 64 percent of the obsessive-compulsive individuals remained significantly improved.

Among the phobic individuals, 55 percent had maintained or had proceeded beyond their treatment gains.

TREATMENT

The mean duration of a complete course of multimodal therapy is approximately 50 hours (i.e., about a year of therapy at weekly intervals). Acutely disturbed people or those with special problems (e.g., work or family crises) may require more frequent sessions, but once a week is often the best frequency in order to give people sufficient time to do the recommended homework. Fewer than 30 percent of the clients seen at the various Multimodal Therapy Institutes seem to require, or are willing to undergo, as much as 50 hours of therapy. While some clients may require extended support and trust building and therefore remain in therapy for several years, the majority favor short-term therapy (15 to 20 sessions). Multimodal therapy also lends itself extremely well to crisis intervention. Moreover, when clients learn to monitor each area of the BASIC I.D., self-management seems to be greatly enhanced.

Various treatment formats have been applied. Outpatient individual psychotherapy is perhaps the most frequent, although when the interpersonal modality becomes the focus of attention, spouses and other family members are usually seen as well. Thus, what often starts out as one-to-one psychotherapy may immediately shift to couples therapy or family therapy, or the client may be invited to join a group. These decisions are based entirely on the therapist's assessment of who or what appears most likely to benefit the client, and their implementation depends on the concurrence of the client and the willingness of significant others to participate. Thus, the well-trained multimodal therapist is capable of treating individuals, couples, families, and groups. On some occasions, as many as 20 multimodal therapists have formed a *multiple psychotherapy* format to treat one client, or one couple, in several brainstorming sessions. When a staff member at one of the Multimodal Therapy Institutes encounters a particularly difficult or challenging case, the therapist is encouraged to invite the client to a multiple therapy meeting. On the age-old principle that if 2 heads are better than 1, 10 or 20 heads may be 5 or 10 times better than 2, most of these brainstorming sessions have been constructive. Of course, some clients are terrified at the prospect of being seen by so many therapists at one time and reject the idea of multiple therapy. (The obviously poor cost-effectiveness ratio is offset by the fact that this is an excellent training opportunity.)

Regardless of the specific treatment format, multimodal therapy encompasses: (1) specification of goals and problems, (2) specification of treatment techniques to achieve these goals and remedy these problems, and (3) systematic measurement of the relative success of these techniques. In essence, this boils down to eliminating distressing and unwanted responses throughout the BASIC I.D. and also overcoming deficits that exist in any of these modalities.

It is worth reiterating the main procedural sequences followed in multimodal therapy.

1. Information from the initial interviews and the life history questionnaire results in a modality profile (i.e.,

a systematic list of problems in each area of the client's BASIC I.D.).

2. The therapist, usually in concert with the client, selects specific strategies to deal with each problem area. If treatment impasses arise, a second-order BASIC I.D. is carried out (i.e., the unresponsive problem is reexamined in each of the seven modalities).

3. Generalized complaints, such as anxiety and panic attacks, are usually dissected into modality firing orders. Thus, some clients create anxiety by dwelling on negative sensations that lead to catastrophic thoughts followed by terrifying images (an SCI sequence), whereas others may commence with negative self-statements followed by distressing images that result in unpleasant sensations (a CIS pattern). Appropriate techniques are selected to deal with each distressing element in turn.

It is worth repeating that in multimodal therapy, attention to what is traditionally called transference and countertransference phenomena— what we simply regard as the examination of client-therapist relationship variables—takes place only when there is reason to suspect that therapeutic progress will ensue. Sometimes, treatment impasses are due to specific client-therapist interactions that need to be addressed, but when therapy is proceeding well, why bother to examine the therapeutic relationship?

In multimodal marriage therapy, the couple is usually seen together for the initial interview, and the main presenting complaints are discussed. Each partner is given the life history questionnaire to take home and fill out independently. An individual session is then arranged with each one for the purpose of examining the completed questionnaire and constructing an initial modality profile. Thereafter, the treatment processes are tailored to the individuals and their unique dyadic requirements (see Brunell, 1985; Lazarus, 1981, pp. 165–86).

Participants in multimodal groups construct their own modality profiles, which serve as a blueprint for the specific gains they wish to derive. Groups can be particularly helpful in dispelling various myths (consensual validation tends to carry more weight than the views of one person, even if that person is a highly respected authority). When interpersonal deficiencies are present, group therapy can provide a more veridical training milieu. Groups lend the opportunity for vicarious or observational learning and offer a rich variety of modeling opportunities. Roleplaying, behavior rehearsal, and other enactments are enhanced by the psychodramatic nuances that groups provide. Lonely and isolated individuals particularly tend to benefit from group therapy, especially when the group provides a springboard for the development of friendships. Extremely hostile, paranoid, deluded, or severely depressed individuals are excluded from multimodal groups because they are usually too disruptive. Similarly, people who are locked into pervasive obsessive-compulsive rituals have responded poorly in multimodal groups. These people are better treated individually or, preferably, in marital or family contexts.

The use of standardized tests is not a usual procedure, but certain problems may necessitate their application. Intelligence tests (especially with children) may augment the appreciation of specific cognitive abilities and deficits. Neuropsychological assessment may shed light on matters of organicity, and tests of aptitude and special abilities may also be used to good effect with certain clients. The test that is most frequently used is a structured, interactive, projective procedure called the *deserted island fantasy technique* (Lazarus, 1971, 1981). In essence, the client is asked to describe what he or she imagines might transpire if on a deserted island for six months in the company of a companion (a congenial person unknown to the client). As clients describe their fantasies about their island sojourn, the therapist is usually able to discern several important facets. The presence or absence of the ordinary give-and-take of personal interaction emerges quite clearly. Some clients are unable to picture themselves suspending their hostility, aggression, or depression. One easily detects those instances where people are especially afraid of close contact. Evidence of autistic thinking may emerge. Direct questions concerning the evolution of friendship on the island can provide important clues about the way in which the therapeutic relationship should be structured. Many additional insights tend to be gained. An entire chapter has been devoted elsewhere (Lazarus, 1981) to this technique.

The application of multimodal therapy to inpatient settings is beyond the scope of this chapter. The interested reader is referred to the book edited by Brunell and Young (1982), which contains a wealth of information about designing, planning, and implementing multimodal treatment programs with hospitalized psychiatric patients.

MANAGEMENT

Setting

Tastefully and comfortably furnished waiting rooms and offices tend to have a positive placebo effect. Some of the Multimodal Therapy Institutes provide soft background music from FM radio stations or cassette tapes in the waiting and reception areas. It is impressed upon the receptionists that they play a crucial role in setting the emotional tone and interpersonal ambience of the institute. They are schooled in putting clients at ease, allowing them to feel comfortable, and they are told to offer tea or other beverages if clients are early or if the therapist is running overtime. Similarly, their telephone manner is required to be tolerant, polite, and patient.

The consulting rooms are carpeted, relatively soundproof, and furnished with armchairs. Books, plants, and artwork create a homelike atmosphere. Most of the therapists seem to prefer no desk between the therapist and the client. There is usually a couch or a recliner (for the practice of relaxation, biofeedback, imagery exercises, or hypnosis). Many of the offices have blackboards or flip charts, which multimodal therapists often use in underscoring a point. The foregoing reflects the educational emphasis that underlies the orientation. Clients are encouraged to have notepads and writing materials at hand. Following Albert Ellis' example, many clients are encouraged to tape-record each session and to study the recordings as a homework assignment between meetings.

Most clients are referred by friends and relatives who have benefited from multimodal therapy. Physicians, attorneys, and other professionals are also important referral sources. Advertisements and public lectures are somewhat unpredictable in terms of referrals. In this regard, weight-reduction groups have been the most cost-effective.

While the majority of sessions are held in the therapist's office, the flexibility of multimodal procedures leaves open a variety of other settings. In dealing with certain clients who do not show some improvement in a short period of time, Fay and Lazarus (1982) emphasized that it may be helpful to shift the locus of therapy outside the office, such as outdoor walking sessions or a session in the park, or, under certain circumstances, a home visit by the therapist. The use of ancillary personnel is also often found to facilitate extensive in vivo work. Thus, nurses, psychiatric aides, teachers, parents, and other paraprofessional volunteers may expedite desensitization, provide reinforcement of adaptive responses, and offer helpful modeling experiences.

Relationships

It is worth reemphasizing that, in keeping with individuals' needs and expectancies, multimodal therapists see relationships with clients on a continuum. Some clients thrive when the relationship is formal, rather distant, and businesslike. At the other extreme, some clients require close, warm, and empathic bonding. The multimodal therapist is not likely to foster dependent, romantic, or other deep attachments because much of the therapy remains task-oriented. Of course, some people are bound to develop elaborate fantasies and project upon the therapist strong feelings of love and/or hate, but we find this the exception rather than the rule. When it does occur it may well become an important therapeutic focus.

It is widely held that people enter therapy with implicit (if not explicit) expectations and that the effectiveness of therapy is often linked with these expectations. If the therapist's personality and approach are very much at variance with the client's image of an effective practitioner, a therapeutic impasse is likely to result. This, however, should not be construed as a passive and inevitable process. Clients' expectations can be modified by the therapist. Many clients, for instance, expect the therapist to "cure them" and seem unprepared to take responsibility for the treatment process and outcome. In these instances considerable therapeutic skill and artistry may be required to elicit the client's active cooperation. The most elegant outcomes often depend on a reasonable degree of congruence between the client's BASIC I.D. and the therapist's BASIC I.D. When inappropriate matching results in an absence of rapport, it is often advisable to effect referral to a more compatible resource instead of insisting that the client-therapist difficulties can or should be worked through.

Multimodal therapists make extensive use of bibliotherapy. If a picture can be worth a thousand words, a well-chosen book can be worth more than a dozen sessions. When a book is recommended to a client, he or she is asked to read it carefully, to underline points that seem important, and perhaps even to summarize it in a notebook that can be kept for ready reference. The readings are discussed during the session so that the therapist can ascertain what impact the book has had and any ambiguities can be clarified. Similarly, audiotherapy (the use of cassette recordings) is also a most useful therapeutic adjunct.

Fees are on a sliding scale depending on income and third-party coverage, among other considerations. Trainees may see clients for no fee in order to obtain supervision from experienced therapists. All in all, we try to avoid incurring economic hardships for our clients in exchange for "mental health"!

CASE EXAMPLE

BACKGROUND

A 33-year-old woman presented with a fear of becoming pregnant, hypochondriasis, and several somatic symptoms —headaches, chest pains, and gastrointestinal distress. A complete medical evaluation disclosed no organic pathology. She also suffered from severe premenstrual tension—becoming irritable, bloated, anxious, and dysphoric a few days before menstruating and experiencing almost incapacitating dysmenorrhea. Her gynecologist had prescribed analgesics, but she was "frightened of taking pills."

She had majored in mathematics at college and was working as a computer programmer. Her husband, a successful company president, had expressed a strong desire for children over the previous three years. "For the first five or six years of our marriage, neither of us wanted to have kids, but when Bill became very successful at work, he seemed to look for other outlets. That's when I realized that pregnancy, childbirth, and that whole scene terrifies me."

For the past two and a half years she had been in therapy with a psychologist. The client was most articulate about the treatment areas they traversed. "We explored my relationship with my mother, my father, my brother, and we also looked into my general home atmosphere.... We spoke a lot about attachment and separation.... It was very interesting." The client realized that what was interesting was not necessarily effective, and after reading a newspaper article, she consulted a behavior therapist who attempted (unsuccessfully) to desensitize her to her fears of pregnancy. "I think he hypnotized me and I was to see myself going through the whole pregnancy, including the labor and delivery." She acknowledged having fewer negative anticipations, but her overall clinical status remained essentially unchanged. Her brother advised her to try multimodal therapy. His senior partner's wife had mentioned that their son and daughter had both benefited from multimodal therapy after failing with other treatment approaches.

Main Problem Areas

The foregoing information was obtained during the initial interview. The life history questionnaire (Lazarus, 1981), was completed and returned before her second visit. The following modality profile was drawn up:

Behavior:	Excessive cigarette smoking; insufficient exercise
Affect:	Anger/resentment/hostility (seldom directly expressed); fear (of pregnancy)
Sensation:	Headaches; palpitations; stomach pains; tremors; chest pains; menstrual pain
Imagery:	Death images; not coping; failing
Cognition:	Perfectionistic; false romantic ideas; overconcerned about parental approval

Interpersonal: Resorts to passive-aggressive tactics (spiteful), especially with husband

Drugs/Biologicals: May require medical intervention for menstrual dysfunction

During the second session, the modality profile was discussed and the client indicated that her most distressing problems were numerous sensory discomforts that she feared were symptoms of organic disease (despite reassurances from physicians). Exploration of her death images resulted in graphic pictures of her succumbing to a heart attack. Thus, "fears heart attack" was added to her profile under *Affect*.

TREATMENT

It became clear immediately that the client's modality firing order almost invariably followed an SICA sequence (Sensation-Imagery-Cognition-Affect). First, she would observe sensory discomforts, whereupon she would dwell on them, thereby intensifying untoward pains and bodily tensions. Unpleasant and frightening images would then become intrusive. For example, she would recall vivid scenes of her maternal grandmother suffering a fatal heart attack when the client was 15 years old. Her negative imagery would lead her to label herself organically ill. "Instead of ignoring it and going about my business, I start thinking of all the things that could be wrong with me." Her unpleasant images and negative cognitions culminated in severe bouts of anxiety. In keeping with her modality firing order, the following treatments were applied:

1. Biofeedback was administered by means of an EMG apparatus attached to her frontalis muscles. She was given relaxation training cassettes for home use.

2. Associated imagery was employed. She was asked to relax, close her eyes, and picture her grandmother's heart attack. When the image was vivid and clear, she was asked to focus on any other images that emerged. As each image was attended to, a pattern began to take shape. She appeared to have overidentified with her grandmother, but on an accelerated time frame. Thus, many of her physical complaints and infirmities paralleled those that her grandmother had suffered and finally succumbed to in her late 70s. Time projection was employed wherein she imagined herself going forward in time, remaining free from organic disease until she reached her late 70s. She was advised to practice the time projection exercise at least twice daily for 5 to 10 minutes each time.

3. Positive self-statements were implemented. "If I do take after my granny, I too will enjoy good health until I'm about 75. So I'll start worrying 40 years from now." These positive self-statements were to be practiced in conjunction with the time projection images.

The foregoing procedures were administered in two sessions. She arrived for her next session feeling "weepy and depressed" although she was not premenstrual. Exploration of her feelings was unproductive and it seemed appropriate to carry out the deserted island fantasy. Five distinct themes emerged:

1. She would inevitably be disappointed with her island companion: "I just know that I will feel let down."

2. She felt that someone would have to be in charge. (Strong, overcompetitive tendencies became evident.)

3. Boredom would lead her to engage in compulsive projects.

4. She would withhold information from her island companion—she would not disclose all relevant aspects of her life. (This led the therapist to speculate about important matters that were being kept from him.)

5. She would never initiate any acts of affection but would always wait for the companion to do so. (She attributed her inhibitions in this area to her father, who showed affection "only when he was good and ready." She claimed that, as a young child, she learned that spontaneous acts of affection had punitive consequences when her father happened to be in a bad mood.)

The relevance of her island fantasies to ongoing life situations was clear-cut. She felt let down by her husband, who was less affectionate, less nurturing, than she desired. She was inclined to compete with him and tried, unsuccessfully, to take charge of his life. She never initiated sex or engaged in acts of spontaneous affection, although she craved greater warmth and caring. She frequently felt a childlike rage toward her husband, much of which was expressed in passive-aggressive and essentially indirect ways. Yet she felt a desire to achieve a close and loving relationship with him. Further clarification of her wishes indicated that her reluctance to have children was not due to phobic anxiety of the childbirth process. "I think my real hang-up is that kids will take Bill away from me even further than he is already." She had come to realize that before feeling able to make an emotional investment in a child, she would have to feel more secure within herself and in the marriage.

Therapy then focused on assertiveness training with special attention to (1) the direct expression of anger and resentment (instead of her indirect, spiteful, manipulative responses), and (2) making requests, particularly asking for attention and affection. Role-playing and coping imagery (in which she pictured herself withstanding rejection and behaving rationally) were helpful facilitators of overt action.

Approximately two and a half months after her initial consultation (eight sessions), some progress was evident. Her gains across the BASIC I.D. were as follows:

B She had stopped smoking.

A She expressed feelings more openly and more frequently.

S She reported feeling more relaxed and was less bothered with physical discomforts.

I She was obtaining clear coping images of herself living a long and healthy life.

C She was somewhat less perfectionistic.

I. She was taking emotional risks with her husband (e.g., asking for his affection).

D. She had seen her physician again and this time had agreed to take medication for her menstrual difficulties.

A week later, the client mentioned that the physician had prescribed a diuretic to be taken five or six days prior to menstruation together with oxazepam (15 mg. twice a day). On the first day of menstruation she was to take zomepirac sodium tablets for pain, as needed. (This combination of drugs proved highly effective.)

At the start of the ninth session she suggested going for a walk instead of meeting inside the office. "I feel like talking today," she said, "I'm not in the mood for hypnosis, or imagery, or stuff like that. The Herrontown Woods are less than five minutes away. Can we spend about half an hour on one of the trails?" Whereas traditional therapists would probably be disinclined to leave the professional confines of their offices, multimodal therapists tend to be more flexible in such matters. Initially, client and therapist admired the scenery, and then the client asked the therapist for his views on extramarital relationships. Was this a proposition? The therapist very much doubted it. He explained that he had no fixed rules, that he was neither blindly for nor universally opposed to extramarital sex. The client then revealed that she had been having an affair for the past year and a half. She had taken courses in computer science and had become sexually involved with her instructor, with whom she enjoyed "coffee and sex" once a week. She derived a good deal of flattery and attention from this clandestine relationship. The therapist inquired if this was having an adverse impact on her marriage, whereupon she insisted that one had nothing to do with the other. The therapist's insinuation that her affair was perhaps partly based on her wish to get even with her husband for his lack of emotional support and nurturance met with denial. She appeared eager to drop the subject. The topic switched to her use of coping imagery. Additional material from the deserted island fantasy test was also discussed.

At this juncture, therapy sessions were scheduled every two weeks, so that she had time to practice her imagery exercises and other homework assignments. She continued to make progress for a month and then began having palpitations, chest pains, and tension headaches. After some evasive comments, she admitted having stopped using the relaxation cassettes, the time projection images, and the cognitive self-statements, and she had also reverted to her unassertive (but aggressive) stance vis-à-vis her husband. The following dialogue ensued:

Client: If you're mad at me and want to yell at me, I won't blame you. Go ahead.

Therapist: It's your life. You've got the tools to make it better. I can't force you to use them. Do you want me to yell at you? What good will that do?

Client: You're angry with me. I can tell.

Therapist: It sounds like you want me to get angry with you. What's happening? Did you decide to have a relapse in order to spite me? Is this some kind of test to see if I care? Or are you annoyed with me and you don't want to give me the satisfaction of having helped you?

Client: I've never seen you like this. You sound like Bill.

Therapist: That's a good observation. I feel you set me up the way you tend to set him up. It seems like some kind of test. But whatever is going on, it is not direct, honest, frank, or positive.

Client: Okay. I'll do the relaxation and all the rest of it.

Therapist: Not for my sake, I hope. Stop looking for my approval, or your father's approval, or anybody's approval. Do what's best for *you.*

Client: Arguing with you is like arguing with Bill. I can't win. You're both too smart, too well educated. You both think very fast on your feet.

Therapist: It's interesting that you feel we are arguing, and I am intrigued by the way you have bracketed me with your husband.

Client: I think I've always felt that Bill is too good for me. He is intellectually superior, his earning power is astronomical compared to mine.

Therapist: This brings us back to your overcompetitive feelings and it also shows me something else that was not apparent—you have a terrible self-concept.

Client: It took you this long to realize that?

Therapist: I never appreciated its full extent. We really need to do something to raise your self-esteem. [Pause.] I wonder if it would be a good idea one of these days for me to meet with you and Bill.

Client: What for?

Therapist: To upgrade the marriage.

Client: I would prefer you to meet with Bill alone so that you can get to know him first before seeing us together.

There were no further setbacks. In each dimension of her BASIC I.D. the client diligently addressed the relevant issues and carried out the prescribed exercises. We reverted to weekly sessions and dwelled heavily on the false cognitions that led to her self-abnegation. The husband was seen only once. The therapist impressed upon him that the client desired a much more intense level of intimacy and emotional support and reassurance. The husband was under the false impression that his wife's disinclination to have children was due to her own career aspirations. A brief discussion cleared up this misconception. The therapist explained the client's competitive reactions as a cover-up for her feelings of insecurity and advised the husband to perceive them as cries for love and support from him.

Eight months after the initial interview, therapy was discontinued by mutual consent. The client casually mentioned that she had terminated her affair.

RESOLUTION AND FOLLOW-UP

About four weeks after therapy had ended, the client called to say that she was pregnant and felt "very pleased" about it. During the brief telephone conversation the client added that she felt "infinitely more relaxed and self-confident" and said, "I'm so assertive

these days that I even put my father in his place."

Approximately a year later she called for an appointment. Her baby boy was about four months old and she was delighted with motherhood. She had maintained all of her gains and added that since the birth of her son, her menstrual pains had cleared up, although she still took oxazepam a few days before her period. The reason she had made the appointment was to discuss the pros and cons of returning to work. As a result of the session, she decided to take a year's leave of absence and to take evening courses to maintain viability in the job market and ward off boredom.

SUMMARY

Multimodal therapy is a comprehensive, systematic, and holistic approach to psychotherapy that seeks to effect durable change in an efficient and humane way. It is an open system in which the principle of technical eclecticism encourages the constant introduction of new techniques and the refinement or elimination of existing ones, but never in a random or shotgun manner. The major emphasis is on flexibility. There are virtues in using not only a variety of techniques but even a variety of therapists. The client always comes first, even if it means referring him or her to someone else. Multimodal therapists subscribe to no dogma other than the principles of theoretical parsimony and therapeutic effectiveness.

Assessments and interventions are structured around seven modalities summarized by the acronym BASIC I.D. (behavior, affect, sensation, imagery, cognition, interpersonal relationships, and drugs/biological factors). This framework allows the therapist to take into account the uniqueness of each individual and to tailor treatment accordingly. The emphasis is constantly on who or what is best for this individual (couple, family, or group). By assessing significant deficits and excesses across the client's BASIC I.D., thorough coverage of diverse interactive problems is facilitated.

The therapist's role and the cadence of client-therapist interaction differ from person to person and even from session to session. Some clients respond best to somewhat austere, formal, businesslike transactions; others require gentle, tender, supportive encouragement. Two specific procedures that seem to enhance treatment effects are *bridging* and *tracking*. (Bridging is a procedure in which the therapist deliberately tunes into the client's preferred modality before branching off into other dimensions that seem likely to be more productive. Tracking is a careful examination of the firing order of the different modalities.)

The BASIC I.D. framework facilitates the roles of artistry and science in clinical intervention. For example, a recursive application of the BASIC I.D. to itself (a second-order assessment) often helps to shed new diagnostic light and helps to overcome some seemingly recalcitrant problems. A graphic representation of the BASIC I.D. in terms of a *structural profile* is most illuminating in couples therapy. Examination of each specific modality and its interactive effect on the other six readily enables the therapist to shift the focus of attention between the individual and his or her parts to the person in his or her social setting.

In general, the trend in current psychotherapy is toward multidimensional, multidisciplinary, and multifaceted interventions. Rigid adherents to particular schools seem to be receding into a minority. Multiform and multifactorial assessment and treatment procedures have become widespread. We believe that the multimodal (BASIC I.D.) framework permits the clinician to identify idiosyncratic variables and thereby *not* fit clients to preconceived treatments. It also offers an operational means for speaking the client's language. Apart from its heuristic virtues, the multimodal structure readily permits an examination of its own efficacy. While all multimodal therapists are eclectic, all eclectic therapists are not multimodal therapists.

ANNOTATED BIBLIOGRAPHY

Brunell, L. F., & Young, W. T. (Eds.) (1981). *Multimodal handbook for a mental hospital.* New York: Springer.

This book is a practical guide to the use of multimodal therapy in mental hospitals, residential facilities, day hospitals, and other complete care centers. The book includes comprehensive details on goals and procedures for various treatment modules, from art and occupational therapy to social and problem skills training. Discussions focus on essential phases of patient assessment, program design, treatment, and evaluation of patient progress and the hospital system. Specific chapters transcend clinical, case-oriented considerations and address large-scale applications of multimodal procedures. The eight authors have pointed the way to more efficient and effective therapeutic interventions with people who are often given little more than custodial care.

Keat, D.B. (1979). *Multimodal therapy with children*. New York: Pergamon Press.

The artistry and technical repertoire of an effective child-therapist involves specific skills that are not required by a clinician who is gifted with adults. To reach certain children, the therapist must be equipped with numerous techniques, including games, stories, and songs, and have a flair for communicating in special ways. This book shows how an imaginative clinician applies the BASIC I.D. to many problems and disorders of children.

Lazarus, A.A. (Ed.) (1976). *Multimodal behavior therapy*. New York: Springer.

This is the first book in which the BASIC I.D. is explicitly employed in the assessment and therapy of clinical cases. The 17 chapters are divided into two parts. The first 7 chapters deal with theoretical and clinical foundations, and the remaining 10 chapters consist of clinical reports and case studies. The 12 authors show how the multimodal format is applied by therapists of different personalities and backgrounds. Specific problem areas are delineated—depression, anxiety, obesity, sexual inadequacy, mental retardation, and other disturbances in children and adults. Specific techniques are incorporated into the multimodal framework (e.g., paradoxical therapy and the use of hypnosis).

Lazarus, A.A. (1981). *The practice of multimodal therapy*. New York: McGraw-Hill. (An updated edition will be available through Johns Hopkins University Press, 1989).

This book is pragmatic and focuses on the common clinical situations confronting most psychotherapists. It spells out exactly how to conduct a thorough and comprehensive assessment. An attempt is made to integrate knowledge from diverse orientations into a coherent approach. The book is essentially a condensation of the author's own experience, the recorded experience of others, and scientific data. Transcripts from actual sessions and vignettes of typical transactions provide rich clinical material. The book also contains a glossary of 37 separate therapeutic techniques.

CASE READINGS

Breunlin, D. C. (1980). Multimodal behavioral treatment of a child's eliminative disturbance. *Psychotherapy: Theory, Research and Practice, 17*, 17–23.

This case shows how even with highly targeted treatment goals, a multimodal approach can prove most advantageous.

Briddell, D. W., & Leiblum, S. R. (1976). The multimodal treatment of spastic colitis and incapacitating anxiety: A case study. In A. A. Lazarus (Ed.), *Multimodal behavior therapy* (pp. 160–169). New York: Springer.

Difficult cases often respond to the structured and very thorough multimodal interventions.

Keat, D. B. (1976). Multimodal therapy with children: Two case histories. In A. A. Lazarus (Ed.), *Multimodal behavior therapy* (pp. 116–132). New York: Springer.

When working with children, the multimodal framework offers a comprehensive and systematic context, but special expertise is required above and beyond the BASIC I.D.

Lazarus, A. A. (Ed.) (1985). *Casebook of multimodal therapy.* New York: Guilford.

This book describes 14 different case studies in a variety of settings and situations.

Lazarus, A. A. (1989). The case of George. In D. Wedding and R. J. Corsini (Eds.), *Case studies in psychotherapy.* Itasca, IL: F. E. Peacock.

This case shows multimodal therapy in action and illustrates the treatment of a client who had been unresponsive to many different types of treatment.

Popler, K. (1977). Agoraphobia: Indications for the application of the multimodal conceptualization. *The Journal of Nervous and Mental Disease, 164,* 97–101.

One of several cases that demonstrates how multimodal assessment is crucial if treatment outcomes are to be long lasting.

REFERENCES

Aigen, B. P. (1980). The BASIC I.D. obsessive-compulsive profile. Doctoral dissertation, Graduate School of Applied and Professional Psychology, Rutgers University.

Bandler, R., & Grinder, J. (1976). *The structure of magic: A book about communication and change (Vol. 2).* Palo Alto, CA: Science and Behavior Books.

Bandura, A. (1969). *Principles of behavior modification.* New York: Holt, Rinehart and Winston.

Bandura, A. (1977). *Social learning theory.* Englewood Cliffs, NJ: Prentice-Hall.

Bandura, A. (1978). The self-system in reciprocal determinism. *American Psychologist, 33,* 344–358.

Bandura, A. (1986). *Social foundations of thought and action: A social cognitive theory.* Englewood Cliffs, NJ: Prentice-Hall.

Bertalanffy, L. von (1974). General systems theory and psychiatry. In S. Arieti (Ed.), *American handbook of psychiatry (Vol. 1)* (pp. 1095–1117). New York: Basic Books.

Brentano, F. (1972). *Psychology from an empirical standpoint.* New York: Humanities Press. (Original published 1874.)

Brunell, L. F., & Young, W. T. (Eds.) (1982). *Multimodal handbook for a mental hospital.* New York: Springer.

Brunell, L. F. (1985). Multimodal marital therapy. In D. C. Goldbert (Ed.), *Contemporary marriage* (pp. 354–373). Homewood, IL: Dorsey.

Buckley, W. (1967). *Modern systems research for the behavioral scientist.* Chicago: Aldine.

Burnham, W. H. (1924). *The normal mind.* New York: Appleton.

Clark, D. M. (1986). A cognitive approach to panic. *Behaviour Research and Therapy, 24,* 461–470.

Corsini, R. J. (Ed.) (1981). *Handbook of innovative psychotherapies.* New York: Wiley.

Dryden, W., & Golden, W. (Eds.) (1986). *Cognitive behavioral approaches to psychotherapy.* London: Harper & Row.

Edwards, S. S., & Kleine, P. A. (1986). Multimodal consultation: A model for working with gifted adolescents. *Journal of Counseling and Development, 64,* 598–601.

Eimer, B. N. (1988). The chronic pain patient: Multimodal assessment and psychotherapy. *Medical Psychotherapy, 1,* 23–40.

Ellis, A. (1962). *Reason and emotion in psychotherapy.* New York: Lyle Stuart.

Fay, A. (1978). *Making things better by making them worse.* New York: Hawthorn.

Fay, A., & Lazarus, A. A. (1981). Multimodal therapy and the problems of depression. In J. F. Clarkin & H. Glazer (Eds.), *Depression: Behavioral and directive treatment strategies* (pp. 169–178). New York: Garland Press.

Fay, A., & Lazarus, A. A. (1982). Psychoanalytic resistance and behavioral nonresponsiveness: A dialectical impasse. In P. L. Wachtel (Ed.), *Resistance: Psychodynamic and behavioral approaches* (pp. 115–132). New York: Plenum.

Ferrise, F. R. (1978). The BASIC I.D. in clinical assessment. Doctoral dissertation, Graduate School of Applied and Professional Psychology, Rutgers University.

Frankl, V. E. (1960). Paradoxical intention: A logo-therapeutic technique. *American Journal of Psychotherapy, 14,* 520–535.

Frankl, V. E. (1978). *The unheard cry for meaning.* New York: Simon & Schuster.

Galin, D. (1974). Implications for psychiatry of left and right cerebral specialization. *Archives of General Psychiatry, 31,* 572–583.

Gerler, E. R. (1979). Preventing the delusion of uniqueness: Multimodal education in mainstreamed classrooms. *The Elementary School Journal, 80,* 35–40.

Greenburg, S. L. (1982). Using the multimodal approach as a framework for eclectic counselor education. *Counselor Education and Supervision, 22,* 132–137.

Haley, J. (1973). *Uncommon therapy.* New York: Norton.

Haley, J. (1976). *Problem solving therapy.* San Francisco, Jossey-Bass.

Herink, R. (1980). *The psychotherapy handbook.* New York: Meridian.

Howard, G. S., Nance, D. W., & Myers, P. (1987). *Adaptive counseling and therapy: A systematic approach to selecting effective treatments.* San Francisco: Jossey-Bass.

Jacobson, N. S. (1987). *Psychotherapists in clinical practice: Cognitive and behavioral perspectives.* New York: Guilford.

James, W. (1890). *Principles of psychology.* New York: Macmillan.

Judah, R. D. (1978). Multimodal parent training. *Elementary School Guidance and Counseling, 13,* 46–54.

Keat, D. B. (1979). *Multimodal therapy with children.* New York: Pergamon Press.

Kimura, D. (1979). The asymmetry of the human brain. *Scientific American, 228,* 70–78.

Kwee, M. G. T. (1978). Gedragstherapie en neurotische depressie. In J. W. Orlemans, W. Brinkman, W. P. Haaijam & E. J. Zwaan (Eds.), *Handboek voor gedragstherapie* (pp. 182–202). Deventer: Van Loghum.

Kwee, M. G. T. (1979). Over de ontwikkeling van een multimodale strategie van assessment en therapie. *Tijdschrift voor Psychotherapie, 5,* 172–188.

Kwee, M. G. T. (1981). Towards the clinical art and science of multimodal psychotherapy. *Current Psychological Reviews, 1,* 55–68.

Kwee, M. G. T. (1984). *Klinische multimodale gedragstherapie.* Lisse, Holland: Swets and Zeitlinger.

Kwee, M. G. T., & Roborgh, M. (1987). *Multimodale therapie: Praktijk, theorie, en onderzoek.* Lisse, Holland: Swets and Zeitlinger.

Lawler, B. B. (1985). An interrater reliability study of the BASIC I.D. (multimodal assessment). Doctoral dissertation, Graduate School of Applied and Professional Psychology, Rutgers University.

Lazarus, A. A. (1956). A psychological approach to alcoholism. *South African Medical Journal, 30,* 707–710.

Lazarus, A. A. (1958). New methods in psychotherapy: A case study. *South African Medical Journal, 32,* 660–664.

Lazarus, A. A. (1965). Towards the understanding and effective treatment of alcoholism. *South African Medical Journal, 39,* 736–741.

Lazarus, A. A. (1966). Broad spectrum behavior therapy and the treatment of agoraphobia. *Behaviour Research and Therapy, 4,* 95–97.

Lazarus, A. A. (1971). Behavior therapy

and beyond. New York: McGraw-Hill.

Lazarus, A. A. (1973). Multimodal behavior therapy: Treating the BASIC I.D. *Journal of Nervous and Mental Disease, 156,* 404–411.

Lazarus, A. A. (1976). *Multimodal behavior therapy.* New York: Springer.

Lazarus, A. A. (1978). *In the mind's eye: The power of imagery for personal enrichment.* New York: Rawson. (Reprinted 1984, Guilford.)

Lazarus, A. A. (1981). *The practice of multimodal therapy.* New York: McGraw-Hill. (Updated paperback edition, 1989, Johns Hopkins University Press.)

Lazarus, A. A. (1982). *Personal enrichment through imagery.* New York: BMA Audiocassettes.

Lazarus, A. A. (Ed.) (1985). *Casebook of multimodal therapy.* New York: Guilford.

Lazarus, A.A. (1988). The practice of rational-emotive therapy. In M. E. Bernard & R. DiGiuseppe (Eds.), *Inside rational-emotive therapy.* New York: Academic Press.

Mann, J. P. (1985). A study of the interrater agreement of therapists using the BASIC I.D. profile as an assessment tool. Doctoral dissertation, Department of Psychology, Western Kentucky University.

Margraf, J., Ehlers, A., & Roth, W. T. (1986). Panic attacks: Theoretical models and empirical evidence. In I. Hand & H. U. Wittchen (Eds.), *Panic and phobias.* Berlin: Springer-Verlag.

Meichenbaum, D. (1977). *Cognitive behavior modification.* New York: Plenum.

Mendels, J. (1974). Biological aspects of affective illness. In S. Arieti & E. G. Brody (Eds.), *American handbook of psychiatry (Vol. 3)* (pp. 491–523). New York: Basic Books.

Nathan, P. E., & Harris, S. L. (1980). *Psychopathology and society* (2nd Ed.) New York: McGraw-Hill.

Nieves, L. (1978a). *The minority college student experience: A case for the use of self-control.* Princeton, NJ: Educational Testing Service.

Nieves, L. (1978b). *College achievement through self-help.* Princeton, NJ: Educational Testing Service.

Norcross, J. C. (1986). *Handbook of eclectic psychotherapy.* New York: Brunner/Mazel.

O'Keefe, E. J., & Castaldo, C. (1980). A multimodal approach to treatment in a child care agency. *Psychological Reports, 47,* 250.

O'Keefe, E. J., & Castaldo, C. (1981). Multimodal management: A systematic and holistic approach for the 80s. *Proceedings of the Marist College Symposium on Local Government Productivity.* Poughkeepsie, NY.

O'Keefe, E. J., & Castaldo, C. (1981a). A multimodal approach to treatment in a child care agency. *Child Care Quarterly, 10,* 103–112.

Olson, S. C. (1979). A multimodal treatment of obesity using Lazarus' BASIC I.D. Doctoral dissertation, Department of Psychology, University of South Dakota.

Paul, G. L. (1967). Strategy of outcome research in psychotherapy. *Journal of Consulting Psychology, 31,* 109–118.

Pearl, C., & Guarnaccia, V. (1976). Multimodal therapy and mental retardation. In A. A. Lazarus (Ed.), *Multimodal behavior therapy* (pp. 189–204). New York: Springer.

Ponterotto, J. G. (1987). Counseling Mexican-Americans: A multimodal approach. *Journal of Counseling and Development, 65,* 308–312.

Ponterotto, J. G., & Zander, T. A. (1984). A multimodal approach to counselor supervision. *Counselor Education and Supervision, 24,* 40–50.

Rabkin, R. (1977). *Strategic psychotherapy.* New York: Basic Books.

Ridley, C. R. (1984). Clinical treatment of the nondisclosing black client: A therapeutic paradox. *American Psychologist, 39,* 1234–1244.

Roberts, T. K., Jackson, L. J., & Phelps, R. (1980). Lazarus' multimodal therapy model applied in an institutional setting. *Professional Psychology, 11,* 150–156.

Rosen, R. D. (1977). *Psychobabble.* New York: Atheneum.

Rosenblad, L. V. (1985). A multimodal assessment of perception and communication in distressed and nondistressed married couples. Doctoral dissertation, Department of Psychology, Rutgers University.

Rosenthal, D. (1974). The genetics of schizophrenia. In S. Arieti & E. B. Brody (Eds.), *American handbook of psychiatry (Vol. 3)* (pp. 588–600). New York: Basic Books.

Salter, A. (1949). *Conditioned reflex therapy.* New York: Farrar, Strauss.

Sank, L. I. (1979). Community disasters: Primary prevention and treatment in a health maintenance organization. *American Psychologist, 34,* 334–338.

Shevrin, H., & Dickman, S. (1980). The psychological unconscious: A necessary assumption for all psychological theory? *American Psychologist, 35,* 421–434.

Sperry, R. W., Gazzaniga, M. S., & Bogen, J. E. (1969). Interhemispheric relationships. The neocortical commissures: Syndromes of hemisphere disconnection. In P. J. Vinken & G. W. Bruyn (Eds.), *Handbook of clinical neurology (Vol. 4).* Amsterdam: North-Holland.

Tyrer, P. J. (1982). Anxiety states. In E. S. Paykel (Ed.), *Handbook of affective disorders.* New York: Guilford Press.

Watzlawick, P., Weakland, J., & Fisch, R. (1974). *Change: Principles of problem formation and problem resolution.* New York: Norton.

Weeks, G. R., & L'Abate, L. (1982). *Paradoxical psychotherapy.* New York: Brunner/Mazel.

Woody, R. H. (1971). *Psychobehavioral counseling and therapy: Integrating behavioral and insight techniques.* New York: Appleton-Century-Crofts.

Zeig, J. K. (Ed.) (1982). *Ericksonian approaches to hypnosis and psychotherapy.* New York: Brunner/Mazel.

Zilbergeld, B. (1982). Bespoke therapy. *Psychology Today, 16,* 85–86.

Zilbergeld, B., & Lazarus, A. A. (1988). *Mind Power: Getting what you want through mental training.* New York: Ivy Books.

14
Three Other Approaches

A. ASIAN PSYCHOTHERAPIES
B. PSYCHODRAMA
C. BIOENERGETICS

BUDDHA, Afghanistan

A

Asian Psychotherapies

ROGER WALSH

There is a growing recognition that Western psychologists may have underestimated the psychologies and therapies of other cultures. Certain Asian disciplines contain sophisticated therapies, and experimental studies have demonstrated their ability to induce psychological, physiological, and psychotherapeutic effects. An increasing number of Westerners, including mental health professionals, now use Asian therapies. Benefits include new perspectives on psychological functioning, potential, and pathology, as well as new approaches and techniques. In addition, the study of other cultures and practices often has the healthy effect of revealing unsuspected ethnocentric assumptions and limiting beliefs, thus leading to a broader view of human nature and therapy.

Psychotherapies address three major levels of health and development: pathological, existential, and transpersonal. As this book demonstrates, Western psychologists have devised sophisticated maps of pathologies and techniques for alleviating them. Recently

Westerners have begun to focus more on existential issues—such as meaninglessness, isolation, and freedom—that all of us face simply by virtue of our existence as human beings. Existentialists frequently regard these issues as unresolvable and suggest that the best we can do is to endure them with courage and authenticity.

Transpersonal therapies agree with the prescription for courage and authenticity. However, they claim that these issues are resolvable—more accurately, transcendable—by a transformation of one's state of consciousness and sense of identity, such as can occur through meditation. Techniques such as meditation have traditionally been conceived of as religious but can now be understood psychologically.

Asian psychologies focus primarily on existential and transpersonal levels and little on the pathological. They contain detailed maps of states of consciousness, developmental levels, and stages of enlightenment that extend beyond traditional Western psychological maps. Moreover, they claim to possess techniques for inducing these states and conditions. However, Asian psychologies lack the West's sophisticated understanding and detailed analyses of areas such as early development, psychodynamics, and psychopathology, and until recently had little to offer to those suffering severe psychological disturbances.

The two classic families of Asian psychotherapies are meditation and yoga. *Meditation* refers to a family of practices that train attention in order to bring mental processes under greater voluntary control. This control is used to cultivate specific mental qualities, such as awareness, concentration, joy, love, and compassion. The ultimate aim of these practices is deep insight into the nature of mind, consciousness, and identity and the development of optimal states of psychological well-being and consciousness.

Yoga refers to a family of practices with the same aims as meditation. However, yogas are disciplines encompassing ethics, life-style, body postures, breath control, and intellectual study in addition to meditation. In the West the best known practices are the body postures of Hatha yoga, which have frequently been taken to be the totality of yoga. In fact, they comprise only one aspect of a far more comprehensive training.

It has sometimes been argued that these Asian practices cannot really be considered psychotherapies because the essence of psychotherapy, as defined in the West, is the helping interaction, yet much meditation and yoga practice can be done alone. This argument seems to ignore the wide range of relationships possible in both Western and Asian therapies.

On the Western side, one can find therapies in which the patient is completely dependent on the therapist. At the other extreme is self-therapy, which Freud used on himself in his attempt to gain self-understanding, an understandable venture since there were no other psychoanalysts available at that time. Some Western therapies, such as psychoanalysis, foster transference. Others, such as behavior modification, try to minimize it and to substitute an instructor-student relationship.

The spectrum of relationships is almost as broad for Asian therapies. Some foster transference, others minimize it; in some the relationship is primary, in others definitely secondary. However, instruction and assistance from a skilled helper is regarded as essential in all Asian practices which are never entirely solitary. These considerations justify inclusion of Asian practices among those we call psychotherapy.

HISTORY

PAST HISTORY

The origins of meditation and yoga can be traced back almost 3000 years. Until recently very little was known of these practices in the West, and what was known was frequently misunderstood and dismissed. As late as 1946 a well-known psychiatrist proclaimed meditation to be "an attempt at psychological and physical regression to the condition of intrauterine life ... a sort of artificial schizophrenia" (Alexander et al., 1946). However, since the 1960s there has been an explosion of popular, professional, and research interest in meditation and yoga.

CURRENT STATUS

Although originally employed in the East for work at existential and transpersonal levels, considerable clinical and research data suggest that meditation and yoga may also be effective for reducing pathology. Thus, while significant numbers of Westerners employ these techniques for their traditional benefits, others use them for more modest and immediate benefits, such as relaxation, stress management, or a heightened sense of psychological well-being, or for managing specific psychological or psychophysiological disorders.

Several hundred experimental studies of meditation and yoga indicate that these therapies are effective for a wide range of disorders. Many studies report that meditation reduces both generalized anxiety and specific phobias. Clinical research indicates that drug and alcohol use may be reduced in those who practice meditation. Hospitalized psychiatric patients may also benefit from daily meditation. (For reviews of these therapeutic applications, see Shapiro [1980, 1982] and Shapiro and Walsh [1984]).

Psychophysiological benefits also occur. Meditation has been employed successfully for rehabilitation after heart attacks; to treat irregular heartbeat, bronchial asthma, and insomnia; to reduce high blood pressure; and to help with the management of chronic pain.

Positive effects have also been noted in healthy nonclinical populations. Several studies suggest that meditators change more than controls in the direction of enhanced confidence, self-esteem, sense of self-control, empathy, and self-actualization.

Perhaps the most startling finding is that meditation may enhance longevity. A geriatric population taught meditation not only scored better on objective tests of psychological functioning

and subjective measures of well-being than did any of three matched control groups, but also had a significantly lower mortality rate (Langer, 1988).

It is therefore clear that meditation has therapeutic potential. However, many studies are flawed by methodological problems, and several studies suggest that meditation may be no more effective for clinical disorders such as anxiety or high blood pressure than are other self-regulation strategies, such as relaxation training and self-hypnosis. On the other hand, some subjects have reported meditation to be more meaningful, pleasurable, and relaxing than other strategies. Patients most likely to benefit from meditation for psychological or psychophysiological problems are probably those who are less severely disturbed and already possess a sense of self-control.

Therapists who practice meditation and yoga themselves may also experience benefits, including enhanced therapeutic effectiveness. Several studies have shown that meditation increases perceptual sensitivity as well as empathic sensitivity and accuracy. The deep insights that meditation provides seem to foster understanding of, and compassion for, the painful experiences of others. These effects may be particularly valuable because research suggests that traditional training programs in the health sciences do little to enhance empathy and may even reduce it (Lesh, 1970).

In Asia the current status of meditation and yoga remains unchanged: these techniques are practiced by tens of millions of people and are regarded as essential practices for advanced psychological and religious development. Their relationship to religious goals has become psychologically understandable in terms of altered states of consciousness. Research in this area has brought the startling recognition that parts of the world's great religions can be viewed as methods for inducing altered, and especially transcendent, states of consciousness (Wilber, 1981).

Behind the better known practices of many religions, one often finds a core of disciplines such as contemplation, meditation, and yoga. These practices are used to induce states of consciousness embodying desired qualities, such as emotions of love and compassion, states of peace and joy, reductions of greed and anger, and motives of generosity and service. Consequently, aspects of both Western and Eastern religious life, such as meditation and yoga, can now be understood in psychological terms. Research studies have begun to lend support to these ideas. In one study, for example, Rorschach tests of advanced meditators showed "no evidence of sexual or aggressive drive conflicts" (Brown & Engler, 1986).

The classic Asian practices of meditation and yoga are the most widely used of all therapies, with perhaps 100 million practitioners worldwide. Meditation has been more thoroughly researched than all therapies except behavioral therapies, and several good reviews of this research are now available (Kutz, Borysenko & Benson, 1985; Shapiro, 1980, 1982; Shapiro & Walsh, 1984). Wilber, Engler, and Brown (1986) provide more technical analyses of the experiences and stages of meditation and yoga. Several reviews describe integrations of Asian and Western therapies, especially in the field of transpersonal psychology (Goleman, 1988; Vaughan, 1986; Walsh & Vaughan, 1980; Wilber, 1981). Reviews of Morita and Naikan therapies

are also available (Ishiyama, 1986; Reynolds, 1981).

For those who wish to learn to meditate, helpful books include Benson (1976), Goldstein (1983), LeShan (1975), Levine (1979), Shapiro (1978), and Ram Dass (1978). The classic yoga text is Patanjali's millenia-old *Yoga Sutras* (Johnson, 1984). Although some progress can be made alone, the guidance of a good instructor/teacher/therapist is extremely valuable. A slightly dated list of meditation centers is available in Ram Dass (1978).

THEORY

Asian therapies stem from and lead to views of human nature, mind, psychology, and consciousness that in some ways differ markedly from traditional Western assumptions. In this section we shall compare the Asian model with the traditional Western paradigm, examine the mechanisms involved in producing the effects of meditation and yoga, and briefly survey Morita and Naikan therapies.

THE ASIAN MODEL

Consciousness

Around the turn of the century, William James remarked: Our normal waking consciousness ... is but one special type of consciousness, whilst all about it, parted from it by the filmiest of screens, there lie potential forms of consciousness entirely different. We may go through life without suspecting their existence; but apply the requisite stimulus, and at a touch they are there in all their completeness. ... No account of the universe in its totality can be final which leaves these other forms of consciousness quite disregarded. (1958, p. 298)

Asian psychologies agree fully. They describe a broad spectrum of these states unrecognized by Western psychology and provide detailed descriptions and techniques for attaining them. Perceptual sensitivity and clarity, concentration, sense of identity, and emotional, cognitive, and perceptual processes all vary with states of consciousness in predictable ways.

Some states are said to be functionally specific, while a few are true higher states. *Functionally specific states* are those in which certain functions are improved while others are less effective. For example, yogic *samadhi* states marked by deep calm and concentration may be conducive to introspective exploration but not to social interaction. True *higher states* are defined as those that possess the capacities present in the usual condition, plus heightened or additional ones (Tart, 1986; Walsh & Vaughan, 1980).

If higher states of consciousness exist, then, contrary to the typical Western assumption, our usual state must be less than optimal. This is exactly the claim of the Asian psychologies, which describe our usual state as hypnotic or dreamlike. Trained observation reveals that our minds are usually filled with a continual flux of unrecognized thoughts, images, internal dialogues, and fantasies that distort and reduce awareness, resulting in unappreciated trance states (Tart, 1986). As in any hypnotic state, the trance and its attendant constriction of awareness may not be recognized.

At times all of us daydream and become lost in fantasy. Asian psychologies claim that these fantasies are significantly more pervasive, distorting, and befogging than we realize. Their extent and consequences remain unrecognized because, like psychological defense mechanisms, they are partially self-masking. The result is said to be *maya*: an unrecognized, encompassing, illusory distortion of perception and experience that remains unrecognized until we subject our perceptual-cognitive processes to direct, rigorous scrutiny, as in meditation.

Thus, the "normal" person is considered to be usually "asleep," "dreaming," or in a "consensus trance" (Tart, 1986). When a dream is especially painful or disruptive it becomes a nightmare and is recognized as psychopathology, but because the vast majority of the population dreams, the usual more subtle forms remain unrecognized. People who eradicate this dream are said to have "awakened," and this awakening, known as *liberation* or *enlightenment*, is the aim of Asian therapies.

To some extent these concepts are an extension rather than a denial of Western psychology and psychiatry. Research (Langer, 1988) has shown that we have less awareness of our own cognitive processes than we usually assume and that we suffer from a broad range of usually unrecognized cognitive-perceptual distortions and automaticities (unconscious automatic habits). Asian psychologies suggest that these distortions and automaticities can be reduced and awareness enhanced by meditative training, a claim now supported by studies of perceptual processing in advanced meditators (Brown & Engler, 1986; Brown, Forte & Dysart, 1984).

These claims do not have to be taken on faith. Those willing to undertake intensive training in observation of their own mental processes—such as in a week of intensive meditation—can easily test the claims for themselves. All Asian therapies recommend personal testing because any thorough understanding requires direct experience. Some previously skeptical behavioral scientists have been shocked into acknowledging the full potency of these disciplines only after personal experience (e.g., Shapiro, 1980; Tart, 1986; Walsh, 1977).

Psychopathology

Ideal psychological health is considered tantamount to enlightenment in Asian psychology. Consequently, most Asian philosophers agree with Abraham Maslow (1968), who said, "What we call 'normal' in psychology is really a psychopathology of the average, so undramatic and so widely spread that we don't even notice it (p. 16)." The roots of this pathology, both individual and social, include addiction (craving), aversion, and ignorance (unconsciousness and misunderstanding of one's mind and true nature).

Asian psychologies point out that addiction can occur not only to food and drugs, but to practically anything, including external possessions and internal emotions, beliefs, and self-images. Indeed, the Buddha claimed that all suffering is rooted in addiction. It is an interesting challenge to try to find examples of psychological pain in one's own life that do not reflect addiction.

The mirror image of addiction is aversion. Whereas with addiction, happiness is dependent on possessing something, with aversion it is dependent on avoiding it.

The mind ruled by addiction and aversion is said to be a slave to every situation and environment in which it finds itself, constantly involved in a never-ending search to get what it wants and avoid what it fears. Happiness is said to be dependent on, and limited to, those occasions when the world is lined up to match one's particular pattern of addictions and aversions. From this perspective, psychological pain is a feedback signal indicating the existence of addictions and aversions and the need to relinquish them. Asian psychologies consequently claim that psychological health and happiness are dependent not so much on the satisfaction of addictions and the avoidance of aversions as on reducing and becoming free of them.

Psychological Health

For Asian psychologies the ideal of health is enlightenment or liberation, rather than adjustment to, or compromise with, psychodynamic and existential givens. The means for attaining health include the reduction of the pathogenic factors of addiction, aversion, and ignorance. However, mental health is also defined in positive terms. Consequently, Asian therapies cultivate and strengthen specific healthy qualities, such as mindfulness, love, compassion, concentration, and calm.

For people in whom these healthy qualities have been cultivated, and addiction and aversion reduced, compassion and selfless service are said to become major motives (Walsh & Shapiro, 1983). This Eastern claim for a correlation between psychological maturity and service parallels several Western concepts, such as Alfred Adler's social interest and Erik Erikson's generativity. Abraham Maslow (1967) claimed that "self-actualizing people are, without one single exception, involved in a cause outside their own skin." (p. 282).

THERAPEUTIC MECHANISMS

A large number of mechanisms are involved in producing the effects of meditation and yoga. In this section we will examine those proposed by both Western and Asian psychologies.

The first of these Western mechanisms is dehypnosis. When we observe our minds carefully we find that we spend considerable time lost in fantasies that seem real at the time. This can be regarded as a type of hypnosis. When we develop concentration and awareness, we can recognize these fantasies for what they are: only fantasies. For example, a meditator may shift from believing that he or she is scared to simply being aware of, and unaffected by, a fearful fantasy. If the process of becoming lost in fantasies is regarded as a form of hypnosis, then the meditation process of recognizing thoughts and fantasies for what they are may be seen as dehypnosis (Tart, 1986).

Other psychological mechanisms that have been used to explain the effects of meditation include relaxation, habituation and desensitization to formerly stressful stimuli, and the deconditioning of old habits. A variety of cognitive mechanisms may also be involved, including the expectation of positive benefits. Physiological explanations have included reduced metabolism and arousal, changes in hemispheric lateralization (a shift in the relative activity of the two cerebral hemispheres), and brain-wave changes and autonomic nervous system changes (Shapiro, 1980).

Several Asian psychologies contain models to explain how therapeutic effects are produced through meditation. One Buddhist model based on mental factors (qualities of mind) is particularly useful in making comparisons with Western psychotherapeutic practices. Seven of these factors, the so-called seven factors of enlightenment, are regarded as particularly important for health (Goldstein, 1983).

The first is mindfulness, a precise, conscious awareness of the stimulus being observed, which might be regarded as a refinement of the psychoanalytic observing ego. The remaining six mental factors are divided into two groups of three arousing qualities and three calming qualities. The three arousing factors are effort (energy, arousal), investigation (active exploration of experience), and rapture (delight in the awareness and exploration of experience). The three calming factors are concentration (the ability to maintain attention on a specific object), calm (tranquility and freedom from anxiety and agitation), and equanimity (the capacity to experience stimuli without disturbance).

Western therapists have emphasized the arousing factors of effort and investigation. Less appreciated is that sensitivity and insight can be enhanced by a complementary development of concentration, calm, and equanimity. Optimal effects occur when all seven factors are cultivated in a balanced, mutually facilitating manner (Goldstein, 1983).

Acceleration of psychological development beyond conventional levels is another mechanism now being explored in the West. Some Western developmental psychologists have argued for the existence of stages of cognitive, motivational, and moral development beyond conventional norms. Several theoretical and experimental studies now suggest that advanced meditators and yogis may attain these higher stages (Wilber, 1981; Wilber et al., 1986).

INNOVATIVE ASIAN PSYCHOTHERAPIES: MORITA AND NAIKAN

Morita is a Japanese therapy designed for the treatment of anxiety, especially in patients characterized by anxious self-preoccupation, perfectionistic self-expectations, social phobia, and extreme dislike of their symptoms. Treatment consists of four components: *acceptance, reattribution, dereflection,* and *active engagement*. Patients are taught to accept and reinterpret their symptoms (what Western behaviorists call reattribution) not as signs of weakness and inadequacy, but rather as reflections of strong ideals. They are also taught to participate fully in life without waiting for their anxiety to dissipate. Through engagement, attention is directed away from the self (a process Victor Frankl calls dereflection) and, secondarily, anxiety is reduced. Morita therapy has produced a large literature that has significantly influenced Japanese psychotherapy and good success rates have been reported (Ishiyama, 1986).

A second Japanese therapy, Naikan, is adapted from a more intensive Buddhist practice and consists simply of intensive reflection on past relationships. Clients reflect specifically on three things: what other people have done for them, what they have done for others, and the difficulties they have caused others. The aim is to foster recognition of human interdependence, of how much we have received from others, how much gratitude is due them, and how little we have demonstrated this gratitude. Along with a confrontation with guilt and unworthiness comes the recognition that one has been loved and appreciated in spite of weaknesses and failings. The result is usually an upwelling of gratitude and a desire to contribute more. Little formal research has been done on Naikan therapy, but case reports document success with a variety of neuroses and personality disorders, the most noteworthy being with convicts and alcoholics (Reynolds, 1981).

METHODOLOGY

The intensity and degree of commitment required to use meditation or yoga for intensive exploration and growth are far greater than that required by their use as more modest self-regulation strategies. For an individual committed to deep self-transformation, meditation and yoga are best viewed as components of an encompassing shift in attitudes, thought, speech, and behavior aimed at the deepest possible transformation of mind, awareness, identity, life-style, and relationships. Meditative and yogic training are usually accompanied by shifts in life-style so that all one's behavior, overt and covert, facilitates the growth process.

The first shift is a commitment to ethical behavior. Asian therapies recommend refraining from lying, stealing, sexual misconduct, killing, and taking mind-clouding intoxicants. Traditionally this is said to lead to "purification," in which counterproductive motives and behavior are gradually winnowed away. In Western behavioral terms this would be seen as the extinction of disruptive habits by the prevention of undesired behavior.

Ethical behavior is not to be confused with externally imposed moralism with a right-wrong, good-bad perspective. No meditator can long remain unaware that unethical behavior is motivated by such states of mind as greed, anger, and aversion, that unethical behavior reinforces these states, and that they in turn disrupt the mind. The end result of unethical behavior is that the mind is left more agitated, anxious, and trapped. Ethicality is therefore seen not as something imposed from without but as something sought from within for its direct benefits to self and others.

The cultivation of generosity and service to others is recommended as a way of reducing self-centeredness and egotistical desire. Practitioners may also be drawn to a life of voluntary simplicity. With deepening practice, meditators increasingly recognize the disrupting effects of greed and attachment and find themselves better able to generate positive feelings that formerly depended on external stimuli. Thus they may experience less need to own the latest and biggest car, boat, or appliance, and instead, find greater pleasure in a deepening sensitivity to the moment-to-moment flow of experience, with each moment increasingly becoming a source of rich and multifaceted stimulation.

For most people meditation and yoga are slow, cumulative processes, and beginners should be cautioned that there may be a period of weeks before the benefits of brief daily practice are clearly evident. Meditation and yoga are skills and, as with any skill, the initial phase is usually the least rewarding. However, perseverance brings increasing benefits.

Most people begin meditating with short sessions of 20 to 30 minutes, once or twice a day. Others begin with a retreat in which they engage in more or less continuous practice for a period of days or weeks under careful supervision. While it is possible to make some progress unaided, any deep practice is greatly facilitated by the guidance of a teacher-therapist.

Meditation practices can be subdivided into two main categories: concentration and awareness. Concentration meditations aim especially at developing the ability of the mind to focus attention without distraction on specific objects, such as the breath, an emotion, or sound. Awareness meditations, on the other hand, aim at examining the nature of mind and exploring any experiences that occur.

In concentration meditation, one attempts to fix attention on a specific stimulus, such as one's breath. However, attention remains fixed for a remarkably short period and the individual is soon lost in fantasy. When this is recognized, one's attention is brought back to the breath and maintained there until lost again. This rapidly results in a startling and disconcerting recognition: We have little control of attention. Most beginning meditators, including Western trained psychotherapists, are astonished to find how much of their lives and mental processes are unconscious and automatic.

It is worthwhile to try the following exercise to appreciate the power and extent of this automaticity. Set an alarm for a minimum of 10 minutes. Then take a comfortable seat, close your eyes, and turn your attention to the sensations of breathing in your abdomen. Try to concentrate on the sensations continuously as the abdominal wall rises and falls. Focus your attention carefully, precisely, and microscopically on the sensations that arise and pass away. Do not let your attention wander for a moment. If thoughts and feelings arise, let them remain, but continue to focus your awareness on the sensations of the breath.

While you continue to pay close attention to the sensations, start counting the breaths from 1 to 10, and after you reach 10, go back to 1 again. However, if you lose count or if your mind wanders from the sensations of your breath, even for an instant, go back to 1 and begin again. If you get distracted or lost in fantasy, just recognize what has happened and gently bring your mind back to your breathing and start counting once more. Continue this process until the alarm tells you to stop; then estimate how much of the time you were actually fully aware of the experience of breathing.

Most people will find that only a very small percentage of their time was spent fully aware of the sensations of breathing. With prolonged practice, concentration gradually improves and, as it does, a number of beneficial experiences begin to occur, such as calm, equanimity, and joy.

Although the practice of concentration can be useful and pleasurable, some Asian traditions view concentration more as a facilitator of awareness meditation than as an end in itself. Insight or awareness practices do not fix attention on a single object but rather allow the mind to explore whatever experiences arise. In doing this the first level of insights that develop might be called psychodynamic, and the individual will recognize patterns of thought and behavior such as might be noticed in traditional psychotherapy. However, as meditation deepens, the significantly enhanced capacities of concentration, calm, and equanimity allow deep insights into the nature of mental processes. This level of insight brings an illumination of how the mind is constructed. One begins to see, for example, the way a single thought or desire may rise into awareness and

modify emotion, perception, and muscle tension patterns. One therefore begins to develop insight into the fundamental nature and effects of such mental processes as thought, motivation, and perception.

With increasing practice the range and intensity of experiences continue to increase and eventually exceed anything experienced in daily life. Yet at the same time calm and equanimity also increase so that this greater range of experiences can be observed and allowed with less and less disturbance, defensiveness, or interference. The individual identifies more and more with the calm observer or witness of these experiences rather than with the experiences per se and, in doing so, experiences a deep sense of peace and freedom.

Occasionally some of these experiences may be disturbing—for example, the occurrence of anxiety, tension, anger, and changes in perception of self and reality. These may sometimes be quite intense. However, symptoms are usually short-lived and disappear spontaneously. Consultation with a therapist familiar with both Asian and Western therapies may be particularly helpful in such cases. In many instances these difficulties seem to represent a greater sensitivity to, and emergence of, previously repressed psychological memories and conflicts. Thus the initial discomfort of experiencing them may be a necessary price for processing and discharging them.

These are the procedures common to most meditation and yoga practices. In addition, numerous yogic techniques are designed to elicit specific qualities and skills. The following two very brief descriptions of skills (which until recently Western psychologists usually considered impossible) merely hint at the remarkable range of practices and powers of mind that Asians have discovered in their 3000-year-long exploration of our inner universe.

The first is the cultivation of love, especially unconditional love, or *agape*. Once preliminary skills such as concentration and calm have been mastered, then specific emotions can be cultivated. For example, the mind can focus intensely on the image of a love object, and the resulting emotion can then be intensified and extended to encompass all people. This is very different from the common Western assumption that love is an emotion largely outside our control that can encompass only a very few people.

"Lucid dreaming," an actual sleep state in which subjects know they are dreaming, is a 1200-year-old Tibetan Buddhist yoga for training and exploring the mind. However, in the West, lucid dreaming was either ignored or dismissed as impossible until Stephen LaBerge (1985) demonstrated its existence and similarities to ancient Tibetan accounts. LaBerge's induction techniques are freely available so that now one can develop this ancient yogic skill and investigate the nature and powers of the mind, all in the comfort of bed.

SUMMARY

Asian psychotherapies include a variety of techniques: the oldest and most widely used are meditation and yoga. Across centuries and cultures they have led to the highest levels of human development, and after 3000 years they remain the world's most widely used psychotherapeutic techniques. With their recent introduction to the West several million Westerners have joined tens of millions of Asians in these practices. However, in the West their most popular application has been for relaxation and stress management rather than for the deeper psychological insights and altered states of consciousness traditionally sought in the East.

Experimental research has clearly demonstrated psychological, physiological, and chemical effects of meditation and yoga, as well as significant psychotherapeutic benefits. However, it remains unclear whether these techniques are necessarily more effective for the management of clinical disorders than are techniques such as relaxation training and self-hypnosis.

Both research findings and ancient Asian claims challenge some fundamental assumptions and paradigms of Western psychology. For example, the Asian claim that our usual state of consciousness is less than optimal runs counter to our basic assumptions that our usual state is best. Similarly, Asian therapies suggest the existence of true higher states of consciousness and claim that these can be achieved through training. A growing network of concepts and data points to the validity of some of these claims. Clearly, Asian therapies have significant implications for both psychological theory and therapeutic application.

Asian psychotherapies may offer several advantages over other clinical interventions. First of all, meditation and yoga are inexpensive. The practitioner is independent of location and instruments and can practice as much or as little as desired. In fact, there may be relatively little need for professional time and energy once the basic practice has been established. There are also multiple applications, as these therapies are useful for certain clinical problems as well as for psychological growth. Both therapists and clients may find them beneficial. They can be a useful adjunct to more traditional therapies, casualties are rare, and they are often very enjoyable. Of course, Asian tradition suggests that the ultimate test of any theory is experiential. Their response to questions about the validity and effectiveness of these disciplines remains the same today as it has been for millenia: "To see if this be true, look within."

REFERENCES

Alexander, F., French, T. M., & Bacon, C. L. (1946). *Psychoanalytic therapy: Principles and applications.* New York: Ronald Press.

Benson, H. (1976). *The relaxation response.* New York: Avon.

Brown, D., Forte, M., & Dysart, M. (1984). Visual sensitivity and mindfulness meditation. *Perceptual and Motor Skills, 58,* 775–784.

Brown, D., & Engler, J. (1986). The stages of mindfulness meditation: A validation study. Part II. Discussion. In K. Wilber, J. Engler & D. Brown (Eds.), *Transformations of consciousness: Conventional and contemplative perspectives on development* (pp. 191–218). Boston: New Science Library/Shambhala.

Goldstein, J. (1983). *The experience of insight.* Boston: Shambhala.

Goleman, D. (1988). *The meditative mind.* Los Angeles: J. Tarcher.

Horney, K. (1942). *Self analysis.* New York: Norton.

Ishiyama, F. (1986). Morita therapy. *Psychotherapy, 23,* 375–380.

James, W. (1958). *The varieties of religious experience.* New York: New American Library. (Original published 1902.)

Johnson, C. (1984). *Yoga sutras of Patanjali* (7th ed.). New York: Brothers of Life.

Kutz, I., Borysenko, J., & Benson, H. (1985). Meditation and psychotherapy, *American Journal of Psychiatry, 142,* 1–8.

LaBerge, S. (1985). *Lucid dreaming.* Los Angeles: Tarcher.

LeShan, L. (1975). *How to meditate.* New York: Bantam Books.

Langer, E. (1988). Minding matters: The consequences of mindlessness/mindfulness. In L. Berkowitz (Ed.), *Advances in Experimental Social Psychology* . New York: Academic Press.

Lesh, T. (1970). Zen meditation and the development of empathy in counselors. *Journal of Humanistic Psychology, 10,* 39–74.

Levine, S. (1979). *A gradual awakening.* New York: Anchor.

Maslow, A. (1968). *Toward a psychology of being (2nd ed.).* Princeton: Van Nostrand.

Maslow, A. (1967). Self actualization and beyond. In J. Bugental (Ed.), *Challenges of humanistic psychology* (pp. 279–286). New York: McGraw-Hill.

Ram Dass. (1978). *Journey of awakening: A meditator's guidebook.* New York: Doubleday.

Reik, T. (1948). *Listening with the third ear.* New York: Farrar, Straus.

Reynolds, D. (1981). Naikan psychotherapy. In R. J. Corsini (Ed.), *Handbook of innovative psychotherapies* (pp. 544–553). New York: John Wiley.

Shapiro, D. H. (1978). *Precision nirvana.* Englewood Cliffs, NJ: Prentice Hall.

Shapiro, D. H. (1980). *Meditation: Self regulation strategy and altered states of consciousness.* New York: Aldine.

Shapiro, D. H. (1982). Overview: Clinical and physiological comparison of meditation with other self-control strategies. *American Journal of Psychiatry, 139,* 267–274.

Shapiro, D., & Walsh, R. (Eds.) (1984). *Meditation: Classic and contemporary perspectives.* New York: Aldine.

Tart, C. (1986). *Waking up: Overcoming the obstacles to human potential.* Boston: New Science Library/Shambhala.

Vaughan, F. (1986). *The inward arc.* Boston: New Science Library/Shambhala.

Walsh, R. (1977). Initial meditative experiences: Part I. *Journal of Transpersonal Psychology, 9,* 151–192.

Walsh, R., & Shapiro, D. H. (Eds.) (1983). *Beyond health and normality: Explorations of exceptional psychological wellbeing.* New York: Van Nostrand Reinhold.

Walsh, R., & Vaughan, F. (Eds.) (1980). *Beyond ego: Transpersonal dimensions in psychology.* Los Angeles: Tarcher.

Wilber, K. (1981). *No boundary.* Boston: New Science Library/Shambhala.

Wilber, K., Engler, J., & Brown, D. (Eds.) (1986). *Transformations of consciousness: Conventional and contemplative perspectives on development.* Boston: New Science Library/Shambhala.

JACOB L. MORENO, 1889–1974

B

Psychodrama

ADAM BLATNER

Psychodrama is a method of psychotherapy in which clients are helped to enact situations dramatically in individual, family, or group settings. Scenes from the past, present, or future, imagined or real, are given intensity and relevance by being acted as if they were occurring at the moment. Special techniques, such as *role reversal*, the *mirror*, the *double*, etc., serve to bring out unspoken feelings and half-denied attitudes. The roleplaying process offers a wealth of diagnostic clues because habitual verbal defenses are circumvented. In the process of working out solutions to problems, clients have an opportunity to discover their capacity for creativity.

While classical psychodrama is a powerful technique that should only be conducted by professionals specifically trained in the method, psychodramatic *methods* may be adapted for use in individual, family, or milieu therapy settings, and with a wide range of problems and clients. Their use is compatible with a number of psychodynamic, cognitive, and behavioral approaches. Psychodrama is no

panacea, sufficient unto itself—it works best in the hands of those who are well-grounded in professional judgment, yet open to applying an eclectic methodology in treatment.

Psychodrama differs from drama therapy in that the former focuses on specific problems of individuals while the latter addresses the more general processes of developing spontaneity and evoking people's self-awareness in groups. Psychodramatists are primarily clinically trained psychotherapists who have added on this subspecialty, while drama therapists have their primary background in the theater. Both psychodrama and drama therapy use the medium of aesthetic expression, and their practitioners, along with the other creative arts therapists, recognize that the vitality and creativity produced is a valuable agent of healing (Landy, 1986).

Roleplaying, a direct outgrowth of psychodrama, has applications not only in psychotherapy (Corsini, 1967; Kipper, 1986), but also in education, management, and other settings. Often the terms are used interchangeably, but in general psychodrama uses roleplaying to gain a more in-depth exploration of emotions, while roleplaying in itself emphasizes working out an effective behavioral response.

The principles of psychodrama have great relevance for psychotherapy. They serve to remind mental health professionals of the potential for healing associated with creativity, spontaneity, physical action, excitement, mutuality, imagination, playfulness, flexibility, self-expression, and a willingness to expand one's vitality by including the powerful channels of poetry, dance, song, music, drama, and art. These rich resources for vitality represent innate connections to the best part of childhood and are filled with pleasure. Consequently, these qualities become intrinsically rewarding and can be useful motivators in treatment. Most importantly, however, they enhance personal autonomy, identity, effectiveness, and hopefulness.

HISTORY

Psychodrama was originated and developed by Jacob L. Moreno, M.D. (1889–1974). A fascinating and complex person, Moreno was also a major pioneer of group psychotherapy, social psychology, and improvisational theater. Moreno was not only a psychiatrist but also a philosopher whose vision of an integrated approach to social as well as individual treatment has only recently found a receptive historical zeitgeist. His early influences included the work of the philosophers Henri Bergson and Charles Sanders Peirce. Interested in understanding the phenomenon of children's make-believe play, Moreno observed and tested his methods with groups of children in the parks in Vienna. The results of these experiences convinced him of the importance of spontaneity as part of the creative and vitalizing processes of life.

Moreno attended the University of Vienna from 1907 to 1917, first as a student of philosophy, then of medicine, the field in which he received his degree. Vienna during that time was engaged in a renaissance of the arts and sciences. Moreno fully entered the intellectual ferment, and during this period, originated such innovations as the self-help group, the beginnings of *sociometry* (a method in which groups can give feedback about their interpersonal preferences, and which came to be a part of modern sociology), and an early form of existentialism, emphasizing such concepts (and coining such terms) as *here and now* and *encounter*. He experimented with how to restore and develop spontaneity and creativity in a variety of situations and chose the context of theater in which to promote these philosophical and psychological explorations. However, Moreno believed the traditional theater was not appropriate because he found it burdened by lack of spontaneity due to rehearsed productions and memorized scripts, which reflected the separation of the creative act of the playwright and the performance of the actor.

While serving as a general practitioner in 1921 in a suburb of Vienna, Moreno, along with a group of actors with similar ideals, began his experimental "Theater of Spontaneity." He later dated this as the beginning of psychodrama, because over the next several years the therapeutic implications of improvisational drama became increasingly apparent to him. In his theater, he reintroduced and developed the method of improvisation as a renewal of the field of drama. His goal was to help people rediscover the aesthetic implications of the events and adventures of their own lives. However, because postwar Europe could not support his dream of a therapeutic theater, he decided to emigrate. Even though the focus of Moreno's work in subsequent years addressed the more limited applications in treating mental illness, he never lost his dream of helping society as a whole develop more effective forms of practical democracy, interpersonal freedom, and interactive creativity.

In 1925, Moreno came to the United States, where he gradually began to develop active group methods. He introduced the term group psychotherapy at a meeting of the American Psychiatric Association in 1932, and in 1936, opened a sanitarium in Beacon, New York. In his experiments with interpersonal approaches to psychotherapy, he introduced the ideas of cotherapy (implicit in the technique of the auxiliary) and marital and family therapy, and worked with the phenomenology of the patient, a form of existential psychotherapy (Compernolle, 1981). In 1942, he opened an institute in New York City and offered open sessions where many professionals visited and enriched their own conceptual frames of reference. That year he started the first professional organization devoted to group psychotherapy, the American Society for Group Psychotherapy and Psychodrama. During the 1950s Moreno promoted group psychotherapy in all its forms, including family therapy and the therapeutic community. He was also instrumental in supporting innovations in the creative arts therapies and the applied social sciences, organizing in-

ternational conferences and writing prolifically.

In 1949, J. L. Moreno married Zerka Toeman. Both of them taught and traveled extensively, and she carried on her husband's work after his death. At the time of this writing, she is the foremost exponent of psychodrama. In addition, hundreds of other directors of psychodrama now work and teach throughout this country and around the world. During his life, Moreno was the major author of scores of articles and books and the editor of several journals about psychodrama and its related approaches. Since 1970, other authors have published a number of important books, including those by Blatner (1989, 1988b), Greenberg (1974), Yablonsky (1975), Starr (1977), Goldman and Morrison (1984), and Kipper (1986).

At present, psychodrama has become a significant part of a number of hospital treatment programs, but it remains on the periphery of traditional psychiatry and psychology in this country. Nonetheless, applications of psychodramatic methods are found in the work of therapists of every discipline. Psychodrama is often integrated with other therapeutic methods; examples are described in books by Leveton (1984) and Nicholas (1984). Active approaches in psychotherapy have become more acceptable, in part because the way was paved by psychodrama. For example, the technique of the action sociogram has become a recognized part of family therapy (where it's called "family sculpture"). Aspects of the human potential movement and the encounter group were derived from Moreno's earlier work; in addition, psychodramatic methods have applications in personal growth settings, and, in a modified form (as sociodrama or roleplaying), in schools and community organizations. In a number of other countries psychodrama has become part of the mainstream of therapeutic process, especially in Sweden, Germany, Argentina, Brazil, New Zealand, Australia, and Japan.

THEORY

J. L. Moreno was among the pioneers of *role theory*, which has become one of the major approaches within the social sciences. However, in contrast to its tendency to be used simply for descriptive purposes, Moreno emphasized its potential for encouraging creative change. Always thinking in terms of practical application, Moreno believed that roles should be continuously reevaluated, experimented with, and shifted around. In this sense, role theory becomes a heuristic, clinically relevant approach (Z. Moreno, 1987).

The concept of *role* implies a separation between the actor and the performance, and when people are able to thus disidentify themselves from those complexes of expectation, habit, and reciprocal communications that constitute their various roles, they begin to develop *role distance*. In clinical situations, role distance gives patients perspective and allows them to consider alternatives to the assumptions inherent in their situations. From this viewpoint, they are helped to redefine, expand, and realign their expectations of themselves and others. In the sense of mental flexibility, psychodrama generates an essentially playful context, although serious and painful matters are often addressed. The result is the development and strengthening of that part of the patient's psyche that observes, chooses,

makes a working alliance with the therapist, individuates, connects with ideals and aspirations, and expresses what both Roberto Assagioli and Otto Rank called the *"will."*

Role theory has other advantages. The metaphor of role is relatively easily understood, and the variety of roles that can be described include the broadest range of human experiences, such as spirituality, fantasy, dreams, art, and temperament. Role theory is also a general framework that can integrate many of the insights of other psychologies. For example, it grants that in some roles Jungian ideas may be more clinically illuminating, while in other roles the concepts of Wilhelm Reich, Aaron Beck or Murray Bowen may have more relevance.

A special advantage of role theory is that it is the most useful framework—and psychodrama the most useful method—for exploring the realm of *interpersonal phenomena*. This area reflects a level of complexity distinct in quality and dynamics from the psychology of individuals or of larger groups (Blatner, 1988b). Family systems theories come closest to addressing this dimension, but the interpersonal field also includes other social relationships. Relevant factors include how roles are distributed, how fixed they are, and the freedom or ability to comment on their complexes of expectations, hidden rules, associated emotions, etc. In other words, role theory builds a bridge between individual and social psychology.

A corollary of this psychosocial focus in psychodrama is the idea that role theory can be used to help people understand each other. Empathy is trainable when the concept of role is used as a lens for considering one aspect of another person's situation at a time. Gradually, using the technique of *role reversal* (discussed more fully below), patients can be helped to relinquish their tendencies toward egocentricity. Moreno meant his concept of encounter to include not only a more honest and direct level of dialogue, but also a willingness to appreciate the other's point of view. In this sense, psychodramatic methods are useful in developing what Alfred Adler considered the key to mental health, a quality he called "social interest" (Adler, 1930).

Psychodrama implicitly encourages an expansion of one's role repertoire. By shifting roles freely and enjoying playing several roles on several levels simultaneously (such as the role of observing the process while enacting the role involved in the task), a sense of vitality is added to therapy. The contribution of psychodrama to psychotherapy resides in its powerful methodology, which demonstrates that healing comes not only through reconditioning, learning, or insight, but also through the sense of empowerment as patients discover their own capacity for creativity. Here, too, psychodrama serves as a methodology for implementing the insights of Otto Rank's approach to therapy (Lieberman, 1985). Furthermore, creative activities are self-reinforcing: the more people discover their ability to be creative, the more confidence they develop that they can use these sources of creativity in times of need.

Moreno discovered that the practical key to everyday creativity was spontaneity and that methods that foster spontaneity increase the patients' progress in therapy. Spontaneity does not refer to mere impulsivity, but rather to a fresh and effective response to a challenging situation. It is the opposite of fixations, addictions, or habitual or compulsive patterns of thought. Many forms of individual and social psychopathology may be viewed as a loss of spontaneity, an unwillingness to think creatively.

The principle of *physical activity* offers several benefits in psychotherapy: (a) the kinesthetic cues aroused in movement and the freeing up of the breath and voice evoke a host of preverbal associations; (b) the sense of being active helps to counter the sense of helplessness and passivity, with their attendant feelings of guilt and shame, which tend to be associated with the demoralization found in psychiatric problems; (c) reintroduction of the rich dimension of nonverbal communication in enactments can be worked with both diagnostically and therapeutically; and (d) physically moving from place to place on stage when taking different roles symbolically compartmentalizes the different facets of a problem and helps to reduce confusion.

The principle of *concretization* engages patients in specifying their problems in dramatic form. Vague abstractions, often used as subtle defenses, are converted into specific scenes. By reanchoring patients in their experiences, the therapist and group are aided in understanding the problem and can engage in more effective help. What Alfred Adler called "the private fictions," those internalized minidramas of secret desires, fears, expectations, and symbolic triumphs, can be reevaluated in the externalization process of psychodrama. With the support of the therapist and the group, and the recognition in the present moment that old strategies are no longer adaptive, new approaches to the problem can be devised.

The development of channels for *sublimation* (using one's energy more constructively and creatively) through the use of psychodrama helps patients begin to release their neurotic patterns by working out alternative ways of achieving satisfaction. Psychodrama, in fostering self-expression of the voice, body, and imagination, allows for metaphorical resolution of internal conflicts. The creative arts therapies also provide effective treatment using this principle. The therapeutic dynamics of psychodrama provide a vehicle for healing by serving as play therapy for adults. The dramatic context provides the benefits of a fail-safe laboratory, a supportive place for experimentation with new behaviors. The vividness of the method and its similarity in essence to the psychodynamics of play—the symbolic resolution of seemingly paradoxical elements—lend a sense of pleasure and reintroduce humor to the process (Blatner & Blatner, 1988a). This element of fun is a powerful motivating factor, for it counters tendencies in psychotherapy to stay overly focused on the client's pain. While an expression of concern is appropriate, too much can discourage hopefulness and attendant resources for change.

Catharsis, a major factor in psychological healing, is a fundamental element in psychodrama. It involves the freeing of psychic energy that accompanies an expansion of consciousness (Blatner, 1985). As the psyche includes previously disowned parts of itself, the energies previously exerted in the service of repression become available for more conscious utilization. In addition, there is a sense of relief in reuniting with an important part of the self that had been previously hidden or disowned.

Psychodrama aims not only at a rediscovery of the various aspects of the self, but also at developing constructive ways of utilizing these dimensions. Referring to this principle, Moreno noted that every catharsis of abreaction should be followed by a catharsis of integration. (Therapies aimed simply at abreactive catharses may have been less effective because they lacked the component of developing healthy behaviors to replace the unhealthy ones.) When people discover that they can be accepted by a group or find a meaningful role in the world, a catharsis of belonging occurs —which may also include spiritual or transpersonal experiences. The unique focus of psychodrama in encouraging the expansion of the self in a group setting creates an opportunity for synthesizing the needs for both individuation and belonging.

By demanding a holistic involvement from the therapist, psychodrama functions not only as a method for developing insight, but also as a method of experiential learning, which facilitates personal growth for the therapist as well as the patient. Furthermore, the techniques have applications in many nontherapeutic contexts and thereby also serve the goals of prevention and social development.

TERMINOLOGY

Moreno described five basic elements in psychodrama.

1. The *director* orchestrates the enactment.
2. The *protagonist* is the client who is the focus of the psychodramatic exploration. A special term is needed because in an enactment, protagonists may play themselves, their mothers, or

several different parts of themselves, or they may even step outside the scene and act as observers. In all these shifts of role, the protagonist remains the focus of the director's and the group's concern. Later in group therapy sessions other clients might become the focus of attention, and during their enactments they would become the protagonists.

3. The *auxiliary* is anyone who helps the protagonist by playing a supporting role. The auxiliary (also called *auxiliary ego*) may portray the protagonist's employer, sibling, a figure in a dream, or even an abstract entity, such as the government. For example, assume the protagonist is in a scene with an employer, played by an auxiliary. If role reversal is used, the auxiliary then takes the role of the protagonist while the protagonist takes on the role of employer. The auxiliary can also take the role of the double for the protagonist, a technique described more fully below.

4. The *stage* refers to a designated area for the enactment. It is generally beneficial to use a separate area rather than to play the scene in the midst of the group. By providing a separate place for dramatic action, the protagonist is reminded that the events in the enactment are clearly different from verbal interchanges. Moreno designed and installed special stages at his own institutes, and some hospitals have created stages for psychodramatic work. Enactments are usually conducted in an area cleared of chairs in a group therapy room.

5. The *audience* refers to the other people present besides the director, the protagonist, and the auxiliaries. In psychodrama, the role of the audience shifts during the course of a session, with some members becoming auxiliaries while others become protagonists. Sometimes the audience plays an active role, giving feedback, encouraging, making sound effects, or calling out pertinent evocative phrases at the request of the director. (This technique is termed the *chorus*.)

METHODOLOGY

A typical psychodramatic instruction is, "Don't tell us, show us." With this phrase, the patient is encouraged to plunge into a situation at a more intense and committed level of experience, *acting as if* instead of *talking about*. "Show us what happened with your family," "Show us the conflict you're having within yourself," and "Show us what you'd like to be doing in 10 years" are, respectively, the techniques of *enactment, multiple parts of self,* and *future projection*. Scenes from the past, present, or future may be set up; concretizing issues in this way cuts through defensive tendencies toward vagueness and circumstantiality.

The key to authentic work in psychodrama is spontaneity, which is developed gradually, using the principle of *warming up*, usually through structured experiences. Warm-up techniques are used to generate group cohesion and involvement from the very beginning. In addition, they may be applied to help patients become sensitized to a particular issue. For example, nonverbal interactions, art therapy activities, sensory awareness methods, guided imagery, theater games, and brief roleplaying of situations that will challenge the participants' spontaneity can give a shared experience and introduce material they can further explore.

Another principle is *encounter*, a dialogue in the present moment, having the patient speak directly to significant others in his or her life (either in reality or with another person played by an auxiliary). Another form of encounter can occur between the different parts of the protagonist's self (Watkins, 1986). Some patients' sense of confusion can be productively reframed as a conflict in which the different parts of themselves interrupt each other too much. By externalizing internal dialogues and separating voices, issues can be clarified. Sometimes a client can play both parts in an encounter—the technique of *monodrama*, using an empty chair as the site of the imagined other.

There are some advantages in using an *auxiliary* because another person's reactions tend to evoke more spontaneity from the protagonist. Also, the use of the auxiliary allows transferences to be directed at the original or more relevant figure in the patient's life (e.g., parent, spouse, teacher, previous therapist, etc.) played by the auxiliary, while the therapist becomes a mediator. The protagonist is able to explore more intense feelings in the heat of the spontaneous interaction. The auxiliary can employ the evocative medium of touch, expressed through a tug on the sleeve, a squeeze of the hand, or a hand on the shoulder. Additional auxiliaries may play roles of other figures in the scene, so there may be several people on the stage at a time.

In the technique of the *double*, an auxiliary plays the role of the protagonist's inner self, helping to express and clarify his or her unspoken thoughts. The double usually plays a supportive role for the protagonist. However, once a sense of alliance is developed between the two, the director may coach the double to include some mild provocation or confrontation to facilitate the clarification process. The double technique offers a type of interpretation phrased in terms of "I" messages, and in words consistent with the patient's self-system. The protagonist is explicitly instructed to correct any of the double's statements that feel inaccurate. This creates a mutuality in which the double helps the protagonist express in an enactment what might never be spoken in the course of an ordinary exchange.

The heart of psychodrama is the technique of *role reversal*. It is an operationalized approach to the golden rule, aimed at helping patients to develop empathy for others and to transcend tendencies toward egocentricity. There is value inherent in the expectation that a patient will learn and exercise this skill. In this technique the protagonist is directed to change parts and take the role of the other person—the parent, employer, friend, etc. The art of this technique lies in the therapist-director's ability to gently warm up the protagonist to the experience of the other's role through interviewing the protagonist as if he or she were the other person.

This technique may be used to portray the behavior of the other person, with an emphasis on such components as voice tone, pacing, or intensity, and such nonverbal elements as posture, facial expression, or gestures. These can be revealing and cathartic if the client is able to vividly communicate to the group the impact of the other person's manner. At a deeper level, role reversal can be used to help patients understand the feelings or attitudes of the other people in their lives. The technique of role reversal has other applications in psychotherapy and education.

Another principle in psychodrama is the incorporation of *surplus reality.* The term refers to that dimension of psychological experience that transcends the boundaries of physical reality. Phenomenologically, people have relationships with others who are deceased, children who have never been born, God, hallucinatory figures, religious personages, etc. These are often as important in a patient's psychodynamics as relations with actual people. In psychodrama, encounters with these significant psychological figures can be externalized and enacted. In this sense, as Moreno noted, psychodrama is the theater of truth, because the full truth of a person often encompasses not only what has actually happened, but, of equal importance, what has never happened and perhaps could never happen in reality.

Surplus reality can be utilized in several ways. One example is the technique of *act fulfillment,* in which the protagonist is helped to experience a corrective emotional experience. Many patients suffer from acute or chronic trauma that has left them with residual feelings of powerlessness, shame, and a secret sense that this is the way life has to be. Reenactment of the traumatic situation breaks through layers of denial and allows for a catharsis of owning the experience. This may then be healed by replaying the scene with a more satisfactory con-

clusion. The victim of abuse, for example, is helped to protest, to become empowered to seek effective protection, and then, using the technique of the reformed auxiliary, given a chance to create a more benign relationship with the aggressor.

Moreno actively used surplus reality as a vital resource in healing. He once said to Sigmund Freud, "You analyze [people's] dreams. I try to give them the courage to dream again" (Moreno, 1946, p. 6). In this sense, psychodrama offers patients an opportunity to envision life with more faith, to reinvest emotionally in the future. (Patients are often demoralized and frequently repress their hopes for a pleasant future as much as they repress desires and thoughts in the present and the past.) Moreno developed the *future projection* technique as a way of encouraging patients to become more explicit in their goal setting. It involves portraying scenes that are hoped for or anticipated. A variation of this is *role training,* a type of behavioral rehearsal, used to help a patient prepare for an event such as a date, an employment interview, or an encounter with a relative. Using coaching, modeling, videotaped or verbal feedback, and other techniques, the patient is allowed to repeat the enactment until satisfactory options are developed.

Many other techniques are used in psychodrama, and all can be modified and adapted for use with diverse populations and in a variety of contexts. All psychodramatic approaches aim to involve patients in their ability to imagine, think, and behave in an as-if context and to engage in dramatic play as a resource for insight, behavioral practice, expansion of consciousness, and healing.

SUMMARY

Psychodramatic methods can be used to enhance the effectiveness of many other therapies, because their principles address a number of dimensions of human experience that are important factors in healing and personal growth. Psychodrama was developed in the 1920s and 1930s by J. L. Moreno in conjunction with his pioneering activities in group psychotherapy and applied social psychology (i.e., sociometry). His techniques have been integrated into many of the more directive forms of therapy in the last several decades. Specific techniques such as role reversal, dialogues between parts of the self, act fulfillment, and role-playing can become valuable parts of any therapist's repertoire of skills.

Moreno's emphasis on creativity and spontaneity deserves to be considered a major contribution to psychology. Indeed, his clinical orientation to role theory can serve as an integrative approach that may help to create an intellectual foundation for a more eclectic psychotherapy. Psychodramatic methods have a unique capacity to integrate many dualities of human experience—the rational and the imaginative, reality testing and emotions, action and reflection, future and past, and playfulness and seriousness. Utilizing the fullest potential of the group, interpersonal relationships, and the innate capacity of certain activities to generate spontaneity as a source of creativity, therapists can use psychodramatic methods to help their patients become more fully integrated by becoming more whole. Part of this healing is the inclusion of the qualities of excitement, playfulness, and the arts that are associated with creativity and spontaneity, because they add the quality of enjoyment to those aspects of therapy that involve an adventure of self-discovery and reconciliation. It was this insight that led Moreno to have written as his epitaph, "Here lies the man who brought laughter and joy back into psychiatry."

REFERENCES

Adler, A. (1930). *The science of living*. London: Kegan Paul.

Blatner, A. (1989). *Acting-in: Practical applications of psychodramatic methods*. New York: Springer. (First published, 1973.)

Blatner, A. (1985). The dynamics of catharsis. *Journal of Group Psychotherapy, Psychodrama, and Sociometry, 37*(4), 157–166.

Blatner, A., & Blatner, A. (1988a). *The art of play: An adult's guide to reclaiming imagination and spontaneity*. New York: Human Sciences Press.

Blatner, A. (1988b). *Foundations of psychodrama: History, theory, and practice*. New York: Springer.

Buchanan, D. R. (1984). Psychodrama. In T. B. Karasu (Ed.), *The psychiatric therapies, Part 2: The psychosocial therapies* (pp. 783–799). Washington, DC: The American Psychiatric Association.

Compernolle, T. (1981). J. L. Moreno: An unrecognized pioneer of family therapy. *Family Process, 20*, 331–335.

Corsini, R. J. (1967). *Role playing in psychotherapy*. Chicago: Aldine.

Farrell, D. (1976). Group techniques with hospitalized patients. In A. Wolberg, L. Wolberg & M. Aronson (Eds.), *Group psychotherapy, 1976—An overview*. New York: Stratton.

Fine, L. J. (1978). Psychodrama. In R. J. Corsini (Ed.), *Current psychotherapies* (2nd Ed.). Itasca, IL: F. E. Peacock.

Goldman, E. E., & Morrison, D. S. (1984). *Psychodrama: Experience and process.* Phoenix, AZ: Eldemar Corp.

Greenberg, I. A. (Ed.) (1974). *Psychodrama: Theory and therapy.* New York: Behavioral Publications.

Kipper, D. A. (1986). *Psychotherapy through clinical role playing.* New York: Brunner/Mazel.

Landy, R. J. (1986). *Drama therapy: Concepts and practices.* Springfield, IL: Charles C Thomas.

Leveton, E. (1984). *Adolescent crisis.* New York: Springer.

Lieberman, E. J. (1985). *Acts of will: The life and work of Otto Rank.* New York: The Free Press.

Moreno, J. L. (1934). *Who shall survive? A new approach to the problem of human interrelations.* Washington, DC: Nervous & Mental Disease Publishing Co.

Moreno, J. L. (1946–1969). *Psychodrama (Vols. 1–3).* Beacon, NY: Beacon House. (For materials published by Moreno relating to psychodrama, write: Beacon House, Inc., Welsh Road & Butler Pike, Ambler, PA 19002.)

Moreno, J. L. (1988). *The essential Moreno: Writings on group method, psychodrama, and spontaneity* (Edited by Jonathan Fox). New York: Springer.

Moreno, Z. T. (1978). Psychodrama. In H. Mullan & M. Rosenbaum (Eds.), *Group Psychotherapy (2nd Ed.)* (pp. 352–376). New York: The Free Press.

Moreno, Z. T. (1987). Psychodrama, role theory, and the concept of the social atom. In J. Zeig (Ed.), *The evolution of psychotherapy.* New York: Brunner/Mazel.

Nichols, M. P., & Efran, J. S. (1985). Catharsis in psychotherapy: A new perspective. *Psychotherapy, 22*(1), 46–58.

Nicholas, M. W. (1984). *Change in the context of group therapy.* New York: Brunner/Mazel.

Starr, A. (1977). *Psychodrama: Rehearsal for living.* Chicago: Nelson-Hall.

Watkins, M. (1986). *Invisible guests: The development of imaginal dialogue.* Hillsdale, NJ: L. Erlbaum Assoc./The Analytic Press.

Yablonsky, L. (1975). *Psychodrama: Resolving emotional problems through role-playing.* New York: Basic Books.

ALEXANDER LOWEN

C

Bioenergetic Analysis

ALEXANDER LOWEN

Bioenergetic analysis is a method of psychotherapy that integrates work with the body into the analytic process. The process aims at helping people understand who they are and why they function as they do. True understanding means more than just acquiring an intellectual knowledge of one's background and motivations. It involves a deep awareness defined as a connection to the events of one's life and to the forces that impel one to action in the present. This connection is made by getting in touch with the body, which is the repository of one's life's experiences. One gets in touch with the body by feeling what goes on in it. This is accomplished in bioenergetic therapy by mobilizing the body through certain active techniques. However, being an analytic therapy, bioenergetic analysis uses most analytic techniques to help in this objective. Dream analysis, slips of the tongue, transference and its associated resistance, and character analysis are all important aspects of bioenergetic analysis.

Work with the body is based on the concept that the more energy a person has, the more alive he or she is, which is translated into more movement, feeling, and thinking. Energy produces movement, which creates feelings and leads to thinking. This formulation is depicted in Figure 14.1, which illustrates the hierarchy of personality functions.

By improving a person's energy processes, all functions above the base are affected: spontaneous movement is increased, more feeling develops, and

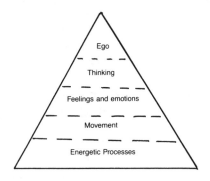

FIGURE 14.1
HIERARCHY OF PERSONALITY
FUNCTIONS

there is a corresponding gain in awareness and understanding. This is working from below. One can also affect all functions from above. Psychoanalysis, working from above, will affect all functions too, but one has a greater leverage working from below—i.e., from the body side. However, to limit the therapeutic program to working solely with the body or the mind is to handicap the process. Working with both body and mind is like walking on two legs, whereas an approach limited to the mind only (or the body only) is like hopping on one leg alone.

The way to modify energetic processes is through breathing and movement. Energy is produced in the body by the metabolism of food. In effect, food is burned in the body to produce energy, just as fuel is burned in an engine. This process requires oxygen. One can limit the amount of energy produced by decreasing either food (fuel) or oxygen. If one increases the amount of food without increasing the available oxygen, there is no increase of energy and the excess food becomes fat. If there is enough food, increasing oxygen immediately produces more energy. Body oxygen is increased by increasing the depth and fullness of respiration. Helping a person to breathe more deeply is one of the active techniques employed in bioenergetic analysis. However, this can pose a problem because increasing a person's energy leads directly to more movement and more feeling, and the feelings evoked may be painful or frightening (e.g., murderous rage).

One learns early in life that holding one's breath can suppress painful or frightening feelings. Restricting the depth of one's breathing reduces the intensity of all feeling. The mechanism for the diminution in breathing and the suppression of feeling is the blocking of spontaneous movement through muscular tension or rigidity. Thus, every chronically tense muscle in the body reflects an inner conflict between an impulse or feeling and the expression of that impulse or feeling. A tight jaw may hold back impulses to bite, and the person will be unaware of these impulses because the inhibition of the movement blocks the perception of the feeling. A tight throat may hold back impulses to cry or scream. Tense shoulders represent the inhibition of impulses to reach out or strike out. A pelvis that is relatively immobile, due to unconscious tension in the muscles surrounding that structure, will decrease the strength of the sexual discharge. These tensions also act to reduce respiration. A tight throat reduces the amount of air flowing in and out of the lungs. A tight abdomen limits the depth of breathing at the same time that it reduces belly feelings: namely, belly crying, belly laughing, and sexuality. A rigid chest wall may cut off any awareness of the feeling of heartbreak, but at the same time it reduces the fullness of respiration.

Chronic muscular tension immobilizes the body, which reduces feeling by deadening the person. Aliveness is inversely proportional to rigidity. A dead person is a stiff; a stiff person is emotionally dead. In bioenergetic therapy one comes to sense personal rigidity and deadness and gets in touch with suppressed feelings through deeper breathing and movement. The ability to accept, integrate, and express these feelings appropriately requires considerable *talking* between therapist and client. About one-half of therapeutic time is spent in discussing problems, feelings, and behavior. In this respect bioenergetic analysis is like any other effective psychotherapy; it differs by adding another important dimension to the therapeutic process.

HISTORY

Bioenergetic analysis was developed in 1953 as an offshoot of the work of Wilhelm Reich, which he called character-analytic-vegetotherapy. Reich, a psychoanalyst, was a member of the Vienna Psychoanalytic Society from 1921 to 1934.

Alexander Lowen was a patient of Reich in 1942. At that time Reich had incorporated working with the body into the analytic process. As an analyst Reich had observed that patients held their breath when they were resisting the full and free expression of their thoughts. Watching his patients as well as listening to them, he realized that there was functional identity between the way patients used their bodies and the way they used their minds. He recognized that a person's character is expressed physically and psychologically in identical terms. He stated that while there is an antithesis between body and mind, there is also a functional identity.

Reich emphasized the role of sexuality in the neuroses. He saw sexuality and the orgasm as the energy regulators of the body. The life process runs counter to the second law of thermodynamics in that it produces surplus energy—that is, more energy than the organism needs for its own survival. This excess energy is channeled into the sexual or reproductive process. Reich stated that the function of the orgasm was to discharge the excess energy of the organism. Theoretically, when all excess energy is discharged, there is no energy left for anxiety or

other neurotic symptoms. This translates into the proposition that neurosis is inconsistent with full and complete orgastic responses. Unfortunately, it is the nature of neurosis to prevent such responses and so, in practice, one cannot cure neurosis by focusing solely upon sexuality. But this relationship between neurosis and sexuality is so direct that to the degree that neurotic attitudes are worked through, sexuality improves and orgasms become more complete and more satisfying. To the degree that sexuality improves, neurosis diminishes.

Reich conceptualized energy as a literal force operating at a physical level; in contrast, Freud's concept of libido was metaphysical and mental. Reich postulated that the energy operating in the living organism was a special energy, which he called *orgone energy* (from org-anism). Whether or not one agrees with Reich about this special energy, there is no doubt that a biological energy powers all living functions. Every neurotic character structure represents a reduction in an individual's energy level and a restriction upon the natural flow of that energy through the body.

Bioenergetic analysis is a true development of Reich's work that has enlarged and extended Reich's views. The need to separate from the Reichian movement grew out of the dogmatic position that his followers maintained. They believed that Reich had said the final word, and they made no allowance for change in theory or practice. In contrast, bioenergetic analysis introduced the following changes:

1. Pleasure was emphasized more than sexuality without denying the great importance of sexuality. The overall concept of pleas-

ure includes sexual pleasure and fulfillment.

2. The introduction of the concept of grounding broadened Reich's approach to the body and the personality. In Reichian therapy the patient lies on a bed. In bioenergetic analysis many positions are used, especially standing, which allows one to get a better sense of one's legs and the ground that is one's basic support. How one stands can be analyzed, and one's ability to stand secure and firm can be developed through appropriate exercises.

3. Concomitant with grounding, physical exercises were developed that permitted patients to be active participants in the therapeutic program. Because many of these exercises can be done at home, the patient can be more independent of the therapist than in most other psychotherapies.

4. This emphasis upon the physical side of the therapy is not at the cost of analytic work. Bioenergetic analysis insists upon the thorough analytic working through of personality problems. The phenomena of transference and resistance are as important in bioenergetic analysis as they are in all psychoanalytic work.

Today bioenergetic analysis is widely practiced in many countries. Located throughout the world are more than 40 centers that offer formal training programs to qualified professionals. These centers or local societies are affiliates of The International Institute for Bioenergetic Analysis, located in New York, which coordinates teaching, holds conferences, and publishes a clinical journal titled *Bioenergetic Analysis.*

THEORY

A primary theoretical concept of bioenergetic analysis is Reich's concept of the unity and antithesis of all living processes. *Unity* refers to the fact that the organism functions as a whole. Every disturbance affects the total person. Thus there can be no distinction between mental and physical illness, or between mental and physical pain. If a person has heart disease, the *person* is ill, not just the heart. Similarly, if a person suffers from anxiety, depression, a phobia, or a compulsion, the body is affected as well as the mind. A physical trauma affects the psyche just as a psychic trauma affects the body. The pain of a child's unfulfilled longing for its mother is not just a mental pain; it is physically structured in the tension and constriction of the throat and mouth as the areas of the body through which that longing would be expressed in a cry or in reaching out to suck or kiss. Evidence of this tension and constriction is proof of the early trauma and its persistence into the present.

The principle of unity also states that the whole body is affected by trauma. The unfulfilled longing of a child disturbs its breathing, its sense of security in its legs, and its self-confidence. Every trauma upsets the basic pulsatory movements of the body. These are the overall expansions and contractions of the organism (which on this level functions like a single cell) and the longitudinal wave-like movements that flow up and down through the body. This expansion and contraction can be clearly seen in the beating of the heart and the in-and-out movements of breathing. The longitudinal flow is seen in the peristaltic movements of the intestines, the sphincters, and the blood vessels. Pulsation is a quality of every cell in the body. When the pulsation is strong, life is strong. At death all pulsatory activity ceases. When pulsation is full and free, a person experiences a feeling of joy and pleasure in his or her body. Any disturbance of these natural pulsatory movements causes a loss of pleasurable feeling and, if intense, produces pain.

The quality of the body's pulsation is most manifest in its breathing, which combines the movements of expansion and contraction with those of the longitudinal wave. Breathing is not limited to the lungs, where the exchange of gases takes place with the outside air. Instead, the whole body participates in respiratory movements. Breathing is accompanied by a wave that begins deep in the pelvis and moves upward to the mouth. In breathing out the wave is reversed. Given that breathing is disturbed in all emotional or neurotic problems, one can determine the existence of these problems from the nature of the respiratory disturbance. As a patient's problem clears up, breathing becomes easier and deeper. When breathing becomes totally free, the problem disappears.

The antithetical aspect of the living process is best reflected in the relation between mind and body. The unity between them doesn't alter the fact that each influences the other and that on a superficial level there is a duality in human nature. Respecting this duality allows recognition that a person's conscious attitude has considerable influence on his or her total functioning. This allows the therapist to introduce *values* into any discussion of human behavior. Although one may be aware that a person's or a society's values are in part determined by unconscious forces, one must accept that they can to some degree be consciously altered in the interest of a better life. Making more energy available to the patient through bioenergetic work with the body facilitates these changes for the better.

Knowing that the body *is* the person (and that its form and movement reveal the personality and contain the history of the person) makes it possible for a bioenergetic therapist to make a tentative diagnosis of the character structure that defines an individual's habitual way of being.

According to bioenergetic analysis theory, there are five major types of character structure: schizoid, oral, narcissistic, masochistic, and rigid. These types are based on libidinal organization and ego development as manifested in the body. The following is an outline of these types:

1. The *schizoid* character structure is characterized by a tendency to split and dissociate. Thinking is split off from feeling. This is manifested on the body level by a lack of good connection between the head and trunk. In many of these individuals the neck is elongated; in others, the head is tilted away from the line of the body. With training this split can be easily recognized. This dissociation between head and body means that a person doesn't feel connected to his or her body. In a severe case, it may result in the phenomenon of depersonalization. In the schizoid personality one also sees a split between the upper and lower halves of the body, manifested by a severe contraction in the region of the waist or a lack of proportion and harmony between the two halves of the body. The

schizoid personality is characterized by a fear of falling apart if one lets go, countered by the need to hold one's self together through tension in all the joint muscles.

2. The *oral* character structure stems from a deprivation of nurturing and support in early infancy and is associated with a fear of abandonment. Fear of abandonment is most manifest in thinness, lack of support in the legs and feet, and underdevelopment of the musculature. The oral character has a strong tendency to be dependent, which can be denied through pseudo-independence. The oral character holds on to self through strong tension in the shoulder girdle and in the legs to prevent falling, which would symbolize being left alone and abandoned.

3. The *narcissistic* character structure is complex. It stems from an early childhood relationship in which the child was seduced by the parent into an intimacy that made the child feel special but in which the child was also used by the parent. Because the seduction was sexual, although not acted out, the child denies feeling as a way to prevent the danger of incest. From being special the child develops a sense of superiority and grandiosity. To be superior the narcissistic person has to hold self above others. This is reflected in the body as an over-development of the upper half and a relative weakness in the lower half. The narcissistic character structure holds self up through strong tensions in the legs and back.

4. The *masochistic* character structure develops in a child who was nurtured but forced to be submissive to the parent. The masochist holds in all feelings through tension in the muscles that control the outlets at the upper and lower ends of the body. Mas-

ochistic attitudes are often associated with early toilet training—the need to hold in and the fear of letting out. On the body level, the masochist is heavy and muscularly overdeveloped, with the main tension in the flexor muscles, which results in a collapse of the body's erect posture.

5. The *rigid* character structure, phallic-narcissistic in the man and hysterical in the woman, is characterized by a straight erect body with considerable pride. However, the erect posture is maintained through a rigidity of the back muscles that denotes an attitude of holding back. This holding back by the rigid character stems from early experiences of being humiliated by the parent of the opposite sex at the time in the oedipal period when the child felt a sexual interest in that parent.

Character types are neither pure nor individualistic. Many persons show a mixture of tendencies and belong to two or more types. In addition, no individual can be understood fully in terms of character type alone because it is only the framework for the clinical picture. As in working with a jigsaw puzzle, one starts with a border and slowly fills in all the pieces. The pieces of the clinical picture emerge as the person gets in touch with the body and, through it, with the experiences of life. Slowly the pieces are filled into the right places, and when nearly all are in, the picture emerges with unexpected clarity for both the patient and the therapist. Each insight, no matter how obtained, is a piece of the puzzle.

Seeing this picture clearly makes the character structure an objective reality for the patient and allows him or her to dissociate from it. At this point there is a major change in the personality, but this major change is also the culmination of many minor changes that have occurred as a result of the insights developed in the course of therapy. These changes are also related to increases in the person's energy level, in aliveness, and in feelings of pleasure.

One of the key elements in producing this change is the analysis and working through of the oedipal situation. Character structure becomes definitively set in that situation as a way of dealing with sexuality. Because character structure is a limitation upon being, it is also a limitation upon sexuality. In the course of working through the characterological issues, sexual feelings increase, with a corresponding increase in sexual pleasure.

No therapy is ever complete, and no one can be restored to a state of innocence. Therapy ends when an individual can take on personal responsibility for continued growth and when he or she has the necessary tools and techniques to promote that growth. Bioenergetics offers these tools through the special body exercises it teaches the patient.

METHODOLOGY

Bioenergetic analysis adds an entirely new dimension to psychotherapy: work with the body. The patient's bodily expression is studied to determine problems and conflicts in his or her personality. There is always an accord between what the body reveals and what the patient tells. Thus, if the patient complains about being depressed, that complaint can be related to the patient's depressed energy level and functioning. The patient whose breathing is shallow can be shown that she is not allowing any feeling to be expressed. The patient who complains of

sexual problems can be shown that he has severe tension in the pelvis that reduces sexual potency. Most patients are not aware that their problems are manifested in their bodies until it is pointed out. Once this understanding is established, it becomes possible to work in a bioenergetic way with the patient.

There are four dimensions to bioenergetic analysis: (a) understanding and working with muscular tension, (b) analyzing association, behavior, and transference, (c) understanding energy dynamics, and (d) focusing on the role of sexuality. All bioenergetic therapists are cognizant of these four dimensions, but their emphasis upon each varies according to their background and experience. Many focus strongly upon the psychological, with some attention to the body because it is the source of feeling. Others do more body work, largely aimed at the expression of feelings. However, all bioenergetic analysts note areas of contraction and tension, interpret the contraction, and then mobilize the body through breathing and movement to release the contraction. Each contraction is blocking a flow of excitation either upward into the head and eyes or downward into the pelvis, genitals, and legs. Pain is always involved in this blocking. On one level, the holding or the contraction is a maneuver to diminish pain, the pain of an unfulfilled longing or desire, the pain of a hurt or humiliation, or the pain of loss or frustration. The contraction diminishes the pain by reducing feeling and by numbing the person to the pain. One *deadens* the area. Releasing the holding is first experienced, therefore, as painful. The surge of an energetic force (blood) through a constricted area is painful. But after release has occurred it is experienced as pleasure. No one can achieve any significant characterological change without experiencing the pain of change. Normal growth is not painful, but therapy deals with distorted or blocked growth and development, and with removing obstacles to growth.

Bioenergetic therapy, although its primary focus is upon the body, is a combined approach that works with both the body and the mind. The proportion of time spent on body work and analysis is approximately equal. In the initial interview, the therapist will spend the first half-hour listening to the patient's complaints and story, asking questions about the present situation and background, and studying facial expression, body attitude, and voice, all of which provide information about the patient's personality. Still more information can be obtained from a study of the form and motility of the body itself. How a person sits, stands, breathes, and moves all reveal problems and conflicts.

Once the relationship between the psychological and the physical is established, the patient knows that his or her body will have to change if personality is to change in a significant way. If the body is too rigid—that is, if one holds back feelings—the body will have to soften. If feelings are held in by muscular tensions that tend to compress the body and close the outlets, these tensions will have to be reduced to allow the expression of feeling. But changing the body in a significant way is a tremendous task. In almost all cases, positive but superficial changes occur rather quickly with bioenergetic therapy. The initial mobilization of the body through deeper breathing

and bioenergetic exercises often evokes long-suppressed feelings. The patient may experience sadness, which can in turn lead to crying or anger, which may be expressed in hitting the bed. The patient may sense a degree of fear that was previously denied and may experience vibrations that provide new bodily sensations. This initial response to bioenergetic therapy is like the opening of a door to an exciting new world of feeling and being. It often produces welcome changes in behavior. At best it provides a foundation of understanding and trust for the more difficult task that lies ahead.

In working with the body, two principles are paramount:

1. Any limitation of motility is both a result and a cause of emotional difficulties. Limitations arise as the result of unresolved infantile conflicts, but the persistence of the tension creates present-day emotional difficulties that clash with the demands of adult reality. Every physical rigidity interferes with and prevents a unitary response to situations.

2. Any restriction of natural respiration is both the result and the cause of anxiety. Anxiety in childhood situations disturbs natural respiration. If the anxiety-producing situation persists and is prolonged, the disturbance of respiration becomes structured in thoracic and abdominal tension. The inability to breathe freely under emotional stress is the physiological basis for the experience of anxiety in such stressful situations.

Unity and coordination of physical responses depend upon the integration of the respiratory movements with the aggressive movements of the body. To the degree that respiration and motility are freed from the restrictions of chronic tensions, the physical functioning of the patient will improve. To that degree, contact with reality on the physical level will expand and deepen. But this will happen only if there is a concomitant and corresponding improvement in the patient's grasp of reality on the psychic and interpersonal levels. One should not be misled, however, by seeming improvements in a patient's functioning on the psychic and interpersonal levels that are not accompanied by an analogous improvement in physical functioning.

Through special movements and body positions, patients in bioenergetic therapy gain a deeper contact with their bodies and a better feeling for it. From this contact and feeling they begin to understand the relation between their present physical state and the experiences of infancy and childhood that created it. Clients learn that denial of the body is a rejection of a need for love; this denial is used to avoid hurt and disappointment. They learn to interpret rigidities as defenses against overwhelming rage and to sense that immobility stems from a deep-seated fear of aggression. Given the opportunity to express rage by pounding or kicking the couch, and given the chance to voice negativity, patients discover that they will not be abandoned or destroyed for expressing feelings. Through the acceptance of their bodies and its feelings, individuals broaden contact with all other aspects of reality.

Because the body is the base of all reality functions, any increase in a person's contact with the body will produce a significant improvement in self-image (body image), interpersonal relationships, the quality of thinking and feeling, and enjoyment of life.

With this energetic understanding, one proceeds to interpret holding or contraction in terms of suppressed feelings. Because feeling has been suppressed, the patient is unaware of it. However, the nature of the holding (body language) identifies the feeling. Generally the feeling can be brought to consciousness by activating expressive movement.

For example, a jaw that is tightly held by tense muscles may hold back impulses to bite. Having a person bite on a towel can activate these impulses so that the suppressed desire to bite becomes conscious. A tightly contracted throat inhibits the expression of crying or screaming, but the person may not be conscious of this inhibition until he or she tries to cry or scream. Rigid shoulders may block impulses to strike out in anger. Often getting the person to hit the bed with his or her fists evokes a feeling of anger. Similarly, one can identify a lack of sexual aggressiveness in an individual from the immobility of the pelvis. However, the ability to read the language of the body is not easily or quickly acquired. Considerable training and experience are necessary to develop this skill to a high level of competence.

Interpreting different patterns of tension in separate body parts (mouth, eyes, shoulders, pelvis, feet, etc.) is much like reading words. Even though one can read words correctly, it doesn't follow that one can make sense of the words. To make full sense, words must be interpreted in the context of a sentence, a paragraph, and even a chapter. Each body has a unique expression that reveals the individual's personality and character. The character structure can be seen as a type that facilitates understanding and communication, but one can't do therapy with a type. Therapy deals with a very specific individual, and it is that specificity that one must understand from a reading of the body. The parts make sense in terms of the whole, but the whole cannot be determined from the parts. Only when we understand an individual in these terms do we have a grasp of his or her problems, and only within that frame of reference does the work on the parts or segments become fully productive.

SUMMARY

If therapy is a voyage of self-discovery, it should be conducted by a guide who has personally made this voyage. A therapist cannot help patients advance beyond the point where he or she has personally gone. However, too many therapists have failed to confront their character structure on a bodily level. This follows from the observation that they have not made any significant changes in their own body structure. Consequently, their knowledge of character structure is more theoretical than experimental. The result is that they count solely on awareness to modify personality. In fact, awareness and insight *can* do this to a limited degree and on a superficial level. However, insight is only a window through which one can see the reason for some aspect of behavior. Knowing the *why* of behavior does not strongly influence the *how* of behavior. To believe otherwise is to ignore the energetic factor.

Energetic considerations dictate that deep change involves continuous work at the breakthrough level. This is the level at which pain and fear are encountered. Fear stems from the fact that breakthrough often occurs together with breakdown. The old structure must crack and crumble so that a freer mode of being can develop. Successful therapists have experienced some of these breakdowns in their own growth and can attest to the pain and fear that accompany this process. One can appreciate the reluctance of many therapists to bring patients to the breakthrough point because they fear the possible breakdown that may occur. Yet this process, however painful, may be necessary if true therapeutic change is going to occur.

Bioenergetic analysis, with its appreciation for the physical as well as the mental aspects of human experience, provides a theory for explaining human neuroses, a typology for classifying character structure, and a balanced therapy for treating patients with psychological problems. It builds on the work of Wilhelm Reich, but goes beyond Reich in both formulation of clinical issues and treatment techniques. It is analytical in nature but expands on traditional analytical methods by incorporating specific body and breathing exercises into the therapeutic hour. Body work suggests new directions for analytical therapy, and insights gained in analysis are used to formulate hypotheses to pursue in body work. Bioenergetic analysis uses these reciprocal and complementary sources of information to provide a comprehensive and balanced psychotherapy.

REFERENCES

Lowen, A. (1958). *The language of the body.* New York: Macmillan.

Lowen, A. (1965). *Love and orgasm.* New York: Macmillan.

Lowen, A. (1967). *Betrayal of the body.* New York: Macmillan.

Lowen, A. (1970). *Pleasure: A creative approach to life.* New York: Penguin Books.

Lowen, A. (1972). *Depression and the body.* New York: Penguin Books.

Lowen, A. (1975). *Bioenergetics.* New York: Penguin Books.

Lowen, A. (1977). *The way to vibrant health.* New York: Harper & Row.

Lowen, A. (1980). *Fear of life.* New York: Macmillan.

Lowen, A. (1984). *Narcissism: Denial of the true self.* New York: Macmillan.

Reich, W. (1972). *Character analysis.* New York: Orgone Institute Press.

Reich, W. (1970). *The function of the orgasm.* New York: Farrar, Strauss.

Appendix

SCREENING FOR MEDICAL REFERRAL

Robert L. Taylor

Psychological symptoms are not always caused by psychological problems—they may also result from organic dysfunction. Instances of psychological symptoms that are caused by physical malfunction create a critical diagnostic issue for therapists and counselors (Taylor, 1982). An outstanding example of such a situation occurred in the case of the American composer, George Gershwin, who was treated in psychotherapy by a psychoanalyst who had two M.D. degrees: one earned in Europe and one from the United States. Gershwin actually had a brain tumor which the psychoanalyst did not suspect. Only upon autopsy was the cause of Gershwin's aberrant behavior discovered.

Persons suffering from medical conditions may seek counseling or therapy for what they presume are psychological problems, just as individuals with psychological problems may seek out medical care, assuming their distress has a biological origin. The therapist's challenge is to recognize telltale clues of possible underlying organic cause. Skill in assessment and referral requires a practical understanding of a few basic principles.

Failure to detect masquerading medical conditions can result in misguided therapy, frustration for both the client and the professional, unnecessary expense and, in certain cases, even death. Few moments in a therapist's professional life are more disturbing than when he or she discovers that a psychodynamic or behavioral explanation has been applied erroneously to symptoms of a brain tumor, thyroid disorder, or other organic condition. The best insurance against this possibility is to learn to identify psychological masquerade.

A sound approach to psychological masquerade starts with avoiding *clinical traps*. The first of these, failing to consider the possibility of a masquerading condition, is perhaps the most common and the most serious pitfall. Rigid clinical assumptions often prevent therapists from seeing the obvious. Pertinent observations are neglected in favor of evidence that supports a favorite clinical hypothesis, such as "borderline personality," "repressed anger," or "faulty family communication." Skill at detecting psychological masquerade depends on the ability to avoid prematurely accepting "obvious" psychological explanations.

A second pitfall is created by the tendency to assume that "psychological" symptoms necessarily imply psychological causes. They do not. Anxiety, depression, paranoia, and obsessive-compulsive disorders are often, but not always, the products of psychological conflict. Identical symptoms can result from a surprisingly large number of medical conditions.

Equating psychotic behavior with schizophrenia or related psychoses is another common pitfall. In the absence of solid evidence to the contrary, any instance of psychotic behavior should be considered organic until proven otherwise. Psychotic behavior complicates the clinical picture of a host of medical conditions, including viral encephalitis, head injuries, brain tumors, petit mal epilepsy, hypercalcemia, drug intoxications, heart disease, and diabetes.

AN APPROACH TO RECOGNIZING PSYCHOLOGICAL MASQUERADE

ALERTING CLUES

Alerting clues are factors that should be noted by the counselor or therapist as indicators of possible psychological masquerade. A single alerting clue is not compelling evidence for organic disease, but it should heighten the clinician's suspicion. Alerting clues are *additive*: the more there are, the greater the case for an underlying medical condition.

No history of similar symptoms. The initial episode of psychological distress deserves special scrutiny. If a person has never before reacted to the stresses and strains of living with noticeable mental and emotional changes, other possible causes should be carefully considered.

No readily identifiable cause. In the absence of a major life stress, psychological symptoms should make a therapist uneasy, particularly when these symptoms appear suddenly. Personal conflict or traumatic life crises can precipitate powerful psychological reactions, but, usually the cause is readily apparent. In contrast, masquerading organic conditions often arise "out of the blue."

Age 55 or older. Statistically, older people are at greater risk for organic mental disorders. Approximately 50 percent of initial psychiatric hospitalizations for people 55 years of age or older have an organic basis. Higher rates of disease and injuries combined with a greater propensity for adverse reactions to medications make older people particularly susceptible to organic mental symptoms.

Chronic physical disease. Chronic disease puts a person at double jeopardy for psychological masquerade. First, the diseased system itself is susceptible to failing and causing secondary brain dysfunction. Second, people with chronic disease typically take medications—often more than one—with the increased risk of adverse mental and emotional reactions.

Drug use. Drugs (including alcohol, street drugs, and prescription and nonpre-scription medications) are the number one cause of organic mental disorders. With addicting drugs, psychological symptoms can result from intoxication and—once addiction has occurred—from withdrawal. It is also important to remember that drugs like caffeine, nicotine, and a host of over-the-counter preparations are psychoactive and can produce unexpected psychological effects.

PRESUMPTIVE CLUES

Presumptive clues indicate a strong probability of organic brain disease. They should be considered hard evidence for an organic mental disorder and justify prompt referral for medical evaluation.

Symptoms of brain syndrome. The brain syndrome is not a disease per se. It is instead a variable clinical picture related to cognitive dysfunction. The symptoms signal a serious impairment in brain functioning that can result from a brain tumor or seizure disorder, but equally as well from heart disease or liver failure. The important point is that brain syndrome is *not* usually present in psychological reactions. The recognition of brain syndrome is presumptive evidence of an organic mental disorder and further diagnostic procedures are required. *One or more of* the following five cognitive deficits accompany brain syndromes: inattention, disorientation, recent memory impairment, diminished reasoning, and sensory indiscrimination.

Inattention refers to severe inability to concentrate or attend for even a few minutes. When asked to repeat five numbers, the inattentive client becomes distracted and is usually unable to do so, even when given a second opportunity.

Disorientation refers to a deficit in understanding temporal and spatial relationships. The disoriented client is unable to identify the month or year or to locate correctly where he or she is at any given moment. Surprisingly, people who are severely disoriented can often hide this fact as long as they stay close to home and maintain their routine.

Whereas long-term memories from childhood may be well preserved in a person with brain syndrome, recent memory fails. Recent memory operates in the recall of experiences five to ten minutes after they have occurred. It can be tested clinically by having the client attempt to recall four items (e.g., book, car, rose, pencil) after five minutes. Repeated failure at this task is suggestive of brain syndrome.

Diminished reasoning refers to profound restriction of the ability to solve problems. Simple calculations provide an excellent screening test for diminished reasoning. What remains if you subtract 14 from 32? How many eggs are there in 2½ dozen? Of course, the ability to reason varies tremendously from one individual to another; thus, in framing appropriate screening questions, the clinician should always keep in mind the person's prior level of intellectual functioning.

Sensory indiscrimination results from the inability to focus on certain sensory inputs while excluding others. A person suffering from brain syndrome may flounder in a state of sensory overload. The client becomes confused and is likely to make sensory misinterpretations. Strangers may be mistaken for old friends or street sounds mistaken for familiar sounds at home.

Manifestations of brain syndrome commonly but not invariably occur in organic mental disorder. The clinician must also be alert to other presumptive clues.

Head injury. The most baffling cases of head injury are those in which the client has no recollection of being injured. This frequently occurs with alcohol and drug intoxication. It is essential for the clinician to closely observe for external signs of head trauma and to carefully scrutinize cases of alcoholism or drug abuse with an abrupt onset of psychological symptoms. Keep in mind that symptoms from head injury are delayed for days or even weeks.

Change in headache pattern. Headache is a common complaint usually caused by muscle tension related to stress. However, *a marked change* in headache patterns suggests an underlying organic condition. Headache is the first manifestation of brain tumor in one out of five cases. It can also be associated with a variety of other brain disorders, including cerebral infections, subdural hematomas, and communicating hydrocephalus.

Visual disturbances. Any visual deficit of recent onset seen in conjunction with psychological symptoms suggests brain impairment. Whereas total loss of vision is obviously readily identified, partial visual loss often goes undetected even by the person affected. Repeated accidents, such as scraping the car when driving into narrow spaces or bumping into the sides of doorways, suggest a partial loss of vision.

Speech deficits. Speech deficits fall into two groups: disorders of mechanical production and disorders of word usage.

Dysarthria falls in the first group and refers to difficulty articulating words. A common example is the garbled speech of a drunk. A similar deficit is seen in a host of neurological disorders and can be mistaken for psychotic speech. However, despite the bizarre images and irrational thought found in functional psychosis, the mechanics of speech itself are unaltered.

In contrast to dysarthria, aphasia refers to the loss of word comprehension or usage. One form—fluent aphasia—closely mimics psychotic language. Typically, aphasics find it difficult to keep on track. They tend to speak in a circular, tangential fashion, making up words as they go to overcome their inability to select appropriate words. These fabricated words are often reminiscent of the neologisms found in the speech of persons suffering from schizophrenia. In the absence of intoxication, the sudden breakdown of normal speech and speech comprehension in an adult suggests aphasia and requires a complete neurological examination.

Abnormal body movements. Psychological symptoms and abnormal body movements occur together in many organic mental disorders. For example, a person's ability to walk is compromised in vitamin B-12 deficiency, brain syphilis, acute and chronic alcoholism, drug intoxication, and normal pressure hydrocephalus. All of these conditions are commonly associated with mental and emotional changes and can easily be mistaken as psychological, especially if the difficulty in walking is overlooked.

There are other abnormal body movements, such as tics and jerks, for which the therapist should be alert. In the early stages, subtle abnormalities in movement may be the only indicators of a neurological disorder. This is true in masquerading conditions such as Parkinson's disease.

Huntington's chorea, Wilson's disease, Tourette's syndrome, multiple sclerosis, and tardive dyskinesia.

Changes in consciousness. Organicity should always be part of the differential diagnosis when there is a major alteration in consciousness—namely, excessive sleepiness, lapses in consciousness, or total loss of consciousness.

The sleepiness caused by medical conditions can be relentless and the client may report a history of falling asleep repeatedly during the day. This tendency to sleep is aggravated by the consumption of even small amounts of alcohol or tranquilizing medications.

Lapses in consciousness are momentary disruptions that can be mistaken for the thought blocking seen in psychotic states. More often then not, however, recurring lapses indicate seizure activity.

Several clues crucial to the clinical recognition of psychological masquerade have been discussed. By watching for them, a therapist minimizes the likelihood of mistaking a masquerading medical condition for a psychological problem.

REFERENCE

Taylor, R. L. (1982) *Mind or body: Distinguishing psychological from organic disorders.* New York: McGraw-Hill.

Glossary

The following abbreviations are used to indicate primary associations: (A) Adlerian Psychotherapy; (B) Bioenergetics; (BT) Behavior Therapy; (CT) Cognitive Therapy; (E) Existential Therapy; (FT) Family Therapy; (G) Gestalt Therapy; (J) Analytical Psychotherapy; (MMT) Multimodal Therapy; (PA) Psychoanalysis; (PC) Person-Centered Therapy; (PD) Psychodrama; (RET) Rational-Emotive Therapy; (TA) Transactional Analysis.

Abreaction (PA). The reliving of painful emotional experiences in psychotherapy, usually involving conscious awareness of previously repressed material. *See also* Catharsis.

Act Fulfillment (PD). Reenacting a traumatic situation correctively, producing more satisfactory results.

Activity Scheduling (CT & BT). Setting up routine activity in order to offset inertia.

Actualizing Tendency (PC). An innate human predisposition toward growth and fulfilling one's potential.

Adapted Child (TA). An ego state with two functions, either conforming or rebelling. One's Adapted Child is highly complex and contains one's script.

Adult (TA). An ego state that is analytical, rational, and nonjudgmental; the objective part of the personality that solves problems and obtains information.

Agape. Unconditional love for humanity (literally, "love between friends").

Aggression (G). The basic biological movement of energy extending out from the organism to the environment. Aggression is required for assimilation, love, assertion, creativity, hunger, humor, discrimination, warmth, etc.

Agoraphobia. An excessive fear of open spaces and/or leaving one's own home.

Aha! (G). Awareness of a situation in which a number of separate elements come together to form a meaningful whole; sudden insight into the solution to a problem or the structure of a situation.

Anal Phase (PA). Freud's second phase of psychosexual development, extending roughly from the ages of 18 months to 3 years, in which most libidinal pleasure is derived from retaining and expelling feces.

Anima (J). The feminine component of the male personality.

Animus (J). The masculine component of the female personality.

Antisuggestion (A). *See* Paradoxical Intention.

Antithesis (B). The dual nature of mind and body; processes working in opposite directions.

Aphasia. An organic speech deficit involving difficulty understanding or using language.

Applied Behavior Analysis (BT). A form of behavior therapy, closely tied to Skinner's philosophy of radical behaviorism, that stresses observable behavior rather than private events and uses single-subject experimental design to determine the relationship between behavior and its antecedents and consequences.

Arbitrary Inference (CT). Drawing conclusions without supporting evidence or despite evidence to the contrary.

Archetypes (J). Primordial images that serve as the building blocks of the collective unconscious. Examples include the Wise Old Man, the Earth Mother, the Anima, the Animus, and the Shadow.

Assertion Training (BT). A treatment procedure designed to teach clients to openly and effectively express both positive and negative feelings.

Assimilation (G). The process of breaking something into component parts so that these parts can be accepted and made part of the person, rejected, or modified into suitable form.

Audience (PD). Any people present during an enactment other than the therapist, protagonist, and auxiliary.

Autoeroticism (PA). Obtaining gratification from self-stimulating a sensual area of the body.

Automatic Thoughts (CT). Personal notions or ideas triggered by particular stimuli that lead to emotional responses.

Automaticity. Engaging in behaviors without being aware of doing so, or operating on "automatic pilot."

Autonomy (CT). A personality dimension based on the needs to be independent, to be self-determining, and to attain one's goals.

Auxiliary (PD). A person who aids the therapist or client in enacting a particular scene.

Awfulizing (RET). Seeing something inconvenient or obnoxious as awful, horrible, or terrible.

Basic Encounter (PC & G). One member of a group's responding with empathy to another member's being genuine and real.

BASIC I.D. (MMT). An acronym that groups together the fundamental concerns of the multimodal therapist: Behaviors, Affective processes, Sensations, Images, Cognitions, Interpersonal Relations, and Drugs (i.e., biological functions).

Basic Mistakes (A). Myths used to organize and shape one's life. Examples include overgeneralizations, a desperate need for security, misperceptions of life's demands, denial of one's worth, and faulty values.

Behavioral Experiments (CT & BT). Testing distorted beliefs or fears scientifically in real-life situations (e.g., having a shy person initiate a conversation to see what actually happens).

Behavioral Medicine (BT). Applying learning-theory techniques to prevent or treat physical problems (e.g., pain reduction, weight loss).

Behavioral Rehearsal (CT & BT). Practicing an emotionally charged event and one's response to it prior to its actual occurrence.

Bridging (MMT). A procedure in which the therapist purposely tunes in to what the client wants to address, then gently channels the discussion into more productive areas.

Broad-Spectrum Behavior Therapy (MMT). The treatment approach, based on learning theory, that was advocated by Arnold Lazarus prior to development of multimodal therapy.

Catastrophizing (RET & CT). Exaggerating the consequences of an unfortunate event.

Catharsis (PA). The expression and discharge of repressed emotions; sometimes used synonymously with *abreaction*.

Character Structure (B). One's habitual way of being or common way of behaving; the five major types are oral (dependent, fearful of abandonment), schizoid (thought and emotion split off from one another), narcissistic (sense of superiority), masochistic (submissive, fearful of emotional expression), and rigid (unable to give, holding back).

Child (TA). A basic ego state that consists of feelings, impulses, and spontaneous acts; as a function of learning history, this ego state can take the form of the Adapted Child or the Natural Child.

Childhood Neuroses (PA). Various symptoms (e.g., nightmares, phobias, tics) produced by conflicts in the first six years of life.

Classical Conditioning (BT). A form of learning in which existing responses are attached to new stimuli by pairing those stimuli with those that naturally elicit the response; also referred to as *respondent conditioning*.

Cognitive Behavior Modification (BT). A recent extension of behavior therapy that treats thoughts and cognition as behaviors amenable to behavioral procedures. Cognitive behavior modification is perhaps most closely associated with the work of Aaron Beck, Albert Ellis, and Donald Meichenbaum.

Cognitive Distortions (CT). Pervasive and systematic errors in reasoning.

Cognitive Restructuring (BT & RET). An active attempt to alter maladaptive thought patterns and replace them with more adaptive cognitions.

Cognitive Shift (CT). A systematic and biased interpretation of life experiences.

Cognitive Triad (CT). Negative views of the self, the world, and the future that characterize depression.

Cognitive Vulnerability (CT). Individual ways of thinking that predispose one to particular psychological distress.

Collaborative Empiricism (CT). A strategy of seeing the patient as a scientist capable of objective interpretation.

Collective Unconscious (J). That part of unconscious material that is universal in the human species, in contrast to the personal unconscious that is determined by individual personal experience. The collective unconscious contains symbolic access to archetypes.

Conditional Assumption (CT). An erroneous "if-then" interpretation of events that leads to an erroneous conclusion (e.g., "*If* one person dislikes me, *then* I am not likable").

Confluence (G). A state in which the contact boundary becomes so thin, flexible, and permeable that the distinction between self and environment is lost. In confluence, one does not experience self as distinct but merges self into the beliefs, attitudes, and feelings of others. *Confluence* can be healthy or unhealthy.

Congruence (PC). Agreement between the feelings and attitudes a therapist is experiencing and his or her professional demeanor; one of Rogers' necessary and sufficient conditions for therapeutic change. *See* Genuineness.

Consensus Trance (Asian). View of the normal waking state as dreamlike, lacking real awareness.

Contact (G). Basic unit of relationship involving an experience of the boundary between "me" and "not-me"; feeling a connection with the "not-me" while maintaining a separation from it.

Contamination (TA). A breakdown in maintaining separate boundaries among the ego states (e.g., child-state fantasies seeping into the Adult state and creating unrealistic interpretations of the world or actual delusions).

Convictions (A). Conclusions based on personal experiences and perceptions, usually biased because each person's perspective is unique.

Coping Imagery (MMT). A technique that pairs relaxation with images of successful self-control in previously anxiety-eliciting situations.

Counterconditioning (BT). Replacing a particular behavior by conditioning a new response incompatible with the maladaptive behavior. Counterconditioning is one of the explanations for the effectiveness of systematic desensitization.

Countertransference (PA). The activation of unconscious wishes and fantasies on the part of the therapist toward the patient; the tendency to respond to patients as though they were significant others in the life or history or fantasy of the therapist.

Courage (A). The willingness to take risks without being sure of the consequences; necessary for effective living.

Critical Parent (TA). An ego state that is critical, judgmental, and fault finding. The Critical Parent may also be assertive and self-sufficient. *Contrast with* Nurturing Parent.

Decatastrophizing (CT & RET). A "what-if" technique designed to explore actual, rather than feared, events and consequences.

Decentering (CT). Moving the supposed focus of attention away from one's self.

Decision (E). The bridge between wishing for something and taking action to see that it happens; often difficult to make because every "yes" choice means saying no to another possibility.

Defense Mechanisms (PA). Methods used by the ego to fight off instinctual outbursts of the id and superego. Examples include repression, projection, and reaction formation.

Deflection (G). A means of blunting the impact of contact and awareness by not giving or receiving feelings or thoughts directly. Vagueness, verbosity, and understatement are forms of deflection.

Dehypnosis (Asian). Eliminating the assumption that fantasies are real, e.g., recognizing thoughts as thoughts rather than identifying with them.

Dementia Praecox. An antiquated term for schizophrenia.

Dereflection (Asian). Directing one's attention away from the self.

Determinism (PA). The assumption that every mental event is causally tied to earlier psychological experience.

Dialogue (G). Genuine, equal, and honest communication between two people; the "I-Thou" relation.

Dichotomous Thinking (CT & RET). Categorizing experiences or people in black-and-white or extreme terms only (e.g., all good vs. all bad) with no middle ground.

Dichotomy (G). A split in which a field is experienced as comprising competing and unrelated forces that cannot be meaningfully integrated into a whole.

Director (PD). The person who manages a scene, usually the therapist.

Discriminative Stimulus (BT). A stimulus or set of stimuli that signify that reinforcement will (or will not) occur.

Disorientation. Inability to correctly identify time and place (e.g., dates and locations).

Double (PD). Playing someone else's inner self.

Double Bind (FT). A situation in which a person receives simultaneous contradictory requests or demands such that any action taken leads to at least partial failure.

Drama Therapy (PD). Use of theater techniques to gain self-awareness or increase self-expression in groups.

Dual-Instinct Theory (PA). The notion that humans operate primarily in terms of pervasive and innate drives toward both love and aggression. *See also* Eros *and* Thanatos.

Dynamics (PA). Interaction among one's basic drives and urges.

Dysarthria. Organic speech deficit involving difficulty with the mechanical production of language.

Early Recollections (A). Salient memories of single incidents from childhood; used as a projective technique by Adlerian therapists.

Eclecticism. The practice of drawing from multiple and diverse sources in formulating client problems and devising treatment plans. Multimodal therapists are technical eclectics (e.g., they employ multiple methods without necessarily endorsing the theoretical positions from which they were derived).

Ego (PA). That part of the mind that mediates between external reality and inner wishes and impulses.

Ego States (TA). Three structural ego states represent distinct and independent levels of psychological functioning: Parent, Adult, and Child. They are capitalized to distinguish them from parents, adults, and children.

Egogram (TA). A visual representation of one's personality using a bar graph to display the amount of energy emanating from the five functional ego states: Critical Parent, Nurturing Parent, Adult, Free Child, and Adapted Child.

Eigenwelt (E). One level of the way each individual relates to the world. *Eigenwelt* literally means "own world" and refers to the way each of us relates to self.

Electra Complex (PA). Erotic attraction of the female child for her father, with accompanying hostility for her mother; the female equivalent of the Oedipus complex.

Elegant Solution (RET). Solutions which help clients make a profound philosophical change that goes beyond mere symptom removal.

Emotive Techniques (RET). Therapy techniques that are vigorous, vivid, and dramatic.

Empathic Understanding (PC). The ability to appreciate a client's phenomenological position and to accompany the client as he or she progresses in therapy; one of the necessary conditions for therapeutic change.

Empathy. Accurately and deeply feeling someone else's expressed emotions, concerns, or situation.

Enactment (PD). Showing (rather than verbalizing) an important life event.

Encounter (PD). Present dialogue between two persons, or two aspects of the same person, either in reality or with one part played by someone else.

Encounter Group. A small number of people who meet (sometimes only once, sometimes on a weekly basis for a specified time) to truly know and accept themselves and others.

Equanimity (Asian). The ability to experience any stimulus without disturbance.

Eros (PA). The life instinct, fueled by libidinal energy and opposed by Thanatos, the death instinct.

Ethicality (Asian). Internally based emphasis on moral or principled behavior.

Exclusion (TA). A situation in which one ego state is so dominant that other states have very little influence (e.g., an irresponsible dreamer's Child is so strong that the Adult's reality and logic have no influence).

Existential Isolation (E). Fundamental and inevitable separation of each individual from others and the world; can be reduced but not completely eliminated.

Existential Neurosis (E). Feelings of emptiness, worthlessness, despair, and anxiety resulting from inauthenticity, abdication of responsibility, failure to make choices, and a lack of direction or purpose in life.

Existentialism (E). A philosophical movement that stresses the importance of actual existence, one's responsibility for and determination of one's own psychological existence, authenticity in human relations, the primacy of the here and now, and the use of experience in the search for knowledge.

Experiencing (PC). Sensing or awareness of self and the world, whether narrowly and rigidly or openly and flexibly. Experience is unique for each person.

Extinction (BT). In classical conditioning, extinction refers to repeated presentation of the conditioned stimulus without the unconditioned stimulus and the resulting gradual diminution of the conditioned response. In operant conditioning, extinction occurs when reinforcement is withheld following performance of a previously reinforced response.

Facilitator (PC). An individual who aids a group in going the direction they choose and accomplishing their chosen goals without doing harm to any member.

Factors of Enlightenment (Asian). Seven mental qualities important for psychological well-being: mindfulness, effort, investigation, rapture, concentration, calm, and equanimity.

Family Constellation (A). The number, sequencing, and characteristics of the members of a family. The family constellation is an important determinant of life-style.

Feedback (FT). The process by which a system makes adjustments in itself; can be positive (restoring a previous balance) or negative (destroying or preventing balance).

Fixation (PA). A strong attachment to a source of gratification in infancy that persists into adulthood.

Formative Tendency (PC). An overall inclination toward greater order, complexity, and interrelatedness common to all nature, including human beings.

Free Association (PA). A basic technique of psychoanalysis in which patients are asked to report, without structure or censure, whatever thoughts come to mind.

Free Child (TA). That part of the personality that is spontaneous, eager, and playful. People who possess too much Free Child lack self-control.

Functionally Specific States (Asian). States of consciousness in which particular abilities such as introspection, are increased, while others are reduced.

Fusion (ET & FT). In existential therapy, the giving up of oneself to become part of another person or a group; a particular attempt to reduce one's sense of isolation. In family therapy, a relationship that allows no boundaries among family members, no separate sense of self. Fusion is observed in schizophrenic families and considered highly maladaptive.

Future Projection (PD). Demonstration of what one sees going on in life at some specified time in the future.

Games (TA). Stereotyped and predictable patterns of behavior based on transactions that are partially ulterior and result in negative payoffs for the players. Games have names like "Kick Me," "Rapo," and so on, and are classified as first, second, or third degree, depending on the seriousness of their consequences.

Gemeinschaftsgefühl (A). A combination of concern for others and appreciation of one's role in a larger social order; usually translated as "social interest."

Generalization (BT). The occurrence of behavior in situations that resemble but are different from the stimulus environment in which the behavior was learned.

Genital Stage (PA). The final stage of psychosexual development, usually attained in late adolescence, in which sexual gratification occurs through intercourse and is not limited to specific body areas.

Genogram (FT). A three-generation structural diagram of a family system.

Genuineness (PC). The characteristic of being real and true to oneself; lack of pretense, social facade, or refusal to allow certain aspects of one's self into awareness.

Graded-Task Assignment (CT & BT). Starting with a simple activity and increasing the level of complexity or difficulty in a step-by-step fashion.

Grounding (B). The use of many body positions, especially standing, to help patients get a better sense of their basic posture and support.

Hidden Agenda (TA & Others). The actual goal of an interaction between people (as in a game), which is different from what superficially appears to be the goal.

Higher States (Asian). States of consciousness containing normal mental capacities plus additional, heightened ones.

Holism (A). Studying individuals in their entirety, including how they proceed through life, rather than trying to separate out certain aspects or parts, such as studying the mind apart from the body.

Homework. Specific activities to be done between therapy sessions.

Hot Cognitions (CT). Powerful and highly meaningful ideas that produce strong emotional reactions.

Hysteria (PA). An early term for conversion reaction, a disorder in which psychological disturbance takes a physical form (e.g., paralysis in the absence of organic disturbance). Many of Freud's theories grew out of his experience in treating hysterical patients.

Id (PA). The sum total of biological instincts, including sexual and aggressive impulses. At birth, the id represents the total personality.

Imagery Reactor (MMT). An individual who responds to the environment predominately in terms of images, usually auditory or visual.

Inattention. Severe inability to maintain concentration.

Inclusion (G). Putting oneself as completely as possible into another's experience without judging or evaluating, while still maintaining a separate sense of self.

Individual Psychology (A). An approach to understanding human behavior that sees each person as a unique, whole entity who is constantly becoming rather than being, whose development can only be understood within a social context.

Individuation (J). A human instinct directed toward self-fulfillment and wholeness.

Inferiority Complex (A). An exaggeration of feelings of inadequacy and insecurity resulting in defensiveness and neurotic behavior. It is usually, but not always, abnormal.

Inferiority Feelings (A). Sometimes seeing oneself as inadequate or incompetent in comparison with others, with one's ideal self, or with personal values; considered universal and normal. *Contrast with* Inferiority Complex.

Intensive Group (PC). A small number of people who come together for a brief but condensed period (e.g., a weekend) to engage in special interpersonal experiences that are designed to expand awareness of self and others.

Interlocking Triangles (FT). Basic units of family relationships consisting of a series of three-person sets of interactions (e.g., father-mother-child; grandparent-parent-child).

Internal Frame of Reference (PC). A view or perception of both the world and self as seen by the individual, as distinguished from an observer, psychotherapist, or other person's point of view.

Introjection (G). Accepting information or values from the outside without evaluation; not necessarily psychologically unhealthy.

Irrational Beliefs (RET). Unreasonable convictions that produce emotional upset (for example, insisting that the world should or must be different from what it actually is).

Isolation (G). A state in which the contact boundary is so thick, rigid, and non-permeable that the psychological connection between self and environment is lost and the person does not allow access from or to the outside. *Isolation* can be healthy or unhealthy. *Contrast with* withdrawal.

Isolation (PA). Separating thoughts or memories from any emotion associated with them so that they become neutral in tone.

Latency Period (PA). An inactive time in psychosexual development that follows the phallic stage and lasts till puberty.

Leaning Tower of Pisa Approach (FT). A variation of paradoxical intention in which a therapist exacerbates a problem until it falls of its own weight and is thereby resolved.

Libido (PA). The basic driving force of personality in Freud's system. It includes sexual energy but is not restricted to it.

Life-Style (A). One's characteristic way of living and pursuing long-term goals.

Life Tasks (A). The basic challenges and obligations of life: society, work, and sex. The additional tasks of spiritual growth and self-identity are included by Rudolf Dreikurs and Harold Mosak.

Locus-of-Evaluation (PC). The place of a judgment's origin, its source; whether the appraisal of an experience comes more from within the individual (internal) or from outside sources (external).

Logotherapy (E). A therapeutic approach developed by Viktor Frankl emphasizing value and meaning as prerequisites for mental health and personal growth.

Lucid Dreaming (Asian). A sleep state in which people know they are dreaming.

Magnification (CT). Exaggerating something's significance.

Marital Schism (FT). A situation in a marriage that results in poor relationships and psychological separation, usually due to the inability of one of the marriage partners to break a tie with the parental home.

Marital Skew (FT). A marital relationship characterized by one spouse's excessive dominance.

Maya (Asian). An illusory and encompassing distortion of one's perception and experience that is not recognized as such.

Mediational Stimulus-Response Model (BT). A behavioral model that posits internal events, such as thoughts and images, as links between perceiving a stimulus and making a response.

Meditation (Asian). Practices designed to train attention and bring various mental processes under greater voluntary control.

Mindfulness (Asian). Clear objective awareness of an ongoing experience.

Minimization (CT). Making an event far less important than it actually is.

Mirror (PD). A person who imitates a client's behavior and demeanor so that the client can more clearly see him- or herself in action.

Mitwelt (E). One way in which each individual relates to the world, socially and through being with others; the age we live in, our age, our own times, the present generation, our contemporaries.

Modality Profile (MMT). A specific list of problems and proposed treatments across the client's BASIC I.D.

Monodrama (PD). One client's playing both parts in a scene by alternating between them.

Morita (Asian). A Japanese therapy for treating anxiety by redirecting one's attention away from the self.

Motility (B). Movement or activity; an essential principle in working with the body. Any limitation of movement both results from and causes emotional difficulties.

Multiple Parts of Self (PD). Physically acting out internal conflicts.

Multiple Psychotherapy (A). A technique in which several therapists simultaneously treat a single patient.

Musturbation (RET). A term coined by Albert Ellis to characterize the behavior of clients who are absolutistic and inflexible in their thinking, maintaining that they must not fail, must be exceptional, must be successful, etc.

Mystification (FT). A pattern of confusion, chaotic, and unclear communication, or doubletalk, sometimes seen in schizophrenic families.

Naikan (Asian). Japanese therapy using intensive reflection on past relationships to increase social and interpersonal contributions.

Narcissism (PA). Excessive self-absorption, self-concern, or self-love arising from psychic energy vested in oneself.

Natural Child (TA). A form of the Child ego state that is impulsive, spontaneous, and creative. Contrast with Adapted Child.

Negative Reinforcement (BT). Any behavior that increases the probability of a response by terminating or withdrawing an unpleasant stimulus. Negative reinforcement always increases the likelihood of the future occurrence of the behavior it follows.

Neurosis. A dated but common term referring to a variety of relatively mild disorders in which the patient distorts (but does not deny) reality.

Neurotic Anxiety (E). A state of fear or apprehension out of proportion to an actual threat. Neurotic anxiety is destructive or paralyzing and cannot be used constructively. Compare with Normal Anxiety.

Nonpersonal Unconscious (J). See Collective Unconscious.

Normal Anxiety (E). A sense of apprehension appropriate to a given threatening situation which can be faced, dealt with, and used creatively. Compare with Neurotic Anxiety.

Nurturing Parent (TA). A personality ego state that is warm, supportive, and caring. Contrast with Critical Parent.

Oedipus Complex (PA). Erotic attraction of the male child for his mother, accompanied by hostility toward the father. See also Electra Complex.

Ontological (E). Concerned with the science of being or existence.

Operant Conditioning (BT). A type of learning in which responses are modified by their consequences. Reinforcement increases the likelihood of future occurrences of the reinforced response; punishment and extinction decrease the likelihood of future occurrences of the responses they follow.

Oral Phase (PA). The earliest phase of psychosexual development, extending from birth to approximately 18 months, in which most libidinal gratification occurs through biting, sucking, and oral contact.

Organ Inferiority (A). Perceived or actual congenital defects in organ systems believed by Alfred Adler to result in compensatory striving to overcome these deficits.

Organismic Valuing Process (PC). Making individual judgments or assessments of the desirability of an action or choice on the basis of one's own sensory evidence and life experience.

Orgone Energy (B). An actual physical force that powers all human functions, including the psychological; proposed by Wilhelm Reich.

Overgeneralization (CT & RET). Constructing a general rule from isolated incidents and applying it too broadly.

Paradoxical Intention. A therapeutic strategy used in a variety of systems in which the client is instructed to engage in and magnify the very behaviors of concern.

Payoff (TA). Bad feelings experienced by one person deliberately created by another person playing a game.

Persecutor (TA). Someone seen as being unfair to or overly critical of another; one of three possible roles in a game. *See also* Victim *and* Rescuer.

Persona (J). A disguised or masked attitude useful in interacting with one's environment but frequently at variance with true identity.

Personal Unconscious (J). The surface layer of the unconscious, consisting largely of subliminal perceptions and repressed experiences. *Contrast with* Collective Unconscious.

Personalization (CT). Taking personal responsibility for negative events without supporting evidence of personal involvement.

Phallic Phase (PA). The third stage of psychosexual development in which libidinal gratification occurs through direct experience with the genitals. This phase occurs between the ages of three and seven and involves a desire to possess the parent of the opposite sex and to replace the parent of the same sex. *See* Oedipus Complex *and* Electra Complex.

Phenomenology (A, G & E). A method of exploration that primarily uses human experience as the source of data and attempts to include all human experience without bias (external observation, emotions, thoughts, and so on). Subjects are taught to distinguish between current experience and the biases brought to the situation. Phenomenology is the basic method of most existentialists.

Pleasure Principle (PA). The basic human tendency to avoid pain and seek pleasure, especially salient in the first years of life. *Contrast with* Reality Principle.

Positive Reinforcement (BT). Any stimulus that follows a behavior and increases the likelihood of the occurrence of the behavior that it follows.

Presence (G). Therapists sharing their own experiences, thoughts, and feelings with patients; genuinely "being with" a patient.

Projection (PA & G). Attributing to others unacceptable personal thoughts, feelings, or behaviors.

Pseudomutuality (FT). An artificial closeness in some families that fosters dependency and a loss of self-identity.

Psychoanalysis (PA). A system of psychotherapy closely tied to the work of Sigmund Freud and his followers. The techniques of psychoanalysis include free association, dream analysis, and working through transference issues.

Psychoanalytic Situation (PA). The standard way psychoanalysis is conducted, i.e., the patient lies on a couch, with the analyst seated out of the patient's view, and expresses whatever comes to mind while the analyst listens objectively and interprets what the patient says.

Psychological Masquerade. Apparent psychological symptoms actually caused by physical or organic conditions.

Punishment (BT). An aversive event likely to terminate any behavior that it follows.

Racket Feelings (TA). Habitual patterns of emotion (e.g., sadness, fear, or anger) that people engage in over and over throughout their lives. Games are played to emphasize racket feelings (mad, sad, scared, confused, and so forth).

Rapture (Asian). Delight in the awareness of experience.

Reaction Formation (PA). A defense mechanism through which an individual replaces an anxiety-eliciting impulse with behavior that is the exact opposite of the initial impulse.

Reality. Psychologically, an individual's private world, but socially and more generally, a group of perceptions or "facts" with substantial consensus about their meaning.

Reality Principle (PA). The guiding principle of the ego, the reality principle permits postponement of gratification in order to meet the demands of the environment or secure greater pleasure at a later time. *Contrast with* Pleasure Principle.

Reattribution (CT). Assigning alternative causes to events; reinterpreting one's symptoms.

Regression (PA). A defense mechanism involving a return to an earlier stage of development to obtain gratification.

Reinforcement (BT). The presentation of a reward or the removal of an aversive stimulus following a response. Reinforcement always increases the future probability of the reinforced response.

Repression (PA). A major defense mechanism in which distressing thoughts are barred from conscious expression.

Rescuer (TA). Someone who rushes to the aid of another who has not been justly dealt with; one of three possible roles in a game. *See also* Victim *and* Persecutor.

Resistance (G). The reluctance of people to know, show, or own aspects of themselves. Resistance can be healthy as well as unhealthy.

Resistance (PA). Reluctance or failure of the patient to be fully engaged in the process of psychoanalysis; usually an unconscious process.

Respiration (B). Breathing; an essential principle in working with the body. Any restriction in breathing both results from and causes anxiety.

Respondent Conditioning (BT). See Classical Conditioning.

Retroflection (G). A contact boundary disturbance in which a person substitutes self for the environment and does to self what he or she originally did or tried to do to others. Retroflection is the chief mechanism of isolation and is not necessarily unhealthy.

Role Distance (PD). An increase in objectivity about an event that comes from playing a part connected to or associated with it.

Role Reversal (PD). Playing the part of an important other person in one's life in order to get a better perspective.

Role Training (PD). Rehearsing an anticipated situation so that the response is appropriate in the actual situation.

Roleplaying (PD). Acting the part of someone or something else.

Samadhi (Asian). Yogic state of consciousness marked by deep calm and concentration.

Schemas (CT). Strategies or ways of thinking comprising core beliefs and basic assumptions about how the world operates.

Scripts (TA). Basic existential decisions about one's life plan made at an early age regarding one's self and others.

Second-Order BASIC I.D. (MMT). Focusing on a particular aspect of the BASIC I.D. to get more detailed information; useful for diagnosis and for breaking impasses in therapy.

Selection Abstraction (CT). Basing a conclusion on a detail taken out of context and ignoring other information.

Self-Actualization (PC). A basic human drive toward growth, completeness, and fulfillment.

Self-Concept. One's own definition of who one is, including attributes, emotions, abilities, faults, etc.

Self-Instructional Training (BT). A technique, described most completely by Donald Meichenbaum, for replacing self-defeating thoughts with self-enhancing cognitions.

Self-Regard (PC). That aspect of the self-concept which develops from the esteem or respect accorded oneself.

Sensate Focus (BT). A series of exercises used in sex therapy and designed to reintroduce clients to receiving and giving sensual pleasure.

Sensory-Reactor (MMT). An individual who interacts with the world primarily in terms of the five basic senses.

Shadow (J). That aspect of the unconscious that contains the opposite of what we feel ourselves to be. The shadow is that part of ourself to which we are not sufficiently well related.

Social Interest (A). The feeling of being part of a social whole; the need and willingness to contribute to the general social good. *See also* Gemeinschaftsgefühl.

Social Learning Theory (BT). A system that combines operant and classical conditioning with cognitive mediational processes (e.g., vicarious learning and symbolic activity) to account for the development, maintenance, and modification of behavior.

Sociometry (PD). A method in which groups give feedback about their interpersonal preferences (e.g., attraction or repulsion).

Sociotrophy (CT). A personality dimension characterized by dependency on interpersonal relationships and needs for closeness and nurturance.

Socratic Dialogue (CT). A carefully constructed series of questions designed to arrive at logical answers to and conclusions about a hypothesis.

Splitting (G). A situation in which a person splits off part of self as a polar opposite. When aware of one pole, the person is oblivious to the other. For example, an individual may split into competent and incompetent selves and vacillate between these roles. A split is one form of a dichotomy.

Stimulus Control (BT). Arranging the environment in such a way that a given response is either more likely or less likely to occur (e.g., buying only one pack of cigarettes per day in order to decrease the likelihood of smoking).

Strategic Intervention Therapy (FT). An approach to family therapy employing specific strategies, plans, and tactics in order to force changes in behavior.

Strokes (TA). Recognition from others. Strokes can be positive (warm fuzzies) or negative (cold prickles).

Structural Profiles (MMT). A quantitative assessment of the relative involvement of each of the elements of the BASIC I.D.

Structural Theory (PA). Freud's later model of the psyche which maintains that one's psychological makeup comprises three parts, each having specific functions. *See also* Id, Ego, Superego.

Structuralism (FT). An approach to family therapy, associated with Salvador Minuchin, that emphasizes the importance of the nuclear family and seeks to change pathological alliances and splits in the family.

Stuck-Togetherness (FT). A situation observed in schizophrenic families in which roles and boundaries are blurred and no family member has an identity distinct from the family.

Subjective Reasoning (CT). Believing that feelings are the same as or equivalent to facts.

Superego (PA). A portion of the personality structure that grows out of the ego and reflects early moral training and parental injunctions.

Support (G). To provide the psychological, physiological, social, or material aid needed to initiate, terminate, regulate, and maintain contact-withdrawal as needed by the person or the environment. People are self supporting to the degree that they are the chief agents in initiating, terminating, regulating, and maintaining contact-withdrawal and do so based on self identification. For example, knowing what one wants and being able to appropriately ask for it is self-supporting.

Surplus Reality (PD). Psychological experiences involving other than physical reality (e.g., spiritual events, relationships with deceased people that still have an influence, hallucinations).

Symbiosis (TA & Others). A relationship in which two people, often a mother and her child, become so intertwined that it is impossible to find a boundary between them.

Symbolization (PC). A process of allowing a life event or experience into one's consciousness or awareness and interpreting it in terms of the self-concept; may be straightforward, distorted, or prohibited altogether.

Synthesis. Making a whole from elements or parts; constructing the overall meaning of a situation from many different aspects of it.

System (FT). A complete unit made up of interconnected and interdependent parts operating in a stable way over time.

Systematic Desensitization (BT). A step-by-step procedure for replacing anxiety with relaxation while gradually increasing exposure to an anxiety-producing situation or object.

Thanatos (PA). An instinct toward death and self-destruction, posited by Freud to oppose and balance Eros, the life instinct.

Token Economy (BT). A program that provides people with short-term reinforcement for specific behaviors by allotting tokens (poker chips or points) that are accumulated and later exchanged for privileges or desired objects.

Topographic Theory (PA). Freud's earliest model of psychic functioning, which emphasized mental functions operating at various depths or levels of awareness *See* Unconscious.

Tracking (MMT). A careful examination of the firing order of the BASIC I.D. modalities to facilitate more effective sequencing of the treatment procedures.

Trading Stamps (TA). Treasured feelings, whether positive or negative, that can be traded in for other experiences (e.g., a "free" depression earned by repeatedly being abused).

Trait Theory. The belief in stable and enduring personality characteristics.

Transactions (TA). The basic unit of human communication; any exchange between the various ego states of two or more individuals. Transactions may have an overt social level and a covert psychological level.

Transference (PA). The therapy situation in which the patient responds to the therapist as though he or she were a significant figure in the patient's past, usually a parent.

Trust (PC). Basic faith in oneself and others as being growth-directed and positively oriented.

Umwelt (E). A way of relating to the world through its biological and physical aspects; one's relationship with nature and the surrounding world.

Unconditional Positive Regard (PC). A nonpossessive caring and acceptance of the client as a human being, irrespective of the therapist's own values. One of Rogers' necessary and sufficient conditions for therapeutic change.

Unconscious. A division of the psyche; the repository of psychological material of which the individual is unaware.

Unity (B). Mind and body functioning as a whole; an imbalance in one area affecting all other areas as well (e.g., physical illness having an effect on psychological well-being or anxiety having an effect on the body).

Vicarious Learning (BT). Learning through observation and imitation. Synonym: modeling.

Victim (TA). Someone seen as being unfairly treated or having a difficult time because of other people's actions; one of three possible roles in a game. *See also* Persecutor *and* Rescuer.

Voluntary Simplicity (Asian). Self-motivated choice to live more simply and to deemphasize material goods.

Warmth (PC). Positive and real feelings of acceptance toward another.

Will to Power (A). Individual striving for superiority and dominance in order to overcome feelings of inadequacy and inferiority.

Withdrawal (G). Temporary withdrawing from contact while maintaining a permeable contact boundary. *Withdrawal* can be healthy or unhealthy. *Contrast with* isolation.

Work (G). The process of exploring by phenomenological focusing in order to increase awareness. One can work in any setting and can focus on any theme (here and now contact, life problems, developmental themes, spiritual concerns, creativity and emotional expansion, dreams, belief systems, etc.).

Yoga (Asian). Disciplines dealing with ethics, life-style, body postures, breath control, intellectual study, and meditation.

Zeitgeist. The spirit of the times; the prevailing cultural climate.

Name Index

NAME INDEX

Subject Index

THE BOOK'S MANUFACTURE

Current Psychotherapies,
Fourth Edition, was typeset by
Compositors, Cedar Rapids, Iowa.
The typefaces are Melior and Melior Bold
for text and display.
Printing and binding by
Arcata Graphics, Kingsport, Tennessee.
Cover and internal design by John B. Goetz,
Design & Production Services Co., Chicago.